Organizational Behaviour

Daniel King and Scott Lawley

OXFORD

UNIVERSITY PRESS

OXFORD
UNIVERSITY PRESS

Great Clarendon Street, Oxford, OX2 6DP,
United Kingdom

Oxford University Press is a department of the University of Oxford.
It furthers the University's objective of excellence in research, scholarship,
and education by publishing worldwide. Oxford is a registered trade mark of
Oxford University Press in the UK and in certain other countries

British Library Cataloguing in Publication Data

Data available

ISBN 978–0–19–960309–1

Printed in Italy by
L.E.G.O. S.p.A. – Lavis TN

Acknowledgements

The writing of this book has been supported by many people. The pedagogical approach that underpins it is based on our previous six years of teaching at Nottingham Trent University. Therefore we would like to thank the thousands of students that we have had the pleasure of teaching over the last few years on the Foundations of Managing and Organising module at the University. Teaching you has been the inspiration for this book as we have sought to find ways of communicating our fascination with organizational behaviour to hundreds of students a year and make the subject come alive through our running case study. Similarly we would like to thank our colleagues at NTU who we have had the pleasure of teaching alongside and who have helped us develop the ideas that led to the foundations of this work. We would also like to thank Harry Barton for his support of us throughout this project: for his encouragement, and for enabling us to take the ideas we have developed during our teaching into this textbook.

At OUP we would like to thank Fran Griffin for initially sparking the idea that the way that we taught could be converted into a book and for her continual support and enthusiasm for the project and development of many of the ideas; Ben Pettitt for his work at keeping us on track with the tight publishing deadlines and being a constant source of support throughout the writing process; Sian Jenkins for her attention to detail throughout the copyediting stage; and Fiona Goodall for her work on the ORC. We would also like to express our gratitude to the many reviewers for their valuable comments and insights, their ability to understand the concept underlying this book, and their suggestions for its development.

We would also like to thank the many people we interviewed for the creation of this book, including Joe Greenwell, the Chair of Ford in Britain, and Stephen Hester, CEO of Royal Bank of Scotland. We are grateful to Emma Morris and James Scott for their work on the vodcasts throughout the ORC.

Daniel would like to thank Steph for her continual support throughout the process of writing the book and is looking forward to spending more time with her, Saffron, and Josh! Their sacrifice of weekends and holidays throughout the last two years has been considerable and it would not have been possible to write without their understanding. He would also like to thank his parents for their continual support in so many ways, and his friends—many of whom he has not been able to see as much as he would like in recent times!

Scott would like to thank colleagues past and present for their ideas and inspiration over the years, and all friends and family for their support during the writing of this book.

How to use this book

Running case: too much to do and not en

Nina Biagini, Junction Hotel's maître d' looks at the pile of na
the restaurant opens at 5pm; 400 glasses also need to be cl
be polished. 'We are never going to be ready for tonight's Ro
the top of our game with all these business leaders coming',
to herself, 'what with our busy season coming up, this place i
We need help.'

Feeling anxious that the restaurant will not be ready in tim
of hands. 'What?', Weaver blasts down the phone, 'we can't aff

Running case:

The fictional running case is set in Junction Hotel, and presents organizational problems and theories in a familiar context. We see issues from multiple perspectives and discover that there is often no 'one best way' to do things. The running case is closely integrated with the theories discussed in each chapter.

Real life case: the upside-down badge

Jobsworth stories where officials have implemented rules that s
petty and where people have been punished for seemingly m
infringements of the rules often make the news.

For example, in 2011 a pensioner with a disability
Nottinghamshire, UK, was fined £35 for parking in a disa
parking bay with the relevant accreditation badge displayed i
windscreen, but upside down (BBC News, 2011).

On one hand, the rules state that the badge must be legible. Fo

Real life case boxes:

Organizational behaviour theories are played out in the real world every day. Contemporary examples from a range of sources (including businesses such as Vodafone, public sector institutions like the Metropolitan police, and not-for-profit organizations such as food cooperatives) help you make the link from theory to reality.

Employability skills: the recruitment and s

This chapter relates personality to the recruitment and selec
valuable insight into the processes used when you apply for er
vacation work, for a placement, or when you graduate and beg

While this chapter concentrates on personality, it is useful to
of recruitment and selection ahead of applying for jobs. Unders
the ways in which they match applicants to jobs, and, importa
dates are all things which will give you a head start. Your univer
ture on the subject and will be able to offer advice.

Study and employability skills boxes:

Each chapter contains skills tips to help boost your grades and your employability. These are linked to topics being discussed in the book, and further reinforce the relevance of organizational behaviour to real life.

Theory in context: responding to the rise o

The rising interest in organizational culture occurred at a poir
nomic superpower was being challenged by the rise of Japanes
was challenged by Honda's smaller, more efficient bikes (Ouch
    The Japanese culture was seen as key in their success. For ins
a story of a 'Honda worker who, on his way home each eve
blades on all the Hondas he passes. He can't stand to see a fla
some US workers were seen as purposely destructive. For ex
would go home at night chuckling to himself about the thing

Research insight: 'We recruit attitude', Calla
2002. 'We recruit attitude': the selection and s
centre labour. *Journal of Management Studie*

In a study of recruitment and selection in a call centre, Callag
while technical skills, such as numeracy and using a keyboard a
process is given to personality. In particular, a positive, energet
humour during calls are seen as aspects of good customer se
tomer service that may differentiate the company from others
emotional labour in service industries in Chapter 16).

 Imagine if your university library building close
would it have on the rest of the university and h
keep the university running?

 Visit the Online Resource Centre for furth

Open and closed systems

A further distinction in the nature of a s
(Jackson and Carter, 2007: 211).

Review questions

1. Describe the main features of the planned approach to c
2. Explain how the planned approach to change addresse
   surface'.
3. Analyse how organization development helps bring abou

Apply

4. How might the three-step model have been used to impl

Further reading

Schein, E. 2010. *Organizational culture and leadership.* Jossey Bas
    Popular management writer and consultant, Schein provides a goo
    agement viewpoint. He offers ways to understand culture and prac

Peters, T. J., and Waterman, R. H. Jr. 1982. *In search of excellence*
    Harper Row, London.
    An early, influential book in management circles on the role of cult
    given that it has been subject to substantial criticism for both its me

Smircich, L. 1983. Concepts of culture and organizational anal
    339–358.

Theory in context boxes:

Where do theories about organizational behaviour come from? What influenced the theorists' thoughts and the resulting theories? The wider contexts of society, technology, politics, and economics are considered, and you are encouraged to critically analyse theories to deepen your understanding.

Research insight boxes:

The body of academic literature on the subject of organizational behaviour is vast. This feature highlights seminal research articles that made a significant contribution to the topic. The full reference is provided so you can follow up your textbook reading with further research.

Stop and think questions:

These short, reflective questions appear throughout the chapters and encourage you to consider the topics in light of your own experience.

Review questions:

At the end of every chapter section review questions help you assess your understanding of the central themes and your readiness to progress to the next part of the topic.

Further reading:

To take your learning further, reading lists have been provided as guides to finding out more about the issues raised within each chapter and to help you locate the useful academic literature in the field.

How to use the Online Resource Centre

www.oxfordtextbooks.co.uk/orc/king_lawley/

The Online Resource Centre that accompanies this book provides students and registered adopters of the textbook with ready-to-use teaching and learning materials. These resources are free of charge and designed to maximize the learning experience.

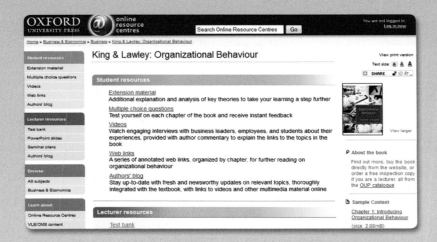

Author blog:

The authors will provide fresh and newsworthy updates on relevant topics, thoroughly integrated with the textbook, with links to videos and other multimedia material on the Internet.

For students

Videos:

The world of work can sometimes seem far removed from the theories being discussed in the textbook. Business leaders, employees, and students are interviewed about their experiences, and an author commentary on each video clip explains the links to topics in the book.

Extension material:

Additional explanation and analysis of key theories which go beyond what is covered in the textbook are available to help you to take your learning a step further.

Multiple-choice questions:

A bank of self-marking multiple-choice questions has been provided for each chapter of the text and includes instant feedback on your answers, cross-referencing the textbook to assist with independent self-study.

Weblinks:

A series of annotated weblinks, organized by chapter, has been provided to point you in the direction of important material on organizational behaviour.

For instructors

Seminar plans:

A suite of fully developed seminar plans has been prepared for use in class. Activities are based around extension material from the running case and additional real-life case studies and video clips.

Test bank:

A fully customizable resource containing interactive multiple-choice questions accompanied by answers and feedback with which to test your students.

PowerPoint slides:

Customizable PowerPoint slides have been included for use in lecture presentations. Arranged by chapter theme, the slides may also be used as hand-outs in class.

Contents

Detailed contents

Part 2: Managing groups and teams   121

Part 4: Managing the organization   335

Introducing organizational behaviour

Transitions and new beginnings

Why read this introduction?

This chapter answers two key questions.

1. What am I studying? It will give you an overview of the key themes within organizational behaviour (OB) to help you understand what they are and give you an overview of how they connect. It is useful to read this as it will give you a good understanding of the key theories you will cover and the underlying disciplines that they are based on.

2. How do I study OB? Studying OB is not simply taking in a series of theories that can then be reproduced in an essay or an exam. To gain a higher grade and really understand OB requires the ability to think critically, to question your own assumptions, and to be able to apply the theory to real-life contexts. Throughout this chapter we will look at some of these skills and how you can develop them, including the importance of critical thinking, the transition to degree level, and some top tips that will help you succeed in this subject.

Introducing organizational behaviour

> **Running case:** Transitions and new beginnings—Simon Chance starts his reign
>
> It is 7:45 am and Simon Chance, the newly installed Chief Executive of Junction Hotel and president of Second-Chance Consortium sits at his desk surveying his group's latest acquisition.
>
> The Second-Chance Consortium has just bought Junction Hotel, an upmarket, city-centre hotel with a proud tradition of strong customer service and a traditional approach. In its heyday people would flock to the hotel for its high-class service, great food, and friendly, but formal, approach. Those days, however, are long gone and the hotel has undergone numerous changes of ownership. With paint peeling off the walls, worn carpets, and an antiquated computer system, Chance knows that Junction Hotel is in need of some real investment.
>
> Chance's office is a bit like Junction Hotel—faded glory. A dark green leather chair from the 1940s sits in the corner—stylish but uncomfortable. Instead, Chance decides to use a chair from Ikea—not the most elegant design, but far more practical. The room is oak-clad, but some of the wooden panels are loose and a couple now have gaps in between them, 'I must fix that', Chance muses. 'This place is a mess, nothing works properly. I am sure we can turn it around'.
>
> The Second-Chance Consortium is a venture capitalist company specializing in turning failed businesses into profitable enterprises. Led by Simon Chance, a former footballer who retired because of injury, Chance reinvented himself as a business entrepreneur. Teaming up with his former agent and self-styled *business guru* Phil Weaver, Chance has led the consortium for six years, starting with the local football team and gradually building up a portfolio of successfully transformed firms. Chance feels confident that he can make the hotel a success. 'They just need strong leadership and a good strategy', he thinks. 'I am sure that we can succeed here'.

At first glance running an organization seems a straightforward operation. If you watch a television programme you might get the impression that all you need is the right product, marketing, and finance and you will make money and be successful. Equally, you might look at your own boss or the manager of a football team and think, 'why don't they just tell them to get on with it—if I was in charge we could quickly sort it out'. Yet, in practice, OB is more complicated.

Organizations can be difficult, challenging places, largely because they involve people. People can be unpredictable and complex as they have their own agendas (desire to be seen as a success, fear of failure , etc.), beliefs (e.g. this is the right way to do things), identities (e.g. I am an accountant and this is how I do things), practices, and habits, all of which shape how they act.

To manage, or even work alongside, people you need to be able to understand how they think, what motivates them, what increases their commitment, how to organize them, and how to ensure they act in an ethical and sustainable way (Figure 1.1). Working with, and managing, people, therefore, is likely to be one of the most difficult and challenging things that you do.

Figure 1.1 The way individuals are managed.

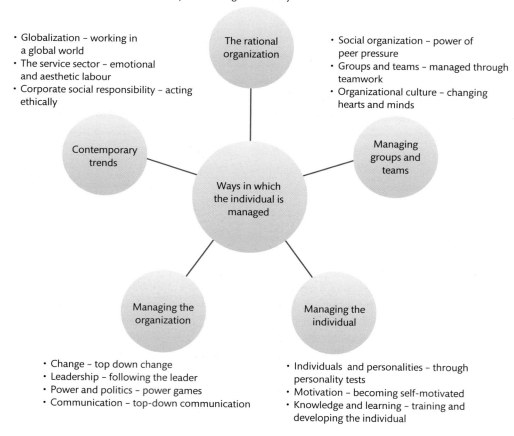

- Bureaucratic procedures – following rules and regulation
- Taylorism – following set work procedures
- Rational organization today – Rational principles spread throughout society

The rational organization

- Globalization – working in a global world
- The service sector – emotional and aesthetic labour
- Corporate social responsibility – acting ethically

Contemporary trends

- Social organization – power of peer pressure
- Groups and teams – managed through teamwork
- Organizational culture – changing hearts and minds

Managing groups and teams

Ways in which the individual is managed

Managing the organization

Managing the individual

- Change – top down change
- Leadership – following the leader
- Power and politics – power games
- Communication – top-down communication

- Individuals and personalities – through personality tests
- Motivation – becoming self-motivated
- Knowledge and learning – training and developing the individual

People are, therefore, at the heart of this book; particularly how they are managed, motivated, trained, led, and communicated with. At the individual level we examine their personality, motivation, and learning; at the group level, how they are managed through teams and groups; and, at the organizational level, how they are led, impacted by power and politics, and the organization's culture.

OB is also about how organizations are structured and run through systems and procedures, as well as how they relate to the wider, globalized world. Furthermore it is about society—or, more precisely, the impact that organizations have on the people that work for them, the communities around them, and society as a whole. It examines how organizations operate globally and also impact, for good and ill, society and the planet.

To study OB, therefore, is to really begin to understand how and why things happen at work, what is the most effective way of achieving things, and what impact this has on the people that work for organizations and the societies in which they operate.

Running case: Understanding the complexity—our fictional case study, Junction Hotel

From:	Phil Weaver
Sent:	2 September
To:	Simon Chance
Subject:	Junction Hotel Report

Hi Simon

I have done a full survey of the hotel, looking back at its accounts for the last five years and surveying the building, kitchen and staff. Having stayed in the hotel overnight as part of the mystery shopper exercise I found the staff courteous and friendly, but the systems slow and cumbersome. Checking-in took 20 minutes as they had lost my registration details, and we had to walk to the restaurant in order to pay my bill as the 'machine was not working'. The rooms were comfortable and fairly clean, but did seem to be of an inconsistent standard. I must say that the food at the restaurant was excellent and shows real class, but service was slow.

Overall, this hotel shows potential but there is much to improve. They are quite disorganized, some staff seem unmotivated and unclear in their tasks, and the service, while polite and professional, is not what you would expect.

Speak soon

Phil

Chance turns to the main report. The Second-Chance Consortium always create a comprehensive report when they take over a failing venture and collect good management data so that they can work out what to improve. Chance reads about the hotel's history and is interested to learn that back in its heyday, Junction Hotel hosted some stars from the stage and screen, its restaurant won awards, and it had successful conference facilities. As he reads more of the report, however, his mood changes. 'This won't be a quick fix', he thinks, looking in detail at the problems that Weaver identified: poor systems, unmotivated staff, erratic schedules, no clear identity or purpose to the hotel, and running at a loss for the last five years. 'We need to sort this place out', Chance thinks staring out of the window. 'I'll get Weaver on the phone and work out our plan'.

What do you think are the key challenges that Simon Chance faces in transforming Junction Hotel?

Visit the Online Resource Centre to read the full report.

The complexity of organizations is often best understood in the context of familiar situations. In this book we will do this through our innovative fictional running case study, Junction Hotel. Instead of seeing theories as dry abstract models, in this book we use them as ways to make sense of the challenges the characters face. Through this case study we will learn about the hotel's characters, their personalities, backgrounds, experiences, and the dilemmas they face. We will see their emotions, reactions, and different interpretations of the same event.

Applying theory to real situations is suggested by learning theorists, such as Kolb and Gibbs, to be far more effective. It helps us understand real dilemmas and challenges that managers, workers, or society face. Just think of it this way: a manager does not try to motivate their staff because it says that they should do it in a textbook; rather, motivation becomes an area of interest because they are facing a problem that they want to solve. Therefore, to gain a richer understanding of OB we need to explore how these interventions would occur in practice. So, as you read the theory in this book try relating it to your own experiences, cases you know from real life, and to our fictional case, Junction Hotel.

What is organizational behaviour?

So, what is involved in running and working in organizations? This book will be divided into five themes, each with their own focus and issues.

1. The rational organization.
2. Managing groups and teams.
3. Managing the individual.
4. Managing the organization.
5. Contemporary trends.

As we will see, these themes offer us a different perspective on what goes on within organizations and how to manage them (Figure 1.2).

Theme 1: the rational organization

Chapter 2: Bureaucracy

Chapter 3: Taylorism

Chapter 4: Rational organization today

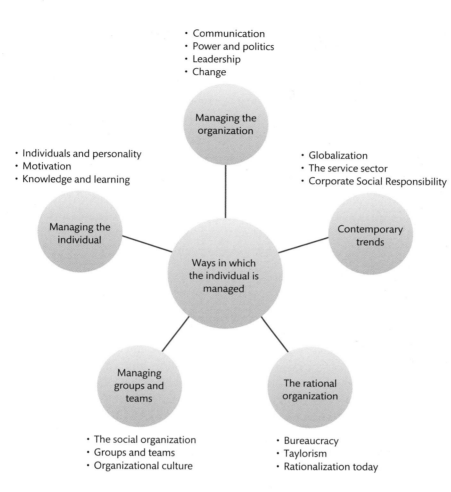

Figure 1.2
Key themes in organizational behaviour.

- Communication
- Power and politics
- Leadership
- Change

Managing the organization

- Individuals and personality
- Motivation
- Knowledge and learning

Managing the individual

- Globalization
- The service sector
- Corporate Social Responsibility

Contemporary trends

Ways in which the individual is managed

Managing groups and teams

The rational organization

- The social organization
- Groups and teams
- Organizational culture

- Bureaucracy
- Taylorism
- Rationalization today

Running case: 8:15 am Phil Weaver discusses his report with Simon Chance

'We need systems and procedures', Weaver states boldly to Chance, 'like we did at the football club, to make this place run like clockwork.' Weaver animatedly discusses his plans with Chance. 'I've been looking at the booking-in procedure, I'm sure we could make it run quicker by streamlining it. Also, the cleaners seem to be getting away with murder—working slowly without set targets or procedures', he continues hardly taking a breath.

Getting out a grid drawn on a sheet of A3 paper, Weaver lays out targets for every individual and department, with measurements for every aspect of the hotel—from customer satisfaction through to room cleanliness. 'It's another Weaver masterplan', Chance declares excitedly. Impressed, Chance picks up a document entitled 'Streamlining food production', which has detailed step-by-step guides to peeling carrots through to cooking chicken. 'I've only just started', Weaver states. 'I think we should work on the cleaners first. I'm sure that we could come up with detailed ways of doing everything in this hotel to make it run more efficiently.'

Bureaucratic The process of bureaucracy, sometimes used in a derogatory sense.

For well over 100 years, managers have dreamed of creating rational, logical, and efficient organizations. As we will examine in Chapter 2 by creating **bureaucratic** procedures, policies, and practices they aim to create standardized, predictable, and efficient organizations so that management gain maximum control and efficiency over workers.

This ambition for control was exemplified by Fredrick Taylor. As we will see in Chapter 3, Taylor (1911) believed that through scientific analysis he could discover the *one best way* of performing every task and through this approach create a more efficient, productive, and rational way of working.

As we will examine in Chapter 4 such an approach continues to underpin so much of what we do today, from fast-food chains, such as McDonalds, and hotels like Travelodge to the way in which you take out your library books. This rational approach has come to dominate the thinking of much of Western capitalism. Indeed, sociologist George Ritzer (2011) has described our society as **McDonalized**, where the principles of the fast-food restaurant, and therefore rational production, have come to dominate more and more parts of society.

McDonaldization (of society) The principles of efficiency, calculability, predictability, and control by which fast-food restaurants are managed and organized, as applied by Ritzer to other contemporary organizations.

This approach has brought with it many positive features, with vast improvements in productivity enabling mass production and has dramatically cut the cost of most consumer goods, making cars, televisions, clothes, and furniture highly affordable to many people.

But while these techniques of organization design achieve efficiencies, they are not without human costs—they can be boring, predictable, and routinized, and an imbalance of power between management and workers is created. It also transfers knowledge and power from the workers to the managers, and creates systems that reduce the worker to a small cog in a very large machine. As Marxist theorist Harry Braverman (1974) argued, this rational approach de-skills the workers and leaves them dehumanized in the process.

Theme 2: managing groups and teams

Chapter 5: The social organization

Chapter 6: Groups and teams

Chapter 7: Organizational culture

Running case: Meg Mortimer prepares herself for the board meeting (8:20 am)

Meg Mortimer sits at her desk in the little cubbyhole-cum-office behind the reception desk busying herself for the new day. 'I've seen it all before', she thinks, as she prepares herself for the staff-wide meeting that morning. 'These new owners will come in with their grand plans and new procedures and try to lay their mark on the hotel, but they are not going to take us away from what we really are', she thinks to herself, 'a caring and considerate hotel based on traditional quality service.'

Mortimer, the second longest-serving member of the Junction Hotel team, started life as a cleaner and has worked through every position in the hotel to eventually become one of the senior managers. 'Owners come and go', she thinks, 'but the Junction Hotel way will outlive any of them.'

While the principles and practice of the rational or formal organization continue to be highly popular, over the last eighty years there has been increasing recognition of the influence that the informal side of the organization has on actual practice. The informal organization sits beneath the surface, impacting what goes on in quite powerful, but often invisible, ways.

We will start with the **Hawthorne studies** in Chapter 5 and examine how they claimed to have 'discovered' that people are social beings who are influenced by the *social norms* of their peer group. Elton Mayo (1949) proposed that organizations should be seen as social spaces rather than machines, full of people with feelings and desires.

Chapter 6 will develop this view illustrating how **groups and teams** have become increasingly important ways of managing people and increasing productivity. However, teamwork can be challenging, as it often fails to work as effectively as it might. Models such as Belbin's theory of group membership (2010) present techniques to make teams more effective.

Finally, in Chapter 7 we look at the social phenomenon of organizational culture—the behaviours, language, stories, and symbols of an organization that are enacted through the groups and teams within the organization. Again, we will see that culture is something that organizations seek to manage, but, some argue, it is to a large degree beyond their control.

> **Hawthorne studies** A series of studies which ran from 1924 into the late 1930s. Widely credited with discovering the human side of the organization.
>
> **Group** A collection of people with a sense of shared identity and something in common but *not* with a shared purpose
>
> **Team** A group who meet together with a common purpose and some degree of mutual interdependence

Theme 3: managing the individual

Chapter 8: Individuals and personality

Chapter 9: Motivation

Chapter 10: Knowledge and learning

Running case: Linda Wilkinson, Domestic Manager, arrives at work (8:30 am)

Linda Wilkinson makes her way hurriedly across the car park of Junction Hotel, grabbing hold of her briefcase. 'Flipping traffic,' she mutters under her breath, 'the school run will be the death of me.' As she rushes past the boardroom window, she notices a man in his mid-50s staring into the distance. 'Is that Simon Chance,' she wonders to herself, 'the new owner of Junction Hotel, and who's he with?', looking at a smaller, earnest man pointing aggressively at some charts. As she does so, she catches a glimpse of herself in the window. Tall, blonde, and still quite elegant—or so her friends tell her—the 40-something mother of two notices the vomit stain left on her jacket's left shoulder by Sam, her youngest, as she dropped him off at nursery this morning. 'Grrrrh', she declares, slightly louder than she had intended. 'This is the last thing I need today', she mutters. Her slight outburst alerts the man who looks up at her. Trying to subtly hide her shoulder Wilkinson smiles positively at him even though today she feels anything but positive. 'This is a big day', she thinks to herself, 'I need to make a good impression and present myself as the manager-in-waiting.'

In the third theme we focus our attention on individuals within the organization and how they are managed. We begin in Chapter 8 by looking at theories of **personality**—what are the traits that make us all different and can they be measured? We see how managers use such theories to create 'personality tests' that are used in procedures such as recruitment and appraisal.

> **Personality** A set of characteristics and behaviour displayed by any individual.

Seeing people as having differences is also important when examining what motivates people to work harder; what motivates workers is the subject of Chapter 9. Maslow's hierarchy of needs (1943) is a familiar tool for analysing human **motivation**, but we discover that motivation is, in fact, a much more complex phenomenon—individual differences can relate not only to factors of personality, but also to the social factors that they bring in from their life outside the workplace.

Finally, we turn our attention to **knowledge and learning** in Chapter 10. We will see that in the knowledge-intensive economy how knowledge is developed, captured, and distributed is an increasingly vital aspect that differentiates successful firms from those that fail. What, though, do we mean by knowledge? Is it a set of facts that can be learned or is it something that we acquire through experience?

Theme 4: managing the organization

Chapter 11: Change

Chapter 12: Leadership

Chapter 13: Power and politics

Motivation The will and desire that a person has to engage in a particular behaviour or perform a particular task.

Knowledge and learning An aspect of organizational behaviour which emphasizes the importance of information, understanding and practical skills for organizational success. In particular it examines the capacity of the organization to share this knowledge in effective ways.

Running case: 10:00 am Simon Chance meets all the staff

At 10:00 am Chance, followed closely by Weaver, walks purposefully into the conference room, reaches the podium, and surveys his expectant audience. All the staff of Junction Hotel are gathered, somewhat nervously, to hear from their new owner and Chief Executive Officer.

Chance starts by introducing himself, his consortium, and why they bought the hotel. He says that it has a proud tradition of quality customer service, but the world is changing and the hotel needs to change with it. He, with all their help, is going to transform this place, to bring it back to its former glory.

'Junction Hotel is going to feel like a new place', he goes on to say, 'a new culture where hard work gets rewarded and the best people succeed. This is a clean slate for everyone and I am going to set the hotel on a new course.'

'This is an exciting time for all of us', Chance continues warming to his theme, 'but let's be under no illusions, it is going to be challenging. Some of you are going to find the changes that we put in place difficult. Some of you might not even want to come with us in this new direction. I respect that. But we have a direction', he warned, 'and we will not be blown off course.'

'Over the next few months we will all need to pull together. Working together, I'm sure we can make Junction Hotel great again.'

Weaver then got up, unravelled his A3 sheets, and started to lay out the new direction for Junction Hotel.

Change The process by which an organization changes in practices, processes, culture, etc. in a planned or emergent fashion.

Our fourth theme focuses on how the organization as a whole is managed. In a sense, the whole book is about organizational **change**, but we particularly focus on this topic in Chapter 11. We will see through that chapter that there are two major models of change: the emergent and planned approaches. While these focus predominantly on the role of the senior managers in organizations, we will see that how the rest of the staff respond to that change is critical in the organization's success. We also look at how theories of individual learning and development contribute to successful change and development on an organizational scale.

This brings us on to the issue of **leadership** and followership in Chapter 12. Leaders are seen as powerful people, vital for the success of the organization. While numerous theories have sought to identify what makes a great leader, recent theory has focused on the importance of followers for organizational success.

Far from the rational organization we begin the book with, Chapter 13 will examine the more messy realities of organizational life, where organizational decisions are products of **power games and politics** between competing people (e.g. senior managers) or interest groups (e.g. workers and managers).

Our final chapter under this theme is communication. We will see that communication is fraught with difficultly and represents a major challenge to effective organization.

Theme 5: contemporary trends

Chapter 14: Communication

Chapter 15: Globalization

Chapter 16: The service sector

Chapter 17: Corporate social responsibility

Running case: the meeting ends and all the staff leave the conference room (10:48 am)

As they filter out of the meeting, Graham Effingham, Junction Hotel's award winning chef, goes on his phone and posts a quick blog post on his site. This is where he goes undercover and says what is really going on in the hotel, but without ever saying exactly where it is.

Just come out the staff meeting with our new owners—arrrgh what a load of old clap-trap. I won't say the name of the new owners but all I can say is I think they have no chance.

They gave us all this talk about transforming the business, making it a place that people will be proud to come to and we would all feel excited by working for it. How it would be a hard journey, but if we all stick together (which I read as following what they say) then we will all be a success.

Nonsense—we've all been through this before with the last owners; it won't last. This lot, though, say they have a plan. The owners side-kick had all these charts and tables about how we compare to other hotels—the man has an obsession with graphs and stuff, I can tell you. He kept on comparing us to more 'efficient' hotels, like Travelodge, saying that we can learn from them, or this European one Etap. It seems like a race to the bottom, I can tell you. Sounds like they are trying to turn us into a sweatshop!

Then, as we all left, we were given our department's A3—a set of targets that we are meant to achieve over the year. Mine is to cut the cost of the food by 30% and make it 23% quicker. 23% quicker, what the hell does that mean? I have to come back in a few weeks with a plan as to how we will do this and keep the costs 'reasonable', otherwise they are going to look into getting our food from one of these catering suppliers. They only do processed food, not the direction we want to go!

In the final theme we turn our attention to the contemporary issues that face organizations. We start, in Chapter 15, by looking at the theme of **globalization**. As the recent global

---

Leadership The process of leading or influencing the behaviour of others. In the broadest definition, it can be carried out by anyone in the organization.

Power games and politics The process where one individual or group tries to gain advantage or get another individual or group to do things that they might otherwise not intend to do.

Globalization Defined in many different ways, globalization is where activities take place on an increasingly global scale.

recession has demonstrated, we live, perhaps more than ever, in a highly interconnected and integrated world. Large multinationals have grown to become hugely powerful—in some cases bigger than many countries. However, the globalized economy brings with it its own challenges for management. As Hofstede (1980) noted, national culture still remains strong and presents multinational companies with significant challenges in managing the differences between cultures.

Chapter 16 looks at the rising **service sector**, which, in some senses, represents a continuation and, indeed, intensification of the rational approach we saw in the first theme. However, because it is customer facing it carries the additional challenge of emotional and aesthetic labour in which employees have to manage their feelings and appearances.

The recent financial crisis and corporate scandals have put the spotlight on our final theoretical chapter, **corporate social responsibility** (CSR). We will see some of the key ethical challenges that organizations face, how they respond to them, and the criticisms that campaigners and activists have about these responses.

Service sector Non-manufacturing industries, such as retail, leisure, transport, finance and media.

Corporate social responsibility A contested term with different interpretations but generally taken to be social and environmental responsibility corporations have towards their stakeholders.

Organizational behaviour— an interconnected discipline

Running case: (11:15 am) Weaver and Chance meet again in the boardroom

'Well that went well', said Weaver in a confident way, 'I think we really hammered home our message. This place needs a good shake-up and we're the people to do it. With our new targets and management practices Junction Hotel is going to be a very different place in a years' time when we have transformed them'.

Meanwhile, Linda Wilkinson is less jubilant as she talks to Meg by reception. 'They talk very positively', Linda says with a sense of despondency, 'but they cannot just come here and impose their views on us like that.'

In our final chapter we draw all the issues together and look forward to the future challenges that face organizations. We will see that, while we have discussed all these topics as discrete entities, in practice they are highly interconnected and rely on each other.

It is, therefore, important to be aware of the connections between the themes as you read the chapters and prepare to write your essay or answer your exam.

Key underlying theories

As will be apparent from the discussion OB covers a wide range of issues. To cover these issues it draws on a wide range of underlying disciplines (Figure 1.3).

- Sociology explores how society shapes people. It helps us understand that no action takes place in a social vacuum and helps us appreciate how individual experiences are part of broader society.

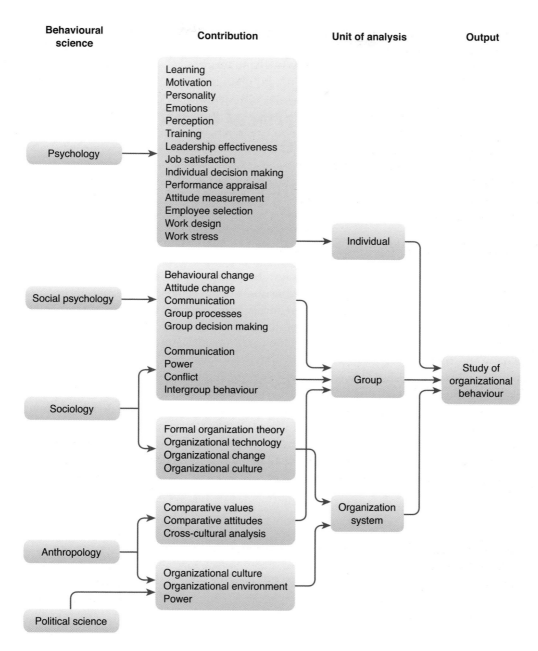

Figure 1.3
The underlying disciplines.

Source: Robbins, Stephen P.; Judge, Timothy A., *Essentials of Organizational Behaviour*, 10th Edition, © 2010., p. 5. Reprinted by permission of Pearson Education, Inc., Upper Saddle River, NJ.

- Psychology seeks to measure, explain, and sometimes change human behaviour. It is often considered the science of the mind.

- Social psychology bridges sociology and psychology, and tries to understand the impact the group has on the outlook of the individual.

- Anthropology examines rites and rituals that shape how groups and cultures work.

- Political science examines the role of power within organizations.

Visit the Online Resource Centre for deeper analysis of the underlying theories.

It is important as you read through the book to be aware of the significance of these underlying theories and how they shape OB theories. As you gain more understanding of OB you will be able to distinguish between these underlying theories.

The importance of critical thinking and multiple perspectives

Why there are no right answers in organizational behaviour

While they represent different theoretical disciplines, all the theories within OB attempt to explain human behaviour, and human behaviour is complex and subjective.

First, people do not act in predictable ways, share the same outlook, or always behave as we would expect. Secondly, it is difficult to measure human behaviour scientifically because it is not controllable like, for instance, chemicals; people are not standardized or predictable. Thirdly, the different theoretical traditions each have their own questions, areas of interest, and debates, and, consequently, look at different features of organizational life. Finally, the 'right answer' depends on the beliefs about society in whose interests organizations should serve—either managers/shareholders or employees/society (we have more to say about this in the following sections).

Consequently, within OB there are *no right answers*. This does not mean that the theories presented here are incorrect or that they are based on poor reasoning. In fact, there are many fascinating and insightful accounts of the subject. Rather, there are *no definitive answers* to the issues that we discuss. This makes OB a fascinating, although potentially somewhat complex, subject.

Real life case: executive pay

The importance of different beliefs can be illustrated through the current debate over executive pay. In recent years this has become a hot topic in business, the media, and among organizational theorists, causing considerable controversy. The average pay of executives of FTSE100 companies (the top 100 companies quoted on the UK stock exchange) in 2010/11 was £3.5 million, up 32% from the previous year (http://blog.manifest.co.uk/2011/05/5053.html).

Perspective 1: business leaders deserve their money

Many from within the business community have spoken in favour of high pay. They argue there is a 'war for talent' (Peacock, 2010), with top people able to travel anywhere in the world; therefore, firms have to pay competitive salaries and bonus packages in order to attract and retain the best people. Business leaders, such as Royal Bank of Scotland's Stephen Hester (Source: Author interview with Stephen Hester, Royal Bank of Scotland, February 2012), argue that they do not decide their own salaries and they ▶

are merely getting paid what the market demands (see Chapter 12). Holders of this perspective argue that business leaders have a lot of responsibility and their decisions are critical in the long-term success of a firm.

Perspective 2: executives are overpaid and create a divided society

Increasingly, there are many protest groups, unions, religious leaders, some academics, and politicians challenging the amount that these top business leaders get paid. They claim the significance of business Chief Executive Offiers are overestimated and they are paid disproportionately high for what they do. Critics of high executive pay argue that these executives are paid, on average, some 120 times more than their employees, 35 times more than hospital consultants and 162 times more than the average teacher (High Pay Commission, 2011). Such high pay levels create imbalances, and inequalities create an unfair society. Furthermore, the committees that decide on these pay levels are often made up of people who come from similar backgrounds and are not representative of the shareholders, employees, or wider society. As such, they approve levels of pay that most people would not find acceptable.

What are your initial views on these two perspectives? Which one do you think is right? Why? What is it that leads you to this perspective? Why do you think you hold that view?

You may have a view on each of these, but they are both correct in their own regard. We cannot really choose which we think is our preferred approach until we see the assumptions that underlie them (summarized in Table 1.1).

Here we see, by analysing these positions, that the views expressed arise because they hold fundamentally different assumptions about the world. Your job, therefore, in conducting this analysis is to understand these underlying assumptions first and then make a judgement based upon them. It is only by actually understanding these assumptions that it is possible to really make a judgement on the validity of the positions that theorists hold.

Table 1.1 The underlying assumptions of the two perspectives

	Perspective 1	Perspective 2
Role of leader	Managers have the right to manage. Leaders are central to directing the organization	The over-emphasis on leaders downplays the key role that the rest of the employees play
Hierarchy	The leader is the key person within the organization, and can make the difference between success and failure	The role of the leader is overstated and we tend to fetishize the leader as the saviour of the organization when, in reality, they are dependent on their employees
Purpose of organization	Organizations should exist to make profit for shareholders	Organizations should exist to create freedom, autonomy, and fulfilment for everyone involved
Overview	Ultimately, Perspective 1 believes in the free market and capitalism, and executive pay is justified if it improves the share price	Ultimately, perspective 2 rejects the assumptions of the free market, arguing that wider issues, such as the impact on society should be considered

The importance of analysis

It would be easy to read the preceding section and think 'well anything goes in this subject. If there are no right answers then it is just about opinion and all I need to do is put forward my opinion, as it is as valid as anyone else's'. While tempting, we believe such a perspective is dangerous for a number of reasons. First, the ideas developed in this book are based upon years of research built up through numerous investigations, theoretical reflections and analysis, and argued through many lectures, articles, and books. They are, therefore, more than simply opinions, but built on reasoned arguments and investigations into actual practice. Secondly, they draw on (as we have seen in the preceding section) a variety of different underlying perspectives that are built on deep theoretical foundations. These are more than simply personal opinions or gut reactions, but reasoned arguments based on fundamentally different ways of thinking about and discussing the world. Finally, as we will explore in more detail in the following sections, these perspectives are built on wider theoretical reflections about the nature of societies and the role that organizations should play in them.

Study skills: the difference between personal opinion and academically informed perspective

My opinion:

- using own taken-for-granted assumptions
- based on gut reaction and personal opinion
- I think that. . . .

Academically-informed perspective:

- challenge received opinion and taken-for-granted assumptions
- based on theoretical reasoning, evidence, academic literature, and evaluation of competing perspectives
- based on the evidence we can see that. . . .

Therefore, while at first glance informed critical analysis might seem like simply stating your own opinion, in practice developing an academically-informed perspective is more rigorous, thoughtful, and evidence-based. While your personal opinion might, therefore, be a starting point, given that it begins with common-sense assumptions rather than evidence and theory, you should be prepared to reconsider these views. Indeed, often the best essays are by students who have read and really engaged with the academic arguments.

OB as an area to study is therefore what we sometimes call *contested*. There are multiple perspectives because the issues that we are interested in cannot be 'solved' in any straightforward way and, consequently, it is an area of constant debate. The skill of a good analyst is to uncover these underlying assumptions, and to see how they inform the research and how it differs from alternative perspectives. One of the central study skills that you will need throughout your time studying OB (and at university as a whole) is to be able to uncover the key underlying assumptions that inform the theories.

The need to develop critical thinking

Developing your critical thinking skills is a long-term process of acquiring skills and also a mindset of approaching the world in a different way. As we can see from the real life case here it can be highly beneficial as it helps you to think more deeply and to be more innovative in your approach—something that employers throughout the world are increasingly looking for.

Real life case: innovative thinking in Singapore

The need to always be right and to find the right answers is increasingly being criticized in countries like Singapore. While for a long time their approach has been hugely successful in attracting multinational firms and making the country prosperous because 'Singaporeans are hardworking, loyal, and well-educated' (Economy Watch, 2011a), as the economy has developed questions are increasingly being raised about their ability to undertake more creative and innovative jobs. Recently, Steve Wozniak (Apple's co-founder) suggested that a rigid education system could stifle creativity and innovation, for example: 'Singapore, teachers and employers are caught up with "the right answer", instead of the journey to get there and the creative solutions to other problems.' Wozniak's statement suggests that their education system, which praises students when getting the right answers, is, therefore, less able to prepare them for the more innovative thinking that creative jobs require. Being innovative and being able to solve complex problems (which people often produce) requires the ability to be prepared to think differently, to question one's assumptions, and to be able to cope with uncertainty and doubt.

One of us (Daniel) discovered this when teaching in Singapore. At the end of a week of intensively teaching OB to a group of Singaporean undergraduates, one of them came over to say that they both loved and hated the course. It made them think differently and question what they knew, and at the same time made them feel uncertainty and doubt. Studying OB can get us all to feel this way.

Source: Economy Watch (2011a, 2011b).

So how do I develop critical thinking skills?

Teaching yourself to question things and also to learn in a different way can be a difficult, but exciting, process. At university your lecturers will want you to demonstrate a higher level of critical analysis than you may have encountered before and also a different approach to thinking. Rather than simply recounting the strengths and weaknesses of particular theories, they will be looking for you to look at the wider implications for our understanding of broader issues in society. This requires deeper thinking and engagement, opening yourself up to competing perspectives and interpretations of the world, and a readiness to engage in complex ideas. This can be particularly challenging given, on the surface, OB seems little more than 'common sense'.

One example of the value of critical and analytical thinking is that it encourages us to go beyond these general assumptions to really examine the implications of these theories, not just for management practice, but for society as well. This moves us not to simply ask pragmatic questions, such as how things are done, but also wider ones, such as in whose interest they are conducted. This requires alternative ways of thinking.

Real life case: thinking outside the box

One of our students describes how she has struggled with wanting to find the *right* answer. 'I am a bit of a perfectionist really and I want to know the answers. At A level I studied History—where there were a lot of dates and facts, Law—where there were many cases, and Business (where there was a lot of accounting)—where there were right answers. At university, studying organizational behaviour, I have realized that there are no right answers and I need to think outside the box.'

You might find studying OB difficult and challenging, particularly if you come from a scientific or mathematics background, which tend to have 'correct' and 'true' answers. For many students this desire for the right answers and *anxiety* about getting the wrong answer leads them to want to memorize and learn facts about theories, as these seem more certain and understandable. For instance, we have seen countless students put in details about when key theorists were born and when they died, or long descriptions of a theory, presumably believing this is the 'correct information'. However, it demonstrates very little understanding and often has a negative impact on their grade.

To really develop critical thinking requires asking different types of questions and focusing on different areas (Figure 1.4).

At the surface level is **description** (Figure 1.5). At this level you simply describe the theory, giving details of what it is, how it works, and its basic concepts. You will discuss the basic facts, models, or theories, and you will need to show familiarity with the theories, but little more.

However, this level largely involves repeating back the theory. You do not need to do much thinking as you are merely reproducing what you have been told in lectures or in this book. You need this level as it is the foundation for the subject, but you need to remember it is not enough at degree level.

The next level down is **explanation**, comprehension, and **evidence**. At this level you show that you really understand the theory, its relevance to the question, and to real life practice. To do this you can apply the theory to an organization and show the implications for organizational practice. You can also identify the relevant points of the theory to the actual question asked. This shows a far deeper level of understanding as it takes a stronger appreciation of what the theory entails in order to apply it to practice.

While this level shows a greater level of insight, it does little to question the assumptions that underpin the theories. It simply takes things for granted and does not show the deeper level of thinking that is necessary to make judgements about a theme.

Description A piece of writing that describes the theory or case study with little attempt at providing analysis. Often considered more superficial and therefore in student coursework results in lower grades.

Explanation In academic writing the ability to explain a theory or perspective.

Evidence In academic writing, support for claims made.

Description	Recalling and describing the theory: Multiple choice questions, facts, recall, definitions, and models
Explanation	Applying to real life and own experience, and what the theory means for organizations in practice
Analysis	Considering strengths and weaknesses, exploring alternative viewpoints and the underlying assumptions
Critical analysis	How the theory challenges our fundamental understanding of OB. In whose interest is the theory?

Figure 1.4 Levels of critical thinking.

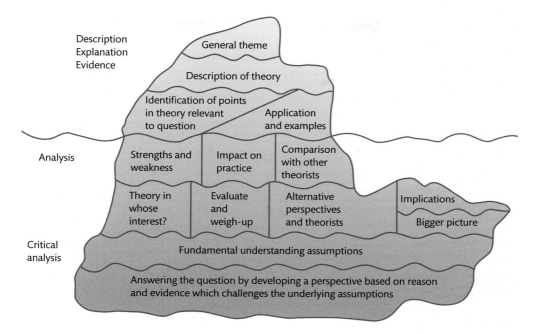

Figure 1.5 The critical thinking iceberg.

Dropping below the surface is where we begin to **analyse** the theory. This level looks at the theory's strengths and weaknesses, identifying the advantages and disadvantages of the theory, or the benefits and drawbacks that the theory offers. This form of analysis is common at post-16 qualifications (e.g. A level) and demonstrates a stronger appreciation of the theory itself and how it works in practice.

The deepest level of **critical analysis** includes synthesis, comparison, evaluation, and creativity. It requires a much higher level of thinking because it does not merely assume that the theory is correct, but looks as much at what the author does not say and who it impacts. Because of its greater complexity and more advanced level of understanding, this approach often gets higher marks. To achieve this you need to really understand the theory and its implications, read between the lines, and not accept things at face value, but to question everything. This also involves judgement, weighing-up of the relative merits of the theory, and then drawing conclusions to see if the perspective offered is fair and valid.

To develop your critical thinking, the following questions are useful when reading academic theory:

- What are its strengths and weaknesses?
- How does it compare with other theories?
- What evidence is it based on and is it reliable?
- What are the implications of the theory to practice?
- What are the underlying assumptions?
- Whose interest does it serve?
- What is its implication to answering the question?

As we can see, to really get to the heart of the issue and understand its significance we need to go beyond merely describing a theory and seek to understand its underlying assumptions.

Analyse Widely associated with deeper intellectual thinking it is the process of breaking things down into their constituent parts, investigating the underlying cause or basic principles.

Critical analysis To question the underlying assumptions of a perspective. In OB this may have particular emphasis on how power and inequality occur.

Degree-level analysis

Throughout this discussion you may have thought that much of this talk of analysis is familiar to you, as you have heard the terms analysis, evaluation, and application. While post-16 (A level) uses these terms, we require deeper and more engaged thinking to do well at degree level.

For instance, at post-16 *analysis* often consists of describing the strengths and weaknesses of a particular theory, and may compare it to other theories; at university, we are after a deeper examination of the implications of the theory to the fundamental assumptions of the discipline. Table 1.2 summarizes these differences.

Table 1.2 The differences between post-16 and degree thinking

	Post-16	Degree level
How you use the theory	Reproduce material taught and show you understand which theorists are relevant	Digest the material and demonstrate understanding of its implications
Markers are looking for	Correct answers to hit the mark scheme	A critical response to the literature
Use of theory	Show understanding of the theory and both sides of the argument	Making an argument by writing within a school of thought, and using accepted concepts and theoretical tools
Analysis is	Strengths and weaknesses of a theory	Questioning the underlying assumptions and their implications for the question
Evaluation is	Demonstrating understanding, comparing and weighing-up of both sides of the argument	Providing own response to the question based on the theories in question
Material used	Given specific texts to investigate	Go out and undertake your own research
Paragraph structure	Key points, quote to back up, and then evaluate	Links together to make an overall argument that fully answers the question

Ultimately, at degree level, the emphasis is on making an argument, based on theory, that responds directly to the question asked.

Real life case: making the transition to degree-level analysis

Having recently received back comments on her assignment for her OB module, one of our students has come to realize that the type of analysis required at degree level is deeper than she had previously been asked to do for A level. 'Having read the assignment I thought that I was doing analysis by listing the strengths and weaknesses as we were asked to do at A level. I now see that this was only part of what analysing means and you want us to think a lot deeper at degree level.'

The central intention here is that you will become independent critical thinkers who are able to develop arguments through critical analysis of others' positions.

Critical thinking: mainstream and critical views

Critical thinking can also mean a political view that asks you to question the underlying assumptions and values of theories for the purposes of understanding and challenging their impact on society, e.g. workers, the environment, and is seen in opposition to mainstream theory. (Used in this sense, this is often called the 'critical management studies perspective'.)

The **mainstream**, or dominant view, represents the *general established management thinking* about management. It is primarily interested in creating theory that helps understand management practice better and generally to improve it. The mainstream perspective assumes organizations exist to make profit and that the goal of management theory is to achieve performance, efficiency, productivity, order, and control. Furthermore, it supports hierarchy, managers' right to manage, and the idea that firms exist primarily for shareholders.

The **critical** view argues that these mainstream views systematically favour *elite* interests at the expense of *disadvantaged* groups, for instance managers over workers; men over women; profit over society; and economic growth over the environment; arguing that this limits freedom of all (Grey and Willmott, 2005). The critical perspective suggests that there is a 'dark side' to organizations that these mainstream accounts rarely discuss.

While the critical perspective might seem negative, its proponents would argue that it is aiming at a more positive society. The critical perspective argues organizations *should* exist for freedom and fulfilment, creativity and expression, and for the benefit of society, not just for shareholders. Critical perspectives therefore aim for emancipation (freedom from slavery). This form of critical thinking can be hard—it challenges many of our basic assumptions of the world, but it can also be highly transformative.

> **Mainstream** The dominant or accepted view that emphasizes managers' right to manage and the central objective of organizations to make profits for shareholders.

> **Critical** (as in 'critical management studies') A critical perspective , among other things, draws on Marxist theory and seeks to challenge the assumptions of mainstream management theory by stressing the impact that it has on employees and society.

For whose benefit should the theory of OB be written? Management? Shareholders? Employees? Customers/Clients? Society?

Study skills: questioning taken-for-granted assumptions

When reading a theory, instead of taking the ideas for granted, the following questions can give the essay a more critical perspective.

- What are the underlying perspectives presented in the text?
- What are the taken-for-granted assumptions contained (but not expressed) in the theory?
- Whose interests are being served by this perspective?
- What issues are being glossed over or downplayed?
- What are the implications for power and control?
- What are the effects of the theory on people, society, and the planet?
- What other perspectives have been downplayed or ignored by this theory?

Employability Skills: the importance of critical thinking

Most people who study business and management degrees do get a job. Yet, often we do not really consider what we need to do in order to achieve this. As an employer has stated in a fairly recent report: 'Academic qualifications are the first tick in the box and then we move on. Today we simply take them for granted' (Brown et al., 2003: 120). Therefore, while getting a good degree is essential, on its own—in this increasingly competitive market—it is not enough.

So, what is it that employers are looking for? While there can never be a definitive list, some of the common requirements of graduate recruiters are:

- professionalism or work ethic
- oral and written communication
- teamwork and collaboration skills
- critical-thinking or problem-solving skills
- generic skills rather than subject-specific skills
- abstraction (theorizing, using models, metaphors, and formulae)
- systems thinking (seeing the part in the context of the wider whole)
- experimentation (intuition and analysis)
- collaboration (communication and teamwork skills).   Reich (1991, 2002)

You might be reading this and be thinking 'but I have just got to university why should I be thinking about this now?'. Our experience, having been students ourselves and talking to thousands of students through teaching, is that your time at university goes by very quickly. While the next three or four years may seem a long way off, this time will fly by and you will wonder what you did with your time at university. Our key advice is that you start thinking about this stuff **now**. You will find that your first year will pass very quickly and you will miss a golden opportunity that this first year at university presents: to begin to acquire the skills, experiences, knowledge, and self-awareness that will help develop you as a person and as a future employee. There are countless things that you could be doing to boost your experiences so that you are a step ahead when it comes to getting a job.

So how do you start building your employability? Throughout this book we will have a number of employability prompts to get you started thinking about these issues. You should then follow them up with material found in the Online Resource Centre, which will point you in the direction of further reading, activities, and advice that will enable you to construct your CV, and gain skills and experience to help you get ahead. These include:

- self-test questionnaires
- video interviews with employers, students, and recent graduates
- employability tips
  - things to be thinking about now
  - short exercises to do now
- much more advice, and pointers to other websites and material.

The links between study skills and employability skills

While we often think that the skills we need to study are different from those that we will use in a work situation, the links between the two are surprisingly similar, as we can see in Table 1.3.

Table 1.3 The similarities between study skills and employability skills

	Study skill	Employability skill
Time management	Many assignments due at the same time A lot of study time and therefore personal responsibility Juggling paid employment, studying, clubs and societies, and personal responsibilities	Working on numerous projects in which you have to manage your own time and that of others
Synthesis of a lot of complex information	Reading dozens of academic articles and pulling out the key themes, arguments and positions of the authors	Reading numerous reports, background briefings, and market research, and being asked to make sense of it
Working with ambiguous briefs	Getting an assignment brief and needing to work out what you need to do to get a good grade	Being given a loosely-defined task and be told to 'get on with it'
Writing for different audiences	Studying different modules with their various approaches to academic work such as referencing, analysis, and styles	Writing for different managers, your staff, and to clients—all of which have different requirements

Therefore, as you go through your university career it is valuable to develop these study skills as they are often transferrable to a work situation.

Visit the Online Resource Centre for more information on transferable skills.

Employability and study skills: keeping a journal with evidence and examples of the skills you have developed at university and outside, and a diary to reflect what you are learning

When you apply for most graduate jobs you will need to fill in an application form which will ask you for *evidence* that you have hit a number of requirements, such as teamwork, taking initiative, or project management. One way that you can significantly improve your chances is to keep a record of *actual examples* of you meeting any of these criteria. This could be through assignments at university— teamwork, working with different nationalities; or external activities, such as being involved in the football club (planning and organizing as you arrange matches and transport).

Studying OB is particularly useful in this regard as the subject matter deals with many of the key skill areas that you will need at work. Therefore, as you read on topics such as motivation, leadership, and teamwork consider your own experiences and how you can demonstrate examples of actual practice.

Throughout this book we will also offer study skills which offer you opportunities to develop your abilities as a student. As you go through your course it is really helpful to keep a diary in which you can honestly and openly reflect on what you would like to achieve in your working life and how you would like to get there.

Chapter summary

Running case: the day draws to a close

Simon Chance's office (5.50 pm)

As early evening approaches, Simon Chance opens his diary and starts making a few notes to himself about his reflections on his first full day at Junction Hotel. The staff seemed friendly and generally professional, and seemed to take the meeting well. That chef though (Effingham he thinks he's called), looked a bit of a livewire and will need keeping an eye on. Everything here feels slightly chaotic, unmanageable even, Chance considers. Everyone goes about their jobs OK, but from where he is sitting they are not working effectively. It will take some doing to kick this lot into shape.

The bar (10.00 pm)

As the kitchen staff's shift ends, Effingham, Josh, and Toby are sitting round the bar enjoying their evening 'nightcap'. 'What do you think about this new owner?', Josh asks Effingham. Effingham snorts, 'same old management clap-trap, if you ask me. They come out with all these phrases and buzz words, "blue sky thinking, A3s, gold standard customer service", but they don't have a clue what it's really like'. Toby butts in, 'Yeah, I'd love to see him prepping for evening service or doing the breakfast run, then tell me all that management speak really means anything'. 'Yes', Josh smiles, 'it's us who run the show really'.

As we have seen organizations are fundamentally about people, and people can be complex and make organizational life messy. Rather than being rational and logical places, as we often like to believe, they can be full of emotion—pain, joy, excitement, disappointment, hope, fear, and anxiety—competing ambitions, and different perspectives. As such, instead of seeing the theories as abstract and separate from real life, OB is best understood by relating to and applying concrete experience and practice. Our running case study, Junction Hotel, therefore gives you an insight into how theories can play out in practice.

As a consequence, there are no right answers within OB as it is a subjective discipline, born out of various theoretical disciplines and subject to different social and political perspectives. Therefore, to study OB effectively requires critical thinking and questioning, the ability to understand different perspectives, and to seek to challenge your own assumptions.

It is also heavily linked to real practice. The employability and study skills therefore bring some of these issues to life as you develop your abilities for your university and employment career. Keeping a diary and working through the exercises in the book and the Online Resource Centre will help you to maximize your experience and gain a fuller understanding of the subject.

Further reading: to develop your study skills

Cottrell, S. 2011. *Critical thinking skills: developing effective analysis and argument*. **Palgrave Macmillan, Basingstoke.**
This popular study skills book gives some really useful material on the importance of critical thinking and offers practical, as well as theoretical, ideas on how to improve in this area. Reading this will be useful, not only in studying this subject but also to other subjects on your degree course.

Bowell, T., and Kemp, G. 2002. *Critical thinking: A concise guide*. **Routledge, London.**
Another popular study skills book that stresses how to develop and build arguments. It looks at how to assess the strengths of an argument and how to develop your own.

Gallagher, K. 2010. *Skills development for business and management students*. **Oxford University Press, Oxford.**
This study skills guide provides useful ideas on how to develop your all-round skills as a business and management student, including teamwork, presentation, and reading skills.

Bibliography

Belbin, R.M. 2010. *Team Roles at Work*. Butterworth-Heinemann: Oxford.

Brown, P., Hesketh, A., and Williams, S. 2003. Employability in a knowledge-driven economy. *Journal of Education and Work* 16(2): 107–126

Economy Watch. 2011a. The trouble with the Singapore workplace. Available at: http://www.economywatch.com/economy-business-and-finance-news/the-trouble-with-the-singapore-workplace.21-07.html (last accessed 15 June 2012).

Economy Watch. 2011b. Would Apple ever have been created in Singapore? Available at: http://www.economywatch.com/economy-business-and-finance-news/would-apple-ever-have-been-created-in-singapore.10-03.html (last accessed 15 June 2012).

Grey, C., and Willmott, H. (eds) 2005. *Critical Management Studies*. Oxford University Press: Oxford.

High Pay Commission. 2011. *Cheques with Balances: Why Tackling High Pay is in the National Interest*. Final Report of the High Pay Commission.

Hofstede, G.H. 1980. *Culture's consequences: international differences in work-related values*. Sage Publications: Beverly Hills, CA.

Knights, D., Willmott, H. 1999. *Management lives: power and identity in work organizations*. Sage: London.

Manifest. 2011. CEO performance and pay – the weakest link. Available at: http://blog.manifest.co.uk/2011/05/5053.html (last accessed 23 November 2012).

Maslow, A.H. 1943. A theory of human motivation. *Psychological Review* 50(4): 370.

Mayo, E. 1949. *The Social Problems of an Industrial Civilisation*. Routledge: London.

Peacock, L. 2010. War for talent resumes as salaries climb *The Daily Telegraph*. 5 August 2010. Available at: http://www.telegraph.co.uk/finance/jobs/7929183/War-for-talent-resumes-as-salaries-climb.html.

Reich, R. 1991. *The work of nations*. Simon and Schuster: London.

Reich, R. 2002. *The future of success*. Vintage: London.

Ritzer, G. 2011. *The McDonaldization of Society*. Pine Forge Press: Thousand Oaks, CA.

Taylor, F.W. 1911. *The Principles of Scientific Management*. Harper: New York.

Part 1
The rational organization

Rational organizational design and bureaucracy

From direct to impersonal control

Chapter overview and learning outcomes

By the end of this chapter you should be able to:

- describe the main features of bureaucratic organization

- explain how bureaucracy is a form of rational organizational design that helps managers to control organizations as they grow in size

- analyse the negative effects of bureaucracy that Weber described as an 'iron cage'

- describe dysfunctions of bureaucracy, such as red tape and the bureaucratic personality

- analyse the balance between the positive effects of bureaucracy that make large-scale organization possible, and its dysfunctions and negative effects.

List of key theorists

Max Weber	A sociologist who observed the increasing dominance of bureaucracy within society, noting its technical achievements, but also its negative impacts on people
Henri Fayol	An industrialist known for outlining a rational, structured approach to bureaucratic organizational design and administration

List of key terms

Bureaucracy	Official aspects of an organization, such as the hierarchical structure, rules, procedures, and paperwork which allow control to be exerted over the whole organization
Rational organizational design	As championed by Fayol, the design of bureaucratic features in the most technically efficient way so as to achieve the organization's goals
Iron cage of bureaucracy	A phrase which summarizes Weber's critique of bureaucracy and rationality, suggesting that it is inescapable and leads to monotonous, dull routines

Introduction

Running case: 'A disorganized mess'

Simon Chance likes order and being in charge, but after a week with the management team he had inherited after taking over at Junction Hotel, he feels frustrated. 'This place is a disorganized mess', he thinks to himself, 'no one seems to know what they are doing—it's unmanageable.'

The lack of formal organization is highlighted when Chance asks Meg Mortimer, the general manager, for an organization chart. 'Organization chart?', she says with a surprised tone, 'no we don't have one of those, I know everyone here personally and we work together as a friendly little group.'

Mortimer has been at the hotel for 25 years, from when it was a small organization. Although the hotel has grown and new staff have been taken on, she still tries to manage with a personal touch, as if it were still a small group of staff.

Chance soon realizes, however, that Mortimer delegates much of the hands-on management to her deputy, Linda Wilkinson. Wilkinson's role has grown over the years to include responsibility for the reception area, the cleaners, the waiting staff, the maintenance staff, and the fitness centre employees. Wilkinson also processes stock orders and similar paperwork—something she generally does in a rush whenever she finds some time.

While concerned about Wilkinson's workload, Chance also notes that Mortimer can't resist interfering in these everyday decisions, particularly with 'her girls': the cleaners and the reception staff. 'I know their jobs inside out', Mortimer explains, 'I used to be a cleaner and was the main receptionist here for years!'

Chance decides to speak to Linda Wilkinson, who seems a little stressed. 'I feel sometimes that I run the place on my own, it's a lot for one person to do.' Chance presses her on Mortimer's interference: 'Meg feels that she needs to be involved in everything', Wilkinson continues, 'don't get the impression I don't value her input, but sometimes I would like to be left alone to get on with it'.

Chance notes that Wilkinson becomes more stressed when the conversation turns to the restaurant staff. 'The waiters are supposed to be managed by me. However, Graham Effingham . . . well, he thinks they work for him.'

Head Chef, Graham Effingham, confirms the confusion over restaurant roles. 'I have official control over the chefs, but not the waiters. What's the point in that, especially when Linda is so overworked already? So, I tell the waiters what to do anyway—it gets the job done. Sometimes they don't like it and they go moaning to Linda when I shout at them, but needs must. They must be confused about who exactly is their boss, though. I wish I could just run the whole restaurant without any outside interference.'

Chance starts to feel that things don't run as smoothly as Mortimer has suggested, sensing further problems with the role of David Hunter. Hunter, an old friend of Mortimer's, works part-time maintaining the company accounts. Mortimer often confides in Hunter and trusts his advice—he often chips in with his thoughts on running the reception area and procedures for stock ordering. 'To be honest', chortles Hunter, 'who gets bonuses and pay rises is pretty much on my say-so.' Again, Wilkinson resents this interference in her work.

While Mortimer's presence seems to hold the hotel together, Chance can't help thinking that there are simmering tensions, many caused by a lack of a clear structure, with blurred roles and responsibilities. Furthermore, there is a lack of clear rules and procedures, and paperwork in the files is far from ordered. While Mortimer gives the hotel a veneer of being well-organized and managed, underneath the surface it is ad hoc and dysfunctional.

With a meeting with his team of investors imminent, and a clear instruction from them to get a grip on the hotel and make it profitable, Chance realizes that he needs to bring some coherent management and organization to the hotel.

Control: from small- to large-scale organizations

It may seem to be a statement of the obvious, but organizations need to be managed and organized in order to function effectively. Organizations are meant to be orderly places, in which managers at the top are in charge and staff do what is required of them—anything other than this may be seen as *dis*organized.

French industrialist Henri Fayol was one of the people who laid the foundations for our common-sense view of what orderly managing and organizing entails. In Table 2.1, Fayol (1949) provides a useful initial definition of the five main functions that managers perform.

Table 2.1 Fayol's five functions of management (1949)

Planning/forecasting	Looking to the future, trying to calculate and predict future circumstances (such as demand, competitors, etc.), and acting so as to be able to respond to this
Organizing	Building up the necessary structures, resources, and people to best meet the needs and goals of the organization
Coordinating	Bringing together the structure, human, and resource elements of the organization to act in harmony and towards the goals of the organization
Commanding	Giving orders and directions to people within the organization to maintain activity towards achieving the organization's goals
Controlling	Checking and inspecting work—monitoring and surveillance of work done rather than direct command

How well do you think Fayol's five functions of management are being carried out in the Junction Hotel case?

Real life case: the hairdressing salon

Many organizations that we encounter—the convenience store, the car workshop, the local café—are small-scale, independent organizations with a handful of employees. Think of a typical hairdressing salon. It will be independently run by an owner, who is also a hairdresser, employing a team of four or five stylists.

Informal management in a salon.

Managing this small group is done informally, performed daily on a face-to-face basis. It is a highly personal style of management. The owner will know all employees personally and by name. Rotas, holidays, and similar scheduling tasks will be sorted out in conversation and by informal negotiation between the owner and the team. The owner will know the personalities and characteristics of their staff, knowing who to reward as a good worker and, likewise, who might need a quiet telling-off from time to time.

The personal style of management described might work for a small enterprise with a handful of employees, but what if the hairdresser becomes successful and opens a second branch, then a third and a fourth? What if it grew to 100 employees, for example, or 1000, or even became a multinational enterprise employing tens of thousands of people across different continents? Could this personal style of management still be maintained?

Many of Fayol's functions of management involve the management of people. In a small-scale organization, this can be done on a direct, personal, face-to-face basis by the owner in direct conversation with the workforce. The larger an organization becomes, employing more and more people, the more difficult it is to manage and organize in this way.

Direct control by one individual owner/manager at the top of the organization is no longer possible—the organization would become unmanageable and disorganized. This chapter examines how, as an organization grows in size, managers need to adopt more indirect, **impersonal control**, using, in particular, the bureaucratic structures and procedures which make up **rational organizational design**.

Rationality suggests that the structures and procedures of the organization are designed logically and methodically to achieve the organization's aims in the most efficient manner possible. Such impersonal, rational forms of organizational design and control are termed bureaucracy.

Aspects of bureaucracy

Bureaucracy refers to the formal structures and procedures that facilitate the management of an organization, in particular as a solution to the problem of diminishing control as an organization outgrows personal, face-to-face management.

Bureaucracy derives from the French word *bureau*, meaning 'office', and refers to what we might call the 'official' or formal side of the organization. In the following three sections of the chapter, we examine three particular aspects of bureaucracy.

- A **hierarchy**, or structure of offices develops, with each level reporting to the level above and commanding the level below. Management is thus delegated from one level to another rather than one manager at the top trying to control the whole organization single-handedly. This hierarchy is often represented as an organization structure or chart, with each position within referred to as an **office** and the person holding the position as an official.

- Rules, procedures, and policies are instructions, usually written down, which govern activity across an organization. All officials must act in accordance with the rules, procedures, and policies that relate to the office they hold.

- Paperwork, such as forms, **records**, and timetables are all used within a bureaucratic organization to present and collate information about its people and processes in a manner that can be accessed and handled quickly and efficiently. Such paperwork makes up office work—filing, processing records, etc.—and is now done more and more through computer technology rather than using paper.

A double-edged sword?

What are your initial thoughts and reactions when you hear the word 'bureaucracy'?

Direct control Face-to-face control of workers by a manager or owner.

Impersonal control Control of workers that is not done face to face, for example through delegation or through rules and procedures.

Rational organizational design The design of organizational structures and activities in order to achieve the organization's goals in the most technically efficient manner. Rational organization suggests an organization which is designed logically and systematically, even scientifically, so as to achieve its aims.

Bureaucracy From the French *bureau*, meaning office; bureaucracy covers official, formal elements of rational organizational design, such as the hierarchical organization structure, the rules and procedures, and the official paperwork, which exert impersonal control over the organization.

Hierarchy The levels and ranks of an organization. Any one level reports to the level immediately above and commands the level immediately below.

Office A defined role within an organization.

Records Information held by the organization relevant for bureaucratic functioning, including information about workers.

Elements of bureaucracy have existed for centuries, for example in the ranks and strict rules and regulations of armies (Morgan, 2006: 21) or in the hierarchical nature of religious organizations.

Visit the Online Resource Centre to see further examples of bureaucracies.

However, in the early 1900s, industrialization in the Western world saw the widespread emergence of large-scale organizations (see Thompson and McHugh, 2009: 19–27), for example the development of the factory system, as will be examined in Chapter 3. This saw the refinement of bureaucracy into a particularly efficient form (Ritzer, 2011: 24).

Fayol, who was managing and writing at this time, certainly saw bureaucracy as an issue of rational, technical design—achieving the optimum combination of a number of bureaucratic elements for the organization to achieve its aims. Max Weber, a sociologist writing at around the same time, also noted the technical efficiency of bureaucracy in achieving the aims of an organization, but was also critical of its effects upon humans and society. He saw it as trapping people in monotonous routines, taking away people's autonomy, and ensnaring us all in its 'iron cage' (Weber, 1968).

Study skills: theory in its historical context

It is useful to be able to contextualize theory—to understand the historical period that it came from and how other theories and practices developed from it. While much of the theory in this chapter developed in the early 1900s, in future chapters we draw out the relevance for contemporary organizations.

Sometimes the date of publication of a text does not give the exact date of when it was written. It may refer to an edition published subsequent to the first edition, for example. Similarly, it may refer to a translation. This is the case with Fayol and Weber in this chapter. While they originally wrote in their own languages (French and German respectively) in the early 1900s, the translations into English did not appear until decades later.

Thus, references to Fayol (1949) and Weber (1968), for example, refer to publication dates in the English translation rather than when the first texts were actually published. It is useful to understand the distinction between when a text is actually written and its date of publication.

Bureaucracy tends to be associated with negative connotations, such as red tape, inflexibility, and unthinking, petty officialdom. Bauman's (1989) analysis of the role of bureaucracy in making possible the Nazi holocaust of World War II brings out further sinister consequences of bureaucratic organization and control.

We thus examine bureaucracy in the latter part of this chapter as a 'double-edged sword'. On one hand, bureaucracy allows for great achievements to take place—the large-scale organizations that we know today, and all that they achieve, would not be possible without bureaucracy. On the other hand, it brings considerable problems and dysfunctions of its own.

Review questions

1. Describe the five main functions of management according to Henri Fayol.

2. Explain why face-to-face management becomes more difficult as an organization grows in size.

3. Describe the main features of bureaucratic organization.

Bureaucratic structure and hierarchy

Running case: mapping the structure at Junction Hotel

Chance calls in Phil Weaver—a friend and trusted colleague from the football club that he ran. Weaver has a reputation as a fixer—his hard-headed, no-nonsense attitude is needed to bring some order and organization to the hotel. He will be seconded to work two days a week at the hotel to 'shake things up a bit'. While he will have a roving trouble-shooter role within the hotel, he will take a particular interest in the restaurant and the fitness centre, as these are areas that Chance wants to develop and make more profitable.

With Mortimer unable to provide an organization chart for the hotel, Chance and Weaver begin their work to bring organization to the hotel by sketching out the current organizational structure. As best they can, they try to show where each person fits into the structure—who reports to whom and what authority each person has. Their first attempt is shown in Figure 2.1.

Some problems are apparent immediately:

- too many chiefs at the top—there are too many levels of hierarchy with just one person occupying each level. Mortimer and Chance both seem to be running the hotel, and bringing in Weaver results in another level of management at the top

- Hunter assists Mortimer, but his actual role in the hierarchy is ill-defined—he seems to 'float around' at the side—the same can be said of the newly-introduced Weaver, who is assisting Chance.

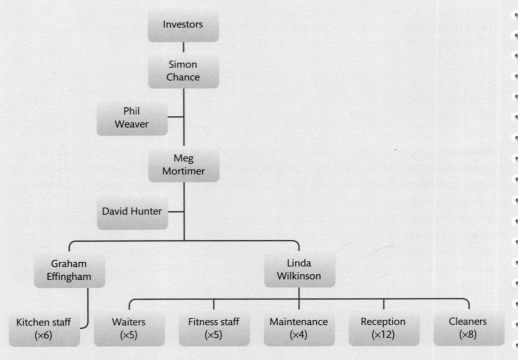

Figure 2.1 The current structure at Junction Hotel.

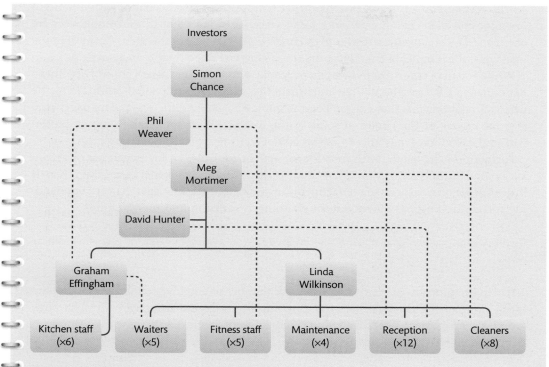

Figure 2.2 Unofficial structure in practice at Junction Hotel.

- Linda Wilkinson seems to be overburdened with supervisory responsibility (34 people) in addition to the other tasks she performs.

While this chart outlines the official structure and associated roles and responsibilities at Junction Hotel, it doesn't tell the full story. People are acting in unofficial capacities not shown by the chart. Chance takes the original diagram and adds a series of dashed lines to show areas of control and supervision that are not officially defined, but which happen in practice (see Figure 2.2).

Mortimer intervenes regularly in the supervision of reception and cleaning staff. Hunter also tries to influence reception procedures, while Weaver now has responsibility for the development of the fitness centre. It is unsurprising that Wilkinson, although having a huge amount of official responsibility, is confused as to her exact power and authority within the hotel. This is shown with the waiting staff, in particular, where lines of authority are confused between Wilkinson and Graham Effingham. Effingham himself seems to have the future of his restaurant in the hands of Phil Weaver, even though the official organization structure suggests the restaurant is under Effingham's control.

Overall, there is a picture of confusion, with ill-defined, blurred roles and responsibilities coupled with an unevenly distributed hierarchy that is too narrow at the top and too wide at the bottom.

Chance and Weaver begin to think about restructuring the hierarchy.

The first element of bureaucracy that we examine is the official structure or hierarchy. A hierarchy develops as a response to the problem of maintaining control over people in an organization as it grows in size. Figure 2.3 illustrates such a situation.

Span of control The number of workers controlled by a manager at any one particular level in a hierarchy.

Delegate To give a task to somebody else to perform on your behalf.

Organizational structure The roles and positions in an organization, often organized horizontally and vertically in the form of an organization chart diagram.

The starting point is similar to the earlier hairdressing salon scenario, with a handful of employees managed directly on a face-to-face basis. But what if more employees are taken on? The organization moves to the middle position where the **span of control** of the manager—the number of employees that they supervise directly—has increased.

While a span of control of five was manageable, a much larger span of control becomes a handful, and stretches the abilities and capabilities of any one individual. Maintaining the personal relationships that existed beforehand is a lot more difficult—the manager may even be unsure of the names of some of the workers. Indiscipline and disorganization within the workforce may arise from this lack of control.

Furthermore, managing with such a large span of control is an inefficient use of a manager's time. If time is spent mired in issues of discipline and personal issues then there is little time for other aspects of managing the organization. The manager may be commanding and controlling, but how about the planning, organizing, and coordinating?

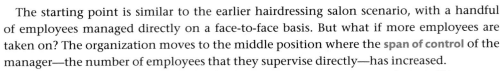

If you were the manager of an office of 100 people, how would you command and control all of those workers on a day-to-day basis?

To solve the problem of control over a larger number of employees, managers will relinquish some of the personal, face-to-face control and instead **delegate** control through layers of management beneath them. The final part of Figure 2.3 shows the development of **organizational structure** and hierarchy:

Figure 2.3 Structure and hierarchy develop as an organization grows in size.

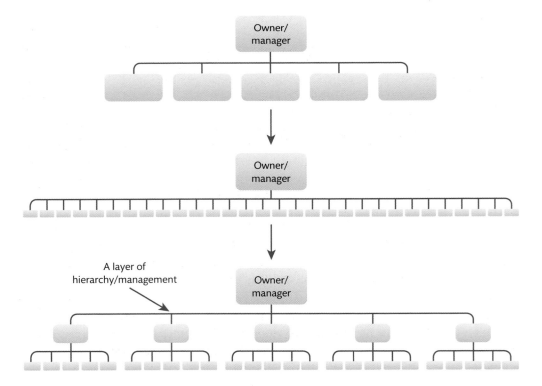

- there is a level of management between the owner and the other workers
- day-to-day tasks, such as supervision, discipline, and calculating pay are now delegated to the level of managers below
- commands need only be issued to managers at the level below, who will then pass the command down the hierarchy
- the owner no longer needs to even see, or have any contact with, the workers at the lower level
- the owner returns to a manageable span of control of five, as do each of the managers below.

When the span of control is too much at any one level, a further level of hierarchy can be introduced. In theory, and indeed in practice, this extension of levels of hierarchy will extend to organizations of any size. From a small factory to a multinational corporation, the principle of control through the hierarchical structure remains the same, only the number of levels differs. The larger the organization, the more levels of hierarchy will exist.

Between each of the levels in the hierarchy there is still personal, direct, face-to-face control. But, as orders and commands pass down the hierarchy, a form of control which is impersonal, indirect, and at-a-distance emerges.

The hierarchical structure of the organization allows the owner control of the organization, albeit a form of control that now passes down through the levels of the hierarchy. It can also be seen as an efficient form of control in that the owner only needs to deal with the level of management below, freeing time for other management tasks to be performed.

Vertical and horizontal differentiation

The development of hierarchy creates **vertical differentiation**. Employees are separated and differentiated vertically from one level of the hierarchy to the next.

However, experience tells us that managers may also be differentiated by the specific responsibilities that they have within the organization. **Horizontal differentiation** occurs across the organization chart as different branches of the hierarchy are assigned different functions. Thus, horizontal differentiation is also known as functional differentiation.

Be they the head of the maths department in a school, the area sales manager for Europe in a manufacturing organization, or the director of finance for a local authority, managers are identified both by their level in the hierarchy and the specific area of the hierarchy over which they have responsibility. Horizontal differentiation might exist by:

- product, service, or area of activity—schools are organized according to subjects taught; local authorities are structured into areas for services, such as housing, social services, etc.
- specific function performed—manufacturing companies are often structured into departments for functions such as sales, marketing, production, human resources, finance, etc.
- geographical area—multinationals are structured along continental lines (e.g. European division, African division); an exporting company might be based in one country, but be structured according to the areas where it sells its products (e.g. UK sales, Scandinavian sales, etc.).

Vertical differentiation The process whereby a hierarchy creates a number of different layers of management within an organization.

Horizontal/functional differentiation The process whereby different parts of the hierarchy are grouped according to criteria, such as the function performed, the geographical area served, or the product or service provided.

Figure 2.4 A typical factory organization.

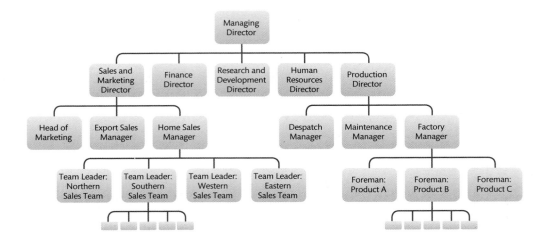

In practice most organizational structures will be a mix of these, with different means of horizontal differentiation at different levels of the vertical hierarchy. Figure 2.4 shows a typical factory organization. Here, we see higher levels of the organization organized by function (sales and marketing, finance, etc.), home sales organized geographically (northern, southern, etc.), and the factory floor organized by product (Product A, B, C, etc.).

There is no one correct way in theory or practice in which any organization should be differentiated both horizontally and vertically. Different types of structure will be more appropriate in different circumstances.

Real life case: Vodafone's organizational structure

Vodafone is a multinational telecommunications group. Beneath the Chief Executive Officer (CEO), it is organized both by function (e.g. group finance, group human resources) and by geographical areas (Vodafone, 2011). There are individual national divisions, which have their own particular organization structures.

The structure gives a clear line of command and control that can go from the CEO at the top down to an assistant in a mobile phone store in Spain (or any of the other countries in which the company operates). While the CEO may never meet the vast majority of workers in the global organization, the structure still allows for command and control over the whole workforce.

Visit the Online Resource Centre for a link to Vodafone's structure chart and examples of different organizational structures.

Compare the differences in the structures shown on the Online Resource Centre. Can you describe the structures using such terminology as 'span of control', 'hierarchy', 'horizontal differentiation', etc.?

Roles and relationships

Running case: the new structure

A management team meeting is convened and Chance hands out a sheet of paper outlining the new structure (see Figure 2.5).

Outlining his rationale for the new design, Chance makes the following points:

- the structure creates defined roles. Previously, people have taken on tasks because of who they were or who they knew, or had simply fallen into doing different jobs over time. Now, the role will take precedence, with staff being allocated to appropriate positions. Each role will have a written job description which will outline precisely the tasks to be performed

- Chance will assume a more hands-on role as General Manager. Beneath him, the managerial workload will be split more evenly, with new positions and levels of hierarchy being created

- a Front-of-House Manager will have all responsibility for the reception area, including reception staff and porters. Given Meg Mortimer's tendency to concern herself with reception matters, she is deemed most appropriate for this role. From the receptionists and porters, there will be a promotion within each team to the positions of Head Receptionist and Head Porter, each reporting directly to Mortimer

- cleaners and maintenance staff will be the responsibility of a Domestic Manager, a role to be filled by Linda Wilkinson. Promotions within each of the two teams—cleaning and maintenance—will create another layer of hierarchy. Wilkinson will now have a definite and manageable workload. The lines of authority drawn out also mean that Mortimer no longer has a legitimate cause to interfere in the work of the cleaners

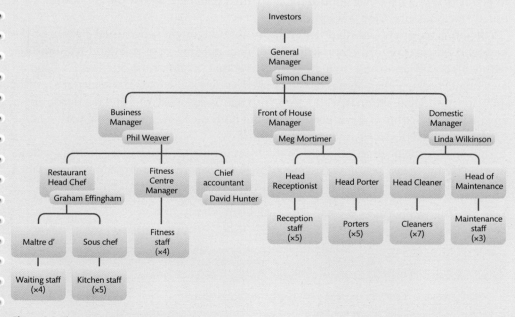

Figure 2.5 The new structure at Junction Hotel.

- Phil Weaver will fill a new role of Business Manager, with responsibility for finance, marketing, and business development. The restaurant and fitness centre will fall under this part of the structure, as will the position of Hotel Accountant. Graham Effingham will remain as the Head Chef of the restaurant, with a Sous Chef and a Maitre d' forming a further level of hierarchy over the kitchen and waiting teams respectively. This clears up the confusion over who manages the waiting staff, placing them firmly under Effingham's control. One of the fitness centre staff will be promoted to manager of the fitness centre. Finally, David Hunter will report to Phil Weaver as Chief Accountant; his 'cosy' relationship with Mortimer will be broken up. Both Weaver and Hunter's uncertain roles within the organization are now clear and definite.

Looking at the changes made to the Junction Hotel structure, how would the changes improve the running of the hotel? Who do you think would be happy or unhappy with the changes made, and why?

Official A person who fills a particular role in an organization. When working in that role, a person is said to be working in an official capacity.

Each position on the organization chart represents a role to be carried out by a person—the office indicated is to be held by a person acting in an **official** capacity. As such, the bureaucratic structure maps out the relationships between people acting in different official roles within the organization.

Lines of authority are shown—the structure demonstrates who a worker is controlled by and, likewise, who a worker has control over. It also shows the limits of such authority, namely who a worker has no legitimate authority over and to whom a worker is not answerable.

Horizontal differentiation specifies each role even further, with the specific task associated with each role defined. Positions within a bureaucratic structure will often have a written **job description** attached, which outlines the level or grade within the hierarchy of that position, and the specific tasks and duties that the office holder would be expected to perform. If you have ever applied for a job, then you'll know that the application pack usually includes such a job description.

Job description A document which outlines the formal duties and activities that the holder of a particular office will be expected to perform, and their place within the overall organizational structure.

The job description and tight definition of roles highlight a particular feature of the nature of bureaucratic structure. It is able to map out the set of roles and relationships within an organization and facilitate control over that organization, often with a diagram on a single sheet of paper. Alongside this broad overview it also exerts influence at a level of quite intricate detail within that structure, with tightly specified roles and relationships for any one person within it. Bureaucracy maps out both the large-scale general nature of the organization and the small-scale specifics within.

The existence of job descriptions indicates that bureaucracy needs more than just a structure to operate. In fact, written rules, procedures, and paperwork are equally as important a part of bureaucratic functioning and control as the hierarchy and structure.

Visit the Online Resource Centre to see examples of job descriptions.

Review questions

1. Describe what is meant by hierarchy in an organization structure.

2. Explain how hierarchy allows control to be exerted over a whole organization.

3. Explain the differences between direct and impersonal control.

Bureaucratic standardization—rules, policies, and procedures

Running case: implementing procedures

Running the organization is much more straightforward with the new structure in place. However, while Chance has delegated authority throughout the hierarchy, managers are implementing that authority in different ways and some staff are starting to complain that this is unfair.

- Meg Mortimer is authoritative, but is seen to have her favourites when it comes to taking breaks or being able to leave early to deal with family issues. They also seem to be first in line when any opportunities for extra shifts or overtime come up.

- Linda Wilkinson is seen as a soft-touch—cleaners and maintenance workers are taking extended breaks and seem to be allowed to leave early for spurious reasons. If workers are off sick, Linda takes their word for it, not insisting on any form of medical note. She doesn't keep a record of illness, leaving others in the organization to suspect that people are getting away with taking 'sickies'.

- Graham Effingham rules the restaurant with an iron rod, bawling out waiters and kitchen staff directly, and not going through the managers below him. He is unsympathetic to people who are off sick and often insists people work through breaks if there is a busy shift. If a shift extends beyond the set hours, Effingham sees this as a part of the job and does not award any extra money for overtime. He is even known to dock pay if he feels that work is not up to scratch.

Chance decides that, to even out conditions across the workforce, rules and procedures will be created and implemented. Two documents, entitled 'Pay and Working Hours procedures' and 'Disciplinary policy', are sent to the three managers below Chance, who are asked to implement the policies immediately.

The Pay and Working Hours policy specifies a standard working day with defined hours and break times. Employees will sign in and out at the start and end of the day, and for all breaks taken. Managers will send this data weekly to David Hunter who will calculate pay and prepare pay packets. Absence will be reported directly to Hunter who will get employees to provide appropriate evidence upon their return.

The Disciplinary policy specifies expectations of staff behaviour, and a series of set offences with appropriate standard punishments is created. Chance wants to take discipline out of individual managers' hands as they seem to make up their own rules, which is at the heart of a lot of the unfairness felt by workers. Any disciplining of staff will, therefore, be referred to Chance directly in accordance with the new rules.

How might managers react to having to follow rules and procedures just outlined in the Junction Hotel case?

Bureaucratic structure is supplemented and enhanced by another aspect of bureaucracy: **rules, policies, and procedures**. Their aim is to standardize behaviours and activities throughout the organization, such that control is implemented in the same way at all levels across and up and down the hierarchy.

While the bureaucratic hierarchy allows the owner to control the organization in an indirect and more efficient manner, it can also be seen that there is a risk that at each level of the hierarchy control is lost because of the way in which that control is *implemented* at

Rules, policies, and procedures Formal instructions that govern how particular activities in an organization are to be performed.

Table 2.2 Examples of rules, policies, and procedures in organizations

Grievance	Policies which outline how workers themselves may pursue grievances—areas in which they are unhappy with how they are being managed
Finance	Procedures relating to expense claims, outlining what workers might legitimately claim (e.g. car mileage or transport costs), and a standard allowance for these
Equal opportunities	Policies that ensure equality of treatment on grounds such as gender, race, age, sexual orientation, and disability
Appraisal and promotion	Procedures for monitoring the standard of work that employees do, often done in a standardized appraisal procedure on an annual basis. Such a procedure can then feed into decisions on promotion or pay increases
Recruitment and selection	Policies may cover aspects such as where a job is advertised, criteria for selecting candidates, and types of evidence required to demonstrate that candidates meet different selection criteria (see Chapter 10 for more on specific recruitment and selection techniques to match personalities to job descriptions)

levels below. Are all managers following their orders to the letter or are individual managers acting as they please? If workers hear that they are being treated unfavourably compared with other workers it can cause unrest and disruption.

Thus, pay rates and scales are an example of a rule or procedure which may be implemented to standardize the way in which remuneration is offered across a whole organization. In some cases, pay scales are even standardized across a whole industry sector (e.g. in education, local government, and the health service). Payment rules and procedures extend beyond pay itself into other terms and conditions, such as working hours, holidays, sick pay, pension entitlements, etc., and take **discretion** out of individual managers' hands.

Discretion The ability of an individual to act according to their own independent judgement, rather than being told exactly what to do.

There are many other areas within modern-day organizations where activities will be controlled by a set of rules, or a policy or procedure which standardizes behaviour across the organization. See Table 2.2 for some examples.

 What type of rules and procedures do you have to follow in your workplace? Do they help or hinder you in your work?

Here, we see an extra dimension of bureaucratic control. Not only is control delegated down through the hierarchy, but the autonomous action of any manager within that hierarchy is also now taken away. Instead, managers are controlled by adherence to the written rules and procedures. For the owner, this gives increased control and a standardization of behaviour across the organization.

In some cases, requirements for bureaucratic rules and procedures come not just from a desire for management control, but also from a legal imperative. This is the case in the UK, where workplace legislation (much of which originates at the level of the European Union) covers aspects of workplace management, such as equal opportunities, health and safety, and disciplinary aspects (e.g. unfair dismissal and workplace bullying). Many bureaucratic procedures in workplaces are thus as much about ensuring compliance with such laws as they are about enforcing management control.

 Visit the Online Resource Centre for further examples of rules, policies, and procedures.

The work involved in implementing bureaucratic procedures relating to the human side of the organization leads to sections of the organization being devoted to this aspect of organizational functioning. Thus, there is a whole organizational function, alongside functions such as marketing, production, and finance, that deals with **human resource management**.

In Chapter 4, with the example of the McDonalds restaurant chain, we see how such standardization even takes place globally, not just with human resources policies, but with set instructions and procedures for performing particular work tasks.

Human resource management (HRM) The part of an organization, and the study of organization, which concentrates on policies and procedures relevant to the management of people within the organization (sometimes known as personnel management).

Review questions

1. Describe what is meant by rules, policies, and procedures.
2. Explain why rules and procedures are needed to standardize behaviour across an organization.
3. Analyse the effect that rules and procedures have on managerial discretion.

Bureaucratic records and paperwork

Running case: for the record

Charged with running the new payroll and absence system, David Hunter is beginning to find the paperwork something of a burden. He is used to writing down information in a notebook as and when he receives it. Now, with clocking-on records and absence reports coming in daily, and pay cheques to prepare weekly, Hunter is becoming overwhelmed.

Some managers scribble their daily records on to a scrap of paper, others lay it out as a well-ordered spreadsheet. There is no common format and storing the scraps of paper in his notebook makes it increasingly difficult for Hunter to access and process payroll and absence information as more and more of it comes in. When asked for details of any specific employee, he finds he is wading through a mass of paper and this is taking up more and more of his time.

Hunter decides that a standard system of record keeping is needed. Opening a filing cabinet, he allocates a folder to each employee. On the front of each he creates a standard template to record details of the employee—name, address, date of birth, tax code, and any other relevant information. Furthermore, each employee is allocated an employee number.

A set of forms is created—one where managers can record clocking-on and clocking-off details for each employee, one for reporting absences, and one to record any disciplinary incidents. For each of these, the first box to be filled in is the employee number. Hunter can then file the forms immediately when received and access them rapidly when required.

The forms help Hunter to manage the payroll process much more efficiently; however, Simon Chance spots a further benefit. Every so often he asks Hunter to send up the file of a particular employee. Even if Chance doesn't know the employee personally, he can read the file and get a good picture of their working history, e.g. their absences, time taken on breaks, and disciplinary issues.

Even though the employees may be distant and unknown to Chance within the structure, their employee record makes them instantly visible to him.

What control over individual workers does the record keeping at Junction Hotel give to the managers?

Paperwork Official documentation and record keeping within an organization.

Pro-forma A type of paperwork, sometimes called a form. It is a blank template with standard fields for different types of relevant information, which is filled in as a means of capturing information for the records of an organization.

While rules and procedures standardize aspects of workplace control, such procedures both necessitate, and are facilitated by, the keeping of records and **paperwork**. This is the final aspect of bureaucracy that we examine.

Bureaucratic paperwork is typified by the **pro-forma**—a set of fields and boxes that represent some aspect of the organization. For instance, employees will be represented in an organization as a set of fields and boxes on a form, each of which records a piece of information relevant to the organization. Such record keeping serves two purposes for management in controlling the organization.

- First, many of the rules and procedures outlined in the previous section require information about the organization and its workers in order for those rules and procedures to be implemented. A payroll policy needs information about the hours worked by each employee; an absence policy needs to record frequency and reasons for absence, etc. If this information were unstructured (e.g. scribbled on scraps of paper) it would be difficult to manage. Thus, a pro-forma standardizes the information to be stored and, as such, makes it easy to access, retrieve, and use in implementing the policies that it supports.

- Secondly, a by-product of such record keeping is that a record is kept of an employee's activities that can be accessed at a later date. As such, it allows added control through surveillance and monitoring of employees. While an employee might be 'lost' within a large organizational structure, referring to their records allows management to still cast an eye over their activity and exert control if, for example, there is a problematic absence record. (See Chapter 4 for a discussion of control through surveillance and the Panopticon.)

Real life case: the UCAS form

UCAS is the organization which handles applications for UK universities.

In dealing with the thousands of university applicants each year, UCAS has the problem of ordering a complex mass of individuals. They could ask people to turn up at their premises to discuss their university application but this would overwhelm their premises by the sheer weight of numbers and there is no way that an individual staff member could remember each potential student with whom they had had discussions. They could ask people to write a letter of application stating any relevant details. This would prevent the premises from being swamped, but how would they collate thousands of letters? Say they wanted to find all applicants for Midwest University. Or say they wanted to find all applicants for Geography degrees. Or all applicants over 25 years old. It would mean sifting through and examining closely every single letter among thousands to find the relevant details. Nothing would ever get done.

So, to make this task manageable, UCAS uses a number of bureaucratic mechanisms—the UCAS form, in particular. Rather than writing unstructured letters, UCAS structures each individual in the shape of the UCAS form. Each individual is represented by the different fields and boxes that they fill in on the form: age, predicted grades, gender, preferred universities, preferred courses, etc. Now, the mass of individual applicants is represented and structured in a way that makes their ordering, and, ultimately, allocation to different universities, possible. What was previously unmanageable is now manageable—it is the bureaucracy that allows information to be managed efficiently and, ultimately, for control to be exerted over the mass of student applicants for that year. ➤

USE BLOCK CAPITALS ON PAGE 1

UCAS APPLICATION FOR ENTRY IN **2013**

Attach your application fee and stamped, addressed acknowledgement card here with a paperclip

YOU MUST READ *HOW TO APPLY* BEFORE COMPLETING THIS FORM
Return completed form to: UCAS, PO Box 28, Cheltenham, Glos GL52 3LZ, UK

IMPORTANT
You must complete all the red sections, marked with an asterisk (*). Your application will be delayed if you do not do so.

1 PERSONAL DETAILS Title* Male (M)* Female (F)* Your date of birth* D D M M 19 Y Y Age on 1 September 2013 Y Y M M

Surname/family name*

First/given name(s)

Preferred first name

Postal address*
Line 1
Line 2
Line 3
Line 4
Postcode (UK only)
Country* (not UK)

Mobile phone number

Home phone number (including STD/area code)

email

Home address (if different from above)
Line 1
Line 2
Line 3
Line 4

Postcode (UK only)
Country (not UK)
Previous surname/family name at 16th birthday (18)

2 ADDITIONAL DETAILS
Fee code*
Student support arrangements
Disability/special needs (including dyslexia/medical condition*)

Occupational background* (22)
Parents' higher education
Enter ✔ if you **want** to receive correspondence in Welsh where available

Time in care
Representative's name (30)
Relationship (30)

Area of permanent residence* (30)
Country of birth* (30)
Residential category*

Nationality* (30)
National identity* (UK applicants only)
Ethnic origin* (UK applicants only)
Date of first entry to live in the UK* D D M M Y Y

Start date | Duration | School year | Location | Sponsor
Activity 1 M M Y Y
Activity 2 M M Y Y

3 CHOICES IN ALPHABETICAL ORDER OF INSTITUTION CODE NAME

(a) Institution code name*	(b) Institution code*	(c) Course code*	(d) Campus code*	(e) Start date*	(f) Further details only if requested on Course Finder (20)	(g) Point of entry	(h) Live at home*	(i) Defer entry*
				D D M M Y Y				
				D D M M Y Y				
				D D M M Y Y				
				D D M M Y Y				
				D D M M Y Y				

If you have applied to any of the above institution(s) before, enter your most recent UCAS application number or Personal ID (if known)

4A SCHOOL, COLLEGE, CENTRE AND UNIVERSITY EDUCATION* (40 per line)

	PT, FT or SW	From* MM YY	To* MM YY
		M M Y Y	M M Y Y
		M M Y Y	M M Y Y
		M M Y Y	M M Y Y

4B HIGHEST LEVEL QUALIFICATION ACHIEVED*
Honours degree level or above qualifications
Below honours degree level qualifications
I will have no formal qualifications

Form Number   Figures in brackets = maximum no. of characters, including spaces, allowed   * Mandatory information   Page 1

The UCAS form.

© Universities and Colleges Admissions Service.

How does the use of a pro-forma at UCAS allow records to be processed efficiently (e.g. saving time and effort)?

The UCAS case shows how bureaucracy functions in both ordering and managing vast numbers of people, but also allows the record of any one individual within that mass to be pinpointed immediately. As such, bureaucracy can be used as an instrument for ordering and governing populations of whole countries.

Government bodies and organizations exist as massive bureaucracies, processing information and paperwork about their populations, with the intent of ordering and controlling that population in one way or another.

In the UK, the Driver and Vehicle Licensing Agency (DVLA) maintains records for all licensed drivers and their vehicles. Such records control who can and cannot drive, and even manage the exclusion of individuals from driving based on penalty points accrued or a lack of car taxation. Similar giant, national bureaucracies keep records or our tax details and health records, etc. Privately-owned, commercial record-keeping organizations, such as Experian in the UK, keep similar records, for example about the financial history of an individual, for use in credit checks.

Visit the Online Resource Centre to see more on organizations that maintain records.

The use of bureaucratic techniques to manage a vast number of people is at the heart of so many organizations. Each individual is represented in a 'highly caricatured yet immediately available form' (Poster, 1995: 91). The paperwork and the records caricature an individual according to a standard set of entries on a pro-forma, which, at the same time, makes them visible, and their records easy to pinpoint and access within a mass of similarly constituted individuals. As such, this adds to the power of bureaucracy.

Employability skills

In a world of 'information overload' (see Chapter 14 on 'Information, communication, and technology'), managing information is a vital workplace skill. Where previously this tended to be done in physical files and folders, there are now various forms of software which can help with the tasks of storing information, categorizing it, and making it available for easy retrieval at a later date. This might be for project management or for organizing your own notes.

Without such a level of organization and categorization of information in the workplace it is easy for information to become a confused mass. Even something as straightforward as email allows the creation of virtual folders so as to be able to keep information in a more manageable and easily accessible form.

Review questions

1. Describe how bureaucratic records are used to control the populations of entire countries.

2. Explain how a pro-forma helps to standardize bureaucratic records.

Apply

3. What would happen if government bureaucracies such as the DVLA didn't exist?

The power of bureaucracy: large-scale control and rational design

Running case: great work

Phil—what you've done is great. Such simple ideas, but they give me so much control!

The various aspects of bureaucracy allow an organization, as it grows in size, to remain ordered and controlled rather than descending into chaos. With face-to-face control becoming more difficult, if not impossible, control is implemented through impersonal elements, such as the structure, rules, and paperwork. In that bureaucracy can achieve this control across large scale organizations, even national populations, it creates tremendous organizational power.

It is difficult to think of organizations which do not have elements of bureaucracy to one degree or another: structure, rules, procedures, paperwork, etc. It underpins all large-, medium- and probably small-scale organizations that we know today—bureaucracy is 'ubiquitous and inevitable' (Watson, 2002: 239).

The ordering and controlling power of bureaucracy makes possible many achievements of organizations that we take for granted, but which, without bureaucracy, would simply be beyond human capability. Quite simply, the organizations that we know today would be incapable of operating without bureaucracy.

Research insight: The railway timetable, Chia, R. 1995. From modern to postmodern organizational analysis. *Organization Studies* 16(4): 579–604.

Chia (1995) examines the vast power of a simple bureaucratic instrument—a railway timetable, which can order trains, passengers, and workers across a whole country. Think also about timetables in the context of your own university studies and how they direct both you and the university staff from hour to hour.

One sheet of paper can represent the organization by structuring it and breaking it down in terms of space (different rooms), time (different time slots during the day), and people (allocated to different timetable slots). This small sheet of paper exerts power and control over vast numbers. Without the timetable it would be impossible to run a university—it would be a mass of people milling around without direction (i.e. anarchy).

Fayol, bureaucracy, and the principles of management

As noted previously, bureaucratic structures, rules, and paperwork have existed for centuries; however, the particular power that they have brought to organizations since the early 1900s comes, in part, from the rationality of the design of bureaucratic structures, as promoted by the likes of Fayol.

Table 2.3 Bureaucratic techniques and Fayol's five principles of management (1949)

Planning/forecasting	Standard rules and procedures make behaviour and actions more predictable across the organization and thus easier to plan for. Paperwork and records give data which can be used for forecasting, e.g. planning staffing requirements
Organizing	A structure is created to meet the needs of the organization, and encompass the vertical and horizontal levels of hierarchy needed to achieve the organization's aims. Tightly defined job roles and recruitment procedures allow the development of an appropriately qualified workforce
Coordination	Standard procedures (e.g. for pay) make it easier to coordinate activities across the organization (e.g. through a payroll department). The bureaucratic structure and rules make clear what each person does and how they relate and report to each other across the organization
Commanding	Command is delegated through the hierarchical levels of bureaucratic structure. Rules and procedures tell people what to do without a human commanding presence being necessary
Controlling	Paperwork means that records of employee actions are kept, which can be used to monitor work performance and associated issues, such as absence

Table 2.3 shows how the different elements of bureaucracy can be seen to allow Fayol's five functions of management to still be exerted as an organization grows in size and scale.

Fayol's work on bureaucratic organization design went along this rational route in that he saw it as playing an important part in achieving organizational goals in the most efficient manner possible. In other words, rational organizational design is about finding the most direct and efficient means to achieve organizational ends.

Fayol expanded his five general functions of management to create his general principles of management.

Theory in context: Henri Fayol and the profession of management

Henri Fayol (1841–1925) was a French mining engineer who became a manager. Having turned around a failing mine (Wren, 2001), he suggested that good management was a consequence of following a set of general principles. Regardless of the person holding an office, following such principles would ensure efficient management across the organization. In his 1916 work, *Administration Industrielle et Generale*, (English translation, 1949), he set out these principles.

Management became a profession in itself, with the training of managers becoming as important as training for production skills or other functions in the organization, such as finance. In Chapter 3 we encounter Taylor, a fellow management pioneer. Unlike Taylor, who concentrated on making individual work tasks more efficient, Fayol was interested in efficiency *at the level of the organization overall*.

However, work by both Fayol and Taylor was the basis for what became known in the UK as the **Classical Management School** (see Smith and Boyns, 2005)—a form of management that emphasizes rationality and searches for the 'one best way' to manage an organization. This is opposite to the disordered, ad hoc, and chaotic form of organization that might exist were it not for bureaucracy.

Classical Management School A set of theories of management which draws upon rational methods of managing and organizing. Having developed from the early 1900s, it encompasses a number of theorists and practitioners who advocated 'one best way' of management. Examples of management styles and techniques which the school draws upon include Fayol from this chapter, and Frederick Taylor from Chapter 3.

The principles of management numbered fourteen in total, although Fayol suggested that this was flexible—any principle that helped efficient management and control could be included. The principles promote the use of bureaucratic structures. Examples from his list include:

- a division of work where all tasks are specialized (as with vertical and horizontal differentiation), creating specific roles within the organization
- unity of command where each worker answers to only one manager, not several
- centralization, with **delegation** down through the ranks
- equity of treatment for all employees, as seen with rules and procedures
- order—everything to be in the right place at the right time, as seen with timetables
- subordination of interests—individual interests are secondary to those of the organization as a whole.

Visit the Online Resource Centre to see Fayol's full list of principles.

Delegation Passing a job, task, or order down to lower levels of a hierarchy.

The power of bureaucracy seems to come from its rational approach to managing and organizing—not just in preventing disorder, but in making possible large-scale control and coordination that would otherwise be impossible without rational, bureaucratic instruments. However, rationality is a contested term—it has different meanings depending on your perspective. This contested nature is something we will encounter in the next section when we examine some of the critiques of bureaucracy.

Review questions

1. Explain how bureaucracy allows Fayol's five functions of management to be exerted over large-scale organizations.
2. Describe what is meant by the Classical Management School.

Weber and the critique of bureaucracy

Running case: What happened to the magic?

Chance feels that the new procedures enhance his power over the organization, standardizing both worker and managerial behaviour. However, while Chance is pleased with his work, reactions are hostile. What seemed perfectly rational to Chance as a means of running the organization efficiently is not necessarily perceived in the same way by others.

Meg Mortimer feels that she has been demoted, having to take her place alongside Linda Wilkinson in the hierarchy. The tightly written job descriptions limit her sphere of influence within the hotel and she is not happy that she will no longer be working closely with her friend, David Hunter.

Linda Wilkinson is somewhat disappointed. Although her workload will be reduced, she takes it as a slight on her performance that many areas she had managed are being taken away from her.

Graham Effingham is apoplectic—why does he find himself now a level below Linda Wilkinson in the hierarchy? Chance tries to reassure Effingham that the restaurant will be run almost as a separate unit under the guidance of Phil Weaver, and that the appointment of a Maître d' and Sous Chef means, in fact, that Effingham has as many levels of hierarchy beneath him as Wilkinson and Mortimer. Effingham is still not happy, however, muttering about his reduced status within the organization.

Overall, there is a general lack of morale developing among the staff, especially as more and more policies and procedures are introduced to the hotel. Chance takes Meg Mortimer to one side to ask what the problem is.

'It's the work here', replies Mortimer, 'there's too much drudgery. I have to fill in numerous forms—rotas, pay sheets, absence reports. I feel like I'm suffocating in paperwork. I spend most of my time in that back office but I need to be around people—that's how I get my buzz. And it's the same with the receptionists, too. We have to go out there, and be cheerful and welcoming to customers, but that spark has been extinguished.

'Last week you gave us another form to fill in, monitoring water usage for your environmental audit. I'm sure it's a great cause but it just adds to the drudgery. We are expected to go out there and create magic— really create the atmosphere for the customers. But how can we when the magic has gone?'

While bureaucracy may increase the power and control of organizations and managers, and their ability to operate on a large-scale, it does not come without consequences. Such consequences form the heart of the critique of bureaucracy from Max Weber. While Weber appreciated the power and technical efficiency of bureaucracy, he was also wary about its increasing dominance and negative effects within society.

Theory in context: Max Weber and the study of organizations

Max Weber is synonymous with bureaucracy. However, while he wrote in the early 1900s (at the same time as Fayol) it should be noted that *Weber was not a manager like Fayol* and thus had no interest in implementing bureaucracy within organizations so as to increase efficiency and control within them, *nor was he a management theorist*.

As a sociologist, Weber was interested in a wide range of aspects of society (MacRae, 1974)— economy, religion, and music being examples. One interest (Weber, 1958) was in forms of authority and control within society, which led him to analyse bureaucracy in terms of its characteristics, its power, and its effects on people and society.

It is sometimes suggested that Weber's work has met with a 'strange fate' (Perry, 1992) in management and organization theory, being viewed only in terms of how is can help organizations be managed more efficiently rather than recognizing the negative effects that he identifies. Thus, when Weber (1968) speaks of an 'ideal type' of bureaucracy, it is seen in some quarters almost as some form of blueprint for the design of organizations in a similar, technically-efficient sense to that suggested earlier by Fayol.

The value of Weber's contribution, however, is found in his critique of bureaucracy, its dominance in society, and the effects that it has upon society.

Weber's (1958) studies of society led him to conclude that society at the time was moving from a grounding in tradition and religion towards rational, formal structures, such as bureaucracy. This was reflected in how authority operated in society. Where once power came from tradition (such as a hereditary position) or from the charisma and personality of an individual leader, Weber noted that authority was coming more from bureaucratic forms of authority, which he described as **rational–legal authority**.

Rational–legal authority According to Max Weber this is power that is legitimated by rules and procedures associated with an office rather than by traditional or charismatic means.

Rational-legal authority is where authority comes not from tradition or the charisma of an individual, but rather the authority that they have from the office they hold. Authority comes from the bureaucratic rules associated with that position. (See Chapter 12 on 'Leadership' and Chapter 13 on 'Power and politics in organizations' for more about power and authority in organizations.)

Noting the increasing dominance of rational, bureaucratic organizational forms within society, Weber (1968) outlined features of an 'ideal type' of rational, technically-efficient bureaucracy, including:

- functional division of labour (horizontal differentiation)
- hierarchical structure (vertical differentiation)
- rules and regulations
- impersonality—the separation of working lives from personal lives
- unbiased decision making, including recruitment, selection, and promotion.

The ideal type contains some now familiar aspects of bureaucracy and, indeed, has some aspects in common with Fayol. However, rather than being a prescription for efficient organizational design, Weber's model was a hypothetical abstraction of features he had observed in a number of bureaucracies. While noting it as a technically efficient 'ideal type', Weber did not suggest that his model was necessarily the right way to manage and organize.

Formal and substantive rationality

For Weber, the **formal rationality** of the ideal type is but one type of rationality. It is a technical form of rationality which finds the most efficient means to achieving ends. *But this does not mean that pursuing those ends is rational in more human terms.* Weber proposed another form of rationality—**substantive rationality**—to take account of the effects of actions in human and ethical terms.

> **Formal rationality**
> Technically efficient means of achieving particular ends without thinking of the human or ethical consequences.
>
> **Substantive rationality**
> Rationality from a human and ethical perspective—if something is formally rational and efficient it does not make it substantively rational when considering its human and ethical consequences.

Research insight: Modernity and the Holocaust, Bauman, Z. 1989. *Modernity and the Holocaust.* Polity Press, Cambridge.

In a compelling account of the Nazi Holocaust, Zygmunt Bauman (1989) asks how individuals working in death camps, where prisoners were killed in mass extermination chambers, could bring themselves to commit such horrific acts. His answer lies in the nature of bureaucracy.

By dividing labour, and giving individuals just a small, tightly-defined role in the overall organization, they became blinkered to the end result. In an organization with many levels of hierarchy, commands given from the top can seem very distant and impersonal from the bottom—orders and their consequences come without a human face.

Thus, workers in death camps saw only their one small part in the process (it might be recording a name in a log book) rather than the overall end result.

Bauman's work on the Holocaust reflects some of the dehumanizing aspects of bureaucracy that will be encountered later in this chapter. It also highlights different forms of rationality. In terms of formal rationality the Nazi death camps were perfectly rational—with a task set of killing many prisoners *en masse*, it achieved the most technically rational way of achieving this. But how can it be rational in human terms for an organization to exist to pursue such an ethically abhorrent act in such a ruthless and efficient manner?

The case of the Holocaust highlights Weber's distinction between formal and substantive rationality. While something may be formally rational, i.e. technical and efficient, it does not make it substantively rational, i.e. in human and ethical terms.

The Holocaust is a dramatic example, but we can think of examples in organizations today. In Chapter 17 (Corporate social responsibility) we examine contemporary organizational arrangements that can be seen as ethically dubious, for instance by creating pollution or using sweatshop labour in the developing world. These may be formally rational in that they are the most efficient ways for an organization to operate, but are they substantively rational in terms of their effects upon humans or upon the environment?

Such issues also highlight Bauman's idea of individuals within an organization being distanced from the end result of that organization's activities. Does a sales assistant in a UK clothes shop feel personally responsible for the sweatshop conditions in which the clothes they sell were produced? Does a forecourt cashier in Sweden feel responsibility for pollution caused by oil spills on the other side of the planet? In both cases, the worker is a part of the same organization that created the problem, but their roles are so tightly defined and so distanced from the end results that they can potentially continue with a clear conscience.

 Have you, in a workplace, ever performed a task that you thought to be wrong but continued because you were following orders or rules?

Disenchantment—the loss of magical elements

Disenchantment
For Max Weber this was a loss of 'magical elements' in society, and suggests some of the dehumanizing elements of bureaucracy.

Weber noted a more general issue of substantive rationality, namely its negative effects on people and society. In particular, Weber (1958) noted that, as society moved from religious and traditional views of the world towards more formal, bureaucratic procedures—both in religion and society generally—there was loss of the 'magical,' enchanted elements in life. This removal of 'magical' elements in life was termed **disenchantment** by Weber. The magical is replaced with the rational, formal, and procedural.

While written originally about the loss of magical elements in society generally, disenchantment is often interpreted as a dehumanizing and stifling effect of bureaucracy. It brings with it monotonous, repetitive routines; people unable to act independently but instead bound by rules and procedures, becoming unthinking and detached from their work.

 Have you ever done work that you have found repetitive, dull, and monotonous? How would you have made it more interesting?

Such disenchantment can be seen in the way in which following set rules and routines makes life predictable, rather than being spontaneous and creative, people simply follow rules.

The iron cage of bureaucracy

Iron cage of bureaucracy Max Weber's observation of the increased presence of bureaucracy in society and its potential to trap people in its routines and procedures.

The phrase with which Weber (1958) is most commonly associated is the **iron cage of bureaucracy**. This stems from Weber's caution about the prevalence of bureaucracy within society and its potential negative effects.

How many aspects of your life are not governed by bureaucracy—rules, procedures, paperwork, timetables, etc.—in some form or another? How easy is it to escape from its influence?

For Weber, bureaucracy, even when he was writing in 1922, was coming to dominate more and more aspects of people's lives and of society in general. Thus, the iron cage gives a sense of people being trapped—small, insignificant elements in large-scale organizations.

Such critiques of bureaucracy, which see bureaucracy as sinister and inhuman—an 'invisible enemy' (Bell, 2008: 65) that dominates people through its unquestioning, faceless rules and procedures, leaving people with very small, meaningless jobs and routines to pursue—are often seen in artistic and fictional portrayals of bureaucracy.

Theory in context: the critique of bureaucracy in *Brazil*

In the dystopian film *Brazil* (dir. Gilliam, 1985), a typographical error on a form (caused by a fly landing on a typewriter) leads to the wrong person being arrested (Bell, 2008: 84). The film follows a low-level government employee who tries, with increasing frustration, to reverse the error. A powerful visual metaphor within the film is of the office exploding, scattering its paperwork across the landscape below. The arrested character tries to escape, but the flying paperwork catches up, covers him, and suffocates him.

Have you ever tried to get an error corrected by a large scale organization?

The film *Brazil* resonates with Weber's concept of the iron cage, highlighting both the unquestioning nature of the rules and procedures of bureaucracy, its dehumanization —literally suffocating a character in paperwork—and the inability to escape from bureaucracy.

The film also portrays bureaucracy's inflexibility and unquestioning nature in reversing something once it is formalized in paperwork. Such inflexibility suggests another area of critique beyond that of Weber—namely that bureaucracy may not *in practice* be efficient.

Review questions

1. Describe what is meant by rational-legal authority.

2. Explain the main problems that Weber found with bureaucracy.

3. Analyse the difference between formal and substantive rationality. How can the Holocaust be viewed in terms of these two forms of rationality?

Apply

4. Which of Weber's critiques of bureaucracy applies most to the 'drudgery' encountered at Junction Hotel and why?

Dysfunctions of bureaucracy

Running case: unintended consequences

Chance had thought that his rules, procedures, and paperwork would bring about a standardization and uniformity of behaviour among the Junction Hotel workforce. However, in practice, he finds a number of unexpected consequences.

- The fitness centre manager meticulously completes the paperwork related to attendance. On occasions, this leads to the fitness centre opening late as he tries to complete paperwork by the deadlines set.

- Effingham is upset at not being able to shout at staff. He feels it is part of the nature of kitchen work. In protest, he follows the disciplinary procedures to the letter, sending staff to Chance for the most minor infringements. At one point, all of the kitchen staff are waiting outside Chance's office to be disciplined while the kitchen lies empty with a restaurant full of unhappy customers waiting for their food.

- Meanwhile, the lax regime of Linda Wilkinson seems to continue. It is rumoured that she has told staff not to bother clocking in and that she will cover-up any absences when she fills out the paperwork. She feels that this creates good staff relations, but also makes her own life easier—she doesn't have to spend time calculating absence rates and can get on with other management tasks.

- Check-in times at Reception have increased, despite the introduction of new procedures. It seems that the receptionists are so frightened that Mortimer will pick up on any deviation from procedures that they're following them to the letter, even when common sense suggests otherwise. On one occasion, a couple who, to all eyes, appeared to be over 70 years old were asked for proof of their year of birth to qualify for a pensioners' discount. As the woman reached for her bus pass, she strained her back and was taken to hospital, vowing loudly never to return as she was stretchered out past the, by then, massive queue in the foyer.

Looking at all the delays caused by the procedures, Chance wonders whether he is achieving efficient control over the organization after all. To his eyes, it seems like a return to the ad hoc dysfunctionality that he has tried to avoid.

While Weber presented a number of critiques of bureaucracy, he still noted the technical efficiency of the 'ideal type' of bureaucracy, albeit an ideal type that came with significant social consequences.

Remember, however, that Weber's ideal type was a hypothetical model, created without observing the workings of actual organizations. A number of organizational studies uncovered a difference between the ideal type of bureaucracy and how bureaucracies actually function. They found that, rather than being rational and efficient, bureaucracies either had unintended, inefficient consequences, or that their rules were ignored in the name of the smooth running of the organization. Many of these **dysfunctions of bureaucracy** are still encountered today.

Dysfunctions of bureaucracy Unintended consequences of bureaucracy which lead to it not functioning in the efficient manner for which it is designed.

Red tape

The term **red tape** suggests negative connotations of rules and regulations getting in the way of an organization achieving its goals or where an organization puts in place a prohibitive amount of form filling and 'check boxes' that must be ticked. Rather than promoting efficiency, bureaucracy has the opposite effect.

Red tape is typically characterized as where paperwork and rules and procedures create extra work—they get in the way rather than helping with the work that people have to do. This is a typical source of contention in many professions—the feeling that paperwork and form filling prevent people from doing their actual job.

Two recent major reports in the UK have suggested that excessive bureaucracy—adherence to rules and regulations, and the constant need to complete paperwork and provide data and information—was actually getting in the way of people doing their front-line work in both the police force (Berry, 2010) and in social work (Munro, 2010). In the latter case, a problem arises where the burden of paperwork takes social workers away from one of the important tasks that they are meant to perform, namely protecting vulnerable children.

> **Red tape** An un-intended consequence of bureaucracy, where rules and paperwork get in the way of work and activities, rather than helping tasks to be performed efficiently.

Real life case: the Red Tape Challenge

At the time of writing, the UK government was engaged in a public consultation over unnecessary rules and regulations which get in the way of organizations achieving their aims (Department for Business, Innovation and Skills, 2012). The 'red tape challenge' invited businesses to suggest regulations that were unnecessary burdens and a hindrance. The following extract from their website shows the balance between bureaucracy and rules that are needed, and those that become red tape:

'Good regulation is a good thing. It protects consumers, employees and the environment, it helps build a more fair society and can even save lives. But over the years, regulations – and the inspections and bureaucracy that go with them – have piled up and up. This has hurt business, doing real damage to our economy. And it's done harm to our society too. When people are confronted by a raft of regulations whenever they try to volunteer or play a bigger part in their neighbourhood, they begin to think they shouldn't bother.'

Source: Department for Business, Innovation and Skills (2012).

Visit the Online Resource Centre for a link to the Red Tape Challenge.

The bureaucratic personality

Many of us may have encountered a 'jobsworth': an official who follows rules to the letter rather than thinking of the bigger picture or more reasonable outcomes. The jobsworth follows rules rigidly and inflexibly—to do otherwise is 'more than my job's worth'.

Real life case: the upside-down badge

Jobsworth stories where officials have implemented rules that seem petty and where people have been punished for seemingly minor infringements of the rules often make the news.

For example, in 2011 a pensioner with a disability in Nottinghamshire, UK, was fined £35 for parking in a disabled parking bay with the relevant accreditation badge displayed in the windscreen, but upside down (BBC News, 2011).

On one hand, the rules state that the badge must be legible. Following the rules to the letter, it was correct to issue the fine. However, the overall aim of the rules is to prevent people without the correct accreditation parking in a disabled bay. Here, we can interpret a mismatch between the spirit and aim of the rules, and their rigid implementation.

Source: BBC News (2011).

Disabled parking bay sign.

An unquestioning adherence to rules is an example of what Merton (1940) termed the **bureaucratic personality**. The rules are seen as important above all else, to the extent that 'conformity with the rules interferes with the achievement of the purposes of the organization' (Merton, 1940: 563). Rather than being guided by what would be of benefit to the organization overall, or to a particular client or customer of the organization, a bureaucratic personality suggests simply doing as one is told by the rules and procedures.

A similar unflinching adherence to rules and procedures is encapsulated by the phrase **trained incapacity**, which describes people so reliant on rules and procedures that they become inflexible and unable to act in any other way. If something new or different happens, they are so set in their ways that they are unable to adapt and deal with the change.

> **Bureaucratic personality** A tendency to follow rules to the letter rather than seeing the wider picture and making more common-sense judgements.

> **Trained incapacity** Where people are so used to their behaviour being controlled by bureaucratic rules and procedures that they become inflexible and unable to think for themselves and show initiative.

Theory in context: 'computer says no'

A recurring sketch on the BBC comedy *Little Britain* depicts an office worker, variously working in a bank, travel agency, or hospital, who feeds information from customers into a computer which then makes decisions on her behalf. The catchphrase 'computer says no' depicts the clerk having no human input into the decision—it is all a result of information and procedures encoded within the computer system. When asked if decisions can be changed, she proves to be inflexible—unable to do anything beyond what the computer says. The character is portrayed as dehumanized, almost robotic, and is an example of the 'bureaucratic personality'.

 Visit the Online Resource Centre for links to video clips of the show.

As with red tape, the bureaucratic personality suggests that, rather than being technically efficient, bureaucracy can have the opposite effect and hinder an organization in achieving its aims. Indeed, a common form of industrial action is the **work to rule**. By following rules and procedures to the letter, work is actually slowed down dramatically—the instruments of bureaucracy are used against the organization.

> Work to rule A form of industrial action where workers follow rules, regulations, and instructions precisely—this often results in the speed of work slowing considerably.

Bending the rules and exercising discretion

You may have heard the phrase 'rules are meant to be broken'. Many bureaucracies operate *despite* their rules—if people followed them to the letter they would get in the way of the organization running smoothly, creating too much red tape or inflexibility. In this respect, people are seen to operate not with a bureaucratic personality, but by interpreting and bending the rules where necessary.

Blau (1963) studied workers in a US business law enforcement agency. He found that workers would make informal adjustments to formal rules and requirements if it helped to get the job done or if the formal requirements were getting in the way. Workers who bent rules actually got jobs done more efficiently and achieved organizational goals better than those who followed rules to the letter.

Lipsky (1980) noted that discretion is required by social work professionals in applying rules in different cases. He suggests that they deploy a form of 'street-level bureaucracy', judging each case as it comes and in its own context, rather than applying rules to the letter. It is a more contextual flexible application of rules and procedures than that of the rigid bureaucratic personality. Barton (2003) notes a similar exercise of discretion in police work. While the purpose of police work is ostensibly to enforce rules (or in this case laws), at street level officers use their own judgement and discretion in which laws to apply and when. The best end result might come from a 'quiet word' rather than applying a particular law to the letter, which could inflame a sensitive situation.

The ultimate in bending rules is where they are ignored. Gouldner (1954) suggested that where rules are imposed and seen as unnecessary there might exist a **mock bureaucracy**—the rules exist on paper but are ignored in practice. Sometimes the phrase 'we have a policy' suggests that the policy exists but is not necessarily followed.

> Mock bureaucracy A situation where policies and rules exist, but are ignored.

The inflexibility of bureaucracy

The examples in this section all show a distinction between the ideal type of bureaucracy and bureaucracy in practice whereby its rules, structures, and paperwork are used more flexibly. As we have seen, this flexibility can be necessary in order to get the job done—a rigid adherence to bureaucratic rules and procedures leads to dysfunctions, such as red tape and the bureaucratic personality (see Morgan, 2006: 26-27, for more on where bureaucracy may or may not be appropriate).

Review questions

1. Describe the different dysfunctions of bureaucracy.

2. Explain what is meant by bureaucracy being inflexible.

Apply

3. In the Junction Hotel case, what type of bureaucratic dysfunctions can you see in the different actions of staff at the hotel?

Evaluating bureaucracy: a double-edged sword?

Bureaucracy can be seen as something of a double-edged sword. On one hand, it makes possible management and activity on a large scale that would otherwise be beyond human capability. The vast majority of the organizations that exist today would not be possible without bureaucracy. On the other hand, bureaucracy has negative aspects, both in its dehumanizing effects upon people and its dysfunctions.

That most, if not all, organizations employ some form of bureaucracy is a testament to its undoubted advantages:

- it not only allows for Fayol's five aspects of management (planning, organizing, commanding, coordination, and control) to take place, but it allows for them to be done efficiently on a large scale
- it solves the problem of keeping order over an organization as it grows in scale
- it creates clear roles and responsibilities, outlining clear lines of authority and the limits of that authority
- it allows for information about individuals in organization, even whole populations, to be stored in a form that is easily manageable
- it ensures **impersonal fairness** within the organization, for example with equal opportunities. Rules and procedures that are in place are intended to bring about equality and fairness in how workers are treated as much as it brings about control for management (see du Gay, 2000).

Impersonal fairness
The idea that standardized bureaucratic procedures treat people equally and avoid the personal prejudice and preferences that individual managers might have.

These advantages, however, come at the expense of some considerable disadvantages of bureaucracy:

- what might be rational in formal terms may not be substantively rational—bureaucracy is ethically neutral and simply a means to an end
- it can create negative human consequences—its routines and procedures are dehumanizing and disenchanting; in Weber's terms, encasing society and people in an 'iron cage'
- its inflexibility creates inefficient dysfunctions, such as red tape and the bureaucratic personality, such that bureaucracy might be circumvented rather than adhered to rigidly.

The death of bureaucracy?

An overall critique of bureaucracy is that its inflexibility leaves organizations unable to adapt and change, for instance to changes in the law, in the actions of competitors, or in the demand for a product or service (see Chapter 11 for more on organizations and change management, and Chapter 10 for the 'organizational learning' perspective where the emphasis is on developing creative, autonomous workers rather than workers simply following rules). This might not have been such a problem when Fayol and Weber were writing, when the world that organizations faced was seen to be more stable.

In Chapter 4 we see a move from bureaucracy to post-bureaucracy. In response to a more dynamic, fast-changing world, organizations have developed more flexible structures and means of dealing with rules and paperwork than that suggested by the rigid, ideal type. From this perspective, dysfunctions have made bureaucracy, at least in the form described by Fayol and Weber, obsolete in the contemporary world.

However, it is wrong to proclaim the 'coming death of bureaucracy' (Bennis, 1966). Bureaucracy is used in all organizations in one form or another, even if it is not in the rigid type described by Fayol and Weber. In Chapter 4 we also see how contemporary organizations not only make use of bureaucracy, but also that it is used in, arguably, a more intensive way. In Chapter 16 (discussing the service industry) we see that rational forms of control are more than prevalent in the modern-day service industries.

Computers and bureaucracy

Bureaucracy is now usually performed by computers rather than paperwork in filing cabinets. Given that bureaucracy is as much about holding and processing records and information as it is about structure, it is a task at which computers are adept. Indeed, the language used to describe how computer information is organized uses bureaucratic imagery, with 'files' and 'folders' an allusion to the paperwork of bureaucracy and its storage.

Traditional filing system.

The bureaucratic power of organizations is helped greatly by the information processing power and speed of computers. Chapter 14 looks specifically at information and computer technologies. However it is worth noting here how computers not only enhance the power of bureaucracy, but their use in organizations very much reflects and enhances bureaucratic procedures. Furthermore, in a world dominated by computer networks, bureaucracy plays a role in ensuring that information communicated between computer networks is stored in a standardized format (Kallinikos, 2004: 18).

Computers also aid the monitoring and control function of bureaucracy. Paperwork and records store data about people, as do computer databases—at an organizational or governmental level. Such surveillance and its implementation through computer technology are explored in Chapter 4.

Early models of bureaucracy can be seen as somewhat inflexible and dated. However, aspects of bureaucratic design and functioning similar to these are a necessary part of the workplace today, as will be seen in subsequent chapters.

Further reading

Morgan, G. 2006. *Images of organization*. Sage Publications, Thousand Oaks, CA.
See Chapter 2 'Mechanisation takes command: Organizations as machines' for an overview of bureaucracy and how it fits in with other aspects of rational work design.

Pugh, D.S. 2008. *Organization theory: selected classic readings*. Penguin Books, London.
  Contains extracts of original writings from Weber and Fayol (and other chapters relate to other theories in this book).

Smith, I., and Boyns, T. 2005. British management theory and practice: the impact of Fayol. *Management Decision* 43(10): 1317–1334.
  A history of Fayol's work and how it has been adopted in the UK.

For the two reports mentioned in this chapter which examine red tape and bureaucratic dysfunctions in UK social work and policing see:

Munro, E. 2010. *The Munro Review of Child Protection*. Department for Education, London. Available at: http://www.education.gov.uk/munroreview/firstreport.shtml.

Berry, J. 2010. *Reducing Bureaucracy in Policing*. Home Office, London. Available at: http://www.homeoffice.gov.uk/publications/police/reducing-bureaucracy/reduce-bureaucracy-police.

Bibliography

Barton, H. 2003. Understanding occupational (sub) culture—a precursor for reform: The case of the police service in England and Wales. *International Journal of Public Sector Management* 16(5): 346–358.

Bauman, Z. 1989. *Modernity and the holocaust*. Polity Press: Cambridge.

BBC News. 2011. Nottingham pensioner fined £35 for 'upside down' badge. Available at: http://www.bbc.co.uk/news/uk-england-nottinghamshire-13891422 (last accessed 27 March 2012).

Bell, E. 2008. *Reading management and organization in film*. Palgrave Macmillan: Basingstoke.

Bennis, W. 1966. The coming death of bureaucracy. *Think Magazine* Nov-Dec: 30–35.

Berry, J. 2010. *Reducing bureaucracy in policing*. Home Office, London.

Blau, P.M. 1963. *The dynamics of bureaucracy; a study of interpersonal relations in two Government agencies*. University of Chicago Press: Chicago.

Chia, R. 1995. From modern to postmodern organizational analysis. *Organization Studies* 16(4): 579–604.

Department for Business Innovation and Skills. 2012. Red tape challenge—home. Available at: http://www.redtapechallenge.cabinetoffice.gov.uk/home/index/ (last accessed 27 March 2012).

du Gay, P. 2000. *In praise of bureaucracy: Weber, organization, ethics*. Sage: London.

Fayol, H. 1949. *General and industrial management*. Pitman: London.

Gilliam, T. 1985. *Brazil*. 20th Century Fox.

Gouldner, A.W. 1954. *Patterns of industrial bureaucracy*. Free Press: Glencoe, IL.

Kallinikos, J. 2004. The social foundations of the bureaucratic order. *Organization* 11(1): 13–36.

Lipsky, M. 1980. *Street-level bureaucracy: dilemmas of the individual and public services*. Russell Sage Foundation: New York.

MacRae, D.G. 1974. *Weber*. Fontana: Glasgow.

Merton, R.K. 1940. Bureaucratic structure and personality. *Social Forces* 18(4): 560–568.

Morgan, G. 2006. *Images of organization*. Sage Publications: Thousand Oaks, CA.

Munro, E. 2010. *The Munro review of child protection*. Department for Education, London.

Perry, N. 1992. Putting theory in its place: the social organization of organizational theorizing. In: Reed, M., and Hughes, M. (eds.) *Rethinking organization*. Sage: London, pp. 85–101.

Poster, M. 1995. *The second media age*. Polity Press: Cambridge.

Ritzer, G. 2011. *The McDonaldization of society 6*. Pine Forge Press: Thousand Oaks, CA.

Smith, I., and Boyns, T. 2005. British management theory and practice: the impact of Fayol. *Management Decision* 43(10): 1317–1334.

Thompson, P., and McHugh, D. 2009. *Work organisations: a critical approach*. Palgrave Macmillan: Basingstoke.

Vodafone. 2012. Organisation structure. Available at: http://www.vodafone.com/content/index/investors/management/organisation_structure.html (last accessed 23 November 2012).

Watson, T.J. 2002. *Organising and managing work: organisational, managerial, and strategic behaviour in theory and practice*. Financial Times/Prentice Hall: Harlow.

Weber, M. 1958. *The Protestant ethic and the spirit of capitalism*. Scribner: New York.

Weber, M. 1968. *Economy and society; an outline of interpretive sociology*. Bedminster Press: New York.

Wren, D.A. 2001. Henri Fayol as strategist: a nineteenth century corporate turnaround. *Management Decision* 39(6): 475–487.

Rational work design
Cutting costs, increasing control

Chapter overview and learning outcomes

By the end of this chapter you should be able to:

- describe the principles behind Taylorist and Fordist rational work design
- explain how Taylorism and Fordism contributed to control over the workforce and the creation of more efficient forms of working
- analyse the effects that Taylorism and Fordism are said to have upon workers by reducing them to 'cogs in a machine,' including the critiques by Marx and Braverman
- explain the legacy of Taylorism and its prevalence in working methods today, such that they have been described as 'the most enduring social change of the 20th century' (Donkin, 2001: 159).

Key theorists

Frederick Winslow Taylor	An industrialist and one of the prominent pioneers of efficient, rational work design, Taylor developed the system of 'scientific management'
Henry Ford	Also an industrialist and pioneer of rational management techniques, Ford created systems of mass automobile production with his innovation of the moving assembly line
Frank and Lillian Gilbreth	Husband-and-wife team and associates of Taylor, who developed the time and motion study
Karl Marx	A political philosopher who commented on the inequalities of power between capital and workers
Harry Braverman	A follower of Marx who formed the deskilling thesis that criticized the loss of craft skills under rational production methods

Key terms

Rational work design, rational production	The techniques developed by Taylor and Ford, among others. Work is designed to achieve maximum efficiency and organizations and workers are the tools used to achieve this efficiency
Capitalist working relationship	The relationship between capitalists, who pay wages, and labour, who work in return for those wages
Scientific management, Taylorism	The techniques pioneered by Frederick Taylor whereby work is broken down into small tasks which are then measured precisely and designed to be performed in the most efficient manner possible

Fordism	Rational work design, pioneered by Henry Ford, where work is designed for maximum efficiency. The worker remains stationary in front of a moving assembly line and repeats the same task
Efficiency	Getting more output from the same amount of resource input, e.g. time, money, labour
Deskilling	From the work of Braverman (1974), this is the loss of craft skills and expert knowledge experienced by workers when their jobs are simplified to fit in with rational work design
Alienation	From the work of Marx (1894/1981), this is a number of ways in which rational work design impacts workers negatively, isolating them from their skills, the final product, and their co-workers

Introduction

Running case: the bottom line

Simon Chance is worried. Junction Hotel is not breaking even and there are rumours of a budget hotel opening nearby. Furthermore, Chance is presented with a report by his investors, which makes for grim reading.
The executive summary states:

- having weathered a recession, the hotel industry is suffering—corporate customers are reducing spend on hotels

- prices need to come down to remain competitive and for the hotel to stay in business—*to afford that price reduction, Junction Hotel needs to reduce its costs*

- budget hotels are aggressively cutting costs, for example by removing free toiletries.

Chance has a dilemma. Junction is a luxury hotel—if they cut corners then customers will complain and the hotel will lose its reputation. At the same time, low cost competitors are taking business away from them.
Chance calls in Business Manager Phil Weaver, who has overseen many efficiency drives in his career. Weaver looks over the accounts and declares: 'You know, your biggest cost isn't shampoo or wallpaper or anything like that. Your biggest cost is your wage bill. That's the bottom line—it's losing you money and making you uncompetitive. *There's a lot of waste and inefficiency*.'
'There are plenty of opportunities to reduce your wage bill and still get the same job done. I've stayed here before and seen your cleaners stood around gossiping. Tell you what: let me have a closer look at what they do—I bet I can make them much more productive and bring down the wage bill.'
Chance looks queasy, 'I don't know', he says. 'They do a good job—I wouldn't want to rock the boat. I don't think they would like you interfering in what they do.'
'The problem is you haven't got a clue what they do!' retorts Weaver. 'If you want this hotel to survive then you need to take *control*. It's not that you are just paying your cleaners—they are taking you to the cleaners! Let me have a go at getting them to work for their money.'

Cost is a concern for all managers. In the recent recession, both companies and governments have been making 'efficiency drives', taking 'austerity measures', slashing budgets, and taking other actions in order to cut costs. The justification for government is to 'cut waste', 'reduce the deficit', and produce more 'efficient public services' at better 'value for money'. Businesses have also had massive cost-cutting exercises, which they claim are needed to cope during difficult economic times—possibly even to stay in business.

We all like our money to stretch as far as it can, especially when on a tight budget. Think about how you minimize your own personal costs—shopping around, using comparison websites, and taking advantage of 'happy hours' and 'two-for-one'-type offers. All of these allow us to get more from our hard-earned money.

Even in times of economic growth, control of costs is an issue for business. Reduced costs can mean that lower prices can be charged (giving a competitive advantage) or increased profits can be reaped, leading to increased shareholder dividends. As will be seen in Chapter 4 (*Rationalization in contemporary organizations*), there are contemporary business models, such as those of Travelodge and Ryanair, which focus on price competition through intensive cost reduction. In Chapter 15 (*Globalization*), we see how international competition can undercut costs at home.

> **Theory in context:** Wedgwood and costs
>
> Cost control is not just a recent issue. In the eighteenth century, the pottery industrialist Josiah Wedgwood identified costs as a major area of measurement and control in setting market prices for his goods. Beforehand, pricing had been a result of educated guesswork, which had led to Wedgwood making a loss. While Wedgwood was a one-off pioneer in his own day, costs are now a major area of control for companies and organizations (Hoskin and Macve, 1986: 124; Morgan, 1990: 103–6; McKendrick, 1970).

One of the largest costs, if not *the* main cost for most organizations, is labour—the amount spent on wages (Simpson, 1999: 52). In this chapter, we examine how **rational work design** is applied to the **labour process** in order to create workers who are more cost effective. In other words, through the design of work itself, workers do more for the wages they are paid—they are more efficient and more productive.

Rational work design, as we will see in Chapter 4, is pervasive in today's workplaces. However, it developed from a period of rapid industrialization and the development of the factory system in the Western world around the early 1900s. Industrialists, such as Frederick Taylor and Henry Ford, designed work to be as efficient as possible. While Taylor and Ford are synonymous with rational work design (the terms **Taylorism** and **Fordism** being used, respectively, to describe their scientific management and assembly line innovations), they share the key features of rational work design with many other innovators of their time, which we summarise as:

- work is seen as a means of achieving a clearly defined end
- work is designed so as to achieve this end in the optimum or most efficient possible manner, both in terms of time and cost

Cost The amount in wages and materials that it costs to produce a good or provide a service.

Rational work design The design of work tasks to achieve maximum efficiency and reduce costs.

Labour process How work is designed and controlled by management.

Taylorism The work process designed by Taylor, associated with the division of labour into small tasks, which are then redesigned to be performed as efficiently as possible.

Fordism The use of a moving assembly line to mass produce goods.

- work is designed in a scientific manner, using measurement and calculation, as if designing a machine
- work is broken down into simplistic, repetitive tasks which take little or no skill to perform—a **division of labour**
- waste is designed out of the work process.

Division of labour
Breaking down a job into more simplistic, individual tasks.

While rational work design might make workers more efficient and cost-effective, we will see that this comes at a cost. Workers are subject to increased managerial control and monotonous, simplistic work which leaves workers' skills superfluous to requirements. The chapter will examine critiques of rational work design from Karl Marx and Harry Braverman, examining the considerable resistance encountered when implementing such techniques.

Thus, rational work design is seen not just as a technique for reducing the cost of labour, but also as a technique which attempts to exert control over workers. This struggle for control stems from the nature of the capitalist working relationship.

The capitalist working relationship: cost and control

Running case: Amy Turtle

Amy Turtle is in her mid-50s and has been a cleaner all her working life. She has been with Junction Hotel for ten years, and before that she was self-employed for twenty years. While she had enjoyed the independence of working for herself, she took on the position during a time when her client list was dwindling, and opted, instead, for a regular salary rather than the risk and hassle of managing her own business.

Her relationship with Linda Wilkinson is good—they are both old-timers at the hotel. With Wilkinson being busy enough with other tasks, she happily leaves the cleaning side to run itself, trusting Turtle to keep her eye on things. It's as if Turtle is still managing herself and, indeed, she resents any attempt by management to interfere in her cleaning work.

During her time at Junction Hotel, Turtle has developed a reputation as being a knowledgeable cleaner and a formidable character. She brings much experience and knowledge into the workplace, and is very much the 'queen bee' among the cleaners. Sometimes, she even brings in her own cleaning products to try out—she likes nothing more than the challenge of a new or mysterious stain to tackle.

Turtle socializes with the older cleaners and is a matronly presence with the younger ones. In the reorganization she is promoted to Head Cleaner. This very much reflects a role she has held informally for many years, whereby she is part supervisor—instilling fear in the younger cleaners who might stray—and part champion, sticking up for 'the girls' when necessary and taking their concerns to the management.

Rational work design needs to be understood in the context of changes that the early factory system brought about in the early 1900s. Prior to the factory system, manufacturing work was often based around the individual family household—the backyard workshop or furnace was commonplace (see Thompson and McHugh, 2009: 20). The work had a number of features which may seem unusual today other than for people who are self-employed:

- workers owned their own **means of production**—tools, equipment, etc.
- workers were independent and autonomous, i.e. they were their own boss—they decided their own working time, the amount they would sell goods for, the amount they would take as a wage or reinvest in the business, etc.

While many workers today might crave such independence, it comes with a degree of risk. The individual worker is exposed if, say, equipment breaks down and needs expensive repairs, or if orders drop suddenly. Furthermore, such production is inefficient—it doesn't take advantage of **economies of scale**, that is to say each piece of equipment or capital investment is not used to its optimum.

The factory system took advantage of economies of scale. Rather than having individual workers, each independently investing in their own small-scale equipment, a factory brought together a group of workers in one space, operating large-scale equipment (see Simpson, 1999: 48). The initial outlay on equipment might be more expensive, but for the number of workers that can use that equipment it works out less than each of them buying their own equipment individually.

The shift to the factory system brought about a new working relationship.

- Workers no longer owned their own means of production. Factories required massive capital outlay, beyond the means of any one individual worker. Factory owners, either wealthy individuals or a group of shareholders, were, thus, capitalists, providing that initial outlay and owning the means of production.
- Capitalists paid a wage to workers who would work in their service within the factory. Workers lost their previous independence and autonomy—their working hours would be dictated and their tasks set, and they would have no control over the price of goods or investment decisions, etc. Their role was simply to turn up and do a day's work.

Thus, the **capitalist wage-labour** relationship is an exchange (Figure 3.1). The capitalist who owns and invests **capital** in a company pays a wage to workers. In return for this wage, workers supply their **labour**.

Means of production
Tools, premises, and other property used to manufacture goods.

Economies of scale
Cost reduction that comes from producing a product in large amounts.

Capitalist wage-labour relationship The relationship between capitalists, who pay wages, and labour, who work in return for those wages.

Capital Investment in a business to set up the means of production, often used as a term to refer to business owners or capitalists who make that investment.

Labour Any person who works in return for a wage; the term is used to refer to such workers collectively.

CAPITAL

£

LABOUR

Figure 3.1 The Capitalist wage-labour relationship.

The capitalist wage–labour relationship gives rise to a need for management. Workers are directed in what to do, what time to arrive, when to leave work, etc. All of this needs to be implemented by management. But where would management appear in Figure 3.1? On one hand, management are the agents of capital, doing their bidding in directing workers. On the other hand, managers are not owners. Just like the people they direct and control, they too are wage labourers.

Tensions in the capitalist wage–labour relationship

This relationship between capital and labour, fairly new at the time of the factory system, might seem like a simple exchange, but a fundamental tension lies at its heart: capital and labour want different things, and have different priorities.

Capital has an interest in getting the most work for the wages they pay, i.e. in obtaining maximum efficiency. This means the employees working to their maximum possible output and not wasting time and effort. It is here that such techniques as rational work design act in the favour of capital by maximizing what effort they get for their labour costs.

However, as we saw in Chapter 2, what might be rational from one perspective may not be from another. Workers have an interest in not being worked necessarily to the optimum, but in taking regular breaks, having holidays, and paid sick leave, etc. All of these conflict with the capitalist's desire to maximize effort in return for the wage (Figure 3.2).

As we will see, from a Marxist perspective the capitalist working relationship becomes one of a battle of control between two conflicting sets of interests as much as it is an exchange of effort in return for wages—one which can result in conflict and resistance. **Industrial action**, such as strikes, is often a result of disagreements over aspects of the capitalist working relationship, such as pay and working conditions, etc.

In the following sections we see how rational work design was used by Taylor, Ford, and their contemporaries not just as a means of gaining **efficiency** for the wages paid, but also as a means of asserting control from the side of capital in the wage–labour relationship. The Marxist critique, examined later in the chapter, recognizes how conflict might be an inevitable outcome of such control given the tensions inherent in the relationship.

Industrial action Any action taken by workers in a dispute between capital and labour.

Efficiency The minimization of cost, doing the same for less input of time and money.

Figure 3.2 Conflict in the capitalist wage–labour relationship.

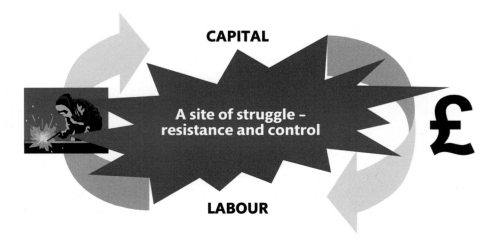

Review questions

1. Describe the main features of the capitalist wage–labour relationship.
2. Explain why the factory was '. . . a revolutionary organisational form' (Simpson, 1999: 48).
3. Analyse why workers might want different things to capitalists in the wage–labour relationship.

Apply

4. How does the position of Amy Turtle relate to the capitalist wage–labour relationship (a) before and (b) after she joined Junction Hotel? Do you think that the hotel is getting the most from her for the wages that they pay her?

Frederick W. Taylor: efficiency and control

Running case: initial observations

Phil Weaver shows his notebook, in which he has made his initial observations of the cleaning process, to Linda Wilkinson.

Amazing—no method or routine. Cleaners put in pairs, given list of rooms to do then left to get on with it—all of them approach the task in different ways and have had different training in how to clean. Lots of gossiping—with each other and with guests. Turtle might tell the younger ones off but she covers up for them in front of management—she looks after her own first. Best of all—they deliberately speed up the morning shift to get an extra 30 mins gossiping time over lunch. If they can work that quickly they should be doing more. Problem is, no management to be seen—there's no control over them: they are a law unto themselves.

Wilkinson gives him a knowing smile and replies, 'Phil, don't you think I realize that. Thing is—they are happy, the job gets done, and I get an easy life'. Weaver, however, is getting more and more frustrated: 'That's 30 minutes when they could be doing something else—30 minutes you are paying them for.' 'Look', says Wilkinson more seriously, 'I learned my lesson a few years back. I did ask Amy whether they would be able to squeeze a few more rooms in before lunch but she blinded me with science—told me how long different processes would take. She outlined different ways of tackling different stains, all built up from her years of experience, and talked about the dangers from various different bacteria if she didn't clean properly and thoroughly. In the end, I gave up.'

'This is nonsense!', yells Weaver. 'You have no control over these workers. If anything, they control you and, as a result, you are getting far less out of them than is possible for the wages you pay.'

'Let me have a look at this more closely', says Wilkinson.

Taylor's rational work design innovations transformed how organizations operated, and still have a major impact on how we live and work today. His *Principles of Scientific Management* (Taylor, 1911), developed in the early 1900s' Philadelphia steel industry, identified a set of techniques that came to be known simply as 'Taylorism'.

For Taylor, as suggested by the term **scientific management**, there was a *science* of management and the organization was to be managed as if it were a machine. An industrial engineer by training, he saw management problems just like mechanical and engineering problems. In the words of his biographer, Taylor saw the world through the eyes of both an economist and an engineer (Copley, 1923a: xviii).

Scientific management
The use of scientific techniques to design work to be as efficient as possible.

In this respect, Taylorism is often seen as being simply about efficiency, minimizing waste and increasing output. However, such attempts at efficiency are directed within the capitalist wage–labour relationship at people rather than machines. And, while Taylor wanted to design organizations like machines, people do not necessarily behave in the same, precisely-controllable manner.

Theory in context: Taylor's obsessions

Bahnisch (2000) notes that a number of commentators have written about the 'obsessional' and 'neurotic' nature of Taylor's personality, and his desire for control. His meticulous attention to detail crossed over into aspects of his private life, such as positions for sleeping and steps to be taken when dancing.

Taylor addressed his hobby of golf in a similarly meticulous and obsessional manner. He devoted time to designing a putter that would give the optimum performance (Copley, 1923b), although his double-handled invention never caught on. He also turned his attention to the ideal standard form of grass for putting greens, experimenting with growing grass in his own garden and analysing the impact of 23 different variables on the quality of grass grown (ibid).

It is this obsession and attention to detail that he took into his workplace experiments, and which feed into many management techniques that exist today.

Taylor's 'problems' of control over labour

When Taylor first began working in a factory environment, he viewed the existing approach to work as rather amateurish, governed by traditions and habits—all of which were controlled by the workers. The management, Taylor thought, had little control over what was happening and did little to influence the work process.

 Visit the Online Resource Centre for more information on the early factory systems.

In *Principles of Scientific Management*, Taylor (1911) identifies a number of problems with how work at that time was organized, which indicate that his concerns were as much about control as they were efficiency. In that people do not behave and are not easily controlled like machines, this presented a number of problems of control over labour which, for Taylor, got in the way of the efficiency that he craved.

Non-standard and unpredictable labour

In the Philadelphia steel industry, where Taylor worked, there was a mix of people within his factory. They came from different craft traditions, each with their own ways and means of performing jobs; furthermore, many had a variety of cultural backgrounds, languages, and, indeed, attitudes to work (Jaffee, 2001: 51; Thompson and McHugh, 2009: 29). Workers could certainly not be seen as standard units that would behave and be controlled in the same way as would components in a machine.

Craft knowledge and power

Craft knowledge is where workers have specialist expertise in the work that they do. This was a problem for Taylor because it meant that they held power over him as a manager. He

Craft knowledge
Knowledge of a particular skill, often the result of a long period of training or apprenticeship.

did not know the work as intimately as his workers and, thus, when he asked a question about how long a process would take or how much it would cost he relied, to a large extent, on them being truthful about their expert knowledge.

Workers would use their craft knowledge to create a **rule of thumb** (Taylor, 1911: 16)—the estimate that workers would give for the time a job would take. This was the workers controlling the work process—they could blind management with science, take longer to do tasks, and even demand higher wages because their skills were not easily replaceable.

Have you ever had to take your computer to be repaired? When you are given a quote for the amount that the repairs will cost and the time that it will take, how much of a position are you in to argue back and negotiate? The engineer has an advantage over you because of their expert knowledge, which you cannot dispute.

> **Rule of thumb** A rough estimate of the time needed to perform a task, based on a worker's expert knowledge of that task.

Soldiering

Taylor believed that a typical worker was inherently lazy, lacking the motivation to work other than picking up a wage at the end of the day: '. . . this man plans to do as little as he safely can . . . to do not more than one-third to one-half of a proper day's work'. (Taylor, 1911: 13).

However, while this natural individual **soldiering** (ibid: 13) was one thing, the fact that workers were organized in tightly-knit gangs led to a more systematic form of soldiering, with pressures from co-workers to 'underperform'. Using their expert knowledge and the 'rule of thumb' they could cover for each other, overestimating to management the time that it would take to complete a job and thus improving their own conditions of work by making more time available, leaving room for breaks, and thus not working to the optimum.

> **Soldiering** Techniques used by workers to create time for themselves during the working day. Soldiering means that workers are not working at the most efficient level possible.

From Taylor's perspective, the drive to control workers for greater efficiency and his frustration with workers' own control over the work process was understandable. However, looking back at the nature of the capitalist working relationship it is also understandable why workers wanted to maintain and exert that control—they maintained autonomy over the pace and nature of their work, earned extra time in the form of breaks, and generally helped to maintain some balance in their side of the working relationship. It was with Taylor's innovations in scientific management that this balance would be changed more firmly in favour of management.

Review questions

1. Describe what is meant by craft knowledge? Explain how this gives workers power over management.

2. Explain how human labour presented a problem for the ways in which Taylor wished to control an organization.

3. Analyse what you think were Taylor's central assumptions about how an organization should be managed?

Apply

4. How do you think Taylor would view the power held by Amy Turtle and the cleaners at Junction Hotel?

Scientific management: finding the 'one best way'

Running case: the one best way

Weaver observes the cleaners, running about with a clipboard, timing workers with a stopwatch, and measuring the distances they walk from room to room. He even sets up a video camera to record cleaners as they go around a room. When he plays it back, he can make further detailed measurements of the work process, analysing the pictures with some specialist computer software.

He starts taking cleaners to one side to practise different movements, demonstrating a series of basic moves which they should perform every time they clean a toilet, and constantly measuring and refining the moves to make them more and more efficient, and reduce the time taken to clean one toilet.

Similar routines are devised for such tasks as making beds, replacing towels, and for cleaning all parts of the room. In each case, the task is broken down into a set of pre-defined movements which Weaver then refines to make more efficient. In all cases, wasted movements are to be eliminated—including stopping and gossiping mid-way through a shift.

Everything has its right place in the room—the TV remote, the kettle, sachets of tea and coffee, writing paper, etc. with the aim of standardizing the process and removing any variability in the job.

Weaver also suggests that equipment and fittings could be designed to make the process even more efficient. Items would be laid out on the trolley in the order in which they would be placed in the room, for example toiletries first, and tea and coffee second. Trolleys should be big enough to accommodate all the linen and equipment needed so as to avoid wasteful trips down to the laundry or the store cupboard to reload.

Eventually, following all of his observations and work redesigns, Weaver presents the 'one best way' to clean a room, proudly written down in a training manual given to all cleaners. Whereas a room previously took an average of 30 minutes to clean, Weaver sets a target of 15 minutes per room.

One best way Rational management techniques that propose one most efficient way to perform any task.

Taylor firmly believed that for any job there was **one best way** to perform it. The four principles of scientific management that he outlined not only increased the efficiency with which a job was performed, but also put power in the hands of management by understanding exactly what work people did to make a product and creating the standard one best way for workers to then perform that task. The four principles, which we will examine in turn in this section, are (based on Taylor, 1911):

- *work is broken down into small, repetitive actions—a division of labour.* These are analysed scientifically, through a time and motion study, and redesigned so that they are performed to their optimum efficiency with minimal waste
- *workers are selected scientifically* for each role with the most suitable workers then being trained so as to work to the optimum efficiency
- *division of work between management and workers*, with management taking responsibility for the design and planning of the work
- *cooperation* between management and the workforce to achieve the task in hand.

The division of labour

Scientific management begins by breaking a job down into a series of simple repetitive tasks—a division of labour. A worker ceases to manufacture a product from start to finish, for example making a whole wheel. Instead, the worker is one of many who perform one repetitive and simplistic task in a chain, for example inserting a spoke in a wheel.

Have you ever assembled a piece of flat-pack furniture? Even though you may have no previous experience or skill in furniture-making, the way in which the job is broken down into small, manageable tasks with a set of basic instructions means that you are able to assemble your new bookcase. Now imagine that you and a group of friends had 100 flat-pack bookcases to assemble. What would be the most efficient way to do this? Would you each sit and make bookcases individually from start to finish, or would you use a form of division of labour, where each of you specializes in just one task, performing that one task on each of the bookcases?

Taylor was neither the first nor the only person to use the division of labour, but the degree to which he then scientifically analysed the work process marks him out.

Visit the Online Resource Centre for a description of Adam Smith's observation of the division of labour.

Taylor was interested in designing work that eliminated waste movements and created the most efficient way to perform a task. This might be through instructing workers on what moves to make, or designing machinery and the physical layout of the factory to minimize waste movement. Work was designed like a machine and workers were managed as if they were a part of that machine, using precise, scientific measurement and calculation.

Taylor was a pioneer of the **time and motion study**, a technique still used in modern day organizations. This involved closely observing and measuring every movement made by a worker using a stopwatch and measuring tape for every movement made.

The most famous example of this given by Taylor (1911: 43ff) was the story he recounts of the Dutch labourer, Schmidt, in *Principles of Scientific Management*. He speaks (in mostly disparaging terms) of how he observed this labourer's movements in shovelling pig iron— a very basic task—and redesigned the work to be performed at the optimum efficiency. At the Bethlehem Steel Works, where these observations took place, the number of pig iron-handlers required for the same task was reduced from 600 to 140 (ibid: 71)—representing a massive reduction in labour costs. In return for this punishing and monotonous work, Taylor increased pay, but by a level which was more than offset by the efficiency gains.

> Time and motion study Rational work design where tasks are measured and timed, and redesigned to maximize efficiency.

The Gilbreths: time and motion study

The work done by Schmidt was very basic, unskilled labouring. However, the same principles of scientific management could, according to Taylor, be applied to any task in hand. Taylor cites with approval the work of his contemporaries Frank and Lillian Gilbreth, who studied the work of bricklayers. They looked not just at the motion of bricklaying, but also the position of the bricks and tools next to the bricklayer so as to further decrease waste motion. They were reported to have designed the process of laying one brick from an initial observation of eighteen individual moves down to just five. The resulting efficiency gain saw bricklayers move from laying 120 bricks per hour to 350 (Taylor, 1911: 81).

The Gilbreths were, arguably, the experts at time and motion study, extending it into a number of different areas—not just factory work but also retail work and office work, such as typing. In their quest for measurement and efficiency, and using a grid and stopwatch, they filmed people performing their work and then analysed and re-designed their movements to enable them to perform their tasks more efficiently (Price, 1992: 61).

Theory in context

As with Taylor, the Gilbreth's brought their desire for efficiency into their home life. Two of their twelve children wrote a book about their home life (Gilbreth and Carey, 1949), which was made into the Hollywood film *Cheaper by the Dozen* (Lang, 1950). Among anecdotes of home life in the book, the children were invited to submit sealed bids for household chores, such as washing-up. Furthermore, a gramophone player was placed in the bathroom so that family members could listen to language-learning records—no time was to be wasted time.

After the death of Frank Gilbreth, Lillian Gilbreth performed similar work in department stores, introducing time and motion studies to work that requires a greater variety of movement than a simple, repetitive task (Graham, 2000).

The time and motion study will be familiar to many workers today, sometimes masquerading under such names as 'Organization and methods'. The same ideas apply—work is observed, measured, and timed with the aim of eliminating waste movements. Either the job itself is redesigned, or the equipment and layout are redesigned so as to eliminate such movement. The redesign can be quite practical, for example a bank worker who has to constantly walk to a safe at the back of the office could have the safe moved closer to save time and effort (and thus increase their efficiency). A whole science of **ergonomics** is devoted to making the working environment adapt as efficiently and conveniently as possible to the humans who will use it.

Ergonomics The design of workplace environments and tools to best fit the movements of the human body.

Study skills: time-management

As a student you may see the need to be efficient with money, but are you also efficient with your time? Do you work out any particular methods for tasks such as cleaning a room, making a meal, or writing an assignment which help you to complete them more quickly and avoid wasting time?

A key study skill is time-management: the ability to plan time around your university work and other competing demands, such as work and social life. Many of our students who have not done as well as they have hoped on essays will openly admit that poor time-management contributed to their poor grade.

Time-management isn't just about not starting an essay the night before a deadline. It involves getting materials for the essay, which can involve a wait for library books. It also involves knowing the availability of tutors and when they are available to help—they are unlikely to be able to answer questions at the very last minute, for example.

Scientific selection of employees

Taylor's design of work went beyond work and equipment. He also believed that particular people were better 'fits' for different jobs. In a sense, with work designed like a machine, certain people made better 'components' for different types of work. Referring back to Schmidt, it is obvious from Taylor's own work that this hefty individual was better suited for the work he did than others might be. Thus, for Taylor, a **scientific selection**, and training, of individuals for jobs was just as important as the work design itself.

Scientific selection
Defining the precise
characteristics of the
ideal candidate for a job.

Workers work, managers manage

This idea of workers simply 'fitting in' is shown by a second aspect of the division of labour under scientific management. While there was a *horizontal* division of labour on the shop floor (i.e. a division of work tasks) there was also a *vertical* division of labour between management and workers (see Figure 3.3). This builds on the bureaucratic organization structure developed in Chapter 2 in that it now shows where knowledge of the production process resides within that structure.

Management do all the planning—the work measurement, work design, and so on, and the workers then do simply as they are told. There is a separation between the mental work, the thinking, and the physical work on the shop floor. In other words, there is a **separation between planning and doing**. Taylorism began to introduce levels of management based around the work design—functional foremanship meant that supervisors were assigned to specific tasks rather than the more informal and ad hoc arrangements under the internal contracting system.

Separation of planning
and doing Tasks
designed by manage-
ment, with workers
having no input other
than to perform those
tasks.

Workers and managers cooperate

A final aspect of scientific management, as described by Taylor, is that it requires the cooperation of workers and management. However, as we see in the next section, such cooperation is more a relationship of control and, furthermore, one where Taylor encountered resistance, rather than cooperation.

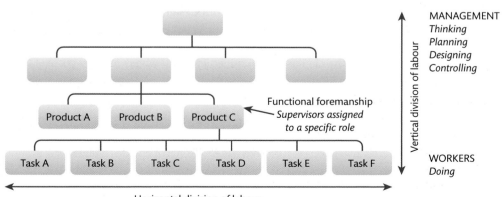

Figure 3.3 The horizontal and vertical division of labour.

Review questions

1. Describe the four principles of scientific management.

2. Explain how time and motion study increases efficiency.

3. Analyse what is meant by a 'separation of planning and doing'.

Apply

4. Think of an organization that you know. Are there any areas where scientific management principles are applied or are there any areas where scientific management principles might improve efficiency?

The fall and rise of Taylorism

Running case: resignation letter

Dear Linda,

With great regret, I am writing to offer my resignation from my job at Junction Hotel.

I used to have a job here where I had great pride in my work. I felt part of a family and felt valued, both for my knowledge and my experience.

Now I feel completely demoralized, and would rather opt for early retirement than continue to work here.

I feel so sorry for the other girls—they are not happy. They have no control over what they do and when. Everything is dictated to us, there's no room to breathe. And as for all of that checking up—it feels like we're in the army on parade. I used to love this job—now every task is simply given to us step by step.

Best wishes

Amy

Today, there are few workplaces that do not employ Taylorist techniques to some extent; indeed, as will be argued in Chapter 4, rational work design is alive and well, and more prevalent and intensive than ever. However, it was not always so; indeed, there was initial resistance to Taylorism from both workers and factory owners. In part, this came from the nature of the work, but also the degree to which it enabled managers to exert control.

Control through Taylorism

It was not just efficiency that was increased by scientific management. The rational work design that he pioneered also gave a solution to the problems of control over labour that he had earlier encountered.

1. *Standardization.* By designing and defining precisely the nature of work, down to its most basic movements, Taylor was able to increase uniformity and predictability—work was

standardized, minimizing the variable nature of human labour that Taylor so feared. It no longer mattered that people came from various craft traditions, all with their own particular ways of performing a task. With a tightly-defined and prescribed task much of this variability in the labour force could be overcome.

2. *Individualization.* Rather than work being organized in gangs under the patronage of a subcontractor, workers were now individualized, that is to say they had the one task that they performed, having been selected and trained for that task. Again, this regained some control for Taylor as he was able to bypass the soldiering and control which came from groups of workers.

3. *Surveillance.* Individualization brought about another type of control—a more internalized form of control. Whereas workers underwent direct supervision, it is not difficult to see that if a worker is assigned to one small element of the work process and that element is defective or not being produced to speed, the culprit is easy to single out (see Panopticism, surveillance, and control in Chapter 4).

4. *Knowledge.* The power that workers had from their craft knowledge was effectively rendered redundant. Atomizing the work process means that workers only have knowledge of their one small part of the job. The separation of planning and doing means that knowledge of the overall process resides with the management—those who do the calculations and then plan the work process. So, the control that workers had over the pacing and other aspects of their work are now gone and are held by management.

5. *Skill.* Similar to knowledge, the level of skill required to perform a job is diminished greatly by scientific management. Previously, managers relied on the craft skills of workers which meant that workers were valuable and often irreplaceable—a source of power. With skill replaced by a simple, repetitive task, workers become more expendable—they can be replaced easily by other unskilled labour. Again, this gives greater bargaining power to management.

Resisting Taylorism: workers and managers

Running case: the showdown

Phil Weaver is summoned to Simon Chance's office, where he stands with Linda Wilkinson. Chance is enraged: 'What have you started here? We've got our best cleaner resigning, the rest of them are unhappy. We all used to get on so well, now it feels like civil war'.

   'Maybe so', replies Weaver, 'but I've done what you asked—they are working more efficiently and with such routinized jobs they are easy to control'.

   Wilkinson is uncomfortable. Yes, there is more control over the cleaners, but it seems to be Weaver who is exerting it, not her. She can see much more trouble ahead.

During Taylor's lifetime, evidence suggested that the adoption of his techniques was piecemeal rather than swift adoption across the board (Clegg et al., 2005: 21). Workers were keen to defend their craft traditions (see Braverman (1974) on deskilling). In the UK this combined with factory owners and a ruling class, who preferred a conservative approach to maintain stability and avoid upheaval in the workplace, rather than going for wholesale change and adopting Taylor's more 'modern' techniques (Whitston, 1997: 2).

Workers, factory owners, and even governments, had their own doubts about rational working techniques. In 1912, the US congress launched an inquiry into Taylorist techniques following a strike at the Watertown Arsenal, a munitions factory where such techniques were being used (see Kanigel, 1997: 459–484). The report from the inquiry declared Taylorism to be a failure, with time and motion studies being banned in all US defence plants.

It is perhaps surprising given the fame of Taylor's techniques today that he was, in fact, eventually sacked from his position at Midvale. Although he had brought about efficiencies in production, they came at a price—notably industrial unrest, which, as we will see later in the chapter, also beset Henry Ford's assembly line (p. 83). For the factory owners, the hassle of this unrest simply wasn't worth the efficiency gains.

Taylor spent the rest of his time as a consultant, taking his scientific management ideas into other workplaces and industries.

The rise of Taylorism

Running case: all hands on deck

As if things aren't bad enough for Weaver, most of the cleaners have walked out in support of Amy Turtle. Simon Chance and Linda Wilkinson are facing rooms that need cleaning and no cleaners to do the work. 'You've got a lot to answer for Weaver', snarls Linda.

'Right', says Weaver. 'You two get a couple more of the management team, roll your sleeves up and we'll show the cleaners a thing or two.'

Despite not being experienced cleaners, Weaver is able to demonstrate the cleaning routines from the cleaning manual. 'All of the knowledge of cleaning is in here', he states, 'no more relying on Amy and her experience.'

They quickly pick up the simple tasks and set to work cleaning the hotel rooms from top to bottom. And, to their surprise, they learn the tasks fairly easily, getting the job done in not much less time than the usual cleaning team.

A potential crisis is averted. Chance knows that the management can't do this every day—he needs to patch things up with the cleaners—but, at the same time, he sees the value in Weaver's techniques—anyone can now do this work.

From such an initial slow take-up, and outright resistance and controversy, the techniques of Taylorism gained ground in the USA so as to become 'conventional wisdom' (Whitston, 1997: 2) in management by the end of World War I.

Indeed, wartime was a time where its benefits could be demonstrated. As the (male) workers in the factories were away fighting, the women at home were the people who came to work in factories which produced guns, tanks, and other machinery needed for the war effort. They were unskilled, but, given the deskilled nature of Taylorist work, were able to be productive with little training. Taylorism could now claim to have been used for patriotic purposes (Kanigel, 1997: 487). Despite the considerable criticism faced by Taylorism, Grey (2005: 41) points out that it also created the tanks which overcame Nazi Germany.

Different countries embraced Taylorism in different ways. Often it had to blend in with their own national culture. Thus, within the USA, the UK, France, Germany, and even Russia and Japan, Taylorist techniques came to dominate the factory floor, albeit taking different routes and time spans to be implemented (Copley, 1923a: xx–xxii; Nelson, 1992: 16ff).

Visit the Online Resource Centre for more detail on the effects of national cultures on Taylorism.

The spread of rational work design was aided by the development of Henry Ford's assembly line.

Review questions

1. Describe the ways in which Taylorism allows management to exert control over workers.
2. Explain how Taylorism was not taken up instantly by all organizations.
3. Analyse why management might be resistant to Taylor's techniques.

Apply

4. Do you think Taylorist techniques are beneficial for the cleaning department at Junction Hotel or do they cause more disruption than good?

Henry Ford and the assembly line

Running case: the laundry factory

Weaver looks for further areas of the cleaning work process that he can redesign, including automating the laundry room, where towels and bed linen are laundered each day. However, he realises that operations at Junction Hotel are on too small a scale to justify such an outlay on equipment. He begins to think that he has done all that he can to make the cleaning side of the hotel as cost-effective as possible when an email from an old golfing partner arrives in his inbox.

To: phil_weaver@junctionhotel.com
From: bob.smith@laundromation.co.uk

Subject: Of interest???

Phil—long time, no speak. I hear you are in the hotel business—my new venture might interest you, especially as far as your laundering costs go. How about a round of golf next week and then I'll show you around?

Bob

Weaver visits his friend's new business, Laundromation, which is effectively a factory for processing laundry on a large scale. Clients, such as local hotels, leisure centres, and restaurants, have their dirty linen picked up by Laundromation and, in return, a fresh batch of clean linen is delivered. The task is *outsourced* to the laundry factory.

Inside the factory, Weaver looks around in admiration. At one end, vans dump dirty laundry into a chute where it goes on to a conveyor belt. Workers place the laundry into giant washing machines then into driers. As dry, clean laundry emerges from the driers, workers remove and sort it—there is an individual conveyor for each type and size of laundry, along which workers stand and fold each item as it passes. Workers are trained, in a Taylorist fashion, how to fold an item in the speediest fashion possible and they become expert at this. A worker can spend the entire day standing in one position folding the same types of towel.

At the end of each conveyor belt the products are stacked so that van drivers can pick up individual orders easily, load them on to a trolley and then into the van for delivery.

'You see', says the factory owner, 'by creating a laundry factory on this scale I can do the job a lot more efficiently. Think what you spend on wages, laundry equipment, etc. and all the hassle of having to supervise your cleaners. I can do it for you at less cost. On this scale I can do the job far more cheaply per towel than you could ever do in-house'.

Assembly line An automated conveyor that moves a product in front of workers who perform a small, repetitive task to each product that passes before them.

From a manager's perspective Taylorism made great gains, increasing efficiency and shifting control firmly in favour of management. These changes in control and efficiency are taken even further by Henry Ford's development of the moving **assembly line**.

At first glance there are many similarities between Taylor's scientific management and the assembly line Ford used to manufacture the Model T car at his Detroit plant in 1913. While there is nothing to suggest that Ford and Taylor ever met, these two industrialists were both working in the USA in the early part of the twentieth century and were certainly aware of each others' work. Ford faced the same issue of variability in the workforce as Taylor; indeed, much of Ford's workforce was made up of immigrant labour from Europe, many of whom did not speak English but could be trained easily to perform this very basic and standardized work (Beynon, 1984: 36).

However, while Taylor split the work process into its component parts, Ford's innovation was to then place these tasks in the order they needed to be completed and create the *moving* assembly line for his Highland Park car plant in Detroit. In other words, while Taylor's attention focused on a specific task performed by an individual, *Ford's interest was in a whole sequence of tasks which went into the manufacture of a finished product.*

Theory in context: development of the assembly line

Ford's inspiration for the moving assembly line came from butchery. On a visit to an abattoir, an aide of Ford witnessed the way in which carcasses were dismembered in sequence. With the fresh carcass hanging from a pulley, it was moved along in a line in front of various butchers who each took their own particular cut of meat in turn—not so much an assembly line as a disassembly line.

Ford realized that the assembly line allowed each butcher to become specialized in one particular task. However, unlike Taylor's system, by being on a pulley the carcass would come to the worker, rather than the worker travelling to it. This made the process quicker and more efficient. Ford wondered whether the process could be reversed and applied to making products. Placing his workers in two lines in the order of which component they added to the car, Ford had a chassis mounted on a trolley which was wheeled slowly in front of the workers who, in turn, did their small part in putting the car together—the prototype for the automated moving assembly line (Donkin, 2001: 147–8).

The extent of the breakdown of a task exceeded that of Taylor. For instance, even the job of inserting a nut and bolt could be broken down (one man inserts a bolt, one man places a nut on to the bolt, and one man tightens the bolt). Components were designed so as to facilitate easy and speedy assembly in this manner.

The moving aspect of the assembly line increased efficiency. Workers did not have to move from the spot to perform their tasks—the work simply passed by in front of them. The assembly line system is also sometimes termed a 'flow-line' system. Work flows along the line and at each point the worker performs a highly specialized task, often with machinery specially designed for that one specific task (e.g. tightening a nut on a wheel) (Figure 3.4).

A modern assembly line system.

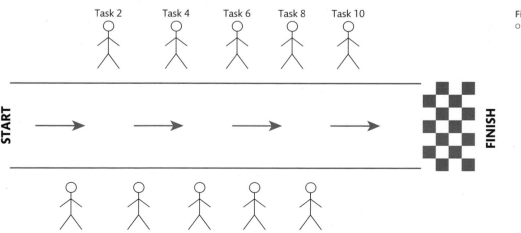

Figure 3.4 Efficiency on the assembly line.

Think back to the earlier flat-pack example. How could you organize mass production of such furniture using assembly-line techniques? How much more efficient would this make the process?

The Fordist assembly line certainly increased the efficient production of the model T. The first model Ts—made by stationary assembly in 1909—were produced at a rate of approximately 14,000 a year at a cost of $950 per car. By 1916, and the move to a fully automated assembly line, over half a million cars were being made with cost being reduced to $360 per car (Donkin, 2001: 148).

The Model T Ford.

Ford's system worked because his main product, the model T car, was highly standardized. Ford is famously reported to have said of the Model T: 'Any customer can have a car painted any colour that he wants so long as it is black' (Ford and Crowther, 1922: 71). The standardized nature of the product, in this case the colour, is vital to the efficiency gains made by the assembly line—too many variations and the line has to be stopped and started again, e.g. to set up a different colour of paint. The fewer variations there are in the product, the more costs are kept down.

Fordism and mass production

Mass production
The production of a large volume of a standardized product, often making use of an assembly line.

Mass consumption
Large-scale purchasing of a product by consumers within society.

The Fordist system can only operate under large economies of scale, known as **mass production**. Think of the costs involved in setting up the car factory and all of its specialized equipment—the assembly line is a large-scale, capital-intensive undertaking. Such an initial capital outlay requires massive costs per unit if only a few cars are produced.

But mass production needs people to buy the cars. Part of Ford's revolution was to create a change in society, as well as the workplace, towards **mass consumption**. Cheaper mass-produced cars were more affordable to the public, thus increasing the demand for them. Beforehand, car ownership was out of the financial reach of many—especially the unskilled workers who made up Ford's workforce. Now, with cars retailing for below $600 (Raff and Summers, 1987: 64), and with Ford encouraging a savings scheme among his workers, car ownership by the masses was possible.

Mass production and consumption is a legacy that endures from Ford; indeed, mass-produced objects constitute so much of our daily lives that Donkin describes Taylorism and Fordism as 'the most enduring social change of the 20th century' (Donkin, 2001: 159). It is not just cars, but most electrical items, computers, and clothing that are produced and consumed en masse using the assembly line system or some form of derivative.

Real life case: surgical assembly lines

It is not necessarily unskilled work that can be subject to an assembly line process. In 1985, a Moscow eye surgeon, Syvastoslav N. Fyodorov, developed an assembly line technique for performing cataract operations, going as far as to describe his clinic as a 'medical factory'. Rather than a conveyor belt, patients on trolleys are moved along as different parts of the process are performed. Similar techniques have been used in India with the resulting efficiency savings making vital healthcare procedures available to a largely poor population. The techniques are also being extended to procedures such as heart surgery.

   With medical procedures there is a limit to how much the assembly line can be used. Only the most basic, standard procedures are amenable to this. Whereas the Fordist factory led to deskilling, the skills of the surgeon are still needed for more complex cases.

Sources: Shmemann (1985); Matthews and Nemtsova (2006) and Morris (2010).

Food production on an assembly line.

While its origins are in heavy industry, the assembly line has been applied to many other tasks which have repetitive, standardized elements. Food production often follows an assembly line pattern, for example the supermarket sandwich originates from a standardized component—the triangular piece of bread (The Food Programme, 2010). In white collar work, the idea of a 'paper factory' has also emerged, where administrative tasks, such as processing forms, move along a series of stages where simplistic operations are performed at each (Baldry et al., 1998).

Just how much of an impact does the assembly line have on your everyday life? What items that you are wearing or using in your home, workplace, or place of study have been mass-produced on an assembly line? Without the assembly line we would not have affordable cars, computers, or electrical goods, etc. In other words, our modern way of life would be unrecognizable.

Review questions

1. Describe the main features of the assembly line.
2. Explain how the assembly line draws upon, but also intensifies, the techniques of Taylorism.
3. Analyse why Fordism needs mass production and consumption to make its efficiency gains.

Apply

4. What modern-day industries can you think of that use assembly line techniques?

Rational production: the Marxist critique

Running case: cogs in a machine

Babs Davies is off to clean again, but is looking to work elsewhere.

Babs Davies: I used to love working at Junction, now I don't even feel like a human being there.

Debbie Smith: Feel the same, since they let that consultant in there's no room to breathe—everything is watched and we're ordered about. Feels like I'm under a microscope all the time. And the work is just boring now. I feel like my soul has been taken away from me.

Andy James: You've got it lucky, try coming to work at Laundromation—hot, steamy, folding the same towels day in day out: that's soulless for you.

Babs Davies: Well, if the rumours are true I might be looking for a job there. Weaver wants to outsource half of our work to you—there's going to be job cuts if that's the case.

Debbie Smith: Tell me about it love, feel like we're just cogs in a machine these these days.

Fordism offers many of the forms of control seen under Taylorism in a more intensified form. The speed of work on the assembly line was controlled simply by the *speed of the line itself*; workers would have to perform their individual tasks as and when each car appeared in front of them. The system ties workers more than ever to being a part of the machine, to the point of controlling them to remain at the line and perform their task, not pausing or taking un-authorized breaks for fear of their one unperformed task being detected later down the line.

Go back to the five features of Taylorist control earlier in the chapter. How do you think the Fordist assembly line intensifies each of these five forms of control? How would you feel working under such circumstances?

The intensification of work by Ford was not without its problems. Ford also recognized that work in his factories was monotonous and dehumanizing. Indeed, Ford had to pay a decent wage to get people to work in his factories. Whilst subject to certain stringent qualifying conditions, the $5 day far exceeded the $2.34 that unskilled workers could previously hope to earn (Raff and Summers, 1987: 69).

These problems were not isolated within the factory gates. They had a resonance in wider society, as reflected in various artistic media of the time.

Theory in context: cultural critiques of Ford

Charlie Chaplin's (1936) silent film *Modern Times* is a satire on the human effects of assembly line work. In a memorable scene, Chaplin's worker performs a repetitive task as the speed of the line is increased. Hypnotized by the repetitive task and unable to keep up with the speed of the line, Chaplin is carried along into the heart of the machinery. The imagery is deliberate—Chaplin's character has been reduced, literally and figuratively, to being a 'cog in the machine'.

A similar negative view of the factory system and its effects upon individuals was presented by the Mexican artist Diego Rivera. Commissioned by Henry Ford to produce a set of murals for the Ford

> headquarters in Boston, Rivera produced a set of paintings where the imagery of the machine was dominant, the people reduced to small, sullen, expressionless beings. Ford was so incensed by this portrayal of his factory system that the murals were destroyed, never to be exhibited.
>
> In the novel *Brave New World*, Aldous Huxley (1932) presents a world where people are in danger of losing their own identity—a world run by a god named Henry Ford. In this novel it is not cars that are mass produced, but humans themselves. At the lowest levels of society are 'epsilons'—humans produced as workers in mass bundles.

In all three of these cases, common critiques of Ford and Taylor are that humans lose their individuality, their humanity even, in the face of organizations which are run as massive machine-like entities. What is rational in terms of organizational efficiency is not necessarily rational in terms of the effects upon humans themselves. The observations of the likes of Chaplin, Rivera, and Huxley suggest a mode of organization that is inherently **dehumanizing**—workers become components in a larger industrial machine. Beynon's (1984) study of work on the Ford production line has many quotes from workers talking not just about the boredom of the work, but its complete lack of interest and meaning (compare it with the meaning and identity that people take from work in Chapter 9).

> **Dehumanization** Work that reduces people to part of a machine-like process, ignoring their human attributes. Widely associated with rational work design that was criticized by Harry Braverman.

Rational production: Marx's critique of capitalist production

Running case: on strike

Midshires Gazette

Fresh walkout leaves laundry factory in a spin

Laundry services company, Laundromation Ltd, has suffered from the latest in a series of walkouts over working conditions. Problems began on last night's night shift when workers downed tools, bringing a halt to all activity in the plant.

Laundromation provides contract laundry services to a number of local organizations, including hospitals, sports centres, and hotels. It is understood that over half of today's scheduled deliveries have not taken place.

Simon Chance, the owner of Junction Hotel, said: 'This is the third time this month it has happened. We're left with no towels, no clean linen, no tablecloths—how are we supposed to run a hotel? It feels like we're hostage to the poor industrial relations at Laundromation.'

Andrew Rook, head of the regional branch of the Collectivity union, outlined the reasons for the actions: 'Work has been increasingly intensified. The conveyors which carry the laundry to workers are being speeded up week by week as the company takes on more contracts. We're being expected—forced—to work harder for no extra money.'

Bob Smith, Managing Director of Laundromation said, 'We are sorry for the disruption this is causing to our valued customers. I should point out that this action is being organized by a few militant workers in one small section of the factory. At Laundromation we pay highly competitive wages. I would have expected that workers would be grateful of a full order book in such difficult economic times and would work to make sure that we retain our current customer base.'

Karl Marx saw the desire for efficiency as an inevitable part of the capitalist working relationship. In competitive markets, with capitalists demanding high returns on investment in order to keep investors and shareholders happy, the pressure is on managers to reduce all costs, including labour, meaning that work needs to be as efficient as possible. A Marxist view suggests that this causes a conflict of interest: the accumulation of profits is done at the expense of workers who see their conditions of work and rewards from the capitalist working relationship deteriorate.

Surplus value Profit that capitalists gain over and above the wages they pay to workers.

Karl Marx (1964) suggested that the capitalist working relationship produced **surplus value**. By working more efficiently workers help to increase profits, but this is enjoyed by capitalists rather than the workers themselves. Conversely, workers experience, through the pursuit of efficiency, a deterioration in their own conditions of work, and see their craft skills depleted and replaced with monotonous, repetitive, and dehumanizing tasks.

For Marx, this relationship is fundamentally unequal. Whereas workers previously owned their own means of production, determined their own pace of work, and how much they took from the business for their efforts, these terms—wages, hours, and working conditions—are now set by management. Management have the power to do this because they are acting on behalf of capital—the power of the money, property, and equipment tied up in the business. Each individual worker relies on this for their wage—effectively their ability to live, eat, and be housed. However, should they object to the working conditions and wages set they are effectively powerless—management have the ability to hire and fire.

Have you ever worked in a job where you have felt unhappy with something, such as pay, working hours, the type of work you have to do, or your relationship with your boss? How much power have you felt (or not felt) to do something about it? What might have given you more power in the situation?

Marx and alienation

Karl Marx (1894/1981) took a different view of the nature of workers than that of Taylor and Ford. Rather than being naturally lazy, workers were, for Marx, naturally creative—they had a desire to transform the world around them. Furthermore, work was, for Marx, fundamentally a social rather than an economic activity. Factory working systems, however, laid to waste a lot of this human potential, trapping them in dull, monotonous working routines, often in isolation from other workers.

Alienation In capitalism, the estrangement of people from a number of human qualities, noted particularly by writers such as Marx and Braverman as a consequence of rational work design.

The result, for Marx (1894/1981), is that there are a number of negative effects upon workers, which he terms **alienation**.

1. Workers are alienated from the product. Rather than having a defining role in planning and creating the product, they only play one small part in the production process, with planning done by the capitalists. The worker may not even see the end product, and may not have a role in selling and realizing the profits.

2. Workers are alienated from the production process. Work becomes a series of dull, repetitive, meaningless tasks performed solely for money. There are no intrinsic rewards in the job. Craft skills become redundant as work is deskilled.

3. Workers are alienated from the human species or their 'human essence'. Work is dehumanizing in that the natural human desire for creativity is taken away and workers become 'cogs in a machine'.

4. Workers are alienated from other humans. Work becomes an economic transaction in return for a wage rather than a social activity. Workers are individualized in the production process and also separated from management.

Braverman and deskilling

Such a waste of human potential is echoed in Braverman's (1974) **deskilling** thesis. At a basic level this means a degradation in the nature of work, from workers having highly valuable craft skills to being reduced to performing monotonous tasks requiring no skill whatsoever. Deskilling is something that Braverman witnessed first-hand as a worker in the print industry, seeing his own skills replaced by new technology (see Chapter 14 for more on deskilling in the print industry).

Braverman (1974) suggested two particular areas of deskilling:

* organizational deskilling represents the overall knowledge of the production process being held by management and taken away from the brains of the workers
* technological deskilling represents the means by which the design of tasks removes the need for workers' skills; indeed, it can even replace them with technology and thus lead to job losses.

As with Marx, for Braverman the pursuit of efficiency inevitably led to deskilling and the degradation of work. For both it creates a conflict of interest between workers and capital—a fundamental tension at the heart of the capitalist working relationship.

How much knowledge and skill do you need to perform a task on a production line? How much would you know about other tasks which go into making the overall product? How would you feel working on a production line being told what to do all day?

> **Deskilling** The obsolescence of workplace skills caused by rational work design or the introduction of new technology.

Conflict in the capitalist working relationship

Marx's conclusion is that such alienation and the inequality of the capitalist working relationship leads, inevitably, to conflict between capital and workers. The formation of **trade unions**, which are able to take **collective action**, such as **strikes**, can be seen as an attempt to reintroduce collective power to the workforce—power which was lost through the control mechanisms of Taylor and Ford.

Ford's factories were certainly plagued by industrial unrest and unionization was heavy in his factories (see Beynon, 1984). Even with the $5-a-day wage, the boring, monotonous work was still resisted fiercely. The nature of his production system left it vulnerable to the so called 'spanner in the works'—with all parts of the work process interdependent in a line it only took a problem in one small area to bring production to a halt.

Strikes, sabotage, and even riots were commonplace. Ford himself had an abrasive approach to industrial relations. Beynon (1984: 49) described how, in one period of industrial unrest and rioting, Ford considered arming the non-striking workers with the intention of them turning on the strikers.

Visit the Online Resource Centre for more detail on attempts to reintroduce collective power.

> **Trade unions** Membership organizations which collectively represent the interests of a group of workers.
>
> **Collective action** Any form of resistance against management taken by a group of workers.
>
> **Strike** A form of collective action where workers withdraw their labour.

Resistance doesn't necessarily take the form of organized action, such as strikes. If people opt out of the job—resigning, looking for work elsewhere, etc.—this too is a sign of resistance against the organization. When Ford wanted to add 100 people to the line it was necessary to hire 963 people because initially they were skilled mechanics who did not like the unskilled task of simply pulling the lever on a machine (Crawford, 2006: 20). Ford's plants had, on average, a labour turnover rate of 370%—almost four people a year for each position (Raff and Summers, 1987: 63). In other words, each job changed hands every ten weeks.

In this section we have seen that the introduction of rational production techniques came at the cost of a great amount of conflict. In the final section we assess this against the possible advantages of such production techniques.

Review questions

1. Describe what is meant by alienation.
2. Explain why work in Ford's factories might be described as 'dehumanizing'.
3. Analyse what Marx means when he says that the capitalist working relationship favours the side of capital.

Apply

4. What examples of industrial action have you seen recently in the news. What are the reasons for why such action has taken place?

Evaluating rational work design

Running case: some positive reactions?

Phil Weaver is in an ambiguous position in the eyes of the management at Junction Hotel. His work with the cleaning department has demoralized the workforce to the point that it caused the crisis of the walkout. And yet these same techniques created the means by which the management have been able to cope with the crisis.

On further analysis, some cleaners have not joined in the walkout and later claim that they don't mind Weaver's techniques.

'Look—I know exactly what I have to do', says one cleaner. 'When Turtle ruled the roost you were open to her moods and she undoubtedly had her favourites. Now I know just what to do and how my work will be judged, full stop. I much prefer it that way—it's not open to personalities.'

Another cleaner, a student, adds: 'I don't want to come here and think. I'm just after a bit of extra cash to get through my studies. Work now is great—I just come in and get on with the job. There's no hassle.'

While rational working techniques are subject to much critique, in many ways they mirror how we often routinize tasks in our own lives (Morgan, 2006: 26). Maybe you take part in sports—how do you learn to perform that sport better? Are there advantages to be gained from breaking down movements into smaller parts and analysing them so as to be able to perform them more effectively? Perhaps you have a job around the house, such as making the bed—do you devise a standard routine, with each stage of the process performed in a particular order, that helps you to perform it more efficiently?

In this section we examine both the advantages and disadvantages of rational work design.

Employability skill: work simulation

Many job selection processes, especially at assessment centres (see Chapter 8) involve some form of practical work simulation. So called 'in-tray exercises' involve dealing with a series of tasks that might be encountered during the job itself.

The chances are that the task will not be deskilled and repetitive, as with Taylor and Ford's work. Nevertheless, the assessors may well be looking for you to devise some sort of system and routine for dealing with the tasks as you go along. Do you, for example, group together similar tasks so that they can be dealt with more efficiently together? If you have a complex task to repeat several times, do you break it down into more manageable stages?

Such routines show a methodical and efficient way of working rather than taking each task randomly and without any forethought into how it will be performed.

Not all workers react negatively to rational work designs, such as Taylorism and Fordism. In Chapter 9 we will see that some people prefer a straightforward task, whereby they can come into work, do a clear and simple job without having to put in too much thought, and collect their wage at the end of the day.

Furthermore, the standardization and simplification of rational work design can be seen to have a number of positive effects for workers.

- Simplifying the task opens up work to people who might otherwise have been unable to participate in the job market. Both Taylor and Ford employed unskilled workers. In the case of Ford's factories we have seen that many of the workers spoke different languages, but could still learn quickly the simple tasks undertaken in his factories.

- The nature of Taylor's work also opened up work to people with disabilities who may previously have been unable to find work. Work and task design is used by contemporary organizations to ensure compliance with relevant legislation concerning the employment of people with disabilities (see Equality and Human Rights Commission, 2011).

- Rational working methods bring in an element of fairness. Where previously the conditions of work, pace and standard of work expected, payment, and even being hired or not were open to the whims of individual managers, now they are standardized and formalized, and can be applied equally across the workforce. In this respect, there is a link between rational work design and the bureaucratic rules and procedures examined in Chapter 2.

Rational work design: advantages and disadvantages

Running case: denouement

Simon Chance sits down a few months after the walkout and analyses the situation.

The cleaning department will never be the same again. Where once it had larger-than-life characters who had Junction Hotel running through their veins, now it has part-timers and students walking around like robots. Yes, they are more compliant, easy to control, and easy to replace if they become uncontrollable, but a little something has been lost.

At the same time, Chance realizes that his wage bill is considerably reduced. Rooms are being cleaned much more quickly. There is the odd short-cut being taken and there are a few more complaints from guests, but, overall, the job is being done.

Chance feels there are lessons to be learned for the rest of the hotel. Efficiencies need to be spread, but Chance decides to minimize the overall influence of Weaver as his methods are too extreme and the consequences on the workforce too great. But, at the same time, there are areas throughout the organization where rational work design can be used to some extent to make things more efficient.

For Gareth Morgan (2006: 26), Taylorism is seen as a strength when there is a straightforward task performed in a stable, unchanging context, and where precision is important. In other words, Taylorism and similar rational work designs are ideal when there is a very machine-like environment in which the tasks are performed. This includes having people within the work process prepared and happy to work as if a part of a machine.

While Morgan saw rational work design as being fine for stable working environments, equally its rigidity makes it difficult for coping with changing circumstances or where a large variety of different products rather than one standard product are produced. In Chapter 4, we will see how, with such a changeable environment existing in the modern day, rational techniques such as Taylor's and Ford's are seen by some people to be somewhat unsuitable and out of date. This does not, however, mean that rational work design has necessarily been superseded. Indeed, we will see in Chapter 4 that in modern-day organizations, such as the fast-food restaurant, the techniques of rational work design and the bureaucratic procedures that we saw in the Chapter 2, are alive and well, and more intensified than ever.

Review questions

1. Describe the circumstances in which Gareth Morgan suggests rational work design works best.

2. Explain how rational organization can be seen to increase fairness in the workplace.

Apply

3. Can you think of any tasks in your own life to which you apply rational techniques?

Chapter summary

Rational work design encompasses techniques from, among others, Taylor and Ford. Taylor's scientific management addressed issues of organizational control and efficiency by meticulously breaking down the work process into small, discrete tasks. These tasks were then analysed scientifically—through measurement and calculation—and redesigned to be as efficient as possible. This made the process more efficient and gave management much more control over workers—a process intensified by the moving assembly line of Henry Ford.

However, as observed by theorists, such as Marx and Braverman, and writers and dramatists, such as Huxley and Chaplin, rational production also had negative effects. It created boring, monotonous work, and also loaded the capitalist working relationship heavily in the favour of management. Skills gained through craft knowledge, apprenticeships, and experience became worthless and degraded as deskilling took place, with the knowledge of the overall production process moving from individual workers to levels of management.

The overall advantages and disadvantages of rational work design are summarized in Table 3.1.

Table 3.1 Advantages and disadvantages of rational production techniques

Advantages	Disadvantages
Increase in production efficiency when there is a simple, standardized product to be produced	Inefficient and inflexible for product ranges with plentiful variation or where market conditions require rapid changes
Increase in control over a large number of factory workers	Workers lose autonomy and control over their day-to-day activities
Tasks and expectations for workers are clear, simple, and unambiguous	Workers lose craft skills and expertise
Workers can participate in the labour market regardless of skill, experience, or language	Work is dull, monotonous, and unfulfilling
Fair treatment/equality of opportunity—workers are hired and paid according to pre-existing standards; minimizes potential for favouritism that existed with previous factory systems	Can be inefficient if the alienating and intensive nature of work causes widespread resistance
Provides efficient goods or services in times of need (e.g. war, poverty)	Interdependence of work tasks leave the assembly line prone to a 'spanner in the works'
Allows goods to be mass produced at a price that would otherwise be unaffordable to the public	Humans are reduced to being 'cogs in a machine'

Further reading

A lengthy but thorough introduction to the life and work of Taylor.

Beynon, H. 1984. *Working for Ford*. Penguin, Harmondsworth.

Considers the developments of Taylor and Ford, bringing in a critical edge to examine the de-skilling and degradation of work.

Crawford, M. 2010. *Shop class as Soulcraft: An inquiry into the value of work*. Penguin, Harmondsworth.

Donkin, R. 2001. *Blood, sweat and tears: the evolution of work*. Texere, New York.

Kanigel, R. 1997. *The one best way: Frederick Winslow Taylor and the enigma of efficiency*. Little, Brown and Company, London

Bibliography

Bahnisch, M. 2000. Embodied work, divided labour: subjectivity and the scientific management of the body in Frederick W. Taylor's 1907 'Lecture on Management'. *Body and Society* 6(1): 51–68.

Baldry, C., Bain, P., and Taylor, P. 1998. Bright satanic offices: intensification, control and team Taylorism. In: Thompson, P., and Warhurst, C. (eds) *Workplaces of the future*. Macmillan: Basingstoke, pp. 163–183.

Beynon, H. 1984. *Working for Ford*. Penguin: Harmondsworth.

Braverman, H. 1974. *Labor and monopoly capital: the degradation of work in the twentieth century*. New York: Monthly Review Press.

Chaplin, C. (dir.) 1936. *Modern Times*. United Artists.

Clegg, S., Kornberger, M., and Pitsis, T. 2005. *Managing and organizations: an introduction to theory and practice*. Sage: London.

Copley, F.B. 1923a. *Frederick W. Taylor, father of scientific management*, Vol. 1. Harper and Bros: New York.

Copley, F.B. 1923b. *Frederick W. Taylor, father of scientific management*, Vol. II. Routledge/Themmes Press: London.

Crawford, M.B. 2006. Shop class as soulcraft. *The New Atlantis*. Summer 2003: 7-24.

Donkin, R. 2001. *Blood, sweat and tears: the evolution of work*. Texere: New York.

Equality and Human Rights Commission. 2012. At work–making reasonable adjustments. Available at: http://www.equalityhumanrights.com/advice-and-guidance/your-rights/disability/disability-in-employment/at-work-making-reasonable-adjustments/ (last accessed 28 November 2012).

Ford, H., and Crowther, S. 1922. *My life and work*. Garden City Pub Co.: Garden City, NY.

Gilbreth, F.B. Jr., and Carey, E.G. c.1949. *Cheaper by the dozen*. William Heinemann: London.

Graham, L. 2000. 'Lillian Gilbreth and the mental revolution at Macy's, 1925–1928. *Journal of Management History (Archive)* 6(7): 285–305.

Grey, C. 2005. *A very short, fairly interesting and reasonably cheap book about studying organizations*. London: Sage.

Hoskin, K.W., and Macve, R.H. 1986. Accounting and the examination: a genealogy of disciplinary power. *Accounting, Organizations and Society* 11(2): 105–136.

Huxley, A. 1932. *Brave new world. A novel*. F.P. Chatto & Windus: London.

Jaffee, D. 2001. *Organization theory: tension and change*. McGraw Hill: Singapore.

Kanigel, R. 1997. *The One Best Way: Frederick Winslow Taylor and the Enigma of Efficiency*. Little, Brown and Company: London.

Lang, W. (dir.) 1950. Cheaper by the Dozen. Twentieth Century Fox.

Marx, K. 1964. *Economic and philosophic manuscripts of 1844*. International Publishers: New York.

Marx, K. 1894/1981. *Capital: a critique of political economy*, Vol. 3 (transl. David Fernbach). Penguin: London.

Matthews, O., and Nemtsova, A. Medical meccas: eye surgery assembly line. *Newsweek International*, 30 October 2006. Available at: http://www.highbeam.com/doc/1G1-153298203.html (last accessed 20 July 2012).

McKendrick, N. 1970. Josiah Wedgwood and cost accounting in the Industrial Revolution. *The Economic History Review* 23(1): 45–67.

Morgan, G. 1990. *Organizations in society*. Macmillan: Basingstoke.

Morgan, G. 2006. *Images of organization*. Sage Publications: Thousand Oaks, CA.

Morris, C. 2010. 'Production line' heart surgery. *BBC News* (2 August 2010). Available at http://www.bbc.co.uk/news/health-10837726.

Nelson, D. 1992. Scientific management in retrospect. In: Nelson, D. (ed.) *A mental revolution: scientific management since Taylor*. Ohio State University Press: Columbus, pp. 5–39.

Price, B. 1992. Frank and Lillian Gilbreth and the Motion Study Controversy 1907–1930. In: Nelson, D. (ed.) *A mental revolution: scientific management since Taylor*. Ohio State University Press, Columbus, pp. 58–76.

Raff, D., and Summers, L. 1987. Did Henry Ford pay efficiency wages? *Journal of Labour Economics* 5(4): 557–586.

Schmemann, S. 1985. Moscow eye doctor hails assembly-line surgery at clinic. *New York Times*, 2 July 1985. Available at: http://www.nytimes.com/1985/07/02/science/moscow-eye-doctor-hails-assembly-line-surgery-at-clinic.html (last accessed 20 July 2012).

Simpson, I.H. 1999. Historical patterns of workplace organization: From mechanical to electronic control and beyond. *Current Sociology* 47(2): 47–75.

Taylor, F.W. 1911. *The principles of scientific management*. Harper: New York.

The Food Programme. 2010. BBC Radio 4, 17 October 2010 [radio programme].

Thompson, P., McHugh, D. 2009. *Work organisations: a critical approach*, 4th edn. Palgrave Macmillan: Basingstoke.

Whitston, K. 1997. Worker resistance and Taylorism in Britain. *International Review of Social History* 42: 1–24.

4 Rationalization in contemporary organizations

Chapter overview and learning outcomes

By the end of this chapter you should be able to:

- describe Ritzer's McDonaldization and other examples of contemporary forms of rationalization

- explain how post-Fordism and post-bureaucracy are examples of a trend away from rationalized forms of organization in contemporary society

- explain how computer technology allows rational techniques to exert increased control and surveillance in organizations, such as in call centres

- analyse the different degrees to which rationalization is used in different contemporary organizations, and the extent to which this is desirable for different organizations.

Key theorists

Daniel Bell	American sociologist who suggested that the economy was moving away from manufacturing towards a 'post-industrial' society
George Ritzer	American sociologist who examined the hyper-rationalized techniques of the fast-food restaurant, using the term 'McDonaldization' to describe their use in many contemporary organizations
Michel Foucault	French philosopher who used the prison metaphor of the Panopticon to examine how power is exerted through the surveillance methods that rational management techniques in organizations produce

Key terms

Rationalization	Methods for increasing the efficiency of work, drawing on techniques of bureaucracy (see Chapter 2) and of rational work design, such as Taylorism and Fordism (see Chapter 3)
Post-industrialism	A perspective which suggests that, in response to a more changeable and unpredictable environment, organizations are moving away from rationalization to more flexible forms of managing and organizing. Encompasses both post-bureaucratic and post-Fordist perspectives of management
McDonaldization (of society)	A perspective (Ritzer, 2011) which recognizes the continued use of rationalization in contemporary organizations, as typified by the work design of the fast-food restaurant
Panopticon	Based on a seminal prison design, a metaphor for the levels of control and surveillance in contemporary rationalized organizations

Introduction

Running case: the business trip

Heading down to London for a business trip, Simon Chance thinks about the degree to which he can introduce rationalization at Junction Hotel. Do nothing, and the hotel becomes disorganized and wasteful—ultimately it may not even survive if work-related costs are not kept under control. Go too far and workers become like robots, demotivated because of boring repetitive work. In a business where guests and workers are constantly in contact, this would not give the best impression. 'Rationalization has efficiency benefits', thinks Chance, 'but at the end of the day we're not a factory, we're a hotel—and a luxury hotel at that.'

Chance decides to make his trip a fact-finding mission about rationalization in other hotels and organizations. Arriving at his first hotel, a luxury hotel, he begins to write some notes.

Hit the jackpot here, this hotel is top-end luxury, a massive room with two balconies overlooking a park.

Service at reception is polite and attentive, although all done through a standard computerized procedure, with a key card eventually being issued. At least the staff aren't identikit—they are always happy to pass the time of day, no matter how trivial the request.

So, here I am sat on the balcony. Interesting that, though well-turned out, the rooms use identical furnishings. Indeed, they are identical across the chain—I've stayed in another of these elsewhere. It doesn't detract though, it's good quality stuff.

Just ordering breakfast for tomorrow—very similar to most other hotels. I hang the order on a pre-printed form on the door. And the cleaning seems to be pretty much as we designed it back at Junction, all quite efficient. But they do take time to put a lovely little tuck into the end of the toilet roll . . .

A life of luxury?

To what extent does the luxury hotel use rationalization? Are there any areas where you think it would be inappropriate for their area of the market?

In the previous two chapters on bureaucracy (Chapter 2) and rational production (Chapter 3), you could be forgiven for thinking this a book about history rather than contemporary management. Rational techniques in those chapters emerged from the heavy industry of the early 1900s: the bureaucratic structures and techniques, as witnessed by Weber, or the methods of efficient production developed by Taylor and Ford. In this chapter we ask if such *historical* ideas are still relevant *today*?

The chapter begins by examining post-bureaucratic and post-Fordist theories, which suggest that today's world is different—it is no longer dominated by manufacturing industry and is much more dynamic and changeable. It is suggested that the **rationalization** of Taylor and Ford's era is no longer appropriate for this contemporary world.

However, while such movements away from rationalization have been evidenced over the past decades, it would be hasty to suggest that it is obsolete. Rationalization is present today, just as it was in the Industrial Revolution, in industries other than the manufacturing settings in which it originally flourished, and often in more intensified forms. In this chapter we examine a number of examples of contemporary rationalization.

Rationalization Work that is designed to achieve maximum efficiency and reduce costs, encompassing aspects of bureaucracy and the scientific design of work.

- George Ritzer has noted that the McDonalds restaurant chain is a hyper-efficient organization which uses rationalized techniques that have their roots in scientific management, bureaucracy, and the assembly line. The organizational techniques of the fast-food restaurant are found in many modern-day organizations, to the extent that Ritzer (2011) has suggested that today's society is 'McDonaldized'.

- Many organizations also employ their own particular models of cost-cutting and minimization. We examine examples of contemporary efficient organization such as 'no frills' and 'value engineering'.

- As much as rationalization is about *efficiency*, we also saw in Chapters 2 and 3 that it allows management to exert *control* over the workforce. Computer technology allows contemporary organizations to exert such control even more intensively. Michel Foucault's (1977) metaphor of the Panopticon is used to examine the means by which rational organization is used to control and exert surveillance over contemporary organizations, which we apply to the example of the call centre.

When first formulated in the Industrial Revolution, rationalization was very much presented in a **one best way** formulation. This chapter concludes that while there may no longer be 'one best way' to manage and organize, and while rationalization may not be appropriate for all organizations, it is still ever-present in the contemporary organizational world.

> **One best way** Rational management techniques that propose one most efficient way to perform any task.

The demise of rationalization?

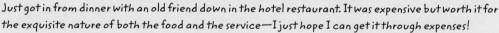

Running case: the hotel restaurant

Just got in from dinner with an old friend down in the hotel restaurant. It was expensive but worth it for the exquisite nature of both the food and the service—I just hope I can get it through expenses!

The maître d' showed us to our seats. Even though he was obviously serving others, he had a gift when at the table of making it seem like we were the only customers in there.

The food was outstanding and, having ordered, the chef actually came to the table to ask just how we wanted it cooked. Although the menu set out the dishes on offer that day, the chef was able to customize the dish for each of our individual requirements. He chatted to us about how he operated the kitchen:

'Nothing is set in stone,' he said, 'it's not just that customers might want different things, sometimes a particular food will be unavailable at market, or out of season, and I have to be ready to change the menu around at the drop of a hat. Not just me—all of the kitchen staff have to be ready to react as and when necessary. All of that comes from training, knowing our food, and having a passion for cooking.'

With my professional hat on, I asked the maître d' a bit more about how the place was managed. 'Not very much,' was the reply, 'they try to keep rules and regulations to a minimum. We're all encouraged to meet up, try out new ideas, make suggestions—anything that helps improve what we offer to customers. Overall, we're trusted as professionals with expertise and an interest in our work. The chef actually makes sure that the staffing of different shifts is always changed around so that people don't get stuck in their ways. Instead, we are always learning and sharing ideas with different people.'

As I left, I couldn't help thinking about the restaurant at Junction. Could we keep Graham Effingham forever, or is this the sort of thing he aspires to? Certainly, if we did anything to downgrade his restaurant and the quality of food and service, he'd be off.

How is management in this example different to rational forms of management encountered in Chapters 2 and 3? What benefits does it bring to the restaurant?

In the previous two chapters, ideal-type bureaucracies and Taylor's scientific management have been presented as examples of a one best way approach to managing and organizing. However, it has also been suggested (see Chapter 3) that such 'one best way' approaches are only valid in certain circumstances, for example with a standard product and stable environmental conditions.

Environment The world outside of an organization which can have an impact upon that organization.

We first examine the idea of an organization's **environment**, and the impact that it has. We see that the environment facing organizations has become more unstable and changeable since Fordism and Weber's theories of bureaucracy were first formulated, and examine trends from Fordism and bureaucracy towards more flexible post-Fordist and post-bureaucratic theories of management.

However, we also see that while the nature of organizations and their environments may have changed, arguments for post-Fordism are accompanied by arguments for neo-Fordism, where rationalization is still used, in some cases in more efficient forms than when the first assembly lines were developed.

The organization and its environment

The concept of the organizational environment suggests that organizations are not hermetically-sealed; they interact with, and are affected by, things going on around them. The **PEST model** (Figure 4.1) splits the environment into four sectors:

PEST model A model which breaks an organization's environment into four sectors: political, economic, social, and technological.

- political—government policies and laws
- economic—e.g. the state of the economy, demand, exchange rates, etc.
- social—consumer tastes, fashions, and opinions
- technological—current technology and innovation.

The environment impacts organizations, who might have to react and make changes. For example, in many countries, a factor in the political sector of the environment has been to ban smoking in public places. This has forced changes upon a number of organizations, such as pubs and restaurants that have had to create, for example, outdoor smoking areas (see Chapter 11 for more detailed examples).

Figure 4.1
The PEST model.

The impact of the environment is the starting place for an argument which suggests the retreat of rationalized forms of organization.

The contemporary environment

An initial example of an attack on the one best way approach can be seen in the set of theories developed around the 1970s, known as **contingency theory** (e.g. Thompson, 1967; Woodward, 1958). These studies took Weber's ideal type of bureaucracy (see Chapter 2) as a lead, but concluded that rather than one ideal type, there were a number of different 'ideal types' of bureaucratic structure and functioning, depending on the environment facing the organization. Environmental variables, such as uncertainty, the technology used by an organization, and the size of the organization, demanded different types of bureaucratic organization—organizational design was about making the best 'fit' between the organization and its environment. While contingency theory moves away from one 'ideal type' of bureaucracy, it is still quite rational in its focus, matching the ideal organizational structure to a set of variables.

In the 1980s, much greater shifts in the nature of the environment facing organizations were in evidence. Western economies moved from a manufacturing focus to a **post-industrial** society (Bell, 1973), one which is dominated by service industries (see Chapter 16) and, more recently, where information technologies mean that information and organizational activity takes place at instantaneous speed through global networks (see Chapter 14).

The contrast between the contemporary environment and that facing Weber, Taylor, and Ford is described by Clegg and Baumeler (2010) as a shift from the static, unchanging nature of 'iron cages' of bureaucracy to a world that is fast-moving, changeable, and in constant flow. Rather than being static and stable, Bauman (2000) describes our contemporary world as a fluid world of **liquid modernity**.

With such a turbulent, dynamic, changeable, and uncertain environment, one best way approaches begin to creak at the seams. They can be seen as dinosaurs—inflexible and slow to react. In contrast, more flexible, nimble organizations are able to cope better and gain advantage in such situations. It is thus suggested that there has been movement from bureaucracy to post-bureaucracy, and from Fordism to post-Fordism.

 Visit the Online Resource Centre for more detail on the contemporary environment.

From bureaucracy to post-bureaucracy

Traditional **bureaucracy**, as described in Chapter 2, with its rigid structures and fixed rules and procedures, might provide certainty and predictability, but it is not quick to react. Orders have to be passed through several levels of hierarchy. A need to change a procedure rapidly may run up against inflexible rules. Given the more changeable nature of the environment, Bennis, as far back as 1966, predicted the 'coming death of bureaucracy' (Bennis, 1966).

A move towards **post-bureaucratic** forms has seen organizations attempt to design structures which are more flexible and which minimize the dysfunctions of bureaucracy, such as

Contingency theory Suggests that the best structure for an organization is determined by factors such as environmental uncertainty, the organization's size, and the technology that the organization uses.

Post-industrial A move in society and economy away from the dominance of manufacturing, towards a more flexible, service-based economy.

Liquid modernity Bauman's characterization of modern day society as dynamic, changeable, and flexible.

Bureaucracy From the French *bureau*, meaning 'office', bureaucracy covers official, formal elements of rational organizational design, such as the hierarchical organization structure, the rules and procedures, and the official paperwork, which exert impersonal control over the organization.

Post-bureaucracy/ post-bureaucratic organization A trend away from rigid, bureaucratic rules and structures in organizations towards more flexible and less hierarchical, rule-driven organizations.

Red tape An unintended consequence of bureaucracy, where rules and paperwork get in the way of work and activities, rather than helping tasks to be performed efficiently.

Trained incapacity Where people are so used to their behaviour being controlled by bureaucratic rules and procedures that they become inflexible and unable to think for themselves and show initiative.

Matrix structure An organizational structure that combines a traditional functional hierarchy with separately-managed project teams that draw people from across different functional departments.

red tape, where rules get in the way of people doing their work, and **trained incapacity**, where strict rules and regulations mean that people do not think for themselves and are unable to change and adapt to new situations (see Chapter 2).

Matrix structures

An example of a move away from the traditional bureaucratic hierarchy is the **matrix structure** (see Figure 4.2). While there are heads of different departments, such as finance or sales, there are also heads of different projects. A project might be any task or area of focus for the organization, such as a particular product or service that the organization offers. For example, in Figure 4.2 project A might be the development of a new project. There is a head of the project who coordinates staff from across the production, finance, and sales departments to bring their particular knowledge and expertise to that project.

The matrix organization means that, rather than being in one fixed work group, people move between different teams. More knowledge and information can be shared across the organization as people shift between teams (see Organizational Learning in Chapter 10) and specialists with particular knowledge can be brought into particular project groups where they are needed.

The matrix organization shifts away from bureaucracy in that it breaks one of Fayol's principles of management (1949, see chapter 2): that of unity of command, where people have just one line manager. While this moves away from the rigidity of bureaucracy, it also brings the danger of confusion as to who is in charge of any one individual and that individual having divided loyalties between their different 'bosses'.

The post-bureaucratic organization

While the matrix structure begins to introduce some elements of flexibility to organizational structure, post-bureaucratic organizations are those which go even further in

Figure 4.2 A typical matrix structure.

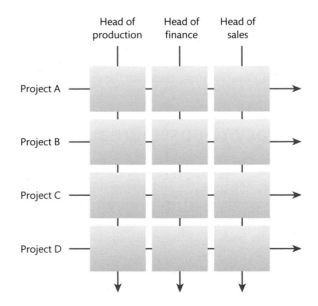

minimizing bureaucratic structures, and rules and regulations. The aim of such organizations is to promote creativity, innovation, and rapid response among their workers when required.

The goal of such organizations is to focus on the competencies of their workers and how they can be used for particular tasks, rather than fitting people into official positions or roles with strict definitions of what they should be doing during their working day. Furthermore, the post-bureaucratic organization tries to foster dialogue and discussion among its workers in order to share ideas and innovations.

Real life case: Oticon—the 'spaghetti organization'

Oticon, a Danish technology firm specializing in hearing-aid equipment, is often held up as an example of what a purely post-bureaucratic organization might be like.

- All paperwork is scanned when first received and stored on computer. The paper itself is shredded and, as a symbol of the intent to remove paperwork, the shredded paper is put into a clear plastic chute that passes from roof to floor in the middle of the canteen.

- There are neither job titles nor fixed roles. Departments and similar examples of bureaucratic structure are removed, and in their place are 'projects' into which any interested people from any part of the organization might contribute.

- Formal offices and dividing walls have also been removed; even fixed desks no longer remain. Instead, workers have their own trolley which contains their computer and other essential items.

In Oticon we can see a move away from formal structures and towards movement and fluidity—rather than structure, the organization is interlinked like spaghetti. As people move around with their trolleys, they are more likely to speak with other members of staff, share ideas, and come up with new innovations. Rather than working in pre-existing departments and within a pre-existing structure, people cluster together to work on particular projects. Rather than being directed top-down, workers are left to self-organize.

Burnes (2000: 319–27), Jaffee (2001: 161–2), and Larsen (2002).

What elements of bureaucracy have Oticon removed? How do you think the firm operates without them?

While the lack of rules and structure at Oticon may seem unusual compared with many of our working lives, a similar lack of rules and structure can be seen in the Googleplex, the headquarters of Google (see Chapter 11). In both cases, these are organizations that wish to promote technical innovation and respond rapidly when change is needed, and not have rules and structures getting in the way.

Is a post-bureaucratic form suitable for all organizations? Are there some types of organization where it would not work?

Employability skills: the post-bureaucratic worker

Working for a post-bureaucratic organization such as Oticon or Google might seem like an ideal job—very few rules, the ability to work on projects that you like, and, in the case of Google, the ability to turn up to work at whatever time you want in the morning (p. 366)—it's very different to working the regular 9 to 5.

Such work, however, has its own pressures. There is often a pressure to perform—to demonstrate the ability to innovate by coming up with the goods. And with such a lack of formal control and rules a lot of self-discipline is required in order to keep focused on tasks relevant to work.

Qualities which would suit a post-bureaucratic organization, such as flexibility, problem-solving, and team working are often stated in job adverts. What examples could you give of these to an employer, how could you, for example, demonstrate creativity or a 'capacity to innovate'?

From Fordism to post- and neo-Fordism

In the 1980s, many Western economies were in recession. Manufacturing was in decline and the service sector became more dominant. Furthermore, new computer-technologies were able to produce goods in a more customized way than the mass-produced assembly line, and tastes in consumption were also becoming more fragmented towards niche and specialist markets, rather than standardized, mass-produced goods.

At the same time, the economy of Japan was becoming more successful. Western organizations, including Ford, began to look at Japanese forms of organization, which were much more successful in comparison.

One response to these changes has been a move away from the traditional Fordist assembly line, where work is highly controlled and jobs are fragmented into small tasks which require little skill. **Post-Fordism** is seen as a break with the deskilling and highly-controlled nature of Fordism and Taylorism, instead valuing the skills and knowledge of workers and allowing them autonomy in how they organize their work.

While post-Fordism doesn't suggest any one particular form of organization, a number of examples of managing and organizing demonstrate post-Fordist characteristics.

> **Post-Fordism** A break away from Fordism and towards management techniques which use the skill of workers and grant autonomy to workers, emphasizing communication and competencies, rather than command and control.

- In Sweden, Volvo moved away from the assembly line to manufacturing cars in small teams. Workers received training in a wider, and deeper, level of skills, and the teams largely managed themselves, with representatives from teams also involved in decision-making at a higher level in the organization (Rehder, 1994).

- Flexible specialization (Piore and Sabel, 1984) was observed in clothing manufacturing in Italy, where an industry would cover a geographical area, but within which were small, specialist firms of trained workers, concentrating on high-quality, niche production.

- Ford themselves introduced elements of work organization that can be described as post-Fordist. As we will see in Chapter 10, Japanese firms welcome suggestions and input from shop-floor workers, whereas the traditional Fordist model is one where workers are at the bottom of a hierarchy and do as they are told. In the 1980s, Ford instigated an 'After Japan' programme, to move away from top-down management and engage workers in participative management, whereby they had a say in decisions, and in team work, with cross-functional teams as would be found in a matrix structure like the one we saw earlier in this chapter. The intention was to generate trust and cooperation, moving away from the Fordist 'management by fear' (Starkey and McKinlay, 1994).

Visit the Online Resource Centre for more analysis of these examples.

Post-Fordism or neo-Fordism?

Real life case: you could have your lunch off the floor

When you think of a car factory what do you imagine? Noise, dirt, oil, grease, mess? Certainly our popular perception leads us to the impression that car manufacturing is quite a dirty and messy environment. This view is wrong. In our interview, Joe Greenwell, the Chairman of Ford in Britain states: 'Don't think of the car industry as some grubby manufacturing environment . . . there are no grubby manufacturing environments anymore . . . you could have your lunch off the floor. It is a very different, uncluttered, quiet, air-conditioned environment where technicians abound and there is a very high degree of automation'.

This is not just at Ford but throughout the car industry. For instance, Volkswagen's Phaeton factory in Dresden, Germany is called Gläserne Manufaktur—the factory made of glass. This transparent factory has glass walls so that the whole production process can be seen. The process is so clean the floors are made of Canadian Maple and the workers even wear white overalls (see AutoMoto TV, 2010).

All the parts come in on a tram and are then delivered to the appropriate location by robots guided by magnets. The entire floor is a giant conveyor belt moving very slowly. Each workstation is powered via the floor. The whole process is also computerized so that it monitors everything that goes into the vehicle and will even know if a single screw is missing and when the car is ready to go to the next stage. The car is even moved round by a machine to suit the technician's body as they put in the parts.

Car manufacturing has come a long way in 100 years.

Source: Author interview with Joe Greenwell, Ford in Britain, 2012.

Visit the Online Resource Centre to view videos of modern car factories in action and for the full interview with Joe Greenwell.

While trends away from the rationalization of Fordism have been observed with post-Fordism, **neo-Fordism** suggests Fordism being developed in ways which draw from Japanese techniques, but retain the drive for efficiency of traditional Taylorism and Fordism.

In neo-Fordist organizations, computer technology helps to control large volumes of production, but rather than Fordist, standardized products, the technology allows for changes to the set-up to be made quickly. Thus, neo-Fordist organizations combine mass production and economies of scale with the ability to react more flexibly than a Fordist assembly line.

With neo-Fordist organization comes a ruthless desire for efficiency and the minimization of waste. Techniques such as **lean management** are a development of the Japanese

Neo-Fordism A form of rational organization which combines Fordist efficiency and control with the ability of computer technology to introduce flexibility into the work process.

Lean management A contemporary form of Taylorist rational organization that attempts to eliminate waste or anything that does not add value from organizational processes.

Just-in-time management A form of management that tries to promote efficiency by reducing the amount of stock that an organization holds, with components delivered as and when needed.

just-in-time system, whereby components are delivered as and when necessary, rather than wasting space in store rooms (Jafee, 2001: 135ff). In this case, computer technology helps with the process of tracking such components. Work tasks are designed to be efficient and to minimize waste with the same degree of calculation and precision as Taylor's scientific management. Again, computer technology assists with this.

Workers have a better working environment than the traditional noisy, dirty factory. Furthermore, they often have a wider variety of tasks than the one repetitive task of the traditional assembly line. Instead, they engage in job rotation or job enlargement (see Chapter 9). However, in a manner similar to their counterparts from the traditional Fordist assembly line, they often perform repetitive and tightly-controlled tasks, with little autonomy over their own work.

Summary

In this section we have seen two contemporary and seemingly contradictory trends:

- on one hand, post-bureaucracy and post-Fordism suggest a 'retreat from rationalization' and a movement towards more flexible forms of organization with skill and autonomy returned to the workers
- on the other hand, neo-Fordism achieves flexibility through technology, but this technology is used to make work processes efficient and to exert precise control over the tasks that workers perform.

While both trends are able to co-exist, we see that rationalized techniques are still very much in existence in contemporary organizations. They may not follow the 'one best way' prescription of Industrial Revolution era rationalization, but the drive for efficiency still exists—in many cases in more intensified forms. The following three sections of the chapter examine contemporary rationalization in organizations. In examples such as the fast-food restaurant and the call centre we see elements of neo-Fordism—a variety of tasks are performed by workers, but these tasks are designed to be performed as efficiently as possible and the workers are highly controlled.

Review questions

1. Describe the main changes in the environment facing organizations since the time of Taylor and Ford.
2. Explain what is meant by post-Fordism and post-bureaucracy.
3. Analyse the differences between post-Fordism and neo-Fordism in the way that they have developed Fordism in the contemporary era.

Apply

4. How would you describe the work at the luxury restaurant in the case study in terms of post-Fordism and post-bureaucracy?

Fast-food restaurants and 'McDonaldization'

Running case: the fast-food restaurant

At the moment, I'm sitting in a fast-food restaurant. It wasn't planned but I'm running a bit late, so I stopped here to grab a quick lunch. The contrast between this and last night's dining experience couldn't be more pronounced.

Went up to order my food—it felt like I was talking to a machine and it seemed like the till they were using was feeding them lines to say. There certainly didn't seem to be any thought going on between the assistant's ears; indeed, at one point I ordered a black coffee and was asked 'Do you want milk with that?'.

I observed as my order was put together. With burgers being deposited down chutes and fries being scooped into cartons, my meal was eventually presented on a tray—it felt like I was the last station on an assembly line.

It's not the most comfortable dining experience ever. I am sitting on a hard plastic chair, having to share a table with other (not well-behaved I hasten to add) diners. A cleaner is going around mopping the floor and actually mopped under my chair as I was sitting on it!

Well, I am getting out of here as quickly as possible—can't believe I am expected to even deposit my rubbish in the bin myself. Do they not have waiters here?

Still, it did the trick of getting me fed as quickly as possible, and the cost is not a fraction of what was spent last night. I can only imagine what would happen though if I tried to go back to our place and suggest Effingham run his restaurant like this—he would erupt!

Rather than being a relic of the past, for George Ritzer (2011) rationalization is something that is alive and well in contemporary organizations. The prime example of this, Ritzer suggests, is the McDonalds fast-food restaurant, a global organization which employs rational techniques to the optimum for the rapid, mass-production, and service of food. For example:

- putting together a burger is broken down into small, repetitive tasks which can be learned easily and rapidly by untrained staff, in a similar manner to Taylorism. A burger is 'assembled' from simple components in a manner similar to Fordism (Ritzer, 2011: 55)

- the service encounter, where orders are taken, is often done according to a pre-planned set of steps, often with the till giving operators lines to say or prompting them as to what they should ask the customers (ibid: 102–3)

- manuals outline procedures for almost all aspects of work within the organization (ibid: 105–6, 119); for example, there are step-by-step instructions on how to perform a mundane task, such as cleaning a toilet

- much of the work of management involves implementing bureaucratic rules and procedures that come centrally from the organization (some of which are identical in all restaurants worldwide) or filling out predesigned forms for such things as pay and stock ordering.

In outlining these familiar, rationalized techniques, but in a fast-food restaurant rather than a factory setting, Ritzer describes **McDonaldization** as 'the extension of rationalised techniques from Weber and Taylor onwards' (Ritzer, 2011). There are few levels in the organization which escape this intensive and pervasive cocktail of rationalization.

McDonaldization (of society) The principles of efficiency, calculability, predictability, and control by which fast-food restaurants are managed and organized, as applied by Ritzer to other contemporary organizations.

Characteristics of McDonaldization

For Ritzer (2011: 14–16), there are four particular principles that characterize the organization of fast-food restaurants, all of which can be seen to have their origins in rationalized techniques of bureaucracy and scientific management (see Chapters 2 and 3 for more explanation of these):

- *efficiency* is finding the optimum way of getting something done with as little waste as possible in the shortest amount of time and with the least cost input in terms of wages and resources, as was the basis for Taylorism and Fordism
- *calculability* is an emphasis on what can be measured and calculated so as to achieve that efficiency, as with Taylor's time and motion studies
- *predictability* is about standardization and the elimination of variability. This may be through standard products and work processes, as with Taylorism and Fordism, or through bureaucratic rules and procedures
- *control* is getting workers to do what is required of them through bureaucratic rules and hierarchy, but also by making work as simplistic as possible and, where possible, replacing humans with technology.

In this section we examine these four principles as Ritzer applies them to the fast-food restaurant.

Efficiency

Fast-food restaurants have efficiency inscribed in their DNA—not just in the production of food, but at just about every level and function of the organization. It is even a part of the language and marketing of the restaurant (*fast*-food, *express* tills, etc.). Efficiency not only benefits the company, it is what customers come to expect from a fast-food restaurant—speedy and efficient service.

Every task is designed to be as efficient and as least wasteful as is possible. Think about the process of putting together a burger and, in particular, the role of the folding box into which it is placed (based on Ritzer, 2011: 55–57):

- the two (pre-sliced) halves of bread for the burger are placed in each half of the box
- on top of the bottom half are placed the meat, sauces, (pre-shredded) lettuce, and other items
- in a final flourish of efficient work design, the box is closed—there is no need to place the bread on top of the burger, the act of closing the box simultaneously, and with no extra time or effort, also puts the bread in place.

This may seem a trivial example, saving just fractions of a second, but the aim of a fast-food restaurant is to serve people quickly and in volume. If fractions of a second are saved not only in closing the box, but at all stages of making a burger, and this is replicated thousands of times during a day, then the fractions of a second add up to big efficiency savings.

Similar efficiency can be found in the service encounter, where the till is designed to make processing the order and communicating it to kitchen staff as efficient as possible. There is a separate button for each item on the menu, no need to waste time training staff to know the prices of different items or to look it up on a separate menu.

Real life case: working for free at a fast-food restaurant

When you go to a fast-food restaurant, think about how you actually do some of the work and, furthermore, do that work for free.

Within the restaurant you act as waiter, taking your own tray of food to the table, and as a cleaner, emptying your tray into a bin. This is all work which would otherwise take up the paid time of members of staff. In some fast-food restaurants, there are 'express' tills where the customer keys in the order, pays by card, and then collects their food. Yet another job—that of the till operator—is now performed for free by the customer.

All of this helps the restaurant to run more efficiently; indeed, getting work done for free rather than paying a wage is, perhaps, the ultimate in efficiency and cost-saving.

Source: based on Ritzer, 2011: 73–77.

How do you feel about performing work for free at a fast-food restaurant? Can you think of any other organizations where you do similar work for free?

Efficiency also comes from simplifying the product range in a similar way to Henry Ford limiting his Model T car to one colour so as to avoid halting the production line to change the paint set-up (see Chapter 3). Unlike a high-class restaurant where a meal is chosen and cooked individually, a fast-food restaurant has a limited number of products and options. While it is possible in a fast-food restaurant to order a burger without, for example, gherkins, it requires the burger to be produced individually away from the main 'production line'. While this may be done occasionally, if every customer wanted a similar customization, it would take more time and the process would become less efficient.

Calculability

Is a fast-food restaurant the type of restaurant that you would go to in order to impress a business client or, perhaps, for a romantic first date? Certainly, it would be difficult to emphasize the quality of a fast-food restaurant compared with, say, a Michelin-starred restaurant. Not only is the food of the Michelin restaurant in a completely different league, there is also a difference in the quality of the experience. You would not be expected to clear away after yourself in a Michelin-starred restaurant, nor would there be someone cleaning the floor underneath your table as you eat!

For Ritzer (2011: 81), if quality cannot be marketed, then fast-food restaurants emphasize quantity—the amount that you get for your money. This can be seen in the names of products—the Big Mac, the Whopper, the Supersize menu.

Real life case: 'Supersize Me'

The documentary film *Supersize Me* (dir. Spurlock, 2004) focused on the health impacts of eating nothing but fast-food. The film-maker, Morgan Spurlock, ate nothing but McDonalds food for a month and when asked if he wanted to 'supersize' a meal he would have to agree.

The film saw how his health declined as a result of this. McDonalds, in response, claimed that their food is not meant to be eaten at all meals and should be part of a balanced diet (McDonalds, 2004).

Calculability also extends to work design in fast-food restaurants—hardly surprising given their origin in Taylorist techniques based around measurement and calculation. While much of the work process is based around calculating the optimum efficiency with which to perform a task, the emphasis on what can be measured can also be seen with 'live' orders on a screen behind the service area, with a clock ticking to show how long has elapsed since the order was taken.

Predictability

Many of you may have travelled abroad and found yourself in an unfamiliar environment where you don't know the language, the local customs, or the local foods. The sight of a set of golden arches on the front of a McDonalds restaurant can be a welcome sign of familiarity, where the nature of the food is known instantly—even ordering is simple as a phrase such as 'Big Mac' is universal.

Ritzer (2011: 98) suggests that McDonalds restaurants exhibit predictability—a lot of what they do is identical, whether the restaurant be in Birmingham, Beijing, or Berlin. Such predictability comes about as a result of using the standardized routines and work patterns of bureaucracy:

- the interiors of fast-food restaurants for any one chain often look very similar—what Ritzer describes as 'predictable settings'. The predictable setting is not just about marketing and image; there are efficiencies from buying fixtures and fittings in bulk, and from having a standard design for a restaurant rather than employing individual designers each time (see also the global standardization of organizational environments in Chapter 16)

- as we have seen, fast-food restaurants have a standard range of products and the procedures for making these products are also standardized. Furthermore, conditions are placed on suppliers for the potatoes, meat, etc. that they provide. The end result is that there is a predictable and familiar range of products which look and taste identical wherever they are consumed (ibid: 39)

- the behaviour of employees, who are all trained using the same manuals and procedures, is also predictable from one restaurant to another (ibid: 166–7).

Many fast-food restaurants are global organizations, and so there is predictability and standardization on a global scale—the same settings, products, and behaviours worldwide.

(However, see Chapter 15 for examples of where McDonalds do have to adapt for national markets.)

Control

McDonaldization exhibits Taylorist control (see Chapter 3) and also bureaucratic control through its meticulous use of manuals and procedures for tasks throughout the organization.

Ritzer (2011: 119) outlines further areas where control is exerted and the independent, autonomous activity of workers is minimized. As much as possible is pre-prepared before it even reaches the restaurant, for example the aforementioned pre-shredded lettuce, so there is less for workers to do and fewer mistakes that they can make.

A major aspect of control is exerted by replacing 'human with non-human labour' (Ritzer, 2011: 117ff)—getting a machine to perform the task where possible. For example, the judgement on the length of time to cook fries is not left to humans as it may be with a trained chef; instead, a timer beeps to tell the operator when to remove the fries (ibid: 119). As previously seen, technology at the till takes away human judgement from the service encounter, prompting the till operator what to say or ask next. The express till replaces operators completely with a machine.

Control in a fast-food restaurant.

The 'McDonaldization' of society

The four aspects of McDonaldization connect with each other to produce a form of contemporary rationalized organization that is efficient on a global scale. Even small elements of the work process that might go unnoticed can contribute to this process. Think of the scoop that is used to place fries in a carton—it contributes to all four aspects of McDonaldization:

- it is an *efficient* way of transferring fries to the carton
- it *calculates* the portion size that goes into the carton
- it allows *predictability* in that the same portion size is served every time
- it *controls* the worker, preventing them from producing variable portion sizes each time.

When Ritzer refers to the 'McDonaldization of society' he does not mean that society is becoming overrun with fast-food restaurants, but that the rationalized organization and management techniques found in fast-food restaurants are found in *many other* types of contemporary organizations worldwide. McDonaldization, for Ritzer, is thus defined as:

> The process by which the principles of the fast-food restaurant are coming to dominate more and more sectors of American society as well as the rest of the world.   (Ritzer, 2011: 1)

Examples of McDonaldized organizations

There are many other types of organization that can be described as McDonaldized, displaying similar characteristics of efficiency, calculability, predictability, and control to those found in fast-food restaurants. For example:

- banks employ standardized procedures and have similar, predictable branch settings. Efficiency is gained from getting customers to do work for free through online banking and cashpoints. Technology controls and performs many tasks, such as balance transfers or paying bills, which used to be done by cashiers in handwritten ledgers (Ritzer, 2011: 69)
- multiplex cinemas have a standard, predictable appearance across a chain, and are efficient by maximizing the number of screens within the building. Again, the customer does some work, and technology takes control through online and automated ticket booking
- Parker and Jary (1995) describe McDonaldization in universities, where courses are divided into standardized modules and assessments, such as multiple choice assessments, which are designed for speed and efficiency, often using technology, such as a scanner, to mark the assessment.

Visit the Online Resource Centre for more examples of McDonaldized organizations.

What other examples of McDonaldized organizations can you think of? How do they display characteristics of efficiency, calculability, predictability, and control?

Study skills: university rules and procedures

There was a time when universities were exclusive organizations that very few people could hope to reach. Students would have regular one-to-one tutorials with eminent professors, discussing academic issues and work in depth.

Nowadays, such a situation exists only at the very top institutions. Mass higher education means that many more people are able to go to university, but it also means that there is less personal contact with tutors—contact is in larger seminar groups that are timetabled automatically.

As with other organizations as they grow in size, universities have to use bureaucracy and rationalized techniques to manage the organization. Parker and Jary's 'McUniversity' (1995) reflects this rationalization.

Part of the rationalization of university life involves a wide range of rules and procedures, for example:

- exceptional circumstance procedures for dealing with illness or similar problems
- degree classification procedures for bringing together module marks into a final degree classification
- assessment briefs and marking schemes
- academic misconduct procedures, e.g. for dealing with plagiarism.

Many of these rules and procedures are there to help students, and most have an impact on their academic achievement. It often surprises us that many students are unaware of even basic procedures, such as the requirements for an essay, yet alone what to do if an extension is needed because of illness—many never read the undergraduate handbook that is given to them at the start of their studies!

Being aware of the various procedures that affect your life as a student is a great help in getting the most out of your studies—understanding exactly what is required of you, what help and assistance is available to you, and how your work will be assessed, allows you to focus your studies much more clearly.

The 'iron cage' of McDonaldization

While Ritzer first described the concept of McDonaldization, this does not mean that he supports or advocates it as a form of management and organization. Indeed, Ritzer echoes Weber's concerns with the **iron cage** of rationality (see Chapter 2) to suggest that there now exists an 'iron cage' of ever-present McDonaldization. Following Weber, Ritzer (2011: 115) cautions against the 'irrational' aspects of rationality—the difference between what might be formally rational for an organization in terms of efficiency and what is substantively rational: the effects in human terms.

Ritzer (2011: 148–49) uses Weber's concept of **disenchantment**—a loss of the 'magical aspects' of life, as more and more organizations and aspects of life become standardized and routinized. An example or symptom of this today can be found in campaigns against 'identikit' high streets, where the same chains, rather than independent retailers, can be seen in high streets across the country—the implication being that in being standardized, individual towns lose something of their character (Judd and Kirby, 2005).

> **Iron cage** Max Weber's observation of the increased presence of bureaucracy in society and its potential to trap people in its routines and procedures.
>
> **Disenchantment** For Max Weber this was a loss of 'magical elements' in society, and suggests some of the dehumanizing elements of bureaucracy.

Deskilling and McJobs

Restaurant work is often linked with high levels of skill and even artistry. Top chefs train for years to get to their level and have a great deal of personal pride and identity linked to their work. A further critique of McDonaldization parallels Braverman's (1974) **deskilling** thesis which critiqued the loss of workers' skills under Taylorism (see Chapter 3).

Fast-food restaurants deskill food production. No longer is it a highly-trained art form; instead, it involves performing a repetitive task which can be learned in a couple of hours. As with Taylorism, knowledge of the overall production process rises to the management levels which design the overall work process. Individual workers are left with a very limited knowledge of one very simplistic task and their autonomy is reduced, as is the amount of control that they can exert—a troublesome worker is easily replaced, and their replacement can be trained and put in place within the day.

> **Deskilling** The obsolescence of workplace skills caused by rational work design or the introduction of new technology.

Such is the impact on the nature of work in fast-food restaurants, the phrase **McJobs** (Etzioni, 1986) has entered the common parlance to describe simplistic, repetitive jobs with little job satisfaction, often performed by younger workers in the service sector (although see Gould (2010), who suggests some benefits for workers of 'McJobs', including the ability to work flexible hours around an individual lifestyle).

> **McJobs** Deskilled jobs found particularly in service industries, such as the fast-food restaurant.

Summary

McDonaldization outlines some characteristics that are prevalent in many contemporary organizations, not just fast-food restaurants, and makes the link between rational techniques in such organizations and those developed during the Industrial Revolution. However, we should be cautious of taking the phrase 'McDonaldization of society' to apply to *all* contemporary organizations. Indeed, a volume by Smart (1999) outlines a number of instances where resistance against McDonaldization takes place—we will see some examples of these in Chapter 15.

In the following section we examine some further models of contemporary rationalization.

Review questions

1. Describe the four main features of McDonaldization.

2. Explain how McDonaldization is a development of more traditional forms of rationalization, such as bureaucracy and scientific management.

3. Analyse how McDonaldization can be seen to bring about a trade-off between quantity and quality.

Apply

4. What aspects of McDonaldization can you see in organizations with which you are familiar?

Contemporary models of rationalization

Running case: budget hotel

I'm now in a budget hotel and, after the luxury of the previous hotel, this is a bit of a shock to the system.

At check-in, the queue extended to the front door and was managed by a temporary aisle of the sort used outside nightclubs.

Customer service was perfunctory—there was a job to do in processing the queue as quickly as possible. The check-in process was efficient. Despite the long queue, I soon had my key card, which gave me access to the lift and, finally, my room.

The room was almost identical to other rooms that I've experienced in this budget chain. It's interesting to see no door on the wardrobe—it certainly cuts costs: fewer raw materials to make the things in the first place, no moving parts to require repair should they go wrong, and no door for the cleaners to have to open and reach inside.

Tea and coffee was provided. The small kettle was hard-wired into the wall. Next to it were receptacles for the tea/coffee sachets—almost to a preset size so that the cleaners can just drop in the required amount very quickly. There was soap, but no other toiletries—I had to purchase those for myself from reception.

Food was to a set menu—not very much choice, just a standard, and limited, range and served in the bar area. Reception staff seem to double-up as bar and waiting staff.

Check-out required no human interaction; the key card was simply dropped into a slot on the reception desk. Had I wished to store baggage I would have needed to purchase a token and then place it myself into a set of lockers put aside for the purpose. Normally, hotels will store left-luggage for free; here, it is an optional paid extra—and I had to go and collect it for myself.

Obviously, this place reduces its costs well, but I'm not sure we could go this far with Junction Hotel—the service and luxury is what our customers want.

Can you list the methods by which the budget hotel saves costs?

Many organizations that we use on a regular basis run on a rationalized business model of saving costs and increasing efficiency—in some cases their main business strategy is cost minimization in order to compete on price. In this section we examine some examples of these, such as supermarkets, no-frills airlines, budget hotels, and flat-pack furniture retailers.

All of these could be described as 'McDonaldized' in Ritzer's terms and do exhibit some of the characteristics of McDonaldization. However, each also has their own particular ways of implementing rationalized techniques, which are worthy of examination in their own right. While this section does not cover all examples of contemporary rationalization it highlights rationalization in a number of familiar organizations.

'No-frills' rationalization and value engineering

There was a time when air travel was seen as glamorous—the province of celebrities and the well-off. Now, it is relatively cheap thanks to the development of budget airlines such as Ryanair, EasyJet, and German Wings.

Such airlines are described as **no-frills** airlines. While they may cut costs in the labour process, their main cost-cutting strategy is to simply eliminate costs that are not essential to providing the basic service of a seat on a plane. If a customer incurs any further optional costs, they pay for them as and when. Where previously the price of an aeroplane seat would include extras, such as a meal and a baggage allowance, budget airlines strip the offering down to the most basic necessities at the lowest price possible.

A similar pricing and cost minimization model is found in the budget hotel industry. Davis (2007) notes how a budget hotel company, such as Travelodge, engages in **value engineering**—a meticulous analysis of where costs are incurred and whether they can be pared down.

No-frills A model of organizational cost reduction which offers a basic product, charging customers for anything extra to this basic offering.

Value engineering A form of cost analysis that compares the cost of an item or process against its perceived value.

Real life case: value engineering at Travelodge

Famously, Travelodge does not offer shampoo in its rooms—it means that they save on the cost and are able to offer the room at a lower price. If people want shampoo or similar optional extras, they can buy them at an extra cost. Travelodge's own website gives the reasons for this:

- Our hotels are equipped with **everything you need for a good night's sleep**.
- Unlike other hotel companies we don't provide a trouser press, chocolates on pillows, toiletries or other unnecessary items.
- **We keep things simple and consistent** because we understand that all you want is a restful place to sleep. This keeps our costs down and therefore we can offer rooms for much less than other hotels.

Source: Travelodge, 2012.

Visit the Online Resource Centre to see a variety of ways in which hotels use 'no-frills' offerings.

Are there any other industries or organizations where you have seen a 'no-frills' model in operation?

Flat-pack rationalization

Many of us have had the experience of putting together a piece of flat-pack furniture; indeed, the first days of moving into student accommodation can involve hours spent with a screwdriver in hand, components laid out across the floor, trying to interpret the diagrams which tell you how to put together a wardrobe, computer desk, or similar item.

Flat-pack furniture is most associated with the Swedish global retailer IKEA, whose standardized stores offer the same standard range globally, although the flat-pack technique is used by other manufacturers and retailers.

Other than the standard range offered, there are rationalized aspects of flat-pack furniture which allow costs to be minimized and the product to be sold much more cheaply than high-end bespoke furniture (see also Ritzer, 2011: 18–20).

- As we saw in Chapter 3, flat-pack furniture is designed to be packed as small, individual parts which can be assembled easily, just as Taylor designed work tasks. The customer does the actual work of assembling the goods themselves, so saving the manufacturer the costs of assembly, and there is no need for the expensive skills of trained furniture-makers at any point in the process.

- Tasks are simplified so much that the instruction sheet can be provided simply as a set of diagrams rather than words. This means that exactly the same package is stored in all countries, there is no need to translate and print different instruction booklets for each country. Economies of scale are global.

- It is not just products that are standardized. Standard components, such as shelves and screws, can be used across a number of products.

- Being able to flat-pack the furniture saves on storage space and space on delivery vehicles, and thus further saves costs (IKEA, 2003). Companies like IKEA work to shave fractions of a millimetre off the size of their packaged goods so as to maximize the number that can go into a delivery vehicle; thus, the transportation costs per unit drop.

Barcode technology and rationalization

When you go to the supermarket, you may see the barcode on each of the products as a type of electronic price tag. While this is true, the barcode allows a supermarket to do far more than calculate prices at the till. Much of the rationalization in supermarkets is a result of the technology associated with barcodes, allowing the supermarket to make efficiencies and reduce costs in a number of ways (see also Ritzer, 2011: 74–75).

The ubiquitous barcode.

- The barcode is printed on each individual product by the manufacturer and so the work of pricing-up individual items does not need to be done in the supermarket. When a price change is required, the price can simply be altered on the computer system. In fact, it can be done not just for one store, but for all stores across the country—a massive efficiency gain in terms of the time that it would take nationally to apply labels to all individual products.

- Rather than keying in individual prices for items, the supermarket cashier simply waves the goods in front of a barcode reader. The checkout often has a conveyor belt—it is as if the cashier is simply one part in an assembly line that begins with the customer placing goods at one end and packaging them at the other.

- The act of scanning the barcode not only adds up the total bill for the customer, it simultaneously reduces the store's inventory for that product. There is much less need for stocktaking to be done by staff and, indeed, stock ordering can be done automatically by the computer system. The simple act of passing a product in front of a till feeds into a national distribution and supply system.

- Self-service tills have become commonplace in supermarkets, with the customer doing the work of a cashier and scanning the items for themselves. In future, it may be that barcodes can be replaced by radio-frequency tags—these have the capabilities of barcodes but with the added advantage that they need not be scanned individually: a whole trolley can be 'read' in one go.

The example draws from large-scale supermarket chains. Which of the techniques and characteristics mentioned have you experienced in other, possibly smaller, stores?

While the use of a barcode and associated computer technology enhances the capabilities of a supermarket in getting a large and increasing volume of customers through the store as efficiently as possible, it also leaves it vulnerable. If one area of the rational system is disrupted then it can stop the system overall from functioning.

One such disruption, which is probably familiar to many of you, can happen with barcodes. A customer is being served at a till. On one item the barcode is ripped and cannot be read by the scanner. The customer knows the price of it and the cashier also knows the price. But, the only way that it can be input is by scanning the barcode—without it the transaction cannot take place. During this time the customer, and anyone else in the queue, is made to wait and become frustrated by what seems to be a rigid following of procedure rather than having the issue resolved in the quickest way possible.

When working well, the barcode produces an efficient system, but the demands of the system are such that, when it breaks down, it can suffer from similar issues of 'red tape' as seen in Chapter 2, where the system and its rules and procedures actually get in the way of work being done efficiently.

Barcodes, information, and tracking

Real life case: Ebuyer

Many online retailers have warehouses from which their orders are despatched—a massive operation for some of the larger companies.

Ebuyer, a UK-based electronics retailer, demonstrates how it can deliver orders the following day if they are ordered up until 11 pm. At the heart of this efficient process is its partly-automated warehouse, where goods can be picked out within 15 minutes, travelling along conveyor belts, with the barcode being scanned at all stages as a means of tracking the product.

Source: Ebuyer, 2007.

 Visit the Online Resource Centre to view a video of what goes on in the warehouse.

Barcodes are not just used as a type of product label in supermarkets, they can be used for tracking a product or a person. When a parcel is delivered to your house, the courier may scan a barcode on the label—this barcode will have been scanned at several points on its journey as a means of tracking the product. You can even follow its progress for yourself by typing in the order number on the courier's website.

While this allows for an efficient handling of products for despatch, tracking a product also allows an organization to track where the worker handling that product has been and how efficiently they are working. It allows for surveillance and control over the workers.

It can lead to an intensification of work. Hencke (2005) notes how in some warehouses, workers have computers strapped to their arms which direct them to the next product to pick up. In a Taylorist sense, wasted movement can be minimized—the computer system can identify the nearest worker to the product so that it can be retrieved in the quickest time possible.

Rather than just accessing existing information on a database, barcodes and computer systems allow for information to be generated about a worker's performance, and allow for control to be exerted over that worker. It is to these issues of surveillance and control in the contemporary rational organization that we turn in the next section.

Review questions

1. Describe how the organizations in this section cut costs and create efficiencies.

2. Explain how barcodes facilitate both efficiency and control.

Apply

3. Thinking about all of the organizational examples in this section, to what extent do they display the four characteristics of McDonaldization?

Panopticism, surveillance, and control

Running case: the credit card statement

MIDTOWN BANK

Credit card statement	S. CHANCE (Business a/c)	Card No. 4567 887 999988
Date	**Vendor**	**Amount**
1/2/2011	Midtown Trains Online Booking	57.89
1/2/2011	Hurryup.com Hotels Online	70.00
1/2/2011	Budgetshack	34.00
5/2/2011	Marks & Spencer (St Pancras)	5.50
5/2/2011	House of Fraser (Oxford Street)	120.00
5/2/2011	City casino, Leicester Square	100.00
5/2/2011	Bunny's Soho	120.00
5/2/2011	Luxhotel restaurant	180.00
6/2/2011	Fastburgers, Euston Road	4.00
6/2/2011	Budgetshack Hotels	20.99
7/2/2011	Mr Florists	23.00

How much of Chance's business trip can we retrace from this credit card statement? Is there anything on here that he may wish to hide (and does this explain the final entry on the list for when he got home)?

The French philosopher Michel Foucault (1977: 228) is renowned for his statement that '. . . [P]risons resemble factories, schools, barracks, hospitals, which all resemble prisons . . .'. Foucault doesn't mean that people are kept under lock and key when in school or in hospital, his quote refers to how all of these organizations exert power and control through the use of **surveillance**.

Foucault suggests that an early prison design which permits surveillance, the **Panopticon**, is a model on which similar types of surveillance and control are exerted in organizations more widely. Although Foucault died before the advent of call centres, we will examine them as an exemplar of such panoptic power within organizations.

From within Foucault's work, we find some parallels with the way in which control is exerted in the rational organization, whose design facilitates surveillance over people within organizations. This surveillance is intensified by computer and database technology.

Surveillance The observation, either overt or covert, of people to gain information about them or to exert order and control over them.

Panopticon A prison design that allows surveillance to take place efficiently over all prisoners, used as a metaphor for surveillance and control in organizations as a whole.

Foucault and the Panopticon

> **Research insight:** Discipline and punish, Foucault, M. 1977. *Discipline and punish : the birth of the prison.* New York: Pantheon Books.
>
> The French philosopher Michel Foucault (1926–84) was not interested specifically in organizational issues, but was interested in how control and order were maintained historically in society as a whole.
>
> Foucault begins with a gruesome description from 1757 of Damiens the regicide (murderer of the king) being hung, drawn, and quartered in Paris. Today, says Foucault, control and punishment in society are not so torturous and direct; instead, power operates by more subtle means, and this power operates at the level of individual organizations and institutions.
>
> The exemplar of this is the prison design of the Panopticon, which exerts power not directly and physically, but through more indirect means of surveillance. The design of the Panopticon, according to Foucault, is a blueprint for power and surveillance in many organizations that we encounter, and are a part of our daily lives.

The Panopticon is an architectural design for a prison building originally proposed by legal and social reformer Jeremy Bentham (1748–1832). It was built so that cells were arranged in a circle around a central watch tower.

In the Panopticon, every prisoner is instantly *visible* and thus open to surveillance (the word surveillance links with the idea of visibility—*surveiller* being the French word for 'watching over'). Its design means that at any one time a prisoner can be selected and observed from the central tower. The prisoner does not know at any one moment whether they are being observed, but the fact that they *might* be observed at any given moment makes them behave as the guards would wish—control is internalized within the prisoner.

The design of the Panopticon allows for a massive efficiency gain in terms of staffing the prison. One guard can maintain order over hundreds of prisoners from the central watch tower, rather than many guards needing to exert direct control over the prisoners. Thus, the Panopticon encompasses two aspects of rational organization—efficiency and control.

 Visit the Online Resource Centre for more detail about the original Panopticon.

The modern-day Panopticon

The same type of power through surveillance operates in modern-day CCTV systems. When we are in a store or town centre covered by CCTV cameras, we do not know if the pictures are being observed at any one time, but it is the fact that they *might be* which makes us behave. Again, we internalize control and power rather than having it exerted upon us face to face.

Modern day surveillance.

The image of a security guard sitting in front of a bank of CCTV screens, showing different areas of the store or town centre is perhaps not too different to the prison guard in the Panopticon looking at a grid of individual cells. In both cases, an efficient system to exert power and control is in place. The advantage that CCTV has over the Panopticon is that even if the security guard misses something as it happens, it is preserved on film to be looked at later. Technology can thus be seen to enhance the power and surveillance abilities of the Panopticon.

Think about how you are controlled when you drive. A speed camera may not even be loaded with film, but you are not to know this as you approach it. To what extent does the speed camera make you internalize power and control? Are speed cameras a form of modern-day Panopticon?

Organizational Panopticons

In a prison setting, the structure of the Panopticon allows for surveillance to be exerted that brings about two benefits which, no doubt, would interest managers in other types of organization.

* It allows for control to be exerted over the organization where otherwise chaos and unpredictability might ensue.
* It allows for this to be done in a highly efficient manner.

Maybe it should come as no surprise that Bentham based his idea for the Panopticon as a prison on an idea that his brother—a factory owner—had for redesigning his own factory (Hume, 2004: 270). Just as control over a large number of prisoners presents an organizational problem, so might control over a large number of workers in a factory.

Production systems based around Taylor's ideas, such as the assembly line, or the McDonalds restaurant, can be seen to display panoptic principles. Workers are given individual, simplistic tasks. This improves the efficiency of the production process, but also helps to increase surveillance over each individual worker. If a product is being made with component number 49 incorrectly attached, it does not take much to locate the cause of the problem—it is the worker whose sole job is to attach component 49.

The call centre as an organizational Panopticon

A rationalized, efficient form of contemporary organization that has been described as operating in a manner similar to a Panopticon (Fernie and Metcalf, 1988) is the call centre. Whenever we interact with many large-scale organizations by telephone (our bank or insurance company, for example) more often than not this call is handled by a call centre— a part of the organization designed specifically for dealing with telephone calls, or even by an outside organization that is subcontracted to handle calls.

The **call centre** is a model of rationalization that handles a large volume of telephone calls in as efficient a manner as possible. Calls are automatically directed to operators—the operator does not pace their own work. When a call is finished, the system automatically directs the next call to them. In some respects it is similar to the assembly line—the pace of work

Call centre An organization or department set up to handle a large volume of telephone calls, often managed efficiently using rationalized techniques.

is dictated by the line or, in this case, the computer system. Work is passed before the worker and has to be attended to there and then—there is no room for a rest or a breather.

Such intensive work regimes are further controlled by the degrees of surveillance within the call centre, which exhibit a number of characteristics similar to the Panopticon:

- the physical layout of a call centre—workers having their own individual booths is visually remarkably similar to the layout of the Panopticon. Workers can be watched, as with the guard in the Panopticon, so anyone leaving their booth for a cigarette or toilet break can be spotted instantly

- while an operator might be tempted to deal with a rude customer by telling them in no uncertain times where to go, they are prevented from doing this by the possibility that a supervisor may be listening in to their conversation. As with the Panopticon, this is not a constant, direct, face-to-face level of control—it is the fact that at any one moment the supervisor might be listening, which leads the operator to internalize power and control, and behave accordingly

- call data is recorded electronically—targets for the number of calls handled per hour can be set and reviewed on a computer printout by a supervisor. To increase the efficiency of a call centre, the target number of calls per hour can be increased—similar to increasing the speed of the assembly line. Computer data can also be used to review and monitor performance. For example, data can indicate the time spent away from the computer. There are instances where a maximum toilet time is given and the computer data can monitor if people take longer (Hencke, 2005).

While not all call centres control and monitor workers to such an extent, and there are examples of how such a system can be resisted (see Bain and Taylor, 2000), the potential for electronic monitoring and surveillance leads Fernie and Metcalf (1998) to describe the call centre as an 'electronic panopticon', where supervisory power has been 'rendered perfect'.

In what ways in your life in general, beyond the workplace, are you under surveillance? How can your behaviour be observed even after it has taken place?

The electronic Panopticon and 'dataveillance'

The final aspect of control created within the call centre—the use of electronic data—makes a link back to bureaucratic control (the keeping of records) and rational work design (the calculation of standards and workplace targets). Panoptic power becomes not just about physical observation, but also about how information is generated and recorded about workers, and used to judge their performance, especially when stored in an electronic, computerized form (Simpson, 1999: 69).

The ways in which organizations generate data information about people, putting them into categories and measuring them against targets, was an interest of Foucault—especially where such targets are used as a means of control.

Visit the Online Resource Centre to read more on how data can be used as a means of control.

Real life case: credit ratings

Many of us are used to having our credit rating checked when we apply for a loan, for example, or sign up to a mobile phone contract, but do you know how such ratings are calculated?

Credit rating agencies are companies that hold masses of data about all individuals—especially their financial history. They have records of credit cards held, loans taken out, and other financial products held. Furthermore, they have records of how well people have kept up with their payments—do they have an unblemished record or have they missed several months of payments in a row? (Lewis, 2002.)

From all of this data held, the credit rating agency is able to exercise surveillance in that they can see your entire financial history and from that make decisions about whether or not you are a worthy credit risk.

In the contemporary world we are used to a lot of information being generated and held about us. As we will see in Chapter 14, vast amounts of data are held in computer networks and shared between organizations. Terms such as **dataveillance** and the **electronic Panopticon** are used to describe the ways in which data can be used by organizations to exert control and surveillance over individuals in a manner similar to the Panopticon. Such control and surveillance has two important aspects:

Dataveillance
Surveillance brought about by examining electronic data which is held about individuals.

Electronic Panopticon
The ability to monitor our lives through the amount of electronic data and records held about us.

- anything that we do that is recorded on a computer system—websites visited, tweets sent, etc.—is potentially discoverable at a later date. Politicians have found this to their cost when emails that they thought were private are uncovered months later and leaked to the press (e.g. Pearse, 2012). It also means that anything which links to a computer system is recorded—bank withdrawals, credit card payments, card swiped through door entry systems, etc. There is a lot of electronic data held about us that could potentially come back to haunt us

- such data can not only be used for surveillance—to find out what we have been doing— but can also be used to make decisions about us. While credit-rating agencies assess our creditworthiness, insurance companies use data to assess the degree of risk that we pose as drivers, for example, comparing us with data held on other individuals (Poster, 1995).

The Panopticon thus shows how surveillance and control affects us not just in the workplace, but that it is used to exert power and surveillance over us by organizations in society generally. While the Panopticon was first conceived of as a rationalized prison design centuries ago, Foucault shows how its surveillance and ordering mechanisms are just as relevant to rationalized organizations today.

Review questions

1. Describe how the Panopticon exerted control over prisoners.

2. Explain how surveillance is used as a means of power and control in contemporary organizations and society.

3. Analyse what Foucault meant by saying that prisons are a blueprint for power and control in many other organizations.

Apply

4. What examples of surveillance in your own workplace or university can you identify?

Chapter summary

Running case: the email

From: Simon Chance
To: Management Team
Subject: A tale of two hotels

Colleagues,

As you know, I have been away on business and, during that time, I stayed in two contrasting hotels. One is a luxury outfit like our own, the other was a cheap and cheerful budget hotel.

I've attached a report with my reflection on the two. In brief, as you may expect, the budget place has more examples of rationalization in order to gain efficiency. Now, that's great for costs, but it's at the expense of the overall experience. Of course we can't go down that route as a luxury hotel.

However, even the luxury place still rationalizes to an extent—it's a matter of finding where it's feasible and appropriate.

So, I want all of you to look at your areas of responsibility and send me back a report detailing where rationalization is possible and where it would simply ruin things.

Thanks,
Simon

Simon Chance is considering the extent to which he will bring in rationalization to Junction Hotel. As a hotel with a luxury reputation, to what extent do you think rationalization is appropriate for the organization overall?

In this chapter we have seen two different trends describing the degree to which rationalization is found in contemporary organizations:

- on one hand, there are post-Fordist and post-bureaucratic models which adopt more flexible, less rigid, and less controlled models of organization, and which can be seen as a trend away from rationalized forms of managing and organizing

- at the same time, neo-Fordism, McDonaldization, panoptic surveillance, and other contemporary forms of organization have shown that rationalization is still used today, in some cases in more intensive and widespread form than in the days of Taylor and Ford, when it was first developed.

These two trends are not mutually exclusive—they coexist and, thus, there are a variety of forms of organization which use different degrees of rationalization. Rather than a 'one best way' approach to rationalization, it is a matter of using rationalization in the most appropriate way for any one particular organization (see Morgan, 2006: 26–27).

For example, post-bureaucratic forms of organization are appropriate in an organization where creativity and innovation require workers to have autonomy and flexibility. But,

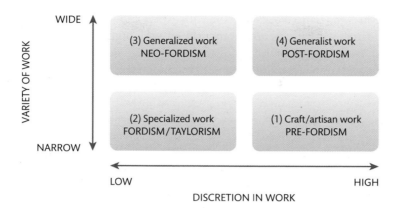

VARIETY OF WORK

WIDE

(3) Generalized work
NEO-FORDISM

(4) Generalist work
POST-FORDISM

(2) Specialized work
FORDISM/TAYLORISM

(1) Craft/artisan work
PRE-FORDISM

NARROW

LOW   HIGH

DISCRETION IN WORK

Figure 4.3
Work categorization framework.

© John Bratton, Peter Sawchuk, Carolyn Forshaw, Militza Callinan and Martin Corbett, *Work and Organizational Behaviour*, published 2010. Reproduced with the permission of Palgrave Macmillan.

for a fast-food restaurant, which requires conformity and the ability to do a simple task repetitively in order to operate efficiently, it would be wholly inappropriate—a fast-food restaurant does not want its staff to spend time being creative and devising new menus! And, while some people may want the convenience and efficiency of a fast-food restaurant, at other times people desire the much less rationalized approach, and the greater attention to individual detail and quality of a Michelin-starred restaurant.

Figure 4.3 brings together in one framework, different categories of work, and the degree to which that work is rationalized. The diagram locates type of work according to:

- *variety of work*—does a worker do a wide variety of tasks, or just a small number—even just one—repetitive task?

- *discretion in work*—the degree of control that a worker has over their own work. Do they have high discretion, with a large amount of autonomy and independence, or low discretion, where their work is very tightly controlled?

The diagram shows how different types of work coexist, displaying different degrees of rationalization. For example, we could relate the framework to the food industry, showing how different types of work in that industry relate to the types of work in the four quadrants.

1. Pre-Fordism is craft or artisan work, where a worker exercises a skill or craft on a small scale. They work independently, and so have high discretion, and work on a small variety of tasks. An example might be a dairy farmhouse kitchen, where one person makes a small amount of speciality cheeses.

2. Fordist production is specialized work. A single task is performed and workers are highly controlled, and so have low discretion. Some food factories mass produce food on assembly lines. A worker on such a line may have just one, repetitive job, for example sprinkling icing sugar on to cakes as they go past on the line.

3. Neo-Fordist production is generalized work, where a worker performs a wide variety of general tasks, but tasks which are simplistic and highly controlled, and so the worker has low discretion. A fast-food restaurant would be an example of this: a worker rotates between jobs such as serving customers, cleaning tables, and making burgers, but each of these jobs is designed to be simplistic and highly-controlled.

4. Post-Fordism is generalist work. A person with expert knowledge performs a wide variety of tasks and does so relatively autonomously, i.e. with high discretion. The head chef of a restaurant is an example of this, using their knowledge and expertise to produce any of a wide variety of dishes, creating the menu themselves each day.

The example listed shows the variety of work in an industry, but Noon and Blyton (2002: 166) suggest that such a variety can be seen even within one organization. Can you find examples for each of the four types of work shown in Figure 4.3 in Junction Hotel or in a similar type of workplace?

In this chapter we have examined the differing degrees of rationalization that exist in contemporary organizations and how these exist alongside trends away from rationalization. Moves towards, and away from, rationalization will also be reflected in future chapters, for example:

• perspectives such as the learning organization (Chapter 10) and emergent change (Chapter 11) lean towards a more post-bureaucratic, less rationalized view of organization, where organizations need to be flexible in order to respond rapidly to change and maintain competitive advantage. Furthermore, perspectives that emphasize the social side of the organization (Chapter 5) and the importance of groups and teamwork (Chapter 6) move us away from the rationalized view of organizations as machines and people as cogs within them

• Nevertheless, by examining work organization in the service sector (Chapter 16), global standardization and subcontracting (Chapter 15), and the issue of sweatshop labour in factories in the developing world (Chapter 17), we see examples where rationalization is still prevalent and widespread.

Further reading

Noon, M., and Blyton, P. 2007. *The realities of work: experiencing work and employment in contemporary society*. Palgrave: Basingstoke, New York.
Chapter 6 is a good overview of Fordism, post-Fordism, and neo-Fordism.

Ritzer, G. 2011. *The McDonaldization of society: an investigation into the changing character of contemporary social life*. Pine Forge Press: Thousand Oaks, CA.
The classic, and accessible, overview of the McDonaldization thesis.

Gould, A.M. 2010. Working at McDonalds: some redeeming features of McJobs. *Work, Employment & Society* 24(4): 780–802.
Presents arguments for and against 'McJobs'.

Fernie, S., and Metcalf, D. 1998. *(Not) hanging on the telephone: payment systems in the new sweatshops*. Centre for Economic Performance, London School of Economics and Political Science: London.
A study which likens call centres to the Panopticon and also looks at the Panopticon concept itself.

Bibliography

AutoMotoTV. 2010. Volkswagen Phaeton: Die Gläserne Manufaktur Dresden Available at: https://www.youtube.com/watch?v=sFV5EnsRgvw (last accessed 28 November 2012).

Bain, P., Taylor, P. 2000. Entrapped by the 'electronic panopticon'? Worker resistance in the call centre. *New Technology, Work and Employment* 15(1): 2–18.

Bauman, Z. 2000. *Liquid modernity*. Polity Press, Blackwell: Cambridge, UK, Malden, MA.

Bell, D. 1973. *The coming of post-industrial society; a venture in social forecasting*. Basic Books: New York.

Bennis, W. 1966. The coming death of bureaucracy. *Think Magazine* Nov–Dec: 30–35.

Bratton, J. 2010. *Work and organizational behaviour*. Palgrave Macmillan: Basingstoke.

Braverman, H. 1974. *Labor and monopoly capital: the degradation of work in the twentieth century*. Monthly Review: New York.

Burnes, B. 2000. *Managing change: a strategic approach to organisational dynamics*, 3rd edn. Financial Times/Prentice Hall: London.

Clegg, S., and Baumeler, C. 2010. Essai: From iron cages to liquid modernity in organization analysis. *Organization Studies* 31(12): 1713–1733.

Davis, E. 2007. Value engineering, *BBC News* (21 May 2007). Available at http://www.bbc.co.uk/blogs/thereporters/evandavis/2007/05/value_engineering.html (last accessed 29 November 2012).

Ebuyer. 2007. An order from Ebuyer. Available at: http://www.youtube.com/watch?v=G1aNPfNEGRQ (last accessed 29 November 2012).

Etzioni, A. 1986. The fast-food factories: McJobs are bad for kids. *The Washington Post* (24 August 1986).

Fayol, H. 1949. *General and Industrial Management*. Pitman: London.

Fernie, S., and Metcalf, D. 1998. *(Not) hanging on the telephone: payment systems in the new sweatshops*. Centre for Economic Performance, London School of Economics and Political Science: London.

Foucault, M. 1977. *Discipline and punish: the birth of the prison*. Pantheon Books: New York.

Gould, A.M. 2010. Working at McDonalds: some redeeming features of McJobs. *Work, Employment & Society* 24(4): 780–802.

Hencke, D. 2005. AA to log call centre staff's trips to the loo in pay deal. *The Guardian* (31 October 2005).

Hoskin, K.W., Macve, R.H. 1988. The genesis of accountability: the West Point connections. *Accounting, Organizations and Society* 13(1): 37–73.

Hume, L.J. 2004. *Bentham and Bureaucracy*. Cambridge University Press: Cambridge.

IKEA, 2003. From supplier to store. Available at: http://www.ikea.com/ms/en_GB/about_ikea/press_room/distribution.pdf (last accessed 29 November 2012).

Jaffee, D. 2001. *Organization theory: tension and change*. McGraw Hill: Boston, MA.

Judd, T., and Kirby, T. 2005. Clone attack/ The two sides of high street UK. *The Independent* (7 June 2005).

Larsen, H.H. 2002. Oticon: unorthodox project-based management and careers in a 'spaghetti organization'. *Human Resource Planning* 25: 30–37.

Lewis, M. 2012. Credit rating: How it works and how to improve it. MoneySavingExpert.com. Available at: http://www.moneysavingexpert.com/loans/credit-rating-credit-score (last accessed 29 November 2012).

McDonalds. 2004. McDonald's UK position on 'Super Size Me' press release. Available at: http://web.archive.org/web/20071012135323/http://mcdonalds.co.uk/pages/global/supersize.html (last accessed November 29 2012).

Morgan, G. 2006. *Images of Organization*. Sage Publications: Thousand Oaks, CA.

Noon, M., and Blyton, P. 2007. *The realities of work: experiencing work and employment in contemporary society,* Palgrave: Basingstoke, New York.

Parker, M., and Jary, D. 1995. The McUniversity: Organization, management and academic subjectivity. *Organization* 2(2): 319.

Pearse, B. 2012. Jeremy Hunt should quit over 'hacking advice' email, says Ed Miliband. *The Guardian*. 21 May 2012. Available at: http://www.guardian.co.uk/media/2012/may/12/rebekah-brooks-jeremy-hunt-email.

Piore, M.J., and Sabel, C.F. 1984. *The second industrial divide: possibilities for prosperity*. Basic Books: New York.

Poster, M. 1995. *The second media age*. Polity Press: Cambridge.

Rehder, R.R. 1994. Saturn, Uddevalla and the Japanese lean systems: paradoxical prototypes for the twenty-first century. *International Journal of Human Resource Management* 5(1): 1–31.

Ritzer, G. 2011. *The McDonaldization of society 6*. Pine Forge Press: Thousand Oaks, CA.

Simpson, I.H. 1999. Historical patterns of workplace organization: From mechanical to electronic control and beyond. *Current Sociology* 47(2): 47–75.

Smart, B. 1999. *Resisting McDonaldization*. Sage: London.

Spurlock, M. 2004. *Supersize Me*. Palisades Tartan (UK).

Starkey, K., and McKinlay, A. 1994. Managing for Ford. *Sociology* 28(4): 975–990.

Thompson, J. D. 1967. *Organizations in action*. McGraw Hill: New York.

Travelodge. 2012. Everyday low prices – how we do it. Available at: http://www.travelodge.co.uk/everyday_low_prices/#question1 (last accessed 29 November 2012).

Woodward, J. 1958. *Management and technology*. HMSO: London.

Part 2
Managing groups and teams

Discovering social organization

The Hawthorne studies and the human side of the organization

Chapter overview and learning outcomes

By the end of this chapter you should be able to:

- describe the basic features of the Hawthorne experiments
- describe how the Hawthorne experiments challenged many of Taylor's views
- explain how the Hawthorne experiments led to the foundations of modern organizational behaviour (OB), moving away from the mechanical perspective to the social side
- describe the power of the informal organization
- analyse whether the results of the Hawthorne studies increase worker *freedom* or *control* over workers.

Key theorists

Elton Mayo	Seen as the founder of human relations and a key figure in the Hawthorne studies. One of the founders of OB
Fritz Roethlisberger and William Dickson	The writers of the largest account of the Hawthorne studies comprising over 600 pages of highly detailed analysis of the research
Mary Parker Follett	Alongside Lillian Gilbreth, she was a key female early-management theorist. She was a political scientist, social work pioneer, speaker, and advisor to leaders concerning the relations between workers and management
Daniel Bell	A key social theorist after World War II, who wrote extensively about post-industrialization and its impact on society. Provided a key critique of Mayo

Key terms

Social organization	The underlying belief that the social relations between people are a key factor in shaping how people act in organizations
Hawthorne studies	A series of studies which ran from 1924 into the late 1930s. Widely credited with discovering the human side of organization
Human relations	Born out of the Hawthorne studies, human relations aims to understand and prescribe changes in workplace behaviour based on the importance of group norms, communication, and supervisory skills

Introducing the social side of the organization

Running case: too much to do and not enough time

Nina Biagini, Junction Hotel's maître d' looks at the pile of napkins piled in front of her: 250 to fold before the restaurant opens at 5pm; 400 glasses also need to be cleaned and then all the sliver cutlery needs to be polished. 'We are never going to be ready for tonight's Rotary International meal and we need to be on the top of our game with all these business leaders coming', she thinks. 'This is just the start of it', she says to herself, 'what with our busy season coming up, this place is going to be carnage if we don't get it sorted. We need help.'

Feeling anxious that the restaurant will not be ready in time, Biagini phones Weaver to get an extra pair of hands. 'What?', Weaver blasts down the phone, 'we can't afford more people. Look, I'll get you help today, but I can't keep baling you out like this . . . I'll tell you what,' he continues, in a calmer manner. 'I'll come down and work out how to make this process more efficient so this doesn't happen again.'

Weaver feels confident he can achieve the same efficiencies for the restaurant as he did for the cleaners. So, sitting in his office, he devises detailed napkin-folding instructions, including starching the cloths before they are used, how to sit them in the right way to minimize movement, and how to fold them in the exact order. 'One hundred and twenty napkins folded an hour per person . . . easy!', he concludes.

Excited with his new procedure Weaver is confident this will increase efficiency, thereby making prep-time stress-free. However, when he shows it to the restaurant team the reaction is not as he hoped. 'We're not robots', Naomi and Saffron complain. 'Weaver should try doing this job day in, day out and see if he can do it. We get tired and it's cold in here—not like in *his* office, which is comfortable with the radiator on.'

Social The human side of the organization, in particular the relations between people at work.

This chapter is about the importance of the human side of the organization. It tells the story of a fundamental transformation in management theory and practice from a Taylorist view (see Chapter 3), which saw organizations as purely mechanical, formal, measureable, and rational machines, to one that revealed the significance of informal relations between people. This view, which we will call the *social side* of the organization, has led to the interest in the importance of teamwork, organizational culture, motivation, and leadership—all of which feature heavily throughout the rest of the book. In other words, this chapter is about the introduction of a new way of thinking about organizations that stresses the importance of the informal, human side of the organization.

The findings from the Hawthorne studies have been credited with humanizing management practice. People are not nameless cogs in the machine, following rules and procedures in mechanical, predictable, and routine ways. Rather, to work effectively, people should feel wanted and part of the team, and be treated as human beings. According to this view, the informal group, rather than a problem as Taylor assumed, becomes a resource used by management to increase productivity. Consequently, to be productive it is possible—indeed, essential—to treat people as human beings. Management can, therefore, be humanized—humanity is restored.

This chapter is about one of the most important pieces of research to introduce this way of thinking. The Hawthorne studies, particularly as they were popularized by Elton Mayo, are widely credited as introducing this way of thinking to a large management and academic audience. It introduced a revolution in thinking and a change in attitudes, presenting what seemed like a magic cure—an end to conflict between the worker and the manager, producing harmony and progress, paving the way for a different agenda for management.

At the time it sent shockwaves across business circles, fundamentally challenging both management practitioners and the emerging university Business School. To our twenty-first century eyes, however, the idea that the social side of the organization is important, that we are influenced by peer pressure, that teamwork is important, and that employees respond better when managers pay attention to them is unlikely to shock. They have become an accepted part of management thinking and practice. This chapter is about the emergence of a new way of thinking and its continued importance for management today, showing how these ideas arose.

Chapter outline

This chapter starts with describing the key studies in the Hawthorne series. As you will read, these started with assumptions that would fit comfortably within a Taylorist framework—that the levels of lighting and worker fatigue impact employee output. However, as the studies progressed, the researchers began to realize the importance of the informal behaviour of the group. These findings lead to a change in assumptions in how to manage people.

These highly influential studies, however, have been the subject of criticism in terms of their research methodology, interpretation of findings, and whether they are really as beneficial to the worker as they claim to be. The latter part of the chapter will examine these criticisms, drawing attention to the political and social consequences of the Hawthorne studies, particularly Mayo's interpretation of them.

The existence and strength of the criticisms of the Hawthorne studies presented however, should not detract from the positive benefits that the findings of the Hawthorne studies have presented to management theory and practice. In comparison with the dehumanizing impacts of Taylorism, an awareness of the significance of the human side of the organization certainly presented a step forward. However, from the workers' point of view, as we will argue in this chapter, it still offers a way that management can control workers—potentially in ways that we do not even see.

Background to the Hawthorne studies: from the mechanical to the social

The Hawthorne studies were a series of six experiments carried out between 1924 and 1932 at the Western Electric Company in Cicero, on the periphery of Chicago, IL, USA. It has been considered one of the most significant pieces of research in the history of OB, not only

Table 5.1   The dates of experiments in the Hawthorne studies

No.	Name	Dates	Description	Findings
1	*Illumination*	1924–April 1927	Tested how different levels of light impacted productivity	No clear correlation between lighting levels and output
2	*Relay I*	April 1927–June 1929	Assessed the impact of rest periods on productivity	No clear correlation between rest periods and output
			Tested fatigue and monotony thesis	No clear correlation between fatigue and output
3	*Relay II*	August 1928–January 1929	Tested effects of wage incentive on output	No notable increase in output from wage incentive but not sustained
4	*Mica Splitting experiment*	October 1928–September 1930	Duplicated relay assembly room, but without wage incentive	Same pattern for first year then declined. Output more to do with **psychological** issues than wage incentives
5	*Interview program*	September 1928–February 1929, extended into 1931	Link between morale and supervision, improvements in employee–supervisor relations and the attitude of staff	Workers often have obsessive and irrational views. Social groups have powerful influence over the actions of individuals
6	*Bank wiring observation*	November 1931–May 1932	The role of the group in determining output	The informal group is key to impacting behaviour

Psychological Arising from the mind or emotions.

for the depth of research, but also because of the implications it holds for our understanding of management theory and practice today.

The Hawthorne works was a large factory, which has been described as being like a small town with over 29,000 (over 40,000 at its peak) employees. They made telephones and telephone equipment, and needed a number of highly-skilled workers to put together the fiddly systems. It was one of the first, and remains one of the biggest, pieces of research of its kind. The main experiments and their findings are shown in Table 5.1.

While the Hawthorne studies are closely associated with Elton Mayo, the fullest account is provided by Fritz Roethlisberger, a professor at Harvard, and William Dickson, the Chief of Employee Relations at the Hawthorne Works. Their book *Management and the Worker* (1939) provides a highly detailed (over 600 pages) and often fascinating account of every experiment, including the methods used, the often surprising reactions of the staff, the questions that the perplexing results raised for the researchers, and how the research led to alternative interpretations of management problems and potential solutions. We will concentrate on the key events, interpretations, and debates.

Visit the Online Resource Centre for a full account of the research. It is worth reading about this research in some depth as much of its significance lies in the detail.

The experiments

Experiment 1: testing the link between lighting levels and output—the illumination experiments

Running case: Weaver explores the impact of heating

Looking at the results, Weaver is concerned that the restaurant team are not as effective as he thought they could be. On paper, they should fold at least 120 napkins an hour, but they are still only folding 80. Weaver feels confused and decides to investigate further.

Visiting the restaurant, Weaver starts to watch how the restaurant team work, noting their body movements, the way they arrange the napkins and glasses, and the way they perform their tasks.

'It is a little cold in here', he thinks, 'I wonder if they can't move their fingers properly.' Asking Nina Biagini why this is, she states that when there are no customers they do not have heating. Weaver thinks this might be the cause of their slow work. Inspired by his time and motion studies, he starts recording the output and heating on a graph, asking them how they feel about the temperature as he does it. 'If we can find the right temperature', he thinks to himself, 'then we can maximize the output.'

In 1924, a small group of researchers aimed to uncover the links between lighting levels and employee output. By trying to create a 'science of seeing' they thought they would discover the optimum levels of lighting needed to maximize productivity and, owing to their funding from General Electric—one of the world's largest manufacturers of light bulbs—the research would also lead to increased sales of light bulbs to industry (Donkin, 2001: 165).

This research, conducted just over a decade after Taylor had published *The Principles of Scientific Management*, was set firmly within the scientific management tradition. Indeed, 'Taylorist', Alexander Church, a supporter of scientific management, had already stated his belief that poor lighting caused a strain on workers and that high-intensity lighting lifted workers' spirits. Frank Gilbreth (see Chapter 3) was also worried that the reflection on surfaces caused tiredness among workers (Donkin, 2001: 165). Thus, the first research shared Taylorist assumptions that physical conditions are an important area for *scientific* research.

Aiming to improve efficiency, they believed that creating the right inputs (in this case physical conditions) would increase output (the workers' productivity). Armed with measurement devices to assess the strength of lighting and record sheets to measure output, the researchers recorded the levels of lighting, and set about monitoring and adjusting the levels of lighting and output.

The assumption that the correct physical conditions, such as lighting, can improve employee output is widely held today. Many offices are designed to be 'light and airy', maximizing the amount of natural daylight and supplementing it with suitable artificial light, where necessary, believing that it energizes the workers.

How important do you find the levels of lighting to your feelings of energy, well-being, and levels of productivity?

The researchers fully expected to find a pattern between the lighting levels and output; however, the results shocked them. Instead of seeing a direct correspondence between light levels and employee output as they expected, the 'output [levels] bobbed up and down' in rather confusing ways.

Unable to find a link between lighting and output, they became more scientific and set up a **control group**, for which they kept lighting levels the same, and an experiment group, for which they adjusted the lighting. However, again, to their bafflement both groups' productivity went up in 'almost identical magnitude' (Roethlisberger and Dickson, 1939: 16). Lighting, it seemed, did not matter. Still trying to establish

A modern office designed to maximize daylight.

a link they set up a third experiment in which they reduced the lighting to levels where the workers 'were hardly able to see what they were doing' (ibid: 17). Even at this level efficiency remained high. At one point they even said that they changed the light bulbs for brighter ones when they had not and productivity went up.

The researchers, particularly as recounted by Roethlisberger and Dickson (1939: 17), therefore began to question their original assumption that lighting was an important component to productivity, concluding it was 'more "psychological" than real'. They needed to look for other factors involved in increasing productivity.

Control group Used in scientific research, a control group does not receive any intervention and therefore is seen as representing the population as a whole. The control group is used as a standard of comparison to the research group who do receive intervention.

Review questions

Explain

1. Why did a focus on lighting levels reflect Taylorist assumptions?

Explain

2. Why did the researchers conclude productivity was more psychological than real?

Experiment 2: testing the link between fatigue and output—the Relay I assembly test room

Running case: if it's not heating then what is it?

Weaver meets Nina Biagini to discuss the preparations for the busy Christmas period. 'We are making some improvement but the level of heating does not seem to make any difference', Biagini states. 'Yes, it is odd', replies Weaver, 'I mean you would have thought that when we dropped the heating back to the original level their performance would have dipped again. There must be more we can do. In a couple of weeks' time we are going to have three sittings a day, so we are going to have to work extra hard to keep up.'

'But we will never be able to achieve that', Biagini responds. 'They barely keep going for two hours, let alone for four. They get exhausted doing the same thing over and over again.'

Suddenly, Weaver has a brainwave. 'Exhaustion you say. I think you might be on to something.'

As the initial experiment suggested, lighting was only a minor factor in employee output. The researchers, continuing in a scientific mindset, believed there must by other physical factors that impacted productivity. Their next assumption was that fatigue must impact productivity, as they held the common-sense assumption that tired workers would produce less. They therefore aimed to discover scientifically the ideal balance of work and rest.

The role of fatigue was already a subject of much research with concern that operators, particularly the munitions workers of World War I, working seven days a week with only one day off per month were often so tired that they were found asleep at their lathes (Gale, 2004).

The researchers took a group of six women, who were making telephone circuits, from the large factory and put them in a special unit to study them. Trying to control the experiment scientifically they decided that the women needed to be highly experienced so productivity increases could not be attributed to improvements in skill, but as result of what they were testing—the balance between work and rest. Crucially, for their later findings, they also decided to make the research environment as friendly, cooperative, and natural as possible so they could get closer feedback on the results. We will return to why this was significant in section *The importance of group norms*.

Theory in context: gender in the Hawthorne studies

One of the fascinating aspects of the Hawthorne studies is the role that gender played. Throughout Roethlisberger and Dickson's (1939: 182) account they referred to the six women in the relay assembly room as 'girls'. The language that they used indicates it was not a relationship of equals.

As with many aspects of working life at the time, men decided levels of pay, hours, or even if women could have a job. In this experiment it was men who decided that the women should work in a separate special room away from the large factory; it was men who decided that the women were talking too much; it was men who decided when it was acceptable for the women to talk; it was men who carried out physical examinations and asked questions as to the women's eating habits, bedtimes, and activities outside of work; and it was men who decided the meaning of the discussions that the women had. Indeed, as Marks argues, when the research was intrusive, it was the women who were investigated, whereas when they decided to avoid manipulation the researchers decided to select men as their subject matter (Marks, 1999).

This gendered relationship even extends to the language that the researchers and commentators used. For instance, Elton Mayo (1933) argued that it revealed the existence of 'Social man', which replaced the previous assumption of 'Economic man'. While you may dismiss the use of *man* in this context as semantics, as simply a difference in the meaning of the word, the choice of words reflects the assumptions that were prevalent at that time—that the world of work revolved around male assumptions of the world. We will be using the more gender-neutral 'social person' for the remainder of this chapter, as it represents a more inclusive perspective.

Review question

Analyse

1. Analyse the implications of the early research being conducted by men studying women.

The work the women did was mind-numbingly boring. For instance, to put one of the relays together, the worker had to perform thirty-two separate operations for each hand and to make one every minute for nine hours a day for five and a half days a week. They had little hope of promotion or even variation in the job (Gillespie, 1991).

Imagine that you did this kind of work—how would you feel? How would you cope with the monotony?

The primary objective of the research was to discover the ideal pattern of work and rest. To test this they started by keeping everything constant for a few weeks and then experimenting with different break periods. Table 5.2 shows that by the eighth period they had started shortening the working day and then, by the eleventh period, even removing the Saturday morning shift.

To their surprise they discovered that regardless of how long the rest periods were or when they were taken, output constantly rose. Even when they returned to the original pattern output was higher than ever. The researchers concluded, contrary to their assumptions, that there was no simple correlation between output and rest patterns.

So why did the output levels not correspond to the rest periods? To find the answer the researchers devised a number of hypotheses, such as better lighting and ventilation, reduction in overall fatigue, reduction in monotony of work, and increased pay.

Centring on their hypothesis that fatigue was the most important factor, the researchers went to some lengths to test the physical condition of the workers. This included regular physical examinations of the workers' blood pressures and **vascular skin reaction** to test their level of fatigue. They even compared the results with marathon runners believing that stamina was vital for work.

While they still assumed that physical conditions were important, they also began to notice—which became important for later studies—that the atmosphere and mental attitude in the group improved. At first, they had prevented the women from talking, but as the study continued they allowed them to talk to each other more. Indeed, the researchers felt they needed to create a more harmonious atmosphere in order to undertake the tests they wanted. They came to realize that the 'girls' enjoyed the less formal test room with no formal bosses present and increased freedom. Over the course of the study they noticed that antagonism

Vascular skin reaction
A white line on the wrist created by a blunt instrument which disappears more quickly when the person is fatigued.

Table 5.2 Rest patterns

Period	Rest pattern	Period	Rest pattern
I	Standard	VIII	As VII stop 4:30
II	Standard	IX	As VII stop 4:00
III	Standard	X	As VII
IV	2 × 5 minutes	XI	As VII Sat. am off
V	2 × 10 minutes	XII	Standard
VI	6 × 5 minutes	XIII	As VII
VII	1 × 15 and 1 × 10 minutes		

between the group members was replaced by banter and joking. Attendance improved and they worked well together. The women, by being allowed to talk, managed to overcome some of the monotony of the job and found a way of working that best suited them.

What do you think about these tests? Are they a good way of capturing this information or do they treat people more like robots?

Real life case: fatigue at work today

While the Hawthorne studies rejected the fatigue hypothesis as the key to productivity, research continues to investigate it today. A recent survey has claimed nearly 40% of Americans experienced fatigue over a two-week period, costing employers an estimated $101 billion a year (Ricci et al., 2007). Clearly, fatigue continues to be a central concern for business.

Experiments 3 and 4: testing the link between pay and output—Relay II and the Mica Splitting experiment

The second relay experiment and the Mica Splitting experiment shifted the focus of the Hawthorne studies dramatically. For the first time the researchers began to examine the *psychological* and *social* factors that influenced how people behaved, rather than just the *physical* ones. They therefore became interested in what made them a team and how individual behaviour arose out of the nature of the group. It was, therefore, a shift in focus from the individual to that of the group.

Workers in the relay assembly department. © Baker Library Historical Collections, Harvard Business School.

This change in focus laid the foundations for an area of research known as '**Human Relations**', an academic school of thought which examines the *social relations* between people, the *motivation* of workers, and the impact that *employee satisfaction* has on output and productivity. Rather than seeing workers as 'cogs in the machine', this approach saw workers as social beings, with a need for belonging within the group. This approach acted as a precursor to modern day *human resource management*.

However, these two experiments did not begin by examining the social relations between group members; rather, they held another Taylorist assumption: that pay levels would increase output—an attempt to establish a link between another set of inputs (bonuses) and output.

Human Relations A movement emerging out of Organizational Development that studies the behaviour of people in groups.

At first it seemed that their assumptions were correct because after giving the workers a bonus, output rose sharply. However, to their puzzlement, this rise did not continue. The results, though, proved to be inconclusive, as the experiment had to be cut short. Other groups in the factory got wind of the scheme and felt it was unfair that this 'social group' were getting preferential treatment and they 'wanted similar consideration' (Roethlisberger and Dickson, 1939: 133). Fearing upset, the rest of the factory managers demanded that the experiment was ended—showing the importance of social factors.

The researchers continued their investigations into whether increased output could be attributed to a wage increase; therefore, in experiment 4—the *Mica Splitting Test Room*—they tried replicating Relay II, but without the bonus scheme. To their surprise the first year results mirrored Relay II with a sharp increase in productivity, even without the bonus. However, in the second year output declined. The researchers believed this was because rumours were spreading that jobs were to be transferred to another city, concluding that the employees' 'fears and anxieties so completely overshadowed the experimentally introduced changes' (ibid: 153). This suggested to the researchers that it was not wage incentives that impacted their performance, but the employees' attitudes (e.g. fear of job loss). Again, we can see the importance of social factors.

As pay did not seem a significant factor, the researchers began to consider other explanations. What mattered more was employees' morale, their relationships with their supervisors and each other, and their personal backgrounds. Most importantly, they concluded that the Relay Assembly Test Room was a '"group" story' where the members acted as a team, did not have bosses, but cooperated and worked together. Whereas they thought that the Mica Splitting Test Room 'was a story of "individuals"' who were self-sufficient and did not feel the need to work together (ibid: 156). They thought that individual behaviour was 'rooted in [shaped by] their personal and social background' (ibid: 171). In other words, the Relay experiment was successful because the members cooperated and saw themselves as part of a team, whereas the less successful Mica Splitting Test Room subjects were individuals who did not bond.

 Why do you think the researchers at the Hawthorne studies began to see the importance of the relationship between group members to their overall levels of productivity?

Experiment 5: interview programme—discovering the importance of a personal life

Running case: listening to the staff

Faced with the confusing results from Weaver's experiments Nina Biagini is asked to interview the restaurant staff and find out how her team feel about working in the restaurant.

'Right Isabella, I have been asked by the senior management team to find out the level of staff satisfaction at Junction Hotel. We want to have a happy team, as well as a productive one, so today I want to know your views of working at Junction Hotel. Don't worry, your views will be kept anonymous—we just want to know what you think.'

A little taken aback, Isabella smiles at Biagini. 'Oh, me, well', pausing before laughing nervously, 'how long have you got!' Isabella begins by cautiously saying that she really enjoys working for Junction Hotel: 'they are all good fun', and, 'supportive when you're having a bad day, although I didn't like Weaver watching us like that'. She then goes on to say that she is finding life at home a little hard at the moment: 'there's always so much to do and I feel a little harried', she confesses to Biagini. She's just fallen out with her son and isn't talking to her husband—'he's just so distant' she says with a faraway look in her eye. Listening to all this Biagini starts to feel a little uncomfortable—'I feel more like a counsellor than a manager', she thinks. Rounding off the discussion, Isabella turns to Biagini—'oh, sorry, I hope I didn't go on to much. Thanks so much for listening'.

Having established the importance of the social side of the organization, the next set of experiments began exploring employees' attitudes to work. Undertaking a large interview programme, the researchers thought that gaining an insight into how employees viewed work and their relationship with their supervisors would unlock ways of increasing productivity. What they found, however, was that it was the interview itself, particularly being listened to, that the employees really responded to.

The researcher team conducted one of the largest investigations of employee attitudes ever undertaken with an enormous 10,300 interviews lasting between 30 minutes and 1.5 hours, all of which were fully transcribed. This was a very time-consuming task as, on average, an hour-long interview can take at least five hours to transcribe. This produced hundreds of pages of detailed personal information, providing an amazing insight into the mindset of these ordinary American workers during the 'Great Depression'. Even today the size and level of detail of this study is hard to match, and it gave a comprehensive insight into the lives of ordinary workers.

The researchers took the thousands of comments and sorted them into categories, such as work conditions, attitudes to supervisors, and the nature of their jobs, and divided them into favourable and unfavourable groups. They discovered the workers disliked certain working conditions, such as washrooms and the smoke and fumes, but strongly approved of the benefit plan and vacations. Men seemed more interested in economic security, whereas the women were more focused on working conditions. This, they thought, would help the management understand how workers felt and therefore how to manage them.

However, the researchers were surprised (and often frustrated) that the interviewees would become fixated on what they considered irrelevant issues in their personal lives. Employees would recall personal events, sometimes from years before, with full emotion as though it was yesterday. The researchers surmised that doing repetitive factory work gave 'a great deal of time for preoccupation' (Roethlisberger and Dickson, 1939: 133), resulting in the workers being 'obsessive' and 'irrational'. This brooding on their personal lives, they considered, made the workers less productive.

Eventually, though, rather than dismissing their home lives, the researchers began to see that what happened at home shaped employees' experiences at work. For instance, being treated unfairly by a supervisor at work at the same time as feeling unfairly treated at home (e.g. by a husband) made them over-react to the criticism (ibid: 310–11). The researchers concluded that supervisors need to understand people's home situations to manage them better. Furthermore, being part of a group with 'human comradeship and social conversations' (ibid: 324) helped employees manage their emotions.

These interviews revealed that workers' personal backgrounds and experiences shape how they perform. Unlike Taylorism—where the worker was little more than a cog in a machine—the Hawthorne studies revealed the importance of understanding employees' personalities and, most significantly, of them working in groups.

Real life case: listening to your staff can reduce their stress

According to the Chartered Institute of Personal Development (CIPD), stress is now the biggest cause of workplace absenteeism, overtaking the physical problems of back strain and cancer (Peacock, 2011). During the recession this increased owing to fear of job losses and the increased pressure of work. To counteract this, CIPD researcher Dr Jill Miller stated that managers could help relieve the stress by listening to their staff. Speaking on the BBC's Today programme (BBC News, 2011), in a move that echoes the findings of the Hawthorne studies, she said in times of increased stress increased communication was important: 'even if people do not

Attentive managers can help reduce stress.

have all the answers to tell employees, managers can still be there to be supportive and to be really talking about employees worries, and this reveals the key role for line managers'.

Sources: CIPD (2011); Peacock (2011) and BBC News (2011).

Do you think it is realistic to expect that employees always separate their personal life and working life? Do you think managers manage better when they understand their staff's personal lives?

Experiment 6: Bank Wiring Observation Room— the power of the group

Running case: slow down, you'll put us out of a job

'Hey speedy, what are you trying to do—put us all out of a job?', Isabella jokes to Naomi as she sees Naomi's napkin-folding rate on the whiteboard in the staff room. 'One hundred and twenty-five an hour . . . you'll kill yourself working as hard as that.'

Group norms The unwritten rules that shape behaviour.

The final set of experiments produced some of the most startling results to academics and managers at the time. It revealed that the informal group, by producing **group norms** and informal rules, controlled behaviour and output more powerfully than rewards (e.g. bonuses) or supervisory influence. In other words, it was the discovery of the power of the informal, social organization.

The researchers' interest was sparked in this area because, during the interview pro-gramme, employees that were seen as working too hard were called 'dumb', picked on, given nicknames, and excluded from social activities by their fellow employees. In one particular case the supervisor, rather than praising and trying to protect the productive worker (as rationally he should), feeling powerless and believing the productive worker caused disharmony, gave him extra jobs to reduce his output.

The idea that workers were systematically restricting output was hardly a shock. Fredrick Taylor called this phenomenon 'soldiering' (Chapter 3), arguing that workers systemati-cally tried to restrict their output. However, the investigators decided that rather than try-ing to get rid of these informal behaviours, they would investigate them.

The researchers decided to watch closely the behaviours of one particular group. This time the group was all male: nine wiremen who placed wires in the correct location (a skilled job); three soldermen who solder the wires (a less skilled job); and three well-educated inspectors who tested the units to make sure there were no errors. The researchers wanted to investigate these two themes:

- Does the group restrict output and, if so, how?
- What is the relationship between the supervisors and the group?

The role of the group in restricting output

Officially, each worker was meant to make 7,200 units per day, for which they would receive a bonus. However, surprisingly from the viewpoint of the researchers, they seemed to restrict their effort.

Investigating further, the researchers discovered informally that the workers believed making between 6,000 and 6,600 units a day represented 'a day's work'. While those that did not produce enough were 'bawled' at by the supervisors, if they made above the (unofficial) average they were excluded from the group and nicknamed 'Shrimp', 'Runt', 'Slave', and 'Speed King', and even '**binged**' to indicated they were breaking group norms. As one worker put it, those that 'loaf along are liked better than anybody else' (Roethlisberger and Dickson, 1939: 418). The workers' personal relationships were highly complex, full of tension, animosity, teasing, and, at times, physical violence (Figure 5.1).

Binged A phrased used during the Hawthorne studies meaning flicking the ear or arm of the person working too hard.

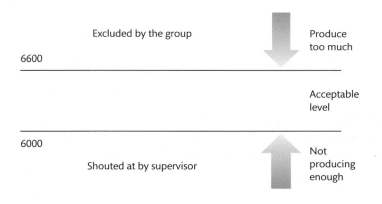

Figure 5.1 Pressure on employee to perform.

6600 — Excluded by the group — Produce too much

Acceptable level

6000 — Shouted at by supervisor — Not producing enough

From this observation the researchers stated the group had the following informal rules.

1. You should not turn out too much work. If you do, you are a 'rate-buster'.
2. You should not turn out too little work. If you do, you are a 'chiseller'.
3. You should not tell a supervisor anything that will react to the detriment of an associate. If you do, you are a 'squealer'.
4. You should not attempt to maintain social distance or act officious. If you are an inspector, for example, you should not act like one.   (ibid: 522)

Cliques Exclusive groups.

The researchers saw that the group was, in fact, two **cliques** each with different ways of behaving and output levels. In order to fit in with one group, workers had to behave in a particular way (see Table 5.3).

Table 5.3 Behaviour of the two cliques

Clique	1	2
Output	High	Low
Personal behaviour	Sensible	Messing around

They concluded the group internally controlled members' behaviour, but, at the same time, protected them from external management interference. The workers, they thought, were more motivated by their need to belong to the group than what management said to them or financial incentives. In short, the group controlled the behaviour of its members through *group norms*.

The importance of group norms

One of the central findings of the Hawthorne studies, particularly in Elton Mayo's interpretation, was the power of group norms. The group norms provide the rules or standards of conduct that group members have to adhere to in order to fit in. They act as unwritten rules that guide behaviour and help members gain a sense of belonging, providing group members with a framework of how to behave and a shortcut to know how to react to a given situation.

In general, nobody dictates these rules directly; we are left to pick them up through subtle cues from other members, such as jokes at our expense and being excluded from conversations. In particular, we often learn these rules when we break them.

Group norms are powerful because if we want to belong to the group and, in particular, gain high social status within it, we have to stick to them. Very few people violate them as this ultimately means being excluded from our peer group, leaving the individual feeling isolated and without social and emotional support.

Group norms can provide stability to the group by providing an accepted way of behaving. However, they can also be controlling, as there is pressure to go along with the views of the group, even when it might be at odds with your personal views. This can be particularly difficult when working in, say, a sexist or homophobic environment.

Difficult position of the supervisor

Running case: Nina Biagini goes to Phil Weaver's office

'You are still not hitting the targets', Weaver complains. 'They should be able to fold at least 140 napkins an hour if they followed my plan . . . look they are only hitting 80. And look at Naomi, she was folding 125 an hour and now that the chart has gone up she has fallen down to the same level as the rest of them.' Biagini looks downcast. 'It's not as easy as that', she states. 'I just feel powerless in front of them. Naomi is a good worker, but the rest just drag her down to their level.'

'Why don't you just tell them what to do?' Weaver asks. 'It's not as easy as that', Biagini replies, 'you see if I start having a go at them it will make our relationship difficult and really tense. Then, if I want them to do anything extra, like stay at the end of the shift to clear up or deal with a difficult customer, then they will just say no.'

The Wiring Bank Observation Room also demonstrated how weak the supervisor's position was. Because he relied on the group's goodwill to get the job done he had to maintain friendly relations with them. However, as a representative of management he had to keep costs down and keep production levels high. This was particularly evident in how he recorded individuals' work and workers' bonuses. The wiremen pressurized him to record higher figures, but management wanted to keep the records low. If he followed the groups' interest then he was not doing his job properly, but if he tried to impose the management's priorities he faced losing the sympathy of the group, making the working relationship difficult. He was, therefore, under pressure from two directions, as shown in Table 5.4.

Table 5.4 The supervisor's dilemma

Supervisor action	Let them get away with it	Middle ground	Report to foreman
Consequence of action	Not perform task effectively	Try to balance group and management needs	Be a 'grass' and lose the sympathy of the group

The researchers concluded that the supervisor could not change the group purely by the force of their personality. In fact, he was a victim. Indeed, we could argue, following Karl Marx's thought, that the supervisor was as much exploited by capitalism as the workers.

This was demonstrated through the results obtained by the two supervisors during the study. The first supervisor was lax about certain rules and could be considered almost part of the group. His replacement was stricter, more authoritative, and rules- and output-focused. Surprisingly, the group were more productive under the first supervisor.

Roethlisberger and Dickson (1939: 531) believed the workers restricted output for a number of reasons. In part, it was because they did not understand the bonus scheme; they thought the workers also acted 'irrationally', choosing to believe that the management might lay people off as productivity rose, but they had no concrete evidence of this. The workers were not lazy (as Taylor assumed) or in conflict with managers (as Marx assumed), and the supervisors were not ineffective. Such a view 'mistake[s] symptoms for causes and [is] to neglect the social factors involved' (ibid: 548). Their key finding was that the informal group controlled output and behaviour, often in ways that went against the interests of the organization *and* the individual employee.

Review questions

Describe:

1. What are group norms?

Explain:

2. Why should a manager be aware of group norms to be effective?

The implications of the Hawthorne studies

Running case: team meeting

Nina Biagini gathers all the waiters and waitresses together. 'We are the "restaurant team"', she declares. 'If we are going to move forward then we need to work together as a team.' She opens the meeting asking for a 'full and frank' discussion, and airing of views.

The waiters and waitresses begin cautiously, with everyone being respectful but, after 15 minutes, begin to share more of their thoughts and feelings. Nina Biagini, alongside Meg Mortimer, listens attentively to what everyone is saying, nodding throughout the discussion.

At the end of the discussion Nina Biagini thanks everyone for their involvement. 'We are one big team', she states, 'and all need to work together'.

The results of the Hawthorne studies are widely credited with transforming management theory and practice. They challenged the dehumanizing Taylorist approach by showing it was possible, and even desirable, to be concerned with the interest of the workers. They showed the significance of the informal organization and the power of the group in controlling individual behaviour. Most importantly they also claimed to provide a more

Table 5.5 Comparison of Taylorism and the Hawthorne studies

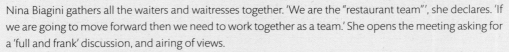

	Taylorism	Hawthorne studies
Focus	Individual	Groups
Labour/capital relations	Conflict	Harmony
Management is:	Dehumanizing	Humane and caring

humane approach to management (see Table 5.5). Particularly in the hands of Elton Mayo, who, as we will see, wrote some of the most influential interpretations of the Hawthorne studies. They shifted attention away from focusing simply on the processes and to trying to understand and satisfy employees' needs. To their supporters they offered a better and more enlightened form of management based around harmony and cooperation. They also laid the foundation for OB today. Most of all they provided a shift in assumption from people as simply economy beings solely interested in their own private benefit, to social beings who want to belong to groups.

The key implications will be discussed in the following sections.

A note on the alternative layout

Observant readers will notice for the rest of this chapter the layout is a little different from the rest of the book. For the remainder of the chapter the headings 'Claim X' and 'Critical perspective X' will be used to assess the Hawthorne studies' research. As with all research and theories, the Hawthorne studies were based on assumptions about human nature and the way that society (should) operate. These assumptions shaped (consciously and unconsciously) the way that the research was carried out, the findings which were considered important, and the way the results were interpreted and presented. By uncovering these assumptions it helps us to better understand the research and judge it for ourselves. We will, therefore, look at each of the key claims that the research was based on (which we will label Claim X) and some of the challenges that later researchers have made to either the research itself or the manner in which it was interpreted (which we will call Critical perspective X).

It needs to be made clear that the existence of these assumptions does not make the research invalid. Indeed, all research and theory is based on assumptions. We are, therefore, focusing on the Hawthorne studies in this chapter and highlighting these assumptions as a way of encouraging you to think more critically about *all* research and theory that you read.

Discovery of the 'social person'

The Hawthorne studies are widely credited with discovering the 'social person'—the underlying belief that people are governed by social needs, such as belonging to a group, rather than economic needs and self-interest, which Taylorism and other rational theories are based upon. This, they argue, explains why the employees preferred to stick to the norms of the group rather than make the rational, economic decision to work a bit harder and receive more pay.

Elton Mayo, one of the key researchers and popularizers of the Hawthorne studies, argued that the classic 'economic man' thesis provided a negative view of human nature. He called it a 'rabble hypothesis', a view which sees humankind as a horde of unorganized individuals motivated solely by self-interest (Mayo, 1949 [1975]). The Hawthorne researchers argued for a richer and more rounded view of human nature, which understands the 'relations of mutual interdependence' between people (Roethlisberger and Dickson, 1939: 569). In other words, they argued for a more complex view of workers' lives, concentrating on personal histories, group interactions, and the bonds that develop between people (Figure 5.2).

Figure 5.2 The fuller understanding of the social person.

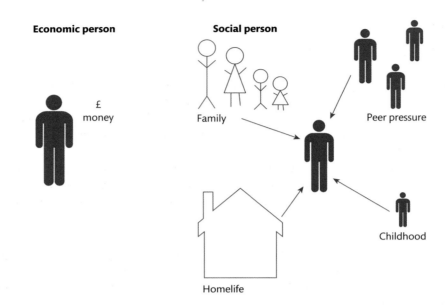

This, therefore, provided a fundamental reconsideration of human nature and a completely different view on how to manage people.

Contribution to OB: This more complex view of workers opened the door to studying organizational culture (Chapter 7), the importance of personality (Chapter 8), and motivation (Chapter 9) as a way of understanding why people behave how they do in organizations. It therefore introduced a richer and more complex view of human behaviour.

Management can harness the power of the group

A key implication of the 'social person' thesis was understanding how the group fundamentally influences individual behaviour and restricts output. This phenomenon had already been identified by Fredrick Taylor, who regularly complained that groups restricted individual output. His solution was to break the power of the group by individualizing tasks. The Hawthorne researchers concluded that although the Taylorist solution might technically 'make the employees more efficient', it would 'unwittingly deprive them of those very things which give meaning and significance to their work' (Roethlisberger and Dickson, 1939: 418): the sense of social belonging.

This 'social person' perspective therefore 'reformulated' management's problems (ibid: 569) by seeing the informal group as 'a necessary prerequisite for effective collaboration' (ibid: 559) instead of a problem. In other words the group could be used to aid production rather than to stop it.

Contribution to OB: This insight has led to considerable attention being placed on the role of teams and groups (see Chapter 6) and the power of group norms—codes of conduct that shape behaviour. It also has implications for leadership and management (Chapter 12) as it draws attention to how to influence the group rather than particular individuals.

There is harmony of interests between workers and managers

The Hawthorne researchers were able to make these bold claims about the power of the group based on their belief that if people were left to their own devices groups *naturally* develop their own spontaneous social organization with their own values and objectivities which would be 'more likely to be in harmony with the aims of management' (Roethlisberger and Dickson, 1939: 418).

This view was strongly pushed by Elton Mayo. He argued that people naturally strive for cooperation and harmony. As evidence for this view he cited the increased output in the Relay Assembly Room claiming it was a result of a 'revolutionized supervisor' who formed a cohesive group of cooperative workers, eager to push production on to a higher level, acting in 'wholehearted cooperation with management' (Mayo, cited in Handel, 2002: 100).

This cooperation, Mayo argued, was feasible because all human action comes from a need for social solidarity; in other words, the need to belong to a group. Consequently, when managers act fairly, workers have no need to complain as they are working for collective interests.

This allowed them to make the following bold claim:

'Producing an article at a profit and maintaining good employee relations are frequently regarded as antithetical [opposite] positions. The result of the studies which have been reported indicated, however, that these two sets of problems are interrelated and interdependent.'

(Roethlisberger and Dickson, 1939: 552).

They therefore stated that they had solved the problems of Taylorism and Marxism. Management and the workers' interests, according to this view, no longer need to be seen in conflict (as assumed by Taylorism or Marxism). Rather, organizations can only be more productive when workers' needs are taken into consideration. Mayo, through the Hawthorne studies, therefore sought to redraw the capitalist working relationship by claiming that workers and management did not need to be in conflict (Figure 5.3).

Contribution to OB: Mayo presents organizations as places of potential harmony and cooperation. However, as we will see in Chapter 13, those from the political Left, such as

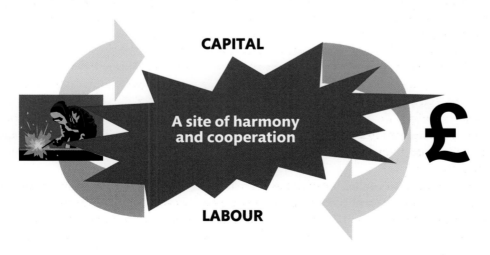

Figure 5.3 Mayo's redrawn capitalist working relationship.

Steven Lukes, disagree by stating that the labour–capital relationship is always fundamentally in conflict—even when it does not appear so at first glance.

The nature of leadership needs to change

One of the fundamental shifts in management practice that the findings of the Hawthorne studies produced was to change the way we see management. While Mayo believed harmony and cooperation could be achieved, he argued that this spirit of cooperation is not inevitable. It requires improved communication with leaders listening to their group. Mayo offers us this prescription:

> 'Before every change of program, the group is consulted. Their comments are listened to and discussed; sometimes their objections are allowed to negative a suggestion. The group undoubtedly develops a sense of participation in the critical determinations and becomes something of a social unit.'
>
> (Mayo, 1933: 39).

According to Mayo, managers, therefore need to work on transforming the nature of the group rather than particular individuals by listening to workers and overcoming any objections.

Contribution to OB: The Hawthorne studies showed the importance of *soft skills* in management and leadership, such as listening to staff and understanding their views before a change is made. It therefore has implications for our understanding of leadership (Chapter 12) and how to manage change (Chapter 11).

Employability skills: the importance of soft skills

The Hawthorne studies demonstrated the importance of managers treating their employees as people: listening to them, understanding group norms, and responding to individual and group concerns. To be an effective manager you need to be able to understand and respond to these 'social issues'. Therefore, as well as gaining the technical qualification of your degree, it is important to develop these so-called soft skills. University offers many possibilities for this, such as group work and seminars where you have the chance to work with others and improve your communication skills; joining clubs and societies where you can join committees, plan events, and learn to work as a team; and volunteering, where you can work with different types of people in the community. Such experiences are not only great for your CV, but also excellent for self-development.

What activities can you do to increase your skills, experience, and confidence in these areas?

An alternative view of human nature

The Hawthorne studies thus produced a fundamentally different way of seeing human behaviour and human nature. Table 5.6 compares this with the rational organization approach.

To the supporters of the Hawthorne studies, they are a symbol of a new way to manage, away from a path of conflict and soul-destroying work by isolated individuals to new practices based on cooperation and harmony, and understanding of employees' needs while still increasing production.

Table 5.6 Difference between the rational approach and the human relations approach

	Rational organization approach	Human relations
Key theorist	Fredrick Taylor	Elton Mayo
Human nature	Economic person	Social person
Acts	In rational best interests	Irrational and governed by sentiment
Employee motivation	Economically-motivated	Socially-motivated by belonging needs
Mentality of researcher	Engineer	Psychologist
Approach to organization problems	Mechanically fix with technical solutions	Social engineer to get people working together
Restrictions to output	Worker laziness Physical condition, e.g. fatigue Soldiering	Power of informal organization in creating norms that regulate behaviour
Solution to output restrictions	Individualize work by breaking tasks down to increasingly simple tasks	Collective collaboration
Management control by:	Managing every aspect of the task and through time and motion studies	Gaining loyalty of the group, shaping its beliefs to work towards common outcomes
Relation output and employee satisfaction	Unrelated—employees are just told what to do, they are all replaceable	Inter-related—employees need to be satisfied to be productive

Contribution to OB: as we stated in at the start of this chapter, these studies represent one of the most significant studies in OB and one of the foundations of the discipline.

Review questions

Describe

1. What are the key implications of the Hawthorne studies?

Explain

2. How did they challenge pre-existing assumptions of management theory and practice?

Critics of the Hawthorne studies

Running case: leaving the meeting

As they filed out of the meeting Naomi was glowing. 'It is really nice to see management taking an interest in us as people. I mean we do a good job here and it is nice to be noticed.' Saffron looked at her in a surprised manner. 'They just want us to work hard and produce more without paying us more, I'm not falling for that one. Do you think they are really that interested in us?'

As we have seen, the results of the Hawthorne studies have been used to claim that people are naturally cooperative, and harmony between management and workers is not only desirable, but also possible. In short, particularly in Mayo's hands, it provided a fundamentally different way of looking at the world.

The Hawthorne studies have been called part of the 'creation myth' of OB—one of the central studies the field is based on. Yet, as scholars of OB it is important that we do not take these findings at face value, but question how the research was constructed and interpreted, its circumstances and background, and what assumptions it was based upon. To do this we need to examine the research methods themselves, the interpretation of the findings, the context of the research, and the background and values of the researchers carrying out the research. The rest of this chapter will carry out this task.

It is important to note that the following criticism made of Mayo and the Hawthorne studies could equally be levelled at other theories, such as Taylorism. All academic theory has inbuilt assumptions upon which they are based and can be examined from alternative 'critical' perspectives. This does not mean that we should discount their findings. While some of these findings were based on small samples and, arguably, the pre-existing beliefs of the researchers, the social side of the organization is undoubtedly a vital component of organizational life. Moreover, although, as we will argue, it potentially gives managers increased control over the workers, it does offer the potential for a more humane form of management than pure Taylorism.

Study skills: the importance of thinking critically—assessing academic theories

Where do your beliefs about management come from? How often do you stop to question them or look for alternatives?

We tend to think that our beliefs about management and organizations are based on common sense. Yet, the views we hold today have not always been accepted. Indeed, a quick examination of the history of management theory reveals that people in other times held quite different perspectives to ours. In fact, our common-sense certainties might seem to them to be highly controversial or even wrong. For instance, fifty years ago many thought women incapable of working in the boardroom. Today, such a view would be unacceptable.

So where do our ideas come from and what influences them? One source is academic research. Not only is it the research itself that is important, but the way that it has been received, interpreted, and used. As such, our beliefs are, in part, a product of past debates, where the winning perspective has become accepted as true and is today's common sense.

However, quite often the origins of the research get lost in time and we are only left with the conclusions that become filtered into practice and accepted without question. In the next section we will argue that it is important that we are aware of this background not only because it gives us a deeper understanding of the theories themselves, but also because it allows us to question their assumptions and challenge the things that we take for granted.

For the remainder of the chapter we will be assessing the Hawthorne studies *analytically*, taking the argument apart by seeing the *assumptions* that they are based upon. We will see whether the ▶

▶ *research methods* and the *conclusions* they drew were valid, and whether the *evidence* they presented stacks up. We will be exploring this *critically* by examining it from other viewpoints and seeing how these alternative perspectives, based on different *assumptions*, may lead to different conclusions. The chapter will lay the foundations for some *debates* which we will examine in the rest of this book.

This chapter aims to encourage you to *think critically*. This means not taking things at face value, being able to weigh-up the evidence, and to understand the implications of a perspective. By doing so its aim is to help you be a better student and also potentially a better manager. By not taking things for granted it will help you learn to think more deeply and not accept things as they are given—to see things from other perspectives and understand the assumptions behind the views people hold.

The assumptions of the Hawthorne studies assessed

Claim 1: workers are naturally cooperative and harmonious, and form groups spontaneously (testing assumptions 1, 2, and 3)

The findings of the Hawthorne studies, and particularly Elton Mayo's interpretation of them, are based on the discovery of the 'social person', who is naturally cooperative and seeks harmony. Mayo based his argument on the experiences witnessed in the first Relay Assembly Room experiment, which he stated saw a smooth and rapid change in the attitude of the staff who became, in his words, a 'team that gave itself wholeheartedly and spontaneously to co-operation in the experiment' (Mayo, 1949: 64).

However, to make this interpretation Mayo was forced to downplay and even ignore key findings that did not fit his perspective. The departments and participants used for the study were specifically selected to be cooperative, and the supervisors tried to make the relationships as smooth and friendly as possible. It cannot, therefore, be assumed that people naturally want to be cooperative.

This selection for cooperation even went as far replacing two 'uncooperative' workers in the Relay Assembly Room experiment who were 'talking too much' and 'lacked attention to their work'. To his funder, Mayo reported that one worker had '"gone **Bolshevik**" and had to be dropped' (cited in Bramel and Friend, 1981: 872). In his account Mayo ignores these features simply saying they 'retired' (Mayo, 1949). They were replaced by two new, enthusiastic employees, both of who were immediately more productive than the ones they replaced.

Mayo also downplayed the significance of the arguments between the workers and managers. Roethlisberger and Dickson's research showed the workers often actively resisted management, slowing down output, and stating that if they had their rest periods back they would increase productivity. Management responded by threatening to take away perks, such as lunch breaks. As Bramel and Friend state:

Bolshevik An insult indicating that a person is a Russian communist; in other words, that they are troublemakers who want revolution.

'The workers were quite consciously adopting a strategy intended to induce the experimenters to return quickly to the preferred conditions. If the workers had in fact had the kind of trust in management's good intentions that Mayo claims, would they have found it necessary to resist the experimenters so actively in this period? The picture we get, instead, is of a group of rather wary workers engaged in a continuing skirmish with management and determined not to be taken advantage of. Rather than become a part of the company "team", they became a team of their own, rather coolly looking out for their own economic interests in an adversary relationship with management, regardless of how much they may have personally liked certain members of the research team.'   (1981: 874)

The increase in productivity, rather than through cooperation, could equally be seen as a result of stern discipline, e.g. replacing difficult staff (Carey, 1967) and the use of coercion, rather than naturally-produced cooperation.

Critical perspective: the Hawthorne researchers, particularly Elton Mayo, were highly selective in what evidence they reported; findings that did not fit their view were ignored.

Study skills: implication of this perspective

We need to be careful in assuming that what people report is the only interpretation of the findings. We should not take research at face value.

Claim 2: workers are more motivated by social needs than financial ones (testing assumptions 1 and 2)

Mayo, and Roethlisberger and Dickson claimed that the group members were more motivated by the need to fit within the group than by financial needs. Concerns that if workers increased production it would lead to others losing their jobs were dismissed as 'irrational' because they stated there was no evidence that this would be true.

However, the research took place in the 1930s, which saw the deepest and most prolonged depression of the twentieth century. During this time there were very high levels of unemployment and little social security, producing mass poverty. Clegg and Dunkerley believe of the Hawthorne studies that 'Restriction of output by voluntary norms was a rational response by primarily economically-oriented agents to the increasingly likely prospect of unemployment' (1980: 131). In other words, there were genuine fears that increasing production would mean that other workers would be sacked as higher production did not necessarily mean higher sales. They were responding rationally to their economic situation.

Also, as Carey (1967) convincingly argues, much of their own data demonstrates the significance of wage incentives in creating increases in productivity.

Critical perspective: the Hawthorne researchers dismissed economic reasons as irrational; however, given the context, the employees' views could be seen as quite logical.

Study skills: implication of this perspective

The ideological position of researchers shapes how they interpret their findings. If you believe economic reasons motivate action then you are more likely to see this. If you believe it is social factors, then this evidence may seem stronger.

Claim 3: the findings of the Hawthorne studies can be replicated in management practice (assumption 5)

The findings of the Hawthorne studies are rightly considered significant because they were one of the first set of experiments to examine real people in a real factory rather than in a laboratory. Therefore, it is claimed that what the researchers discovered can be applied to management practice.

However, the actions of the participants cannot be considered 'natural'. Throughout the study the research subjects were constantly observed, with their level of output recorded every 30 minutes. This form of observation changes behaviour. The implication is that the very act of measuring the output meant that the workers were better able to adjust their output.

The Hawthorne Effect

This phenomenon was labelled the **Hawthorne Effect** by Henry Landsberger. He concluded that the very act of someone observing a person changes their behaviour (Landsberger, 1958). There are two key ways in which this phrase has been used. First, the increase in productivity that is seen to result from psychological and social factors. Secondly, the impossibility of researching what people *actually* do because the very act of observation (and particularly monitoring performance) changes behaviour. The research findings cannot therefore be assumed to represent what people *naturally* do.

Hawthorne effect The very act of observation changes behaviour.

Imagine yourself at work (or writing a university assignment) on a normal day. Now think how you would act if someone watched everything that you did. Would you act the same? Would you still take sneaky breaks, check Facebook, or talk to your friends at work in the same way?

Despite the extent of the research as a scientific experiment it was poorly controlled. One of the key focuses of the research—the changes of human behaviour under supervision—only emerged later in the study, meaning that the researchers had to make assumptions about the workers' early behaviour rather than actively studying it. Equally, in the Bank Wiring Experiment, the researchers did not have a control group and therefore they did not know whether output would have gone up anyway.

The sample size is very small (six for the Relay Assembly Room and thirteen for the Bank Wiring Observation Room). While this gave the researchers unprecedented access and a highly detailed account of workers' daily interactions, it is a mistake to claim that the findings of the research are true for all societies over human history.

Critical perspective: the results of the findings are influenced by the researchers being present and the small sample size. Very large claims have been made on what is a small amount of evidence.

Study skills: implication of this perspective

Because it involves people, any process of social research will be influenced by the way that it is researched and the presence of the researcher. This is unavoidable. Consequently, we need to be aware that research results are influenced by the way the research is carried out.

Claim 4: the research 'discovered' the social person (assumption 1)

Roethlisberger and Dickson present the Hawthorne studies as a *journey of discovery* where they began their enquiry believing in essentially (although never named) Taylorist assumptions, but, because of the evidence, they came to discover 'social man'. However, both Roethlisberger and Mayo had pre-established assumptions which shaped their research findings.

Roethlisberger had a strong disliking of Taylorism, calling its effects 'repugnant'. Wickström and Bendix argue that he used the Hawthorne studies as a platform to provide an alternative scientific basis to management (Wickström and Bendix, 2000). Equally, Mayo (1949) had a strong preference for cooperation and harmony, and a strong disliking of conflict which he saw as a 'social disease'. Even before the Hawthorne studies, he had already concluded that 'Social and psychological ills could be traced back directly to failure to establish stable systems of cooperation. Individuals must feel that their work is socially necessary and must be able to see beyond their group to the society' (Smith, 1998: 231).

Critical perspective: rather than *discovering* the 'social person', both Roethlisberger and Mayo, in particular, had long-held views about the importance of cooperation, harmony, and the need for spontaneous forms of organization. In the Hawthorne studies, rather than revealing 'social man', the social man perspective was the lens through which the research findings were interpreted.

Study skills: implication of this perspective

Academic theories are based on the underlying assumptions set by the theorists which shape the results that they present.

Claim 5: the Hawthorne studies represent a progressive alternative to Taylorism (assumption 5)

It is often claimed by its supporters that the result of the Hawthorne studies is a more humane and holistic approach to managing people. It certainly offers some benefits. Listening and responding to the needs of employees, and focusing on teamwork provides a more rounded view of the worker, and a more supportive and person-centred form of management. However, it has been widely criticized for also being a stronger form of control.

One of Mayo's earliest critics was the sociologist Daniel Bell, who argued that Mayo did little to challenge the key assumptions underlying Taylorism and that the focus should be on increasing productivity. For Bell, all Mayo really did, to quote Bell's title, was *Adjusting Men to Machines* (1947).

Mayo's attention on employees' needs, Bell argued, was just another way of controlling them. He did this, Bell stated, by treating anyone who challenged harmony (for which he meant the manager's view) as evidence of psychological problems. Bell argued, like many other critical theorists, that such harmony was not possible because workers and management have divergent interests. Consequently, the labour/capital conflict cannot simply be solved by improving communication between the workers and managers.

Bell went further by stating that people only work because their human spirit has been tamed and they have been trained to desire consumption rather than meaningful human relations. In an early critique of consumer society he said that we are obsessed with our next purchase. This has resulted in a diminished view of work and social society. 'The belief in man as an end in himself has been ground under by the machine, and the social science of the factory researchers is not a science of man but a cow-sociology' (Bell, 1947: 88). In Bell's view, to offer a true break from Taylorism then, Mayo should have explored how work could be created to expand human freedom and spontaneity. Mayo therefore 'fail[ed] to consider whether work offers other possibilities for the expansion of human spontaneity and freedom' (Waters, 1996: 52).

Bell's view is supported by a recent article by Bruce and Nyland (2011). They argued the Hawthorne studies offered 'a new way to control workers to accept less, while claiming that workers needed psychological counselling about their relations at work that only management could administer' (Bruce and Nyland, 2011: 386).

According to such theorists, the use of psychological counselling offered managers a powerful tool to access the hidden world of employees' unconscious drives and use them for their own purposes. It offers the promise of harmony and cooperation, but only on management's terms and interests rather than on the employees' terms. '[C]ooperation in the Mayo perspective', according to Baritz (1974: 113), 'is the relationship involving happily unorganized (nonunionized) workers who unthinkingly and enthusiastically comply with the wishes of management towards the achievement and maintenance of its economic objectives'.

Theory in context: the philosophical underpinnings of Mayo's theory

Mayo did not restrict his claims on the benefits of the Hawthorne studies to a more considerate form of management—he saw it as a way of *saving* Western civilization.

Modern society, he argued, was characterized by increasing numbers of unhappy people who are fragmented into groups that are 'not eager to co-operate wholeheartedly with other groups' (1949: 7). The root cause of this, Mayo argued, was the industrial revolution. Led by large corporations, it brought rapid changes in technology which, although they produced material comfort, did so at the expense of a 'destruction of individual significance' (1949: 7). Through this the social ties of what Mayo called *established* society—the structures of families, communities, and traditional authority—were broken, producing a new *adaptive society*, which, Mayo argued, had abandoned its traditional effort for cooperation, leading to potential chaos.

According to Mayo, one result of this was that worker unhappiness and industrial disputes have a psychological root, rather than an economic one. He argued an increasing number of unhappy workers had obsessive personalities and did not wish to cooperate. Workers had irrational, or what Mayo called 'non-logical', mindsets. Individual unhappiness was often as a result of their personal lives or childhood which, when not listened to by managers, reinforced their problems. Mayo saw the interview programme as a therapeutic release of pent-up emotion. It gave workers an opportunity to get rid of useless emotion which enabled them to collaborate better with other workers. An interview 'clears lines of communication of emotional blockage' (1949: 72) to allow the development of cooperation and teamwork. ▶

> 'Thus, individual happiness and the social "growth and health" of society are dependent not upon freedom from unreasonable restraint nor upon any rational calculus of pleasure and pain, nor upon the opportunity for self-development, but upon whether or not the individual has a sense of "social function"'.
>
> (Bendix and Fisher, 1949: 313)

The solution to these problems, believed Mayo, was the training of an administrative elite—what we would now call management—who could learn how to manage people. '[C]ollaboration of an industrial society cannot be left to chance' Mayo argued (1949: 8). Current training and research, Mayo argued, had seen considerable advancements in technical expertise (e.g. Taylorism) but social skills had not kept up with this, leading to an imbalance. This administrative elite could be trained in these social skills—which Mayo called the ability to secure cooperation of people—and learn how to manage people.

Review questions

Explain

1. Why do some commentators believe Mayo did not 'discover' the social person? What are the implications of this?

Analyse

2. Why does Mayo's interpretation of the Hawthorne studies results not necessarily produce a more humane form of management practice?

Suppression of industrial democracy

While Taylorism is often demonized as oppressive to, and controlling of, workers, there were a number of theorists, writing at the same time as Elton Mayo, who were seeking to supplement this with industrial democracy. These progressive Taylorists, such as Mary Parker Follett, wanted workers to choose their own representatives and to be involved in management decisions. Having just endangered their lives in defence of democracy in World War I, as John Dewey argued, it seemed ironic that they then returned to a system of 'industrial and economic autocracy' (Dewey, 1982: 85). These Taylorist democratists supported the growth and development of unions (Bruce and Nyland, 2011). Mayo, with the support of Rockefeller money, had a strong distrust of such moves.

'There is another difficulty for me in Miss Van Kleeck's [a member of these progressive Taylorists] approach to the investigation—she seems to assume that a "democratic" method of managing industry is necessarily appropriate . . . If it means that industry is to develop a two-party system and to determine any issues that arise by discussion and compromise then it would seem that such a method would revive and accentuate a situation of class conflict. This is indeed exactly what has happened in Australia—the country that has provided a "shocking example" of how things should not be done in industry.'   (Mayo, 1929 cited in Bruce and Nyland, 2011: 397)

Theory in context: Mary Parker Follett

Mary Parker Follett was one of the earliest management theorists, a writer, speaker, and consultant who, alongside Lillian Gilbreth (see Chapter 3), was one of earliest women to influence OB. She had an interest in social work, psychology, administration, learning, teamwork, and, our interest here, in democracy. Follett argued not only for local government democracy through things like neighbourhood forums, but also for more industrial democracy.

Follett believed that conflict was inevitable, but rather than imposing power 'it is possible [for management] to develop the conception of power-with, a jointly developed power, a co-active, not a coercive power' (Follett cited in Fox and Urwick, 1973: 72). Like Mayo, she believed that managers should work with a group. But unlike Mayo she thought this should be in a role as a facilitator: 'we are beginning to think of the leader not as the man (sic) who is able to assert his individual will and get others to follow him, but as the one who knows how to relate the different wills in a group so that they will have driving force' (Follett cited in Fox and Urwick, 1973: 247).

As Parker and Ritson put it 'Follett offered an impressive spectrum of contributions to management thought that were well ahead of the practices and theories of her day and which anticipated many subsequently emerging management theories and practices' (Parker and Ritson, 2005: 1342–3).

Mayo saw elites, particularly managers, as having the right to manage. Mayo's conclusions to the Hawthorne studies and his 'theory of human relations was based almost entirely on his own political interpretation of worker motivation' (Bruce and Nyland, 2011: 385). Rather than a neutral investigation, Mayo's work could be seen as a highly political attempt to crush moves towards industrial democracy and give elites more power.

Critical perspective: while the Hawthorne studies present a more holistic view of human nature, critics say that Mayo and his colleagues did not challenge the fundamental assumptions of the capitalist working relationship; indeed, arguably, it intensified it. Its aim was the psychological control of the workers. In taking this approach it even diverted attention away from a more democratic form of management.

Study skills: implication of this perspective

It is important to understand the underlying assumptions and politics behind a management theory.

Summing up

While the Hawthorne studies represent a substantial move forward towards a humane form of management practice, we have seen the critics, particularly of Mayo, state that the theories produced are, in fact, a more subtle form of control. Mayo and his colleagues were selective in their evidence, dismissed and psychologized rational alternative perspectives held by the employees, and, rather than changing management control, actually reinforced it. One of the key criticisms is that rather than discovering through malicious research the social side of the organization, these were Mayo's long-held beliefs. It is to this we now turn.

The funding of the Hawthorne studies

Another underlying influence on the Hawthorne studies was the funding they received, and the social and political circumstances under which they were conducted. A large part of the funding for the research, and particularly for Elton Mayo's role at Harvard Business School, was from the Rockefellers—a highly influential and wealthy family of American businessmen. In a recent article, Bruce and Nyland claim 'Mayo could conceivably be considered as a mere puppet or servant of far greater power: the Rockefellers' (2011: 388). They argue that 'Mayo simply and shrewdly tuned into what he believed his benefactor wanted to hear' (2011: 391), twisting his personal biases to meet the needs of John Rockefeller.

Because of the Great Depression, many factory owners were scared that workers and trade unions would try to overthrow capitalism and produce a new society. As a consequence, many business leaders were 'seeking to find a way to resolve industrial conflict without jeopardizing their status as the central locus of organizational authority' (O'Connor, 1999: 120).

According to this view, Mayo used his scientific evidence as a way of justifying the prejudices and interests of his funders (Bruce and Nyland, 2011), and therefore constructed knowledge that aided managers to the detriment of the workers. Indeed, Mayo, Baritz argues, believed that 'America's managers were remarkable men without prejudice'—an 'elite which had the ability and therefore the right to rule the rest of the nation' (Baritz, 1974: 200). The findings of the Hawthorne studies, particularly as popularized by Mayo, were appealing to these ruling elites as it explained social problems as results not of economic inequalities, but as a product of irrational thinking on behalf of the worker. Mayo argued that society needed an 'administrative elite' capable of creating cooperation and producing harmony. Consequently, instead of being undermined by these social problems, these powerful people's interests were actually enhanced by them. It 'presented business leaders both with an insidious means of monopolizing authority in the workplace and the wider community, as well as a justification for this monopoly founded on the assertion that the minds of workers are not suited to management or political decision making' (Bruce and Nyland, 2011: 384). Bruce and Nyland argue that the findings of the Hawthorne studies therefore reinforced the right of managers to manage by demonstrating their need to solve social problems. Mayo's widely criticized pro-management bias, therefore, was, at least in part, a product of the funding he received.

Review questions

Explain

1. What is the relevance of who funds a piece of research?

Analyse

2. What is the significance of the historical context (the Great Depression and post-Word War I) for the way that the Hawthorne studies' findings have been interpreted?

Chapter summary

In this chapter we have explored in some depth the contribution of the Hawthorne studies, particularly as popularized by Elton Mayo. We have seen that these studies have been highly influential in the history of management thought, introducing new ways of seeing organizations as social organizations governed by informal dynamics. These studies laid the foundations for issues such as teamwork, culture, personality, motivation, and leadership, which we will explore in the following chapters.

The Hawthorne studies have certainly offered a more positive view of human nature and a way of managing people. By introducing the social side of organization it opened up management theory and practice to the importance of the informal organization, and showed that it was possible—even desirable—for managers to embrace this side of the organization. This meant that managers no longer had to be restricted to simply looking at processes and managing people through coercive approaches of targets and punishments, but through a more positive view of getting teams to work together. This approach has laid the foundations for teamwork (which we will see in Chapter 6), as well as interest in organizational culture (Chapter 7) and reappraising the role of leadership (Chapter 12).

However, the Hawthorne studies have also been widely criticized for deepening management control over the psychological realm of organizational life, controlling workers' thoughts and feelings—reducing their capacity to resist. By studying people's thoughts and feelings management is able to turn these insights to their advantage by manipulating them towards management goals.

The Hawthorne studies therefore remain one of the most significant and powerful theories in management today. In particular, they raise the question of whether informal or social organization is an area which creates a more humane form of management, or a stronger and more subtle form of control?

Further reading

Roethlisberger, F., and Dickson, W. 1939. *Management and the worker.* **Harvard University Press, Boston, MA.**
Provides the most comprehensive and in-depth account of the Hawthorne studies. It gives very detailed descriptions of the Hawthorne studies from the researchers that led the research.

Mayo, E. 1949 [1975]. *The social problems of an industrial civilisation.* **Routledge, London.**
Mayo popularized the Hawthorne studies to a wider management audience. This book gives a background to many of his ideas, and his broader thoughts on management and society.

O'Connor, E. 1999. The politics of management thought: A case study of Harvard Business School and the Human Relations School. *Academy of Management Review* **24(1): 117–131.**
This provides a really interesting account of the early development of the Human Relations Movement as led by Elton Mayo. It helps explain the social context in which the Hawthorne studies emerged and the part Mayo played in popularizing it.

Bruce, K., and Nyland, C. 2011. Elton Mayo and the deification of human relations. *Organization Studies* **32(3): 383–405.**
This recent article shows the importance of the funding that Mayo received in developing the Hawthorne studies and the influence that it had on the findings.

Bibliography

Baritz, L. 1974. *Servants of power: History of the use of social science in American industry.* Greenwood Press: Westport, CT.

BBC News. 2011. Job stress 'worse in public sector'. Available at: http://news.bbc.co.uk/today/hi/today/newsid_9607000/9607686.stm (last accessed 13 June 2012).

Bell, D. 1947. Adjusting men to machines. *Commentary* 3: 79–88.

Bendix, R., and Fisher, L.H. 1949. The perspectives of Elton Mayo. *The Review of Economics and Statistics* 31(4): 312–319.

Bramel, D., and Friend, R. 1981. Hawthorne, the myth of the docile worker, and class bias in psychology. *American Psychologist* 36(8): 867–878.

Bruce, K., and Nyland, C. 2011. Elton Mayo and the deification of human relations. *Organization Studies* 32(3): 383–405.

Carey, A.1967. The Hawthorne Studies: A radical criticism. *American Sociological Review* 32(3): 403–416.

CIPD (Chartered Institute of Personnel and Development). 2011. Absence management survey. Available at: http://www.cipd.co.uk/hr-resources/survey-reports/absence-management-2011.aspx (last accessed 13 June 2012).

Clegg, S., and Dunkerley, D. 1980. *Organization, class and control.* Routledge: London.

Dewey, J. 1982. Internal social reorganization after the War. In: Boydston, J.A. (ed.) *John Dewey: The middle works, 1899–1924*, Vol. 11, pp. 73–86. Southern Illinois University Press: Carbondale, IL.

Donkin, R. 2001. *The history of work.* Palgrave Macmillan: London.

Fox, E.M., and Urwick, L. (eds). 1973. *Dynamic administration: The collected papers of Mary Parker Follett.* Pitman: London.

Gale, E.A.M. 2004. The Hawthorne Studies – a fable for our times? *QJM: An International Journal of Medicine* 97(7): 439–449.

Gillespie, R. 1991. *Manufacturing knowledge: a history of the Hawthorne experiments.* Cambridge University Press: Cambridge.

Handel, M. 2002. *The Sociology of Organizations: Classic, Contemporary and Critical Readings.* Sage: London.

Landsberger, H.A. 1958. *Hawthorne revisited.* Cornell University: Ithaca.

Marks, S.R. 1999. The gendered contexts of inclusive intimacy: the Hawthorne women at work and home. In: Adams, R.G., and Allen, G. (eds) *Placing friendship in context.* Cambridge University Press: Cambridge.

Mayo, E. 1933. *The human problems of an industrial civilisation.* Macmillan: New York.

Mayo, E. 1949 [1975]. *The social problems of an industrial civilisation.* Routledge: London.

O'Connor, E. 1999. The politics of management thought: A case study of Harvard Business School and the Human Relations School. *Academy of Management Review* 24(1): 117–131.

Parker, L.D., and Ritson, P. 2005. Fads, stereotypes and management gurus: Fayol and Follett today. *Management Decision* 43(10): 1335–1357.

Peacock, L. 2011. Stress overtakes cancer as main form of sickness absence. *The Daily Telegraph* (5 October 2011).

Ricci, J.A., Chee, E., Lorandeau, A.L., and Berger, J. 2007. Fatigue in the U.S. workforce: Prevalence and implications for lost productive work time. *Journal of Occupational & Environmental Medicine* 49(1): 1–10.

Roethlisberger, F., and Dickson, W. 1939. *Management and the worker.* Harvard University Press: Boston, MA.

Smith, J.H. 1998. The enduring legacy of Elton Mayo. *Human Relations* 51(3): 221–249.

Waters, M. 1996. *Daniel Bell.* Routledge: London.

Wickström, G., and Bendix, T. 2000. The 'Hawthorne effect' – what did the original Hawthorne studies actually show? *Scandinavian Journal of Work, Environment & Health* 26(4): 363–367.

Managing groups and teams
From managing the individual to managing the collective

Chapter overview and learning outcomes

By the end of this chapter you should be able to:

- describe why teamwork has become a central feature of organizational life
- explain the link between teamwork and productivity
- analyse the factors needed to produce an effective team
- explain how teamwork can lead to greater surveillance and control
- explain how groupthink can have negative implications on teams.

Key theorists

Meredith Belbin	A British management researcher best known for his team roles
Bruce Tuckman	An American psychologist best known for his categorization of stages of group formation
Jon Katzenbach and Douglas Smith	American management consultants and organizational theorists
Irving Janis	An American social psychologist who pioneered the groupthink theory

Key terms

Groups	A collection of people with a sense of shared identity and something in common but *not* with a shared purpose
Teams	A group who meet together with a common purpose and some degree of mutual interdependence
Groupthink	A psychological phenomenon which limits the range of alternatives being considered because there is an overwhelming desire for consensus
Cohesiveness	Where the group members feel bound together, often feeling as though they share a similar fate
Group dynamics	The underlying (and often unconscious) processes which shape the way group members react to each other

Introduction

Linda Wilkinson walks into the kitchen. 'It's chaos in here,' she thinks, 'not only are they not getting the food out on time, but they are arguing about it as well.'

Despite having an award-winning chef and a great menu, the last few months have seen an increase in customer complaints and, recently, a few negative comments in the local paper. With the reputation that head-chef, Effingham, holds personally, and the hotel being in such a great building, Wilkinson worries that the standard of their day-to-day service is slowly eroding their image.

Looking round the kitchen Wilkinson begins to see why. All the chefs seem to be working very hard, cooking their individual items and putting them on the 'pass' (where the food is checked by the head chef before going out to the customers) when they are done. However, they work in a haphazard order, with some items being completed long before the rest of the table's order is finished, leaving food to go cold.

The tickets (the orders on slips of paper) are also stacking up. Food is going out to different tables at different times, with some customers waiting only 10 minutes and others waiting well over an hour.

Effingham, as the head chef, is barking orders to the chefs Josh, Toby, and Ella, who are doing their best to keep up with the standards he demands. As they cook they present the food to him ready to be served—if it is not up to the standard Effingham expects, he sends it back. 'We are trying to win an award here', he can be heard muttering repeatedly to himself. 'We'll never make it with that standard of food.'

Wilkinson also notices the front of house team darting in and out, picking up plates but looking confused as to what to do with them. 'Where is that one for?' she asks Isabella, one of the most experienced waitresses. 'Umm, Table 17, I think' and she rushes out, only to come back two minutes later looking frantic with the same food.

'What are you doing girl?', Effingham shouts at her. 'That chicken is for Table 7—come on you should know that.'

'But, we've served Table 7', Isabella stammers. 'For goodness' sake', Effingham shouts, 'look it is written here, Table 7.'

Even more worrying is that the waiting team keep taking orders for items that have sold out and then having to return to the customer to take alternative requests. Getting annoyed with each other, the kitchen and waiting staff can be heard from the restaurant shouting at each other.

'This is getting embarrassing', Wilkinson thinks to herself. 'What should be the flagship part of the hotel is disorganized chaos.'

We are regularly in groups and teams. In our personal lives this might be through being in a sports or pub quiz team, or on a student committee. Even organizing a night out with friends requires listening, understanding others, cooperation, and negotiation—essential teamwork skills.

In our working life teamwork is also essential. You may already have worked in shop sales teams or in a team working in a bar. As you progress in your career you may get involved in senior management teams, product launch teams, project teams, marketing teams, or

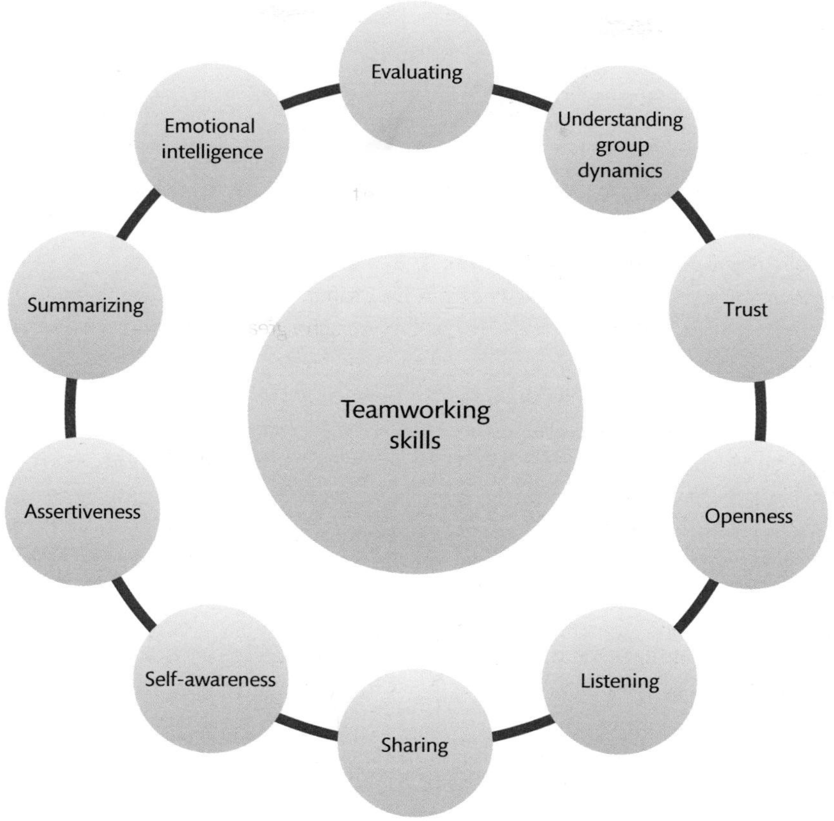

Figure 6.1 Teamwork skills.

training teams. Most jobs have some elements of teamwork and, for many, it is an essential characteristic and essential if you are to be a success. Being a good team member is thus seen as key for your organizational and personal life.

Groups and teams are important as they give us our sense of belonging and identity, and they are often where we gain many of our opinions and values (Figure 6.1). Developing good teamwork has come to be seen as essential element in an organization's success. 'High performance teams' have, for many, become a holy grail, with many claims made about how they increase levels of creativity, problem-solving, output, and employee satisfaction. Indeed, many jobs see teamwork as an essential component.

However getting a team to genuinely work together is difficult and gaining effective teamwork can be fraught with difficulties. People can fall out, not pull their weight, have competing interests and ideas, have personality clashes, and end up as a dysfunctional team where nobody feels a sense of identity or commitment to the collective project. Dysfunctional teamwork is often demonstrated on the TV show *The Apprentice*. The contestants often act as individuals or have a leader who tries to do everything him/herself. When they reach Lord Sugar's boardroom we see the results of the team breakdown: blame, a lack of trust, infighting, and a lack of common vision.

Study skills: doing group-work at university

Often, students dislike group assignments as they find them frustrating and get annoyed with others 'not pulling their weight'. To get around this they often simply divide up the tasks into equal parts and then do them individually, only bringing them together at the end. While this might feel quick and easy it can cause problems because the work is inconsistent in terms of quality and the information presented. Importantly, this approach means many of the benefits of group-work, such as creative thinking, alternative perspectives, and encouragement and support, get lost.

To make group-work more effective it helps to have a shared vision of what the group wants to achieve, and build trust and communication between group members so that ideas can flow freely and new insights can be generated. To work well in a team you therefore have to be skilled at balancing the needs to the task, the team, and individuals.

Teamwork skills take time to develop and university is a good location to practise them. Some of the key things you can work on are listening skills, facilitation skills, and understanding of group dynamics. Writing a reflexive diary on these skills can help you understand better how you act in teams and how you can improve.

Visit the Online Resource Centre for some further practical tips on team working.

The difference between groups and teams

Group A collection of people with a sense of shared identity and something in common but *not* with a shared purpose.

Team A group who meet together with a common purpose and some degree of mutual interdependence.

While in common usage the words groups and teams are often interchangeable, in the academic literature they tend to have quite specific meanings (although not universally agreed). **Groups** cover wider situations, such as a group of friends. Although holding some commonality a group *does not necessarily work together for a common purpose*. A **team** is seen as having a *more specific purpose* and function. They rely *more on each other*, have a greater sense on *collective vision*, and are *mutually accountable*. A summary of the differences is shown in Table 6.1.

Table 6.1 Differences between teams and working groups

Team	Working group
Collectively accountable	Individually accountable
Plan together, collaborate, collectively decide future actions	Share information and different perspectives
Focus on team goals and outcomes	Focus on individual goals and outcomes
Work together on collective tasks	Individual tasks which sometimes are done in connection with others

Employability skill: teamwork

Teamwork is generally seen as a vital skill in many graduate jobs and is often a key requirement on application forms. As a recent Confederation of British Industry (CBI) survey has stated, 25% of businesses do not find graduates sufficiently skilled in teamwork (CBI, 2012: 34). Therefore, while getting a good degree is vital for getting interviews, demonstrating teamwork and interpersonal skills is increasingly essential for getting a job.

University is a good time to build your teamwork experience, particularly through outside activities. Spend five minutes thinking about the activities that you regularly engage in and the teamwork skills that you have developed and those you still need to develop. For instance, you might have organized a charity fundraising night or done a *Duke of Edinburgh's* award, which requires teamwork. For each area can you think of one or two good examples of each?

Visit the Online Resource Centre for more details and some related activities.

What is a team?

The etymology (origin of word) of team is a set of animals yoked together (pulling a cart) emphasizing the *common purpose* and *mutual independence* of the team members.

Within the academic literature there are numerous definitions of teamwork, two of the popular ones are:

The origin of the word team.

> A team is a collection of individuals who are interdependent in their tasks, who share responsibility for outcomes, who see themselves and who are seen by others as an intact social entity embedded in one or more larger social systems . . .
> (Cohen and Bailey, 1997: 241)

> . . . small groups of interdependent individuals who share responsibilities for outcomes for their organization . . .
> (Sundstrom et al., 1990: 120)

Most academic definitions stress the importance of mutual reliance, interdependence, and accountability that group members feel when working together.

Real life case: the Chilean miners

On 5 August 2010 the tunnel to San José mine, Chile, collapsed leaving 33 miners trapped 700 metres underground under around 700,000 tons of rock. Stuck for a world record of 69 days, the first 17 of which were without any outside contact, the miners had to survive in cramped, hot temperatures, which one described as 'like hell, only smaller'.   ◗

▶ With only a tiny amount of food (they did not even have the two days' rations that the mining company were legally obliged to provide), water meant for cooling the machines, and a small amount of power, they had few resources in order to survive. These circumstances could easily have led to infighting as individuals struggled to survive. Instead, they developed into a highly effective team.

They faced many teamwork issues, including personal relationships (imagine being trapped in a space with no light for nearly three months with the same people) and emotional support (think of the emotions you would go through in the first 17 days when you did not know whether you would be rescued). To help them deal with the psychological challenges they arranged themselves in eleven small buddy systems of three people each, with older miners supporting the younger or the more emotionally-fragile ones.

They also had practical challenges. To work together they set schedules and jobs to create a sense of order and teamwork. They ran a mini democracy, voting on the decisions that they took and how to work together. They had to collaborate over their meagre rations—agreeing to eat only when everyone had a fair share.

The *Wall Street Journal* (cited in Arneson Leadership Consulting, 2010) reported that Rose Marie Fritsch, a Chilean psychiatrist, told Chile's *24 Horas* television newscast that a key feature was the miners' 'capacity to organize themselves, to conserve certain structures and stand tall', she said. 'It's evident that they didn't lose their organization or their survival system.' Barrionuevo (2010) reported Dr Jaime Mañalich, Chile's health minister, saying 'They are completely organized. They have a full hierarchy. It is a matter of life and death for them.'

They were led by the foreman Luis Urzua who has been widely credited with motivating the group. In this situation it was not his technical skills that mattered but his capacity to 'rally a team of hungry, anxious men fighting for their lives in a cramped, dark, hot space half a mile below the earth' (McGregor, 2010).

Sources: Arneson Leadership Consulting (2010), BBC (2011a), Barrionuevo (2010), McGregor (2010).

What role do you think teamwork played in the miners' survival? Do you think that they could have survived without cooperation and teamwork? Why was the psychological side important to good teamwork?

The Chilean miners are an extreme case, being thrown together in that situation they had to become a team just to survive. However, we can see similar teamwork issues with people working in organizations. Often thrown together with strangers, business people need to get along, understand each other, and even provide emotional support and encouragement. They need a common vision, sense of trust, and cooperation to work together effectively as a team.

Review questions

Describe

1. Describe the differences between groups and teams.

Describe

2. Describe why teamwork is important.

The variety of teams

So far we have used teams in quite a generic way; however, in practice the nature of teams is quite diverse. Different teams can be placed along a range of different continuums, as shown from left to right in the following tables.

While each of the teams in Table 6.2 is officially a team, some, like the supermarket check-out team, have very little interaction or interdependence, and are a team in name only. Others, like in the hospital theatre, are completely interdependent and require high levels of cooperation.

Table 6.3 shows different levels of formality. The informal group can be a vital place to discover informal rules, careers advice, tacit knowledge (see Chapter 10 for more details) and cultural insights. As you build your career it is useful to spend time developing these networks with others in your field, both within and outside of your company. They can also be places in which you can get mentored and supported as you take the first steps in your career.

Teams can also be fixed and permanent, or more temporary in nature, as shown in Table 6.4.

While the emergence of new technology has increased the possibilities of virtual meetings, many managers still prefer physical meetings, particularly to establish initial contact. However, the rise of technology does save time and reduce carbon emissions (see Table 6.5).

Some teams can be based on location, or can cross national and cultural boundaries, as shown in Table 6.6.

Table 6.2 Independent-to-interdependent continuum

Independent: Same tasks	Independent: Different tasks	Independent: Specialist	Interdependent: Specialist	Interdependent: Same tasks
Supermarket checkout team	**Manufacturing team**	**Hospital theatre**	**Project team**	**Gymnastics team**
While called a team, in practice they act as independent people doing their own tasks with little interaction.	Everyone in the team does their own task in order on the production line.	Each person does their own job but they have to work together as they operate on the patient.	Work together and share information using specialist skills to tackle problems.	All completely dependent on each other.

Table 6.3 Formal-to-informal continuum

Formal team	Semi-formal team	Informal work group	Informal group
Committees, project or sales teams	**Working group around a specific area**	**Conversations around the water cooler**	**Group of sales representatives that meet in the pub**
Established by management, are officially recognized, and have particular tasks or responsibilities.	A team that comes together to work on a particular problem, but are not formally constituted by management.	Gossip, exchange inside information, personal views on events, and career tips.	Fulfil personal needs of friendship and mutual support.

Table 6.4 Permanent-to-temporary continuum

Permanent team: fixed roles and positions in the team	Temporary team: arranged around a specific project and then disbanded
Senior management team	**Construction project**
While the membership of the team might change, the roles and functions are generally quite stable.

They have the advantage of common understandings of how to achieve tasks and understandings of each other. However, this potentially creates challenges, e.g. personality clashes, and deep-seated group dysfunction as the group members are focused on **interpersonal relationships**, as well as the task. | Tackle a specific task or are together for a limited period of time, team members come together around a specific project. For instance on a project basis, bringing in teams of specialists to tackle a problem.

Have to quickly form working patterns and hierarchies, and are therefore often more task-focused. This can make them quite productive, but they do not have the deeper levels of trust and cooperation that established functioning teams can have. |

Interpersonal relationships The way group members relate to each other.

Table 6.5 Physical-to-virtual continuum

Physical meeting	Meeting in temporary locations	Virtual meeting
Domestic management team	**Regional management team**	**An international management team**
Meeting in offices or visits by sales representatives. They are very useful at getting informal information through conversation and establishing rapport.	Meetings in areas like airports. Sometimes business people fly in to an airport, conduct the meeting, and then leave again.	Video-conferencing, email, and use of software like *Microsoft Live Meeting* or *Skype*.

Sometimes team members never meet, as they all work on different parts of the project or in various countries. |

Table 6.6 Domestic-to-multinational continuum

Cross-cultural teams or trans-national teams	Local or regional team
Multinational company	**Domestic company**
From different cultures often across different time-zones, languages, and cultures. These teams increase the pool of expertise and perspectives that can be drawn upon, but face the challenges of cultural differences.	They require less travel, a reduction in project time, less potential communication and cultural differences, but possibly more limited perspective and available talent.

What the team does

Our last categorization is not so much a continuum but three different types of teams. According to Katzenbach and Smith (1993) there are three key categories of teams, those that:

- *do things*—make a product, conduct a service, or market a product
- *run things*—such as managers who devise the organization's strategy and mission statement
- *recommend things*—such as problem-solving teams.

Does teamwork increase productivity?

Running case: Linda Wilkinson meets Graham Effingham

After the service has finished Linda Wilkinson meets Graham Effingham.

'Look Graham we need to get the whole of the restaurant team working together. It is a complete shambles at the moment. You have some skilled individuals but you're not getting the best out of them.'

'We currently have 90 covers a night, we should be doing 130 and have the potential for 180. The food is great but we are getting a reputation for slow and erratic service, and that isn't going to get any better unless we work together. I want us to run a smooth, slick service and produce food that we are all proud of without you all running around like headless chickens.'

Effingham, taken aback, begins to protest. 'How can you say that? I've won awards for my cooking', he retorts, pointing to the plaque on the wall.

'I'm not talking about you as a chef, or the food—which is great', Wilkinson replies calmly, 'but it's the way the whole restaurant is functioning. We're just not getting food out quick enough or in the right order—we're beginning to get a bad reputation.'

'Well it's not me you should be talking to is it?', Effingham responds with a menacing stare. 'The problem isn't the kitchen, it's with them. They cause us chaos. I mean Nina and her lot, they are just completely clueless sometimes. It's like trying to cook blindfold. Not only do they tell the customers wrong things about the food and put in orders for things that we have sold out of, but they even keep changing the menu, allowing customers to change the food. I had Josh last week pulling mushrooms out of the risotto, that's just crazy. They should try cooking for a week!'

Armed with this information Wilkinson goes over to speak to Nina Biagini, the maître d', who is sitting with her team in the opposite end of the bar. 'Ha, is that what he said?', Biagini replies indignantly. 'It's his lot that are in chaos, we can only put on the tables what we are given. Effingham just spends his time shouting at everyone—my guys and girls can't stand being in there. We're the ones having to go and see customers and apologize for the slow service—it's painful sometimes. And then whenever they go in the kitchen they just get shouted at if they dare say anything about speeding things up. My crew are all good people and we like to put customers first. Effingham and the other chefs never have to face customers. I agree with you it's getting bad, but Effingham is the problem. He's more worried about winning awards and his personal reputation than serving ordinary customers.'

Returning to her office, Wilkinson begins to jot down some notes to herself.

It's the restaurant as a whole. The service is a mess, there is no communication between the front of house and the kitchen: things in the wrong order and they get in each other's way. They also drink in separate groups at the end of the night.

Given the prevalence of teams in organizations a central question is whether teamwork actually enhances performance. There are two key perspectives.

Social loafing A term which describes people who, when working in groups, do not work as hard because, often unconsciously, they rely on others to do the task.

Social facilitation The tendency that individuals have to work harder when being watched by others, particularly on simple tasks.

Common sense would suggest that a tug of war team will do better than an individual alone. However, this isn't always the case. Studies have shown that a team of 8 pulls 50% less per person than individuals (Harkins et al., 1980). Harkins et al. claim that when in a team individuals try less—a phenomenon known as **social loafing**.

However, Norman Triplett (1898) looked at cyclists pedalling around a track. He found that those who pedalled around in groups went faster than those that pedalled alone. Cycling in a group increased performance which has come to be known as **social facilitation** theory.

From your experience of being involved in teams do you work harder or slack off? Why do you think this is the case?

The benefits of teamwork: more than the sum of its parts

Since the 1980s there has been explosion of interest in teamwork, with supporters arguing it offers a more productive, creative, satisfying, and empowering way of working (Procter and Mueller, 2000).

Teams are vital for sharing and retaining knowledge. They increase the range of knowledge to tackle a problem, with advocates arguing they produce more accurate and creative answers because team members bring with them a breadth of knowledge perspectives and skills, and challenge each other's views, which leads to better decisions. Also, when one member leaves or is off sick, all of the team's knowledge does not disappear with them.

Real life case: breaking the silos—working in teams in the car industry

In traditional hierarchical organizations (which we saw in Chapter 2) different functions within the business were kept in their distinct groups and rarely worked together. We have seen this perspective in the classic Taylorist model, where the designer works independently from the person actually producing the product. This, though, created what Joe Greenwell, the Chairman of Ford in Britain, calls 'silos'—separate areas which rarely connected with each other. This resulted, he stated, in some communication and design problems, as the designers would design things that could not be manufactured easily. UK car manufacturing 'tended to be silo based' with the associated risk of 'turf wars' and a rather redundant rivalry, particularly between engineering and manufacturing. What began to happen, and now it's close to standard practice, is to have manufacturing engineers co-located alongside product development engineers, both placed at the plant so they can both work together to produce solutions.

As a consequence these 'functional chambers' began to disappear and working in cross-functioning teams has become the norm. In the car industry this move towards stronger teamwork came from the problems of UK manufacturing in the 1970s (the industrial disputes and poor productivity), and the emergence of Japanese manufacturing and productive development processes, such as the Toyota production system, and Total Quality Management. ▶

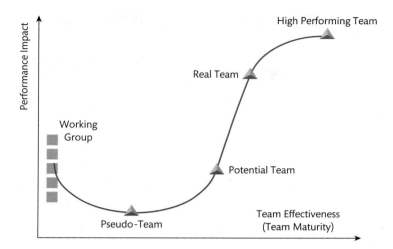

Figure 6.3
Katzenbach and
Smith's teamwork
performance curve.

Source: Katzenbach and
Smith, 1993. Reproduced
by permission of Harvard
Business Publishing.

commonly-agreed working approach, and members are mutually accountable. Katzenbach and Smith believe that the key to achieving a real team is a focus on performance rather than personal chemistry (1993: 61).

4. The *high performance team*. Teams that achieve this level are rare, but highly productive. They are like *real teams*, but with greater levels of trust and commitment to each other's personal growth, professional development, and success. They work on the model that 'if one of us fails, we all fail' (1993: 66). They have interchangeable skills, greater flexibility, shared leadership, a deeper sense of purpose, and even greater humour and more fun. High performance teams have 'a deeper sense of purpose, more ambitious performance goals, more complete approaches, fuller mutual accountability, and interchangeable as well as complementary skills' (1993: 79).

A comparison of high performance and poor performance teams is given in Table 6.10.

Think of teams that you have been involved in—what stage of the team performance curve do you think they are at?

For a group to move to a team therefore requires stronger bonds of cooperation, trust, and interdependence in terms of tasks, knowledge, and cognitive/emotional needs.

Table 6.10 Comparing high performance and poor performance teams (based on Ket De Vries, 1999)

High performing teams have:	Poor performing teams have:
1. Members who respect and trust each other 2. Members who protect and support each other 3. Members who engage in open dialogue and communication 4. Members who share a strong common goal 5. Members who have strong shared values and beliefs 6. Members who subordinate their own objectives to those of the team 7. Members who subscribe to 'distributed' leadership	• A lack of a clear sense of direction • Insufficient or unequal commitment to the group • A lack of skills in key areas • Uncohesive or outright hostility among group members (Katzenbach and Smith 1993) • Unresolved goals • Personal conflicts • Poor leadership

Real life case: the Dutch national football team

A clear example of the importance of teamwork can be seen in sport. For many years, the Netherlands have had some of the most talented football players in the world, particularly in the 1970s when they played 'total football'. Yet, despite their brilliant, breathless football they often lost to inferior opponents in championships and had nothing to show for all their talents. The often-cited cause for their failure was reported to be infighting within the team (in 1974) or because certain players refused to go to the World Cup (1978). They were certainly less than the sum of their parts!

Sources: Rich (2012); Taylor (2010) and Winner (2001).

Building an effective team

Running case: Linda Wilkinson gathers the entire restaurant staff together

'Welcome to the first restaurant team meeting', declares Linda Wilkinson, as she paces up and down in front of the front-of-house and kitchen staff. 'You might have wondered why you're here.' 'You're telling me', Effingham whispers to Toby, who sniggers. 'Well, we felt', says Linda continuing to look directly at Effingham as if to keep him in his place, 'that we really want the restaurant to work together—you are one big team. So today we are launching "Team Junction Restaurant".'

'We all need to work together and act as one big unit if we are going to achieve our mission—providing high quality service to the customer.'

'As members of "Team Junction Restaurant" you all need to work together and rely on and trust each other—if we are to succeed, we succeed together; if we are to fail, we fail together.'

'This is a chair from Malawi, east Africa', Wilkinson continues, pointing to a carved wooden chair. 'What I love about it is it shows everyone doing their job but being part of one big community. Everyone is important, from the lowliest basket carrier to the most senior chief. If you remove any one of them the whole thing would come crashing down—this is how I see "Team Junction Restaurant": one big community.'

As we have seen earlier, teamwork is central to most organizations but is difficult to get right. A group of individuals cannot simply be put together and be expected to become a team, which sadly is often the case (Katzenback and Smith, 1993). So, how do you build a successful team? Unfortunately, despite the numerous attempts by academics, business consultants, and managers to discover a formula to create a well-functioning team, there is no single, quick-fix solution (Katzenbach and Smith, 1993) (Figure 6.4).

Figure 6.4 What makes an effective team?

What makes an effective team

Right people

Technical skills

Teamwork skills

To build an effective team requires finding the right people with the right technical and team-working skills, with a sense of commitment to each other, and then setting the right environment for them to succeed. It also requires the team members to cooperate, trust, and be committed to each other, and to take collective ownership of problems. It is how to develop these aspects that we now turn.

Review questions

1. Explain the difference between the working group and a high-performance team.
2. Explain why Katzenbach and Smith counsel that a working group should not always try to become a high-performance team.

Skills balance

To create a successful team it is essential to have the right balance of the skills and knowledge for the team to carry out the tasks they need to complete. In some settings this will be achieved by having specialists who carry out specific tasks (such as an orchestra where each person carries out one task). In other environments these skills might be spread across the team. Some organizations, such as the UK's National Health Service (NHS), conduct a skills audit matrix to decide whether the team is equipped with the necessary skills. While sometimes the team leader will be able to build the team from scratch, often they are required to develop these skills within the existing team; therefore, it is important to identify potential within the current members' skills potential or gaps that need to be filled by new members.

Visit the Online Resource Centre to see the NHS skills audit matrix in detail.

Have a think about your skills and what you can bring to a team. What are your greatest strengths and how can you use them?

Real life case: Strengthscope™

An example of a tool marketed to business professionals is by Strengthscope™. They offer a tool which allows individuals, teams, and organizations to assess the strengths that an individual team member holds and maps them across the whole team, seeing who has what strength. Rather than looking at technical expertise, such as accounting, they look at work-based strengths, such as courage, emotional control, compassion, decisiveness, self-improvement, and critical thinking. With a skilled facilitator they believe that a team can be made more effective by tapping into the strengths (sometimes hidden in normal working arrangements). Unlike traditional appraisal systems which look at rectifying weaknesses, they seek to build on individuals' strengths in relation to others. They claim that using their system can lead to:

© Strengths Partnership Ltd

- improved team communication, problem-solving, and focus on results
- heightened appreciation of, and respect for, individual differences
- enhanced accountability for delivering team goals
- higher levels of team morale and enhancement
- increased confidence and resourcefulness to overcome performance blockages
- improved understanding of the team's weaker areas and ways to manage or mitigate these.

Source: www.strengthscope.com

Visit the Online Resource Centre for more detail about this tool.

As we will see in Chapter 8 such personality tests should come with a health warning, as some researchers are sceptical of their ability to capture the 'essence' of a personality. They also require considerable levels of trust within the team, as members reveal private information about how they see themselves and how others see them.

Team roles

Running case: teamwork results

Linda Wilkinson stands in front of Team Junction Restaurant. 'Right, each of you has an envelope which contains a report about your team-working skills. There are no superior roles—everyone is equally important. What we need to do is merge you into a team. Over the next week I will be meeting all of you to discuss your role and how we can all work better together.'

'Plant', declares Toby in a slightly puzzled way. 'Oh I get it', he declares as he reads more. 'I always told you I'm creative! What are you Josh?' 'Monitor Evaluator' Josh replies, in a more muted fashion. 'Goody-two-shoes', Toby mocks. 'Effingham, what are you?' 'Shaper', Effingham replies, barely able to hide his smirk. 'Told you I'm the one to get things going round here—right let's get on with some real work and stop this nonsense!'

Team-role theorists argue that in order to get the optimum output of technical skills, a team only reaches its full potential when it has a balance of team roles. The central premise of all these systems is that for a team to function effectively the team needs a number of roles fulfilling. The most popular of these theories is provided by Meredith Belbin (2010), who devised his famous *Team Role Inventory* (Figure 6.5). These different roles are useful for the group as, for instance, the *Resource Investigator* in Belbin's model is often good at kick-starting projects, but loses interest after the initial enthusiasm has passed, whereas the *Completer Finisher* is not as good at these initial phases but can bring a project to completion.

Figure 6.5 Belbin's team role summary descriptions.

BELBIN®

Team Role Summary Descriptions

Team Role		Contribution	Allowable Weaknesses
Plant		Creative, imaginative, free-thinking. Generates ideas and solves difficult problems.	Ignores incidentals. Too preoccupied to communicate effectively.
Resource Investigator		Outgoing, enthusiastic, communicative. Explores opportunities and develops contacts.	Over-optimistic. Loses interest once initial enthusiasm has passed.
Co-ordinator		Mature, confident, identifies talent. Clarifies goals. Delegates effectively.	Can be seen as manipulative. Offloads own share of the work.
Shaper		Challenging, dynamic, thrives on pressure. Has the drive and courage to overcome obstacles.	Prone to provocation. Offends people's feelings.
Monitor Evaluator		Sober, strategic and discerning. Sees all options and judges accurately.	Lacks drive and ability to inspire others. Can be overly critical.
Teamworker		Co-operative, perceptive and diplomatic. Listens and averts friction.	Indecisive in crunch situations. Avoids confrontation.
Implementer		Practical, reliable, efficient. Turns ideas into actions and organises work that needs to be done.	Somewhat inflexible. Slow to respond to new possibilities.
Completer Finisher		Painstaking, conscientious, anxious. Searches out errors. Polishes and perfects.	Inclined to worry unduly. Reluctant to delegate.
Specialist		Single-minded, self-starting, dedicated. Provides knowledge and skills in rare supply.	Contributes only on a narrow front. Dwells on technicalities.

© BELBIN 2011   www.belbin.com

To perform well a team needs a good balance of all these roles. The theory states every person has a series of traits that lead them to have a preference for one particular role, but also has one or two back-up roles should the team demand it.

Each role has strengths and allowable weaknesses, e.g. the price that has to be paid for the strength. For instance, in the Belbin model the *Shaper* role is dynamic and has a strong drive which can push through ideas; however, this can lead to that person offending people's feelings and being provocative.

Each individual discovers their team roles through completing a self-assessment inventory, which can be supplemented by assessments by managers, colleagues, and those you manage.

This approach has become a mini-industry in itself, with many paid-for online assessment exercises, numerous books, games, and group activities based on similar models.

While Belbin is the most famous, others include the *Team Management Systems* (TMS Global, 2012) model and Peter Honey's (2001) five team roles.

 Visit the Online Resource Centre to read more about these models.

According to Fisher et al. (2001), the background of Belbin's model is a combination of the need for clearly defined roles that are matched to specific individuals, drawn from bureaucratic theory (see Chapter 2), and the desire to involve team members in decision-making, which originates in the human relations approach (Chapter 5).

Despite their popularity, concerns exist over their validity and usefulness. Furnham et al., (1993) argue that Belbin's original research was based on limited evidence, and the questionnaires are vague and do not necessarily relate to how people behave within a team. Negative personality traits like neuroticism are not included in the models, despite the fact that they have significant impact on team performance. Most troubling is that they rely on self-reporting, which is not a dependable way to discover how we act. Fisher et al., go as far as to argue it is 'psychometrically unsound' (2001: 142), and Anderson and Sleap (2004) state that it takes little account of gender.

Real life case: team roles in action

Completing these types of personality tests can have powerful effects on people's sense of identity. As a placement student, one of us had a manager who completed a Belbin-style questionnaire and was quite taken by the result:

> 'Daniel, some academics have done some research on me and discovered I am a driver [this particular team-roles version of a shaper]', he said waving a 40-page report. 'I am really dynamic, see things that others do not see and will drive the group onwards. This does mean that I tread on people's toes and can upset people . . . but that's just who I am. You know', he continued reflectively. 'At first I did not believe it, as it did not seem like me. But over time I have realized that it really summed up who I am.'

What is interesting is his response to this 'research', which was actually little more than a self-assessment exercise and a couple of observation exercises. Instead of simply reflecting his team role, he began to identify himself as that character. In other words, instead of discovering the truth about himself, he began to mould himself into the type of team role personality that the report described.

What type of team role do you normally adopt—do you know what this team role is and how you can utilize it to your advantage?

Personality clashes

Running case: tensions rise in the kitchen

Despite Linda Wilkinson's best efforts, on Friday night when service resumes, the tensions between the kitchen and the front of house still continue. Orders keep being misplaced and arguments are breaking out between the kitchen and the waiters. Concerned that the heads of the kitchen and front of house are still at loggerheads, Wilkinson decides she needs to intervene.

'He just thinks he's God's gift', Biagini complains. 'He is more bothered about winning that wretched award than serving customers, it is just not right.' Looking away from Wilkinson, Biagini mutters 'I just can't really cope with him. He's arrogant and loud-mouthed, just not the type of person I can work with. I don't want my team being treated like that.'

Concerned, Wilkinson goes to visit Effingham. 'If you can't stand the heat then you need to get out of the kitchen', he replies gruffly as Wilkinson tentatively raises Biagini's concerns. 'Look, the kitchen is a tough environment, we can't be pussyfooting around being bothered by a waitress's feelings. They should just concentrate on getting the orders right.'

Wilkinson looks on in despair. Despite her best efforts, things seem more difficult than she ever thought.

Even when a team has the right balance of skills and roles some teams fail because of personality differences. The root cause of these clashes, many personality researchers state, is the imbalance of personality traits within the group. What is necessary, they argue, is to get the correct balance of personality characteristics and make sure that no individual dominates. For instance, extraverts can be positive influences, as they are sociable, enthusiastic, energetic, and optimistic. However, Barry and Steward's (1997, cited in Barrick et al, 1998: 381) findings suggest that, '. . . teams may be more effective when there is greater variance among member levels of extraversion, so that complementary roles of leading and following are carried out'. Similarly, high levels of emotional stability can be important to create a well-functioning team as it promotes a relaxed atmosphere, reduces anxiety, and promotes cooperation. However, as is often documented in the creative industries, sometimes a clash of personalities or having a group with heightened emotional sensibilities can lead to more creative work, even if this is difficult to sustain in the long term.

These personality researchers see personality traits as relatively fixed and knowable. They devise complex numerical formulas to capture the personalities within a team and work out their ideal balance (see Barrick et al., 1998 as an example). This offers interesting possibilities for managers when they set up a team.

However, as we will see in Chapter 8, other personality perspectives see personality as more changeable over time (see Chapter 8 for an in-depth discussion of personality traits). There are serious questions as to the validity of reducing personalities down to a set of numbers (as these studies tend to) and whether people act as these computer models predict.

Have you ever fallen out with someone during a team exercise. Why do you think this was and how much of it was down to a clash of personalities?

As we have seen, to become a team rather than a group, the members need to feel they belong together and have a common purpose. Consequently, to be successful team, members need to feel that their fate is tied in with that of the team.

Social identity theory

Social identity theorists (Abrams and Hogg, 2001) argue an individual has two identities: (i) personal identity, which comprises personal and social beliefs, and (ii) group identity, which comprises the benefits of belonging to the team. Ideally, these identities will be aligned, but, if not, the team membership identity should be stronger.

To make this change they argue that individuals need to be 'de-individualized' (Adams and Hogg, 2003), transformed from thinking and feeling like an individual to feeling 'psychologically intertwined with the group's fate' (Mael and Ashforth, 1995: 310). In other words, their primary identity is that of a member of the team rather than as an individual (Tajfel and Turner, 1986). This shifts their outlook from 'my task' to 'our tasks', thus thinking as a team and being committed to the collective output.

Employability skills: creating a team's collective identity

If you take on the role of managing a team one of the central ways that you can get people to work together is to get them to adopt the language and the perspective of the team rather than seeing themselves as individuals.

Therefore, rather than speaking to, or praising, individuals, a team spirit can be encouraged by praising the team collectively and getting them to spend time together, as this collective mentality helps form the bonds within the team.

Things that help are using 'we' rather than 'I', referring to the team as a whole rather than individuals and responding to requests by the team as a whole rather than from one individual.

In short, your role is to develop a team perspective rather than an individual outlook.

Review questions

1. Explain why personality clashes can harm teamwork.

2. Analyse the strengths and weaknesses of Belbin's model.

Tuckman's stages of group formation

Running case: the three-legged race

'Why are we like this', Josh asks quizzically of Saffron looking down at his leg, which is tied to hers. 'It looks like we are about to do a three-legged race', she replies, in an equally confused tone.

'I've gathered you all together', Linda Wilkinson declares, 'to get us all working together'. She looks across at her gathered staff, who are all in a line, in pairs—one from the kitchen the other front of house—with their legs tied together. 'Over the last few months we have been working against each other. Today, we want to be working as a team. In pairs, you need to complete the obstacle course, carrying your uncooked egg and the balloon to the finish line. We have a trophy for the winner and a booby prize of cleaning out the deep-fat fryer for the loser.' With that, she blows her whistle and begins the contest.

At first, the restaurant staff, all feeling a little silly, go through the obstacle course reluctantly, not wanting to be seen as too enthusiastic for what they all collectively feel is a little embarrassing. However, after the first circuit Effingham, shouts 'blow this' and suddenly makes a dash for the front, dragging Biagini with him. 'Come on Nina, you're with the kitchen team now', he shouts as they charge for the front. Sensing the change in attitude Saffron calls to Josh, 'Come on, we can beat them'. Suddenly, the race gets going.

As they go round for the second time Linda Wilkinson looks on in great delight. For the first time the two departments seem to be genuinely working together. For the open parts of the course the more cavalier attitude of the chefs seem to drive them forward whereas when they come to the obstacle section the front-of-house workers guide them through better.

They then move on to a blindfolded obstacle course, where one of the pairs has to guide their partner around the field avoiding various items while the other is blindfolded. Finally, they have to build a tower.

'Well, I've not had so much fun in ages', declares Effingham as they reflect on events in the bar afterwards. 'You know what', he says looking directly at Biagini, 'I was impressed with how you guided me around that blindfold course, you really made it clear what to do'. Biagini smiles. 'You weren't so bad yourself, you really had a good eye for that tower.' Effingham picks up the trophy. 'Yep, we won this together.'

To build this sense of identity organizations often engage in team-building activities, the most famous of which was developed by Bruce Tuckman (Tuckman, 1965; Tuckman and Jenson, 1977).

Tuckman's model lays out the path to high performance. The central concept is that teams have to go through stages in order to become mature and function effectively. A fully mature team, he argued, functions well because they have established norms of behaviour and trust.

Tuckman argued there are two key factors: interpersonal relationships and **task orientation**. These two factors shape the members' behaviours within the team (what we will call group dynamics) and how the team deals with different perspectives, communication, conflict, leadership, and trust (Figure 6.6).

Teams, therefore, go through five stages: forming, storming, norming, performing, and adjourning.

> **Task orientation**
> Focusing on tasks rather than on people.

Stage 1: forming

This is the initial stage in which team members often feel lost, uncertain of how to behave and are looking for ground rules. Tuckman describes this as the orientation stage, as team members are looking to reduce their anxiety and are seeking a leader to tell them what to do. Team members often deal with this anxiety by creating irrelevant discussion on peripheral problems and over-intellectualization of issues to avoid making decisions. At this stage, team members are normally quite polite, although tentative, as nobody wants to say anything that offends others.

Stage 2: storming

This politeness does not last too long as after a while the group members become hostile and begin infighting. At this stage, the group lacks unity and often gets polarized over key issues. Many resist becoming members of the group, seeking to retain their individuality, and conflict arises as the differences between personal goals and group goals are revealed (see social identity theory earlier in the chapter). This often leads them to become defensive, negative, or aggressive, or to withdraw—what Wilfred Bion (1961) calls fight or flight. Members often clash with one another as the 'pecking order' is established. Leaders do not always survive this period.

Stage 3: norming

The norming stage occurs when the group begin what Tuckman calls 'a "patching-up" phase' (Tuckman 1965: 392) and the 'group norms and values emerge' (ibid). This results in group conflicts being resolved and a sense of togetherness, and what Tuckman calls 'we-feelings' emerge. At this stage the group becomes a cohesive unit where the members accept the group and 'idiosyncrasies of fellow members' (ibid: 386). Core here is that the group members want the group to exist and therefore value harmony as central. Emotions are still high at this stage, but they are more focused on achieving the tasks.

Stage 4: performing

At this stage the group has bonded and interpersonal issues are solved, the group structure is accepted, and the group has matured. The group, therefore, is focused on problem-solving. Members provide each other with mutual support and strong interpersonal bonds.

Stage 5: adjourning

This is the stage where the team is dissolved, either because the team members leave or the task is complete. This can be a difficult stage for team members as they will have felt a personal connection with the team and can feel like mourning the death of it.

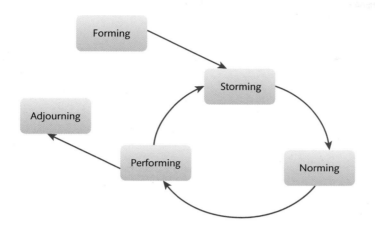

Figure 6.6 Tuckman and Jensen's (1977) team formation.

Recall an experience you have had of being in a team. How closely does Tuckman's model replicate your experiences?

The changing role of the team leader

Not only does the role of the team change over time, but also, as we will see in Chapter 12, how the leader acts also needs to adjust. An effective team leader style will need to act in a *telling* manner to the *forming team* to give them certainty. As they reach the *storming* stage the leader's role is under most threat as they can become the victim of the team infighting. They therefore need to sell the team a vision of the future. In the *norming* stage they need to develop more *participatory* decision-making processes to help the team develop its norms. As the team reaches the *performing* stage the leader needs to *delegate* to the team, as members have increased commitment and experience. Overall, the team leader moves from a position of cop (controlling the team) to coach (facilitating their growth and development).

Real life case: team-building exercises

'Drum circles' have been used as team-building exercises. By taking part in one of these drum circles team members are said to develop synergy, camaraderie, and increased well-being. As one drum circle website (drumcircle.com) states: 'As the team begins to play music together a common language emerges and communication improves. Individuals become a team and the team becomes a thriving community'. Another (activerythmology.co.uk) claims: 'One of the things people learn is how to work together and to do this they first have to listen and respond. They automatically want to make the improvised music sound better, so without realising it they adjust their playing and their relationships to one another. The mixed sounds of a drum circle co-operating to make a harmonious whole is a great metaphor for the benefits of team work building in real life – which can be pointed out in a training exercise if appropriate'.

Drawn from both websites, some of the benefits of drum circles are said to be:

- teach team-building in a unique way
- stimulate creative thinking

- promote cooperation among participants
- demonstrate the individual effect on the larger whole
- encourage clear communication
- develop communication skills
- motivate interaction between participants
- define common ground
- provide a playful vehicle for experiential learning.

Sources: http://www.drumcircle.com/team-building/index.html and http://www.activerhythmology.co.uk/

Have a quick search online to see what other types of team-building activities there are. What claims do these websites make about their effectiveness and do you think they are justified?

Developments of Tuckman's model

Rickards and Moger (1999, 2000) developed Tuckman's model by reducing the five stages to three (Figure 6.7). They argue that between each stage there is a barrier, which acts like a glass ceiling, that needs to be broken to progress.

The first barrier is interpersonal forces, where the group develops its norms. This barrier is weak and so is easy to break resulting in around 85% of teams achieving this. Once they reach the second stage they establish the group and function quite effectively. They do not become a high-performance team or what Rickards and Moger (1999) call the 'dream team' until they smash the second barrier and break out of conventional expectations. Very few groups go through this barrier.

The implication is that it is relatively easy to reach normal performance levels but difficult to reach high performance ones. They suggest training to help the teams break through these barriers.

Observations of organizational practice, however, state that groups do not necessarily follow these stages. Rickards and Moger's own experiences of teams are that they 'never

Figure 6.7 Team development model.

© Rickards, T. and Moger, S., 'Creative Leadership Processes in Project Team Development: An Alternative Tuckman's Stage Model', *British Journal of Management*, Vol. 11, 273–283, 2000, Wiley-Blackwell

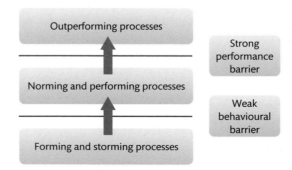

seemed to achieve a satisfactory level of coherence' (2000: 277). Ed Kur goes further, arguing that the linear direction of Tuckman's model is misplaced. He suggests that 'teams move from moderate to high levels of performance, then into dysfunctional conflicts, through self-assessment and back to high performance' (1996: 32). Rather than stages of development building on each other, the team has 'faces', or personalities, which rotate. Therefore, rather than being static 'even the highest performing, most empowered and most productive teams periodically put on the other faces' (Kur, 1996: 33). A team might have a 'performing face' then have a negative experience which makes them reassess their mission (the forming face) before returning to the 'performing face' again.

- *Informing face*: shared mindset, debating, exploring, and testing values.
- *Forming face*: clarifying mission, get to know each other and expectations.
- *Storming face*: confusion and anger with way things are, or misalignment with hopes for the group and what it has become.
- *Norming face*: group rules with a focus on harmony.
- *Performing face*: team with high trust, energy, and innovation (based on Kur, 1996).

One of the great strengths of Tuckman's model is also, arguably, its weakness. It is very straightforward and easy to understand, and this has led it to be applied widely. However, it is too simplistic as it represents group development as clear cut stages. The stages are idealized and they do not necessarily represent what happens in reality.

Theory in context: the background to Tuckman's model

Even though Tuckman's model is very popular, there is very little actual evidence for it. Indeed, it was not based on direct research or even accounts of business practice. Rather, Tuckman created a **hypothesis** based on synthesizing fifty published studies of group development. Many of these studies were based on therapy groups, whose main purpose is to learn from the experience of being in groups rather than, what Tuckman calls, a normal work group which is focused on 'impersonal, intellectual tasks'. The studies of teams in an organizational setting, as Tuckman notes, often miss stage two, as the team is more focused on the tasks than the experiences and social processes involved in becoming a group.

Teams in organization, Tuckman (1965; Tuckman and Jensen, 1977) argues, therefore develop this pattern.

- *Forming*: like in the main study, members are uncertain, but reduce uncertainty by making judgements about each other based on the roles they occupy outside of the team, e.g. other accountants they have met. This, Tuckman concludes, 'is somewhat suggestive of testing'.
- *Storming*: while in an organization there is still some rebellion. Opposition and conflict are not personal as in therapy groups, which most of Tuckman's theory was based on. Therefore, in organizations, teams tend not to go through the storming stage.
- *Norming*: group members discover what they have in common and there is a growth interlocking friendships, roles interdependence, increased harmony, and establishment of group norms. Key task activity is in feeling able to exchange ideas.
- *Performing*: there is positive interdependence and emphasis on task achievement where the group develops its own subculture.

Hypothesis A proposition that needs to be tested.

Why do you think that groups in organizations seem to go through the stages a bit differently to therapy groups?

Consequently, while there are similarities, groups in organizations act in a more muted way than Tuckman's hypothesis suggests. Furthermore, in real life, teams generally have more fluid membership that has evolved over many years and therefore do not go through the cycles that Tuckman describes. Furthermore, groups today are often more diverse, with a wide range of backgrounds leaving Lembke and Wilson to suggest it is 'difficult to apply traditional group dynamics models' (1998: 927) to modern organizational life.

Review questions

1. Describe the five stages of Tuckman's model.
2. Does researching the group processes in therapy groups necessarily translate to work organizations? Why might this matter?
3. What are the implications of Tuckman's model being a hypothesis?

Group dynamics

Group dynamics The processes involved in interaction between group members, with particular emphasis on the tensions, conflicts, and adjustments that occur.

Tuckman's work derives from a theory called **group dynamics**. This perspective argued that groups have their own dynamic, or we might say personality or patterns that exist independently of a single individual. These patterns are powerful forces, as they shape the way that the group and individuals act.

According to group dynamic theory, groups operate at two levels—the task level, the work tasks a group needs to complete—and the group processes, the underlying way the group behaves. These group processes or dynamics exist outside of the conscious awareness of the group members, but shape the way they interact and behave.

Group dynamics theory was named by Kurt Lewin, and developed by, among others, Gustave Le Bon (2008) and Wilfred Bion (1961). Lewin argued 'the group to which an individual belongs is the ground for his perceptions, his feelings and his actions' (Allport, 1948: vii). In other words, the group you belong to provides the basis for how you see the world, what you judge to be acceptable and unacceptable, what you aspire to, and how you interpret events. The group could thus be thought of as a lens through which we interpret the world.

Furthermore, it is argued that it is 'usually easier to change individuals formed into a group than to change any one of them separately' (Lewin 1947: 76, cited in Burke et al., 2008). Therefore, he claimed, the leader should focus on changing the team than any one individual.

Unconscious group dynamics

Some group dynamics theorists stress the importance of the **unconscious** processes that shape the group behaviour. Developing from psychoanalytical theory, such as that of Sigmund Freud and Melanie Klein (see Freud and Riviere, 1927; Likierman, 2001), they argue that the group is shaped by unconscious forces that members of the group are largely unaware of.

Wilfred Bion (1961), one of the earliest to put forward this view, argued that group behaviour occupies the three basic assumptions shown in Table 6.11.

Unconscious From psychology, particularly psychoanalysis, the area of thinking that is not directly available to the conscious mind, and is below the level of personal awareness.

Table 6.11 Bion's dynamics of group behaviour compared with Tuckman's (1965) stages of group formation

Bion's three basic assumptions		Cf. Tuckman's model
Dependency	Group aims for security by looking for a leader to remove all anxieties and solve their problems. The leader is seen as god-like and can do no wrong. If the leader does not miraculously achieve this then they will look for a new leader.	Forming
Flight/Fight	Where the group tries to preserve itself at all costs it either fights or runs away from a common enemy, or directs this energy inwards where the group argues and falls apart. The group ignores all other activities when it is in this phase.	Storming
Pairing	Two people dominate the group and talking to each other is considered by the individuals and group as sexual. The group hopes that they will produce a new leader to save them.	Norming

These three 'basic assumptions' shape the way that the group acts. They create defensive positions that unconsciously protect group members from harm. Bion states they are primitive in origin and provide the emotional energy of the group. They provide an essential conflict within team members between the need to belong and the frustration felt by having to conform. Bion argues that the group needs to mature to become an effective, or what he calls a 'sophisticated' group, where it is more cooperative and not controlled by these basic assumptions. Bion's work draws from psychoanalytical theory and can be difficult to grasp. However, it does alert us to the challenges of creating a well-functioning team, as groups are often shaped by unconscious assumptions that members are only dimly aware of.

Strong bonds: the dangers of a close team

Running case: Team Junction Restaurant sitting together at the end of the night

'Well I must say I'm in shock', Effingham declares to Biagini, 'I really thought that tonight would work, I just can't see why it didn't'. Biagini smiles at him. 'Nor me, it seemed such a good idea—a toga night with all the customers dressing up for Valentine's night with our roman menu and a Venus and Mars waiting team! We had put so much effort into the layout of the restaurant tonight and the statues. With only ten bookings, three of which were couples who did not even dress up, tonight was a disaster. Where did we go wrong? It seemed such a good idea at the team meeting.'

As we have seen, most team theories see a successful team as having strong bonds. Members should see their identity primarily as part of the team, be loyal to each other, committed to the team's purpose, and share similar outlooks. This can be highly beneficial as without competing perspectives decision making is quicker as members do not need to explain what they mean each time a decision is made or try to understand each other's perspective. However, such a close relationship can cause problems.

Over-conformity potentially stifles creativity and growth. With everyone sharing the same basic assumptions different viewpoints do not get debated and therefore opportunities, or risks, can be ignored. Strong teams can therefore have collective beliefs or delusions which results in outside evidence either being ignored or interpreted in such a way as suits the group's interests.

Amanda Sinclair argues that the emphasis on consensus and the assumptions that mature teams are task-focused narrows the definition of what a team is. In particular, she argues that what appears to be consensus is often a result of downplaying division, as political pressure is placed on non-conforming members. 'Behaviour which recognizes and defers to the dominant power-holders in the group is likely to be labelled constructive or task-orientated, while behaviour which challenges that power is labelled disruptive and counter-productive' (Sinclair, 1992: 621).

Groupthink

Have you ever been part of a group thinking it was making a wrong decision but did not speak out? Within academic theory, this is called *groupthink*. Groupthink (Janis, 1971) occurs when powerful social pressures are put upon group members to think in a particular way, or not to voice concerns or alternative viewpoints.

Groups that suffer this problem have a tendency to minimize conflict and therefore do not explore alternative options. They also often stick to agreements that the group has committed to, even if they turn out to be the wrong options. Janis argued that this results in a 'deterioration in mental efficiency, reality resting and moral judgments as a group of group pressures' (1971: 84).

> The more cohesive the group, the greater the inner compulsion on the part of each member to avoid creating disunity, which inclines him [sic] to believe in the soundness of whatever proposals are promoted by the leader or by a majority of the group's members.   Janis (1971: 85)

Theory in context: the background to groupthink theory

Irving Janis devised the concept of groupthink when writing about US foreign policy fiascos, such as the 'failure to be prepared for the attack on Pearl Harbor, the Korean War stalemate and the escalation of the Vietnam War' (1971: 84). The most famous example was the botched *Bay of Pigs* invasion.

The Cuban flag.

The US government was trying to overthrow the Cuban leader, Fidel Castro, but they did not want anyone to know it was them. Therefore, they trained 1400 Cuban exiles to invade the *Bay of Pigs*, as the CIA believed the invasion would cause an uprising in Cuba.

> ⏵ However, the planned uprising did not happen because the invasion was some 80 miles from where people lived. The Cuban exiles were massively outnumbered, without air support, enough ammunition, or even an escape route, leaving most to surrender or be killed. It ended in massive failure.
>
> Some could argue that this was a failure of planning, organizing and thinking. 'How could we have been so stupid?', President Kennedy was heard muttering regularly to himself afterwards, reflecting on the Bay of Pigs fiasco. It was, he said, a 'colossal mistake' which ended in complete failure (Dallek, 2004: 367, 375).

Janis (1971) states that the Bay of Pigs fiasco was a result of groupthink, particularly over-confidence and not accepting evidence to the contrary. According to this theory, the danger is not that the group member will not reveal criticisms, but that they will not even think them, will not carry out careful scrutiny of the ideas, and reject any misgivings that they might have. Groupthink, Janis argued, has the following characteristics:

1. *Illusion of invulnerability*—the group overestimates its power and is over-optimistic, and takes extraordinary risks and ignores warnings.
2. *Constructs rationales to avoid warnings and negative feedback*—being selective with information and discounting ideas that contradict their perspective.
3. *Belief in inherent morality of their group*—morally justified in the actions they take.
4. *Stereotype view of the enemy*—as evil, stupid, or ineffective.
5. *Pressure on opponents*—attack anyone who puts forward an alternative viewpoint.
6. *Self-censorship*—avoids deviating from the group consensus and minimizes personal doubts.
7. *Illusion of unanimity [consensus]*—false view that anyone silent is in agreement and prevents disagreements from arising.
8. *Become mindguards*—protect themselves and the leader of the group by stopping the discussion or not passing on information.

Real life case: groupthink in the city—Barings Bank, Enron, and 2008

There have been numerous examples of groupthink occurring in the financial sector.

- In 1995 Barings Bank collapsed after Nick Leeson, one of their traders, lost them £827 million. He had posted amazing levels of profit but, in reality, was losing hundreds of millions. However, senior managers at the bank did not question his activities or how they were being achieved, and believed what he reported (BBC, 2011b).
- In late 2001, Enron, an American commodities company, went bankrupt despite claiming a profit of over $100 billion the previous year. Enron's board exhibited signs of groupthink and appeared to be one of the last to know about Enron's collapse. The group shared a similar background, felt cohesive, had a superstar culture, and believed that they were changing society. These features meant that they did not ask sufficiently probing questions of how they were operating (O'Connor, 2002; Sims and Brinkman, 2003). ⏵

- The banking crisis of 2008 saw evidence of collective delusion with traders believing that the stock market would always rise and that complicated financial models would continually produce profit. When Paul Moore, HBOS's Head of Regulatory Risk, challenged their practices, saying they were too risky, he was criticized and then sacked (BBC, 2009; The Daily Telegraph, 2009).

All of these financial scandals demonstrate elements of groupthink. Very senior, intelligent, and well-paid people failed to question the practices that they were engaged in.

A recent parliamentary report (UK Parliament, 2010) has argued 'the lack of diversity on the boards of many, if not most, of our major financial institutions, may have heightened the problems of "group-think" and made effective challenge and scrutiny of executive decisions less effective'.

The Chair of the committee, John McFall, argues that a solution is to introduce more women. 'Diversity at the top is one way to challenge potentially dangerous "group-think"' (UK Parliament, 2010).

The result of groupthink is that members look at very few options, fail to consider the costs of decisions, do not take into account what outside experts say, or do not consider how opponents might react. Believing in their own righteousness and invulnerability they can make a decision that might be perceived by an outsider as a bad one (Janis, 1971). For instance, in the Iraq war many members of the Bush administration were convinced that the Iraqis would be so pleased to see them that they would be welcomed with open arms. They failed to consider that many would not like a foreign occupying force and would resist it; therefore, they did not properly plan for the aftermath of the war, with what some commentators have argued to be disastrous consequences (Fox News, 2004; Badie, 2010).

> **Research insight:** The Abilene paradox, Harvey, J. B. 1988. *The Abilene Paradox and other meditations on management.* Jossey-Bass, New York.
>
> The Abilene paradox states: 'Organizations frequently take actions in contradiction to what they really want to do and therefore defeat the very purposes they are trying to achieve' (Harvey, 1988: 19). This occurs when a group collectively makes a decision that actually goes against the preference of any individual. It is a failure to manage agreement and has six stages:
>
> 1. Agree privately as individuals the nature of the problem the organization faces.
> 2. Agree privately as individuals the steps to take.
> 3. Organization members fail to communicate accurately their desires or beliefs to each other, but do the opposite.
> 4. With inaccurate information they make contrary decisions to what they want to do.
> 5. By making counterproductive decisions members become frustrated and angry, form subgroups, and blame each other—particularly blaming leaders.
> 6. This cycle repeats itself and becomes more intensive.
>
> To check that they are not falling into the trap of 'groupthink' Wilkinson suggests that group members should ask each other 'Are we going to Abilene?' to make sure that the decision is really desired by the group.

To overcome groupthink Janis recommends:

1. Encouraging *critical evaluation* in every member.
2. Encouraging an *impartial stance* at the beginning of the meeting to create open-mindedness.
3. *Evaluation groups* for decisions.
4. Discussing decisions with *outsiders* and reporting back.
5. Inviting *outside experts to question decisions*.
6. Members playing *devil's advocate* for key decisions.
7. Considering *rivals' reactions* to a decision.
8. Occasionally dividing into two groups and returning to discuss different perspectives.
9. 'Second chance' meetings to express remaining doubts.

The concept of groupthink therefore makes an important challenge to the underlying ideas of teamwork by warning of the dangers which occur when people share perspectives that are too similar and reject dissenting voices. While the examples that Janis gives are quite extreme in their consequences (potentially costing thousands of lives and billions of pounds), groupthink often occurs on a more mundane level when members of a team, despite their personal misgivings, go along with decisions that outsiders would question. All teamwork requires a balance between coherence/**conformity** and dissent/creativity—the challenge is to get the balance right.

Conformity Everyone in the group thinking and acting in the same way.

Have you been involved in a team that you felt demonstrated elements of teamwork? How did you feel about it and what were the consequences of this? Do you think that Janis's advice is helpful?

Decision making in teams: the risk-shift phenomenon

When we are in groups we tend to take more risky decisions than we do when alone. This is called the 'risk-shift phenomenon'. This occurs because when we are in groups we feel more secure and responsibility is spread across the group, and individual members do not want to let others down. By listening to others in the group more open to risk, individual members move towards greater risk.

Review questions

1. Explain why groupthink happens.
2. Analyse what the implications of groupthink are to our understanding of teamwork.

Does teamwork produce increased freedom?

Running case: clearing up

Isabella phones her boyfriend Steve. 'Hi Steve, it's me. Look I know its Valentine's night and I promised you a night out, but we're having to clear up after tonight's meal. Oh, it was such a disaster, nobody came so we are going to all go out to drown our sorrows. I was involved in the planning for this so I feel I need to help clear up the pieces. Look, I know I'm letting you down, but I really feel I owe it to this lot to stick together. I've got tomorrow night off—I'll make it up to you, I promise.'

One of the great claims made about teamwork is that it gives the potential for greater freedom and autonomy for the team members. As we can see in Figure 6.8, the greater skill level of the team members, the more freedom (or empowerment) the team can have.

Figure 6.8
Empowerment continuum.

Reproduced from *Management*, Daft et al. © 2010, South-Western. Reproduced by permission of Cengage Learning.

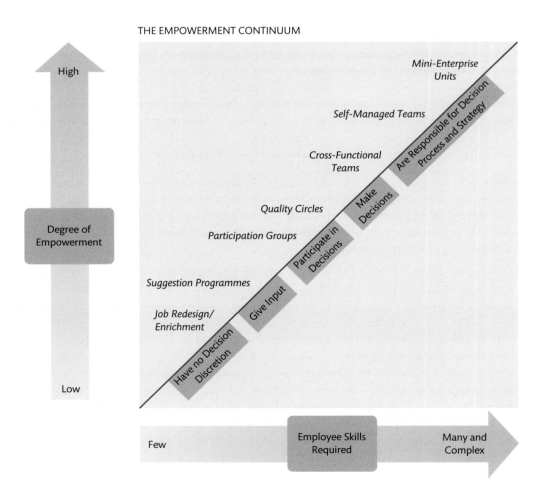

THE EMPOWERMENT CONTINUUM

When team members have low skill levels being part of a team can give greater variety through *job rotation*. In firms such as McDonalds, relatively unskilled workers can change roles, e.g. making chips, then putting burgers together, etc., which makes the job more interesting. This concept, like *job enrichment*, gives the workers more opportunity to use skills and, as Herzberg believed, increases motivation (Paul et al., 1969).

Employees can also be involved in recommending changes through suggestion programmes. These schemes, however, give them little opportunity to implement the changes, as a *recommending team* (e.g. a group of managers) makes the final decision.

A strong level of empowerment can be achieved by employees forming **quality circles** (Marks et al., 1986). Members of these groups are ordinary members of staff (e.g. from production or service delivery) who meet together for a few hours a week or month and discuss solutions to work-related problems. They then present these solutions to management. In doing so they aim for continuous improvement in how they work, from health and safety through to production processes. They therefore combine the *recommending team* and the *doing team*. While quality circles have not lived up to their promise since the 1980s (Lawler and Mohrmann, 1985), they can be effective ways of bringing about improvements lead by the employees themselves.

Interdisciplinary teams or **multifunctioning teams** have, in recent years, become increasingly popular and used in areas such as social services, health, and policing (Schofield and Amodeo, 1999). They are often used in skilled professions and have more autonomy as they can make decisions. Inter-disciplinary teams can be powerful in that they draw together multiple skills and knowledge to tackle complex problems, but they are also challenging to work in as different professions within the team often hold competing understandings of problems and can, therefore, find it difficult to establish a common language.

Such teams draw people in from many different professions, such as doctors, nurses, occupational therapists, mental health nurses, and many others, to talk about a patient, offender, or drug addict, etc., and to make sure that all the different services are sharing information and working together to deliver 'joined up services' rather than piecemeal delivery, which sometimes contradict each other (Robinson and Cottrell, 2005). Within businesses, multi-functioning teams might come together to discuss the launch of a new product or service.

Visit the Online Resource Centre to watch some videos on teamwork.

Empowered or **self-managed teams** have increased autonomy and higher skill levels (Cohen and Ledford, 1994). The key part of these teams is they have the authority to solve their own problems and directly respond to the needs of their customers. These teams do not have managers telling them what to do, but the group makes decisions and has collective responsibility for its actions. This can be done by rotating the leader or by using collective decision-making processes. Self-managed teams can often set their own hours, the planning of tasks, and even their own budgets.

Self-managed teams can be more productive because they can make quicker decisions, create stronger bonds between team members as they tackle challenges collectively, and increase commitment as the team members have more freedom to experiment and have an increased say in how things are run. 'In theory, ownership, responsibility and involvement in the strategic direction [by self-managing teams] are likely to lead to more rapid development and implementation of the strategy by workers dealing directly with customers' (Dunphy and Bryant, 1996: 692).

Quality circles A group of workers who come together, often under the supervision of a leader, to identify, analyse and solve organizational problems.

Interdisciplinary team or multifunctioning team A team of people that is comprised of people coming from different disciplines. This approach can produce a wider perspective and knowledge but can also produce greater conflict.

Empowered The process by which the workers are given greater power and autonomy. Critics suggest this approach also places a greater burden on workers.

Self-managed teams A team, often of professionals or highly qualified people, who manage themselves.

However, such teams can be harder to manage, particularly initially, as it requires managers to be able to trust the team to work well together, be committed to the aims of the team and customers, and skilled in the task that they are doing. It can also be challenging for managers schooled in traditional 'command and control' practices, as it requires a different relationship with the team. It has been described as moving from the 'cop' to 'coach', or 'controlling' to 'involving' (Lawler, 1986). The senior manager's role is to set the parameters for the group, such as its vision, objectives, and key milestones, whereas the team works out the operational details, such as the most effective way to perform the tasks and meet the objectives.

Thus, teamwork proponents argue it simultaneously enables increased organizational performance with improvements in employees' working lives and even solves alienation within society.

Is teamwork a way of enhancing control?

Downsizing Reducing the size of the workforce.

The introduction of self-managed teams can result in **downsizing** by removing layers of management as their responsibilities get absorbed into the team (Dunphy and Bryant, 1996). This reduces the cost of management, but increases the cost of training and development of team members. It can, as we will see, increase the burden on ordinary members of staff as they become more responsible for the delivery of products and services, but often without additional pay. Therefore, it can be seen as an intensification of work as employees come to be seen as more responsible for solving problems—traditionally a manager's domain. Workers are therefore responsible for reaching targets that are not of their own making. Barker (1993), and Sewell (1998) thus argue that it can actually represent a stronger form of control.

Barker argues that, on the surface, *self-managing teams* represent a shift in power from management to workers, who can reach a negotiated consensus about core values and practices. 'Instead of being told what to do by a supervisor, self-managing workers must gather and synthesize information, act on it, and take collective responsibility for those actions' (Barker, 1993: 413).

This can result in increased commitment by employees as they feel responsible for completing a task. As one of the employees in Barker's study states 'Under the old [bureaucratic and hierarchical] system, who gave a hoot if the boards shipped today or not? We just did our jobs. Now we have more buy-in by the team members. We feel more personal responsibility for the product' (1993: 422). Barker describes how this results in team members missing their children's school plays, working weekends, and starting work at 5.00 am to meet production schedules.

While at first glance it might appear that management have given up control, Barker argues that, in fact, it represents a far more subtle and intensive form of control. Team members, he argues, control each other's actions. 'Team members rewarded their teammates who readily conformed to their team's norms by making them feel a part of the team and a participant in the team's success. In turn, they punished teammates who had bad attitudes . . . with guilt and peer pressure to conform' (1993: 425). The control is intensified because it is less apparent who is doing the observation. Barker states in his case that more experienced members of staff watched and disciplined the less experienced, and reinforced the rules and group norms. This resulted in the experienced staff feeling like unpaid supervisors and suffering burnout, and the new staff feeling like they were constantly being watched. This creates a stronger, what Weber called, iron cage (see Chapter 2), but this time not of bureaucracy, but of the discipline of the team.

Teamwork, therefore, could be seen as a way of shifting the responsibility from managers on to the shoulders of staff. Workers have what Sewell (1988) calls *responsible autonomy*. They are given freedom so long as they hit the targets set and use their discretion for the good of the organization. They become responsible for solving organizational problems, often with no additional pay or recognition.

At a deeper level, teamwork changes the outlook of employees: 'management is concerned not only with changing the way in which employees work but also the way they think' (Knights and McCabe, 2000: 1494).

Review question

1. Explain why teamwork can increase freedom *and* control.

Chapter summary

Running case: Josh and Toby are talking in the kitchen at the end of the day's service

'It's not like it used to be', Josh reflects, 'you know when it was just us lot before this "Team Junction Restaurant" thing. I mean, working with the waiting staff is all well and good, but at the end of the day they are not chefs like us really, are they?' Toby smiles back at him. 'Yep, I know what you mean. It's all well and good talking about this as a team exercise, and I would say that we are now working together much more, but they do need to know their place don't they. Let's not just assume that we are all equal here. Chefs are chefs and waiting staff just put food on the table.'

Teamwork has come to be seen by many management theorists and practitioners as a great way of increasing productivity *and* employee satisfaction. When it works well it helps create more imaginative and successful products and services, combining the skills, experience, and different outlooks of people from different backgrounds and areas within the company to gain a wider and more creative perspective. Teamwork is an essential part of organizational life and something that is likely to be key to your future working life.

However, as we have seen through this chapter it can be a challenge. It requires trust, accountability, an openness to other people's ideas, an ability to rely on each other, and to share a common outlook. In particular, to be part of a team requires the ability to forgo an individualistic outlook and to see yourself as part of a team. This can be a painful and challenging process as it can mean giving up personal ideas and putting faith in other people.

Organizational theorists, consultants, and managers have, therefore, spent a lot of time developing models and ideas of how to make teams function effectively. Despite these efforts there still appears no 'magic bullet' to make teams function fully and it can be challenging for even the most experienced manager. As teams form tight bonds they can encounter difficult emotional and psychological experiences that many people try to avoid. As a result, it can be challenging for teams to achieve all the results expected of them.

Teamwork should not be seen in isolation. Other forces, such as culture (Chapter 7), power, and politics (Chapter 13), also come into play and can shape the experiences of a team.

Teamwork, though, can also be thought of as another form of control. Rather than producing autonomous teams it can be seen as a form of surveillance as team members watch each other, controlling each other's effort and output. The manager is, therefore, replaced by team members: ten pairs of eyes rather than just one.

Further reading

Tuckman, B., and Jensen, M. 1977. Stages of small-group development revisited. *Group Organization Management* **2(4): 419–427.**

In his classic text Tuckman describes the key stages of his group formation model. It also provides an interesting insight into the background of the theory.

Katzenbach, J.R., and Smith, D.K. 1993. *The wisdom of teams: creating the high performance organisation.* **McGraw-Hill, Maidenhead.**

Provides an interesting account of how to create a 'high-performance' team from a manager's viewpoint.

Belbin, R.M. 2010. *Team roles at work.* **Butterworth-Heinemann, Oxford.**

Describes one of the most popular teamwork models and gives some practical insight into how the theory works in practice.

Janis, I.L. 1971. Groupthink. *Psychology Today* **5(November): 43–46, 74–76.**

A classic account of groupthink with some interesting historical accounts.

Barker, J.R. 1993. Tightening the iron cage: concertive control in self-managing teams. *Administrative Science Quarterly* **38(3): 408–437.**

Provides an interesting critical perspective on why teamwork can be a stronger form of control.

Bibliography

Abrams, D., and Hogg, M.A. 2001. Collective identity: Group membership and self-conception. In: Hogg, M.A., and Tindale, S. (eds) *Blackwell handbook of social psychology: Group processes.* Blackwell Publishers: Oxford, pp. 425–461.

Allport G.W. 1948. Foreword. In: Lewin, G.W. (ed.) *Resolving social conflict.* Harper & Row: London.

Anderson, N., and Sleap, S. 2004. An evaluation of gender differences on the Belbin Team Role Self-Perception Inventory. *Journal of Occupational and Organizational Psychology* 77(3): 429–437.

Arneson Leadership Consulting. 2010. Leadership and teamwork, underground. Available at: http://arnesonleadership.wsiefusion.net/_blog/Bootstrap_Leadership_Blog/post/Leadership_and_Teamwork,_Underground/ (last accessed 25 June 2012).

Badie, D. 2010. Groupthink, Iraq, and the War on Terror: Explaining US Policy Shift toward Iraq. *Foreign Policy Analysis*, 6(4), 277–296.

Barker, J.R. 1993. Tightening the iron cage: concertive control in self-managing teams. *Administrative Science Quarterly* 38(3): 408–437.

Barrick, M.R., Stewart, G.L., Neubert, M.J., and Mount, M.K. 1998. Relating member ability and personality to work-team processes and team effectiveness. *Journal of Applied Psychology* 83(3): 377–391.

Barrionuevo, A. 2010. Trapped Chilean miners forge refuge. *New York Times*. 31 August 2010. Available at: http://www.nytimes.com/2010/09/01/world/americas/01chile.html?_r=1&hp (last accessed 25 June 2012).

BBC. 2009. The choice. BBC Radio 4. First broadcast 3 November 2009. Available at: http://www.bbc.co.uk/programmes/b00nk2c2.

BBC. 2011a. Chilean miners: 17 days buried alive (BBC 2, 16 August 2011).

BBC. 2011b. The reunion: Barings Bank collapse. BBC Radio 4. First broadcast 7 August 2011. Available at: http://www.bbc.co.uk/iplayer/episode/b0132026/The_Reunion_Barings_Bank_Collapse/

Belbin, R.M. 2010. *Team roles at work*. Butterworth-Heinemann: Oxford.

Bion, W. 1961. *Experiences in Groups: and Other Papers*. Tavistock: London.

Burke, W., Lake, D.G., and Paine, J.W. (eds) 2008. *Organization change: A comprehensive reader*. Jossey-Bass: San Francisco, CA.

CBI. 2012. Learning to grow, what employers need from education and skills, CBI/Pearson, London. Available at: http://www.cbi.org.uk/media/1514978/cbi_education_and_skills_survey_2012.pdf (last accessed 26 November 2012).

Cohen, S.G., and Bailey, D.E. 1997. What makes teams work: group effectiveness research from the shop floor to the executive suite. *Journal of Management* 23(3): 239–290.

Cohen, S.G., and Ledford, G.E. 1994. The effectiveness of self-managing teams: A quasi-experiment. *Human Relations*, 47(1), 13–43.

Daft, R.L. 2001. *Organization Theory and Design*, 7th edn. South-Western Publishing: Cincinnati, OH.

Dallek, R. 2004. *John F Kennedy; An unfinished life*. Penguin: London.

Dunphy, D., and Bryant, B. 1996. Teams: Panaceas or prescriptions for improved performance? *Human Relations* 49(5): 677–699.

Fisher, S.G., Hunter, T.A., and Macrosson, W.D.K. 2001. A validation study of Belbin's team roles. *European Journal of Work and Organizational Psychology* 10(2): 121–144.

Fox News. 2004. 'Group Think' Led to Iraq WMD Assessment. 11 July 2004. Available at: http://www.foxnews.com/story/0,2933,125123,00.html.

Freud, S., and Riviere, J.T. 1927. *The Ego and the Id Authorized* (transl. J. Riviere). Hogarth Press: London.

Furnham, A., Steele, H., and Pendleton, D. 1993. A psychometric assessment of the Belbin Teamrole Self-perception Inventory. *Journal of Occupational and Organizational Psychology* 66(3): 245–257.

Harkins, S.G., Latane, B., and Williams, K. 1980. Social loafing: Allocating effort or taking it easy. *Journal of Experimental Social Psychology* 16: 457–465.

Harvey, J.B. 1988. The Abilene paradox: the management of agreement, *Organizational Dynamics* 17(1): 17–43.

Honey, P. 2001. *Improve Your People Skills*, Chartered Institute of Personnel and Development: London.

Janis, I.L. 1971. Groupthink. *Psychology Today* 5(November): 43–46, 74–76.

Katzenbach, J.R., and Smith, D.K. 1993. *The wisdom of teams: creating the high performance organisation*. Harvard Business School: Boston, MA.

Ket De Vries, M. 1999. High-performance teams: lessons for the Pygmies. *Organizational Dynamics* 27(3): 66–77.

Knights, D., and McCabe, D. 2000. Bewitched, bothered and bewildered: The meaning and experience of teamworking for employees in an automobile company. *Human Relations* 53(11): 1481–1517.

Kur, E. 1996. The faces model of high performing team development. *Leadership & Organization Development Journal* 17(1): 32–41.

Latané, B., Williams, K., and Harkins, S. 1979. Many hands make light the work: The causes and consequences of social loafing. *Journal of Personality and Social Psychology* 37(6): 822–832.

Lawler, E.E., and Mohrman, S.A. 1985. Quality circles after the fad. *Harvard Business Review*, 63(1), 65.

Lawler, E.E. 1986. *High-involvement management. Participative strategies for improving organizational performance*. Jossey-Bass: San Francisco, CA.

Le Bon, G. 2009. *The Crowd: A Study of the Popular Mind*. Classic Books International: New York.

Lembke, S., and Wilson, M.G. 1998. Putting the "team" into teamwork: alternative theoretical contributions for contemporary management practice. *Human Relations (HR)* 51(7): 927–944.

Likierman, M. 2001. *Melanie Klein: Her Work in Context*. Continuum: London.

Mael, F., and Ashforth, B.E. 1995. Loyal from day one: biodata, organizational identification, and turnover among newcomers. *Personnel Psychology* 48: 309–333.

Marks, M.L., Mirvis, P.H., Hackett, E.J., and Grady, J.F. 1986. Employee participation in a Quality Circle program: Impact on quality of work life, productivity, and absenteeism. *Journal of Applied Psychology*, 71(1), 61–69.

McGregor, J. 2010. Luis Urzua: Chile's underground leader. *The Washington Post*. 12 October 2010. Available at: http://views.washingtonpost.com/leadership/post_leadership/2010/10/after-nearly-70-days-the.html (last accessed 24 November 2012).

O'Connor, M.A. 2002. The Enron Board: The Perils of Groupthink. *U. Cin. L. Rev.* 71, 1233.

Paul, J.P., Robertson, K.B., and Herzberg, F. 1969. Job enrichment pays off. *Harvard Business Review*.

Procter, S., and Mueller, F. (eds) 2000. *Teamworking*. Macmillan: Basingstoke.

Rawnsley, J. 1995. *Going for Broke: Nick Leeson and the Collapse of Barings Bank*. HarperCollins: London.

Rich, D. 2012. Netherlands v Germany: Oranje feeling the squeeze. *The Independent*. 13 June 2012.

Rickards, T., and Moger, S. 1999. *Handbook for creative team leaders*. Gower Press: Farnborough.

Rickards, T., and Moger, S. 2000. Creative Leadership Processes in Project Team Development: an alternative to Tuckman's stage model. *British Journal of Management* 11(4): 273–283.

Robinson, M., and Cottrell, D. 2005. Health professionals in multi-disciplinary and multi-agency teams: changing professional practice. *Journal of Interprofessional care*, 19(6), 547–560.

Schnake, M.E. 1991. Organizational citizenship: A review, proposed model, and research agenda. *Human Relations* 44(7): 735–759.

Schofield, R.F., and Amodeo, M. 1999. Interdisciplinary teams in health care and human services settings: are they effective? *Health & Social Work*, 24(3), 210–219.

Sewell, G. 1998. The discipline of teams: the control of team-based industrial work through electronic and peer surveillance. *Administrative Science Quarterly* 43(2): 397–428.

Sims, R., and Brinkman, J. 2003. Enron Ethics (Or: Culture Matters More than Codes). *Journal of Business Ethics*, vol 45:3, 243–256.

Sinclair, A. 1992. The tyranny of a team ideology. *Organization Studies* 13(4): 611–624.

Shaw, M. 1932. Comparison of individuals and small groups in the rational solution of complex problems. *American Journal of Psychology* 44(3): 491–504.

Sundstrom, E., De Meuse, K.P., and Futrell, D. 1990. Work teams: applications and effectiveness. *American Psychologist* 45(2): 120–133.

Tajfel, H., and Turner, J.C. 1986. The social identity theory of intergroup behaviour. In: Worchel, S., and Austin, W.G. (eds) *Psychology of intergroup relations*. Nelson-Hall: Chicago, pp. 7–24.

Taylor, D. 2010. World Cup 2010: Holland hope for harmony from their feuding stars. *The Guardian*. 13 June 2010.

The Daily Telegraph. 2009. HBOS whistleblower Paul Moore: Evidence to House of Commons 'Banking Crisis' hearing. 11 February 2009. Available at: http://www.telegraph.co.uk/finance/newsbysector/banksandfinance/4590996/HBOS-whistleblower-Paul-Moore-Evidence-to-House-of-Commons-Banking-Crisis-hearing.html.

TMS Global. 2012. Available at http://www.tms.com.au (last accessed 26 November 2012).

Triplett, N. 1898. The dynamogenic factors in pacemaking and competition. *American Journal of Psychology* 9: 507–533.

Tuckman, B. 1965. Developmental sequence in small groups. *Psychological Bulletin* 63(6): 384–399.

Tuckman, B., and Jensen, M. 1977. Stages of small-group development revisited. *Group Organization Management* 2(4): 419–427.

UK Parliament. 2010. Report calls for more women in City to challenge group-think. Available at: http://www.parliament.uk/business/news/2010/04/report-calls-for-more-women-in-city-to-challenge-group-think/ (last accessed 25 June 2012).

West, M.A. 2004. *Effective teamwork; practical lessons from organizational research*. Blackwell: Oxford.

Winner, D. 2001. *Brilliant Orange: The Neurotic Genius of Dutch Football*. Bloomsbury Publishing: London.

Organizational culture
The hidden side of the organization

Chapter overview and learning outcomes

By the end of this chapter you should be able to:

- describe what organizational culture is
- describe why organizational culture has become a popular term within management practice and academic theory
- explain how organizational culture shapes the behaviour of organizational members
- explain how managers try to change culture
- analyse the extent to which managers can change culture
- analyse whether managing through culture represents a rise in greater freedom or increased control.

List of key theorists

Tom Peters and Robert Waterman	Popular management writers and consultants who spearheaded interest in organizational culture as a management resource. They argued that organizations need a 'strong culture' to be successful
Edgar Schein	Schein believes that culture is significantly influenced by the founder and leadership, and that by following the ten-step programme it can be changed. Argues that culture has three levels which are progressively harder to access, but are more significant the deeper down they are
Linda Smircich	Sees culture as something that the organization: either • *has*—something that is a possession of the organization that managers (and others can control) or • *is*—an integral part of the organization
Hugh Willmott	A critical management theorist who argues that there is a dark side of organizational culture—a form of slavery and control

List of key terms

Organizational culture	The collective behaviour exhibited by members of an organization, often seen as comprising of values, beliefs, practices, history, and traditions
Mission statement	The stated aim of the organization—often with the intention of inspiring the employees and differentiating them from others
Cultural typology	A classification of the type of organizational culture
Cultural change	Often driven by management or consultants with the intention of making the organization more productive. Sees culture as a possession that management can control

Introduction: learning a new culture—new situation, new rules

Running case: first day nerves

Sue Marshall looks into her mirror, preparing for her first day of work at Junction Hotel. 'What will people be like? Friendly I hope. Am I dressed correctly?' she says, looking down at her new suit. 'Not too formal I hope, but I need to be taken seriously. This is an important job for me.'

She tries to relax, but still feels nervous. 'How should I act when I get there? They seemed quite friendly when I looked round, but you never know. Linda Wilkinson did say they are one big happy family.' Sue hopes this is true, but she's heard rumours about the Head Chef, Effingham. Her friend Isabella said he shouts and swears. 'I do hope that Isabella was just saying that to scare me. I'm not sure if I'll fit in if that's the case. Oh well, only one way to find out . . .'

Think back to when you started a new job, school—what did it feel like, what were your hopes and fears? What were your first few days like? Did anything seem strange in the way people talked or behaved?

Going into any new social situation can be unsettling. We do not know what the people will be like, how to behave, what to wear, and what to say. We often worry whether people will like us and whether we will like them, will we share similar interests—in short, will we fit in?

A key way of fitting in at work is learning the organization's culture. We often do this without even thinking by looking for clues in the appearance of buildings, the company's reputation, and how they present themselves during the interview. We see the culture spelt out in policy documents, mission statements, official histories, induction packs, and dress codes. However, we also look to the less obvious things, such as jokes and stories, subtle put-downs or praise. Through observation we slowly pick up the unwritten rules of behaviour and learn how to fit in. In short, we aim to learn how the culture works.

Employability skills: learning to fit into the organization's culture

People who are successful are often the ones who manage to fit within the company's culture. Put simply, if you want to be seen as a success at work you need to learn and adapt to your organization's culture—it will not adapt to you.

There are a number of things that you can do to fit in better:

- check out the culture before you apply to make sure that you can fit in with it
- when joining spend the first few weeks assessing the culture to pick up clues on how it works, focusing particularly on:
  - the norms and patterns of behaviour, how other people act within the organization
  - the formal *and* informal aspects of culture—do not just follow what the official culture management try to promote, but also be aware of how your colleagues respond to these aspects ▶

- be aware that there is often more going on than first meets the eye and that within different departments there might be more than one culture
- build and maintain strong relationships with key people within the organization, particularly those that can act as mentors and supporters.

However, it is also important not to become too drawn into the culture or to accept it uncritically. An organization's culture can shape your values dramatically, potentially in ways that might go against the personal beliefs you held before joining the organization. Organizational cultures can also lead you into negative perspectives that are counter-productive. Therefore, while it is important to learn and adapt to the organization's culture it is also vital to gain critical distance from it so that you are not drawn into it. Having a friend or a peer from another organization that you can talk to can be helpful in giving you some critical distance from what is going on in your own organization.

At its most basic level *organizational culture* is the way things are done and the values held within an organization. We could see it as the characteristics that make an organization unique. It shapes how individuals behave and think. This has led many managers, consultants, and academics to see organizational culture as a key factor in separating success and failure—a resource to increase performance and commitment.

However, some argue that a strong culture can also have its dark side, acting as a trap, with little room for resistance. This can end up producing what critical theorist Hugh Willmott has called a type of slavery, to 'exploit, distort and drain the dwindling cultural resource of caring, democratic values' (1993: 541).

Throughout this chapter we will debate if managing through culture offers increased freedom or greater (and more insidious) control? Is it a resource that management use or beyond the scope of any individual or group?

What is organizational culture?

Running case: Sue Marshall arrives at Junction Hotel

Sue Marshall arrives at Junction Hotel and walks up to reception. It is smaller than she remembers, she thinks. 'Can I help you?', the smartly-dressed receptionist with understated make-up asks. 'I'm here to start work', Sue replies nervously. 'Oh, you must be Sue—we've been expecting you. I'm Mandy', the receptionist says, breaking out into a broad smile. 'I do hope that you enjoy working here. Come with me.'

They walk at a gentle pace through the corridor and down a hall. The thick-pile carpet gives off an air of quality, thinks Sue as she walks next to Mandy. As they walk Mandy engages Sue in polite conversation. 'She seems friendly enough', thinks Sue. 'I might just fit in here.'

At its simplest organizational culture is 'the way we do things around here' (Deal and Kennedy, 1982: 4). It describes the common practices, attitudes, behaviours, beliefs, and values that are shared between organizational members (Schein, 1985).

Organizational culture could be seen like the organizational glue. Here are some popular definitions:

- 'Culture is the system of such publicly and collectively accepted meanings operating for a given group at a given time' (Pettigrew, 1979: 574)
- 'the collective programming of the mind which distinguishes the members of one organization from another' (Hofstede, 1991: 262)
- 'the basic assumptions and beliefs which are shared by members of an organization, that operate unconsciously, and that define in a basic "taken-for-granted" fashion an organization's view of itself and its environment' (Schein, 2010). Schein also defines culture as 'a set of basic assumptions [that] defines for us what to pay attention to, what things mean' (2010: 32).

However, like many of the subjects in this book, there is no consensus of what culture is, how it operates, or its importance to organizations. Indeed, as Frost et al., as far back as 1991, argued, researchers 'do not approach the phenomena they do study from the same theoretical, epistemological, or methodological points of view' (1991: 7).

Why study organizational culture? The rise of management interest

Running case: Simon Chance attends a business seminar

Simon Chance has just come back from a business seminar *Harness your culture—your secret weapon for success* at his local Business Link. He is excited. The speaker, an influential American, talked passionately about how he turned his food manufacturing business from a small-scale enterprise into a market leader through changing the culture of his firm, focusing on the customer and excellence in everything they did. His enthusiasm was infectious. Anyone can buy machines and set up a business but it takes a strong culture to be a success.

Chance is impressed. He likes the idea of a unified culture where everyone shares the values of high quality and affordable prices. He looks at the leaflet he picked up at the seminar and starts to read it . . .

Why do you think Chance would want to change the culture of Junction Hotel? How would you go about finding what the culture of the organization is?

In 1982 two management consultants, Tom Peters and Robert Waterman, published a book that caused a storm within management circles. *In Search of Excellence* became a global hit, selling over 3 million copies and was commonly seen in boardrooms, airport lounges, and business schools. This phenomenal success led to organizational culture becoming the **buzzword** for businesses.

Buzzword A phrase which is a fad for a period of time.

At its heart was the claim that *excellent* companies had one key thing in common: a strong set of shared values which put the customer at the heart of the operation. Successful firms, Peters and Waterman argued, were defined by strong, unified cultures, a bias for action, being close to the customers, being innovative, being value driven, and giving their staff autonomy in decision making. 'In fact', Peters and Waterman state, 'we wonder whether it is possible to be an excellent company without clarity on values' (1982: 280).

They were not alone in this interest in culture. Indeed since the late 1970s academics and consultants such as Deal and Kennedy (1982), and Geert Hofstede (1991) all argued that organizational culture is central to firms' success. For instance, '[t]o be successful', Tichy argues, 'a company's culture needs to support the kind of business the organization is in and its strategy for handling that business' (1982: 71). As Cameron and Quinn have argued recently, 'Virtually every leading firm you can name, small or large, has developed a distinctive culture that is clearly identifiable by its employees' (2006: 4–5).

Indeed, as far back as the 1960s people like Tom Watson Jr, the former President of IBM, claimed that 'in order to survive and achieve success, [organizations] must have a sound set of beliefs on which it premises all its policies and actions' (1963: 5, cited in Posner et al., 1985: 294). He went on to say these beliefs 'must always come before policies, practices, and goals. The latter must always be altered if they are seen to violate fundamental beliefs' (1963: 72–73). Culture and shared values, therefore, were seen as central for organizational success.

Do strong cultures equal strong performance?

Running case: Simon Chance looks at changingculture.info.uk

Simon Chance looks through the changingculture.info.uk website.

'If your people continue to act and think as they now do, will you be able to achieve the results you need? If your answer is no', the website continues, 'then changing your organisational culture is not simply an option—it's essential. Organisational culture', he reads on, 'can be the difference between success and failure, change or stagnation . . . Changing your culture can drive spectacular results by capitalising on your greatest asset, your people . . . You can change the way that people think and act . . . become more competitive and focused . . . be the best in your field . . . To succeed, you must win the hearts and minds of your staff. changingculture.info.uk develop winning corporate cultures with shared beliefs and passion for the organisation where all the energy of the company pulls in the same direction.'

Great stuff, thinks Chance. The staff seem committed but I'm not sure I have won their 'hearts and minds'? Maybe I should give culture change a go.

Go to the online material and follow the links to culture change consultancies. What claims do they make regarding the impact that they can make on organizational performance? How do they claim they make these impacts?

The interest in organizational culture hung on one central claim: that the right culture increased performance. Some very bold assertions were made to support this. Deal and

Kennedy stated 'we estimate that a company can gain as much as one or two hours of productive work per employee per day' (1982: 15). Similarly, Collins and Porras argued visionary companies outperformed non-visionary companies by about 1500% over 64 years (1994). With results like this, it is easy to see why having a strong culture was seen as vital for organizational success.

The right culture, its proponents claim, increases productivity, creates a shared sense of purpose, increases motivation for staff (Peters and Waterman, 1982), commitment (Deal and Kennedy, 1982), reduces conflict, increases the smooth running of the organization, and produces higher levels of productivity, quality, efficiency, and morale (Cameron and Quinn, 2006). Getting the organizational culture right, they claim, produces successful organizations.

There are many cultural change consultancies who make bold claims. Visit the Online Resource Centre for links to some of them. Why do you think they see culture as so important? Do you think the claims are justified?

Indeed, as Cameron and Quinn argue, while anyone can buy machinery, set up and design production processes and distribution networks, what makes successful organizations stand out is having the right culture (2006). This is even truer in service and knowledge-intensive work, which rely almost entirely on their staff for success.

> **Research insight:** Does organizational culture really make a difference?
> Posner, B. Z., Kouzes, J. M., and Schmidt, W. H. 1985. Shared values make a difference: An empirical test of corporate culture. *Human Resource Management* 24(3): 293–309.
>
> With the rising interest in corporate culture, researchers began to look for evidence that it was really making a difference. This early research asked 6,000 managers (of whom 25% replied) about their personal values and expectations, and how they matched the firms they worked for.
>
> They found that where there was **congruence** between personal and organizational values there was less conflict, more ethical decision making, more satisfaction with work, less tension in home lives, reduced anxiety, increased ability to cope with pressure, and increased productivity and commitment. For instance, those with high value congruence were less likely to take a promotion if they felt unsure about their ability to handle the job.
>
> They advised companies to select, train, reward, and counsel new staff in the light of their shared values to maximize the chances of them fitting in. Managing culture they argued, was, therefore, a key responsibility of managers.

Congruence To correspond or match.

From managing machines to managing dreams: a new way to manage organizations

The focus on organizational culture led to considerable hype that organizations would be transformed. These management gurus presented a tantalizing, almost messianic, vision that businesses could be changed from top down, hierarchical control with all the problems of conflict we saw in Chapters 2–4, to one of harmony and productivity, as workers and management come together around shared values.

Theory in context: responding to the rise of Japanese manufacturing

The rising interest in organizational culture occurred at a point when the USA's position as the economic superpower was being challenged by the rise of Japanese firms. For example, Harley Davidson was challenged by Honda's smaller, more efficient bikes (Ouchi, 1981).

The Japanese culture was seen as key in their success. For instance, Peters and Waterman recounted a story of a 'Honda worker who, on his way home each evening, straightens up windshield wiper blades on all the Hondas he passes. He can't stand to see a flaw in a Honda!' (1982: 37). In contrast, some US workers were seen as purposely destructive. For example, one worker described how 'he would go home at night chuckling to himself about the things he had thought up during the day to mess up the system. He'd leave his sandwich behind the door panel of a car, for example . . . Or he would put loose screws in the compartment of the frame that was to be welded shut' (Cameron and Quinn, 2006: 15).

American business dominance was therefore seen as being under threat, with a new recipe for success needed. The interest in organizational culture could be seen as a way that US firms reasserted their dominance and increased confidence, as Deal and Kennedy put it: 'a strong culture has almost always been the driving force behind continuing success in American Business' (1982: 5).

According to this view, managers' roles had to change fundamentally. They no longer simply controlled 'hard' financial measures, structure, and strategy, but needed to manage 'soft', less measurable aspects of visions and values, mission and purpose, unifying the workplace around core values everyone believed in. Table 7.1 presents a summary of these contrasts.

Managing through culture and values presented a new, more innovative and exciting way of managing. As Tom Peters (2001) later put it, 'soft stuff that determines what really gets accomplished and how well it gets done. It turned out to be a revolutionary message'.

Table 7.1 Rational and cultural management (based on Peters and Waterman, 1982)

Rational management	Cultural management
• Hard	• Soft
• Rational argument based on facts and figures	• Emotional appeal through shared values
• Manage through budgets, strategy, and targets	• Managed through shared values and purpose
• Management control imposed on workers via rules and procedures, and systems of accountability	• Workers control themselves through shared beliefs and values
• Formal communication through newsletters, emails, etc.	• Informal communication through symbols and stories
• Use formal authority structures and hierarchy	• Reliance on informal opinion leaders, traditions, accepted practices, and sense of mission
• Control, monitoring, and evaluation	• Trust, commitment, and autonomy

Theory in context: culture producing a new form of worker

Peters and Waterman (1982) argued that managing through culture would produce a radical alternative to the standard bureaucratic model that stressed rules and regulations, carrot and stick motivation. They thought this would be replaced by organizations where freedom and autonomy ruled, governed through a shared sense of values and purpose. This, they claimed, would produce a different type of workplace and with it a new type of worker.

The idea was simple. By releasing the worker from constraints of bureaucratic standardization and giving them something to believe in, the organizational members would be committed to the mission of the organization and work harder as a consequence. 'The individual', so dehumanized by Taylorism, Peters and Waterman (ibid) pronounced, 'still counts'.

Peters and Waterman offered a vision where workers would love their company and believe in its values. Gone was Taylorism with its standardization and uniformity, top-down command, and control management and its repetitive tasks. In its place was a shared sense of vision and values, mission and purpose.

The workers' personalities and individuality, so disliked by Taylor, would be rediscovered and harnessed for the organization's benefit. They thought a new society could be created around individual autonomy and freedom, governed by shared values. As Sewell later commented 'direct control of the labor process is no longer seen as necessarily the most effective way to realize organizational goals' (1998: 401).

Organizational culture therefore promises that the worker can be productive *and* have increased job satisfaction. The conflict between labour and capital, Peters and Waterman argued, is solved as there is no longer a conflict between the workers' interests and that of the organization.

Such a move was needed, its proponents argued, because the nature of society was changing. Since the 1960s respect for authority began to diminish and workers accepted less hierarchical relations. Indeed, Deal and Kennedy argued that the loss of faith in large-scale institutions, such as government and church, meant that 'corporations may be the last institutions in America that can effectively take on the role of shaping values' (1982: 16).

Review questions

Describe

1. What is organizational culture?

Explain

2. What are the key claims about why organizational culture increases performance?

Analyse

3. In what way does managing through culture shift the manager's role?

How to understand culture

Running case: Chance wonders whether cultural change will work at Junction Hotel

Impressed with the claims that changingculture.info.uk make about the importance of organizational culture, Chance decides to delve a little deeper. 'It would be great to get the staff all sharing the same vision of Junction Hotel and all our energy directed towards the hotel a success', he muses.

'The first thing you need to do', he reads on the website, 'is to diagnose what your existing culture is. Take our free self-diagnostic test', the website suggests, 'and find out what your culture is'. OK thinks Chance, it can't do any harm.

Completing the survey, Simon Chance clicks on the result: 'A Role Culture'. 'Umm . . .', thinks Chance. 'I guess so, although I'm not sure it is really like that. Anyway what can I do with this information?' At the end of the result page Chance reads 'if you want more information and to talk through your result phone this number'. He decides to give them a call.

The consultants explain that the culture survey is only a snapshot of the organization and it is only based on his perspective. 'To really understand what is going on', Mark Wickham continues, 'a full survey of the organization is necessary. This will give you a chance to understand how your staff view Junction Hotel'.

A popular way of understanding and trying to change an organization's culture is to use a cultural classification, also known as a typology. These **typologies** are useful in that they provide a way of quickly capturing an overall impression of the organization and allow it to be compared to other organizations. There is no single 'best culture'. Rather, the role of managers is to fit the organizational culture with the external environment.

> Typologies A system of classification of traits that organizations have in common.

Deal and Kennedy's typology

One of the first such models was provided by Deal and Kennedy (1982). They argued that an organization's culture is a product of the environment in which they operate—in particular the amount of risk key activities carry and the speed of feedback that workers receive. For example, a car sales person generally gets quick feedback (someone either buys or does not buy a car), but the risk of a single transaction is fairly small, producing a work hard/play hard culture. If someone works in a government bureaucracy it has a low risk and slow feedback, producing a process culture. Each of these cultures has their own strengths and weaknesses. It is important to match the culture to the right environment.

Table 7.2 The link between culture and feedback (Deal and Kennedy, 1982)

Work hard/play hard	**Tough-guy macho**
• Fun focused • Performance and action driven • Strong customer focus • Small risks • High energy level • Example – sales and manufacturing	• Quick decision making • High risk – all or nothing • Highly driven people • Individualistic • Competitive – low teamwork • Example – stockbrokers, media, sports and construction
Process culture	**Bet-your-company culture**
• Bureaucratic – clear rules that must be followed • Highly regulated • Often need for precision • Status orientated • Takes years to discover if decision was correct • Example – government bureaucracies	• Long-term outlook • High risk and cost decisions but years before outcome is known • High planning, technical expertise and diligence throughout • Examples – pharmaceutical firm devising a new drug, oil companies

Left axis (top to bottom): Fast — Speed of feedback — Slow

Bottom axis: Low ———— Degree of risk ———— High

Based on Deal, T. and Kennedy, A., *Corporate Cultures: The Rites and Rituals of Corporate Life* (1982). Reproduced by permission of Perseus Books.

Real life case: stockbrokers in a tough-guy macho culture

The financial markets have received considerable attention over the last few years as people have tried to make sense of what caused the financial crisis that hit much of the world in 2008. Some commentators (e.g. Dewatripont and Xavier, 2012; Wilson, 2012) have begun to criticize those who work in 'the City' (of London) and Wall Street (in America) of taking too many risks. They have argued that they take a very short-term approach, gamble unnecessarily with other people's money, and claim bonuses far beyond their true value.

The macho world of the financial markets.

What happened in 2008 would not have been a shock to those that had followed the numerous exposés of the City in recent years. Films, such as Oliver Stone's *Wall Street*, and books, such as Michael Lewis' (1989) *Liar's Poker* and Venetia Thompson's (2010) *Gross Misconduct*, have portrayed working in the City as a high-risk, adrenaline-fuelled, masculine environment where 'greed is good'.

Dealing with millions of pounds of trade of stocks and shares, bonds, and other complex financial products, life in the City is highly stressful, with millions potentially lost in a single day. It is, therefore, high-risk and fast-feedback, producing a *tough-guy macho culture*. Thompson (2010: 54) states the 'broking floor is arguably the most aggressive, male-dominated environment that anyone could work in. Brokers often have to communicate by shouting to be heard above everyone else. Swearing at each other and smashing things is accepted – not officially, of course, but if a broker smashes a phone, no one notices'. ◗

> She also states the work had a strong social element where avoiding 'drinking at lunchtime was virtually impossible' (ibid: 55). As gaining clients was vital to the success of a broker, entertaining them was an essential activity. 'Getting [the powerful clients] to agree to spend an evening with you, or maybe even a weekend, was therefore a contest in itself, with different brokers competing to secure the best clients for the best events. They had seen and done it all before and had the same jaded reaction, even if you offered a VIP helicopter trip to the Monaco Grand Prix' (ibid: 57–58).

Visit the Online Resource Centre for an extended profile of stockbroker culture.

Which of Deal and Kennedy's cultural typologies do you think that stockbrokers fit? To what extent do you think the culture might explain the action of large banks and their role in the financial crisis?

Charles Handy's typology

Another typology is offered by Charles Handy in his book *Gods of Management* (2009). Handy argues that organizations should try to match their type of culture to the external needs of the organization. Again, he offered the following four cultural categories (based on Handy, 2009):

Power culture
- Power and decision making concentrated on the centre, e.g. founder/manager
- Control of centre becomes weaker as firm grows, so normally split into subdivisions
- Tough and competitive environment
- Few set rules, as is more about power and choosing people who think in similar ways
- *Examples*—family firms, new businesses, and small entrepreneurs

Task culture
- Focus on getting the job done
- Temporary project teams to meet task needed, then disbanded
- Expertise is central
- Control through allocation of people and resources
- *Examples*—project management, construction, and advertising

Role culture
- Bureaucracy in its purest form
- Roof—senior management decision making
- Pillars—functional units
- Staff do their roles
- Authority based on position in hierarchy
- Predictable

- Works well in predictable environments, but is difficult to adapt to change
- *Examples*—civil service and high street banks

Personal or cluster culture
- Consensus-management and power is shared
- Individual freedom is key
- Exist for the members
- No collective goal
- Reject formal hierarchies
- *Examples*—self-help groups and architect partnerships

Quinn and Rohrbaugh's competing values framework

Our final framework was developed by Quinn and Rohrbaugh (1983; see Cameron and Quinn, 2006) and is used to assess not only organizational culture but leadership, communication, and employee selection. Like the other frameworks, it divides culture into four distinct types. The key dimensions on the horizontal axis are if the organization is inward-focused on the organization or outward, in favour of customers. The vertical axis shows whether the control is with management (at the bottom) or autonomy is with the staff (at the top). Each of the four therefore represent opposite sets of assumptions.

Table 7.3 Competing values framework

	Flexibility and discretion	
Internally-focused and integrated	**Clan (late 1960s onwards)** • Like a family organization • Shared values and cohesion • Teamwork and employee empowerment, friendly place to work • Customers are partners • Leaders mentors/parent figures Example PeopleExpress	**Adhocracy (information age)** • Ad hoc—temporary and specialized, disbands when the task is complete • No centralized power—power flows from individual to individual • Emphasis on individuality and risk-taking and creativity Examples software development, think-tanks
	Hierarchy (from 1900 onwards) • Bureaucratic culture • Clear lines of decision making • Stable and efficient • Standardized rules and procedures with no discretion • Environment is stable • Leaders are good organizers Examples McDonalds or Ford	**Market (from 1960s onwards)** • The organization functions as a market with competition • Aims to reduce transaction costs • Profit is key; highly results-orientated • Meeting customers' needs • Customers competitive for best price • Leaders are highly competitive Example General Electric
	Stability and control	Externally-focused and differentiated

Adapted from Cameron and Quinn (2006).

It is interesting to note that these cultures also reflect the organizational structure (see Chapter 2) as they involve how decisions are made and how power operates within the organization.

Cultural typologies assessed

Cultural typologies are popular as they provide a quick way of capturing what an organization is like, its strengths and weaknesses, and comparing it to other organizations. However, they should be treated with caution.

They tend to generalize rather than provide specific descriptions of a particular organization. Organizations do not necessarily fit neatly in these categories and in seeking to apply these typologies in a rigid way can lose some of the unique features of that particular organization. These typologies also focus predominantly on the more structural elements of the culture and therefore might miss the more mundane, everyday aspects of organizational life. Their accuracy also depends on the ability of the individual in successfully understanding the culture and matching it to the framework. Finally, they present organizations as having a unified, homogeneous culture and thus miss some of the subtleties between departments or different sites. They therefore provide a useful frame of reference but should only be used as a starting point for analysis.

Visit the Online Resource Centre and complete the culture diagnostic test for an organization you know well. How well do you think it represents the organization?

Review questions

Describe

1. What is a typology?

Explain

2. How might a manager use a cultural typology?

Analyse

3. What are the weaknesses of typologies?

Edgar Schein's cultural iceberg

Schein sees culture like an iceberg, with much occurring below the surface (Figure 7.1). The things near the top are the easiest to change, but have the least significance. The further one goes down the iceberg the deeper ingrained the culture is and the less conscious the participants are of it. These levels are harder to change but have greater impact.

At the top are physical artifacts, such as the building or staff uniforms. They express certain aspects of the culture, but are open to interpretation by the observer. The middle layer

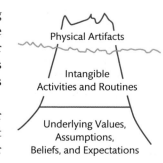

Figure 7.1 Schein's cultural iceberg.

© Schein, *Organizational Culture and Leadership*, 2010, John Wiley & Sons Inc.

Table 7.4 Schein's cultural iceberg (based on Schein, 2010)

Level	Description	Examples	Analysis	Ability to change
Artifacts	What one sees and hears	Physical environment Language Technology Clothing Emotional display Myths and stories about the organization	Visible, but hard to decipher Cannot rely on alone as observer will project their own feelings and reactions	Relatively straightforward but also fairly superficial and therefore not going to change the culture dramatically
Espoused beliefs and values	Beliefs and key practices spoken initially by leader/founder and then validated by the group	What people say in particular situations Mission statements Strategies and goals	Stated assumptions shared by the group Often leave many aspects of behaviour unexplained	The leader can change this level and is good at training new members how to behave
Basic underlying assumptions	Regular solution to a problem, it becomes taken for granted. Preferred solution, any other option inconceivable	Values that guide behaviour Values shared and therefore reinforced Fundamental aspects of life, human nature, nature of truth, importance of family, work, and self-development, etc.	Unconscious and taken for granted that are not discussable. Anything that challenges this produces defence mechanisms	Very difficult to change as are often unconscious and completely taken for granted

© Schein, *Organizational Culture and Leadership*, 2010, John Wiley & Sons Inc.

Intangible Something that you cannot touch.

represents the **intangible** beliefs or values of the organization. Schein believes that these often start from the founder or leader and are passed on to the organizational members through mission statements or strategy. The deepest level holds the strongly held values. Changing them can result in anxiety and defence mechanisms, but 'unless one digs down to the level of the basic assumptions one cannot really decipher the artifacts, values, and norms' (Schein, 2010: 59).

Changing culture is, therefore, a complex process. Because much of culture is unconscious it can be hard to change; however, this is not to suggest that it is impossible to change. Schein argues that by following a ten-step process, cultures can be understood in a single day (2010: 348) and begin changing quickly after that.

Changing culture—a recipe for success

Owing to its importance to organizational performance, many cultural change consultants offer step-by-step guidelines to change culture by:

- diagnosing the current culture
- deciding what needs changing
- transforming the culture to its new way of operating
- entrenching the new culture in the way that the organization works.

The underlying assumption is that culture is management's property, to be controlled and used to enhance performance.

> **Research insight:** Practical guides to changing organizational culture, Cameron, K., and Quinn, R. E. 2006. *Diagnosing and changing organizational culture*. Jossey Bass, London.
>
> Cameron and Quinn offer a popular, and quite practical, guide to changing organizational culture. They offer a range of tools, such as questions, surveys, and instruments for organizational managers to diagnose and change their organization's culture. They offer a framework in which managers can understand the basic assumptions and communication style within the organization.
>
> Their key tips include:
>
> - identifying what can be changed easily
> - changing it and then publicizing it
> - identifying illustrative stories of the type of culture you want to produce
> - measuring change so people know what to focus on
> - holding a funeral for the past approach of the organization and celebrating that past
> - focusing on process.
>
> As we will see in Chapter 11, this approach is quite simple and it is questionable whether change can occur in such a linear approach.

Schein provided an alternative model of changing organizational culture—the ten-step approach, which is outlined in Table 7.5.

Table 7.5 Schein's ten-step approach to changing organizational culture (based on Schein, 2010)

Stage	Heading	Description
1	Obtaining leadership commitment	Changing the culture is a major undertaking, therefore the leadership need to be committed
2	Selecting groups for interviews	Consultant works with leadership to select representative groups, including **subcultures**
3	Selecting an appropriate setting for the group interviews	Comfortable setting with the right equipment
4	Explaining the purpose of the meeting	Leadership set out the key purpose Outside consultant introduced
5	A short lecture on how to think about culture	Explain cultural iceberg and the importance of the organization's history
6	Eliciting descriptions of the artifacts	Ask most recent employee what it felt like entering the organization. All members contribute. Look at issues such as dress code, way of addressing the boss, how people get rewarded (takes about an hour)
7	Identifying espoused values	The consultant explores why they do what they do. Aim is to elicit statements that are commonly agreed (takes about an hour)

© Schein, *Organizational Culture and Leadership*, 2010, John Wiley & Sons Inc.

Subculture A localized culture with its own set of values and behaviours that reflects, but is distinct from, the wider culture.

Table 7.5 (*cont'd*)

Stage	Heading	Description
8	Identifying shared tacit assumptions	Taking the artifacts and espoused values and pushing deeper, particularly where the practices contradict the conscious values (1–2 hours)
9	Identifying cultural aids and hindrances	Break into subgroups and refine understanding of steps 6–8 Explore whether the culture aids or hinders the problem the organization is trying to address
10	Reporting assumptions and joint analysis	Aim for consensus on what is important and implications for what the organization wants to do. Aim to get as clear a view as possible, then explore how to manage culture to achieve the organization's aims (half a day minimum)

(Adapted from Schein, 2010: 340–348)

While there are many models that claim to be able to change culture, as we will see in the following sections, in practice, culture is often more complicated than these recipe book approaches suggest.

The manager changing culture: the role of founders and organizational leaders

Running case: cultural change report

To: s.chance@junctionhotel.net
From: m.wickham@changingculture.info.uk
Subject: Culture change at Junction Hotel – Report
Junction Hotel Current Culture Report

Dear Mr Chance

Many thanks for choosing *changingculture.info.uk*. We are delighted to attach your full report for Junction Hotel's corporate culture. We had a good response rate for the survey, with 73% of staff taking part. The full report gives extensive detail about the culture, but the headline issues are:

- only 23% of staff could name Junction Hotel's mission statement and most of them were managers
- 37% of staff felt that they identified with the hotel
- 76% felt that they enjoyed being part of the hotel
- 27% felt that they were listened to.

Getting the right culture can mean long-term success for your firm, a more committed workforce, higher productivity, and increased job satisfaction. I suggest that we arrange a meeting next week to discuss what contribution *changingculture.info.uk* can offer Junction Hotel.

With very best wishes

Mark Wickham PhD,
changingculture.info.uk – bringing cultural change to UK business, for profits and people

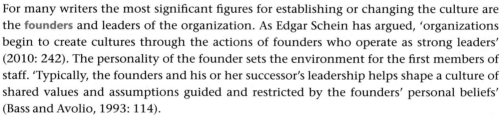

Chance looks at the email in shock—this was not the result he was expecting. He had always thought that people valued working at Junction Hotel and that they shared the same vision, but the survey results seem to be saying something altogether different. He calls in Linda Wilkinson for a chat as she has the ear of the staff.

'What do you think of this, shocking isn't it—don't the staff care?', asks Chance. 'I think . . .' stammers Wilkinson, 'that they value the organization, but not in the same way that you do'. 'Oh', Chance responds somewhat indignantly, 'what do you mean?'. Wilkinson looks up at him. 'Well, sometimes' she responds hesitantly, 'we don't always include them in what we do'. 'So what are you saying?' Chance asks positively. 'That we need a strong shared culture?' Linda looks back somewhat quizzically, 'Yes something like that', she says.

Visit the Online Resource Centre to read the full report.

For many writers the most significant figures for establishing or changing the culture are the **founders** and leaders of the organization. As Edgar Schein has argued, 'organizations begin to create cultures through the actions of founders who operate as strong leaders' (2010: 242). The personality of the founder sets the environment for the first members of staff. 'Typically, the founders and his or her successor's leadership helps shape a culture of shared values and assumptions guided and restricted by the founders' personal beliefs' (Bass and Avolio, 1993: 114).

As the firm grows, the founder's ability to directly influence the staff might diminish, but their influence is often sustained through stories and myths about their actions. These stories can provide the organization with a sense of history, purpose, and a framework within which to operate (see the following sections for more discussion on the power of stories). Founder's stories provide powerful ways to communicate the values of the organization and give the company a sense of tradition and purpose.

> **Founder** The person who established the organization.

Real life case: founders' stories

For some firms the way in which they were founded has taken on almost mythical status. Bill Hewlett and Dave Packard, the founders of Hewlett Packard (HP), one of the world biggest information technology firms and the founders of 'silicon valley', began life in a humble garage. They were innovative in their products and management approach, creating a decentralized and egalitarian system, which has become known as 'the HP way' (Hewlett Packard, 2012):

1. We have trust and respect for individuals.
2. We focus on a high level of achievement and contribution.
3. We conduct our business with uncompromising integrity.
4. We achieve our common objectives through teamwork.
5. We encourage flexibility and innovation.

Both Hewlett and Packard were highly innovative, with a focus on profits, but also charitable activity (giving most of their fortunes away to charity). However in recent times, some have claimed that HP has lost its way (Burrows 2003 and Malone 2007). HP, they claim, has lost its focus on innovation and workers are scolded for working late (Bandler and Burke, 2012). Indeed their new CEO, Leo Apotheker argued that 'HP has lost its soul' (Yarrow, 2011).

How leaders can change culture

Running case: Chance looks for solutions

'So what can we do about this?', enquires Chance of Wickham, the culture consultant. 'Our staff do not seem to share the same passion for Junction Hotel as I do. I thought it was obvious what we stand for', Chance continues. 'We need a few quick hits', Wickham suggests. 'You need to put across your vision for the hotel, show the staff what is important. You are the most important person in the organization. They will follow you.'

Although the organizational founder certainly has significant influence, as they leave or the organization grows, their influence diminishes and the organization's managers gain more influence. In Edgar Schein's (2010: 257) words, leaders 'create the conditions for culture formation'. Similarly, Bass and Avolio (1993: 113) claim 'The characteristics and qualities of an organization's culture are taught by its leadership and eventually adopted by its followers'. Indeed, as Selznick argues, leaders can be seen as the embodiment of organizational values (cited in Schein, 2010).

Schein argues that, given the influence of the leaders, they have to be consistent in their actions otherwise their influence on their followers is diminished. He suggests that they have the following tools to change culture:

Primary Embedding Mechanism
- What leaders pay attention to, measure, and control on a regular basis
- How leaders react to critical incidents and organizational crises
- How leaders allocate resources
- Deliberate role modelling, teaching, and coaching
- How leaders allocate rewards and status
- How leaders recruit, select, promote, and excommunicate

Secondary Articulation and Reinforcement Mechanisms
- Organizational design and structure
- Organizational systems and procedures
- Rites and rituals of the organization
- Design of physical space, facades, and buildings
- Stories about important events and people
- Formal statements of organizational philosophy, creeds, and charters   (Schein, 2010: 246)

Quinn (1984, see Cameron and Quinn, 2006) argues it is important that the leadership style matches the culture in the competing values framework as otherwise they will not be effective.

One of the most powerful ways that leaders can influence their culture is through symbolic acts and powerful stories. These stories have powerful effects in that they transmit the values that the leaders hold and communicate to members what they deem important. As

Smirich and Morgan argue, 'Through words and images, symbolic actions and gestures, leaders can structure attention and evoke patterns of meaning that give them considerable control over the situation being managed' (1982: 263). 'The reason culture is important is because top management can directly influence culture through activities and symbols' (Daft 1986: 486). In other words, leaders, through their actions, can shape the culture of the organization.

Hierarchy	• Coordinator • Organizer • Administrator
Adhocracy	• Entrepreneur • Innovator • Risk-taker
Market	• Decisiveness • Production • Achievement
Clan	• Participative mentor • Facilitator • Parent-figure

(based on Cameron and Quinn, 2006)

Changing layout, changing cultures

Running case: a tour of Junction Hotel

Mandy leads Sue through a tour of Junction Hotel. 'This, obviously, is the front of house. You'll get a chance to meet the girls later—we're a friendly bunch.' Sue notices a computer—which must be for booking in—a board with every room number, and a list. 'Oh, that', Mandy says noticing Sue's attention on it, 'that's for the maintenance team'. 'It's all very organized in here,' Sue comments. 'Oh yes, we like to keep on top of things. In here, this is our office—we call it our cubby-hole. It's not much, but we like it.' Sue looks in amazement: a tiny room with no natural light, one desk with an old looking computer, and a couple of mugs of tea. 'We come here for a gossip', Mandy says with a wink.

Continuing on, Sue is shown some of the plush bedrooms, one with a four-poster bed, the dining room with staff busily preparing for the lunchtime meal, and the kitchen, which is incredibly organized with colour-coordinated chopping boards and lists of the week's meals. They then take a right turn through a door which says staff only and up some stairs. The light flickers on the staircase, the carpet is threadbare, and paint is peeling off the walls. Seeing Sue's face Mandy moves to reassure her: 'Oh, this is just a short-cut to the meeting rooms, we don't let customers or the board come in this way'. 'What about us?', Sue wonders. They proceed through what Sue imagines is the staff room, which has a few old magazines in the corner next to the coffee machine. Back through another door, they return to the plush carpet and are faced with a large oak door with the label Simon Chance's Office on it.

In the office, Sue Marshall looks around at the oak-panelled walls and the luxury deep-pile carpet. In the corner Jenny Hyam, Simon Chance's secretary, sits on a small swivel chair in front of a pine veneer desk—'Ikea', thinks Sue as she assesses the scene. Rows of box files, all neatly ordered are on shelves behind Jenny's desk, colour-coded and alphabetically-arranged. Jenny has a picture of her holding a small child—her daughter Sue assumes—in a pretty red dress. Jenny looks over at Sue. 'He won't be long now', she says calmly. 'Mondays are always a busy day for Mr Chance.'

The oak panelling continues throughout the boardroom, which has a large mahogany table in the centre. Looking down on the room are ten austere-looking men captured in oil paintings with plaques beneath giving their names and dates. The door opens and Simon Chance pops his head round. 'You must be Sue', he says shaking her hand firmly, 'pleased to meet you. I would love to stay and chat but we are making a lot of changes at the moment and I am rather busy, but maybe we can catch up at the end of the month—I'd love to hear your views on the place.' And with that the phone rings and he rushes back into his office.

One of the ways managers try to change the culture is to change the physical surroundings. 'The workspaces themselves usually reflect the style and personality of the organization' (Turner and Myerson, 1998: 1). The design and layout reflect the culture that the organization wants to project to the outside world. It also reflects 'who and what is valued in the organization. For example, arranging offices by rank so that the highest-level executives occupy the top floor(s) and/or the largest and most nicely appointed office space (e.g., corner offices with large windows) and lower-level employees occupy successively lower floors and smaller offices, conveys the message that the organization places a high value on status' (Ornstein, 1989: 145). Overall, the 'Office design might best be analyzed as symbols produced by organizational cultures' (Hatch, 1992: 143).

For instance, the change to open plan is argued by some to lead to greater bonding, team-work, and communication (Ornstein, 1989). However, open plan offices can also lead many staff to feel resentment as such offices produce increased noise and staff sometimes have concerns about loss of status and privacy (Tierney, 2012 and Frontczak et al., 2012).

Real life case: office design in action

Firms like Google present themselves as having bright, colourful, and exciting layouts which enhance creativity, communication, and staff well-being (Google, 2012a). Their virtual tour shows that their offices have features such as bean-bags, good food, table football, an indoor bike lane, yurts and huddle rooms, a climbing wall, and outdoor seating.

Corporate status symbols.

Merchant Banks present very different cultures. They often favour high-rise office blocks, which are often signs of status—for instance, the Burj Khalifa building is the tallest in the world. These images, it can be argued, express the power and authority with status linked to the highest offices. The present a highly formalized, corporate culture stressing trustworthiness, wealth, and power.

Mission statements

It was Mark Wickham from changingculture.info.uk on the phone.

'Do your staff know your values?', asks Wickham inquisitively. 'No, not really', reflects Chance, 'we have a mission statement, but never really communicate it'. 'Then I suggest that you teach your staff your mission statement', Wickham replies. 'This is the best way to get across what your vision of Junction Hotel is. Without a clear vision many firms fail.'

Thinking through this suggestion Chance decides to make the mission statement the central focus of the Wednesday morning team meeting. He wants to make the hotel an upbeat, positive place where people feel good about coming to work and provide a really high quality service.

Wednesday morning team meeting

The restaurant is packed as every member of Junction Hotel had been called in to listen to what Chance has labelled 'mission day'.

'Junction Hotel is a great place to work. It is full of exceptional people with a passion for what they do', Chance begins almost evangelically. 'We have a top class chef, excellent front-of-house team, fantastic support staff, and quality cleaners. But, we do not always work together and see the big picture. So, today I am unveiling our new mission—Gold Standard Service. This will make Junction Hotel stand out from the competition.' Standing in front of the flip chart he unveils the mission statement and stands back to let the staff read it:

Junction Hotel aims to be the hotel of choice because of we completely satisfy our guests.

Through a gold standard service we are committed to making your stay a pleasant experience by making a difference every day.

We aim to continually improve our service and go the extra mile for all our guests.

Covering the tables with big sheets of paper, Chance asks each department's team leader to facilitate a session to think about how they need to change how they work to meet the Gold Standard Service Mission. 'It is important', Chance states, 'that everyone is on board with the mission and knows how they personally, and how Junction Hotel collectively, can meet it. These documents will be fed back to the group via the new monthly newsletter—Junction News.'

Chance ends the team meeting with everyone repeating the mission statement. He says that it will be put up on notice boards and at the start of the next meeting he will pick one member of staff from random to repeat back the mission in front of everyone.

Josh

Just sat through a ridiculous meeting where Chance made us repeat our mission statement over and over again. I felt like we were braying donkeys.

2 seconds ago via Android Like Comment

Do you know the mission statement of your university or the place that you work? Have you ever been told it? How did you react to it?

Mission statements are often presented as one of the key tools for senior managers to change the 'espoused beliefs' of organizational members (level 2 on Schein's iceberg). They became popular during the latter half of the 1980s and are now an almost obligatory feature of most organizations.

Mission statements offer senior management an opportunity to define explicitly the purpose of the organization (Drucker, 1974) and create a vision that all stakeholders (shareholders, employees, customers, and the general public) can buy into. This vision should be uplifting and, by doing so, it is claimed, provide an opportunity for the organization to improve its public image, increase the commitment of the employees, and for senior management to assert their authority over the organization. Finally, mission statements provide a common language for the organization.

Real life case: mission statements

Google's mission is 'to organize the world's information and make it universally accessible and useful' (Google, 2012b).

Starbucks' mission statement is 'to inspire and nurture the human spirit—one person, one cup, and one neighbourhood at a time' (Starbucks, 2012).

The Trades Union Congress (TUC)'s mission statement is to 'be a high-profile organisation which campaigns successfully for trade union aims and values, assists trade unions to increase membership and effectiveness, cuts out wasteful rivalry and promotes trade union solidarity' (TUC, 2008).

The Adidas group strives to be the global leader in the sporting goods industry with brands built on a passion for sports and a sporting lifestyle (Adidas, 2010).

Look up a few mission statements on the Internet and explore what the most common themes are. Would these mission statements inspire you?

One of the important outcomes of developing mission statements is for the senior management to discuss and agree the core organizational objectives. This process forces them to step back from everyday activity and define the purpose of the organization. At times this involves settling competing visions of the organization and setting objectives for the future. Mission statements often state not only business objectives (such as being number one in their field), but also the ethical stance of the organization; many companies stress how they are making a contribution to society. As a consequence mission statements generally are written in uplifting language with the aim of inspiring.

While mission statements have been highly popular with senior management they are not always accepted by the employees. Sometimes many of the employees simply pay lip service to them or do not treat them seriously (Bart, 1997).

Review questions

1. Describe some of the key ways in which managers can try to control culture.

2. Explain why mission statements have become popular.

Rites, rituals, and ceremonies

Running case: Chance welcomes the new recruit

Ending the meeting, Simon Chance looks across at Sue. 'Thank you everyone. As some of you will be aware we have a new member of the Junction Hotel family with us today, I am sure you will join me in our customary greeting', at which point they burst out clapping. 'We also can congratulate Sam, who has been here 25 years as one of our receptionists.' 'You get less for murder!', Effingham shouts out to some people's amusement. 'It is my pleasure', continues Chance undeterred, 'to offer her our Junction Hotel commemorative plaque and a special meal for two at our expense.' Again, everyone claps.

Deeper aspects of the culture are expressed through rites, rituals, and ceremonies. These are formal events, such as the graduation ceremony to mark completion of your degree, or informal activities, such as initiation ceremonies that members of a team do to each other. Rites, rituals, and ceremonies all play an important role in creating and reinforcing an organization's culture.

A **rite**, according to Trice and Beyer, is a 'Relatively elaborate, dramatic, planned set of activities that consolidate various forms of cultural expressions into one event, which is carried out through social interactions, usually for the benefit of an audience' (1984: 655). In other words, rites are events which express important parts of the culture.

> **Rite** A solemn act or procedure to observe an event or occasion.

They describe a number of rites which include *rites of passage*, which occur when someone passes from one life stage to another. For instance Trice and Beyer describe how new army recruits 'receive uniforms and severe haircuts, are taught to make their beds in a ritualized fashion, learn to salute and march, are repeatedly humiliated and told to behave differently than in the past, and are generally stripped of past identities and statuses' (1984: 658).

Another is the *rites of renewal*, which act to reinforce existing social order. For instance, a team-building day helps team members refocus and *renew* their commitment to each other.

The *right of conflict reduction* exists to preserve harmony where there is potential conflict. For instance, union and management negotiate for a pay deal where, publically, each side has tough negotiating stances but, privately, both sides know what the outcome will be. In this situation both 'sets of bargainers may know pretty well throughout the negotiations what the final settlement will be' (Trice and Beyer, 1984: 661–62), but put on an act for their supporters to show that they are tough negotiators.

Our final example is *rites of integration*. These occur to make everyone feel part of the group. For instance, the office Christmas party, where everyone eats and drinks together symbolizing togetherness and organizational members make a special effort to talk to people they normally avoid and 'Otherwise deviant behaviors, such as the acting out of sexual and other attractions, are sanctioned. Such occasions thus provide a break from the strict codes of behavior normally enforced, and they tend to reassert the importance and rightness of these codes by the clearly temporary and exceptional basis on which the usual prohibitions have been lifted' (Trice and Beyer, 1984: 663). However, as Bell and King (2010) point out, some of these rites of integration can equally exclude certain individuals and groups, reinforcing existing power relations and masculine values.

Ceremonies Ceremonies are a formal and symbolic way of celebrating the organizational key values and provide senior management with the opportunity to publically support actions they think are positive.

Universities have many formal ceremonies, such as graduation, when students have finished their degree, inaugural lectures for a new professor, and annual dinners at academic conferences at which people give speeches. In companies, ceremonies are often held as retirement dinners, formal celebrations of promotion, and people winning employee of the month awards.

Unlike planned events, such as ceremonies, **rituals** are more like habits that most members do without thinking. As Ott states, rituals 'are the mundane, systematic, stylized, programmed routines of daily organizational life that tell an alert observer about an organizational culture' (1989: 36).

While they often start for particular purposes '[f]requently, the meanings and purposes of powerful rites and rituals are forgotten and take on lives of their own' (Ott, 1989: 37) and become solely of symbolic importance. They are ways for management to be socialized (i.e. taught to see the world), for employees to know how to behave, and for what is seen as important.

Ceremonies A public act, often planned and formal, which celebrates a particular event, achievement, or anniversary, largely planned by senior management or part of the organization's established calendar. They often have symbolic meaning that emphasizes important aspects of the organization's culture.

Rituals Everyday habits that individuals do without thinking which once had meaning but have gradually become part of the everyday activities of the organization.

Real life case: culture in the banking industry

Paul Moore, former head of Group Regulatory Risk at HBOS said that prior to the credit crunch of 2008 there was a huge focus on targets and a culture of fear if you did not hit them. There was an allegation that one manager created a cash or cabbage competition. If you hit your targets you would get cash put on your desk on a Saturday morning, if you missed them then he would put a cabbage on it—cash or cabbage, in public, every Saturday.

Sources: BBC (2009); Heffernan (2011); and Goodley (2012).

The taste of failure?

How do you think you would feel if you received cash or a cabbage on your desk? What symbol does it give out to the traders? How much have such practices, and the culture it supported, contributed to the financial crash?

Informal or **unofficial** ceremonies, rites, and rituals are done largely between employees and are often tolerated, sometimes condemned, and regularly unknown to management.

Informal or Unofficial culture Culture that is often not known or supported by management but one that many of the employees share. It can be in opposition to official, management-led culture.

A regular informal rite of passage is the initiation ceremony that new recruits are expected to undergo to join an organization. They sometimes involve fairly extreme activities, such as drinking a lot of alcohol or doing something humiliating in front of the rest of the group. These initiation ceremonies are displays of strength and endurance, but can also be practices to humiliate the new recruit and, through this, stress the importance of belonging to the group. They often can be used as ways that workers can express their own culture in opposition to management. For instance, some of our students have told us that members of the university rugby team all go out in their 'speedos' on nights out.

Real life case: student initiation ceremonies

Over the last few years a number of scandals of unofficial UK university student initiation ceremonies have hit the headlines. Stories have come out of students having to drink 30 units of alcohol within 3 hours as part of a university rugby team initiation; those joining the Ferretz, an inter-collegiate (Cambridge) drinking society, have to consume 80 units, beginning with a bottle of gin and finishing with a bottle of port, consumed through a condom; having to eat a 15-course meal with delicacies such as a pig's snout with wasabi sauce and a pint of water with a goldfish swimming inside; and playing vomiting games while saluting an older student dressed in what looks like a Nazi uniform.

As one former student, Natalie Sutton, recalls of her initiation: 'We were told to prepare "bucket juice"—an intoxicating mixture of beer, spirits, alcopops, and wine. We were given OXO cubes to suck as we were paraded, singing and chanting, around the neighbourhood' (BBC News, 2008). Elsewhere another student states that they had to 'eat their own vomit' (Courier Online, 2011).

Sporting clubs and societies often have quite challenging initiation ceremonies. For instance the University of York hockey club initiation ceremony was reported to include having to 'down drinks mixed with dog food and goldfish' (York Vision, 2010). Northumbria University rugby union members have reported being 'systematically humiliated' in a 'team-building exercise'. They claim they had to 'drop their trousers and do press-ups' whilst 'a crowd of people watched from the Students' Union' (Courier Online, 2011). The University of Gloucestershire's hockey team members had 'raw fish . . . stuffed down our bras and we were told to eat a nausea-inducing mixture of cat food, eggs, and breakfast cereal topped with Bovril' (BBC News, 2008). What many participants describe as most troubling is that whilst they did not enjoy the process they completed it without question.

Have you been involved in any initiation ceremony? If so did you feel you had to take part? Did you feel more part of the group afterwards?

While writing this chapter we have been told of stories of where a new recruit in a food processing factory was told to go to the chiller to look for a 'black pudding' and then received a 'good kicking' from Harry, a well-built member of the production team. A student told us about working in a kitchen and how each new waiter would 'get showered' (having a bucket of water poured over their head) by the head waiter. A former nuclear power worker at Sellafield has told us how new recruits used to have their clothes taken away when they went through the showers for the first time and had to walk home in their new uniform.

> **Research insight:** Life in a slaughterhouse, Ackroyd, S., and Crowdy, P. 1990. Can culture be managed? Working with raw material: The case of the English slaughtermen. *Personnel Review* 19(5): 3–13.

In a fascinating, and at times graphic, account, Ackroyd and Crowdy (1990) describe the culture of an abattoir. They found the slaughtermen regularly performed practical jokes on each other, such as filling the boots of someone they considered to be working too hard with blood, at room temperature, so the worker did not notice until they had walked in them all day.

Working with 'raw' material.

The slaughtermen also sprayed blood on their clothes and refused to use the showers. This was in direct defiance of the instructions of management, who stressed the importance of health and safety, and good hygiene. As Ackroyd and Crowdy demonstrate, this was to create a subculture—or what we might see as a counter-culture (a culture in direct opposition to the management)—born out of a strong sense of togetherness and common identity as slaughtermen.

Their case demonstrates the challenges of management in changing culture, a theme we will return to in the following section.

Informal culture

Only joking: the power of stories and jokes

> **Running case:** Sue is warned about Effingham
>
> The meeting ends and Sue goes for coffee with the other receptionist. 'Who was the guy who made the joke about getting longer for working here than murder?', she enquires. 'Oh, that will be Effingham', pipes up Mandy. 'Watch out for him. I don't know if this is true but he once killed a chicken with his bare hands.' 'Really?, Sue replies in a shocked tone. 'No, not really . . . but I wouldn't put it past him', Mandy says with a smirk.

What hidden messages are in this story?

Have you ever heard someone say 'it's only a joke' when they have just said something that could be seen as an attack on someone else. While what they said before may have been interpreted as a 'dig' or even an attack on someone, claiming it to be 'just a joke' allows the speaker to pass off the seriousness of the comment or responsibility for the comment by saying that it was not meant in a negative way. Jokes, as with stories, can, therefore, allow us to say many 'truths' that we would not be able to get away with directly (Martin, 2001: 92).

Hidden in jokes and stories are messages about how to behave and the values of the organization. Managers and leaders sometimes use them to put across explicit messages about how the company wants to be seen. These are often presented as organizational histories on company websites or stories that an organization's leaders tell about themselves.

More commonly, colleagues tell each other and new recruits stories. They can be seen as informal or non-official messages communicating the values of the workforce (which can be different to those of management).

Stories communicate many things. For instance, they can be about people that have done well—organizational heroes—demonstrating values that the employee should follow. They can also be about villains or scapegoats, which act as warnings to the employee about what is considered bad behaviour. Stories also communicate how the organization sees itself such as being cautious or brave, dynamic or steady. They are also based on certain metaphors, such as the organization as a family, school, or prison (Morgan, 2006) that can express the deep assumptions of the organization (see Chapter 11 for other uses of metaphors). Again, these metaphors will not necessarily be explicit, but can be powerful ways of capturing some of the underlying assumptions of the members of the organization. They are particularly useful for new members to learn the informal rules and expectations of an organization.

Real life case: stories told by organizational leaders

One of the powerful ways in which stories are used involve an organization's leader. Often, these stories not only send messages about the character of the leader, but also emphasize particular values or behaviours that are valued within the organization. Sometimes these stories are told informally to new recruits within the first few weeks of joining the organization. On other occasions they are created by the leader specifically to send a message and told at set-piece events (e.g. in speeches), in company literature, or by the leader themselves in conversations. Here are two examples expressing quite different messages.

'A common story at Southwest Airlines describes the CEO working on the baggage line on holidays so that employees can take the day off, illustrating the value that customers are number two and employees are number one at Southwest and "positively outrageous service" applies first to fellow employees' (Cameron and Quinn, 2006: 97).

'At the Revlon Corporation the story is told about Charles Revlon, the head of the group, who insisted that employees arrived for work on time, but seldom arrived himself much before noon. One day Charles wandered in and began to look over the sign-in sheet, only to be interrupted by a receptionist who had strict orders that the list should not be removed. Both insisted that they were in the right until, finally, Charles said "Do you know who I am?", and she said, "No sir, I don't". "Well, when you pick up your final paycheck this afternoon, ask 'em to tell ya" . . . The message here is that rules should be strictly obeyed by most people, but do not apply to those of high status, and should not be enforced where they are concerned' (Brown, 1992: 5).

What messages do you feel are contained in these stories? If you heard them how would you act if you worked for one of these organizations?

Jokes, like stories, are a powerful way in which culture can be communicated. They are said (e.g. Wilson, 1979) to produce a positive, harmonious environment in which employees can freely share knowledge and ideas. They can be used to teach employees the right way to behave, e.g. through subtle teasing to indicate when someone acts in the wrong way.

For example, in describing her experience working as a stockbroker, Venetia Thompson states 'Being given a nickname was a rite of passage; whether racist, sexist, homophobic or just insulting, nicknames were willingly accepted by the recipients and thrown around with little thought as to what was actually being said, or whether it was in violation of some code of conduct in the Company handbook' (2010: 51).

Jokes are, therefore, like stories but with the added advantage that they allow us to say things that we would not otherwise be allowed to, acting as a 'licence' for negative communication (Collinson, 1988). Consequently, through the joke certain home truths can be told and they can be used as a tool for staff to get back at management. Humour can thus create counter-cultures and ways to weaken management's authority (Taylor and Bain, 2003).

Research insight: The impact of humour in the workplace, Collinson, D. 1988. Engineering humour: Masculinity, joking and conflict in shop-floor relations. *Organization Studies* 9(2): 181–199.
Collinson, D. (2002) Managing humour. *Journal of Management Studies* 39(3): 269–288.

David Collinson has written widely on the role of humour in the workplace. In these two influential articles he shows how humour is connected to identity, power, control, and resistance. He describes how workers used humour to control each other, reinforcing particular masculine values and attitudes which virtually everyone went along with—even when they did not believe in those values. It was also used as a way of resisting management, for instance by satirizing authority. Collinson shows how difficult it is for management to break into, and change, these strong cultures.

Breaking taboos—the hidden rules of culture

Running case: Sue breaks a cultural taboo

'Do you remember the time he chopped off all those rabbits heads and put them on the top table', recounts Mandy. 'Yep, and when he pulled the guts out of that duck and threw them across the room when Chance walked in', recalls Sam. 'He's a player isn't he', Mandy declares. 'He seems that way with the waitresses as well', Sue pipes up, trying to join in. 'I saw the way he looked at that blonde.' Suddenly, the room goes quiet and Sue goes red knowing that she has said something wrong. Mandy quickly changes the subject.

'What did I say wrong?', Sue asks Mandy when everyone leaves. 'Oh, its nothing dear', Mandy answers, clearly uncomfortable. 'Just be careful . . . the "blonde" is Simon Chance's daughter.'

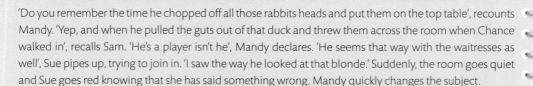

While stories and jokes can give access to the hidden culture, it is only by actually breaking the rules that employees often discover deeper rules. These rules are not actually written down and, indeed, many of the organizational members are not aware that they exist.

Harold Garfinkel has built much of his research on uncovering these rules. In what Garfinkel called 'breaching experiments' he looked at wider cultural rules (throughout society). He asked research participants to breach (step over or break) certain social norms and disrupt shared realities (i.e. the common ways that people think). This is one of Garfinkel's examples:

> The victim waved his hand cheerily.
> (S) How are you?
> (E) How am I in regard to what? My health, my finances, my school work, my peace of mind, my . . . ?
> (S) (Red in the face and suddenly out of control.) Look! I was just trying to be polite. Frankly, I don't give a damn how you are.
>
> (Garfinkel, 1967: 42–44 cited in Feldman, 1995: 10)

Garfinkel's work demonstrates that there are numerous social norms that we often only learn by breaking them. They are important for our understanding of culture in that they allow us access to the hidden, unspoken side of organizational life and the deep values by which the organization operates. Culture, therefore, is not always held in the hands of management, through things like mission statements, and is also not static and fixed. Rather, it can be created continually and recreated through conversations, actions, and meanings expressed by the participants.

Review questions

1. Explain how the underlying values of an organization can be uncovered.
2. Explain what role humour plays in organizational culture.
3. Analyse why the underlying values within an organization are harder to change.

The symbolic side of culture

Running case: Gold Standard Service

Two weeks later.

'Eighty percent of your staff now knows your mission statement', declares Wickham proudly, 'and the Gold Standard Service is ready to be rolled out. How do you feel it is going?'. 'Good, I think we've cracked it', Chance replies feeling that they have achieved his targets.

Most management interventions to change corporate culture focus on the physical surroundings, the espoused (spoken) organizational aims, and stories about the organization's history and actions of the leaders; they rarely go to the deeper parts of the organizational culture (the depths of Edgar Schein's iceberg).

Research insight: Rites, rituals, and ceremonies in practice, Rosen, M. 1985. Breakfast at Spiro's, dramaturgy and dominance. *Journal of Management* 11: 31–48.

In this influential article Michael Rosen provides an excellent account of how these rites of passage, rituals, and ceremonies are played out in practice. He provides a detailed description of the annual 'agency breakfast' for an advertising agency, Spiro's. Held in a luxury hotel all the 'associates' are formally dressed, eating off fine china, being served eggs Benedict by suited waiters—demonstrating an elite image. They listen to speeches which celebrate successes and explain away failure, and celebrate the awards they have won.

Rosen sees this breakfast not simply as an annual gathering, but as an opportunity for management to present certain messages and use symbols to put across key messages. These include being an elite (eating fine breakfasts at a quality hotel—the 'good life' that members aspire to); presenting members with a gift each time they reach five years' working for the company, symbolizing the importance of loyalty; and explicitly stating their values: 'laid-back people have no place in this agency. . . . Drive is what it takes to win. Get drive or get out of the kitchen. . . . I want people who want to win' (1985: 45). Rosen's case demonstrates the importance of being able to read these cultural clues.

To access the deeper parts of the culture requires reaching into areas outside the awareness of most organizational participants (including managers). This involves getting in touch with the symbolic side of organizations—the language, metaphors, and stories. However, culture is also changing constantly and is as much a product of the observer's perception as it is within the organization.

The deepest layer of the culture could be seen as the organization's subconscious. It shapes how organizational members experience the world but they are not always aware of its existence. In order to get to this level of culture, techniques used in psychology and the therapeutic arts are used.

Subcultures and professional cultures

As organizations grow they develop their own subcultures. Subcultures are small groups within the organization that have their own distinctive cultural characteristics, including their own rites and rituals, language, and norms, etc. They can develop informally (social networks) and formally (e.g. departments). In large, multinational corporations they will be based on national differences (see Chapter 15) or different internal histories. Similarly, in chain stores different branches can develop their own distinct cultures based around regional cultures, branch histories, local practices, or the influence of a strong leader. Different departments can have distinct cultures, often produced because of the professions they represent (e.g. accounting might be more cautious than, say, marketing), as well as developing internal histories and cultures.

Real life case: organizational culture at Royal Bank of Scotland

Over the years prior to its near collapse in 2008, the Royal Bank of Scotland grew considerably through buying up other banks and financial institutions not only in the UK, but internationally. The Group spans different business lines (high street and investment banking), as well as different continents (such as Europe, North America and Asia). They also represent different companies with their own backgrounds and histories.

In our interview, Stephen Hester states 'the types of people we have serving customers in our branches in the UK might be completely different from traders sitting in a trading desk in Tokyo' owing to the location, culture, and type of activity. But, he concludes: 'I do not think it is desirable or possible to have a single culture across such a diverse set of inputs. So in the end what you really find is the majority of the culture is specific to the business unit and the geography and its history. Then you have some things that cross businesses and geographies that would be more shared by the senior management team.

Source: Author interview with Stephen Hester, Royal Bank of Scotland, February 2012.

Visit the Online Resource Centre for the full interview with Stephen Hester.

A key reason for subcultures developing is that employees are members of different occupations with their own values and outlooks. As Raelin has argued, many professionals are more loyal towards their profession than the organization they are working for (Raelin, 1986). This can result in a professional being in conflict with the management as their professional objectives might conflict with the specific requirements of the firm. For instance, engineers might be interested in the advancing science, creating an elegant design, or their own pet project, rather than profit for the company. Similarly, in areas like the National Health Service, doctors' aims are often reported (e.g. Robinson, 2012) to be in conflict with a management obsessed with targets. Indeed, management themselves can be considered a subculture with their own language and culture.

The professional or occupational culture is a product of many factors, including the skill, authority, work control, status, and 'education backgrounds, socialization, values, vocational interests, work habits and outlooks' that the employees hold (Raelin, 1986: xiv). The education and professional training that is undergone in order to be equipped to do a job instils certain norms and values that the professional is expected to follow. Newcomers are then informally socialized into the group through meeting with fellow professionals at conferences and networking events, through training, reading trade publications, and the collective identity that the members of these professions share.

Different subcultures can be a challenge for those managing organizations, as they have to work with a range of professionals with their distinct values and ways of looking at the world. In order to be successful the manager needs to understand these different perspectives and find ways to communicate with various subcultures.

Can culture really be managed?

Throughout this chapter we have seen attempts by organizational managers and consultants to categorize, understand, and change culture in order to increase the performance of the organization. They have argued that a strong, i.e. unified, culture performs better, gives the employees a sense of purpose, and increases job satisfaction. However, this view has been heavily criticized.

Merely two years after Peters and Waterman (1982) published their book *In Search of Excellence*, which launched much of business interest in culture, the magazine *Business Week* (1984) printed an article arguing that a third of all Peters and Waterman's 'excellent' companies were now experiencing poor performance. Similarly, many (e.g. Willmott, 1983) have criticized Peters and Waterman's work arguing it lacks conceptual development and did not really investigate the values and beliefs of the staff; rather they took the management rhetoric as true and failed to investigate how it was interpreted by the staff.

Indeed, further questions have been raised recently about the research that underpinned *In Search of Excellence*. In an article for *Fast Company*, Tom Peters states they 'faked the data'. This is not to say they made it all up, but rather than developing a 'scientific' approach, it was developed by gut instinct (Peters, 2001).

Many academics (e.g. Meek, 1988) have argued that the way many of these management gurus have used culture trivializes it by only exploring the aspects that managers can control. They argue that organizational culture is far more complex and richer than simply a tool for management and as a result, the research reduces our understanding of organizations.

Led by Linda Smircich they state the underlying assumption of these mainstream management views is that culture is something the organization *has*, i.e. a possession (1983) that can be changed and controlled. This is from the structural-functionist perspective that aims for unity and consensus (see the Online Resource Centre). Culture is something owned and designed by the top management and available for manipulation (Meek, 1988: 455).

Furthermore, Lynn Meek (1988) has argued that this perspective, while borrowing the language of anthropology, has not used this theory appropriately, has drawn from a very limited range of the literature, and has mutated the theory by over-emphasizing the aspects of unity and control.

The alternative view is that culture is something the organization *is* (Smircich, 1983). This view does not see organizational culture as something separate from the organization

Table 7.6 Culture as something the organization has or is? (Developed from Smircich, 1983.)

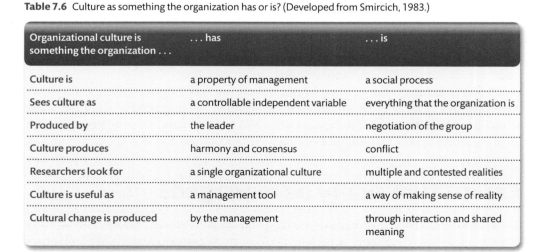

Organizational culture is something the organization . . .	. . . has	. . . is
Culture is	a property of management	a social process
Sees culture as	a controllable independent variable	everything that the organization is
Produced by	the leader	negotiation of the group
Culture produces	harmony and consensus	conflict
Researchers look for	a single organizational culture	multiple and contested realities
Culture is useful as	a management tool	a way of making sense of reality
Cultural change is produced	by the management	through interaction and shared meaning

available for one group (management) to control, but as part of the organization. Culture is thus a root metaphor, a way of looking at the world—everything can be seen as culture. For those of the *is* perspective, culture is not owned by the management: everyone is involved in creating it and no group has power to define it. Rather, it emerges over time and through negotiation (Table 7.6).

The problem of seeing culture as something the organization *has* is emphasized in an account by the academics and business consultants Deal and Kennedy (1984) (who developed the model we saw earlier in the chapter). They describe how after giving a presentation to the board about culture, the chairman claimed it to be the finest presentation he had heard in ten years and then stated to his Chief Executive Officer: ' "George", he said forcefully, "I want a culture installed here next Monday". "With all due respect," we interrupted, "we believe you have a culture here now; that's one of our key points." "Bulls**t!" said the chairman. "We don't have one, and as you pointed out, that's the problem. George, I want a culture here and I want it now—by next week. Your butt is on the line." We left' (1984: 21).

This story illustrates the difficulty of the managerialist perspective. The senior managers thought that culture is something they could simply 'have' and that could be ordered in by the following week, like buying a machine. They failed to see that they already had a culture and, furthermore, that it is not something that management can simply control, but is integral to the fabric of the organization.

Control and resistance

Running case: Is it really Gold Standard?

'Well that was a waste of time', Josh states to Toby on their way out of another Wednesday morning meeting. 'I mean they keep going on about this Gold Standard Service, but I don't see anything different.' 'More than that', says Toby in agreement, 'they keep cutting back on the things that would make a difference to us, like giving more time before serving to get everything ready rather than quizzing us on the mission statement'. Josh smiles at him. 'Well, I pretty-much ignore the whole thing anyway, it's just a fad, it will be a new thing in a couple of weeks—mark my words.'

Hugh Willmott argues that organizational culture is a form of control. By getting employees to believe in the values of the organization and winning their 'hearts and minds', corporate culture, he argues, is 'governance of the employee's soul' (Willmott, 1993: 517) and a way of the employees disciplining themselves. According to Wilmott, because they believe in the organization's mission, employees lose their critical faculties and will accept things that are not in their best interests. Wilmott argues that corporate culture is therefore a way for management to extend their control. Instead of controlling employees' bodies (as in Taylorism—see Chapter 3), corporate culture controls people's hearts, minds, and souls.

Therefore, while organizational culture is presented by its supporters as progressive and more humane (as previously discussed), from this critical perspective it is controlling. The unified culture, presented by those such as Peters and Waterman 'systematically suppresses ideas and practices that might problematize the authority of core corporate values' (Willmott, 1993: 531). Willmott goes on and compares the practices of these strong cultures to totalitarian regimes where alternative perspectives are not tolerated. 'Those who kick against the monoculture [single standardized culture] are "moved sideways" or they are expelled'. As Peters and Waterman put it bluntly: 'The excellent companies are marked by very strong cultures, so strong that you either buy into their norms or get out. There's no halfway house for most people in the excellent companies' (1982: 77).

However, other critical researchers have stressed the ways that employees can resist the overtures of the management and how many do not believe in it. For instance, David Collinson (1992) presents a case study of an engineering firm in the north of England, which was originally a family-run business. The American-run company that has taken over the firm wants to bring about a culture change, from a grimy, complacent, and oppositional culture to one which is more dynamic and based on greater trust and harmony between workers and management. As part of this, they paint the factory walls in a bright white and institute a newsletter. The first newsletter has the headline 'Call Me Barney'—a reference to the new boss's attempt to engender an informal, first-name culture. However, following its publication, a doctored version of the newsletter appeared on the union notice board with the headline 'Bulls**t from Barney' (Collinson, 1992: 13).

Other commentators have also questioned the extent to which employees internalize the culture. They argue that many employees pay lip service to the cultural change programmes and sometimes actively, but often passively, resist the official organizational culture. In other words, they question if employees really believe in these cultural programmes. Professionals, in particular, often believe they have a calling and are thus less likely to tolerate management constraints.

Review questions

1. Explain what the difference is between seeing culture as something the organization is and something it has.

2. Analyse how the view that culture is something the organization is challenges mainstream management thinking.

3. Explain how employees can resist cultural control.

Chapter summary

Organizational culture is presented by many consultants and management academics as a tool that can be used to increase a sense of belonging and commitment to the organization. Its supporters present it as an alternative approach to managing organizations because it moves beyond simply controlling people by telling them what to do, and engages their hearts and minds. Organizational founders, leaders, and managers are seen as central in defining and communicating these values and shaping the way that employees feel and think about the organization. This perspective also stresses the importance of organizational culture as a way of binding together all the members of the organization for a common purpose. Culture is thus something the organization *has* and it *can be managed*.

The opposite perspective argues that culture is something beyond any one individual and is more a product of the group. This perspective emphasizes the collective, shared, and negotiated way in which culture develops. Culture, instead of being something fixed and controlled by managers, is constantly in flux and is interpreted by individual members of the organization. Culture is thus something the organization *is* and *cannot be managed*.

Finally, critical researchers have questioned the social consequences of the cultural change programmes on the well-being of employees. Some see culture as something that controls and conditions employees to the extent that any who resist are excluded. Others have sought to emphasize the way that employees can resist these cultural programmes.

Whichever perspective you take it is widely accepted that culture shapes much of what we say and do, often in ways that we are not conscious of. What organizational culture does demonstrate is that there is much more going on in organizations than we often see on the surface.

Further reading

Schein, E. 2010. *Organizational culture and leadership.* Jossey Bass, San Francisco.
Popular management writer and consultant, Schein provides a good overview of organizational culture from a management viewpoint. He offers ways to understand culture and practical tools to change it.

Peters, T. J., and Waterman, R. H. Jr. 1982. *In search of excellence: Lessons from America's best run companies.* Harper Row, London.
An early, influential book in management circles on the role of culture. Needs to be read with a degree of scepticism given that it has been subject to substantial criticism for both its methodology and findings.

Smircich, L. 1983. Concepts of culture and organizational analysis. *Administrative Science Quarterly* 28(3): 339–358.
This highly influential article provides a rigorous critique of the underlying assumptions of the notion that culture is something that managers can control. Smircich introduces notions from anthropology to offer a richer way of understanding culture.

Willmott, H. 1993. Strength is ignorance; slavery is freedom: Managing culture in modern organizations. *Journal of Management Studies* 30(4): 515–552.
Provides a fascinating critical reading of the corporate culture literature. Willmott argues there is a dark side of organizational culture, as it results in employees disciplining themselves.

Bibliography

Ackroyd, S., and Crowdy, P. 1990. Can culture be managed? Working with raw material: The case of the English slaughtermen. *Personnel Review* 19(5): 3–13.

Adidas. 2010. Corporate Mission Statement. Available at: http://adidas-group.corporate-publications.com/2010/gb/en/group-management-report-our-group/corporate-mission-statement.html (last accessed 24 November 2012).

Allen, R. F., Kraft, C., Allen, J., and Letner, B. 1987. *The organizational unconscious; How to create the corporate culture you want and need.* Human Resources Institute: Englewood Cliffs, NJ.

Alleyne, R. 2009. Shocking Cambridge University initiation ceremonies revealed. The Daily Telegraph, 6 February 2009. Available at: http://www.telegraph.co.uk/education/universityeducation/4538565/Shocking-Cambridge-University-initiation-ceremonies-revealed.html (last accessed 27 June 2012).

Ashby, F.C. 1999. *Revitalize your corporate culture: Powerful ways to transform your company into a high-performance organization.* Gulf Publishing Company: Houston, TX.

Bandler, J., and Burke, D. 2012. How Hewlett-Packard lost its way. CNN Money. Available at: http://tech.fortune.cnn.com/2012/05/08/500-hp-apotheker/

Bart, C. 1997. Sex Lies and Mission Statements. *Business Horizons*, Nov-Dec, 9–18.

Bass, B. M., and Avolio, B. J. 1993. Transformational leadership: A response to critiques. In: Chemers, M. M. (ed.) *Leadership theory and research: Perspectives and directions*. Academic Press: New York.

BBC. 2009. The choice. BBC Radio 4, 3 November 2009 [radio programme].

BBC News. 2008. Initiations: Why I took part in one. Available at: http://news.bbc.co.uk/1/hi/7646891. stm (last accessed 27 June 2012).

Bell, E., and King, D. 2010. The elephant in the room: Critical management studies conferences as a site of body pedagogics. *Management Learning* 41(4): 429–442.

Brown, A. 1992. Organizational culture: the key to effective leadership and organizational development. *Leadership & Organization Development Journal* 13(2): 3–6.

Burrows, P. 2003. *Backfire: Carly Fiorina's high-stakes battle for the soul of Hewlett-Packard*. John Wiley and Sons: Hoboken, NJ.

Business Week. (1984). Oops! Who's Excellent Now? 2867 (5 November). 76–88.

Cameron, K., and Quinn, R. E. 2006. *Diagnosing and changing organizational culture*. Jossey Bass: London.

Collins, J.C., and Porras, J.I. 1994. *Built to last: successful habits of visionary companies*. HarperCollins: New York.

Collinson, D. 1988. Engineering humour: Masculinity, joking and conflict in shop-floor relations. *Organization Studies* 9(2): 181–199.

Collinson, D. 1992. *Managing the shopfloor: subjectivity, masculinity and workplace culture*. de Gruyter: Berlin.

Collinson, D. 2002. Managing humour. *Journal of Management Studies* 39(3): 269–288.

The Courier Online, 2011. Northumbria freshers left intimidated by initiation. Available at http://thecourieronline.co.uk/2011/10/northumbria-freshers-left-intimidated-by-initation/. Last accessed 13 December 2012.

Deal, T. E., and Kennedy, A. A. 1982. *Corporate cultures: The rites and rituals of corporate life*. Penguin Books: Harmondsworth.

Deal, T. E., and Kennedy, A. A. 1984. Tales for the trails: A journey into the existential underbelly of American business. *Hospital Forum*, May–June, 16–26.

Dewatripont, M., and Xavier, F. (eds) (2012). The Crisis Aftermath: New Regulatory Paradigms. Centre for Economic Policy Research: London.

Drucker, P. 1974. *Management: Tasks, responsibilities and practices*. Harper and Row: New York.

Feldman, M. 1995. *Strategies for interpreting qualitative data*. Sage: London.

Frontczak, M., Schiavon, S., Goins, J., Arens, E., Zhang, H., and Wargocki, P. 2012. Quantitative relationships between occupant satisfaction and satisfaction aspects of indoor environmental quality and building design. *Indoor Air*, 22 (2) 119–131.

Frost, P. J., Moore, L. F., Louis, M. R., Lundberg, C. C., and Martin, J. (eds) 1991. *Reframing organizational culture*. Sage: London.

Goodley, S. 2012. HBOS executives 'threatened' colleagues who questioned risk-taking. *The Guardian*. 30 October 2012. Available at: http://www.guardian.co.uk/business/2012/oct/30/hbos-whistleblower-threats-risk-taking?newsfeed=true.

Google. 2012a. Our culture. Available at: http://www.google.co.uk/intl/en/about/company/facts/culture/ (last accessed 26 November 2012).

Google. 2012b. Google's mission is to organize the world's information and make it universally accessible and useful. Available at: http://www.google.com/about/company/ (last accessed 26 November 2012).

Handy, C. 2009. *Gods of Management: The changing work of organisations*. Arrow Books: London.

Hatch, M. 1992. The symbolics of office design: An empirical exploration. In: Gagliardi, P. (ed.) *Symbolics of Corporate Artifacts*. de Gruyter: Berlin, pp. 129–143.

Heffernan, M. 2011. *Willful blindness: Why we ignore the obvious at our peril*. Walker & Company: London.

Hofstede, G. 1991. *Cultures and organizations: Software of the mind*. McGraw-Hill: New York.

Huffington Post, 2012. Freshers' Week 2012: Student Initiation Horror Stories. Available at http://www.huffingtonpost.co.uk/2012/09/03/freshers-week-2012-student-initiation-horror-stories_n_1851788.html (last accessed13t December 2012).

Lawson, M. 2008. Salutes, lies and videotape. *The Guardian*, 4 October 2008. Available at: http://www.guardian.co.uk/commentisfree/2008/oct/04/britishidentity.students (last accessed 27 June 2008).

Lewis, M. 1989. *Liar's Poker*. Hodder: London.

Malone, M. S. 2007. *Bill and Dave: How Hewlett and Packard built the world's greatest company*. Penguin Books: London.

Martin, J 2001. *Organizational Culture: Mapping the terrain*. Sage: London.

Meek, L. 1988. Organizational culture: Origins and weaknesses. *Organization Studies* 9(4): 453–473.

Morgan, G. 2006. *Images of organization.* Sage Publications: Thousand Oaks, CA.

Ornstein, S. 1989. The hidden influences of office design. *The Academy of Management Executive* 3(2): 144–147.

Ott, J. 1989. *The organizational culture perspective.* Brooks/Cole Publishing Company: Pacific Grove, CA.

Ouchi, W. 1981. *Theory Z: How American business can meet the Japanese challenge.* Addison-Wesley: New York.

Peters, T. 2001. Tom Peters's true confessions. Available at: http://www.fastcompany.com/magazine/53/peters.html?page=0%2C3 (last accessed 17 June 2012).

Peters, T. J., and Waterman, R. H. Jr. 1982. *In search of excellence: Lessons from America's best run companies.* Harper Row: London.

Pettigrew, A. 1979. On studying organizational cultures. *Administrative Science Quarterly* 24(4): 570–581.

Posner, B. Z., Kouzes, J. M., and Schmidt, W. H. 1985. Shared values make a difference: An empirical test of corporate culture. *Human Resource Management* 24(3): 293–309.

Raelin, J. 1986. *Clash of cultures: Managers and professionals.* Harvard Business School Press: Boston, MA.

Robinson, S. 2012. GPC warns of 'target culture' as GP commissioning framework revealed. GP Online. Available at: http://www.gponline.com/News/article/1115181/GPC-warns-target-culture-GP-commissioning-framework-revealed/.

Rosen, M. 1985. Breakfast at Spiro's, dramaturgy and dominance. *Journal of Management* 11: 31–48.

Schein, E. 2010. *Organizational culture and leadership.* Jossey Bass: San Francisco.

Sewell, G. 1998. The discipline of teams: the control of team-based industrial work through electronic and peer surveillance. *Administrative Science Quarterly* 43(2): 397–428.

Smircich, L. 1983. Concepts of culture and organizational analysis. *Administrative Science Quarterly* 28(3): 339–358.

Smircich, L., and Morgan, G. 1982. Leadership: The management of meaning. *Journal of Applied Behavioural Studies* 18: 257–273.

Starbucks. 2012. *Starbucks Our Mission Statement.* Available at: http://www.starbucks.ie/about-us/company-information/mission-statement (last accessed 24 November 2012).

Taylor, P., and Bain, P. 2003. Subterranean worksick blues: Humour as subversion in two call centres. *Organization Studies* 24(9): 1487–1509.

Thompson, V. 2010. *Gross Misconduct: My year of excess in the city.* Pocket Books: London.

Tichy, N. M. 1982. Managing change strategically: The technical, political, and cultural keys. *Organizational Dynamics* 11: 59–80.

Tierney, J. 2012. From Cubicles, Cry for Quiet Pierces Office Buzz. *New York Times.* 20 May 2012. Available at: http://www.nytimes.com/2012/05/20/science/when-buzz-at-your-cubicle-is-too-loud-for-work.html?_r=1.

Trice, H., and Beyer, J. 1984. Studying organizational cultures through rites and ceremonials. *Academy of Management Review* 9(4): 653–669.

TUC. 2008. General Council Report to Congress 2008. Available at: http://www.tuc.org.uk/the_tuc/tuc-15225-f0.cfm (last accessed 26 November 2012).

Turner, G., and Myerson, J. 1998. *New workspace, new culture: Office design as a catalyst for change.* Gower Publishing Ltd: Aldershot.

Willmott, H. 1993. Strength is ignorance; slavery is freedom: Managing culture in modern organizations. *Journal of Management Studies* 30(4): 515–552.

Wilson, C. 1979. *Jokes: form, content, use and function.* Academic Press: New York.

Wilson, H. 2012. EU plans curbs on bank risk-taking. *The Daily Telegraph.* 2 October 2012. Available at: http://www.telegraph.co.uk/finance/newsbysector/banksandfinance/9581526/EU-plans-curbs-on-bank-risk-taking.html.

Yarrow, J. 2011. HP CEO Leo Apotheker: 'HP Has Lost Its Soul'. Available at: http://www.businessinsider.com/hp-leo-apotheker-2011-3#ixzz2D9tVzlNU.

York Vision. 2010. York Sport Slams Hockey Initiation. Available at http://www.yorkvision.co.uk/sport/york-sport-slams-hockey-initiation/ (last accessed 13 December 2012).

Part 3
Managing the individual

Personality and individual differences

Chapter overview and learning outcomes

By the end of this chapter you should be able to:

- describe the main features of the nomothetic, ideographic, and social–radical approaches to personality

- describe a variety of models of personality

- explain how personality is measured in organizational settings

- analyse the effectiveness of different selection methods in assessing the personality of candidates for a job.

Key theorists

Carl Gustav Jung	Swiss psychoanalyst who noted the distinction between introverted and extraverted personalities
Katharine Cook Briggs and Isobel Briggs Myers	American amateur psychologists who applied Jung's theory to create the Myers–Briggs Type Indicator personality test
Hans Eysenck	German psychologist who noted the role of emotional stability and instability in personality formation
Raymond Cattell	British psychologist who devised the 16 personality factor model of personality used in workplace selection
Sigmund Freud	Austrian psychoanalyst who outlined ways in which personalities change and develop

Key terms

Nomothetic approach	Views personality as a set of measurable traits or types which can be represented on a static framework or model
Personality testing	The use of questionnaires to measure personality, often used in recruitment and selection in organizations
Ideographic approach	Views personality as complex and unique to each individual, and as something which changes through influences from the world around us
Social–radical approach	Recognizes that rather than just measuring personality, organizations have an effect upon the personalities of their members

Introduction

Junction Hotel

Fitness Centre Duty Manager
Full-time, fixed-term (12 months initially)
Salary negotiable

We are looking for an individual with a big personality to join the team of duty managers at our fitness centre.

Reporting to the Fitness Centre Manager and, on occasions, deputizing, you will be responsible for the day-to-day line management of a team of five full-time fitness centre staff and the recruitment of new staff when necessary.

Working with customers, including delivering personal training sessions, you will also have management and administration responsibilities, including preparation of staff rotas and associated paperwork.

Holding a degree in sports or leisure management, or a related area, you will have at least five years of experience in the leisure and fitness industry, at least two of which should be at management level.

We need an individual who is self-motivated and dynamic, and who can motivate both staff and customers.

Please send CVs and a covering letter to:

Simon Chance
General Manager
Junction Hotel

What do you think would be the ideal personality characteristics for the successful candidate in this job?

To what extent do we go into organizations as individuals with our own distinct personalities? So far in this book, theories of management and organization have paid little attention to the perspective of the individual.

- In the rational organization (Chapters 2–4), the individual is seen as useful only for the precise part they can play on an assembly line, as if they were a cog in the machine. When dealing with a large bureaucracy, such as our bank or even our university, we may feel like the organization sees us as a record on a computer rather than an individual—a feeling summed up in the phrase 'I am a name, not a number'.

- With the social organization (Chapters 5–7), a human aspect of the organization is recognized, but only as a part of a larger group or team. Group dynamics have a powerful influence over individual behaviour and perceptions. Anyone who has played sport may well know the mantra 'there is no "I" in team'—the idea that you put the team before your individuality.

In both of these cases the individual is, in one way or another, reduced to being part of a greater entity. However, as we will see in this, and the following two chapters, organizations do have an interest in managing people at the level of the individual. Theories of motivation and learning, for example, use psychological knowledge to try to understand how the individual mind works.

In this chapter, we use psychological insights to examine the set of characteristics that mark us out as an individual and therefore as different from other people. It is common to speak of ourselves and others as having a **personality** that identifies us as an individual.

> **Personality** A set of characteristics of behaviour displayed by any individual.

Think about yourself compared with your friends and family. What differences in personality can you describe?

We examine three approaches to the study of personality:

- the nomothetic approach sees personality as a set of measurable traits or characteristics, and sorts people into particular **personality types** or scales. Such an approach is most familiar in the workplace in the form of personality tests

> **Personality types** Broad personality groupings which are associated with a set of particular traits.

- the ideographic approach rejects the idea of the personality as a set of traits for being too simplistic and, instead, sees the personality as something much more dynamic and that develops as a result of our experiences and interactions. As such, it sees people as having rich, complex personalities, rather than as fitting into a certain personality type

- a third approach, we suggest, is a social–radical approach, that sees personality and its definition entirely as a product of society and its organizational and power structures. For example, rather than the workplace simply measuring an individual's personality, as in the nomothetic approach, the workplace is a part of an individual's environment which actively shapes their personality.

Throughout the chapter we will see how individual personalities are assessed by organizations when filling a vacancy, i.e. finding someone with the personality characteristics that are felt suitable for that job. It is with this link between personality and the recruitment and selection process that we begin.

Personality in the recruitment and selection process

Running case: whittling down

Chance is met by a deluge of paperwork. Over 200 CVs have been sent in for the job of duty manager and just over half of them seem to be suitable candidates.

Looking at the covering letters and CVs, Chance realizes that he can't use these alone to create a shortlist. Many of the letters simply parrot standard phrases, such as 'I am self-motivated', 'I am dedicated to the task', and 'I work well with other people', but what proof is there to back up these statements?

Chance starts to think about how to whittle down the shortlist and draws up a list of characteristics that a successful candidate will need:

- appropriate qualifications and experience
- well organized to manage rotas and similar paperwork
- calm demeanour in a fast-moving work environment
- good leadership—the candidate needs to motivate and enthuse the team during the course of a shift
- flexibility—needs to be prepared to do different tasks at short notice
- upbeat, motivating personality—especially when greeting customers at reception or engaging them in a personal training session
- able to communicate instructions clearly in a fast-paced atmosphere.

The various qualities are drawn up into a person specification which will be put in an application pack and sent to candidates.

When employers advertise a vacancy, they specify the characteristics that an ideal candidate should have—the degree grades required, the amount of experience in a similar job, the skills that they can offer to the organization, etc. Among these might be characteristics which relate to an aspect of personality—'dynamic', 'conscientious', 'pleasant manner', etc.

> **Research insight:** 'We recruit attitude', Callaghan, G., and Thompson, P. 2002. 'We recruit attitude': the selection and shaping of routine call centre labour. *Journal of Management Studies* 39(2): 233–254.
>
> In a study of recruitment and selection in a call centre, Callaghan and Thompson (2002) note that, while technical skills, such as numeracy and using a keyboard are assessed, the greatest priority in the process is given to personality. In particular, a positive, energetic can-do attitude and an ability to use humour during calls are seen as aspects of good customer service. This is important as it is the customer service that may differentiate the company from others which offer similar products (see also emotional labour in service industries in Chapter 16).
>
> Such characteristics are seen as being innate rather than something that can be learned. As one manager states:
>
> '. . . [W]e recruit attitude. You can tell by talking to someone during interview whether they smile, whether their eyes smile. If you smile during your interview and you are enthusiastic, you'll be OK'.
>
> (Callaghan and Thompson, 2002: 240)

In this section we present an initial overview of how personality characteristics are considered in the recruitment and selection process. While often used together as a phrase, recruitment and selection refers to two distinct phases of the process of filling a vacancy (French and Rumbles, 2010):

Recruitment The process of attracting a pool of candidates for a particular job vacancy.

- **Recruitment** is where the vacancy is publicized in order to generate a pool of applicants, and involves the advertising of jobs and the creation of relevant documentation. The desired personality characteristics are formalized as documents, such as a person specification.

- **Selection** is where the choice is made of who to employ from the field of candidates and, as such, includes such techniques as interviewing, reviewing CVs, and—central to concerns in this chapter—personality tests.

Selection The process of selecting the most appropriate candidate from a pool of applicants for a particular vacancy.

Personality and recruitment

When recruiting for a vacancy, for example in a job advert or on a website, employers will demonstrate the characteristics that they desire in a successful applicant. This might include explicit reference to particular personality characteristics, such as 'outgoing', or might refer to behaviours that imply particular characteristics, for example 'good with customers' implies personality characteristics such as patience and friendliness.

Real life case: 'the Pret behaviours'

On the recruitment section of its website, the British sandwich chain, Pret a Manger publishes a set of 'Pret behaviours' which are expected of all members of the organization and are used to inform processes such as recruitment and appraisal. The behaviours are grouped into three categories:

- passion: pace, pride, ownership, resilience, high standards
- clear talking: straightforward, clear, informal, thoughtful, interesting, sensitive
- team working: fun, caring, sociable, quirky, helpful.

Within these categories are listed behaviours that they 'don't want to see', 'want to see', and 'Pret perfect.' For example, for 'passion' they want to see people who cope well with pressure; for 'clear talking' they want to see someone who is sincere; and for 'team working' it would be perfect to have someone who is charming to other people; but they definitely don't want to see people who are moody or bad tempered.

Visit the Online Resource Centre to see the full list.

Source: http://www.pret.com/jobs/pret_behaviours.htm.

What sort of personality characteristics do you think an ideal candidate for Pret a Manger would have?

A further stage in the recruitment process where personality characteristics may be stated is in the documentation that is sent to interested candidates (or available to download in some instances). Such an application pack usually consists of two documents:

- the **job description** is a description of exactly what task and duties would be expected to be performed as a part of the job
- the **person specification** is a list of knowledge, skills, experience, qualifications, and competencies that a successful candidate would be expected to hold. This might be split into 'essential' characteristics (the bare minimum that a candidate requires) and 'desirable' characteristics (those which might work in a person's favour when making a decision between candidates).

Job description A document which outlines the formal duties and activities that the holder of a particular office will be expected to perform, and their place within the overall organizational structure.

Person specification A formal list of the main requirements for a successful candidate for a particular job.

Again, in these documents there may be references to characteristics, either essential or desired, which relate to aspects of personality. A person specification will also outline the ways in which different characteristics will be assessed, that is to say the selection processes that will be used to match candidates to those characteristics.

Visit the Online Resource Centre to see examples of these documents.

Personality and selection

A number of techniques might be used in a selection process. A CV can be used to assess whether the relevant qualifications are held; references can be used to check up on relevant experience and aptitude tests can measure specific skills such as numeracy. But what about personality characteristics? How would a recruiter assess the personality of a candidate to see that it matches that which is desired and measure their 'enthusiasm' or 'friendliness?'

When you first started at university you will have met many new people and made judgements about their personality upon first meeting them. But how long, with friends, does it take to really get to know every facet of their personality?

Getting to know someone's personality is a lengthy process. We get to know a person and their personality over time. Even with our closest friends we sometimes find aspects of their personality that are new or which surprise us. For recruiters trying to get an idea of a candidate's personality, this length of time is not a luxury that is available.

Assessing large numbers of people can be problematic.

With a large field of candidates, it's simply not possible to get to know each of them well enough to know every aspect of their personality. Even a short interview, where at least candidates are seen in person, gives only a superficial view of personality and the time available for interviews is limited—only a small fraction of the field of candidates will be shortlisted for interview.

In this chapter we will see how techniques such as personality tests and questionnaires are used in the selection process. This is an efficient way of getting a measure of the personality of a large number of candidates, but comes at the expense of the type of data that is produced—rather than the rich knowledge of a personality that we get from knowing somebody personally, it is presented, instead, as an abstract set of numbers and measurements.

The measurement of personality in the selection process thus involves a trade-off between the time available and the richness of the data about a candidate's personality that can be gleaned (see Figure 8.1).

This trade-off relates to the nomothetic and ideographic approaches to personality introduced previously:

- the nomothetic approach suggests that personalities can be represented as a set of standard characteristics and can thus be measured efficiently using instruments such as personality questionnaires

- the ideographic approach sees personalities as rich and complex. Representing personalities though efficient means, such as a personality test, comes at the expense of the richness of personality data gained—the complexity and insight into an individual personality is lost.

In this chapter we will relate a number of methods used in recruitment and selection to the nomothetic and ideographic approaches. Taken in isolation, any one technique of recruitment and selection fares badly in its predictive validity, that is to say how well it predicts performance in the job or gets an accurate picture of personality. Yet, given the costs and time associated with recruitment and selection, it is important for organizations to get it right, i.e. to fit the right person to the vacancy.

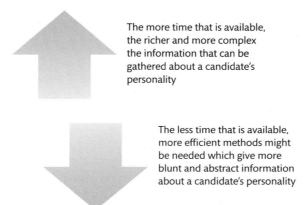

The more time that is available, the richer and more complex the information that can be gathered about a candidate's personality

The less time that is available, more efficient methods might be needed which give more blunt and abstract information about a candidate's personality

Figure 8.1
The personality measurement trade-off.

Employability skills: the recruitment and selection process

This chapter relates personality to the recruitment and selection process, and will, therefore, be a valuable insight into the processes used when you apply for employment—whether for temporary or vacation work, for a placement, or when you graduate and begin your career.

While this chapter concentrates on personality, it is useful to do research and reading into all aspects of recruitment and selection ahead of applying for jobs. Understanding what recruiters are looking for, the ways in which they match applicants to jobs, and, importantly, the reasons why they reject candidates are all things which will give you a head start. Your university careers service will also have literature on the subject and will be able to offer advice.

Visit the Online Resource Centre for suggestions on further research into the recruitment process.

On the other side of the fence, when you are in work, you may, at times, be involved in recruiting and selecting candidates to fill a job vacancy. You may do this as a fully-trained human resources professional; however, in many cases, managers with no formal training are called upon to sit on an interview panel or play a role in the recruitment and selection process. While issues around the accuracy of different selection techniques are important points to note as an employer, the chapter also highlights important issues and legal requirements around unfair discrimination in the recruitment and selection process.

Review questions

1. Describe what is meant by recruitment and selection.
2. Explain how evaluating the personality characteristics of a candidate is a trade-off between efficiency and the richness of personality data gained.

Apply

3. Have a look at a variety of job advertisements, either in print or online. For each advert, consider what personality characteristics are required of the successful candidate.

Nomothetic approaches to personality

Running case: personality test

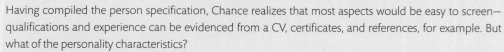

Having compiled the person specification, Chance realizes that most aspects would be easy to screen—qualifications and experience can be evidenced from a CV, certificates, and references, for example. But what of the personality characteristics?

What Chance needs to know is which one of the applicants can really cut the mustard. Who has the personality to manage staff and keep them motivated in a fast-moving environment?

Business manager Phil Weaver advises Chance to get them to undertake a personality test. Using the services of a personality testing firm, a link would be sent to the candidates to fill out a questionnaire over the Internet. The software would then produce personality profiles for all candidates.

'I've used them before, they save a lot of time and effort', says Weaver. 'For a start, they screen out anyone unsuitable—any shy, retiring types will be shown up by the test and we can reject them straight away. We don't even need to look at their profiles—the software will just give a list of people with unsuitable personalities. And for those still in the running, we can use their profiles as extra information to draw up the final shortlist.'

Chance likes this idea—it is an efficient way to deal with the 200-odd applications quickly, leaving him just the most suitable personalities to deal with.

Have you ever undertaken a personality test, either for work purposes or otherwise? What did you think of the results?

Many of us, when younger, will have read the Mr Men and Little Miss books. Each book in this series focuses on a different cartoon character whose characteristics match their name—Mr Grumpy, Little Miss Shy, Mr Happy, etc. The characters' personalities can be summed up by one particular personality characteristic or as it is also known, a personality **trait**.

While our personalities are hopefully not so one-dimensional that we can sum them up with one word, the idea that personality can be described as a set of traits is one with which we are familiar. Indeed, often if asked what a person 'is like' we will respond with a set of adjectives which relate to particular personality traits—friendly, sullen, outgoing, shy, etc.

Trait A characteristic of the person, often considered the behaviour, thoughts, and emotions that the person exhibits considered stable, over time.

Think of a friend or relative—could you produce a list of words to describe their personality? And could you produce a similar list for yourself?

The **nomothetic** approach also sees personality as a set of traits which are organized into a model or framework. There is not an infinite number of adjectives that can be used to describe somebody's personality (as we might do our own unscientific descriptions of the personalities of others). Instead, personalities are classified within the terms of a particular fixed framework. In this section we examine two particular approaches to nomothetic theories of personality:

Nomothetic An approach which views personality as a set of measurable traits or types.

- some theories classify people into broad personality *types*. Associated with each type is a set of personality traits that people belonging to that type are likely to display
- some theories don't group traits into personality types; instead, they start from the traits themselves, usually plotting people on a number of scales between two opposite ends of a particular trait (for example between reserved and outgoing).

In both cases, the nomothetic approach suggests that personality is measurable, using instruments such as personality questionnaires. The personality types and scales are the frameworks on which an individual's personality can be represented and categorized. We will see that such personality tests are used in workplaces for training, development, and, relevant to this chapter, for selecting candidates for a job.

Theories of personality type

Theories of personality type bring together different traits in broad groupings, seeing the traits as being representative characteristics of the broader personality types. As we will see,

Myers–Briggs Type Indicator A personality testing instrument based on the personality types of Carl Jung.

the idea of personality types is used today in the workplace in the popular **Myers–Briggs Type Indicator** (MBTI); however, the idea of categorizing personalities into different types stretches back into antiquity.

Theory in context: Hippocrates and the four humours

In Ancient Greece, around 400 BC, Hippocrates drew out four main personality types from his medical theory of the **four humours**. Blood, phlegm, yellow bile, and black bile were four basic substances, or humours, which Hippocrates believed made up the human body and were associated with certain characteristics and personality types. See Table 8.1 for a description of these. An imbalance in the presence of one of the humours would have effects on both physical health and also on the type of personality type displayed by an individual.

Four humours The four elements that Hippocrates suggested made up the human body and which also divided into four personality types.

Table 8.1 Hippocrates' four humours and associated personality types

Humour	Personality type	Description
Blood	Sanguine	Warm and outgoing, a person who thrives in social environments—lively with few concerns and cares in the world
Phlegm	Phlegmatic	Cool and rational—a controlled, thoughtful, and calm personality
Yellow bile	Choleric	The most volatile of the four personality types, impulsive, excitable, perhaps touchy and bad tempered
Black bile	Melancholic	Reserved and withdrawn—quiet and socially the opposite to sanguine. An anxious temperament, governed by worries, concerns, and even despondency

---

While much of Hippocrates' work has been disproven or superseded, he is seen as being the founder of medicine for his attempt to analyse and classify the workings of the human body. The four temperaments, or personality types, that he outlines give us words that we still use to describe people's personalities today—melancholic, sanguine, phlegmatic, choleric—and which we will see reflected in more recent personality-type classifications.

Can you think of jobs which are particularly suited to the four personality types described? Do you think of personality in such terms today or are there other words that you might use for such personality types?

Carl Jung: introverts and extraverts

Introversion A tendency to focus and gain energy more from within the self rather than externally.

Extraversion A tendency to focus and gain energy externally rather than from within the self.

While Hippocrates introduces the notion of personality types, it is with the work of psycho-analyst Carl Jung that we see the origins of the personality scales and type theories that are more commonly applied in the contemporary workplace. Jung's (1923) *Psychological Types* outlines a distinction between **introversion** and **extraversion** (this is the way it is spelled in psychological theory), which is mirrored in many of the personality types and scales that we will see in this chapter.

Our common-sense understanding of these terms perhaps differs from the depth of Jung's analysis. We tend to think of an extravert as someone who is sociable and outgoing, able to 'work a room' and start up a conversation with people, engaging in small talk. The introvert is more reserved, possibly uncomfortable in social situations, and might seem unsociable and withdrawn.

Certainly these common-sense understandings ring true, but they need to be understood in the context of the specific meanings of Jung's terminology. The basis of Jung's (1923) work is in the relationship between our inner selves and the external world. In effect, there are two particular worlds to which we relate, and we may do so to different degrees:

- the external world is the rational, day-to-day, everyday reality that goes on around us
- the inner world is the world of our own thoughts, dreams, fantasies, etc.

Jung's (1923) theory of introversion and extraversion is about the balance we maintain between these inner and external worlds, and particularly from which of these we gain our energy.

- An extravert thrives on action and being engaged with people—if inactive an extravert can feel restless. *An extravert gets little energy from within, instead getting their energy from others in a social situation.*
- An introvert is capable of, and indeed thrives on, working alone, perhaps doing work that needs consideration or contemplation rather than needing to be a part of a crowd or a team. *An introvert gets their energy from within—social situations drain them of that energy.*

With the example of a person 'working a room', it's not that an introvert is incapable of this; however, they would find that it drains them of energy, while an extravert would get their energy from such a situation. Cain (2012) argues that contemporary workplaces tend to favour the personality characteristics of extraverts more, with working environments, such as open plan offices, and job adverts calling for 'team players' and upbeat personalities. This doesn't mean that an extravert personality is better, simply that working environments suit that side of the scale more, and, indeed, Cain suggests that such environments could miss out on valuable ideas that are generated by more contemplative introverts.

Looking back to the Pret behaviours case, do you think an introvert or extravert personality would best suit those behaviours?

Study skills: lectures and seminars

Cain (2012) suggests that it's not just the workplace that favours extraverts over introverts, but that this is found in schools and universities too. There is a pressure to speak up in class as a way of demonstrating your knowledge and your commitment to the course, and this 'speaking up' is something to which extraverts are more inclined. Does this mean, then, that introverts get nothing out of seminars and are thus at a disadvantage? Let's think about the role that seminars play in your university education.

Lectures give a broad introduction to a topic, highlighting the main areas of importance, but often there is not enough time to go into depth beyond that—they are an invitation to further explore the subject. Furthermore, in a lecture you are usually passive, sitting quietly and taking notes while the lecturer speaks to you, but not engaging any further with the subject matter. ➤

> ⏵ In seminars, you are able to address the lecture topic in more depth, discussing it, and relating it to relevant readings and case studies. You are much more active in a seminar and are not just receiving knowledge, but engaging with that knowledge. A seminar tutor should not need to speak very often, only to keep discussion going and to respond to, and clarify, any points that participants make.
>
> Some people may feel more comfortable than others in speaking up in seminars, but perhaps something to consider—whether you are more extravert or introvert in nature—is that it is the quality of contribution that is important, not the length of time that any one individual speaks. The quality of contribution comes from being prepared—doing the reading and thinking about the ideas presented in the lecture.
>
> Being actively engaged doesn't necessarily mean speaking up all the time as an extravert may do. A person can be engaged by listening and comparing what is being said with their own ideas. However, seminars do need people to speak and contribute in order to work. Just one, carefully considered point or observation can make a big contribution. And Cain suggests that such considered contributions are where introverts excel.

It is not a simple either/or distinction between an individual being either introverted or extraverted, they are two important and complimentary aspects of personality as opposed to mutually exclusive opposites. However, an individual may lean more towards one end or the other on this scale. Jung's (1923) work suggested a complex relationship between an individual's position on the introversion/extraversion scale on the one hand, and two psychological functions on the other: how we perceive the world (sensing or intuition) and how we make judgements about the world (thinking or feeling). These relationships form the basis for one of the most familiar workplace personality instruments—the Myers–Briggs Type Indicator (MBTI).

Myers–Briggs and the application of Jung

While it is now one of the most popular personality profiling instruments in the workplace, the MBTI was developed from an amateur interest in personality types held by Katharine Cook Briggs and her daughter Isabel Briggs Myers. They were heavily influenced by Jung's work on personality types and they used these as a basis for their own classification of personality types, eventually published as the MBTI (Myers, 1962).

The MBTI uses a questionnaire to work out where an individual lies between a set of four personality indices:

- *extraversion/introversion (E/I),* as outlined by Jung, to which orientation are we more inclined when directing our actions and energies—the world around us or our inner selves?
- *sensing/intuition (S/I)*—how do we perceive and gather information about the world around us?
- *thinking/feeling (T/F)*—once we have information, how do we analyse and act upon it, using it to make judgements and decisions?
- *judgement/perception*—how do we deal with, and act upon, the world around us? Do we plan in advance or act in the moment?

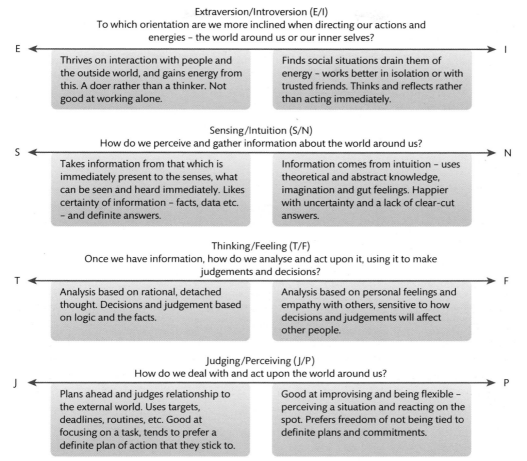

Figure 8.2 The Myers–Briggs Type Indicator (MBTI) personality indices (www.myersbriggs.org).

Modified and reproduced by special permission of the Publisher, CPP, Inc., Mountain View, CA 94043 from the MBTI® Manual by Isabel Briggs Myers, Mary H. McCaulley, Naomi L. Quenk, & Allen L. Hammer. Copyright 1998, 2003, 2012 by CPP, Inc. All rights reserved. Further reproduction is prohibited without the Publisher's written consent. MBTI and Myers-Briggs Type Indicator are trade marks or registered trade marks of the MBTI Trust, Inc., in the United States and other countries.

Figure 8.2 shows these four indices, with examples of the types of behaviour and personality that might be expected at either end.

While people can lie at points along this scale (e.g. a medium preference for sensing, a strong preference for feeling, etc.) the results tend to be presented as a four-letter personality type according to which end of each index an individual is more inclined towards. A person might be an ENTP (Extravert–Intuition–Thinking–Perceiving) personality type, or an ISTP, or an ESTP—or any of the sixteen possible combinations of the letters.

Where do you think you lie on each of the MBTI indices shown in Figure 8.2?

The MBTI instrument is not used as a recruitment and selection tool, but does suggest aptitudes for particular jobs; indeed, one of its earliest uses was during World War II in matching women's personalities to wartime jobs that would best suit them (Myers and Myers, 1995: xiii). As such, it tends to be used more as a developmental tool for individuals. For example, in staff development and training it is used to help people understand their own personality and how they relate to their external world, to their work, and to their colleagues. It is also used for personal development and, given that it matches personality and aptitude for jobs, is a tool used in career development—matching personalities to suitable careers.

A specific link between personality 'temperaments' and specific occupational areas was made by David Keirsey (1988). Keirsey was influenced by the MBTI instrument, sorting the sixteen MBTI combinations into four groups, which correspond to the original personality types of Hippocrates (see Table 8.2). **Keirsey's temperament sorter** then links each of the sixteen MBTI combinations to a particular type of role or occupation.

Keirsey's temperament sorter A personality-testing instrument which relates personality types to suggested occupational roles.

Table 8.2 Keirsey's (1988) temperament sorter

Grouping	Artisan	Guardian	Rational	Idealist
Common characteristics from MBTI	SP (Sensing–Perceiving)	SJ (Sensing–Judging)	NT (Intuition–Thinking)	NF (Intuition–Feeling)
Related Hippocratic group	Sanguine	Melancholic	Phlegmatic	Choleric
Personality types and related occupations	Promoter (ESTP) Crafter (ISTP) Performer (ESFP) Composer (ISFP)	Supervisor (ESTJ) Inspector (ISTJ) Provider (ESFJ) Protector (ISFJ)	Fieldmarshal (ENTJ) Mastermind (INTJ) Inventor (ENTP) Architect (INTP)	Teacher (ENFJ) Counsellor (INFJ) Champion (ENFP) Healer (INFP)

For example, ENFJ is characterized by Keirsey as 'the teacher'. We can see how the different characteristics that make up this personality type would contribute to this role:

- (E)xtraversion—the teacher will be working mainly with groups of people rather than in isolation

- I(N)tuition—Chapter 10 shows that learning comes best from going beyond learning simple facts and instead recognizing patterns and associations, as an intuitive person would do

- (F)eeling—the teacher has a degree of empathy with, and can respond to, students

- (J)udgement—the teacher is able to plan lessons methodically rather than making things up on the hoof.

Interestingly, just one change of letter—from Extraversion to Intraversion—gives INFJ, suggested as 'the counsellor'. Similar teaching skills are required, but here it is in a much more private, individual situation than teaching.

As with the MBTI, Keirsey has an associated personality questionnaire which is used to place people in the relevant groupings (www.keirsey.com has more about the groupings and a test questionnaire).

Visit the Online Resource Centre for more discussion of occupations and the Keirsey groupings.

Trait theories of personality

While type theories sort people's personalities into broad types from which particular traits emerge, **trait theories** see personality traits as the main building blocks of a personality. Usually, traits are arranged in pairs of opposites (e.g. sociable–unsociable) with people scored at some point in between each pairing so as to build up a personality profile. As with type theories, some form of questionnaire is used as the instrument by which these scales are measured. In this section we examine two of the more popular trait theory testing instruments used in the workplace: the **16 personality factor** and the big five personality scale.

> **Research insight:** Eysenck—from types to traits, Eysenck, H.J., and Eysenck, M.W. 1985. *Personality and individual differences: a natural science approach.* Plenum Publishing Corporation, New York.

Similarly to Keirsey, Hans Eysenck (in Eysenck and Eysenck, 1985) made groupings of personality types which mapped on to the ancient groupings of Hippocrates and, similarly to all the modern-day theories of personality examined so far, he made a distinction between extraversion and introversion.

However, Eysenk added another dimension between emotional stability and emotional instability (the latter sometimes called **neuroticism**). Eysenck's two scales were plotted on to a matrix giving four personality types, the quadrants of which map on to Hippocrates' original four humours (see Figure 8.2). Again, this is a classification of personality types that has an associated questionnaire.

Eysenck's work, while still dividing personalities into types, moves us towards trait theories. First, it outlines a set of specific traits within each quadrant (e.g. a stable extraverted person is sociable, outgoing, talkative, etc. in Figure 8.3). Secondly, Eysenck's dimension of emotional stability and instability features alongside the extraversion–introversion scale in many trait theories.

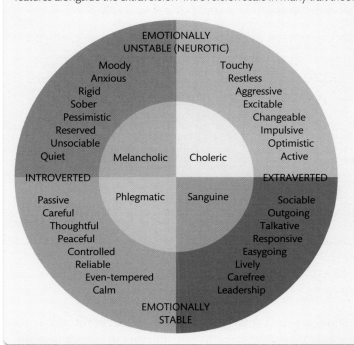

Figure 8.3 Eysenck's model of personality.
Eysenck, H.J. and Eysenck, M.W. *Personality and Individual Differences.* Plenum Publishing, 1985.

Trait theories
Nomothetic theories of personality which see individual traits rather than broad personality groups as the foundations of personality.

16 personality factor
A personality test which measures personality on a set of 16 scales of opposing character traits.

Neuroticism
Emotional instability.

Cattell's 16 PF traits

Cattell's (1966) 16 personality factor (16 PF) theory is one of the most popular personality questionnaires used in selection processes (e.g. Dakin et al., 1994). Cattell analysed questionnaires and the words within them that people used to describe personality (Newell and Rice, 1999: 140), and by grouping similar ideas together, suggested that a personality boils down to sixteen core factors (see Figure 8.4).

These factors are arranged in opposites, for example the 'Dominance' scale ranges between deferential and avoiding conflict at one end, to being dominant and forceful at the other. The scale is normally distributed, that is to say that on any of the scales, approximately a third of the population should be located in the middle band, with numbers tailing off towards the extremities.

Both Jung's extraversion and introversion aspects can be seen in the scale (e.g. factor H—social boldness), as can Eysenck's emotional stability (factor C).

Figure 8.4 Cattell's sixteen personality factors.

Primary Factors

Factor			Standard Ten Score (STEN)										
			1	2	3	4	5	6	7	8	9	10	
A:	Warmth	Emotionally distant from people	+	+	+	+	+	+	+	+	+	+	Attentive and warm towards others
B:	Reasoning	Fewer reasoning items correct	+	+	+	+	+	+	+	+	+	+	More reasoning items correct
C:	Emotional Stability	Reactive, Emotionally changeable	+	+	+	+	+	+	+	+	+	+	Emotionally stable, Adaptive
E:	Dominance	Deferential, Cooperative, Avoids conflict	+	+	+	+	+	+	+	+	+	+	Dominant, Forceful
F:	Liveliness	Serious, Cautious, Careful	+	+	+	+	+	+	+	+	+	+	Lively, Animated, Spontaneous
G:	Rule-Consciousness	Expedient, Non-Conforming	+	+	+	+	+	+	+	+	+	+	Rule-Conscious, Dutiful
H:	Social Boldness	Shy, Threat-Sensitive, Timid	+	+	+	+	+	+	+	+	+	+	Socially bold, Adventurous, Thick-Skinned
I:	Sensitivity	Objective, Unsentimental	+	+	+	+	+	+	+	+	+	+	Subjective, Sentimental
L:	Vigilance	Trusting, Unsuspecting, Accepting	+	+	+	+	+	+	+	+	+	+	Vigilant, Suspicious, Sceptical, Wary
M:	Abstractedness	Grounded, Practical, Solution-Oriented	+	+	+	+	+	+	+	+	+	+	Abstracted, Theoretical, Idea-Oriented
N:	Privateness	Forthright, Straightforward	+	+	+	+	+	+	+	+	+	+	Private, Discreet, Non-Disclosing
O:	Apprehension	Self-Assured, Unworried	+	+	+	+	+	+	+	+	+	+	Apprehensive, Self-Doubting, Worried
Q1:	Openness to Change	Traditional, Values the familiar	+	+	+	+	+	+	+	+	+	+	Open to change, Experimenting
Q2:	Self-Reliance	Group-Oriented, Affiliative	+	+	+	+	+	+	+	+	+	+	Self-Reliant, Individualistic
Q3:	Perfectionism	Tolerates disorder, Unexacting, Flexible	+	+	+	+	+	+	+	+	+	+	Perfectionist, Organised, Self-Disciplined
Q4:	Tension	Relaxed, Placid, Patient	+	+	+	+	+	+	+	+	+	+	Tense, High energy, Impatient, Driven

The big five personality factors

Big five personality scale A personality test which measures personality according to a set of five traits: openness, conscientiousness, extraversion, agreeableness and neuroticism.

The **big five personality scale** (McCrae and Costa, 1990, 1996) is another of the well-known trait theories used in the workplace, and suggests that the number of factors whereby a personality can be adequately represented boils down to five. The big five is also known as the OCEAN scale, OCEAN being an acronym for its five personality dimensions:

- *openness to experience*—the degree to which people are open to new ideas, questioning and imaginative, or prefer existing ways of doing things
- *conscientiousness*—the degree to which people are good, orderly, diligent workers
- *extraversion/introversion*—as with the MBTI, the degree to which a person is outgoing and gregarious, their energies directed externally rather than internally
- *agreeableness*—the degree to which someone is a 'good person'—trustworthy and cooperative—will get along with others in the organization
- *neuroticism (emotional stability)*—as with Eysenck, the degree to which somebody is calm and emotionally stable, or more prone to anxiety and anger.

The main questionnaire for the big five personality test (Costa and McCrae, 1992) runs to 240 questions and takes 45 minutes to complete; however, Gosling et al. (2003) note that a number of shorter questionnaires have been based around the framework, some as short as ten, or even five, questions. The results of big five tests can thus be presented with a range of precision, from detailed percentages which break each factor down into sub-elements, to broad results such as 'mid-agreeableness', 'high conscientiousness', etc.

Nomothetic approaches in recruitment and selection

Running case: the personality test

Chance chooses a personality test based on the 'big five' characteristics. He is asked to think about the ideal candidate for the job, and, in consultation with the testing company that he had employed, an ideal range in each scale is drawn up:

Openness to experience—Mid
Some flexibility needed, but in many respects this is a routine job. Someone too creative might be too disruptive, but someone completely reliant on routine would not be flexible enough when the need arises.

Conscientiousness—High
Needs to be well-organized, for example in putting together rotas and managing the paperwork, and being able to take charge of a shift from start to finish with no one else above them to refer to.

Extraversion—High
Needs to have a very outgoing personality, both in leadership of the team and in being able to motivate them for a shift, and in dealing with, and motivating, customers in the gym.

Agreeableness—High
Needs to be warm and friendly in dealing with customers—most of the time will be spent on the gym floor.

Neuroticism—Mid-to-Low

A bit of nervous energy would be good, but, overall, the gym is a fast-paced atmosphere and the person in charge needs to maintain a sense of calm. This is especially the case as injuries and medical emergencies sometimes need to be dealt with.

The tests are administered. Candidates who are nowhere near the ideal profile are rejected instantly. A list of 20 candidates who match the desired profile, or are fairly close to it, is sent to Chance. Chance looks at the list alongside the original application forms and CVs, and draws up a shortlist of five candidates.

How would you feel if you had been rejected from the shortlist by the method just outlined?

Nomothetic approaches to personality suggest that personality is an objective entity which can be measured and either categorized or plotted out on some form of personality scale as a combination of different strengths of different traits. In the process of recruitment and selection, this suggests that, if a desired personality profile can be outlined for a particular role, in a person specification for example, then personality tests can be used as an instrument to find the most appropriate candidate to match that personality profile.

Personality test A written test whereby the responses to a set of questions are said to provide a measure of personality.

The **personality test** is usually a questionnaire where a candidate selects one of a number of different options for a set of different questions. Some questionnaires will ask candidates to locate themselves on a scale, as in Table 8.3.

Table 8.3 A typical personality test scale question

	Strongly agree	Agree	Neutral	Disagree	Strongly disagree
I enjoy parties and social gatherings					

Such a question would be part of the calculation of a candidate's position on the extraversion/introversion scale—the more strongly a candidate agrees with this proposition, the more likely they are to be extravert in nature. The scale allows neutral responses and there might be some subjectivity in answering, for example how easy is it to tell the difference between agreeing and agreeing strongly?

Other questionnaires might try to force an opinion one way or another, thus the question might be a more simple:

I enjoy parties and social gatherings: YES/NO

or:

Do you tend to prefer:

A quiet night in, or

Parties and social gatherings

This means that neutral answers are avoided, leading to a more definite position on a personality scale. However, it does not allow for subtleties in a personality to be expressed—a person might enjoy parties occasionally, for example, but be equally happy with quiet nights in.

The questionnaires are usually trademarked commercial products for which a company wishing to recruit will pay for the right to use.

Visit the Online Resource Centre for links to these and to some similar tests that you can try for free.

Personality testing assessed

Personality tests provide an efficient means of screening candidates and are thus often used for pre-screening, especially when there is a large volume of applications for a job which need to be whittled down quickly. Thus, a personality test is sometimes administered at the same time as the application, especially in online applications. In other instances a personality test may be used further down the selection process, possibly alongside other selection tools, such as the interview or references.

However, the efficacy of personality tests is a matter of great debate, particularly around their **predictive validity**—the degree to which the result of a personality test accurately predicts the performance of a candidate in the job itself. The results for personality tests suggest that their predictive validity is low, at the most between 30% and 40% (Pilbeam and Corbridge, 2006: 173), and as low as 15% for some self-administered tests (Reilly and Chao, 1983: 32). More positive results emerged from the 1990s onwards, leading to renewed interest in personality testing; however, Morgeson et al. (2007) suggest that the better results come from tests which are customized and specific to a particular job, and that generic, off-the shelf personality tests remain poor in their predictive validity.

There are a number of issues which potentially diminish the predictive validity and usefulness of personality tests, including:

- candidates may fake the answers to a test, giving answers that they think will improve their scores, rather than giving an honest answer (Furnham, 1997; Morgeson et al., 2007)

- the language and assumptions of tests may lead them to have a particular bias, for example Thompson and McHugh (2009: 283) suggest that personality tests are good at finding managers who are '"male, middle-class and middle-aged," and in the West, white'

- Passer et al. (2003) question the extent to which the different traits are independent variables that can be measured, or do they have an effect upon each other?

This final point invites us to question just how realistic personality profiles are as a representation of personalities. They can be seen as reductionist, that is to say they reduce a complex, human phenomenon such as a personality down to a few figures on a set of scales.

Do you feel that human characteristics and emotions can be represented on a numerical scale? How would you feel if you received a Valentine's card stating 'On a scale between love and hate, my feelings for you measure 78.3%'?

This is part of the trade-off in recruitment and selection that we encountered earlier (see Figure 8.1). Personality tests give a snapshot of a personality but they don't give the full picture of the richness of an individual's personality. In this respect, personality tests are often used alongside other techniques that will give further information, especially, as we shall see, in an assessment-centre approach.

> **Predictive validity**
> The ability for a test to predict a candidate's job performance.

An ideographic approach, which we encounter in the next section, would suggest that using more and more techniques, rather than relying on the reductionist personality test alone, would help build up more of a picture of the complexities and richness of individual personalities.

Review questions

1. Describe what is meant by a nomothetic approach to personality.
2. Explain how one of the models of personality in this section represents personality in its framework.
3. Explain how personality tests are used to measure personality in type and trait theories.
4. Analyse why personality tests have a low predictive validity.

The ideographic approach to personality

Running case: the whites of their eyes

The five candidates had been called in for interview. The panel, made up of Simon Chance, Meg Mortimer, Linda Wilkinson, and the current fitness centre manager, Carl Jones, have a discussion beforehand to work out their lines of questioning. They have the candidates' CVs, application forms, and personality test results before them.

Briefing the panel, Chance suggests that the interview would be an opportunity to get a more accurate view of the candidates' personalities, i.e. to see whether it matched with the results of the personality test.

'These personality tests are just figures on a piece of paper. They may give us an overview of what they are like, but we need to confirm that they are accurate. Not only that, there is much more to what people are—what makes them tick—than a few points plotted out on a scale. We need to dig behind that to get a much more rounded picture of what these people are like.'

'A piece of paper isn't enough. We need to see the whites of their eyes.'

For many people, the singer Michael Jackson had an unusual personality. During his life, stories would appear daily in the media alleging the seemingly bizarre goings on in his life. Without passing judgement on Jackson, it is perhaps not too controversial to say that his personality was unique and there will probably never be anyone like him ever again.

To consider a personality like Jackson perhaps brings to the fore some failings of the nomothetic approach:

- firstly, could any personality test and its associated personality scale really put across the true complexity and individuality of Jackson's personality? Do the results on paper get anywhere close to the reality of the person in the flesh?

Michael Jackson.

- secondly, with methods such as MBTI, there are only sixteen possible combinations of personality type (ENTJ, ISFP, etc.). On such a reading, one sixteenth of the world's population would share a personality type with Michael Jackson.

Now, while Michael Jackson might be a particularly far-fetched yardstick by which to measure our personalities, the argument of the **ideographic approach** is that, while our own personalities might be a little more mundane, they are, nevertheless, equally unique. We are all far more rich and complex as individuals than nomothetic, trait theories would suggest.

Do you think that, following MBTI, you share a personality type with one sixteenth of the world's population?

Ideographic approach
An approach which sees personality as complex, unique to each individual, and dynamic.

The personality as dynamic

In the previous section, we encountered a number of theories that saw personalities in static terms, that is to say they were something that could be plotted out on a set of scales or a framework. The ideographic approach suggests that our personality is not so static, that, instead, it is developed and moulded through social interaction. Our personality is adaptable and open to being changed by new experiences.

> **Real life case:** the UK riots
>
> In August 2011, London and other areas of the UK experienced a brief, but intense, period of rioting. While the riots were triggered as a protest against the police killing of a suspect, it seemed, as they spread, that people were taking part in looting seemingly out of enjoyment with no other goal.
>
> In the aftermath and seeking to explain the riots, a distinction came to be drawn in people's efforts to explain what had happened.
>
> On the one hand, it was suggested that the acts of violence were the result of sheer criminality—the suggestion being that this was an innate characteristic of the people involved.
>
> On the other hand, other commentators argued that the rioting came about because of factors such as social deprivation and the influence of gangs. In other words, the behaviour came about as the product of people's immediate environment.
>
> See *The Guardian*'s (2011) set of reports, 'Reading the riots', for more background and analysis of the 2011 riots.

The case of the riots, and the discussion here, is an example of the **nature versus nurture** debate. Are our personalities something that we are born with or do they change over time? In the previous section, the type and trait theories see personalities, to different extents, as a fixed and measurable phenomenon. Eysenck even suggested that personality is so pre-determined that it has genetic and biological elements.

The ideographic approach, however, suggests that our personalities are **processual**—this means that they are not static in the sense that a framework of traits would suggest, but, rather, they are in a continual process of being changed and influenced. Our personalities are always a work-in-progress rather than being a finished article.

Nature versus nurture
The debate between whether our personalities are something natural, i.e. that we are born with, or are nurtured and develop over time.

Processual Always in a process of changing and developing.

Theory in context: Sigmund Freud

The ideographic approach has its roots in the psychoanalytic tradition of Sigmund Freud. Freud is, perhaps, most associated with the stereotypical view of the psychoanalyst, with a patient lying on the couch, speaking to the therapist, talking about their dreams and desires and their past—the analyst analysing this and using what is said by the patient to uncover hidden truths about their state of mind.

Certainly, Freud's psychology is based in a prominent role for our unconscious, inner self, and the role of this in determining personality and behaviour. However, equally important is that personalities develop in an individual way, from childhood onwards. Personalities are not reducible to broad types; rather, each personality is unique and a result of development through environmental factors, i.e. the experience to which we are exposed throughout our lives.

Freud (1927) thus outlines three aspects of the mind that are in battle (or in balance) and which lead to stages of development and problems if unbalanced.

- At the most unconscious level is the *id*—the most basic human drive. This is the irrational and impulsive side of our nature, one which craves instant gratification (and thus is wont to engage in what might be inappropriate behaviour socially).

- At the level of consciousness is the *superego*—this is the environment around us (family, etc.). From this we learn the rules and values of society—it tells us what is appropriate behaviour and what is inappropriate behaviour. The superego is thus about things like upbringing and the influence of societal factors on our development.

- Mediating between the id and superego is the *ego*. For Freud, the ego is absent at birth, but takes shape—at first venturing into the outside world in service of gratifying the needs of the id, but later becoming a balancing factor between the two.

Thus, for Freud, the ego is a vital factor. People function normally when the ego manages its balancing role, but causes personality abnormalities when this role fails to be fulfilled.

Influences on the self

Psychodynamic A description of Freud's approach to personality which sees personality as continually being developed and changed by various influences.

The approach of Freud (1927) is sometimes described as a **psychodynamic** approach—it is rooted in psychology and suggests that personality is dynamic rather than static. Our sense of self and our personality are the product of influences over time—social influences, even unconscious influences.

Rather than a standard set of traits on a framework which can be measured, individual differences are a result of our interactions and experiences in society. While this will be a unique personality development for each individual, it can be seen that there are a number of particular areas of society that will, at different times in our lives, have an influence on our personality—albeit differently for each individual. Examples of such influences that we suggest include:

- *family and upbringing*—a key focus in Freud's work is the early development that our family and upbringing have on our personality. This is where we learn rules, values, etc. as a baby onwards and is thus a very important early formative stage in our personalities

- *school*—going to school brings in more influences: rules, teachers, things learned, and also peer pressure and group dynamics from other pupils

- *university*—for many readers of this book, university will be a major influence on personality at the moment. Some of you will be starting your very first term at university. It's common when returning home after a first few weeks at university to hear people back home say 'you've changed'. The implication is that the new influences and experiences at university have, in some way, changed personality and behaviour

- *organizations and the workplace*—in our careers we will work in several organizations. Like schools and universities, the workplace is a social phenomenon in which we will interact with people and have new experiences, and so organizations themselves are an influence on personality (we examine this later in this chapter under the social–radical approach)

- *social categories*—it's not just specific organizations that have an influence on the development of ourselves as individuals. Categorizations in society also give us a sense of self—possibly with pressures to conform to certain types of behaviour—while at the same time acting as markers of our identity within society. For example, gender not only marks our identity in society, but also produces pressures for certain types of behaviour (e.g. 'boys don't cry'), which carries over into expected workplace behaviours (see, for example, the discussion of women and emotional labour in Chapter 16). Other social categories, such as race, religion, and social class, also have an impact on identity and personality in terms of how we develop as individuals, but also how others see us.

Visit the Online Resource Centre to read more on social categories and the individual.

The list is potentially infinite. If our personality develops from our experiences and interactions, then any aspect of society can, potentially, have an influence on us. In that we all have unique histories of social interaction and influence (we all come from different families, schools, etc.), so the ideographic approach sees every personality as unique, rather than conforming to a standard set of traits.

What organizations, individuals, or societal phenomena could you add to the list just given? How do you think they have influenced your personality?

Problems with the ideographic approach

While the ideographic approach recognizes the individuality of personalities over and above broad personality types or scales, we suggest that this approach does bring some important drawbacks:

- Freud's work has not been used in mainstream management theory to the same extent as we saw with his contemporary, Jung. Its origins are in a clinical setting—the therapist's couch—and it is more concerned with identifying personality problems and focusing on 'abnormal' personalities, rather than identifying general personality types

- the ideographic approach doesn't solve the problem of the time taken to get to understand a personality. Understanding comes from lengthy therapy sessions. Again, is this practical and efficient enough for a workplace recruitment setting? It brings us back to the problem personality tests were meant to solve—the need for efficiency

- where the nomothetic approach can be seen to be too scientific—reducing a personality to something that can be calculated—the ideographic approach is without any form of standardization. Given that personalities are unique and open-ended, our understanding of them is open to interpretation. Different people may perceive the same personality differently and, as we will see in the next section with interviewing, there are many factors that can alter and cause bias in that perception and interpretation.

In many respects, the ideographic approach raises questions, albeit valid questions, about the measurement of personality, rather than offering solutions. It recognizes that nomothetic approaches do not give a measurement of the entirety of an individual's personality, but rather than offering an alternative way of measuring personality it highlights the difficulties in getting such a full measurement. The ideographic approach lays out the complexity of personality rather than offering any hope of measuring that full complexity.

Nevertheless, the ideographic approach does allow us to appreciate the limited nature of information gained about personality in different selection processes. Furthermore, as we will see, it allows us to view the ideal selection process as one of building up information about personality from different sources rather than relying on any one single, limited source.

The ideographic approach and selection

Running case: interview thoughts

As the interviews progress, different panel members react differently to different candidates. Although they won't record it officially in their notes, each has their own reasons for liking or disliking particular candidates.

- Meg Mortimer dislikes one candidate who she felt came across as 'too common' for the hotel.
- Linda Wilkinson looks favourably upon a candidate who comes from her home town.
- Simon Chance takes a dislike to the accent of one of the candidates, which he feels sounds arrogant.
- Carl Jones dislikes a candidate because he had worked at a chain of gyms that he has had a major dispute with.
- Linda Wilkinson is not keen on a candidate who calls her 'Leslie Wilkinson' by accident when they are first introduced.
- Simon Chance is drawn to a candidate who supports the football club of which he is chair.
- Carl Jones feels that a young mother will be unable to juggle parenting responsibilities with commitment to the fitness centre.

The job interview would seem to be a way to make up for the deficiencies of nomothetic approaches, such as a personality test. If a personality test gives just a snapshot of a personality, presented as a few numbers and percentages, then the interview at least allows the selection panel the chance to see people in the flesh and get a better measure of their personality.

The bad news is that the predictive validity of interviews is even worse than that of personality tests (Pilbeam and Corbridge, 2006: 173; Reilly and Chao, 1982: 15). Why should it be that being able to meet and speak to the candidate in person produces even worse results?

Newell and Rice (1999: 159) suggest that many of the problems are due to **interpersonal perception** in the interview process. That is to say, the interpretation of the personality of a candidate can be biased by certain factors:

- the **halo/horns effect** suggests that a positive or negative trait that is picked up early in an interview can then bias the way in which an interviewer perceives an interviewee from then onwards. So, a good initial impression can lead to other perceptions confirming that initial impression, and vice versa for a bad first impression

- similarly, interviewers can be drawn to candidates with characteristics similar to themselves—a sort of halo effect generated by seeing aspects of themselves in the candidate

- the interview can also be subject to **stereotypes** and **discrimination**. In the previous section we saw that race, gender, class, and religion are all aspects of society that feed into the development of our personality and social identity. They can also be factors which bias people's interpretation in an interview. For example, Reilly and Chao (1982) suggest that both race and gender are aspects where negative stereotypes and discriminatory views can affect women and black candidates negatively.

Which perceptual biases do you think are taking place in the running case?

In the latter case such discrimination would not only be unfair, but also illegal if discovered to be the basis for making an appointment. The UK Government's Department for Business and Industry provides guidance on avoiding the perceptual biases listed previously.

Visit the Online Resource Centre to read more on avoiding the biases.

The type of interview described earlier is an **unstructured interview**. Much greater predictive validity comes from **structured interviews** (Pilbeam and Corbridge, 2006: 173), which focus on behaviours relevant to the actual job. Interviewers might ask hypothetical questions, such as 'what would you do in this particular situation?', or questions which draw upon actual working experience, such as 'describe what you did in a particular situation when . . . ?'.

The structure, formality, and focus of a structured interview minimizes the opportunities for perceptual biases to creep in on the part of interviewers; however, it also minimizes the amount to which interviewers are able to get a picture of the personality of the candidate. Newell and Rice (1999: 160) suggest that, while the structured interview is more valid, the unstructured interview still remains the most popular form of interview that is carried out.

Interpersonal perception The way in which one individual perceives the personality of another.

Halo/horns effect The tendency for people to continually reaffirm their initial impressions of a person, whether good or bad.

Stereotype Where a characteristic is attributed to a person because of their membership of a particular social group, e.g. because of race or gender.

Discrimination Where a person is treated negatively and unfairly because of their membership of a particular social group, e.g. because of race or gender.

Unstructured interview An interview with no preset formal structure.

Structured interview An interview with a set format and standard questions, based around job-specific questions.

Informal measures

Running case: informal measures

During a break in interview proceedings, Chance peruses his list of five candidates and decides to undertake a bit of his own detective work.

First, he tries to find them on social-networking sites. Many of the candidates have, sensibly, set their privacy settings high. However, one candidate has left all of their information visible. This was unfortunate as their most status update reads: 'Pulled a sickie today—good times, afternoon in pub for me. Hope I can get out of this job soon, interview tomorrow, fingers crossed!'. Chance finds this bizarre as the candidate had scored well on the 'conscientiousness' aspect of the scale and seemed very sincere in the interview.

Chance also realizes that one of the candidates had previously worked in a gym owned by a former colleague. Chance gives his friend a call and asks about the candidate. 'I was glad to be rid of him', says the friend. 'He had no warmth with customers—he was cold and aloof. I wouldn't employ him if I were you—you'll have the customers leaving in droves.'

Again, Chance finds this strange, as the personality test had scored the candidate high on 'agreeableness' and he had presented himself well in the interview.

Chance feels that his informal enquiries have provided some useful information to add to the selection process, but is left unable to ask the candidates about what he had found out—it wouldn't look good to tell them he'd been snooping around on their Facebook profiles and talking to their ex-bosses.

Perhaps the extent to which managers crave for as much personality data as possibly over and above that which can be provided by formal recruitment methods is shown by the informal measures that managers will engage in. It would be a naïve applicant who thought that informal measures did not take place—phone calls to previous employers and, more recently, checks of social-networking sites should be expected.

Real life case: Facebook as a selection tool

A recent controversy in selection has been the use of Facebook or of online searches by employers trying to find out information about candidates. A candidate who describes themselves as 'serious and hardworking' on an application form might find this declaration undermined by numerous and regular postings of photographs of themselves falling out of nightclubs on their social-networking profile.

Of course, people have become wise to this and any sensible candidate will ensure that their privacy settings make this information private. However, a more recent trend has been for employers to demand Facebook passwords during an interview so that they can then see the full range of information on the profile for themselves, regardless of the privacy settings that the candidate has set.

Sources: Boston Globe (2012), Barrett (2012), Time Magazine (2012).

 What information about you is freely available online and potentially available for current and potential employers to see?

From an ideographic perspective, we can see how social networks and online information provide an insight into personalities that leaves any formal assessment methods lacking. All aspects of a person's life are laid bare—their interests, the comments they have made, and the photographs that they are tagged in.

While people can choose to make this information private, employers requesting passwords is something that Facebook (2012) has described as 'distressing', and they suggest that passwords should not be handed over as it is a violation of the terms of service and compromises the privacy of the information of the candidate's linked friends on Facebook.

Alongside privacy and ethical issues is a consideration of the nature of the data that might be gathered from Facebook and similar social networks. In a study of social-networking sites being used as a part of the selection process, Kluemper and Rosen (2009) make two points about the nature of the personality data provided:

- compared to an instrument like a personality test, social-networking sites give a rich and wide-ranging insight into a person's lifestyle. Kluemper and Rosen (2009) found that such sites could be used to get a good estimation of a personality on the big five scale (see p. 250)

- however, Kluemper and Rosen also caution about the nature of information that is available on such sites. Recruiters are able to find out information about aspects of a person's life which might feed into discrimination and stereotyping: marital status, sexual orientation, religion, etc. This raises legal issues—employers have access, through social-networking sites, to information that cannot be used legally as the basis for selection decisions.

Visit the Online Resource Centre for more on the use of social networking sites in selection and personality assessment.

We can understand the desire of employers to access the wealth of information available online so as to get a greater insight into a candidate's personality, but it is an area that has possible legal issues, with a lot of information irrelevant to the selection decision being made available. A more formal way to increase the amount of information about a candidate for the selection process is through the assessment centre approach.

Getting an overall picture: assessment centres and triangulation

Running case: the new duty manager

The interviews prove inconclusive, with different members of the panel having wildly differing perceptions of the candidates. It becomes apparent that few of the opinions have anything to do with people's aptitudes for the job and, in some cases, they are illegal and discriminatory.

'Only one way to settle this', says Chance, 'let's get them down on the gym floor and see them actually doing the job'.

Each of the candidates is asked to meet with an actual gym member, speak to them, and devise and deliver a workout plan.

Following this the candidates are given an 'in-tray' exercise. Each is placed in front of a computer and given a number of tasks to address: timetabling classes, staff rotas, etc.

Finally, a second interview is offered to the candidates. In this instance, questions are worked out in advance, with each being of relevance to the job or reflecting on the exercise that had taken place.

One candidate above all others shines through. Although his personality test wasn't the best fit, he has done well on the extraversion and agreeableness aspects. The interview and his work with the customers brings this out, and the in-tray exercise shows that he can also apply himself to individual, administrative tasks.

The job of duty manager is offered to David Smith, who accepts.

Pilbeam and Corbridge (2006) summarize research into different methods and their predictive validities (Table 8.4). Taken by themselves, any of the formal assessment methods that we have so far encountered in this chapter score woefully low in predictive validity.

However, by blending methods into an assessment centre approach, a greater predictive validity can be achieved. An **assessment centre** approach doesn't necessarily mean that the selection activity takes place within a specific building of that name. It refers to the fact that no one method is used in isolation, but is blended alongside other methods. The more methods used, the more complete a picture of the candidate is gained.

Assessment centre
A recruitment strategy where different selection techniques are blended in a selection process.

While methods such as personality testing and interviews may still be used, methods that have found to be effective additions to an assessment centre blend include those which are related to the work itself, for example so called 'in-tray exercises', where a candidate actually works through some of the tasks that might be expected of them. For example, in the earlier example of Pret a Manger, one of the techniques used to assess whether or not a person demonstrates the Pret 'behaviours' is to get an applicant to actually spend a day working in one of their stores.

While an assessment centre approach doesn't give a understanding of personality in its full ideographic form, it does draw upon more sources of information than a personality test or an interview alone. Furthermore, its formal nature can avoid the assessors being party to some of the legally-problematic information that more informal methods, while giving a fuller picture of personality, might provide.

Table 8.4 Predictive validities of different selection methods (adapted from Pilbeam and Corbridge, 2006: 173)

1.0	Certain prediction
0.9	
0.8	
0.7	Assessment centres for development
0.6	Skilful and structured interviews
0.5	Work sampling Ability tests
0.4	Assessment centres for job performance Biodata Personality assessment
0.3	Unstructured interview
0.2	
0.1	References
0.0	Graphology Astrology

© *People Resourcing: Contemporary HRM in Practice*, Pilbeam, S. & Corbridge, M., Pearson Education Limited, 2006

Review questions

1. Describe the social factors which have an influence on personality.

2. Explain how the ideographic approach sees personalities as dynamic.

3. Analyse the difference in the assumptions about the nature of personality made by the ideographic and nomothetic approaches.

Apply

4. Think of a time when you have had a job interview—how well did you think the panel were able to judge your personality?

Towards a social-radical approach

Running case: the spark is extinguished

Six months after his appointment, David Smith is seeing out the last of the evening's guests and about to lock up. Simon Chance catches a glimpse of him looking sullen, barely raising his voice to say goodbye to the remaining guests, then slamming the door shut and lamely throwing the keys on to his desk.

This confirms what Chance had been hearing—the bubbly, outgoing, motivated personality that Chance had recruited six months ago has become withdrawn, barely raising a smile during the day. It isn't the best image to project to customers.

Chance is puzzled as to what has happened. All of the recruitment stages—the personality test, the interviews, the situational assessments—had marked Smith out as having the exact personality that they had wanted. And to begin with, he had been just that—it was as if his personality had changed.

Chance calls Smith over to find out what has happened.

'It's the work here', replied Smith, 'there's just too much drudgery. I have to fill in numerous forms—rotas, pay sheets, class timetables, and accident reports. I feel like I'm suffocating in paperwork. I spend most of my time in that back office—just me and a computer. I need to be around people, that's how I get my buzz. I have to just pass on orders to the other guys in the team—they see me as someone who gives them work, not works with them. And it's rubbing off on them, too. We have to go out there and be cheerful and motivate customers, but how can we be when with this work the spark is just extinguished'.

What has been the main influence in changing Smith's personality? Is this a fault of the selection process assessing his personality incorrectly or the organization in changing his personality?

The nomothetic approach saw personality as something which can be measured and sorted into particular types and categories. The ideographic approach saw personalities as more unique and complex, developing as a result of social interaction and experiences. In both cases, however, they see personality as a 'thing', which the organization, in some way, observes and tries to understand.

Both of these approaches also suggest, largely, that personality is a property of the individual, independent of the organization. However, we saw with the ideographic approach that organizations themselves are one of the many societal influences on the self which change and develop our personalities. The workplace thus has a direct effect on the very thing it is trying to measure—personality.

The **social-radical** view that we suggest in this final section brings about a shift in the relationship between organizations and personality. It suggests that the idea of personality as an objective 'thing,' independent of the organization, is problematic. Instead, the organization has a part to play in creating and shaping personalities.

> Social-radical approach The view that organizations have an effect on the personality of their members.

- First, we see personality categorizations as a tool of organizations which come to take on lives of their own and actually have an effect on personalities, rather than simply measuring them. This is symptomatic of how Michel Foucault (1977) saw power operating in society, and so we term this the social part of the social–radical approach.

- Secondly, organizations directly affect personalities and this can be in a negative, as much as positive, way. This negative effect was observed by radical psychiatrist Felix Guattari (e.g. Guattari and Negri, 1990) and we thus see this as the radical aspect of the social–radical approach.

Foucault's critique of categorization

In Chapters 4 and 13 we encounter the work of Michel Foucault, who examined ways in which power operates throughout society. One of Foucualt's (1977) interests, as we saw in Chapter 4, is how power is exercised by categorizing, calculating, and ordering the world around us. We are categorized and labelled as a means of convenience, i.e. it is a simple way of understanding and managing the world. What is important for Foucault is that although such categorizations are shortcuts, they come to take on lives of their own and people identify themselves by these labels.

Think of the results of personality tests—categories like INTJ, ENFP, etc.—these are frameworks that have been created specifically as a way of categorizing personalities in order to simplify them and make measuring them more efficient. But once such tests are administered, it is common that people come to wear them as labels and come to identify with them—people say 'I am an ENTP,' etc. (compare this with the manager in Chapter 6, who takes a Belbin test then starts to live up to the result—the label starts to define not only how the person identifies themselves, but how they actually act). Rather than simply reflecting a personality, the test and its associated label starts to affect and change that personality.

Deleuze and Guattari (1983) build on Foucault's work to examine how psychoanalytical traditions place labels upon people in both nomothetic and ideographic approaches. They would criticize Jung for ordering the personality into certain types and, equally, criticize Freud for his 'ordering role' (Deleuze and Parnet, 2002: 14) in interpreting people's unique personalities.

Felix Guattari worked as a radical psychiatrist in France where he was interested in trying new and different means of treating patients rather than by traditional methods. Guattari treated patients not by labelling them as a particular personality type, as Jung would, nor by labelling them as having some sort of abnormality, as Freud would. Instead, Guattari saw people as having the potential to *become* something else, striving for new experiences and interactions so that their personality can constantly develop.

The radical critique of the effects of organization on personality

The problem for Deleuze and Guattari, and in particular for Guattari, is that the potential of people to strive for new experiences and interactions is often stifled—none more so than by the effects of what organizations actually do and the way in which people are organized.

This is something that we saw in Chapters 2 and 3. Recall the Diego Rivera murals and Chaplin's *Modern Times*. In both cases people were shown as dehumanized, their personalities deadened by boring and monotonous factory work. Weber, too, noted how bureaucracy, with its repetitive routines, led to disenchantment—a loss of the magical elements of life.

Rational modes of organization are thus seen as having a stifling effect upon the personalities of workers. For Guattari, however, there is an alternative and organizations could operate in a way to allow individual potential to be realized. Work which is focused on promoting individual potential and creativity is thus suggested as:

> . . . [A]ctivities in which people can develop themselves as they produce, organizations in which the individual is valuable rather than functional... And redefining work as creative activity can only happen as individuals emerge from stifled, emotionally blocked rhythms of constraint.
>
> Guattari and Negri (1990: 15)

The social–radical view is a complex and critical view of personality which shifts the attention from most of what we have examined in the chapter, i.e. rather than organizations measuring personalities we now see organizations having a direct effect upon people's personalities, more often than not constraining what those personalities could have the potential to be.

The suggestion of the social–radical approach—that organizations should operate in a way that frees individual personalities to reach their potential—may sound idealistic. However, in the following chapters, where we see motivation theories that suggest people should 'self-actualize' and maximize their potential (Chapter 9), and where we see theories of learning that promote the reflective self-development of individuals (Chapter 10), we see people working towards achieving their potential rather than being stifled by the organization.

Review questions

1. Explain how personality types can be seen as putting 'labels' on us.
2. Analyse how organizations can stifle the potential for personalities to develop.

Chapter summary

This chapter has examined two major perspectives on personality and their implications for the assessment of personality in the recruitment and selection process.

The nomothetic approach sees personality as something which is measurable and which can be outlined in terms of models of personality types and/or traits. Such models are the basis for personality testing in organizations, and some of these models are used in the recruitment and selection process.

The ideographic approach sees personality as complex and unique to each individual, and as something which is changed constantly by our interactions with society. It criticizes the nomothetic approach for giving too simplistic a view of personality.

Personality testing in organizations is seen to be of limited use, but, equally, many methods of selection fare badly in their predictive validity. While the use of social networks and other informal methods can gain more insight into personality, the practice is ethically dubious. An assessment centre approach blends selection methods in a more formal setting, and can gain more accurate and valid results in the selection process.

Finally, a social–radial approach takes account of the effect that organizations themselves have upon personality, both in categorizing it in personality tests and in their role as an aspect of society that shapes people's personalities.

Further reading

Bratton, J. 2010. *Work and organizational behaviour*. Palgrave Macmillan, Basingstoke.
Many textbooks cover theories of personality, for example see Chapter 4 of Bratton.

Rees, G., French, R., and Rayner, C., Chartered Institute of Personnel and Development. 2010. *Leading, managing and developing people*. Chartered Institute of Personnel and Development, London.
For an overview that concentrates more on the recruitment and selection process, see Chapter 9.

Cain, S. 2012. *Quiet: the power of introverts in a world that can't stop talking*. Viking, London.
An overview of Jung's introversion and extraversion from the perspective of the introvert.

Kluemper, D.H., and Rosen, P.A. 2009. Future employment selection methods: evaluating social networking web sites. *Journal of Managerial Psychology* 24(6): 567–580.
A case study of the use of social networking sites in the selection process.

Bibliography

Barnett, E. 2012. Facebook passwords 'fair game in job interviews'. *The Daily Telegraph*, 23 March 2012. Available at: http://www.telegraph.co.uk/technology/facebook/9162356/Facebook-passwords-fair-game-in-job-interviews.html (last accessed 18 July 2012).

Boston Globe. 2012. Job seekers getting asked for Facebook passwords (20 March 2012).

Cain, S. 2012. *Quiet: the power of introverts in a world that can't stop talking*. Viking: London.

Callaghan, G., and Thompson, P. 2002. 'We recruit attitude': the selection and shaping of routine call centre labour. *Journal of Management Studies* 39(2): 233–254.

Cattell, R.B. 1966. *The scientific analysis of personality*. Aldine Pub. Co.: Chicago.

Costa, P.T. Jr., and McCrae, R.R. 1992. *Revised NEO Personality Inventory (NEO-PI-R) and NEO Five-Factor Inventory (NEO-FFI) manual*. Psychological Assessment Resources: Odessa, FL.

Dakin, S., Nilakant, V., and Jensen, R. 1994. The role of personality testing in managerial selection. *Journal of Managerial Psychology* 9(5): 3–11.

Deleuze, G., and Guattari, F. 1983. *Anti-Oedipus: capitalism and schizophrenia*. University of Minnesota Press: Minneapolis.

Deleuze, G., Parnet, C., and Deleuze, G. 2002. *Dialogues II*. Continuum: New York.

Eysenck, H.J., and Eysenck, M.W. 1985. *Personality and individual differences: a natural science approach*. Plenum Publishing Corporation: New York.

Facebook. 2012. Protecting your passwords and your privacy. 23 March 2012. Available at: https://www.facebook.com/notes/facebook-and-privacy/protecting-your-passwords-and-your-privacy/326598317390057.

Foucault, M. 1977. *Discipline and punish: the birth of the prison*. Pantheon Books: New York.

French, R., and Rumbles, S. 2010. Recruitment and selection. In: Rees, G., and French, R. (eds) *Leading, managing and developing people*, 3rd edn. Chartered Institute of Personnel Development: London, pp. 169–190.

Freud, S., and Riviere, J.T. 1927. *The ego and the id authorized* (transl. J. Riviere). Hogarth Press: London.

Furnham, A.F. 1997. Knowing and faking one's five-factor personality score. *Journal of Personality Assessment* 69(1): 229–243.

Gosling, S.D., Rentfrow, P.J., Swann, W.B., Jr. 2003. A very brief measure of the big-five personality domains. *Journal of Research in Personality* 37: 504–528.

Guattari, F., and Negri, A. 1990. *Communists like us: new spaces of liberty, new lines of alliance*. Semiotext(e): New York.

Jung, C.G. 1923. *Psychological types: or, The psychology of individuation* (transl. H. Godwyn Baynes). Harcourt Brace: New York.

Keirsey, D. 1998. *Please understand me II: temperament, character, intelligence*. Prometheus Nemesis: Del Mar, CA.

Kluemper, D.H., and Rosen, P.A. 2009. Future employment selection methods: evaluating social networking web sites. *Journal of Managerial Psychology* 24(6): 567–580.

McCrae, R.R., and Costa, P.T. Jr. 1990. *Personality in adulthood*. Guilford Press, New York.

McCrae, R.R., and Costa, P.T. Jr. 1996. Toward a new generation of personality theories: Theoretical contexts for the five-factor model. In: Wiggins, J. S. (ed.) The five-factor model of personality: theoretical perspectives. Guilford Press: New York, pp. 51–87.

Morgeson, F.P., Campion, M.A., Dipboye, R.L., Hollenbeck, J.R., Murphy, K., and Schmitt, N. 2007. Reconsidering the use of personality tests in personnel selection contexts. *Personnel Psychology* 60(3): 683–729.

Myers, I.B. 1962. *Manual: the Myers-Briggs type indicator*. Consulting Psychologist Press: Palo Alta, CA.

Myers, I.B., and Myers, P.B. 1995. *Gifts differing: understanding personality type*. Davies-Black Pub.: Palo Alto, CA.

Newell, S., and Rice, C. 1999. Assessment, selection and evaluation: Problems and pitfalls. In: Leopold, J., Harris, L., and Watson, T. (eds) *Strategic human resourcing: principles, perspectives and practices*. Financial Times/Pitman: London, pp. 129–165.

Passer, M.W., Smith, R., Atkinson, M., Mitchell, J., and Muir, D. 2003. *Psychology: frontiers and applications*. McGraw-Hill Ryerson: Toronto.

Pilbeam, S., and Corbridge, M. 2006. *People resourcing: contemporary HRM in practice*. Financial Times/ Prentice Hall: Harlow.

Reilly, R.R., and Chao, G.T. 1982. Validity and fairness of some alternative employee selection procedures 1. *Personnel Psychology* 35(1): 1–62.

The Guardian. 2011. Reading the riots: Investigating England's summer of disorder. Available at: http://www.guardian.co.uk/uk/series/reading-the-riots,

Thompson, P., and McHugh, D. 2009. *Work organisations: a critical approach*. Palgrave Macmillan: Basingstoke.

Time Magazine. 2012. Job seekers getting asked for Facebook passwords (20 March 2012).

Motivation and the meaning of work

Chapter overview and learning outcomes

By the end of this chapter you should be able to:

- describe the differences between extrinsic, intrinsic, and social factors of motivation

- explain the role and extent of pay in motivating workers

- analyse the role of psychology in understanding motivation, explaining the main contributions

- of behaviourist, content, and process approaches

- explain how social factors, such as identity and orientations to work, contribute to our understanding of what motivates people to work.

Key theorists

Burrhus Frederic ('BF') Skinner	Pioneered operant conditioning which is used in workplace behavioural modification techniques
Abraham Maslow	Developed the hierarchy of needs, which was then used as a theory of workplace motivation
Frederick Herzberg	Suggested that only some job characteristics motivate people in the workplace, while other hygiene factors can only cause dissatisfaction
John Stacey Adams	Developed equity theory, which suggests that people are motivated by comparing their workplace rewards with others
Victor Vroom	Developed expectancy theory, which suggests that people are motivated by actions which help them achieve their desired goals
John Goldthorpe	Suggested that people had different predispositions, or orientations, to work, which influence the meaning and identity people derive from their work

Key terms

Extrinsic motivators	Motivating factors that are a result of an action performed by somebody else
Intrinsic motivators	Motivating factors that are come from within, e.g. a sense of personal achievement
Behavioural theories of motivation	A use of stimulus and response techniques whereby behaviour is altered by a planned provision of rewards and punishments

Content theories of motivation	Theories of motivation which suggest that the content of work be designed so as best to meet the needs which motivate workers; examples include Maslow's hierarchy of needs and Herzberg's motivators and hygiene theory
Process theories of motivation	Theories of motivation which suggest that motivation is a result of individual processes of perception, comparison, and calculation; examples include equity theory and expectancy theory
Social theories of motivation	Theories of motivation which see motivation as part of the role of work in creating meaning and identity for people within society

Introduction

Running case: a sense of lethargy

Meg Mortimer senses something wrong in reception. Not massively wrong—well, at least not yet—but there just seems to be a sense of lethargy: people are sluggish in performing their tasks, with nobody wanting to go the extra mile. Smiles seem forced and the performance of jobs is perfunctory—the job is done but with no great enthusiasm.

Mortimer looks at the reception team on duty today:

- David Morrison—a young porter who, in his spare time, is training to do a triathlon
- Jane Foster—a receptionist who is also undertaking a hospitality course and is tipped for great things within the hotel
- Sue Ridgewell—another receptionist who Mortimer considers to be good, but not as ambitious as Jane
- Steve Long and John McAuley—two students who work part time either as porters or sometimes behind reception.

The reception area is quiet and all that Mortimer sees are the sullen faces of the reception team. What can she possibly do to make these people more motivated towards their work?

How do you feel at the start of a day's work? Are you looking forward to the work, being with your colleagues, and ready to get stuck into the challenges of the day ahead? Or do you face the day with dread, sensing hours of drudgery and boredom in front of you, with only the thought of the pay packet to get you through until the end of your shift? In other words, how much are you motivated by your work?

Motivation, or a 'will to perform' (Brooks, 2009: 80), is the subject of this chapter. If workers have a natural, strong inclination to work and to put plenty of effort into that work, then, perhaps, a part of the job of management is already done. In this chapter we see how

Motivation The will and desire that a person has to engage in a particular behaviour or perform a particular task.

perspectives on workplace motivation have been informed largely by psychological perspectives.

- Pay might seem like the obvious workplace motivator, but we see it as one of many possible workplace rewards. In particular, we distinguish between **extrinsic rewards** that are given by the organization, of which pay is an example; **intrinsic rewards**, such as a sense of achievement, which come more from within the individual worker; and **social rewards** that come from colleagues and co-workers.

- From a behaviourist perspective, **rewards** and **punishments** are used to motivate workers towards some behaviours and away from others. While this may have results, it can be viewed as **coercion** and manipulation, rather than as genuine motivators of behaviour.

- Extrinsic, intrinsic, and social rewards have been integrated into content theories of motivation, which show how individuals are motivated differently. Such content theories include the well-known motivation theories of Maslow (1943) and Herzberg (1966).

- Process theories of motivation see motivation as much more individual, subjective, and changeable. With equity theory and expectancy theory, individuals make their own comparisons and calculations which feed into their levels of motivation.

We suggest that these psychological perspectives, while commonplace in motivation literature, have their shortcomings and do not fully explain workplace motivation. An alternative view of motivation, which we consider at the end of the chapter, comes from looking at the wider social significance of work—the meanings that people attach to work and how this feeds into their identity in society.

Extrinsic reward
A reward that a person receives which is provided by somebody else.

Intrinsic reward
A reward that a person senses for themselves, rather than it being provided by someone else.

Social reward
A reward that comes from the feeling of being part of a group or team.

Reward In behaviourism, a positive response that is received for performing a particular behaviour.

Punishment In behaviourism, a negative response that is received for performing a particular behaviour.

Coercion Behaviour that arises from being forced in some way into performing that behaviour.

Employability skills: find something that you are passionate about

Job adverts often call for 'self-motivated' candidates, but what do employers mean by this? In our interview, Joe Greenwell, the Chairman of Ford in Britain, suggests that a big part of success in a job comes from passion for the work and curiosity about that work.

> If you are going to be successful at anything you need to be genuinely enthusiastic about what you are doing. If you are not enthusiastic about it you are not going to be able to lead people . . . If you want to engender passion in the people you lead you'd better be passionate yourself . . .

> If you are passionate you are also curious. Curiosity is very valuable. If you want to get better at something you need to ask questions, roll your sleeves up and learn and be prepared to get told off and make mistakes.

Source: Author interview with Joe Greenwell, Ford in Britain, 2012. (Visit the Online Resource Centre for full interview.)

If you can demonstrate passion and curiosity about a job to an employer, it is evidence of self-motivation towards that work.

Extrinsic, intrinsic, and social rewards—all about the money?

Running case: triathlon man

David Morrison is a young porter in Junction Hotel. Much of the day is spent standing around reception, following a repetitive routine of opening doors and taking bags up to rooms. He has to do what he is told, when he is told, and he rarely feels challenged at work.

In his spare time he is training for a triathlon, with sessions morning, noon, and night.

In the morning, before work begins, David is in the pool of the fitness centre churning up the lengths towards his target. As he completes the final length, exhausted and gasping for breath from his effort, he looks up to his trainer, who is at the side of the pool: 'good job, 30 seconds less than yesterday'. Morrison smacks the surface of the water with his fist and lets out an almost primal cry of 'Yeeeeesss!'. To say he is pleased with his achievement is an understatement.

All of this effort was done free-of-charge, of course. Indeed, he had to pay quite a lot of his own money for equipment, entry fees, and sports club memberships. And the sponsorship money for the triathlon will all be going to his charity—again, a feeling which makes him proud.

As he emerges from the changing rooms in his porter's outfit, David walks towards reception to perform the one element of the day for which he will actually be rewarded with a wage. His response to starting this part of the day is that he lets out a sigh, feels all of his enthusiasm drain away, and stands in the corner of reception waiting for another day of opening doors and carrying suitcases. He looks up at the clock and can't wait for lunchtime, when he will be back in the pool.

When asked what motivates us to work, the instinctive first response tends to be 'pay'. Work is something that we do for a pay cheque rather than for enjoyment. Certainly, this is the case for many students who have part-time jobs in order to get through university. Working in bars, shops or, occasionally, factories, many of our students have said the pay at the end of the month is the only thing that keeps them turning up for work.

For Frederick Taylor and Henry Ford (see Chapter 3), pay was used as a motivator to get people to do otherwise monotonous and boring work in factories and on assembly lines.

- Taylor believed that workers had a 'natural laziness' (1911: 20)—they were inherently demotivated and thus piece rates (payment for the actual amount of work done) were used to motivate people to work.

- Rather than piece rates, Ford introduced the $5-day. While this was a massive increase from the previous $2.40 a day (Raff and Summers, 1987: 69), it was accompanied by wholesale mechanization and rationalization of the work process, and highly controlled working conditions (Beynon, 1984: 34). Workers disliked the conditions intensely, but the high wage motivated many job-seekers to want to work in Ford's factories.

Both Taylor and Ford had a simple, coercive view of motivation based on the assumption of *homo economicus*—people were motivated by pay and economic reasons alone (see Chapter 5). In this section we examine the link between pay and motivation, but also between other workplace rewards and motivation. In particular, we note two types of rewards:

- pay is an example of an extrinsic reward. It is something external to the individual which is used as a means to motivate them to perform a particular action or behaviour, such as work. Other examples of extrinsic motivators might be promotion, working conditions, perks of the job (such as a company car), etc.
- intrinsic rewards are those rewards which are internal to the individual. Examples include a sense of achievement or a feeling of satisfaction in a job well done. Lawler (1973) suggested that intrinsic rewards could, in fact, be much more powerful motivators than extrinsic rewards, such as pay and promotion.

Motivation and pay—an unclear relationship

The link between motivation and pay is far from clear. It is certainly a major mechanism in the motivation of people in the workplace, but, as Handy (1993: 51) notes, little is known about how it actually works as a motivator. Furthermore, it is far from clear cut that it is the prime motivator in the workplace.

> ### Real life case: footballers' high pay
>
> If you listen to football radio phone-ins on a Saturday afternoon, invariably a caller whose team has lost will start complaining that their players did not seem motivated. 'If I was paid £200,000 a week I would certainly look like I was trying'. Given their astronomical salaries football fans argue that they really should be motivated.
>
> A lack of motivation came to the fore with the case of Carlos Tevez, paid a reported £20 million by Manchester City. This did not stop him from having disputes with the board and putting in transfer requests. At a European match in September 2011, Tevez seemingly refused to go on to the pitch from the substitute's bench when asked to by his manager, although he later claimed this to be the result of a misunderstanding. Much of the discussion after the incident centred on how someone paid so much could be disinclined to do their work.
>
> **Sources:** Taylor 2011a, 2011b; The Daily Telegraph, 2011.

It would seem that high pay alone is not enough to motivate footballers in some instances. Despite the high pay, there was still something missing that meant Carlos Tevez was not motivated to perform on that particular occasion.

Studies into the relationship between motivation, pay, and other types of reward have shown a similar mixed picture.

- Between 1946 and 1992, a series of surveys of US workers showed that praise from managers, interesting work, and good wages are the main workplace motivators, with each of these taking the top position at different times (Wiley, 1997).
- In the SCELI survey (Rose, 1995: 293), 68% of respondents suggested that they worked primarily for economic reasons, while 25% said they worked primarily for 'expressive reasons', and a further 5% for social reasons.
- In a global survey of executives, managers, and employees (Dewhurst et al., 2009), financial rewards, such as bonuses and an increase in base pay, played an important part in motivating workers; however, non-financial incentives, such as praise from a manager,

attention from managers, and being given responsibility, were shown as being slightly more effective motivating factors.

From the various results it would seem that pay has an important role in motivation, but that a word of encouragement or praise from the boss can motivate employees just as much.

Rewards such as praise or interesting work are not as tangible as pay, but they are still extrinsic motivators and management have a role in providing these motivating factors within the workplace. However, such rewards may also contribute to workers gaining intrinsic rewards, such as a sense of achievement or a sense of pride in their work.

Intrinsic motivation—the lottery question

> **Real life case:** lottery millionaires
>
> In March 2012, a syndicate of 12 UK bus drivers shared a £38 million jackpot on the *Euromillions* lottery and instantly quit their jobs, leaving their boss with the headache of replacing a quarter of his work-force (Walker and Jones, 2012).

If you won £10 million on the lottery would you give up work or would you continue to work?

For many of us, our first act on winning the lottery would be to quit our current job—no more of the 9 to 5 routine and answering to the boss. It is certainly an understandable response if people are in a boring, monotonous job, or are unhappy in their work. If the only motivation for work is the pay, then there is no reason to carry on if money is no longer an issue.

However, a different picture emerges if the consideration is whether or not people would give up work *completely*. People might give up their current job but, once a new house and car have been purchased, and multiple holidays have been taken, they might seek out some form of work, or challenge, to occupy them.

The **lottery question** has been posed in numerous surveys and, repeatedly, the answer is that a majority of people would continue to work, either in the same or a different job. In an international comparison, Harpaz (1989) reported that between 68.8% of respondents (in the UK) and 93.4% of respondents (in Japan) said they would continue to work in some form, even if they no longer needed the pay.

In the world of business we see billionaires who have earned amounts akin to a lottery win, but who continue

A life of leisure?

Lottery question
A question which asks whether people would give up work if they had enough money to live without having to work.

to work. Why do the likes of Bill Gates, Richard Branson, and Mark Zuckerberg still work when they have enough money to retire on extremely comfortably? Even if the money is no longer important, there is still intrinsic motivation—from the success of launching new products, perhaps, or a sense of achievement and pride in the company that they have built.

Intrinsic motivation, however, is not just something that motivates the rich. It can be seen to motivate workers who receive a more modest wage packet and, indeed, those who exert effort for no financial reward.

- It is often suggested (e.g. de Gieter et al., 2006) that workers in caring and public-service occupations, such as nursing and teaching, are motivated by intrinsic rewards. Rewards come from an intrinsic sense of satisfaction from caring or doing good for society.

- When people perform voluntary work for free, the lack of pay does not mean that people are demotivated in that work—intrinsic rewards can come from satisfaction or pride in doing good deeds.

- Many of you may do spare-time activities that require work and effort, for example sports, music, or a hobby. Rather than being paid, you may, in fact, incur expense in terms of travel, equipment, and lessons. Again, motivation can be intrinsic—a sense of achievement in scoring a goal or in exhibiting a finished painting, for example.

What activities do you do in your spare time? What motivates you to put in the effort to do them?

Motivation from social factors

Real life case: on the night shift

One of our students, who did a typical student part-time job primarily for the pay, told us of his experiences working as part of a team that stacked shelves in a major supermarket overnight.

The team of shelf-stackers would talk, and laugh, and joke with each other throughout the night shift. Management, adopting a somewhat Taylorist approach, thought that this wasted time and was ill-disciplined. Workers were instructed to stack their own individual shelves and to do so in silence—the only time that they should speak or interact with each other would be during breaks and away from the shop floor.

The result of this new disciplined regime was that productivity went down and workers stacked fewer items during their shift.

While participation in a sports team or a voluntary group might bring intrinsic rewards, for many it is also a social activity, and motivation may, indeed, come from social rewards, such as team spirit or a sense of belonging.

This seems to be the issue in this case. Management's direct control had the opposite effect to what one might expect—productivity actually reduced. In this case it was the social side of the organization that actually motivated the workers in that it helped them through a monotonous, overnight shift—social factors actually increased their motivation to work.

Studies of groups in factory environments (e.g. Ackroyd and Crowdy, 1990; Collinson, 1988) have shown similar evidence of joking and banter, which might seem to be at odds with management's desire for control and efficient work. However, in both cases, the motivation and control within the social group itself led to the amount of work required by management being completed by the group.

These cases illustrate a perspective on motivation which we saw reflected in Chapters 5 and 6, where the importance of the social side of the organization was highlighted. For example, in the Hawthorne studies (see Chapter 5) Mayo suggested that it was the social side of the organization which motivated workers and, in examining groups and teams (Chapter 6), it was demonstrated that group loyalty rather than management control can motivate people immediately.

Extrinsic, intrinsic, and social rewards are all factors which can motivate an individual. In the remainder of the chapter, we examine differing theories and perspectives on how these rewards might be deployed in the workplace by managers wishing to motivate their workforce.

Review questions

1. Describe what is meant by extrinsic, intrinsic, and social rewards.

2. Analyse the role of pay in motivating people to work.

Apply

3. In the running case, what examples of extrinsic and intrinsic rewards motivate David Morrison?

Behavioural theories and motivation

Running case: the smile card

Meg Mortimer asks business manager Phil Weaver to help her increase morale and motivation among her sullen reception staff. 'Easy', he responds, 'just reward them for smiling at customers and engaging with them, and punish them if they don't. That'll get the grins back on their faces'.

Stating that 'if it can be measured, it can be managed', Weaver suggests to Mortimer a 'smile card' reward scheme.

Staff will carry a card with spaces for ticks. A number of 'desirable behaviours' for receptionists are outlined—smiling at a customer, offering information about the local area, etc. If a manager sees a member of staff engage in a desirable behaviour, they will get a tick in the box.

However, there were also a number of undesirable behaviours—being unpleasant to a customer, not offering to help with baggage, etc.—which will attract a 'black mark'.

Once a month the cards will be gathered in. Black marks will be subtracted from ticks and the winning total will get a pay bonus for that month.

Name: _John McAuley_　　　　　　Month: _May_

Desirable behaviours:　　　　　　Black marks:

Date	Behaviour observed	Manager initials	Tick	Date	Behaviour observed	Manager initials	Cross
1/5	Helpful to customer with heavy suitcases	MM	✓	2/5	Passed through reception – ignored guest waiting at desk	SC	✗
3/5	Helped guest with airport taxi	MM	✓				
4/5	Very cheerful with group of tourists	SC	✓				

Figure 9.1 Junction Hotel's smile card.

How well do you think the smile card will tackle issues of morale and motivation among the reception staff?

If someone were pointing a gun at you, would you do what they said? Probably yes, for fear of the consequences. But deep down, would you have been genuinely *motivated* by that gun to the head or would you have been *coerced* into doing what you were told? What if, instead, they offered you money to do something? Would this motivate you to do anything at any time?

In this section we examine an approach to motivation which derived from the psychological tradition of **behaviourism**. Behaviourism is sometimes referred to as a 'carrot and stick' approach. It tries to motivate people's behaviour by providing a reward or incentive for good behaviours (the carrot) and, conversely, a punishment for bad behaviours (the stick).

Behaviourism An area of psychology which suggests that behaviour can be changed through the planned use of rewards and punishments.

If you have a task to do, do you ever use rewards to motivate yourself? For example, if you have an essay to complete you might set a reward, such as a night out or a shopping trip, for completing it.

An effective motivator?

Behaviourism is also known as **stimulus–response** psychology. A stimulus, be it a punishment or reward, is provided as a means to encourage some form of behaviour or response.

In the workplace such stimuli might be the extrinsic motivators examined in the previous section, i.e. the various rewards and punishments which management are able to deploy within the workplace. For example, pay may be the reward for people turning up to work, no matter how monotonous or dehumanizing that work may be. Pay can also be used as a reward in the form of bonus payments for particular behaviours that management wish to encourage.

Pay can also be the basis of punishment, for example the withholding of bonuses or, ultimately, firing a worker. While we may not work at gunpoint, many people may feel a metaphorical gun is pointed at their head as they need to work and earn a wage in order to pay bills and survive.

> **Stimulus–response**
> The underlying relationship of behaviourism, whereby a particular response, or behaviour, is the result of a particular stimulus —either a reward or punishment.

Real life case: punishment and reward in football

It is often the case that professional footballers receive rewards for playing well—a pay bonus for a team that wins the league, for example, or a new, improved contract for a player who impresses during a season.

However, there have also been reports of the stick rather than a carrot being used to punish players for poor performances. For example, Ukrainian football club Dynamo Kiev have a policy of withholding pay from players if the team fails to win a game (Okeleji, 2011) . In the late 1990s, the manager of English club Wimbledon issued a threat of taking players to an opera or making them eat a meal of offal if they ever lost by five goals—the threat seemed to work as they never lost by that margin (Ashdown and Smyth, 2009).

More drastic and disturbing punishments have also been used, for example the Ivory Coast team were sent to a military camp after being knocked out of the early stages of a tournament and were humiliated on television by being shown performing military manoeuvres. The Iraq football team, under the management of the son of Saddam Hussein, were reported to suffer outright torture, such as beatings, scaldings, or being forced to bathe in raw sewage (Ashdown and Smyth, 2009; BBC News, 2010).

In this section we examine how pay and other extrinsic motivators are used as stimuli in behavioural techniques of motivation in the workplace, and to what extent such techniques genuinely motivate workers rather than simply coercing them into performing particular behaviours.

Pavlov and classical conditioning

Running case: grinning like an idiot

From: John McAuley
Been grinning like an idiot all day not a manager here to see me. Then, one frown and Chance suddenly appears putting a black cross on the card.

From: Steve Long
Haha, bad luck mate.

From: John McAuley
I mean, what an idiot Chance is. Feels like he's writing my school report or something.

Imagine that you wanted to stop a particular bad behaviour—biting your nails, for example. One method could be to use a foul-tasting nail varnish. The motivation to stop biting nails comes from the negative association that develops between the behaviour, nail-biting, and the immediate punishment for that behaviour, the unpleasant taste. Behaviour is said to be **conditioned**—the association between stimulus and response leads to a change in behaviour.

This association, and the subsequent modification of behaviour in response to a particular stimulus, is termed **classical conditioning**. While the **aversion therapy** described previously might aim to condition people into stopping a particular behaviour, similar associations can also be used to promote or encourage particular behaviours.

The original experiments in classical conditioning were undertaken by Russian psychologist Ivan Pavlov (Pavlov and Anrep, 1927), who, while investigating the digestive systems of dogs, noticed an unintended result. A dog's natural response is to salivate when faced with the stimulus of a bowl of food. Pavlov began to ring a bell whenever the food was presented. When this had been repeated often enough, Pavlov rang the bell alone with no food present. The dogs, however, would still salivate just at the stimulus of the bell.

In Pavlov's experiments, this conditioned response of drooling would stop if the bell rang and there was no actual food provided. The association between the bell and food became weaker until, eventually, the conditioned response became **extinct**. To maintain the conditioned behaviour, a continuous **reinforcement** of the association between the stimulus and response was needed—the bell had to be rung every time that food appeared.

While classical conditioning might be applicable to humans in clinical settings, such as aversion therapies, its workplace use is limited.

- Punishment needs to be immediate and happen every time a behaviour occurs. In a workplace setting, every example of a negative behaviour would have to be spotted and punished immediately for classical conditioning of that behaviour to take place. In fact, in a workplace setting, punishments can have the by-product of causing anxiety and resentment towards managers, and lowering morale (Villere and Hartman, 1991: 28).

- To motivate workers towards a particular behaviour, management would need to supply rewards continually so as to avoid extinction of that behaviour. Villere and Hartman (1991: 29) suggest that even something as simple as a boss smiling at an employee every morning needs to be maintained—a morning where the smile doesn't occur stands out and can be demotivating.

Conditioning A change in behaviour brought about using stimulus–response techniques typical of behavioural psychology.

Classical conditioning A type of conditioning of behaviour where a reward or punishment accompanies and reinforces every instance of the behaviour to be conditioned.

Aversion therapy A type of classical conditioning whereby a particular behaviour is continually accompanied by a punishment so as to discourage that behaviour.

Extinction Where a conditioned behaviour dies out because the reward or punishment is no longer provided.

Reinforcement In behavioural psychology, the continued encouragement of a behaviour by the provision of a particular reward.

Skinner and operant conditioning

Running case: automatically, all the time

From: meg_mortimer@junctionhotel.co.uk
To: phil_weaver@junctionhotel.co.uk

Subject: Smile cards

Phil,

Not sure about these smile cards—I feel like I have to be in reception all the time to be able to give out ticks on the card. They'll only smile when I'm around.

From: phil_weaver@junctionhotel.co.uk
To: meg_mortimer@junctionhotel.co.uk

Subject: RE: Smile cards

Meg,

No—don't worry about being there 100% of the time. Just make sure you pass through there a few times a day. Reward them every so often and they'll smile automatically all the time.

When we are at work, we don't expect that after every customer served, after every call from a customer handled, or after every pint pulled, the boss will hand us a part of our wages as motivation for us to continue doing that work. Rather than the reward being instant and occurring after every desirable action, as is the case with classical conditioning, we know that a wage comes along at regular intervals—weekly or monthly, for example.

American psychologist B.F. Skinner (1969) developed the ideas of classical conditioning into **operant conditioning**. While Pavlov experimented with dogs, Skinner experimented with animals in an observation box. In one such experiment, if a rat pressed a lever in the box it received a reward in the form of a piece of food.

Skinner discovered that the reward did not need to be provided continuously, but could be intermittent, for example after every fourth press of the lever. Furthermore, he found that rewards that were *variable* rather than *fixed* (i.e. not after every fourth press of the lever, but after 2, then 5, then 4, then 6 presses, for example) were more effective motivators.

In human behaviour, the most effective forms of reinforcement have also been found to be variable, i.e. with an element of surprise and unpredictability. This explains how gambling can become such a powerfully addictive behaviour: 'The potential of winning on the next race keeps gamblers coming back again and again . . .' (Villere and Hartman, 1991: 29). If you knew that a fruit

> **Operant conditioning**
> A conditioning of behaviour which recognizes that rewards and punishments do not need to be continuous, but can be scheduled in a way to still condition behaviour.

Variable rewards.

machine would pay out on every tenth press, there would be no incentive to play the first to ninth spins. But, because the payout ratio is random and variable, there is always the incentive to put more money in the machine and hope that the next spin will be the winner.

Skinner's work has been applied in the workplace by Luthans and Kreitner (1985) as **organizational behaviour modification** (OB Mod). They suggest that fixed and variable **schedules of reinforcement** have different effects in terms of motivating employees into particular types of desired behaviours. For example (Villere and Hartman, 1991: 29):

> **Organizational behaviour modification** The use of operant conditioning techniques in a workplace setting.
>
> **Schedules of reinforcement** A blend of fixed and variable reinforcements designed so as best to reinforce desired behaviours.

- a regular salary, paid weekly or monthly, is an example of a fixed-interval reward—it is provided regularly at a set time. While this might motivate us to turn up and work, it doesn't necessarily motivate us into putting in any extra effort in the workplace from day to day
- variable rewards—such as a bonus, an award, a promotion, or even a pat on the back from the boss—tend to have a higher success rate in motivating workers into specific behaviours that managers wish to encourage over and above what is done simply in order to collect the monthly pay cheque.

 Visit the Online Resource Centre for more on variable and fixed schedules of reinforcement in the workplace.

Operant conditioning thus demonstrates the motivational value of blending different types of reward and reinforcement. The regular salary is important—without it people would not turn up for work; however, blending this with variable forms of reward has a greater effect in motivating specific day-to-day behaviours.

Behaviourism: advantages and disadvantages

Running case: target behaviours

Steve Long is on portering duty, delivering room service to an elderly guest. While engaging her in pleasant chat he notices through the window that Chance is walking into a crowded reception.

Steve instantly cuts off the guest mid-sentence and runs out of the room, slamming the door behind him. Leaving the customer upset and bemused in his wake, he rushes down to reception and starts engaging a group of waiting guests in conversation, showing them some tourist information leaflets, even though they have shown little interest in visiting the local attractions.

As reception empties, Chance walks over with his pen. 'Well done young man', says Chance, placing a tick on Steve's smile card.

Organizational behaviour modification works on a seemingly common-sense principle that '. . . if a particular pattern of behaviour is rewarded, it will occur more often' (Makin and Sutherland, 1994: 6). However, behind this seemingly simple idea lies a pitfall—exactly what behaviour is being rewarded?

If a reward is given, for example, for reaching a particular target, it is behaviours which reach that target which might be motivated rather than the underlying behaviour that the organization is trying to promote. People can often find creative ways to meet those targets that don't necessarily correspond to the initial behaviours desired by management.

For example, Makin and Sutherland (1994) suggest that a way to promote safety-conscious behaviour in organizations could be to reward a lack of accidents. However, rather than motivating people into more safety conscious behaviours, for example wearing safety goggles, a response can be simply not to report any accidents, so as to meet the actual target set. The underlying behaviour change—being more safety conscious—is not addressed, people just engage in behaviours that they think will help them meet the target and get the reward.

Research insight: The target becomes the behaviour, Wray-Bliss, E., and Willmott, H. 1999. Battling with the gods: workers, management and the deities of post industrial management culture. In: Goodman, R. (ed.) *Modern organization and emerging conundrums: Exploring the post-industrial sub-culture of the third millennium.* New Lexington Press, San Francisco, pp. 377–389.

An example of targets not achieving their original aim is seen in Wray-Bliss and Willmott's study of targets in a call centre. A number of calls-per-hour were required to be handled, which was monitored through the computer system (see Chapter 4 for more on this). The system was meant to bring about efficient handling of calls. However, with a target of nine calls per hour, call-centre agents struggling to meet this as the end of an hour approached would make up the shortfall by picking up a ringing phone and hanging up immediately. It would register as a call to help meet the target, but is slamming the phone down on customers a behaviour that the organization would wish to encourage?

At the start of this section, we asked if coercive behaviour, through punishment, genuinely motivates people within or simply alters their behaviour in response to the imminent threat. Even where rewards rather than punishments are used, we can question the ability of behavioural techniques to genuinely motivate deeply rather than simply influence people into particular behaviours for the reward that they bring.

A critique of behavioural techniques is that it sees people in simplistic, mechanistic terms (Martinko and Fadil, 1994: 16). No account is taken of cognitive processes whereby people think for themselves (ibid.)—people are seen almost like robots who respond unquestioningly to various stimuli or rewards. Perhaps this lack of depth of motivation is linked to the fact that behavioural techniques rely on extrinsic rewards and thus simply act at a surface level, ignoring the power of intrinsic and internal rewards.

Nevertheless, behavioural techniques, when applied to the workplace, may have demonstrable effects in some instances, that is to say there are instances where they can be seen to bring about changes in behaviour as seen with Makin and Sutherland's (1994) previous example of accident reduction. While this section has examined behavioural techniques for their contribution to theories of motivation, they have had widespread use in management and organization theory, including in areas relevant to the following chapters:

- in knowledge and learning—behavioural techniques are used to understand how people learn new behaviours (see Chapter 10)

- in change-management—behavioural techniques are one of many techniques that can be used to change the behaviours of workers (see Chapter 11)
- in theories of leadership—behaviourism is used to understand how leaders can shape and condition the behaviour of followers (see Chapter 12).

Overall, behavioural theories provide a 'one size fits all' approach to motivation. For example, if pay is the basis of a reward system, it assumes that everyone will respond in the same way to pay as a motivator. In the next section we see motivation theory taking account of individual differences in what motivates people.

Review questions

1. Describe the main features of classical and operant conditioning.

2. Explain how variable reinforcement has a strong motivational effect on people.

Apply

3. How is the smile card at Junction Hotel an example of organizational behaviour modification? How well do you think it motivates the staff into appearing more lively and engaged with guests in the reception area?

Content theories of motivation

Running case: differences in motivation

Jane Foster has been working at Junction Hotel as a receptionist for five years. She and her partner have not yet had children and they are easily covering their mortgage payments and other outgoings.

Foster receives constant praise for the quality of her work from her boss, Meg Mortimer, and, when Mortimer is away, Foster is the first choice to deputize as the front-of-house manager. She has been singled out as potential managerial material for the future and, as such, the company are sponsoring her to do a part-time degree in hospitality management at the local university on day release.

Mortimer is surprised that Jane has barely participated in the smile card scheme, even not handing in her card on occasions. 'I know when I'm working well and that gives me pride', says Jane. 'I don't need ticks in a box to tell me that.'

Steve Long is a student and is working next to Foster today. His circumstances, however, are different. He is studying full-time for a degree in accountancy. He works part-time in the reception area as a means of supplementing his income—he is finding rent payments hard to meet and needs the money. Mortimer thinks his work is also good, but is surprised that he refuses when she asks him if he would like managerial responsibility. Nevertheless, he has thrown himself head first into the smile card scheme and has twice been the winner, pocketing the bonus cheque.

Content theories
Theories of motivation which suggest that the content of work should be designed so as best to meet the needs which motivate workers.

What motivates you in the workplace may be different to what motivates your colleagues. While one worker is there for the pay, another may be looking for career progression and status. **Content theories** of motivation suggest that managers need to take account of the fact that different things motivate different people.

Behaviourist theories in the previous section used extrinsic motivators to design motivation techniques that were applied equally to all workers in one organization. Content theories recognize that a range of different motivators—extrinsic, intrinsic, and social—may exert a different level of motivation on different people.

Content theories assume that individuals have a set of needs and that the content of work can be designed so as to meet those needs and thus motivate the individual. In this section we examine two widely used content theories—Maslow's **hierarchy of needs**, and Herzberg's motivators and hygiene theory.

Maslow's hierarchy of needs

For many management students and practitioners alike Maslow's hierarchy of needs is overwhelmingly the most familiar model of motivation; indeed, some former business students report it as being one of the few theories that they remember from the entirety of their studies. His ubiquitous triangle (see Figure 9.2) pops up in lectures, training courses, and textbooks such as this.

The allure of this triangle is that it promises a simplistic framework showing the factors which motivate people in the workplace. The problem is that its application in workplace settings is often too simplistic, with many original insights from Maslow either misrepresented or simply removed. Indeed, Maslow did not intend it to be a theory of workplace motivation and suggested that he had not seen proof that it worked in a workplace context (Dye et al., 2005: 1380).

So why are we examining Maslow's hierarchy if it is largely discredited as a model of workplace motivation, even by its own creator?

- First, although his model's efficacy in the workplace is largely disputed, it is something that you will still encounter in studies and in your management career so it is important that you understand the model, its background, and its flaws.

- Secondly, while the way in which Maslow has been used in the workplace might be problematic, this is not to say that Maslow's work is without merit. For instance, he recognizes aspects of workplace motivation that simplistic views, such as the Fordist/Taylorist *homo economicus* or the behaviourist stimulus–response approaches, ignore.

Elements of the hierarchy

In this section, we present Maslow's hierarchy in the important context of his wider psychological interests before examining how it is applied to workplace motivation.

Maslow (1943) suggested that people have five basic needs:

- physiological needs—basic physical needs for survival, such as food and water

- safety needs—a need for safety, physical health, and security

- love and belongingness—social needs, such as being part of a group, interacting with others, and a need for affection

- esteem needs—a need for status, recognition, and self-respect

- self-actualization—a form of ultimate self-fulfilment, the achievement of our ultimate potential and creativity.

Hierarchy of needs Maslow's theory which shows that individuals have a set of needs in hierarchical order, whereby people are motivated by the most immediate unsatisfied need.

Figure 9.2 Maslow's hierarchy of needs.

Self-actualization

Esteem

Social/belongingness

Safety

Physiological

Prepotency One characteristic having dominance over others.

For Maslow, these needs are arranged in a hierarchy of **prepotency** (see Figure 9.2). The most dominant need that will motivate an individual is the most basic need of which they are deprived. Once needs at one level have been satisfied, so an individual will go on to be motivated by needs at the next level upwards. So, if an individual is starving, they will be motivated by the most basic need for food. If people have food on the table then they will be motivated by safety needs, and so on, moving up the hierarchy.

Theory in context: Abraham Maslow

An aspect of Maslow's work that is often missing from management accounts is that his research interests began far away from workplace motivation. He was a primatologist, interested in behaviour among monkeys and much of his research was about patterns of dominance within monkey populations (Cullen, 1997; Dye et al., 2005).

These interests then transferred into an interest in dominance in sexual behaviour in humans. His particular focus was based on interviewing women in their 20s about their sexual desires (Cullen and Gotell, 2002). It is from these streams of research that he developed his hierarchy of needs. In its original form it was not a theory of workplace motivation, but a theory of needs that humans needed to fulfil in order to attain psychological health and well-being.

His interest in dominance in both primates and in sexual behaviour is important here—the hierarchy of needs is essentially a theory of how any one unsatisfied need dominates over others in its motivational effects at any one time.

The hierarchy of needs was not first applied to workplace settings by Maslow, but by Davis (1957) drawing upon Maslow's work. In this reading, different workers will be motivated by different factors, depending on where they are on the hierarchy of needs. For example:

- a worker with not enough money to feed themselves will probably take on any work—they will be motivated by the immediate need to eat (physiological needs)

- a worker who has money for food but is just about managing to cover bills and rent might be motivated by job security to meet these safety needs (shelter, warmth, etc.)

- a worker who is meeting their bills easily will be motivated more by the social/belongingness aspects of the organization—group and team dynamics, and the culture of the organization become important
- as people fulfil their social needs, workers are motivated by esteem needs, such as a desire for promotion within an organization, or recognition of their work, for example by an appreciative word from a manager
- the final aspect of motivation is self-actualization—fulfilment of potential and achievement within the workplace.

Insights from Maslow

Maslow's hierarchy provides valuable insights into human motivation which have relevance to the workplace. In particular, he goes beyond behavioural psychology, which he viewed as too simplistic and having 'no earthly use in any complex human situation' (Maslow, 2000: 7), towards a more multifaceted view of what motivates behaviour:

- it shows that individuals are motivated differently—what works for one worker may not for the other. This provides an important counter-argument to the likes of Taylor who saw pay as a universal motivator. In Maslow's hierarchy pay is one of a number of motivators—it may work at certain lower levels of the hierarchy, but other motivating forces take over as an individual moves upwards
- the hierarchy integrates different types of motivating factors within its framework. Extrinsic rewards, such as pay, are important, particularly at lower levels; social rewards are important motivators at the belongingness level and at higher levels intrinsic rewards, such as achievement and self-respect, become important
- the hierarchy shows that an individual's motivation is not fixed—it is dynamic and people can progress over time. Thus, a student might be motivated by pay in order to meet safety needs of paying rent and bills, but, later in life, a professional might be motivated by esteem needs, such as promotion.

Maslow provides a much more positive view of motivation to simple carrot and stick, or, ultimately, coercive methods. Indeed, in his original work, Maslow placed a strong emphasis on human values showing that people might be motivated by factors other than pay and promotion, such as growth and creativity.

Indeed, the aspect of his hierarchy that Maslow emphasized most was **self-actualization**. He had views about the nature of personality similar to the social–radical approach from Chapter 8 (personality), namely that people had unrealized potential and that it was the role of society, and organizations within society, to help them to achieve this potential (Dye et al., 2005: 1383). Self-actualization is a concept of people reaching their creativity, and a sense of self-fulfilment and achievement in the same way as an artist or musician might do. For Maslow, this could also be achieved in the workplace.

Self-actualization For Maslow, a realization, or actualization, or an individual's ultimate human and creative potential.

Critique of Maslow and the use of Maslow

The critique that we present of Maslow is in many ways a critique of the way it has been frequently applied, or misapplied, by others in the study of management and organizations.

Real life case: Maslow at Tesco

A case study presented by a leading UK newspaper, along with classroom teaching materials, maps the work practices of UK supermarket Tesco on to Maslow's hierarchy.

Examples provided are:

- physiological needs are met by providing regular monthly pay, a restaurant, and lockers for belongings
- formal contracts of employment, and health and safety procedures meet security needs
- social needs are met by team and group-working
- esteem comes from praise for hard work, ensured through the appraisal system
- self-actualization (here renamed self-fulfilment) comes from promotion opportunities, a personal development plan, and fast-track management schemes.

At first sight, this case seems to apply Maslow to Tesco's work practices well—a restaurant surely meets the physiological need for food, for example. But it is a very simplistic application, categorizing a number of practices under Maslow's headings without understanding how people are really motivated by these drives in Maslow's work.

- It ignores the dynamic nature of Maslow's model—it would seem that all motivating forces are acting at once and Tesco is seen to provide for those needs, whereas in Maslow's model it is only the most immediate unsatisfied need that motivates individuals.
- A physiological need for food comes from being deprived of food—a very basic urge. It does not describe people popping casually into the staff canteen for lunch. We assume that Tesco already pay enough for workers to afford food so this more basic need would not be acting as a motivator—it is one which is already satisfied and so the model has been misapplied.
- This application of Maslow underplays the role of self-actualization, even renaming it as self-fulfilment. In Maslow's original work, self-actualization is an ultimate realization of creativity and potential as a human being not simply being on a fast-track promotion scheme.

Source: http://businesscasestudies.co.uk/tesco/motivational-theory-in-practice-at-tesco/.

The argument that can be made against the use of Maslow's theory in the Tesco case is that it has been applied too simplistically and at a surface level, without understanding the deeper insights of his work. This is symptomatic of many of the uses of Maslow's work in management theory.

For instance, in Maslow's work, self-actualization is a healthy state—being at any level below shows that not all basic human needs are met and thus a person is psychologically unhealthy. In management theory, self-actualization seems to become a vague target to aim towards in a career, with workers in the meantime occupying any number of steps along the way. In any of these instances, according to Maslow, the individual would be unhealthy (Dye et al., 2005). Management theory misunderstands the significance of self-actualization.

A further problem with the use of Maslow is that, while it is often presented in management theory as an exact depiction of human motivation or a guideline on how to motivate, in fact it lacks empirical evidence. That is to say its applicability of the theory in workplace reality has not been proven.

Have you ever walked into a workplace at the start of the day thinking about what is motivating you in terms of physiological, safety, belonging needs, etc.? Do you think it is realistic that a worker goes into work thinking along the lines of 'Yesterday I met my esteem needs so today I want to self-actualize'?

Wahba and Bridwell (1976) review a number of studies into Maslow's hierarchy, showing that not even the existence of the five levels of the hierarchy as distinct and separate categories have been proven empirically in the workplace, let alone the idea that people move up from one level to the next. As we saw earlier, Maslow himself stated that he had not seen proof of his theory working in organizational settings.

Furthermore, while there are problems with the application of Malsow's hierarchy in workplace settings, it is also often applied without any consideration of critiques of Maslow's original theory itself.

For example, looking back to Maslow's original studies on domination, Cullen and Gotell (2002: 538) argue that his work is highly gendered in nature. 'Implicit in Maslow's portrayal is an assertion of the naturalness of female submission and the eroticization of male dominance and this assertion, in turn, forms the gendered foundation of the needs hierarchy' (2002: 538). Dye et al. (2005: 1389) note that Maslow is also dismissive of gay men and of black people.

The concept of self-actualization, in Maslow's terms, is thus founded on particular assumptions which privilege white, male, heterosexual ways of being and, furthermore, the concept of self-actualization can be seen as elitist. Maslow suggests throughout his work that not everyone is capable or seems to want to be able to self-actualize (see the collected works in Maslow, 2000). Dye et al., (2005) suggest that maybe this is why the model is so popular in the management context—it suggests management to be an elite capable of self-actualization and, at the same time, dismisses other workers as being motivated by basic, ultimately unhealthy needs.

These critiques of both the misapplication of Maslow and of Maslow's original theory show that while his triangle may have widespread and popular use in management theory, it should be *handled with care*. Certainly, it should not be seen as the one and only model of motivation in itself—many other theories of motivation are discussed in this chapter.

Study skills: models and heuristics

The simplistic nature of models such as Maslow's hierarchy gives them an appeal to students and managers alike—it is a nice idea to think that motivation can be plotted out in such a simplistic framework. Indeed, some students write very poor essays on motivation which see motivation as nothing more than Maslow's hierarchy, ignoring all other theories on the subject.

Models exist as a simple way to present complex ideas. A model is what is known as a heuristic—a way of presenting information or theories in an accessible, easily understandable manner.

The danger is that people rely on these simplified versions rather than looking at the topic in depth. A model is also just one viewpoint on a topic—there may be other models which present the same area of study in a different way and from a different viewpoint.

If using a model such as Maslow in an essay, don't simply repeat it. Think about approaching it in more depth, for example:

- what is the model actually trying to say about the nature of motivation? Don't just draw the triangle—say what each level means and what it implies about how people are motivated

- what assumptions underpin the model? For example, we have seen how Maslow's hierarchy derives from his earlier research about domination and we have noted the importance he places on self-actualization

- what alternative views are there? What other models exist and what do they say that is different or which challenges Maslow's model?

- does it hold up to empirical scrutiny? We have seen how Maslow's hierarchy has not been proven in a workplace setting. Have other models been applied successfully or unsuccessfully in the workplace?

Herzberg: motivators and hygiene factors

Running case: a sense of responsibility

Steve Long has now won three of the smile card bonuses on the trot, and is starting to see the bonus as a part of the regular pay he expects to receive. He has already allocated this month's bonus towards a trip to London to see his friends. He is, therefore, shocked when his friend John McAuley is announced as this month's winner. Having to cancel his trip, Long is unhappy, feeling as though he has had a pay cut.

The contrast with Jane Foster can't be greater. With her degree studies progressing, she is now being given the responsibility of managing shifts in the reception from start to finish, even if Mortimer is around. And, where usually she leaves paperwork in Mortimer's pigeon hole to be signed off, Mortimer has said 'sign it yourself—if you're in charge you have the responsibility'. Foster does all of this, willingly and happily, for the same level of pay as Long.

While Maslow's hierarchy is based in the needs of individuals and then looks at how they might be satisfied in the workplace, Herzberg's motivators and hygiene framework starts with the actual characteristics of the job itself. For Herzberg (1966, 2003), these characteristics of the job can be divided into two distinct groups:

- **motivating factors** are factors that have the potential to increase the satisfaction of a worker. They include achievement, recognition for that achievement, the work itself, having responsibility, and the potential for personal growth (Herzberg, 1987: 9). These are largely intrinsic factors and are factors that are likely to satisfy the higher levels of Maslow's hierarchy

- **hygiene factors** cannot, in themselves, do anything to increase satisfaction; however, this does not mean that they can be ignored. If they are not provided or addressed sufficiently they have the potential to cause dissatisfaction. Such factors are extrinsic factors, such as company policy, supervision, interpersonal relationships, working conditions, job status, job security, and pay (Herzberg, 1987: 9), and are more likely to satisfy lower level needs on Maslow's hierarchy.

Motivating factors
For Herzberg, characteristics of a job which can bring about increases in the job satisfaction and motivation of workers.

Hygiene factors For Herzberg, characteristics of a job which cannot bring about increases in the job satisfaction and motivation of workers, but which can cause demotivation if they are not addressed sufficiently.

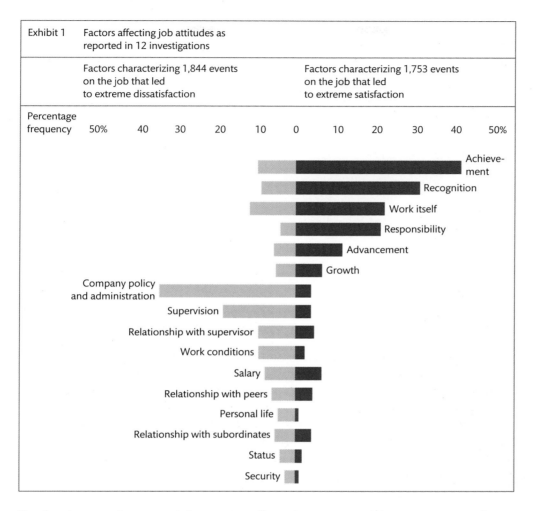

Figure 9.3 Herzberg's (1987) motivators and hygiene model (based on Herzberg, 2003: 87–96).

Reproduced by permission of Harvard Business Publishing.

Herzberg's research was carried out originally with engineers and accountants, and consisted of asking them to name an event at work that had caused them extreme satisfaction or extreme dissatisfaction. The results, shown in Figure 9.3, show the motivating factors at the top of the diagram, providing more instances of satisfaction than dissatisfaction, and hygiene factors at the bottom, showing greater instances of dissatisfaction.

Herzberg's view of pay as a hygiene factor seems to go against our common-sense view of pay—surely a pay rise motivates people? Herzberg (1987: 6) suggests, however, that while a pay rise might motivate in the short term, it only motivates people as far as seeking the next rise. In other words, a pay rise soon comes to be seen as a 'normal' level of pay, which doesn't motivate in its own right. While it provides no extra motivation, if the pay were to be reduced back to its old level it would then demotivate. All that happens, for Herzberg, is that pay levels spiral while adding no additional motivation to workers.

Herzberg and job enrichment

For Herzberg, increased satisfaction comes from the design of work itself in a way that minimizes hygiene factors and maximizes motivators. This suggests a move away from

Job simplification
Where a job is broken down into simplistic tasks, as with Taylorism or Fordism.

Horizontal loading
Increasing the scope of a job by adding elements of work of a similar nature and at the same level of hierarchical responsibility.

Job rotation Where workers alternate between different tasks of a similar nature.

job simplification, as seen with rational work design (see Chapter 3) where work is broken down into simplistic tasks, and towards increasing the intrinsic motivation that workers derive from jobs.

Herzberg (1987) first discusses two forms of job redesign which emphasize the **horizontal loading** of the task. Rather than performing one repetitive task, the worker is given an expanded variety of tasks:

- **job rotation** is where a worker moves between different tasks in the work process rather than sticking to one repetitive task. For example, a worker in a fast-food restaurant does not generally spend the whole of their working life at one task; instead, they will rotate between working on the till, making burgers, and cleaning tables, etc.
- **job enlargement** is where a worker performs several elements of a task at the same time, for example a fast-food worker assembles all elements of the burger rather than just adding the relish.

Would you be any more motivated if you went from one monotonous job to being rotated between four or five monotonous jobs?

For Herzberg (1987: 10), such forms of work do not increase motivation. If two forms of work have zero motivation, then adding them together still makes zero. Instead, he suggests that intrinsic motivators, and thus job satisfaction, will be increased through **job enrichment**. Enrichment comes from **vertical loading**, where more authority and autonomy over the task are given to workers, for example through increasing individual responsibility or the complexity of tasks, and allowing self-directed teams rather than tightly-controlled individuals.

The aim of job enrichment is to increase not just the number and variety of tasks, but also their quality and ability to provide intrinsic forms of motivation. Vertical loading suggests that workers have a part in much more of the work process from start to finish, rather than being just one small 'cog in a machine'.

Job enlargement
Where the elements of an immediate task are increased to take in further elements of a similar nature.

Job enrichment
Where the quality of work is increased through the provision of increased responsibility, autonomy, and variety of tasks.

Vertical loading
Where a job is enriched by adding tasks which would normally be associated with elements of responsibility linked to positions higher in an organizational hierarchy.

Real life case: job enrichment at Volvo

A classic case of job enrichment is the development of Volvo's car manufacturing plant at Uddevalla, Sweden, in the 1980s. The factory floor and organization could not stand in greater contrast to that of the Fordist assembly line. Rehder (1994) states that:

- rather than working individually on a line, workers were divided into six autonomous work groups. Each occupied an area of the factory that was designed to feel as self-contained as possible. The teams would work on four cars at a time, with each car in a different state of progress
- workers were trained in all the skills necessary to build a car and knew how their tasks fitted into the overall production process
- teams had a lot of independence, setting their own work schedules, and even having a say in recruitment when new members of a team were appointed. They also had a say in higher management decisions.

Overall, job enrichment seemed to motivate workers much more than a traditional assembly line—there was a strong team work ethic reported at Volvo.

Source: Rehder (1994).

While job enrichment at Volvo had an effect of increasing motivation and satisfaction of workers, it is something which came at a cost—the production process was around 11% more costly than a traditional car assembly process (Gibson, 1973: 65). While Gibson suggests this can be made up for by the increased productivity and motivation of the workforce, Rehder (1994: 13) notes that following financial pressures and falling sales, the Uddevalla plant was closed by Volvo in 1993.

It's not just cost that management need to invest in if they want to bring about job enrichment—there is time spent training and, ultimately, management have to give away a lot of control—something that would be anathema to managers of a Taylorist persuasion (see Chapter 3). Indeed, for Herzberg, it is a long-term undertaking rather than a quick fix for motivation (1987: 13).

Furthermore, Herzberg's model can be seen to bring about motivation at the equivalent of higher levels of Maslow's hierarchy, designing work to bring about intrinsic rewards. A bias towards these factors could come about owing to his original research featuring white-collar workers. The insight from Goldthorpe later in this chapter shows that some people will work for instrumental reasons—the pay—rather than for any sense of growth or intrinsic reward.

In such an instance, job enrichment (or rotation or enlargement) could, potentially, be seen as a form of intensification of work. For example, workers may not want extra responsibility, especially if there is no extra pay attached to this. Workers would be having to learn and perform extra tasks as part of their work for potentially the same wage.

Again, Herzberg (1987: 13) noted that not all people want job enrichment, nor can all jobs be enriched. We get an idea of how motivation can be increased in some instances by job enrichment, but not a recommendation that this should be applied in all cases.

Review questions

1. Describe the main features of Maslow's and Herzberg's models.

2. Explain the role of intrinsic motivators in both of the models.

3. Analyse the problems in the way Maslow's original theory has been used as a theory of workplace motivation.

Apply

4. Can you use Maslow and Herzberg's models to explain the differences in motivation between Long and Foster in the running case?

Process theories of motivation

We all enter the workplace with different prior life experiences, with different feelings and interpretations of the world. As we saw in Chapter 8, we are all individuals. **Process theories** focus on motivation as a function of individual thought processes, moving from the content of work and static frameworks, as seen in the previous section, to motivation as a far more individual, fluid, and subjective process.

Motivation is based on people's past experiences and the meanings that people attach to those experiences. While content theories might try to explain how people act in relation

Process theories
Theories of motivation which suggest that motivation is a result of individual processes of perception, comparison, and calculation.

to different motivating factors, with process theories the unique and individual ways in which people feel and interpret these factors are also considered.

In this section we examine two examples of process theories—equity theory, where people compare their rewards to others, and expectancy theory, where people evaluate different actions to judge how they will achieve their desired goals.

Adams—equity theory

Running case: it's not fair

Sue Ridgewell, working on reception, has long suspected that her co-receptionist, Jane Foster, got favourable treatment from Meg Mortimer. It was the little snide comments and put downs from Mortimer that did it—nothing serious, but Foster, the blue-eyed girl who was taking the hospitality course, seems to get far more positive comments.

At first, Ridgewell tries to do better, thinking she must be in the wrong and that maybe if she tries harder she, too, will get praise from the boss, but after a while, she realizes that whatever she does there is no praise or reward, and she seems to get fewer ticks on her smile card, even though she feels she is putting in much more effort with the customers.

The result is that Ridgewell stops trying as she sees no point, and is further demotivated by the overall sense of unfairness of the treatment that she receives relative to Foster.

This feeling is compounded when Ridgewell accidentally overhears a conversation behind the reception between Mortimer and Foster. It seems Foster will get more paid time off to do the coursework for her course and other staff will be asked to cover.

Equity theory A process theory of motivation which suggests that people are either motivated or demotivated depending on how they are rewarded in the workplace compared with others.

Inputs In equity theory, efforts and contributions made by an individual to their work.

Outcomes In equity theory, the rewards and results of a person's inputs.

Overheard conversations about pay levels, perceptions that people have a lighter workload, and suggestions of favourable treatment in promotion considerations for some workers—all of these are comparisons that people make between themselves and others in the workplace. **Equity theory** (Adams, 1963), developed from research at General Electric, suggests that such comparisons will affect people's motivation and satisfaction with work.

Equity theory is based on our perceptions of fairness and justice—do we feel that we are getting what we deserve based on the efforts we put in (**inputs**) and the rewards that we get compared with others (**outcomes**). It is very much an individual, subjective level of motivation compared with content theories, for two reasons:

- it is not motivation that comes from the total amount of a reward (e.g. the amount of a pay rise) but from how fairly individuals feel that reward has been distributed

- it is based in individual perceptions of fairness—what one person feels to be fair may be perceived as unfair by another.

As students you are often asked to engage in group work as part of your degree. This can often bring up issues based around fairness and equity when there is a feeling that one group member has not put in the same effort as others—should that member get the same mark as other group members? Are there any instances where you have felt aggrieved at someone receiving the same grade as you for what you perceived to be less effort?

Adams (1963) suggests a number of reactions that individuals might have if they perceive an inequity between inputs and rewards:

* if people feel they are being under-rewarded compared with others, they will feel anger and try to redress the balance, either by negotiating a pay rise, decreasing their level of effort, or engaging in some form of workplace resistance

* if people feel over-rewarded compared with others, they will feel guilt and work harder and, although Adams realizes this is unlikely, take a pay cut.

In both cases, individuals attempt to change either inputs or outcomes to redress the inequity. Adams suggest that other actions may be taken, such as changing the point of comparison (comparing with different people); trying to find reasons and explanations for the inequity or, ultimately, leaving the job.

How realistic this is, is open to debate. There is little evidence, for example, in support of the idea of guilt for over-reward making people work harder. Huseman et al., (1987) suggest that not all people fit into the equity theory model of comparative behaviour.

However, equity theory does indicate that when organizations are designing pay and reward systems, it is in the nature of individuals to make comparisons and that often these can be subjective. People are thus judging the fairness of the system as much as what they will get out of it. If there is a perception that what an individual gets is unfair to them, then it can have a negative effect on motivation.

It is very difficult for managers to control something as subjective as individual perceptions of fairness. Tyler and Bies (1990) suggest, however, that such perceptions can, to some degree, be managed through discussion and explanation by management of changes to pay systems, and by making certain that reward criteria are applied consistently and without personal bias.

For example, Greenberg (1990) studied levels of theft in a US manufacturing plant following a 15% pay cut due to a drop in orders. The theft can be seen as resistance due to a perceived inequity following the pay cut. However, Greenberg found that theft levels were much lower among workers who had been given a detailed explanation for the cut from management than those who had been given a short, inadequate explanation. The discussion and explanation had helped lower the amount of perceived inequity.

Vroom—expectancy theory

While equity theory is based on individual perceptions of fairness, Vroom's (1964) **expectancy theory** examines how individuals link specific actions to how they perceive they will help them achieve specific goals. People will seek out positive rewards or outcomes for themselves, and will pursue behaviours that they *expect* will lead them to that reward.

Expectancy theory suggests three elements which form the calculation of what will motivate people towards a particular behaviour and away from other potential behaviours.

* (E)xpectancy is the belief that a particular effort or action will lead to a particular outcome.

* (I)nstrumentality is the belief that that outcome will attract a particular reward.

* (V)alence is the value that an individual attaches to that reward.

Expectancy theory
A process theory of motivation which suggests that people will be motivated into actions and behaviours that they can link with them achieving goals and rewards that they desire.

For Vroom, the motivational force (MF) of a particular action boils down to a calculation, $MF = V \times I \times E$. Expectancy theory suggests people will be motivated to perform efforts that they believe will be instrumental in them achieving goals and rewards that they value. Similarly, if an effort cannot be linked to a goal they value, or if it is linked to a goal they do not value highly, the motivation to perform that effort will diminish.

Say a person highly desires a pay rise (V). They believe that increased sales figures will be instrumental in them getting that pay rise (I). From experience, they have found that door-step selling generates most sales (E), so the effort to which they are motivated is to go out selling from door to door. Likewise, an effort which doesn't contribute to increased sales, for example helping a colleague to write a report, is something they will not be motivated to perform.

However, a colleague who values good working relationships (V) may find that the respect of colleagues is instrumental in achieving this (I) and would thus be more motivated to the effort of helping a colleague with a report if they believed it would gain respect from that colleague (E).

Why are you reading this chapter now? Can you link it to a particular reward that you desire at some point in the future (e.g. getting a degree, passing a module)?

While expectancy theory considers all forms of rewards, extrinsic and intrinsic, its application in the workplace has tended to focus on designing payment and similar reward systems at an individual level. Where a particular action can be linked with a bonus or pay rise or promotion, it can form part of an appraisal or performance management system whereby specific rewards for the achievement of specific objectives are outlined.

Beyond such systems, we can question, as with many other motivational theories, whether it bears up to empirical scrutiny—does it really match up to the reality of how people are motivated? Certainly, the idea that we manage our behaviours to concentrate on those which bring us a reward is a common-sense one, but do we calculate it in quite the precise, mathematical way suggested by expectancy theory?

Review questions

1. Describe the main features of equity theory and expectancy theory.
2. Explain how process theories see motivation from the point of view of the individual.

Apply

3. What examples can you see of expectancy theory, where people match actions to expected rewards, throughout the running case in the chapter.

Social approaches to motivation: the meaning of work

Running case: the meaning of work

Meg is confused by how differently everyone in the reception area seems to be motivated. Some workers respond well to the smile card scheme, others ignore it but are still good workers. She can't put her finger on exactly what she needs to do to manage the motivation of her staff.

Rather than taking a manager's viewpoint, as Weaver had done with the smile card, she decides to find out what the employees feel and hands out an anonymous questionnaire to all employees. One of the questions, 'What does your work mean to you', gives some differing, yet revealing answers:

- 'Work is a means to an end—I come in, do my shift, take the cheque. Other than that it has no other meaning'

- 'I get a lot out of work and it is really helping me get on in life. I'm really proud to tell people about what I do and the responsibility I have here'

- 'My work is nothing but constant drudgery, I only express myself and get any meaning in life through my sports'

- 'I'm here because my parents told me they were ashamed of me being on the dole—they have been constantly nagging me to get a job'.

Watch any quiz or game show on television, when a contestant is introduced to the audience, more often than not their occupation will be stated alongside their name, age, and where they live. As one of just four facts given in a brief introduction, their work is presented as a key aspect of that person's identity.

This is not just on television—think about when you are introduced to people, at a party for example. One of the first questions asked is about work. Indeed—the centrality of work to life is perhaps encapsulated in the question 'what do you do for a living?'.

For Hughes (1951) work is one of the 'most significant' things by which we are judged in society, and the name of our occupation is both a combination of 'price tag and calling card'. By this, Hughes suggests that the work we do is a significant indication of our value and position within society.

What, if any, judgements or assumptions do you make about people when you hear what job they do?

The approaches to motivation encountered thus far in the chapter have taken a psychological approach—what motivates is determined by a number of stimuli, needs, and perceptions, etc. If management understand these, then they can design work so as to increase the motivation of workers. Taken overall, we suggest that such psychological approaches have a number of problems.

- It is difficult to find empirical evidence for many of these theories—they may appear plausible, but do they reflect the reality of workplace motivation?

- Can broad frameworks of motivation, such as Maslow's hierarchy, ever appreciate the complex, individual nature of personalities, as discussed with the ideographic approach in Chapter 8?
- Overall, motivation to work theories are reductionist and narrow—they boil motivation down to a simplistic framework (e.g. Maslow) or even an equation (expectancy theory).
- Motivation theories tends to focus on just one aspect of the job—reward, satisfaction, etc., rather than having an overall view of both the job and how it links to the outside world.

In this final section we suggest that the motivation also comes from work being an indicator of our identity to the rest of society. Motivation, and the meanings we attach to work, are as much a social phenomenon as they are a psychological one. What, for example, does it mean to be a doctor within society? Or a cleaner? Or to be without work?

Why do we work?

Why do we work at all? Is it out of economic necessity or to gain a sense of identity within society? Part of the reason is the imperative from society to work—it is something that we are expected to do; furthermore, not working is almost seen as a form of deviant behaviour, against the norms of society.

Theory in context: the parable of the talents

The English word 'talent', meaning aptitude or skill, originates in an ancient biblical currency used in the 'parable of the Talents' in the Gospel of St Matthew. A master entrusts his servants with a number of talents. On his return, two of the servants have put their talents to work, doubling their value, and they are duly rewarded. The third has buried his talents in a hole in the ground, gaining nothing, and is punished for laziness. The parable of the talents, from the Christian bible, is about money, but the use of the word talent in English to mean aptitudes suggests an obligation to work and be productive—not to let our abilities and skills go to waste.

Indeed, a duty to work can be seen in the teachings of many major religions. Max Weber (1930) is noted for the notion of the Protestant work ethic, whereby religious salvation comes about as a result of hard work throughout life. Noon and Blyton (2007) note similar work ethics in Islamic, Buddhist, and Catholic faiths. A similar message is given by each—work is good and a religious duty, not working is seen as lazy and contrary to religious teachings.

Although the influence of religious teaching may have diminished in the UK in recent years such work ethics still remain. Thus, the tabloid media scream headlines about 'Dole scroungers' and 'Benefit cheats'—it is as if one were not playing a rightful role in society unless economically productive.

Furthermore, for those excluded from work, especially at a time of recession, stories in the papers are of pity and of their own frustration, again as if being barred from a fundamental aspect of existence and expression within society—the right to work. For example, Kingsley et al., (2011) interviewed young, long-term unemployed people in the UK. While they spoke about the financial problems of being unemployed, they also explained how a lack of work hits at their sense of self-identity within society, giving them less self-belief.

Visit the Online Resource Centre for more insights about the effects of unemployment on self-identity.

For Michel Foucault, who believed that power shapes our view of the world (see Chapter 13) society overall creates the idea that our bodies are working bodies and that it is abnormal if ones inclination is not to work, '. . . the body becomes a useful force only if it is a productive body . . .' (Foucault and Rabinow, 1984: 173).

It is not just in religion and the media that a normal working life is presented. In school and university we are taught and guided towards our ultimate goal of work—even this textbook includes 'employability skills'. In families a common refrain to older children is 'When are you going to go out and get a job?'. From many social and institutional angles, work becomes an obligation or duty. Rather than something for which we are motivated by some form of reward, work has a much more central part in our sense of self and identity, fuelled by a societal sense of obligation.

Orientations to work

The extent to which our working life links with our life in general and gives us a sense of identity within society was investigated by Goldthorpe (1968). In his study of workers in a Luton car factory he noted a particular paradox. On one hand, workers did not seem to be deriving an intrinsic or social satisfaction from their work. On the other hand, workers were not expressing any dissatisfaction with their work, even though they disliked some aspects of it.

Goldthorpe (1968) concluded that such workers had an 'instrumental orientation to work'. Workers saw their work merely as a means to an end. They had no desire for intrinsic satisfaction from the work—they would simply keep their head down, do their shift, and then pick up the pay packet at the end of the week.

Goldthorpe brings a different perspective to motivation. It is not simply a workplace phenomenon with managers manipulating certain rewards; instead, orientations to work have more of a link with our working identity in society. Goldthorpe (1968) suggests three particular **orientations to work**:

> **Orientations to work**
> A perspective which suggests that people have a predisposition to work that is influenced by our lives outside work and the meaning that we attach to work.

- the instrumental orientation to work suggests a strong separation between the working life and non-working life. The only aspect of working life that is carried into the outside world is the pay packet. It is this which—following an instrumental calculation—allows the worker to enjoy the life that they do in the outside world and they desire nothing more from work

- a bureaucratic orientation to work suggests more of a loyalty to the organization—service in return for progress. Meaning and social identity are carried into the outside world—a promotion within the organization is seen as a marker of status and identity in the outside world

- a solidaristic orientation to work is one where meaning, again, is carried outwards into society, but it is a meaning that derives from membership of a group rather than individual status. There is, thus, solidarity between the workers. While there are economic benefits which derive from the organization, loyalty and moral leaning is to the group rather than the organization itself.

Goldthorpe's work shows that professional status contributes to our working identity in the outside world, but that elements in society, such as class, also contribute to that identity. Many accounts of solidaristic group loyalty, for example, link group loyalty in industrial environments to an element of working-class identity (see, for example, Ackroyd and Crowdy, 1990; Collinson, 1988).

> **Work–life balance**
> A balance between work and career on one hand, and wider aspects of life, such as family and leisure time on the other.

A more recent workplace issue is that of **work–life balance**, a desire to achieve a sensible balance between work commitments and private life. The degree to which people achieve this has also been analysed in terms of professional identity (Caven, 2004) and the links with social factors, such as class and gender (Hakim, 2000; Özbilgin, 2011).

Visit the Online Resource Centre to read more about the effects of class and gender on personal identity.

Work and innate creativity

For a final word on motivation and society, we turn to Karl Marx (1867/1990) who, as we saw in Chapter 3, suggested that people are inherently creative—they have a desire to transform the world around them. In a Marxist sense, motivation is thus innate—a very different view of motivation to that of Taylor and Ford seen earlier in this chapter, who saw people as innately lazy.

A similar view of natural human creativity was seen in Chapter 8 with the social–radical approach. People have unlimited potential, it is the nature of work which demotivates them from achieving this rather than workers being disinclined to work.

Ironically, this is the view of people that Maslow held with his self-actualization concept, but which has been written out of the interpretation of Maslow used in management theory. Perhaps if management were able to tap into this aspect of human motivation or design work to enable people to fulfil it, then the whole area of motivation theory, with its associated models and theories, would be rendered obsolete—an important part of management (motivating people to work)—would be covered by the innate motivation of people themselves.

Review questions

1. Describe the three orientations to work suggested by Goldthorpe.

2. Analyse how work provides us with an identity and meaning within society.

Apply

3. What orientations to work do you see in the Junction Hotel staff?

Chapter summary

In this chapter we have seen a number of perspectives on motivation: the behavioural reward and punishment techniques; content theories which suggest that workers have needs which motivate them and for which appropriate job characteristics can be designed;

Table 9.1 Motivation theories and different perspectives on pay as a motivator

Taylorism/Fordism	Pay is the sole motivator for otherwise lazy and unmotivated workers
Behaviourism	Pay is a stimulus—it can be used as a reward or its withdrawal as a punishment to condition people's behaviour
Maslow—hierarchy of needs	Pay motivates differently in different parts of the hierarchy. At lower levels pay is needed to survive. At higher levels intrinsic motivators have more of an effect, although pay could be an indicator of status/esteem
Herzberg—motivators and hygiene factors	Pay is an element that has to be provided in sufficient amounts, otherwise it will cause dissatisfaction. However, pay does not in itself cause any increased motivation
Adams—equity theory	Pay is one basis on which workers will compare themselves against the inputs and rewards received by others
Vroom—expectancy theory	Pay is a reward; however, the degree to which it motivates depends on how much an individual values pay as a reward and how much workers link particular behaviours to receiving that reward
Social theories	Pay may be an indicator of status and working identity in society, but we are also motivated to work because being a working, economically-productive individual is seen as normal and an obligation by society
Goldthorpe—orientations to work	The role of pay depends on an individual's orientation to work. An instrumental orientation might make pay more of a motivating factor, but other orientations, such as bureaucratic and solidaristic, also exist

process theories which suggest that motivation is a result of subjective individual calculations; and social theories which link work motivation with the wider significance of work as a facet of our identity within society.

It seems that any one motivation theory seen in isolation is inadequate—neither Maslow, nor expectancy theory, nor any other theory alone, can explain motivation. However, taken together, theories of motivation outline different facets of what motivates us in the workplace. Perhaps the problem with motivation theory has been that, rather than illuminating different facets of motivation in the workplace, theories have been applied as absolute descriptions and even as 'how-to' lists.

The chapter began by examining the role of pay in workplace motivation, suggesting that this is an important motivating factor in the workforce, but is far from being the only motivating factor. As a summary, we present how different theories of motivation would view pay as a motivator (Table 9.1). While this shows different perspectives on pay, it also gives an insight into the different ways that the theories view motivation overall.

Further reading

Brooks, I. 2009. *Organisational behaviour: individuals, groups and organisation.* Financial Times/Prentice Hall, Harlow.
An accessible introduction to a variety of theories of motivation.

Herzberg, F. 2003. One more time: How do you motivate employees? *Harvard Business Review* 81(1): 87–96.
Herzberg's explanation of his motivators and hygiene theory.

Hughes, E.C. 1951. Work and the Self. In: Rohrer, J. H., and Sherif, M. (eds) *Social psychology at the crossroads; the University of Oklahoma lectures in social psychology*. Harper, Oxford, pp. 313–323.
An examination of the role of work in providing identity within society.

Villere, M.F., and Hartman, S.S. 1991. Reinforcement theory: A practical tool. *Leadership & Organization Development Journal* 12(2): 27–31.
An overview of the use of operant conditioning techniques in the workplace.

Bibliography

Ackroyd, S., and Crowdy, P.A. 1990. Can culture be managed? Working with 'raw' material: the case of the English slaughtermen. *Personnel Review* 19(5): 3–13.

Adams, J.S. 1963. Towards an understanding of inequity. *The Journal of Abnormal and Social Psychology* 67(5): 422.

Ashdown, J., and Smyth, R. 2009. Which teams have been punished for defeats? *The Guardian*. 30 September 2009. Available at: http://www. guardian.co.uk/football/2009/sep/30/teams-punished-defeats-football-questions (last accessed 29 June 2012).

BBC News. 2010. How do you punish a football team? Available at: http://www.bbc.co.uk/news/10402967 (last accessed 29 June 2012).

Beynon, H. 1984. *Working for Ford*. Penguin: Harmondsworth.

Brooks, I. 2009. *Organisational behaviour: individuals, groups and organisation*. Financial Times/Prentice Hall: Harlow.

Caven, V. 2004. Constructing a career: women architects at work. *Career Development International* 9(5): 518–531.

Collinson, D.L. 1988. 'Engineering humour': masculinity, joking and conflict in shop-floor relations. *Organization Studies* 9(2): 181–199.

Cullen, D. 1997. Maslow, monkeys and motivation theory. *Organization* 4(3): 355–373.

Cullen, D., and Gotell, L. 2002. From orgasms to organizations: Maslow, women's sexuality and the gendered foundations of the needs hierarchy. *Gender, Work & Organization* 9(5): 537–555.

The Daily Telegraph. 2011. Carlos Tevez suspended by Manchester City following his refusal to play against Bayern Munich. 28 September 2011. Available at: http://www.telegraph.co.uk/sport/football/teams/manchester-city/8795413/Carlos-Tevez-suspended-by-Manchester-City-following-his-refusal-to-play-against-Bayern-Munich.html.

Davis, K. 1957. *Human relations in business*. McGraw-Hill: New York.

De Gieter, S., De Cooman, R., Pepermans, R., Caers, R., Du Bois, C., and Jegers, M. 2006. Identifying nurses' rewards: a qualitative categorization study in Belgium. *Human Resources for Health* 4: 15.

Dewhurst, M., Guthridge, M., and Mohr, E. 2009. *Motivating people: Getting beyond money. McKinsey Quarterly* November. Available at: http://www.mckinseyquarterly.com/Motivating_people_Getting_beyond_money_2460 (last accessed 29 June 2012).

Dye, K., Mills, A.J., and Weatherbee, T. 2005. Maslow: man interrupted: reading management theory in context. *Management Decision* 43(10): 1375–1395.

Foucault, M., and Rabinow, P. 1984. *The Foucault reader*. Pantheon Books, New York.

Gibson, C.H. 1973. Volvo increases productivity through job enrichment. *California Management Review* 15(4): 64–66.

Goldthorpe, J.H. 1968. *The Affluent worker: industrial attitudes and behaviour*. Cambridge University Press: London.

Greenberg, J. 1990. Employee theft as a reaction to underpayment inequity: The hidden cost of pay cuts. *Journal of Applied Psychology* 75(5): 561.

Hakim, C. 2000. *Work-lifestyle choices in the 21st century*. Oxford University Press: Oxford.

Handy, C.B. 1993. *Understanding organizations*. Penguin Books: London, New York.

Harpaz, I. 1989. Non-financial employment commitment: A cross-national comparison. *Journal of Occupational Psychology* 62(2): 147–150.

Herzberg, F. 1966. *Work and the nature of man*. World Pub. Co.: Cleveland, OH.

Herzberg, F. 1987. One more time: how do you motivate employees. *Harvard Business Review*. September-October 1987: 88–99.

Herzberg, F. 2003. One more time: How do you motivate employees? *Harvard Business Review* 81(1): 87–96.

Hughes, E.C. 1951. Work and the Self. In: Rohrer, J. H., and Sherif, M. (eds) Social psychology at the crossroads; the University of Oklahoma lectures in social psychology. Harper: Oxford, pp. 313–323.

Huseman, R.C., Hatfield, J.D., and Miles, E.W. 1987. A new perspective on equity theory: The equity sensitivity construct. *Academy of Management Review* 12(2): 222–234.

Kingsley, P., Hickman, L., and Saner, E. 2011. What's it like to be young and looking for work in Britain? *The Guardian* (1 November 2011).

Lawler, E.E. III. 1973. *Motivation in work organizations*. Brookes/Cole Pub. Co.: Monterey, CA.

Luthans, F., and Kreitner, R. 1985. *Organizational behaviour modification and beyond*. Scott Foresman: Glenview, IL.

Makin, P.J., and Sutherland, V.J. 1994. Reducing accidents using a behavioural approach. *Leadership & Organization Development Journal* 15(5): 5–10.

Martinko, M.J., and Fadil, P. 1994. Operant Technologies: A Theoretical Foundation for Organizational Change and Development. *Leadership & Organization Development Journal* 15(5): 16–20.

Marx, K. 1867/1990: *Capital, Volume I*. Trans. Ben Fowkes. Penguin Books: London.

Maslow, A.H. 1943. A theory of human motivation. *Psychological Review* 50(4): 370–396.

Maslow, A.H. 2000. *The Maslow business reader*. John Wiley: New York, Toronto.

Noon, M., and Blyton, P. 2007. *The realities of work: experiencing work and employment in contemporary society*. Palgrave: Basingstoke, New York.

Okeleji, O. 2011. Dynamo Kiev players pay for losing. Available at: http://www.bbc.co.uk/sport/0/football/13775725 (last accessed 29 June 2012).

Özbilgin, M.F., Beauregard, T.A., Tatli, A., and Bell, M.P. 2011. Work-life, diversity and intersectionality: a critical review and research agenda. *International Journal of Management Reviews* 13(2): 177–198.

Pavlov, I.P., and Anrep, G.V. 1927. *Conditioned reflexes; an investigation of the physiological activity of the cerebral cortex*. Oxford University Press: London.

Raff, D., and Summers, L. 1987. Did Henry Ford pay efficiency wages? *Journal of Labour Economics* 5(4): 557–586.

Rehder, R.R. 1994. Saturn, Uddevalla and the Japanese lean systems: paradoxical prototypes for the twenty-first century. *International Journal of Human Resource Management* 5(1): 1–31.

Rose, M. 1994. Skill and Samuel Smiles: changing the British work ethic. In Penn, R., Rose, M., and Rubery, J. 1994. (eds) *Skill and occupational change*. Oxford University Press: Oxford, pp. 281–335.

Skinner, B.F. 1969. *Contingencies of reinforcement; a theoretical analysis*, Appleton-Century-Crofts: New York.

Taylor, D. 2011a. Carlos Tevez is finished at Manchester City, says Roberto Mancini. *The Guardian*. 28 September 2011. Available at: http://www.guardian.co.uk/football/2011/sep/28/carlos-tevez-manchester-city-roberto-mancini.

Taylor, D. 2011b Carlos Tevez suspended and fined £500,000 by Manchester City. *The Guardian*. 28 September 2011. Available at: http://www.guardian.co.uk/football/2011/sep/28/manchester-city-suspend-carlos-tevez.

Taylor, F.W. 1911. *The principles of scientific management*. Harper: New York.

Tyler, T. R., and Bies, R. J. 1990. Beyond formal procedures: The interpersonal context of procedural justice. In: Carroll, J. (ed.) *Applied social psychology and organizational settings*. Erlbaum: Hillsdale, NJ, pp. 77–98.

Villere, M.F., and Hartman, S.S. 1991. Reinforcement theory: A practical tool. *Leadership & Organization Development Journal* 12(2): 27–31.

Vroom, V.H. 1964. *Work and motivation*. Wiley: New York.

Wahba, M.A., and Bridwell, L.G. 1976. Maslow reconsidered: A review of research on the need hierarchy theory. *Organizational Behavior and Human Performance* 15(2): 212–240.

Walker, P., and Jones, S. 2012. EuroMillions lottery win buys Corby bus drivers ticket to retirement, *The Guardian* (19 March 2012).

Weber, M., Parsons, T., and Tawney, R.H. 1930. *The Protestant ethic and the spirit of capitalism*. G. Allen & Unwin: London.

Wiley, C. 1997. What motivates employees according to over 40 years of motivation surveys. *International Journal of Manpower* 18(3): 263–280.

Wray-Bliss, E., and Willmott, H. 1999. Battling with the gods: workers, management and the deities of post industrial management culture. In: Goodman, R. (ed.) *Modern organization and emerging conundrums: Exploring the post-industrial sub-culture of the third millennium*. New Lexington Press: San Francisco, pp. 377–389.

10

Knowledge and learning
Developing the individual, developing the organization

Chapter overview and learning outcomes

By the end of this chapter you should be able to:

- describe a variety of theories of individual knowledge and learning
- explain the importance of deep learning, where knowledge is learned from experience and from 'learning to learn'
- describe the importance of knowledge and learning at organizational levels
- explain and analyse the concept of the 'learning organization'.

Key theorists

Michael Polanyi	Recognized that importance of the 'tacit' dimension of knowledge which comes from personal experience, rather than explicit knowledge such as facts and figures
David Kolb	Devised a learning cycle which demonstrated how knowledge is gained through a cycle of experience and reflection
Howard Gardner	Outlined a theory of multiple intelligences, whereby individuals exhibit different types of intelligence, such as logical, musical, or spatial
Ikujiro Nonaka	Suggested that a successful 'knowledge creating company' is adept at transforming tacit and explicit knowledge within its workforce
Chris Argyris and Donald Schön	Suggested that successful organizational learning is that which goes beyond 'single loop' to become 'double-loop' learning
Peter Senge	Outlined a model of the key characteristics of the learning organization
Jean Lave and Etienne Wenger	Noted the existence of communities of practice, and that social groups engaged in learning a common area of knowledge and practice

Key terms

Explicit knowledge	Knowledge which can be expressed to other people as a set of words, facts, diagrams, or instructions
Tacit knowledge	Knowledge which is personal, a form of second nature or knowing things 'off by heart', and which is difficult to explain to others
Experiential learning	Learning which comes from experiences and reflecting on those experiences
Learning styles	Ways in which different individuals approach learning and learn more effectively
Reflective practice	A form of professional development and training where workers reflect on actual workplace experiences and events
Organizational knowledge	Knowledge which is a collective property of an organization rather than belonging to an individual
Organizational learning	Sharing and transferring knowledge so that it becomes a collective property of the organization
Learning organization	An organization which is set up so as to facilitate continual learning at individual and organizational levels
Communities of practice	Social groupings based around a common occupational practice and set of knowledge who develop and share that knowledge among themselves

Introduction

Running case: an alarming experience

Simon Chance has had a busy morning dealing with a full-scale evacuation of the hotel. One of the heat detectors in the restaurant became faulty, setting fire alarms ringing, and all of the guests and staff had to go outside into the car park and wait until the all-clear was given.

Inside the hotel, the maintenance team are having problems. Bob Smith is their expert on the fire alarm system—he knows it inside out and can fix any problems in minutes. Unfortunately, today he is off work sick and nobody else in the team knows how to deal with the problem. Chance sees the remaining engineers standing around the alarm's control panel, flicking through manuals and scratching their heads, but none of them really know what to do—they hadn't had to deal with a problem in the alarm system before.

At great cost, Chance has to bring in an outside engineer, who takes a couple of hours to arrive and a further two hours to fix the problem. In the meantime, he has to deal with a crowd of unhappy guests who are waiting outside with growing impatience.

If you were in charge of training and development of the maintenance team, what would you do to avoid a repeat of this problem?

Do you see the workplace as somewhere to simply pick up a wage or do you see it as more than that, maybe somewhere where you go to develop as an individual? Certainly in the previous two chapters there has been a suggestion that the workplace is somewhere where our personalities develop (Chapter 8) and even where we engage in our highest creative achievements through self-actualization (Chapter 9).

In this chapter we examine how people in organizations develop as individuals and become better at their work by learning and gaining new knowledge from their workplace experience. Knowledgeable workers also benefit the organization. In recent years it has been suggested that knowledge can give organizations a competitive advantage within the economy, especially in certain sectors, such as technology, where constant development and innovation are important.

The chapter thus examines both knowledge (what people know) and learning (how people gain that knowledge).

- First, we look at knowledge and learning at an individual level, drawing a distinction between explicit knowledge, which can be learned off by heart as a set of facts, and a deeper tacit knowledge, which is learned from experience and reflection upon that experience. We also look specifically at management knowledge—what knowledge is needed to be a manager and how do people gain that knowledge?

- Secondly, we move to the level of the organization. The management of knowledge is concerned with how individuals learn, but also with how knowledge, both explicit and tacit, is transferred between people in and across the organization. Knowledge becomes an organization-wide property rather than something belonging to any one individual. We see how organizations that promote the sharing of knowledge become learning organizations, and how this equips them to deal with change and uncertainty.

To conclude, we examine organizational knowledge in a contemporary context, where it can be shared and developed through computer networks and across organizational boundaries.

Individual learning: knowledge, experience, and styles

Running case: training and development

Later in the day, Chance ponders upon the problem with the fire alarm. While there is a lot of knowledge and expertise in the maintenance team, it isn't shared—each person has their own specialist area.

The morning's events have demonstrated how reliant they are on specific individuals who seem to be the only ones who know how to do key tasks. If that person is absent, the task can't be performed.

Chance decides that the maintenance staff need to learn more about each other's specialisms—to have a broader knowledge of maintenance tasks and equipment across the hotel. He sets to work on a training and development programme that will increase knowledge and learning across the maintenance team.

We have all engaged in learning at some point in our lives, whether it is formulas for a maths exam, lines for a play, or new techniques for a sport. By reading this book you are engaged in a learning process. But what does it really mean to have learned something? Is knowledge something as simple as remembering lists off by heart or is there more to it?

In this section we examine individual learning and how we learn. In particular, we examine how **experiential learning** takes us from **surface learning**, where we simply learn a set of facts, to **deep learning**, a richer form of learning where we understand knowledge in its *context* and from our own *experience*, and where we begin to think about the ways in which we learn best and develop our own preferred **learning styles**.

From lists to patterns

Running case: learning rewards

Chance does an audit of the qualifications currently held within the maintenance team, and then offers incentives for people to add to their knowledge and gain more qualifications. Courses in plumbing, gas, and electricity, as well as workshops for particular pieces of equipment, will be offered to the maintenance team, with a bonus paid for each qualification gained. Chance calls this scheme 'learning rewards'.

One of the maintenance staff, Mike Bridges, throws himself into the scheme and gains several certificates from a local college. He is the first person to be called upon when the refrigeration unit in the hotel bar breaks down as he has undertaken a day's workshop with the manufacturers of the refrigeration equipment.

Unfortunately, that knowledge doesn't seem to help him when he is faced with the task of getting the refrigeration unit working again. 'I passed that test six months ago', explains Bridges to bar manager John Vintner. 'Took my bonus and haven't looked at the manual since. I've never actually touched one of these things before, yet alone repaired one.'

What sort of learning do you think the learning rewards scheme promoted? Is it of any use to the hotel?

To help understand the nature of individual learning, we are going to engage in a process of learning ourselves. The Finnish language is a language unlike most other languages and one with which you will probably not be familiar. Have a look at the list of five Finnish words in Table 10.1, and their English translations, and learn them—you will be tested on these later.

How did you go about trying to learn the words? Did you simply read them and commit them to memory, or did

The Finnish flag.

you devise some form of system for learning the words? Did you stop and think about how you have learned a language before or did you dive straight in?

Experiential learning Learning which comes from experiences and reflecting on those experiences.

Surface learning Learning a set of facts in themselves, possibly for the purposes of a test or exam, rather than with any additional depth.

Deep learning Learning that tries to achieve a deeper understanding of, and engagement with, the material being learned.

Learning styles The different ways in which different individuals approach learning.

The particular strategy you adopt says a lot about not only how you go about learning, but also reveals some of the key learning theories.

A behaviourist view of learning

If you were offered a £10 reward for each word you remembered correctly would you be more likely to have learned them by the end of the chapter than without it? Such an approach is underpinned by ideas from **behavioural psychology**. As we saw in Chapter 9, behavioural psychologists argue that people are motivated by rewards and punishments. Learning theorists have adopted these ideas to provide our first learning perspective. Vocabulary tests from school language lessons follow this type of pattern—learn the words and you are rewarded with a good grade, fail to learn them and you may receive a punishment, a detention for example or failing a language module.

Table 10.1   Some words in Finnish, part 1

Tori	Market
Kaupunki	Town
Joki	River
Ulos	Out
Yliopisto	University

> **Behavioural psychology/behaviourism** An area of psychology which suggests that learning can be managed through the use of rewards and punishments.

How much of your learning is motivated by the grade that you will earn?

As we saw in Chapter 9, however, for behaviourist theories to work, the reward needs to be maintained. This suggests that, after gaining the initial £10, people will no longer be motivated to retain the words in their memory. Unless further rewards come along they will eventually forget what they have learned.

With no reward on offer for the Finnish language test other than your own satisfaction at learning the words, let's see how well your learning of the words has gone so far. Without referring back to the original list, can you say the Finnish words for the following English words listed—no cheating and looking back!

- Market.
- Town.
- River.
- Out.
- University.

Whenever we have tried this exercise in a class situation, people have generally remembered very few of the words. The odd person may remember one or two words, but very few people learn and remember all five of the words.

Knowledge as forms and patterns

Perhaps we need to approach the way in which we learn the words differently. Read the descriptions given and, with no need for any form of reward or punishment, we suggest that there is a good chance that you will remember these words not just for the next time you are tested in this chapter, but for days, weeks, months—even years—afterwards:

- the word for market is 'tori.' Margaret Thatcher was a well-known Tory prime minister. Imagine Margaret Thatcher in her blue dress, perfectly styled hair and carrying her handbag, walking around a market looking at all the stalls. A famous Tory is in the market, the word for which is tori

- the work for town is 'kaupunki' pronounced cow-punk-ee. Imagine a cow with a Mohican haircut and a safety pin through its nose—a cow-punk—and it is walking down the main street in your home town. Town is cow-punk-ee

- the word for river is 'joki,' pronouced yok-ee, but let's keep it at the English pronunciation for now—jokey. Imagine you are on a boat cruising along the river, having drinks and everyone is having a good laugh—it's quite a 'jokey' atmosphere on the river. Joki means river

- the work for out is 'ulos' or 'you-loss'. Imagine your team is out of a tournament. Why would the team be out? Because 'you-lost'

- the Finnish word for university is 'yliopisto'—pronounced 'ill-ee-oh-pist-oh'. Imagine waking up at university one morning and you feel ill. Why are you feeling ill? Because last night you had a bit too much to drink. You are at university and you feel ill-ee-oh-pist-oh (by now you should be able to work this one out for yourself!).

Go back to Table 10.1 and test yourself again on the words in Finnish. Did you do better this time? What do you think it is about the way you learned the words this time round that helped you to remember them better?

The type of learning this time is different—it is learning through creating associations and patterns. The importance of associations and patterns is a part of **Gestalt psychology**, a branch of psychology which developed in Germany in the early 1900s. Kurt Lewin, who we encounter in Chapters 6, 11, and 12, was associated with the Gestalt school. His interest was in how individual behaviour was affected by the way people perceive the world around them. Gestalt psychologists as a whole were interested in human perception, and their work has been applied to studies of learning and behaviour.

> Gestalt psychology
> An area of psychology which suggests that we perceive things as forms, patterns, and connections rather than as a set of discrete individual items.

The German word 'Gestalt' translates as 'form', 'pattern', or 'configuration'. Gestalt psychology is thus concerned with how we structure perceptions in memory into particular patterns or forms. Gestalt psychology gives us the familiar saying that 'the whole is different than the sum of its parts' (Koffka, 1955: 176). Think of how we perceive a melody, for example. We don't think about it note by note—a B flat followed by a C—instead, we perceive the song as a whole. It's the same with recognizing a familiar face. We don't think of a friend's face in terms of each individual part—the eyes, nose, etc.—we simply recognize the overall pattern without breaking it down into its constituent parts—the whole is different to the sum of its parts.

Our methods for learning the Finnish words are based on a similar idea and is one which is used in real-life language learning programmes, such as Linkword (see www.linkwordlanguages. com for an example). Rather than take a set of individual words, devoid of any context or familiarity, we have woven them into a pattern of connections that then helps us to recall the words. It is as if we are making the word that we are learning part of an overall story, or part of a 'gestalt'.

You may use similar methods when trying to memorize a list of names or items, perhaps as revision for an exam. Some people use 'mind-maps'—diagrams which show how different ideas connect rather than just trying to learn a list of words. Another trick for memorizing items is where the learner mentally traces out a familiar journey, placing the items to be remembered in locations along the way.

Visit the Online Resource Centre for further examples of learning techniques.

Contextualizing knowledge in this way—as part of a pattern—is an effective way to learn, certainly more effective than learning a simple list of words off by heart. However, in the next section we ask an important question about the quality of the knowledge that has been learned—you may *know* some words in Finnish, but do you *know* how to speak Finnish?

From explicit to tacit knowledge

Running case: a feel for the task

Another of the maintenance staff, Gerry Dawson, walks up to the bar to see the younger Mike Bridges staring blankly at the faulty refrigeration unit.

'Let me have a go', says Dawson, rolling up his sleeves and prodding inside the unit instinctively. 'You might have all your qualifications in there', he says, pointing at Mike Bridges's head, 'but I spent years working in a pub, I used to have to fix these all the time'.

'It's second nature to me, my knowledge of these machines is here', continues Dawson, raising his hands and pointing to his fingers, 'I just have a feel for these things'.

Whether learning a list off by heart or using a more Gestaltist way to remember the list of words, we have, as yet, only learned a list of words. Can you use the words in a phrase or hold a conversation in the language, for example? We do not *know* every aspect of the language because, as yet, we have no *experience* of speaking the language.

The type and quality of knowledge learned is an issue that has been addressed by a number of philosophers of knowledge (e.g. Polanyi, 1958; Ryle, 1949; Russell, 1912). Based on these insights, we suggest three types of knowledge which relate to the example of learning words in a language.

- *Knowledge that*, is knowing a fact, for example that the Finnish word for market is tori.
- *Knowledge how*, is where there is a deeper understanding of how that fact can be used in context. For example, I not only know that the Finnish word for market is tori, I know how to use it in a sentence and how to construct the grammar in that sentence.
- *Knowledge of*, sometimes known as acquaintance knowledge (Russell, 1912), comes from a familiarity with something—the way in which we know a friend rather than the way in which we know a fact. This distinction is not captured well in English, where the same verb 'to know' covers both of these ideas. In French (and many other languages) there are two verbs which translate as 'to know'—*savoir*, meaning to know a fact, and *connaître*, meaning familiarity. Thus, a phrase like 'I KNOW Paris is the capital of France'—a fact—is translated as 'Je *sais* que Paris est le capital de la France'. However, a phrase like 'I KNOW Paris well' indicating familiarity with, and experience of, the city, is translated as 'Je *connais* bien Paris'. In terms of knowing Finnish, knowledge *of* would suggest being a regular speaker of the language. For example, being so acquainted with the language that you know the slang and sayings that people use.

Moving from knowledge *that* towards knowledge *how* and knowledge *of* requires people to actually practise speaking the language, finding out what people really say, making mistakes and being laughed at, and learning from those mistakes. Michael Polanyi (1967) recognizes such a 'tacit dimension' of knowledge—where knowledge is more than just words on a page, it is something which people pick up from experience. Following Polanyi, there is thus a distinction between two types of knowledge:

- **explicit knowledge**—is that which can be codified or written down, and then communicated clearly to other people, for example a set of instructions, a diagram, a reference manual, a list of words, etc.

- **tacit knowledge**—is knowledge which comes from experience—from doing and practising something. It is thus much more of a personal form of knowledge that we carry within us.

We can see how explicit knowledge would relate to knowledge *that* in that it is a simple set of facts that can be stated. We can also see how tacit knowledge relates to knowledge *of*—it is knowledge that can by gained only from doing and experiencing something. Knowledge *how*, the ability to do something, perhaps bridges the two. We can learn how to do something from a set of instructions on a page, but it is through practising and experiencing that action that we really come to know how to perform it—when rather than having to think about it, it becomes 'second nature'.

> **Explicit knowledge**
> Knowledge which can be expressed to other people as a set of words, facts, diagrams, or instructions.
>
> **Tacit knowledge**
> Knowledge which is personal, a form of second nature or knowing things 'off by heart', and which is difficult to explain to others.

Real life case: learning to drive

A major learning experience for many people is learning to drive. It is a learning process which has both explicit and tacit dimensions.

Drivers have to take a theory test before they are allowed to get behind the wheel of a car. This involves learning many aspects of driving theory—what road signs mean, stopping distances at different speeds, how to indicate at a roundabout, etc. This knowledge is learned as explicit knowledge from books, the Highway code, and on websites, etc., following which the learner driver takes the theory test.

But passing a test based on explicit knowledge does not mean a learner then *knows* how to drive—there is another part of learning to drive which involves getting behind the wheel with an instructor and gaining knowledge through the experience of driving. At first a driver will be unsure, driving slowly, and possibly stalling the car often. With practice and experience, driving becomes easier.

Learning to drive has both explicit and tacit dimensions.

A particular development in learning to drive is when tasks that have to be thought about become second nature. Rather than thinking about each gear change in advance, it is done almost without actually thinking about it.

It is this ability and knowledge—knowing how to drive in practice rather than reciting facts from a theory manual—that is tested in the actual driving test.

Think about other common learning experiences in life, for example learning to ride a bicycle or learning to swim. To what extent can these be split into explicit and tacit knowledge? How could you teach someone else to do these activities?

Polanyi (1967: 4) sums up the nature of tacit knowledge when he says that 'we know more than we can tell'. While explicit knowledge can be written down, tacit knowledge is much harder to share because it is so personal and comes only from doing and experiencing something.

This is summed up in the example of learning to drive a car. There is only so much about knowing how to drive a car that an instructor can impart as tacit knowledge—as theory and as a set of instructions, for example. There is a tacit element of knowledge of driving a car, however, that simply cannot be told to other people—they have to learn it from their own experience.

How did you learn to speak your own native language? And how much of that language could you teach to others?

Tacit and explicit knowledge present two aspects of language learning. The vocabulary lists and grammar tables are the explicit knowledge, the building blocks upon which our learning takes place—the knowledge *that*. The knowledge *how* to speak the language and the intimate knowledge *of* the language come from tacit knowledge that we develop personally the more we practise speaking the language—learning comes from experience.

Experiential learning

> ### Real life case: 'Googling' symptoms
>
> Many doctors complain about patients who look up their symptoms on a search engine and enter the surgery already having made a self-diagnosis. It is as if the medical knowledge of a doctor is unimportant given that so much medical knowledge can now be found on the Internet.
>
> However, what the patient is lacking is experience. They may know some medical facts, but the doctor will have trained and been in practice for years. They will have seen patients with similar symptoms, learned from the diagnoses they have made previously, and the occasions when they have made a misdiagnosis. They will have experience of which drugs work best for which patients, and which are less effective.
>
> Thus, an important part of a doctor's expert knowledge comes from experience as much as it does from facts and figures about how a body works.
>
> **Sources:** Alexander, 2012; Paddock, 2012; Tang and Ng, 2006.

The example of medical knowledge shows how knowledge relevant for a particular job can be seen as a blend between facts, or explicit knowledge, and the tacit knowledge that comes from experience—using that explicit knowledge in practice—learning from what works and what doesn't work.

It is often said that we learn from our mistakes. If we do something wrong, we learn from that experience so as not to repeat that mistake in future. However, in this section we see how all experiences—whether a mistake is made or whether we do things well—are a basis for learning when we *reflect* on those experiences.

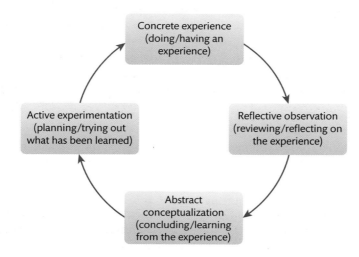

Figure 10.1
Kolb's learning cycle.
Based on Kolb (1984).

Kolb's learning cycle

David Kolb's (1984) learning cycle is a model of **experiential learning**. It suggests learning moves through a continuous cycle between acting , i.e. having an experience and reflecting on that action in a continuous cycle (see Figure 10.1).

Kolb's learning cycle suggests that learning passes through four stages of experience and reflection:

- *concrete experience* is where we do, or have an experience—an action is performed
- *reflective observation* is where we review and reflect on the experience. What went well? What went badly? What could be done better? etc.
- *abstract conceptualization* is where we conclude and learn from our reflections on the experience. After reflection the actor makes links with theory and explicit knowledge—given what went wrong, what theory might help explain this? What explicit knowledge or theory might help to rectify this next time?
- *active experimentation* is planning and trying out what has been learned from the experience. Different options are tried out for next time until the cycle goes back to the next concrete experience and then begins again.

Kolb's cycle shows how tacit and explicit aspects of knowledge link together in the process of learning. This blending together of tacit and explicit knowledge within Kolb's cycle can be demonstrated if we apply it to a specific learning experience. For example, a golf player learning to play and improve their game might go through the stages of Kolb's cycle as follows:

Experiential learning
Learning which comes from experiences and reflecting on those experiences.

Kolb's learning cycle
A model of experiential learning which suggests that people learn through different stages of experience and reflection, and which suggests that people have particular learning style preferences for different parts of that cycle.

- *Concrete experience*: the golfer plays a round of golf and is not happy with her score.
- *Reflective observation*: the golfer thinks back over the round and why it didn't go well. She thinks about different aspects of the game, and identifies her golf swing as the main problem.
- *Abstract conceptualization*: the golfer refers to some explicit knowledge—maybe a golf manual written by an expert, maybe a golf coaching DVD, maybe even a golf class. From this theory and instruction she begins to identify what is wrong with the swing and what could be changed next time.
- *Active experimentation*: the golfer goes to a driving range to put what she has learned about her swing into practice—putting different ideas into action to see which works best with her golf swing.
- *Concrete experience*: the golfer is back on the course and plays another round of golf. The score is a slight improvement from last time . . .
- . . . and so the cycle goes on and each time round the golfer improves her swing more and more.

Applying tacit and explicit knowledge.

Study skills: the role of feedback

How do you use feedback? Do you just read the grade and if it is acceptable put it in your bag and forget about it? Or do you read the feedback and try to learn from it, and apply that learning to your next assignment?

Feedback identifies what you have done well and what you can improve for next time. However, it can only help if you both read it and act upon it. If referencing is identified as a problem, for example, then you can consult referencing guides for next time round or ask a tutor for help. You could even go back to the essay and redo the referencing in the light of the feedback and what you have learned subsequently from referencing guides. This will all help when you come to write your next piece of coursework.

In some respects, the way you use feedback as part of a process of learning as a student has similarities with Kolb's learning cycle. There is the experience—doing the coursework; the reflection—looking at and thinking about the feedback; the conceptualization—looking at guides or asking the advice of a tutor; and the experimentation—trying out things before the next piece of work is attempted.

The feedback plays a vital role in this cycle of development as a student. If you only look at the grade then you miss out on an important developmental opportunity that will improve your future work.

Learning styles

Simon Chance walks into the bar where, by now, the whole maintenance team are standing around looking at the faulty refrigeration unit. Standing back and watching them approach the task, he notes that each of them takes a different approach to the problem.

Some jump straight in and start fiddling with different components to see what will happen. Others stand back for a while, thinking about the problem before actually doing anything with the refrigeration unit.

Furthermore, people consult different sources for information. Some look at instructions in a manual, others look at a circuit diagram of the refrigeration unit, while yet others discuss the problem within the team, asking people about their previous experiences with similar equipment.

Chance realizes that, while he could send his maintenance staff on training courses, when it comes to actually engaging with the actual job there are many differences between how each individual actually learns.

While all stages of Kolb's cycle are an important part of the learning process, he suggests that people prefer certain parts of the cycle to others. People have distinct learning preferences or learning styles. Using the example of our golfer, some golfers may prefer to spend time reflecting on the round of golf, while others may want to get straight to the driving range to start practising and experimenting.

Visit the Online Resource Centre to read more on learning styles.

This section examines different ways in which the different learning styles of individuals have been modelled. In a similar way to personality tests in Chapter 8, many of these frameworks of learning styles also have associated questionnaires through which individuals can measure their preferred learning styles.

Honey and Mumford's learning styles

Kolb's work was developed by Honey and Mumford (1992, 2006) into their **learning styles questionnaire** (LSQ). Figure 10.2 shows the four stages of the cycle of learning, which are similar to Kolb's model (although, unlike Kolb, they have an 'escape route' which recognizes that people sometimes change focus to concentrate on learning something different, for instance someone may stop learning to play the piano and take up the guitar instead).

Each of the stages is linked with one of four particular learning styles:

- activists prefer the actual experience itself—they are doers rather than thinkers. They like action and are prepared to try new things

- reflectors spend time thinking over what they have done. Rather than being in the thick of the action they prefer to stand back and watch and review, seeing a situation from a number of different perspectives

- theorists are rational and logical thinkers who work best with abstract knowledge such as models and theories

> **Learning styles questionnaire** Based on Honey and Mumford's development of Kolb, a questionnaire which ascertains people's preferred learning styles.

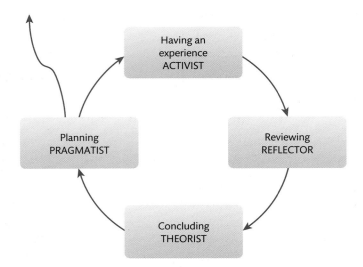

- pragmatists will try out new ideas to see how they work. Rather than trying to theorize, they prefer practical actions.

Can you make any connections between these learning styles and the personality scales in Chapter 8?

The Honey and Mumford learning styles questionnaire is, similarly to personality tests, a set of questions which help locate an individual within these four learning styles. Given that learning is seen as a cycle which needs to pass through all of the stages, it might help an individual to recognize whether they have a tendency to get caught up in one area, for example a reflector might spend too much time thinking about what has happened without progressing further in the cycle and taking practical steps.

The LSQ also allows an organization to see the variety of learning styles that people might have, which can help with training and development in understanding that people learn in different ways. In a similar way to Belbin (see Chapter 6) it also recognizes that in a team people will have different ways of approaching learning that they can contribute to a project or task—some will jump in and get on with the task, while others will sit back and reflect, etc.

Learning styles and multiple intelligences

While Kolb, and Honey and Mumford deal with the link between doing and reflecting, or knowledge and experience, other models of learning styles have pinpointed particular types of intelligence which lead to particular learning preferences.

Howard Gardner (1983) suggested that people exhibit a number of different types of intelligence:

- verbal/linguistic intelligence—the ability to understand and use language to express oneself

- musical intelligence—performing music and understanding musical composition and pitch

- spatial intelligence—an awareness of space and patterns around us
- bodily/kinesthetic intelligence—the ability to do things with the body: sports, arts, etc.
- logical/mathematical intelligence—the ability to perform analytical, scientific tasks
- interpersonal intelligence—the ability to understand, empathize, and work with others
- intrapersonal intelligence—being able to understand ourselves and our feelings.

For Gardner, individuals exhibit these types of **multiple intelligence** in different combinations. Different intelligences predispose us to different tasks or jobs—interpersonal intelligence is good for dealing with people, for example. We can see that some of these intelligences are also more tacit in nature, coming from experience and actually doing things.

The model also highlights areas of ability that we might not initially consider to be a type of intelligence. For example, whilst playing football may not require intelligence in the traditional, academic sense of the word, you may often hear a footballer described as an 'intelligent' player. In knowing how to 'read' a pass, swerve a ball or get into the right position, a football player draws upon kinesthetic intelligence—bodily abilities and movements learned from experience of playing the game—and visual-spatial intelligence, which provides an awareness of the other players on the field and the formation that they fit into.

Gardner's multiple intelligences model does not have an associated questionnaire like so many similar models; however, it does suggest that people are more predisposed to learn tasks and knowledge in different ways. The **VARK model** (Fleming, 2001) (Table 10.2) places the emphasis on how we learn and is tested by an associated questionnaire. It suggests four preferences for how we learn.

> **Multiple intelligences** Gardner's theory that there are different types of intelligence that people possess in different combinations.

> **VARK model** A model and questionnaire which places individuals into one of four preferred learning styles—visual, auditory, reading and writing, or kinesthetic.

Table 10.2   The VARK model (based on Fleming, 2001)

Type of learner	Description
Visual	Learns best from visual clues, e.g. from diagrams, pictures, signs, and symbols
Auditory	Learns best from listening to descriptions and explanations
Reading/writing	Learns best from reading texts and using written notes to organize that knowledge
Kinesthetic (tactile)	Learns best by doing things—actually touching and manipulating objects

Visit the Online Resource Centre for links to the associated questionnaire for the VARK model.

Can you link the learning styles in the VARK model with Gardner's multiple intelligences?

With VARK, we see how different material will appeal more to the learning abilities of different learners. For example, when fixing a car a visual learner might use a diagram of the engine, a reader/writer might look for instructions in a book or on the Internet, and a kinesthetic learner might jump in and see what happens when they touch and play about with different components.

Such intelligences might also be applied to our language example. An auditory learner might learn better from listening to language lessons on a tape, while a reader and writer might prefer to read the language from a book.

The implication of VARK is that people who are teaching and training people need to take account of the fact that people respond differently to different methods and materials of teaching and training. However, the model, and its associated questionnaire, also helps individuals to appreciate for themselves their own learning styles. Many of the models examined in this section, whether VARK, or Honey and Mumford, feed into individual development processes of learning to learn.

Learning to learn: from surface to deep learning and beyond

We have so far seen two broad approaches to knowledge. On the one hand, knowledge is a set of simple, explicit facts that we commit to memory. On the other hand, knowledge is learned in context and through experience and action, so that it becomes a deeper, more personal form of tacit knowledge.

The distinction is echoed in a number of approaches which distinguish between the quality of learning that people undertake (Marton and Säljö, 1976; Pask, 1976). Here, we present a commonly-used distinction between surface learning and deep learning:

- surface learning is simply learning a set of facts off by heart. The learner has no real interest in the knowledge itself; instead, it is a means to an end—to pass a test, for example

- deep learning is where a learner gains a deeper level of knowledge and understanding—not just learning facts, but engaging with the knowledge, making links and comparisons with other knowledge that the learner already has. This might be through using that knowledge in experience, for example, as discussed previously in the chapter so that it becomes a deeper, personal form of tacit knowledge.

Which of the two styles do you think you use in your university work?

Surface and deep learning can thus be compared in terms of the knowledge that is acquired from each, as in Table 10.3.

Table 10.3 Deep learning and surface learning compared

Surface learning	Deep learning
Facts and figures, learning by rote, out of context	Learning as part of a pattern or in context
Knowledge that	Knowledge how/knowledge of
Savoir	*Connaitre*
Explicit knowledge only	Explicit knowledge developing into tacit knowledge through experience (e.g. Kolb's learning cycle)

The difference between surface learning and deep learning can be applied to the earlier example of learning the Finnish language. A surface learner would simply learn the words for the sake of passing an assessment. A deep learner might learn the words, but also try to put them into a sentence, relating them to words already learned, practising them in conversation with others, and even relating them to the culture of the country.

Learning to learn

Models of learning styles have shown us not just how deeper levels of knowledge are acquired, but how people also have preferences for particular learning styles. Gregory Bateson (1973) used the term **deutero learning** to describe levels of learning with greater depth, where the individual not only gains deeper knowledge but engages in a form of self-awareness whereby they learn how to learn.

Again, this can be explained with reference to the Finnish learning example. Earlier in the chapter we learned some words by associating them with particular images and patterns. Learning to learn is where a learner realizes that the system works well for them and applies that same system to another learning situation—learning German, for example, or memorizing a shopping list. Learning to learn involves comparing this with other learning methods to develop an appreciation of what works best for each individual learner.

In a similar vein, Freire (1970) criticizes what he terms **banking education**, where learners are seen as being like an empty bank account, there to be filled passively with 'deposits' of knowledge. Such a type of education does not move beyond explicit knowledge and surface learning. Again, they call for a type of learning that goes beyond the surface and engenders a greater depth of knowledge and creativity in students.

Visit the Online Resource Centre to read more about Freire's theories.

The importance of Bateson's and Freire's contributions is not to dismiss explicit knowledge and surface learning completely, but to see that for individuals to achieve creativity and reach their potential (as mentioned at the start of this chapter) this needs to form part of a process of deeper learning and learning to learn.

Deep learning and learning to learn in the workplace: reflective practice

So far in the chapter we have examined learning at an individual level. In the remainder of this chapter we will see it applied within the workplace. Donald Schön (1983) suggested that professionals in industries such as education, health, and architecture would develop their knowledge and practice of their work better—indeed, into a form of artistry— if they worked as reflective practitioners. **Reflective practice** means that a worker doesn't simply do their job, but, as with Kolb, and Honey and Mumford in this chapter, they see their work as an ongoing cycle of continuous learning, whereby they reflect upon their experiences in the workplace.

In the next two sections of this chapter, we place ideas of reflective practice, deep knowledge, and learning to learn into management and organizational settings.

- First, we examine the job of management itself. How as management students might you 'learn' to be an effective manager and what part does reflective practice play in management knowledge?

Deutero learning
Bateson's conception of a higher level of learning whereby people are aware of how they 'learn to learn'.

Banking education
Freire's critique of learning and teaching styles which see learners as being like bank accounts to be 'deposited' with amounts of knowledge.

Reflective practice
A form of professional development and training where workers reflect on actual workplace experiences and events.

- Secondly, we look at how knowledge relevant to particular organizations, such as technical knowledge, is not only learned by individuals within an organization, but how it is shared across the organization. Schön, along with Chris Argyris (Argyris and Schön, 1978), was a pioneer of organizational learning, whereby organizations themselves 'learn' how to learn and to 'reflect' on that process of learning.

Review questions

1. Describe what is meant by explicit and tacit knowledge.

2. Explain what is meant by a cycle of experiential learning.

3. Analyse the levels of learning and knowledge gained as a learner moves from surface learning to deep learning to deutero learning.

Apply

4. How would you take account of different learning styles in developing a training programme for the maintenance staff at Junctio Hotel?

Reflective practice and management knowledge

What are your expectations of a management degree? It would be a reasonable assumption that, in undertaking a management degree or a similar course, a student would learn and accumulate a certain amount of management *knowledge* that can then be taken into a management career.

In this section we examine what it means to 'know' how to manage, that is to say what is management knowledge? Is it an explicit set of facts and theories, or is it a tacit form of knowledge that comes from experience? Furthermore, if we can pinpoint what is meant by management knowledge, how does someone, for example a student of management, learn this knowledge—how does one learn how to manage?

This short section of the chapter brings a **reflexive** approach to your study of knowledge and learning in organizations. Reflexive means that the chapter is not just describing a set of ideas and theories, rather it invites you as both a current student and potential future manager to locate yourself personally within the subject matter of the chapter.

Reflexivity Where an individual is connected in some way to a text they are reading about or writing, rather than simply looking at a text to which they are completely disconnected.

- As a student, the topic of this chapter—knowledge and learning—is relevant to how you engage in study. Some material in this chapter may be familiar from 'study skills' or 'personal development' sessions at university. For example, you may have taken the VARK questionnaire as a way of understanding your preferred means of learning. The aim of such techniques is to improve your quality of learning as a student, taking you from surface learning to deep learning and deutero learning styles. You are not simply approaching each learning task in isolation, to pass a test for example, rather you think more widely about how you learn best.

- As a student of management, and, potentially, a future manager, theories of knowledge and learning are relevant to the quality of knowledge of 'how to' manage that you will take with you into a managerial career. In this section we see how this links with management knowledge as being tacit and coming from experience, and how students may learn such tacit knowledge in addition to the explicit knowledge gained during their studies.

What is management knowledge?

It is not uncommon for graduate trainees to arrive as newcomers in managerial positions to much suspicion, even sneering, at their graduate status. The insinuation is that these wet-behind-the-ears university types may have all of the knowledge from a degree, but they lack the experience of actually doing management in the 'real world'.

This mirrors the distinction between explicit and tacit knowledge. An amount of management knowledge comes from experience rather than from learning from books.

So, on the one hand, we can see that a management degree outlines a terrain of explicit management knowledge. In defining such management knowledge, we might look at particular theories that are learned—examples in this book might be theories of motivation, rational organizational design, management of groups and teams, and management of change, etc. In other words there is a list of theories, ideas, and models which, together, make up management knowledge.

To see management knowledge just in these terms would, perhaps, follow Freire's (1970) 'banking education' model (Figure 10.3). A student arrives at the start of the degree as an empty vessel and, through lectures, textbooks (such as this), and other sources, is eventually filled with items of knowledge that will equip them to manage. The degree to which you, as a student, have assimilated such knowledge is tested by means such as essays, examinations, presentations, and other assessments. Ultimately, a degree certificate is awarded to

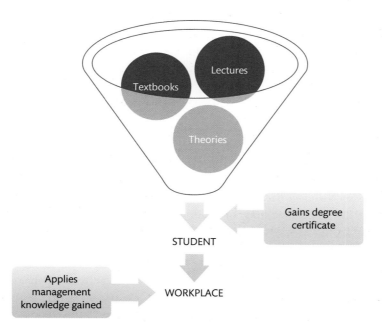

Figure 10.3
Freire's (1970) banking model applied to management education.

prove the amount of management knowledge that a student holds and which they can then go on to apply in the workplace.

But does this accumulation of management knowledge mean that a student *knows* how to manage. Has a student *learned* to be a manager during the course of their degree, with the degree certificate as proof of this? With management knowledge, as with the knowledge of driving a car or learning a language, there is an amount of tacit knowledge that is learned from experience.

Theory in context: origins of 'management'

A tacit dimension to management knowledge is embedded in the origins of the word 'management' as described by Holden and Tansley (2008). It may surprise you to learn that 'management' as a word derives from the training of horses—something which requires skill, but also experience. The word can be traced back to around 1555–1565 to an early Italian word *maneggiare*: to handle, train (horses). In turn, this derives from the Latin word *manus*, meaning hand. The implication is that training horses, while a skilled job that one gets a feel for, is learned by experience and doing. As such, there is a tacit dimension to such knowledge.

The origins of management?

The balance between management as explicit knowledge and management as a more tacit knowledge that comes from experience is also reflected in contemporary definitions of the word *management*. From several dictionaries, the following definitions of 'management' are presented:

- to direct or conduct business affairs
- be successful; achieve a goal
- be in charge of, act on, or dispose of
- to watch and direct
- to dominate or influence
- to continue to get along; carry on: *learning how to manage on my own.*

There is a contrast between managing in the sense of a planned, controlled activity to managing in the sense of coping—managing to cope and get along. This has been reflected in studies of what managers actually do in day-to-day work. Hales (1986) notes a contrast between formal and informal aspects of managerial work—the latter often involving interpersonal skills such as negotiation and dealing with conflict.

Carlsson (1951), in a classic study of Swedish executives, further found that the majority of their working life was spent in conversations—on the phone, in person, etc. This suggests that the majority of management work involves something not necessarily taught on a management degree—it requires interpersonal and communication skills.

As we look into management as both a concept and an activity, we begin to see areas of management knowledge that are learned through experience—interpersonal skills and dealing with the 'messy' side of the organization (the politics, conflict, and negotiation that takes place). While these can be found as content of a management degree, the extent to which they can be taught as explicit knowledge rather than through experience is debatable.

> **Employability skills:** placements and work experience
>
> Many of our students who have done placements in a workplace say that it is only through the experience of the workplace that they have come to fully understand the 'messy' and interpersonal side of the organization.
>
> While a degree programme provides an important amount of theory and skills for management, employers are also interested in 'real world' experience. This is partly the reason why some degree programmes have work placements as a means to locate the explicit knowledge gained at university into a workplace context where students can add to that learning through experience.
>
> Even if you have not undertaken a placement, employers will be interested in what else you have done at university other than the degree itself. Work experience, such as vacation jobs, involvement in running societies or sports clubs, and voluntary work all show evidence of management learning through experience.
>
> This is not to say that your degree work is not important. Remember that Kolb's learning cycle recognizes the importance of both experiential and theoretical knowledge—it is the combination of both which contribute to the learning cycle.

Management as reflective practice

The idea that management learning comes from experience feeds into a lot of training and development programmes. In many management courses, managers are encouraged to become reflective practitioners. Assessment in such courses consists of keeping journals and records of work undertaken, and reflecting on this experience in the light of explicit management theory. Management knowledge is thus seen, as with Kolb's cycle, as a combination of both explicit and tacit elements, and is a knowledge which develops through experience and reflection on that experience.

Such management education aims to equip managers not only with a store of management knowledge, but also with the ability to manage in practice—where managers need to react to events, drawing upon both explicit knowledge and knowledge gained through experience when doing so.

In the next section, we see how knowledge and learning at an organizational level also help organizations to both develop knowledge and be able to use that knowledge to change and react where necessary.

> **Review questions**

1. Describe the explicit and tacit aspects of management knowledge.

2. Explain what is meant by management as reflective practice.

3. Analyse the extent to which a management degree allows a student to know how to manage.

Apply

4. Do you think that you approach your studies as a deep or a surface learner?

Organizational knowledge and learning: the learning organization

So far in the chapter we have seen learning as a process whereby an *individual* adds to their knowledge. In this section we examine knowledge and learning as something that also exists at the level of the *organization*.

Organizational knowledge Knowledge which is a collective property of an organization rather than belonging to an individual.

Organizational learning Sharing and transfer of individual knowledge so that it becomes a collective property of the organization.

Learning organization An organization which is set up so as to facilitate continual learning at individual and organizational levels.

- First, we examine the concept of **organizational knowledge**, the possession of which gives success and competitive advantage to organizations, and even to national and regional economies. We see where knowledge resides and how, as with individual knowledge, it can exist in explicit and tacit forms.

- Secondly, we examine how knowledge is transferred within the organization, a process known as **organizational learning**. For knowledge to be organization-wide, it needs to be transferred between individuals. We examine how this happens, particularly with tacit knowledge, which individuals develop through experience and may find difficult to articulate to others.

- Finally, we examine how organizations that implement and are adept at organizational learning are known as **learning organizations**. Learning organizations not only increase their store of organizational knowledge, but are also seen to be more adept at coping with and responding to a need for change and innovation.

Organizational knowledge

There are sectors of the economy where knowledge and the development of that knowledge are vital for the competitive advantage, and even the survival, of an organization. Think about the mobile phone industry, for example. Consumers eagerly wait to upgrade to the newest smartphones with the latest technical innovations. It is important for companies to stay ahead of the game by developing this knowledge and innovating—those that get left behind can find their market share falling rapidly.

Knowledge-intensive firms Organizations whose main business involves the development and innovation of knowledge.

Knowledge workers Workers employed for their specific knowledge and their ability to use this knowledge to innovate, and develop new ideas and products.

A similar premium on knowledge can be found in industries such as pharmaceuticals, technology, and microelectronics, etc. Companies in such sectors are said to be **knowledge-intensive firms**—a key part of their strategy is the development of leading-edge knowledge. Workers who contribute to this and are valued for their particular knowledge and skills are described as **knowledge workers** (Alvesson, 2004).

Can you think of any other sectors of the economy that could be described as 'knowledge intensive' or professions where workers could be described as 'knowledge workers'?

Visit the Online Resource Centre for some suggestions.

From organizational knowledge to knowing in organizations

Knowledge, however, can be located in all organizations—not just those that are involved in cutting-edge technical innovation. Knowledge of an organization's culture or day to day routines are as much a part of organizational knowledge as specialist skills and expert knowledge.

Furthermore, organizational knowledge is multifaceted—there are different aspects of what, collectively, makes up organizational knowledge. Two dimensions which make up this multifaceted nature are:

1. Is the knowledge located in individuals within the organization or is it more of a collective property of the organization that is shared between people?

2. As with individual knowledge, is the knowledge explicit or tacit (see page 309)?

Blackler (1995) outlines five particular facets of knowledge or, as he describes them, 'images' of knowledge, which we have located along these scales of individual/collective and tacit/explicit in Figure 10.4 (Blackler, 1995: 1023–6).

These five images of knowledge are described in Table 10.4, where we place them in an organizational setting with an example of the types of knowledge that might be found in a restaurant kitchen.

We tend to privilege the embrained, for example, specialist knowledge of a head chef in a kitchen—they are seen as the valued worker upon whose knowledge the organization depends. However, Table 10.4 shows the variety of embodied, encultured, and embedded knowledge that is found within all staff within a kitchen—there are many types and locations of organizational knowledge.

Table 10.4   Facets of organizational knowledge. Based on Blackler (1995)

Type of knowledge	Description	Example
Embrained knowledge (explicit and individual)	The individual knowledge that we hold in our brains which is explicit in nature, equating to 'knowledge that'. It is reflected in an employee's qualifications, for example	*A chef may hold a qualification from catering school, and know a set of recipes or facts about food*
Embodied knowledge (individual and tacit)	The knowledge that comes from actually doing and experiencing a task. This is tacit knowledge that an individual develops—'knowledge how'	*A chef who has made a dish many times will be able to prepare it as if it were second nature*
Encultured knowledge (organizational with tacit and explicit dimensions)	Shared understandings in the organization—the stories, traditions, values, etc. that make up an organizational culture (see Chapter 7). Often it is unwritten and tacit—described simply as 'the way things are done around here', although organizations may try to make cultures explicit by describing them in documents (see Sloan Becker case in Chapter 14)	*Different kitchens have different cultures—expected behaviours and ways of doing things. Some may be noisy and brash, some may be quieter*
Embedded knowledge (organizational with tacit and explicit dimensions)	Knowledge embedded in the routines of an organization. Routines may be formalized and explicit, but also have informal tacit elements. Think of a university timetable—at first you have to consult it regularly; it is an explicit piece of printed knowledge. After a while you get used to your timetable to the point where you automatically go to rooms at the right time—it has become tacit knowledge	*Kitchens have many rigid routines that have to be followed— prepping food before the restaurant opens for business, procedures for taking orders, etc.*
Encoded knowledge (organizational and explicit)	Explicit knowledge found in books, manuals, computer databases, and sets of instructions, in the form of words, signs, symbols, lists, etc. It is also collective as it is knowledge that can be shared and accessed by the whole organization	*A kitchen may have a library of recipe books which have step-by-step instructions for dishes, knowledge which all members of the organization may access*

Figure 10.4 Blackler's (1995) five images of organizational knowledge.

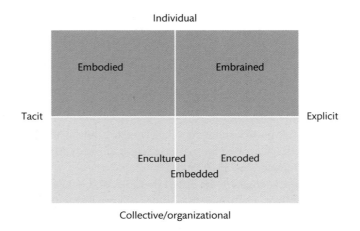

Indeed, for Blackler (1995), to talk of knowledge as a 'thing' misses its dynamic and social nature—it is always changing and is located within, and among, people. Learning and developing knowledge becomes a constant part of organizational activity.

Organizational learning

Running case: learning at the pub

Simon Chance calls in the maintenance manager, George Andrews, to review the training programme.

Chance has taken account of different learning styles among the workforce and realizes how difficult it is to accommodate all of these styles.

He has issued each member of the maintenance staff with a tablet computer which has access to a vast array of documentation—manuals for every piece of machinery in the building, diagrams of circuitry, and even videos from the manufacturers. Staff can access whatever material they feel helps them most.

Furthermore, the tablets give the maintenance engineers access to online forums where they can post their experiences of dealing with different problems for others to read and learn from, and search when they, too, encounter similar problems.

'It's all great', says George Andrews, 'the tablets are really useful and put a lot of information at their fingertips'.

'But, in terms of learning, I think they learn most at the pub on a Friday evening—that's when they really talk among themselves and share experiences of what they've been doing during the week. And, in comparison to providing training and tablet computers, that doesn't cost us a penny.'

Organizational learning is a process whereby an organization increases the amount of knowledge that it holds collectively. Knowledge is *shared*, or *transferred*, between people in the organization, and, furthermore, is transferred between people and the organization itself.

For Nonaka and Takeuchi (1995: 6), the ability for an organization to create knowledge and innovate continually is something which brings competitive advantage. This is noted by Nonaka, in particular, in successful Japanese firms where workers are striving continually to improve the task that they do (see Chapter 7). There is a recognition that workers know their task best—they develop tacit knowledge the more they perform it and, as such, know all the shortcuts and tricks that help them to perform the task better.

The problem for Nonaka is that such tacit knowledge is personal and comes from experience—it is difficult to put it into words in order to share that knowledge with others. As Brown and Duguid (2000: 76) state: 'Actual work practices are full of tacit improvisations that the employees who carry them out would have trouble articulating'. This is similar to earlier examples of individual knowledge—we may know from experience how to ride a bike, but it is difficult to put that tacit knowledge into words in order to share and transfer that knowledge.

Nonaka's model of the *knowledge-creating company* (Nonaka and Takeuchi, 1995, 2007) focuses on the ways in which particular types of knowledge are transferred. For Nonaka, it is the interaction between different types of knowledge—explicit and tacit—that creates knowledge within the organization. Such knowledge can be transferred between explicit and tacit knowledge in four ways (see Table 10.5), which we again illustrate with reference to an example of a restaurant kitchen.

Table 10.5 Knowledge transfer in Nonaka's knowledge-creating company (based on Nonaka and Takeuchi, 1995)

Type of knowledge transfer	Description	Example
From explicit to explicit: combination	Sources of encoded knowledge—manuals, databases, etc. are added to, combined, sorted, and categorized. A library combines a number of different forms of explicit knowledge, sorting and categorizing it in a library catalogue, for example. Such a databank of explicit knowledge, however, does not mean that people necessarily read and learn from it	*A chef has a set of recipe books on a shelf with Indian, Chinese, and French cuisine within. More books are added, covering Italian and vegetarian cuisine. The amount of explicit knowledge has been increased, but this does not necessarily mean that the chef has tried and experimented with any of the recipes in the books*
From explicit to tacit: internalization	As in learning to drive, a learner begins with explicit instructions but continues to practise and reflect on that practice (cf. Kolb's learning cycle) until they have internalized the knowledge—it has become tacit	*A chef takes a recipe—a set of explicit instructions—and makes a dish. She continues to experiment and repeat this until she knows the dish 'off by heart'*
From tacit to explicit: externalization, articulation	An expert or person who is well-experienced in a task attempts to make their tacit knowledge explicit by writing it down as a set of instructions, diagrams, or similar encoded knowledge. The expert is trying to articulate their tacit knowledge to an external audience	*A top chef writes a recipe book featuring instructions on how to make various dishes*
From tacit to tacit: socialization	Perhaps the least controllable form of knowledge transfer as the knowledge remains unspoken—it is never made explicit. Knowledge is acquired through observation and imitation. This might be how cultures are learned—they are absorbed from observation and experimentation rather than being told to people explicitly	*Example: a trainee chef learns from observation under the tutelage of a kitchen's head chef*

At the heart of Nonaka's model is the assumption that the richest form of knowledge is the tacit knowledge that exists within individuals who perform a particular job. However, for the organization to benefit fully from that knowledge it cannot just reside as tacit knowledge within one individual—what if the individual were ill or left the organization, for example? How are other members of the organization meant to learn and develop if the only expert keeps their knowledge to themselves?

The key aspect of knowledge transfer, for Nonaka, is thus how tacit knowledge is made explicit—expressed in words or diagrams, or some form that other people can take on board, practise, and convert to tacit knowledge of their own. Nonaka's model suggests a form of training and knowledge transfer that is still run by the organization itself; however, the transfer of tacit, experiential knowledge has also been observed as more of a social phenomenon which takes place informally among workers.

Real life case: 'war stories'

A classic study by Orr (1996) observed the work of photocopier engineers at Xerox. These are the people who are called out to various clients when photocopiers break down (as they often do).

Using tacit knowledge.

The engineers had knowledge from their training and, furthermore, had encoded, explicit knowledge about each model of photocopier in the form of manuals and diagrams. This, however, was not enough—machines have their own idiosyncrasies and complex problems can emerge that are beyond the instructions in the manual.

Orr discovered that a great deal of the knowledge that workers had was learned from conversations. Engineers developed tacit knowledge from their experience with machines, which they shared in social situations, such as over lunch. Orr described the sharing of 'war stories', where one engineer would tell how they dealt with a particular problem on a particular machine—a knowledge that other engineers could take and apply to similar situations.

Unlike the Xerox engineers, who are based at a head office before being sent out to jobs, some maintenance engineers are based at home and are emailed a set of jobs at the start of the day. What learning opportunities might an engineer in this situation miss out on?

Orr's study shows that explicit knowledge of photocopiers—knowledge from training and the manuals—was enhanced by the sharing, in a social situation, of more individual, tacit knowledge that other workers could then go away and apply. Rather than organizational knowledge, it was a form of knowledge that existed at the level of the group, where they learned from 'war stories' of each others' experiences (Orr, 1996).

Xerox recognized the value of this sharing of knowledge and set up a form of suggestions database where such knowledge could be tapped into and shared across the whole organization (Duguid, 2006; Orr, 1996). (See Chapter 14 for more on information sharing through computer networks.) Such a sharing of knowledge might be familiar to people who have searched online forums if, for example, their car has broken down or if their computer has a virus. The idea is to learn from the experiences that others have posted of how they have dealt with similar situations.

The idea of pooling such knowledge in an organization so that others may use it to enhance their own knowledge and be equipped to deal with particular situations as and when they arise can be seen as part of a strategy of becoming a learning organization.

The learning organization

While organizational learning highlights issues of how knowledge is shared and acquired, the learning organization is concerned with the organizational characteristics which promote and facilitate such learning and knowledge transfer. Organizational learning is thus a feature of the learning organization rather than—as sometimes happens—the two terms being used interchangeably.

By being able to share learning and knowledge, an organization and its members have more abilities at their collective disposal. This goes beyond work-specific knowledge, such as how to fix a photocopier or make a particular recipe, and relates to an organization's capacity to adapt and transform when needed. Competitive advantage comes not just from knowledge as applied to product development, but also the knowledge to be more flexible and adaptable in the face of changing environmental conditions. The organization is seen in biological, evolutionary terms as a 'complex organism' (Senge, 1990: 85) that constantly adjusts in response to its changing environment.

Such an ability to change and adapt is examined elsewhere in the book by two observations about the nature of the contemporary environment facing organizations:

- in Chapter 4 we examined post-bureaucratic organizations, where structures and communication lines are flexible rather than rigid, and where the organization can easily adapt to changes and bring together different configurations of people and knowledge so as to develop further knowledge. The Googleplex was given as an example of a post-bureaucratic organization. We can also see Google as typical of the organizations discussed in this chapter, which place a premium on continually developing knowledge for competitive advantage

- in Chapter 11, we see an emergent approach to change which suggests that, rather than being able to plan change for the future, organizations have to react to events as they happen, as if riding along on the rapids of a river.

Proponents of the learning organization thus emphasize a focus both on the development of individual and organizational learning within organizations, and furthermore, on seeing the organization as being in a continuous process of change and transformation (Pedler et al., 1997; Senge, 1990).

Single- and double-loop learning

Such a level of learning and transformation at the organizational level is addressed by Argyris and Schön (1978). Their concept of single- and double-loop learning has similarities with the difference between surface learning and deep learning at an individual level and is influenced by Bateson's (1973) levels of learning which suggested that increased individual creativity derives from learning to learn or deutero learning.

At an organizational level, a move from surface learning to a more creative and deep form of learning is where an organization as a whole moves from single- to double-loop learning:

Single-loop learning Learning in organizations which merely adapts to achieving a particular goal.

Double-loop learning Learning in organizations which goes beyond achieving a goal to question assumptions behind the goal being set, and that questions assumptions, values, and strategies more widely in the organization.

- **single-loop learning** is where an organization tries repeatedly to solve the same problem or achieve the same goal—a simple form of 'error correction' to ensure that the goal continues to be achieved. For example, an organization might have a sales target for a particular product each year. If it fails to achieve it then it takes steps the following year to correct the problem—hiring new sales staff, for example, or looking at the bonus system. The sales target itself is not questioned

- **double-loop learning** questions the goal itself and the underlying assumptions behind it. It wouldn't just ask how to achieve the target sales, it would ask whether the sales of that product contribute enough to profits to warrant pursuing that goal, whether the market for that product has any future, and even whether targets are a good way to motivate sales staff. In other words, rather than the simple sales target itself, just about everything is up for discussion—an organization's values, policies, and objectives (Argyris and Schön, 1978).

Characteristics of a learning organization

Double-loop learning is thus a more thorough and deep questioning of what an organization does which goes beneath the surface of solving one isolated problem, a questioning which readies an organization for the type of change and adaptability required of a learning organization. For Senge (1990), such a form of learning is part of five characteristics which make up a successful learning organization (see Table 10.6).

The learning organization paints a picture of an organization where there is harmony, trust, and an openness of communication between co-workers, and between workers and management, with all members of the organization unified behind the vision of the organization. To what extent this is realistic or achievable forms the basis for assessing the learning organization.

Table 10.6 Senge's five characteristics of the learning organization (adapted from Senge, 1990: 6–11)

Personal mastery	The organization encourages the personal development and learning of individuals in the organization so that they can reach their potential
Mental models	People are not stuck in old ways of thinking and old routines, and are open to new ideas. People engage in higher levels of learning where goals and assumptions are questioned constantly (as with double-loop learning)
Shared vision	All organizational members have a shared, mutually-agreed vision, which is reinforced through strong and inspiring leadership (see Chapter 12 leadership)
Team learning	People work and learn together in teams with the importance of dialogue and discussion between people being highlighted in a similar manner to the case of the Xerox photocopier engineers
Systems thinking	People think about the organization in terms of relationships and connections (see Chapter 11), with all actions having consequences both inside and outside of the organization. Systems thinking is about seeing how they fit into 'the bigger picture'

Learning organizations assessed

The development of knowledge and learning in organizations has, so far, been presented as a good thing. It gives organizations a competitive advantage in an increasingly knowledge-based economy, and it allows individual workers to develop their potential and creativity, perhaps even moving them towards 'self-actualizing' in their work (see Chapter 9).

The learning organization perspective is a far cry from the Taylorist view of individual and organizational learning presented in Chapter 2. Rather than encouraging learning, Taylor saw individual knowledge as a source of power for workers and a threat to his authority. Taylor's strategy was the absolute opposite of a learning organization—he removed knowledge from workers, placing it all in the hands of management, with individual learning reduced to learning a simple, repetitive task.

However, the view of the learning organization is not without critique; indeed, its vision of harmony in the organization, shared visions, and unhindered individual learning and development is seen by critics as an unrealistic, naïve, or 'utopian' (Coopey, 1998; Driver, 2002) view of how organizations operate. Among many critiques of the learning organization we suggest three broad areas that may prevent the learning organization from being an ideal or achievable form of operating in organizations (see Driver, 2002, for more):

- the assumption of trust, open communication, and a sharing of knowledge ignores the influence of organizational politics (see Chapter 13) where people may choose to retain or restrict access to knowledge as a source of power for their own personal advantage

- it assumes that people have the ability and desire to engage in constant learning and development. As seen with orientations to work (Chapter 9) some people prefer to do repetitive and unchallenging work as a means of simply getting a wage

- while a learning organization may not employ the forms of rationalized control that characterize Taylorism, its shared vision relies on a strong shared culture, which itself can be seen as a form of control (see Chapter 7). The idea of a shared vision also means that there is an element of control that prevents dissent against that vision (see Driver, 2002).

Visit the Online Resource Centre to consider some more critiques of the learning organization.

While the concept of the learning organization is thus open to critique, in the final section we outline how knowledge and learning are still important to the contemporary economy and organizations.

Learning beyond the organization

To conclude this chapter we look at knowledge which is shared across, and between, organizations, rather than residing within the bounds of any one organization. Of course, knowledge does transfer between organizations—when a person leaves an organization and joins another, for example, and takes their particular knowledge with them. The concept of the learning organization recognizes, in fact, the importance of suppliers and other stakeholders that an organization deals with (Pedler et al., 1997).

Here, we briefly suggest three contemporary areas where work-related knowledge is shared across organizational boundaries.

Professional knowledge A common body of knowledge relevant to a particular profession or occupation.

Knowledge clusters Geographical areas where a number of knowledge-intensive organizations in a particular industry are congregated in close proximity.

- **Professional knowledge.** Professions such as medicine, architecture, and law have a knowledge base which is common to all practitioners, regardless of which organization they are based in—knowledge which they need to constantly update. A doctor, for example, needs to know about the latest medical discoveries and opinions, and about the latest drugs and treatments. Thus, there are journals, conferences, email lists, and similar networks through which professional knowledge is shared, potentially on a global scale.

- **Knowledge clusters.** Knowledge clusters occur where a number of organizations engaged in the same industry are located in close geographical proximity. They are able to collaborate with each other, share resources, and benefit from each others' particular knowledge (see Coughlan, 2011). For example, Mediacity in Salford, UK, is a concentration of media-related organizations, bringing together large broadcasters, such as the BBC and ITV, but also smaller, knowledge-intensive companies, for example manufacturers of specialist broadcast equipment or graphic design companies. Another example of a knowledge cluster is where universities set up, or are associated with, nearby 'science parks'. Academics can collaborate and share knowledge with companies and organizations engaged in the same field. For example, computer firm Microsoft has a research facility in conjunction with Cambridge University in the UK (Microsoft Research, 2012).

Open source and online collaboration A form of knowledge sharing and collaboration where computer code is made publicly available and developed collaboratively.

- **Open source and online collaboration.** In Chapter 14 we examine the effects of computer networks on organizations, including the ability for organizations to share knowledge as data through networks. Open source software is computer code which is made freely available so that anyone can apply their knowledge to it and develop it. If you use operating systems such as Linux, many people have applied their knowledge collaboratively to developing such systems—in some cases for free as a hobby, in other cases as part of their work. A similar type of online collaboration can be seen with Wikipedia, where people have contributed their knowledge collaboratively in an open forum to create an encyclopaedia (Mulgan et al., 1995). (See Chapter 14 for more on this.)

Visit the Online Resource Centre for more on materials on learning beyond the organization.

Communities of practice

Communities of practice Social groupings based around a common occupational practice and set of knowledge, who develop and share that knowledge among themselves.

A concept which we can use to unite the three examples is that of **communities of practice**. Lave and Wenger (1991) first used this to note the learning of specific areas of knowledge, especially occupational knowledge, in social contexts. The example of the photocopier engineers earlier in this chapter is an example of a community of practice within an organization—they are engaged in the same area of work, their work is based on a common set of knowledge, and they develop and share that knowledge as a form of social practice.

An organization may consist of many communities of practice within it, not just the photocopier engineers, but also the accountants, the legal staff, and the gardeners, etc. who all learn and develop their knowledge within their social groups.

To what extent is the 'community of practice' perspective relevant to the maintenance engineers in the Junction Hotel running case?

The three examples given are examples of where communities of practice exist across organizational boundaries. For example, with medical knowledge, there may be a community of practice of people involved in treating a particular illness. Although they may all work in different institutions, and even different countries, they are involved in a common practice based on a common body of knowledge which they share and develop in social situations such as conferences.

Collaborators in specific open-source applications can also be seen as a community of practice. Even if some of the collaborators are individuals involved as part of a hobby, it is a shared practice with a common body of knowledge, with knowledge shared and developed often through online social forums, such as discussion boards.

Knowledge as a public or private commodity

Back in 1984, French philosopher Jean-Francois Lyotard noted the increased storage of knowledge in computer systems and networks, something which is examined further in Chapter 14. Lyotard (1984) warned of the dangers of organizations being able to privately monopolize and hoard knowledge. He suggested 'freeing up' the data banks of knowledge to make them publicly available.

While open-source applications can be seen as a 'freeing up' of data banks, for many organizations, knowledge is seen as a valuable possession and is often protected by legal instruments, such as patents and copyrights. At the time of writing, a number of debates were ongoing about the nature of organizational knowledge and its public availability:

- a number of court battles and disputes were taking place over patents in the mobile telephone and computer industries
- the amount of personal knowledge and data held by companies such as Google and Facebook, and how such data may be used commercially, is an ongoing debate, with concern expressed, even at governmental levels
- Harvard University suggested that knowledge in the form of research is a public commodity and that researchers should publish in online sources that do not require payment (Sample, 2012).

We introduce these current debates here briefly at the conclusion of the chapter in order to indicate the ongoing importance of knowledge to organizations and its position as a topic of contemporary debate.

Visit the Online Resource Centre for more on these issues and their subsequent developments.

Review questions

1. Describe the different types of organizational knowledge.
2. Explain what it means for an organization to 'learn'.
3. Analyse the importance of converting tacit to explicit knowledge as a part of organizational learning.

Apply

4. How would Junction Hotel benefit from being a learning organization? What steps have already been taken towards this with the maintenance department? Would there be any negative effects of being a learning organization?

Chapter summary

This chapter has examined knowledge and learning at both individual and organizational levels, and across organizational boundaries. A distinction is made between knowledge being viewed simply as a 'thing' which people and organizations accumulate, and knowledge as more of a dynamic and social process—something which exists through action. It is the latter that is generally viewed as being a better quality and more enduring form of knowledge, a knowledge with depth rather than simply being at the surface level.

For individuals this means developing knowledge from an explicit set of facts to a more personal, tacit knowledge which comes from experience and reflecting upon that experience, and, ultimately, recognizing ones own preferences for learning styles.

For organizations this means working out how to tap into the deep, tacit knowledge of individuals and sharing that knowledge throughout the organization. Concepts such as organizational learning and the learning organization suggest that organizations which excel at this sharing of knowledge, and also take place in deeper, double-loop learning, will gain a competitive advantage, not just through innovation in their particular sector of the economy, but also by being more capable of responding to change and adjusting their operations when required.

The concept of change, and how organizations plan for and react to change, is considered in Chapter 11.

Further reading

Brown, J.S., and Duguid, P. 2000. Balancing act: Capturing knowledge without killing it. *Harvard Business Review* **78(3): 73–80.**
A good introduction to the Xerox photocopier case and how Xerox subsequently tried to tap into the tacit knowledge of their engineers.

Honey, P., and Mumford, A. 2006. *The learning styles helper's guide,* **Peter Honey Publications Ltd, Maidenhead.**

Mulgan, G., Steinberg, Y., and Salem, O. 1995. Wide open: Open source methods and their future potential. Demos. Available at: http://www.demos.co.uk/publications/wideopen (last accessed 3 July 2012).
A report into open source methods, including case studies of Linux and Wikipedia.

Nonaka, I., and Takeuchi, H. 2007. The knowledge-creating company. *Harvard Business Review* **85(7/8): 162.**
Nonaka's overview of knowledge creation and transfer in organizations.

Bibliography

Alexander, B. 2012. Consulting Dr. Google is rarely a good idea. Here's why. NBC News. 20 July 2012. Available at: http://todayhealth.today.com/_news/2012/07/20/12860662-consulting-dr-google-is-rarely-a-good-idea-heres-why.

Alvesson, M. 2004. *Knowledge Work and Knowledge-intensive Firms.* Oxford University Press: Oxford.

Argyris, C., and Schön, D.A. 1978. *Organizational learning.* Addison-Wesley Pub. Co.: Reading, MA.

Bateson, G. 1973. *Steps to an ecology of mind.* Ballantine Books: New York.

Blackler, F. 1995. Knowledge, knowledge work and organizations: an overview and interpretation. *Organization Studies* 16(6): 1021–1046.

Brown, J.S., and Duguid, P. 2000. Balancing act: Capturing knowledge without killing it. *Harvard Business Review* 78(3): 73–80.

Carlson, S. 1951. *Executive behaviour*. Arno Press: New York.

Coopey, J. 1998. Learning to trust and trusting to learn: A role for radical theatre. *Management Learning* 29(3): 365–382.

Coughlan, S. 2011. Battle of the knowledge superpowers. BBC News Online. 28 September 2011. Available at: http://www.bbc.co.uk/news/education-14949538.

Driver, M. 2002. The learning organization: Foucauldian gloom or Utopian sunshine? *Human Relations* 55(1): 33–53.

Duguid, P. 2006. What talking about machines tells us. *Organization Studies* 27(12): 1794–1804.

Fleming, N.D. 2001. *Teaching and learning styles: VARK strategies*. Neil Fleming: Christchurch, NZ.

Freire, P. 1970. *Pedagogy of the oppressed* (transl. M. B. Ramos). Seabury Press: New York.

Gardner, H. 1983. *Frames of mind: the theory of multiple intelligences*. Basic Books: New York.

Hales, C.P. 1986. What do managers do? A critical review of the evidence. *Journal of Management Studies* 23(1): 88–115.

Holden, N., and Tansley, C. 2008. Management in other languages: how a philological approach opens up new cross-cultural vistas. In: Tietze, S. (ed.) *International management and language*. Routledge: London, New York.

Honey, P., and Mumford, A. 1992. *The manual of learning styles*. Peter Honey Publications Ltd: Maidenhead.

Honey, P., and Mumford, A. 2006. *The learning styles helper's guide*. Peter Honey Publications Ltd: Maidenhead.

Koffka, K. 1955. *Principles of gestalt psychology*. Routledge & Kegan Paul: London.

Kolb, D.A. 1984. *Experiential learning: experience as the source of learning and development*. Prentice Hall: Englewood Cliffs, NJ.

Lave, J., and Wenger, E. 1991. *Situated learning: legitimate peripheral participation*. Cambridge University Press: Cambridge, New York.

Lyotard, J.F. 1984. *The postmodern condition: a report on knowledge*. Manchester University Press: Manchester.

Marton, F., and Säljö, R. 1976. On qualitative differences in learning. I—Outcome and Process. *British Journal of Educational Psychology* 46: 4–11.

Microsoft Research. 2012. Microsoft Research Cambridge. Available at: http://research.microsoft.com/en-us/labs/cambridge/ (last accessed 26 November 2012).

Mulgan, G., Steinberg, Y., and Salem, O. 1995. Wide open: Open source methods and their future potential. Demos. Available at: http://www.demos.co.uk/publications/wideopen (last accessed 3 July 2012).

Nonaka, I., and Takeuchi, H. 1995. *The knowledge-creating company: how Japanese companies create the dynamics of innovation*. Oxford University Press: New York.

Nonaka, I., and Takeuchi, H. 2007. The knowledge-creating company. *Harvard Business Review* 85(7/8): 162–171.

Orr, J.E. 1996. *Talking about machines: an ethnography of a modern job*. ILR Press: Ithaca, NY.

Paddock, C. 2012. Dr Google And The Unwise Practice Of Self-Diagnosis. Medical News Today. 23 July 2012. Available at: http://www.medicalnewstoday.com/articles/248145.php.

Pask, G. 1976. Styles and strategies of learning. *British Journal of Educational Psychology* 46: 128–148.

Pedler, M., Burgoyne, J., and Boydell, T. 1997. *The learning company: A strategy for sustainable development*, 2nd edn. McGraw-Hill: London.

Polanyi, M. 1958. *Personal knowledge; towards a post-critical philosophy*. University of Chicago Press: Chicago.

Polanyi, M. 1967. *The tacit dimension*. Routledge & Kegan Paul: London.

Russell, B. 1912. *The problems of philosophy*. Oxford University Press: London, New York.

Ryle, G. 1949. *The concept of mind*. Hutchinson: London.

Sample, I. 2012. Harvard University says it can't afford journal publishers' prices. *The Guardian* (24 April 2012).

Schön, D.A. 1983. *The reflective practitioner: how professionals think in action*, Basic Books: New York.

Senge, P.M. 1990. *The fifth discipline: the art and practice of the learning organization*. Doubleday/Currency: New York.

Tang, H., and Ng, J.H.K. 2006. Googling for a diagnosis—use of Google as a diagnostic aid: internet based study. *British Medical Journal*, vol. 333, 2 December 2002, pp. 1143–1145.

Part 4
Managing the organization

Changing the organization
Planning and emergence

Chapter overview and learning outcomes

By the end of this chapter you should be able to:

- describe a range of triggers to change and resisting factors against change

- explain how change can be messy, causing conflict and resistance

- describe three approaches to the management of change: the naïve, planned, and emergent approaches

- analyse the different perspectives that these three approaches give of the nature of an organization and how it might be changed.

Key theorists

Kurt Lewin	Psychologist whose work on group dynamics has been applied to many areas of planned change, including force-field analysis, the three-step model of change and organization development
Ralph Stacey	Has applied chaos and complexity theories to organizational change
Bernard Burnes	Has analysed the work of Lewin and advocates its relevance to contemporary organizational change
Thomas Cummings and Christopher Worley	Have outlined the wide variety of change management techniques which are used in organizational settings

Key terms

Naïve change	An approach to change which sees the organization in simplistic terms, as if it were a set of building blocks which can be rearranged easily
Planned change	An approach which sees change as planned over a long-term series of steps. Pays attention to human and social aspects of change, which are seen as 'hidden aspects' below the surface, as if the organization were an iceberg
Emergent change	An approach to change which sees the organization as being like a river, in constant flow, and suggests that in such an environment change emerges rather than being planned in advance
Force-field analysis	A technique whereby triggers for, and resistance against, change are plotted on a diagram in order to identify areas on which to focus a change-management programme
Three-step model	Lewin's model whereby a process of change goes through three stages of unfreezing, movement, and freezing
Complexity theory	An emergent approach to organizational change, suggesting that small changes can have unpredictable and potentially limitless consequences

Introduction

Running case: successful change at 'Coral Reef?'

Six months after taking over at the fitness centre, manager Carl Jones is sipping champagne with the hotel's management team in the boardroom. The toast—to the success of the fitness centre. Jones had been brought in as a 'new broom' to turn around the ailing fortunes of the fitness centre. Six months on, the results speak for themselves.

- The centre has been refurbished and rebranded as *Coral Reef*, with the image and ambience of a warm, beach environment.
- Turnover has trebled, and the fitness centre is beginning to make profits and a financial contribution to the hotel.
- The percentage of hotel guests using the centre has doubled from 20% to 40%.
- Full-time membership of the club, from the local area, has doubled.
- A new range of beauty and health services is offered.
- Many more female guests are using the centre where previously the clientele was 95% male.

These achievements, especially the profit figures, are seen as outstanding by Simon Chance. Leading the toast to Jones, he praises his 'authoritative, decisive, and, ultimately, successful programme of change'.

Has Carl Jones been a successful manager of change?

We all encounter change in our lives, whether it is a major decision—to move house or change job, for example—or something as minor as a change of hairstyle. Change might be forced upon us by particular circumstances or something that we do of our own volition.

In organizations, change is any form of effort or initiative undertaken to alter a particular aspect of the organization. This might be to improve the current situation of the organization or, as we have seen with recent economic turmoil, to respond to particular events that necessitate some form of change for the survival of the organization.

We begin the chapter by viewing change from two conflicting perspectives. On the one hand, change might be seen by managers as a reasonable action to take in response to certain triggers or pressures—moving to larger premises, for example, if the current premises are crowded. On the other hand, change can cause anxiety, fear, and upset among the workforce that it affects—the new premises might necessitate a longer commute for the workforce, even resulting in some having to give up their jobs. Rather than being a smooth process, change can be messy, and meet with conflict and resistance.

We present three broad approaches which examine the implementation of change against the backdrop of such conflicting perspectives. These approaches are derived from three particular metaphors or ways of seeing the organization, which we suggest offer different insights into the subject:

- First, we examine a **naïve approach to change** which stems from viewing the organization in simplistic terms, as a set of building blocks. This approach, where managers can change

Naïve approach to change An approach to change which sees the organization in simplistic terms, as if it were a set of building blocks which can be rearranged easily.

the organization by rearranging elements of the organization at will, is one that we suggest is misguided and misses out on many aspects of the organization that are important to the change process.

- Secondly, we suggest that viewing the organization as an iceberg shows that it has hidden depths which affect the implementation of change. Such hidden depths are the human and social aspects of the organization, within which resistance and anxiety can develop. The **planned approach to change** suggests that, using knowledge from behavioural psychology, change can be implemented in a set of steps using techniques which overcome that resistance and bring about attitude change.

- Finally, an **emergent approach to change** sees the organization as a river, constantly in flow. The organization is never still for long enough for change to be a planned process; change is what emerges in the course of events.

The three approaches take us from managers being in absolute control *of* change, to managers almost being controlled *by* change, having to react to events as they happen.

Conflicting perspectives of change: triggers and resistance

> **Running case:** Coral 'grief'
>
> The boardroom celebrations do not extend down to the Coral Reef fitness centre. The long-standing staff have seen their jobs and workplace change out of all recognition in the past six months—changes which have made them unhappy.
>
> Egged on by his colleagues, one of the trainers walks up to the grinning photograph in the fitness centre entrance, underneath which reads 'Carl Jones, Fitness Centre Manager.' He draws on a moustache and spectacles; then, applying his marker pen to the fitness centre entrance sign, 'Coral Reef' is rechristened as 'Coral Grief.'
>
> Later, with the staff having long left the building, Meg Mortimer goes down from the party to check that the fitness suite is locked up. Noticing the doctored photograph and sign she smiles to herself. Of course, she cleans it up before it can be discovered, but after the six months she's had coping with the fallout from Jones's changes, she isn't going to pursue the culprits any further.

When a change takes place, it can be a messy process. People may have different, even conflicting, views and opinions of the change. What might seem like a perfectly rational and necessary change to a senior manager may upset other workers who are happy as they are, or leave them anxious about their job security and working conditions.

In this section we see change as a process that takes place amidst conflicting perspectives across the organization. On the one hand, there are a number of **triggers** which provide an impetus for managers to make a change. On the other hand, reaction to that change might be manifested in different forms of **resistance**.

Planned approach to change An approach to change which sees change as planned over a series of long-term steps. Pays attention to human and social aspects of change, which are seen as 'hidden aspects' below the surface, as if the organization were an iceberg. Closely linked with organization development.

Emergent approach to change An approach to change which sees the organization as being like a river, in constant flow, and suggests that in such an environment change emerges in the course of events rather than being planned in advance.

Triggers Factors which push towards a change taking place.

Resistance Factors which prevent or hinder a change taking place.

Real life case: alternative perceptions of change

A case study of change in a financial services institution (King, 2001) was undertaken by getting employees and managers to draw their perceptions of the change process.

Before the change, the organization was perceived as traditional, secure, and averse to risk, with a 'family' culture that was collective, sharing, and supportive. This safe, but conservative, organization was seen by management as old-fashioned and uncompetitive, so stuck in its ways that it could, potentially, go out of business. The financial services sector was characterized by market deregulation, increased automation and Internet banking, and an increase in the amount and intensity of competition within the market.

A change was undertaken—towards a more dynamic, risk-taking, and sales-driven culture. Targets and charts permeated the organization, with graphs showing sales of mortgages and financial products placed on the wall of the staff room. Management were more visible, with one manager sitting opposite the clock-in machine as people arrived for work.

The change was 'officially' a success. Targets were met and the move to a new sales culture completed. However, many staff left and were replaced with new recruits. Away from the official success story, different perspectives within the organization emerged. The research involved both managers and workers drawing their perceptions of the change process. Away from the official success story, the drawings showed that some employees had a different perception of the change process.

The management perception

A common theme linked management illustrations of the change process—a journey towards a brighter future. One senior manager highlighted the 'baggage' of the organization's past culture dragging it back as it climbed towards its future. It could still go backwards, but if the organization reached the top of the hill it faced a bright future. A branch manager envisaged the organization crossing a bridge towards riches and rewards. Taking that journey would require the right attitude; however, the bridge could be cut and the change prevented by negative attitudes from employees, such as fear and ignorance. Those that complied with the change were portrayed as 'angels', while those that contributed to its failure—through their fear and ignorance—were presented as 'devils'.

The employee perception

Employee drawings suggested a different perception of the change. A long-standing employee of the organization drew small workers on an assembly line, whipped to work harder by an overbearing management and with the targets looming large over the whole organization. A newer employee illustrated herself swamped by the amount of paperwork and a constantly ringing telephone—happy only when the end of the working day came along. In the most dramatic image, an employee, who eventually left, drew a worker shedding tears of money, pushed to this by a ruthless manager depicted as a Nazi.

The drawings illustrated conflicting perceptions of the change. For management, the past was bad and the future good. The change was about the organization growing and developing, and was a rational and purely technical response to environmental pressures within the financial services sector. Management should control the change—any resistance or obstruction of the change was problematic and to the detriment of the organization's future. *They perceived employees that obstruct or resist change as devils.*

For employees, the concern was more with the present situation. They took the change personally, visualizing themselves shrinking in the face of management targets and intensified work regimes. They felt pain and powerlessness, and that they had little choice in what was happening. To them the change was destructive and they felt like victims. *They perceived management implementing the change as Nazis.*

Source: King, 2001.

The conflicting perspectives on the change can be shown as a number of triggers exerting a force for the change to take place (increased competition in the sector, technology, deregulation, etc.), but equally an amount of resistance among the workforce against that change. A swastika to depict a manager is an incredibly powerful, and, indeed, offensive, image to use, but it demonstrates how clearly the workers were upset by the change and how angry they were with the management. *Change can provoke very strong emotions and resistance.*

Triggers for change

Running case: flashback—embarking on change

Six months before the celebrations in the boardroom, Carl Jones had started his first day as the new fitness centre director. His brief: the centre was a loss-maker—it needed to not only hold its own, but to start making money for the hotel. Jones saw two main areas of potential for income growth:

1. External memberships—Junction Hotel offered fitness centre membership to non-residents; however, take-up was low. The fitness industry was highly competitive and dominated by a number of large-scale branded chains. Junction Hotel needed its own, smaller-scale gym to trade on its more personal atmosphere, while matching the offerings of its larger competitors

2. Income from hotel guests—hotel guests could use the gym facilities for free and Jones was not allowed to change this. However, he thought that the fitness centre could provide paid extras for the guests— classes, beauty treatments, etc. Indeed, the fitness centre could become a reason for people to stay at the hotel *per se*, with spa weekend packages being offered.

Jones had started by listing the current features of the gym:

- the fitness centre had no separate identity or brand of its own—it was not marketed within the hotel or externally to the local population

- the décor was somewhat basic (cold, plain walls); the gym had basic equipment (none of the electronic machinery found in competitors' gyms); showers were provided, but no sauna or spa facilities, as found in competitors' gyms

- opening hours—the fitness centre was open from 7 am until 7 pm, and was only fully staffed between 9 am and 5 pm; competitors were open earlier and later

- there was a reception desk at the entrance, which was largely unstaffed, and extras, such as towels, were not provided; staff would be on hand to give advice if asked, although, in practice, this was given mainly to a number of regular members who had devised workout programmes with the staff

- unlike competitors, no exercise classes or lessons were offered. There were two treatment rooms—some of the staff had physiotherapy qualifications and would provide treatments, charging separately for this and pocketing the money themselves. For much of the time, the treatment rooms lay unused—with one of them even being used as an informal staff room

- the five fitness centre staff worked as a team, all working a 9–5 shift, Monday–Saturday, with the centre being unstaffed on Sundays. Work tasks were arranged informally. Tasks included the maintenance and cleaning of gym equipment, pool life-guarding duties, general monitoring of the gym floor and the safety of users, and checking membership cards when people entered—this was the closest there was to any form of reception duties. All staff had a sports science qualification, which they were proud of. No staff uniforms were worn

- the basic nature of the gym floor gave it a 'spit and sawdust' feel. Regular members tended to be male and heavily into weight training. Casual users, such as hotel guests, and people considering gym membership, particularly women, said that they found it intimidating. The staff found no problem with the culture and enjoyed working with the regular members. The fewer new members the better, otherwise it might disrupt the way that things were run.

Jones had started to think of what changes he could make to turn around the fitness centre. At the time, he was working within two financial parameters:

1. There was a healthy budget for investment—equipment, building works, etc. Whatever needed to be done should be done.

2. While the investment budget was plentiful, Jones had to keep increases in running costs to a minimum. Day to day, the fitness centre had to be making a profit. In particular, there was little room to increase staff costs.

What changes would you make if you were in Carl Jones's position?

Triggers for change are forces which give an impetus for a change to occur, whether they are external triggers from outside the organization, or internal triggers from within. Potentially, the number of triggers for change in an organization is limitless.

Senior and Swailes (2010) suggest that external triggers for change can be identified using the PEST (political, economic, socio-cultural and technological) model, as introduced in Chapter 4, to think more broadly about the sectors of the organization's external environment from which these triggers might originate (Figure 11.1).

Some, or indeed all, of these sectors of the environment may be acting on an organization at any one time. For example, in UK universities, triggers from all four sectors of the external environment have, perhaps, pushed universities towards a more commercial and student-focused way of operating, and away from more traditional, academic 'ivory tower' cultures (Figure 11.2).

Figure 11.1 The PEST model and external triggers for change.

Political
- Policies and laws made at an international, national or local level

Economic
- Economic conditions – e.g. growth, competition, interest rates, unemployment levels

Organization

Social
- Social attitudes and values, e.g. towards the environment, healthy eating, equality

Technological
- Technology used in other organizations giving a competitive advantage, consumer desire for new technologies

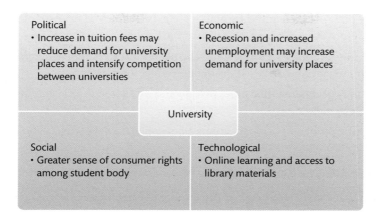

Figure 11.2
Aspects of the external environment acting as triggers for change in UK universities.

The impetus for change can also come from internal triggers—a reorganization or restructuring, for example, may come from a recognition of problems within the organization itself, such as poor communication or coordination between departments. Based on Senior and Swailes (2010: 22) we suggest a number of potential internal triggers to change:

- new senior staff may bring in their own ideas and vision for how the organization should be run—a new broom sweeps clean

- managerial aspirations, whims, and decisions may lead to change

- unions within the organization may bring their own pressure and action for changes

- the politics and power of particular groups, individuals, and coalitions within an organization (see Chapter 13) may be a force towards change

- changes may be required as an organization grows in size, for instance, new premises to cope with the increased capacity

- a redesign of technology, jobs, or even the physical layout of the organization, may bring with it a need for further changes.

Visit the Online Resource Centre for further examples of potential internal triggers to change.

Resistance to change

While triggers and forces for change may exist, change is often resisted strongly by individuals, groups of individuals, or, indeed, by organizational forces as a whole.

As seen in the financial services institution case, change can arouse very strong and powerful human emotions and feelings, which are displayed as resistance to change. Based on Drafke (2009: 431–437) examples of why people resist change might include the following:

- generally, people are not predisposed to change from their everyday routines with which they become comfortable—disruption to routines is not liked

- people may worry about job security or pay issues, i.e. they perceive that they will lose out in some way as a result of the change

- change may disrupt social and informal ties, e.g. being moved from an office with people they enjoy to one where they dislike the people
- people may not recognize or understand the need for the change which is being proposed and which may have a considerable effect upon them
- the change may go against the values held by individuals, e.g. a clash of professional and commercial values
- taking all of the points mentioned, change can create anxiety when people are unsure of what is about to happen.

Visit the Online Resource Centre for further reasons why people resist change.

Inertia A tendency for an organization as a whole to resist change.

Resistance to change may also occur at the level of the organization, where organizational factors cause **inertia**, or a lack of movement. In this chapter we will see that groups and cultures can cause resistance within the organization (the organization as an iceberg), as can the systemic nature of organizations that causes unpredictable knock-on effects (the organization as a river).

At a more practical level, the organization may also be shackled against undergoing a particular change, for example owing to contractual obligations or fixed investments. Furthermore, an organization may simply lack the capability to change. This may be a lack of finance or other resources for the change, a lack of space or equipment, or a lack of capability or skills within the organization's workforce (Senior and Fleming, 2006: 286).

Force-field analysis

Force-field analysis A technique whereby triggers and resistance to change are plotted on a diagram in order to identify areas to focus a change-management programme.

The multitude of triggers and resisting factors show that there are a number of different factors at work in any change situation. The whole situation in any one organization can become very complicated to understand.

Force-field analysis (Lewin, 1943) is a technique which provides a snapshot or overall view of a change situation. The triggers and resistance factors are shown on a diagram (Figure 11.3)

Figure 11.3
Force-field analysis.

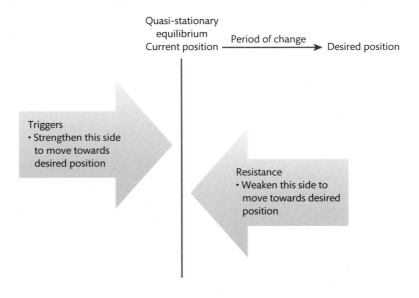

Quasi-stationary equilibrium
Current position —— Period of change ——▶ Desired position

Triggers
• Strengthen this side to move towards desired position

Resistance
• Weaken this side to move towards desired position

as arrows converging on one point—the current position. At this point the organization is in a 'quasi-stationary equilibrium'. To move to a desired situation, i.e. to change, the organization needs to strengthen the triggers to change and weaken the resisting forces.

In the earlier case of the financial services institution, it is possible to plot out the triggers for change and the resistance factors on a force-field analysis diagram (Figure 11.4). In this instance, the triggers, such as deregulation, competition, and senior staff initiatives, are pushing the organization in the direction of a sales-oriented culture. However, these triggers are met by resistance in terms of staff fears, the strength of the current culture, and a dislike of the new working methods, etc.

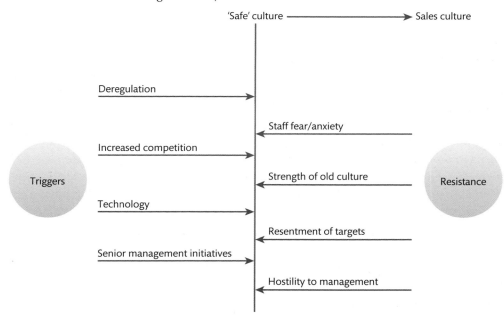

Figure 11.4 Force-field analysis of the financial services institution case.

Force-field analysis derives from the psychology of Kurt Lewin. In Chapter 6 we saw how Lewin analysed the influence of group dynamics, or peer pressure, upon individual behaviour. For Lewin (1943), group dynamics is one of many forces in an individual's **life field** which influence their behaviour. While consisting mainly of psychological forces, this life field may also contain factors from the physical and social world that a person encounters. Such forces can be plotted on a force-field analysis diagram for an individual.

Life field A set of forces, both psychological and material, which influence the behaviour of an individual.

Take, for example, an individual who wishes to give up smoking. A similar diagram can be drawn (Figure 11.5) which shows the triggers pushing the individual towards that change (e.g. family pressure, health concerns, the cost, the unpleasant nature of smoking) pitted against forces resistant to giving up smoking (e.g. its addictive nature, peer pressure in social situations, stress in work and life in general).

There are more triggers than the resisting factors, so will the change happen inevitably? Possibly not as the addictive nature of smoking is a major factor and a considerable weight in preventing the change to being a non-smoker occurring. Another aspect of force-field analysis is that different forces can be given different strengths—such as in Figure 11.6 by showing the different arrows with different weights.

The change to being a non-smoker might come about by attention to reducing the resisting factors, for example by avoiding socializing with the people who smoke or taking some

Figure 11.5 Force-field analysis for an individual giving up smoking.

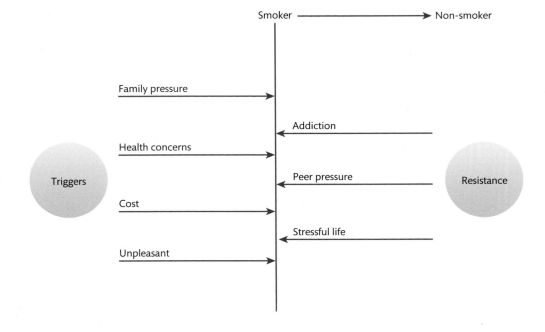

Figure 11.6 Weighted forces in a force-field analysis diagram.

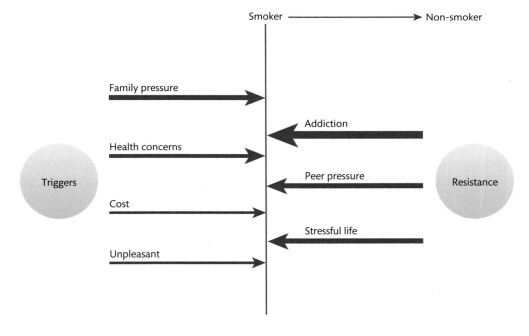

form of treatment for the nicotine addiction. Viewing this situation from the point of view of a government wanting to implement a national programme to stop people from smoking, they might also pay attention to strengthening some of the triggers—increasing the cost of cigarettes, for example, or placing diagrams of diseased lungs on cigarette packets to prompt health concerns (compare these tactics with behaviour modification in Chapter 10).

Although derived from Lewin's work in individual psychology and behaviour, force-field analysis can be used in individual, group, organizational—even societal—situations of potential, or desired, change. In that '. . . any event is the resultant of a multitude of factors' (Lewin, 1943: 293) the value of the force-field analysis diagram is that it provides a snapshot of those factors. It highlights the conflicting factors and perspectives in a change situation, and suggests areas where the implementation of a change management process might focus.

Visit the Online Resource Centre for further examples of force-field analysis diagrams.

Review questions

1. Describe what is meant by triggers for change and resistance against change, giving examples of each.
2. Explain how a force-field analysis diagram plots out the forces working in a change situation.

Apply

3. Can you construct force-field analysis diagrams for a personal change that you have experienced? How would the diagram help you to plan and implement the change?
4. Using the information about the change in the fitness centre, can you draw a similar force-field analysis diagram for the situation facing Carl Jones (see the Online Resource Centre for suggested answer).

Types of change and the nature of the organization

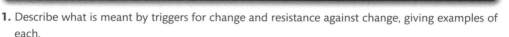

Running case: Jones's action plan

Fitness centre action plan

1. Identity and marketing
   - rebrand as *Coral Reef*—extensive marketing campaign to accompany this.
2. Décor and equipment
   - décor in coral reef style—redesign pool area with tropical island theme and develop part of changing area into health spa
   - redecorate gym and replace equipment—I suggest electronic card-controlled equipment and the card can double-up as the entrance key at reception
   - build extension to create a studio for classes.

3. Customer service
- extend opening: 6 am–11 pm daily, with centre, including reception desk, staffed at all times; towels to be provided at the reception desk, and customers greeted and handed towel on arrival
- staff to maintain presence on the gym floor and pool for safety purposes, but should also welcome and encourage guests.

4. Classes and treatments
- provide beauty and health treatments in the treatment rooms
- no recruitment allowed, so slots within the treatment rooms to be rented to local practitioners— hairdressers, beauticians, etc.
- classes, e.g. pilates in the new studio; pool to offer swimming lessons and aqua aerobics—exisiting staff to do this, but bring in local expertise on a freelance basis as and when needed.

5. Staff
- expected to work flexibly within the 6 am to 11 pm working day, including weekends, according to a rota; staff to always present an upbeat, friendly image
- will promote the paid treatments and classes—some sort of bonus incentive for this
- one qualified member of staff should be on duty at all times. As this will stretch existing staff across the new opening hours, employ local students to work along alongside qualified staff as and when needed.

6. Culture and atmosphere
- *must* change from spit and sawdust to upmarket, tropical luxury—changes to décor will help
- staff to get new uniforms; they are expected to be the embodiment of this culture—motivating people to exercise but, at the same time, creating a relaxing atmosphere
- culture *must* be less aggressively masculine and less intimidating to potential members and hotel guests.

When we speak about 'change' we could be speaking about a whole variety of activities where something is done differently—from a small change in one worker's rota, to a department relocating to a different office, to an overall corporate rebranding. All are examples of change in an organization. Cummings and Worley (2009) suggest four main areas of change management, focusing on different aspects of organizational life:

- *strategic interventions* are major shifts in the overall focus and direction of the organization. Areas of focus might be corporate strategy, products and services offered, culture change, rebranding, or organizational learning
- *technostructural interventions* look at areas of technology and the organization's structure. Examples include the design and division of work, downsizing, bringing in new technology, and redesigning the organization's bureaucratic structure
- *human process interventions* are concerned with human social issues in the organization—how people relate to each other, communication, decision making, and leadership. They are based around group dynamics and team-building activities
- *human resource issues* are focused on people at a more individual level. Examples include performance-management, recruitment, appraisal, reward-management, motivation, and managing diversity.

This list touches on many topics covered in other chapters in this book, and shows that the focus of change is wide and far-reaching; indeed, change is potentially infinite in its scope.

Further categorization can be made in terms of the scale of change small to large scale; from fine-tuning to tuning, and adjustment to departmental or corporate transformation (Senior and Swailes, 2010: 39–41). Senior and Swailes further suggest that the degree of change that an organization faces may be predictable or a complete surprise, depending on the turbulence of the environment (see Chapter 4) that the organization faces.

Taking into account the variety of both types and scale of change, and the differences in the environmental turbulence encountered by the organization, change-management theories tend to divide into two camps: a *planned approach*, which sees change managed through a series of steps from one point to another (as with force-field analysis), and an *emergent approach*, which sees change as more unpredictable, likely to be carried along by the flow of events within the organization and unpredictable influences from the environment.

Change and the nature of organization

What is an organization? This might seem like an obvious question to ask, but we suggest that to understand the nature of change and its implementation, a step back needs to be taken to see the nature of what is actually being changed—the organization itself. Whether change can be planned or whether change is emergent, for example, depends very much on the nature of the organization itself.

In this section we introduce three **metaphors** which provide three different ways of answering the question 'what is an organization?'. These metaphors see the organization as either a set of building blocks, an iceberg, or a river.

> **Metaphor** A figure of speech whereby we try to understand something by suggesting a resemblance to the characteristics of something else.

Study skills: the use of metaphors

Metaphors are ways of visualizing or imagining the world around us in order to gain new insights. For example, Morgan (2006) constructs his whole book *Images of Organization* around different metaphors to understand different aspects of organizational life and theory. One chapter sees 'organizations as machines' as a means of visualizing the rational, Taylorist organization (which we examine in Chapter 2), while 'organizations as brains' is the metaphor used to envisage learning organizations (which we examine in Chapter 10).

The three metaphors used in this chapter—building blocks, iceberg, and river—are different ways in which we can view the nature of what an organization is which lead to different ways of approaching the change process.

The metaphors are not necessarily mutually exclusive—there is no need to choose one as being better or more truthful than the other two. Instead, each uncovers different aspects of an organization's nature—each tells us something different and new about what an organization is. They provide a set of lenses to view and understand the nature of an organization, each of which may inform our knowledge about implementing change over an organization in different ways.

Change agent
A manager, consultant, or other person who instigates and manages change.

The metaphors help us to put ourselves in the place of a manager or consultant who has the job of implementing change within an organization, a so-called **change agent**. They help us to ask four questions about the nature of an organization that inform the nature and implementation of change in that organization:

- Is the *structure* of the organization stable or is the organization constantly changing?
- How does a change agent gain *knowledge* about what is going on in the organization, e.g. when trying to identify and understand the triggers and resisting forces to go in a force-field analysis diagram?
- How does *power* operate in the organization, e.g. what ability does a change agent have to control and bring about change in an organization?
- To what extent is resistance a challenge to power in the organization and how might that resistance be overcome?

Using the metaphors to address these questions leads us to three approaches to change that we examine in the remainder of this chapter (Table 11.1). To the familiar planned

Table 11.1 Metaphors of change and the nature of organization

Metaphor	Description	Related approach to change
The organization as a set of building blocks 	The organization has a solid *structure* that management have complete *power* to control and change at will. Managing change is as easy as rearranging a set of children's building blocks. This takes a very mechanical view of how we gain *knowledge* of the organization and there is little account taken of human elements. *Resistance* to change and to management power is seen as being alien to the organization	Naïve approach to change
The organization as an iceberg 	Like an iceberg, the *structure* of the organization has hidden depths lurking beneath the surface—the human and social aspects of the organization. *Knowledge* of these hidden, human depths is harder to uncover and the change agent relies on human sciences, such as psychology, to understand the organization. *Resistance* is an understandable human reaction to change, but, ultimately, psychologically-informed techniques, which are planned and implemented over a period of time, give management *power* to bring about change	Planned approach to change
The organization as a river 	The organization is in a constant state of flux and flow, like a set of rapids on a river. As such, it is never still long enough to have a stable *structure*. Management has little *power* over an organization that is changing constantly and evading its grasp. *Resistance* is continual—think of trying to paddle against the rapids. *Knowledge* is something that comes from experience and action, from jumping in and riding the rapids	Emergent approach to change

and emergent approaches to change, which we equate to the organization as an iceberg and a river, respectively, we add a naïve approach to change which sees the organization in simplistic terms as a set of building blocks.

Review questions

1. Describe the categories of change outlined by cummings and Worley.
2. Explain how metaphors help us to understand the nature of an organization.
3. Analyse how structure, knowledge, power, and resistance are key features of the organization which influence different approaches to change.

Apply

4. Using Cummings and Worley's categories, what types of change are being attempted in the fitness centre? (Visit the Online Resource Centre for a suggested answer.)

The organization as a set of building blocks: a naïve approach to change?

Running case: letter to employees

Dear Fitness Staff,

As loyal employees of the fitness centre, I'm sure you will be as excited as me by the changes that will transform our centre into a leading gym and health spa facility. From this week the fitness centre will be known as *Coral Reef*. To match the name change we are undertaking a massive refurbishment programme.

It's not just the buildings and equipment that will change, however. We aim to attract new customers and hotel guests with a set of activities and treatments with our new unique selling point of 'tropical luxury'. To make this work we need to change the culture of *Coral Reef* and this can only be done through you—the staff.

For this, we are introducing our 'simply the best' culture change programme. You, as staff, will become 'simply the best' at carrying our new culture in the following ways:

- you will give 'simply the best' customer service, greeting customers when they arrive, smiling at all times, and making conversation with customers on the gym floor

- you will encourage customers to be 'simply the best' by motivating them to achieve their fitness goals and providing encouragement to all customers on the gym floor

- you will become 'simply the best' at generating revenue for *Coral Reef* by promoting our new courses and treatments—each month there will be a bonus for the best at selling.

There will be some changes to working arrangements, with flexible rostering during an extended working day. To cover extra hours, new part-time staff will be brought in along with freelance instructors and treatment practitioners. I'm sure you will welcome them all in due course and help them to also be 'simply the best'.

Best wishes

Carl

How do you think the fitness centre staff will react to receiving this letter?

Imagine yourself as a manager implementing a change. The ideal situation, with the least amount of hassle, would be if you could simply rearrange the elements of the organization as if you were playing with a set of children's building blocks. Our first way of seeing the nature of an organization is that it is like a set of building blocks that fit together and can be rearranged at will.

Perhaps any change that focuses purely on structural or technological features of the organization (see Cummings and Worley's (2009) techno-structural interventions in the previous section) can be seen as taking this building block view of the organization. It is not, however, difficult to criticize this as a naïve view, based on a number of simplistic assumptions that it makes about the nature of an organization:

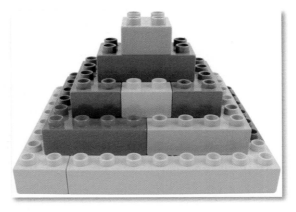

The organization as a set of building blocks.

- the *structure* is simple and solid, where every conceivable element is visible—there are no hidden aspects to the organization
- *knowledge* is simply what can be measured, calculated, or represented as some form of model, equation, or diagram. It is a view of the organization almost as if it were a machine (think of similarities here with Taylor and Ford from Chapter 3)
- management have total *power* over the organization from the top down
- *resistance* has no place in the organization; change is thus a matter of simply issuing orders and commands which will then be followed.

It is a very clean and simplistic view of what an organization is, but we know that organizational life is not this simple—it can be complex, messy, and unpredictable. It fails to note that change is often perceived differently by workers and management, and thus often meets resistance. By paying attention to just the building blocks aspects of the change, management are blinkered to other human and social issues which ensue as a result, and which may be an important aspect between the success and failure of that change.

This is not to say that change involving technostructural elements is naïve and simplistic *per se*—there are times when technology needs to be changed or an organization restructured. Rather, it is the assumption that this is all that needs to be changed while ignoring all human processes and interactions. We could say that it concentrates only on the triggers to change, and remains ignorant of any potential resisting forces, such as the fears and anxieties that often accompany change.

And yet how many managers see their organization in these terms, for example by restructuring a bureaucracy without thinking about how people will fit into the new system? Or, perhaps, by making changes to technology or the buildings without thinking about how people will actually use them or interact within them. Or even announcing a new culture without understanding that the culture has to work through people.

Real life case: Wimbledon FC/AFC Wimbledon

Wimbledon FC, known as the Dons, had a rapid rise to success from being a small, non-league side in 1977, to reaching the top flight of English football by 1985 and winning the FA Cup in 1988. However, the club remained small in terms of its fan base. Along with this, the club retained a special culture, termed the 'crazy gang,' typified by on-field 'hard men', such as Vinnie Jones.

The special culture was part of the experience of Wimbledon for players and fans alike, but the businessmen who ran the club saw other opportunities when Wimbledon reached the big time. Their logic was that there were areas of the country without Premiership football where fans would attend in their droves if they had a nearby club to support, meaning more money in the bank and greater profits. The plan was to move Wimbledon FC to Milton Keynes, a town 60 miles away without its own league football club.

At first sight the move was successful—the club moved to Milton Keynes, renaming itself the Milton Keynes Dons and eventually building its own stadium. What it couldn't take to Milton Keynes, however, were the existing fans and the special culture.

Wimbledon FC supporters were not happy about the prospect of their club being uprooted and taken to another location. Rather than travel to Milton Keynes, the fans set up a trust to create their own alternative football club in Wimbledon, known as AFC Wimbledon:

> Wimbledon supporters set about creating a replacement, a football club which would continue the history and identity of OUR club. Through the hard work and determination of WISA and The Dons Trust, AFC Wimbledon was born, and will continue to live the dream of football in our local community.
>
> Source: Reproduced by permission of Wimbledon Independent Supporters' Association.

AFC Wimbledon had to start from scratch in terms of finding a team, a ground, players and staff, and also in terms of dropping back several divisions to play non-league football. Where it didn't have to start from scratch, however, was in terms of fans and the Wimbledon culture. AFC Wimbledon kept most of the Wimbledon fan-base and regularly attracted larger crowds than the 'official' Wimbledon, now based in Milton Keynes. This was despite the fact that the Milton Keynes side was a professional club in the second tier of English football and AFC Wimbledon was a non-league side several divisions short of league football.

In 2011, AFC Wimbledon gained promotion to League 2, the fourth tier of English football—and one division below Milton Keynes. A situation could occur in the near future where the two clubs are playing in the same league!

Sources: Wimbledon Independent Supporters' Association, 2012; Tynan 2012; Nakrani, 2011; The Guardian, 2004; White, 2003.

The move to Milton Keynes could be seen as a perfectly rational business decision to take advantage of potentially larger crowds and gain more income. However, it can also be interpreted as an example of a building blocks approach to change. The change involves simply the visible, structural elements of the organization—the buildings, league position, and name, etc. It is ignorant or blinkered to other more intangible aspects—the culture, ties with the community, and traditions, etc. Yet, it is these with which the fans identified as being the essence of the club, not the building blocks, such as the ground. It is this aspect over which the management had no power—they could move the building blocks to a new location, but they couldn't get that culture to follow them in the same direction.

Visit the Online Resource Centre to read other examples of naïve approaches to change.

Review questions

1. Describe the main features of the naïve approach to change.

2. Explain how a naïve approach ignores important aspects of the organization.

Apply

3. In what ways could the management of the original Wimbledon be seen to have taken a 'naïve' approach to change? (Visit the Online Resource Centre for more on this question.)

The organization as an iceberg: the planned approach to change

Running case: culture clashes

The new culture was at odds with the spit and sawdust culture that the original staff were used to. They wanted nothing to do with the 'simply the best' culture, and they felt that the constant smiling and upbeat small-talk trivialized their professional qualifications and commitment to fitness. As much as possible they tried to avoid the new culture, making perfunctory smiles only when in view of the boss. The fact that the new rota had disrupted their personal lives, meaning they couldn't work together as a group, didn't help.

Conversely, the new staff—part-timers and freelance instructors—were inducted into the culture from the start and identified with it a lot more. This irritated the older staff, who started to refer to the new staff as the 'grinners'. Two groups emerged who would lunch, socialize, and chat separately. The grinners began to refer to the original staff as the 'oldies'. Contact between them was minimal.

The divisions were more than obvious at a launch night for the new fitness centre. With staff seated (in their oldies and grinners groups) Carl Jones stormed on to a makeshift stage with 'Simply the Best' blaring out over a loudspeaker. After some speeches about the new culture, Jones brought on some staff to model the new uniform. Based around the tropical theme, it consisted of a *Coral Reef* plain top with garish patterned beach shorts.

The oldies looked aghast and their hearts sank—it went against every professional and cultural value that they held. The grinners, however, were jumping up and down and whooping at their 'cool' new uniforms and swarmed Carl Jones to get their hands on their own uniforms to try on.

Think of the trouble than an iceberg can cause for a passing ship. It's not the part of the iceberg that is visible above the surface that causes the problems, it's the vast bulk of the iceberg that is hidden from view beneath the surface of the water that can cause a ship to run aground.

The metaphor of an iceberg sees the organization as having 'hidden depths' that lie 'beneath the surface'. The technical and structural features which make up the building blocks of an organization are merely the tip of the iceberg—the part that is easily visible and perhaps easiest, on first glance, to manage and over which to exert power. Hidden

The organization as an iceberg.

Above the surface

The building blocks of the organization,
e.g. buildings, technology, structure,
rules, procedures

Below the surface

Social aspects, e.g. cultures, group
dynamics

Human aspects, e.g. attitudes, anxieties,
values, feelings, emotions

Figure 11.7 Aspects
of the organization
above and below the
surface.

below the surface, in the bulk of the iceberg, are the more intangible aspects of the organization (Figure 11.7).

These hidden aspects include human aspects, such as anxieties, attitudes, values, and emotions; and social aspects, such as cultures and group dynamics. In a similar manner, Edgar Schein used an iceberg to describe layers and depths of organizational culture (see Chapter 7).

The planned approach to change

While hard to uncover at first, human and social aspects are an important part of the organization and, if ignored, could potentially cause a change management initiative to be met with resistance and potentially run aground. Thus, the iceberg metaphor highlights the following aspects of an organization relevant to the change process, which make up the key assumptions behind the planned approach to change:

- as with the building blocks approach, the *structure* is solid, but also has hidden depths consisting of the human and social elements, which make up a considerable part of the organization 'beneath the surface'

- gaining *knowledge* of the organization means getting 'beneath the surface' to the hidden depths. Psychologically-based techniques are used to get to know and understand this human and social aspect of the organization

- a manager, or change agent, using a set of psychologically-informed techniques, ultimately has *power* to bring about top-down change in the organization. It is not as instant, simple, and neat as the building blocks approach would suggest, but is a wide-ranging and long-term process

- *resistance* is understandable—it is a natural human and social reaction to change. Part of the job of overcoming resistance to change is to understand why it occurs in the first place before implementing a plan to overcome that resistance.

Unlike the naïve approach, the planned approach recognizes that change is not a simple and straightforward process, and that resistance to change can be expected. Given that such resistance resides in human and social aspects of the organization, psychological knowledge and techniques are used to overcome that resistance. To manage change requires a series of carefully planned and managed steps to take an organization, or a part of the organization, from point A to point B.

The three-step model of change

Three-step model of change Lewin's model whereby a process of change goes through three stages of unfreezing, movement, and freezing

Implementing planned change through a series of managed steps is most famously outlined in Kurt Lewin's (1947) **three-step model** of change. For Lewin, the implementation of organizational change follows three broad steps of unfreezing, movement, and freezing.

- Unfreezing is where the current situation is first outlined, perhaps using a force-field analysis diagram, and the organization is shaken out of its current state and prepared for the need for change.

- Movement is where the organization moves and changes slowly towards the desired state.

- Freezing occurs once the change has been achieved—it is reinforced so as to avoid slipping back into the previous way of doing things.

Research insight: Three-step model at British Airways, Goodstein, L.D., and Warner Burke, W. 1991. Creating successful organization change. *Organizational Dynamics* 19(4): 5–17.

During the 1980s, British Airways underwent a major change from being a nationalized, loss-making airline to becoming a private, commercial, profit-making operation. Accompanying this was a change in culture and emphasis, from a bureaucratic, militaristic style to one focused on customer service.

Goodstein and Burke (1991) suggest that the change was achieved by following a three-step pattern. Examples of each of the steps include the following:

- unfreezing from the current state was a achieved through downsizing, bringing in a new top management team, and redefining the purpose of the company as service and not transportation
- movement was brought about through attention to communications, peer support groups, a new training centre, and off-site, team building activities
- freezing, or reinforcement of the change, came from promoting staff who demonstrated the new values, new reward and appraisal systems, and continued development and training.

As with force-field analysis, the three-step model derives from Lewin's psychological background and, in particular, his work on group dynamics. Movement is not as simple as rearranging a set of building blocks; instead, it requires psychological techniques to uncover all of the human emotions and dynamics that are going on beneath the surface and to then begin to change people slowly towards adopting new behaviours.

One of the main techniques developed from Lewin is the **T-group** (or sensitivity training group). A small group of participants learns, with a facilitator, about its own group dynamics and interpersonal processes. Just as the forces at work in an individual's psychology can be plotted out in a force-field analysis, so the intangible values and attitudes that guide group behaviour, and possibly cause resistance, can be identified. By understanding how the group works, it can thus be strengthened and negative behaviours can be changed.

T-group (training group) An activity which aims to get a group to understand and change its dynamics and attitudes.

Organization development

Theory in context: Kurt Lewin and attitude change

Nowadays, Kurt Lewin's work is associated with change in an organizational context; indeed, it is often presented as a set of tools by which management can exert power over an organization. In fact, very little of Lewin's work took place in organizations and, indeed, his political leanings were to the left and to Marxism, rather than towards capitalism and the quest for effective management (Cooke, 1999).

Lewin's background was in social change. As a Jewish refugee from the Nazi regime, his interests were in removing discrimination and promoting harmonious relations within society. His work in America was in attitude change with respect to inter-ethnic relations. It was from this work that T-groups emerged, leading to his foundation of the National Training Laboratories (NTL), a behavioural science institute (Burnes, 2004).

Lewin died in 1947 shortly after the foundation of the NTL. The NTL continued to develop his theories, especially with respect to applying his ideas of social attitude change in organizational contexts.

Lewin's work on group dynamics in society was developed in the context of group dynamics in organizations—a key area of resistance to change and thus an area where management might intervene in change. The group level is the key to successful organizational change; indeed, the T-group is the forerunner of many of the group and team-building activities commonplace in contemporary organizations, as discussed in Chapter 6.

Lewin's work laid the foundation for an all-encompassing approach to change known as **organization development** (OD). While it draws upon the behavioural science knowledge and techniques developed by Lewin, it is combined with other, potentially limitless techniques (see the list from Cummings and Worley earlier in this chapter) to address change at an organization-wide level:

> Organization Development is an effort (1) planned, (2) organization-wide and (3) managed from the top to (4) increase organization effectiveness and health through (5) planned interventions in the organization's processes using behavioural science knowledge.   (Beckhard, 1969: 9)

OD doesn't rule out the type of technostructural interventions addressed in the building-blocks approach, but blends them alongside more psychologically-informed techniques aimed at the aspects of the organization below the surface of the iceberg.

Organization development A wide-ranging set of change management techniques, including techniques which derive from behavioural and Gestalt psychology.

Real life case: the police, institutional racism, and change

UK police forces have recently undergone large-scale, organization-wide attitude and cultural change in response to a problem identified as 'institutional racism'. The term was used in the Macpherson Report (1999), which investigated the handling of the murder of black teenager Stephen Lawrence in London in 1993 and a series of failures by the Metropolitan Police in bringing a prosecution. The report concluded that the police force was not explicitly racist, but institutional racism could be detected at the level of cultures and individual attitudes, defined as:

> The collective failure of an organisation to provide an appropriate and professional service to people because of colour, culture or ethnic origin. It can be seen or detected in processes, attitudes and behaviour which amount to discrimination through unwitting prejudice, ignorance, thoughtlessness and racist stereotyping . . .
>
> (Macpherson, 1999)

Overall, change-management initiatives within the police to counter institutional racism seemed to follow OD lines. On the one hand, there were structural interventions, such as basing the results of police exams on displaying the right attitudes, with failure for displaying discriminatory attitudes. On the other hand, group dynamics were seen as a key area of attention. It was not the case that all individuals were racist, but the prevailing culture at group level allowed racist attitudes to prevail. Police training thus includes diversity training in a situation similar to Lewin's T-groups. Such training highlights individuals' own language and attitudes, and also brings trainees into contact with members of other community groups so as to be aware of their cultures and attitudes (National Police Training Magazine, 2000, 2001).

10 years after the Macpherson Report, the success of change can be evidenced by 67 of the original 70 Macpherson recommendations having been implemented (House of Commons, 2009). While the police force is not completely free of racism, and incidents and concerns still occur, there has been a shift in the culture of the police force since the Macpherson report in 1999, and diversity management is now seen as a critical aspect of managing the organization. That this still follows an OD approach, covering both organization-wide and group-level issues, is shown in a recent Association of Chief Police Officers (2010) document which outlines the main 'strategic themes' for police equality, diversity, and human rights strategy:

- Operational delivery: delivering services that are easy to access and that respond to and meet the needs of all communities

- People and culture: building a working environment that includes everyone and encourages all staff to develop and make progress

- Organizational processes: building equality into the organization's processes and how the service manages its performance.   (Association of Chief Police Officers, 2010: 19)

Visit the Online Resource Centre for links to more case material on police force change, and also a wider discussion of links between change management and culture change.

The attitude and culture change brought about in the police force would seem to have been ideal for the concerns of Lewin, based, as they were, in race relations and social attitude change. However, the case also highlights one of the critiques of Lewin's work and the planned aproach to change. Attitude change, such as that witnessed in the poilce force, does not happen overnight—attitudes and cultures take time to change—in some cases generations.

Thus, a critique of the planned approach is that it is too long-term and slow-moving, a drawn out process which requires consensus amongst groups (Burnes, 2004). In Chapter 4 we saw that the environment faced by contemporary organizations is one which is much more volatile and unpredictable. The idea, posited by the three-step model, that an organization can exist in static 'frozen' states is described by Kanter et al., (1992: 10) as a 'quaintly linear and static' notion, but one which bears no relation to the complex and fast-moving nature of organizational life, where organizations need to be nimble and react quickly to change. Such an environment, where the organization is seen as if it were a river, is examined in the following section.

Review questions

1. Describe the main features of the planned approach to change.
2. Explain how the planned approach to change addresses features of the organization 'below the surface'.
3. Analyse how organization development helps bring about attitude and culture change.

Apply

4. How might the three-step model have been used to implement the change in the fitness centre?

The organization as a river: the emergent approach to change

Running case: unintended consequences

A number of unintended and unpredicted consequences emerged as a result of the change, which had knock-on effects on the hotel and beyond.

- The information technology system at the fitness reception was unable to handle bookings for the freelance treatment providers and for the fitness classes. Eventually, this function was handed over to the main hotel reception, who were not happy with the additional work. Indeed, as bookings became more popular, it got in the way of checking in hotel guests, who started to complain about the waiting times.

- It became increasingly difficult to coordinate the times of freelance treatment providers, as they started to outnumber the two treatment rooms available. Some refused to use one of the rooms as the 'oldies' were still using it as their unofficial room for lunch breaks. As a result, Chance decided to block out three of the guests rooms and use them as treatment rooms—with a loss in revenue for the hotel.

- Reception staff were having to deal with irate fitness customers as the freelancers became unreliable, cancelling bookings at the last minute. Meg Mortimer became more and more exasperated with the situation, especially as she had to deal with one member of staff going off ill with stress as she then had to cover her work.

- The new health spa and showers were installed hurriedly. It turned out that they put a strain on the hotel boiler, which broke down on a number of occassions meaning that there was no hot water for the hotel rooms. As well as bringing more complaints to the already overworked reception, it also meant that laundry had to be outsourced temporarily, at an extra cost.

- As memberships grew, so did the demand for hotel car park spaces. Residents complained (at reception again) about the lack of spaces. More concerned, however, were the local council, who received complaints from residents about overspill car parking on their streets.

Simon Chance had known there were problems and had had to play a mediating role between Meg Mortimer, who seemed to bear the brunt of things, and Carl Jones. Mortimer constantly plotted and briefed against Jones with other managers, but Chance wanted this project to work so supported him, and eventually issued an informal warning to Mortimer that her job would be at risk if she didn't go along with the events. Chance had also had a meeting with the council's residential services division to deal with the parking issues.

If you were going white-water rafting on a river, of course you would plan ahead—working out your route and making sure you had the appropriate safety equipment, etc. But the precise, step-by-step details of the journey are impossible to plan—part of the skill of rafting is reacting *on the spot* to the twists and turns of the water beneath you. No two journeys will be the same, the ever-moving and ever-changing nature of the river is unpredictable:

> You cannot step twice into the same river, for other waters are continually flowing on . . . Everything flows and nothing abides; everything gives way and nothing stays fixed.
>
> Heraclitus c500 BC quoted in Morgan (2006: 241)

The organization as a river.

The river metaphor suggests something which is in constant *flow*, never the same from one moment to the next. As such, it emphasizes the dynamic, complex, and ever-changing nature of organization, with *change as the constant natural state of the organization*. The organization is not a stable entity that is occasionally 'moved around' by management, as with the planned approach—the organization never stays still long enough to be 'unfrozen' and 'frozen'. This gives a radically different view of the nature of the organization to that of the building blocks or the iceberg:

- an organization never stays still for long enough to be described as a *structure*, such as an iceberg or a set of building blocks. Complex, hidden depths exist, but their dynamic nature makes them difficult to even begin to grasp

- it is never possible to have complete *knowledge* of every aspect of the organization to use as a basis for planning owing to the continually-changing nature of the organization—it is always beyond our grasp

- without complete knowledge of the organization, *power* is much more difficult for management to exert. Power is no longer top-down and in the hands of management, but exists within the movement of the organization itself. You may be in charge of the raft, but you are very much controlled by the movement of the river beneath it

- wherever management tries to exert power over an organization it will always meet with natural *resistance*, just as trying to exert power over the course of a river by setting up a dam, for example, will always meet with resistance from the flow of the water. The resistance within the river is always there as a challenge to those who seek to exert power over it.

The emergent approach to change

The metaphor of the river suggests a complex and messy situation for management to deal with, one that is both fast-flowing but with complex murky depths—potentially beyond management knowledge and power. Change is not a discrete period of upheaval planned in advance to take an organization from point A to B; instead, change is the norm and is always present. With the emergent approach, change is managed in a much more ad hoc fashion, reacting to events as and when they occur. Change is what *emerges* along with the flow of the river.

The emergent approach to change is not one specific approach to change, but a number of approaches which recognize the complex and interconnected nature of organizations. Two particular approaches are the processual approach and the systemic approach.

The processual approach to change—political consequences

Processual approach to change An approach to change which emphasizes the messy and political nature of change.

The **processual approach to change** paints change as an 'untidy cocktail' (Burnes, 2004: 989) of individual perceptions and political struggles. As such, this reflects change as a political process. It also emphasizes that there may be no single, individual cause of change and that in the change process there is an interconnectedness and inter-relatedness of individuals, groups, organizations, and society.

Earlier in the chapter we discussed how change causes anxiety and upset. The planned approach would see this as elements of resistance 'beneath the iceberg' to be overcome by psychological means. In a processual approach, human and social elements, such as fear, anxiety, and the power of different groups and subcultures within the organization, become the basis for political battles—rather than being overcome there is active resistance to change (see Chapter 13 for more on these political aspects of the organization).

The systemic approach to change—knock-on effects

Systemic approach to change An approach to change which recognizes the organization as an interconnected system whereby change in one area can have consequences and knock-on effects in other areas.

The processual approach recognizes the interconnectedness of different aspects of an organization. A similar approach comes from an understanding of an organization as a system (**systemic approach to change**) defined by Evered (1980) as 'a set of different parts which combine and work together as an organized whole'.

The different parts are interdependent—if one part of the system breaks down then it can affect the functioning of the system as a whole. Think, for example, of a car. It is a system in that different parts and components function together as a whole. If one of the components fails, the interdependency of the parts of the system means that the system as a whole—the car—can stop functioning.

The organization can be seen as a system—it has a number of different parts (or people, technology, departments, etc.) which are interdependent and which function together as a whole. A change in one part of the organization may have knock-on effects in other parts of the system.

Real life case: the train on platform five

A rail network is an organization that we can also see as a system with a number of inter-related parts. There are tracks, points, signals, trains, and drivers—all elements that work together to make the rail network function overall.

A simple example of the systemic interdependence of the system is when a train breaks down. Rather than being a problem in isolation, the train blocks the track and affects any services behind it.

Such knock-on effects and consequences can amplify in their magnitude. You may well have been standing on a station platform and heard that your service is late because of a signal failure elsewhere in the country—a problem in one part of the system has knock-on effects that have consequences elsewhere.

Source: based on Meek, 2001.

Changing a system

If we see the organization as an interconnected system it follows that making a change will have knock-on effects and consequences, but to what extent can such consequences be managed? The emergent approach would suggest that, rather than managers being in control of the consequences of a change, such consequences are unpredictable and uncontrollable, as if they were being carried along by the flow of the river.

The watchmaker and the surgeon

Collins (1998: 148) highlights the degree to which we can change one part of a system without affecting its overall functioning. We can consider whether the organizational change manager is more like a 'watchmaker' or a 'surgeon'—whether change is a simple mechanical job, or whether the systemic interdependencies make it a much more complex and emergent phenomenon.

- The watchmaker can identify a component which is not working and simply replace it—the system will then begin working again. There is no problem in shutting down the system for a while, making some changes and then restarting it.

- For the surgeon, however, this luxury is not available. Say a heart needs replacing—it's not possible to shut down the body temporarily to do this. The interdependencies it has with the rest of the system means that it must maintain its action for the rest of the system to survive. Thus, the knock-on effects of changing one part of the system have to be considered. Therefore, the surgeon has to make arrangements to ensure that the heart's role within the system (i.e. circulating blood) is somehow maintained while attending to that one component.

While organizational change managers are not surgeons, they have to think about the effects that making a change might have. To return to the rail example, there are often planned engineering works on railways. Unlike a watchmaker, the railway system cannot simply be shut down. The railway manager has to maintain a flow of passengers by providing, for example, alternative bus services or timetabling alternative rail routes.

Imagine if your university library building closed for six months for refurbishment. What effects would it have on the rest of the university and how might the university deal with those effects to keep the university running?

Visit the Online Resource Centre for further discussion on this topic.

Open and closed systems

A further distinction in the nature of a system is between an open and a closed system (Jackson and Carter, 2007: 211).

- A closed system has a distinct boundary around it and operates fully within it—there is no movement across the boundary.
- An open system interacts with its environment—there is movement across the boundary.

As we have seen, and as common sense might suggest, organizations are open systems. They are affected by activity from their environment (think of the PEST model earlier in this chapter and in Chapter 4). In the opposite direction, organizations can affect their own environment. Think of the effects of pollution or an organization creating extra traffic on the streets around it and thus causing those streets to be congested. Many people are affected by, and have an interest in, the activities of particular organizations.

The **Gaia hypothesis** (see Jackson and Carter, 2007: 214) or a 'Systems View of the World' (Capra, 1992) see *all aspects of the world* being potentially interconnected. The nature of organizations as both dynamic and open systems means that the 'ripples and knock-on effects' (Collins, 1998: 149) or 'waves of consequences' (Darwin et al., 2002: 177) of any change or intervention within the system have to be considered. The interdependencies of parts of a system, both inside and out, mean that the consequences of a particular change could, potentially, be limitless. Thus, in Chapter 17, the concept of corporate social responsibility suggests that organizations have a responsibility for the effects of their actions on the world around them—if their activities cause harm to the environment, for example.

Gaia hypothesis
A theory popular in environmental movements where the whole world is seen as an interconnected system.

Chaos and complexity theory—the butterfly effect

The idea of knock-on effects and consequences is mirrored in studies of scientific and natural systems. **Chaos theory** emphasizes the unpredictable and interconnected nature of many scientific systems. Small changes in a natural system can have unpredictable knock-on effects of a disproportionate magnitude.

Lorenz (1972) noted this with his famous question: 'Does the flap of a butterfly's wings in Brazil set off a tornado in Texas?'. A minute change in the natural ecosystem—the air disturbances of a butterfly's wings—has the potential to set up a series of knock-on effects such that it might actually alter weather patterns. Lorenz's **butterfly effect** is perhaps one of the best-known aspects of chaos theory.

Chaos theory
A branch of science which sees natural systems as both ordered, but, at the same time, unpredictable.

The butterfly effect
The suggestion in chaos theory that a small action can have unpredictable knock-on effects of a greater magnitude.

Theory in context: the 'butterfly effect'

Many films use the idea of the butterfly effect as the basis for their plot, i.e. how would things be different now had a small change happened in the past?

- In *Back to the Future* (Zemeckis, 1985), the lead character must ensure that his parents meet in the past, otherwise he will cease to exist in the present day.
- *Sliding Doors* (Howitt, 1998) outlines two very different sets of events that emerge from the simple act of either getting on the tube or taking a taxi.
- In a film that uses Lorenz's terminology, *The Butterfly Effect* (Bress and Gruber, 2004), the lead character played by Ashton Kutcher goes back in time several times to try to change past events for the better. Small changes in the past are found to have amplified into major consequences in the present day, with the character finding himself a prisoner, a college student, and an amputee as a result of small actions he has changed.

Complexity theory has extended the ideas of chaos theory beyond purely scientific systems into systems in general. The recent financial crisis, as examined in Chapter 15 (*Globalization*) is an example of such interconnectedness where a change in one small area—the collapse of one bank—had knock-on effects that led to the near-collapse of the world's financial systems. In a similar manner, complexity theory would suggest that, as a system, small changes in one area of an organization can have disproportionate effects.

Complexity theory
The application of chaos theory to social systems, such as organizations, suggesting that small changes can have unpredictable and potentially limitless consequences.

Real life case: 'Sachsgate'

In October 2008, UK news was dominated by a seemingly trivial affair—a prank call made on a late-night BBC radio show by presenters Jonathan Ross and Russell Brand. During the call, a series of insulting messages were left on the voicemail of Fawlty Towers actor, Andrew Sachs.

The original broadcast attracted little attention, but was picked up in the press a few days later, eventually developing into a storm of complaints and further media coverage that eventually claimed the jobs of Ross and Brand, and the head of BBC Radio 2, Lesley Douglas. Further down the line, comedians now complain that, as a result of compliance regulations brought in since the scandal, their acts are suffering from restrictive regulations in terms of what they can and cannot say.

The original broadcast had not been live and had been referred to Douglas for clearance before transmission. She had not heard the broadcast. Trusting the advice of other staff, she sanctioned the broadcast with a single word, 'Yes', sent from her mobile phone.

Sources: Lawson, 2009; Holmwood, 2009; The Guardian, 2008; Holmwood, 2008; Gibson et al, 2008.

If the text message had said 'No', how different would the consequences be today?

An implication of chaos theory is that long-term predictions in systems are impossible to make (Tsoukas, 1998). Take a system like the weather. We know that weather forecasting is not a precise science. Meteorologists can model the system and have a good stab at predicting the weather for the next few days, but, beyond that, the system is so complex and open to any number of knock-on effects and changes that prediction is impossible, and, indeed, very few forecasters now provide long-range forecasts.

In Stacey's (1992) terms, it is not that the future is *unknown*, it is the fact that the future is inherently *unknowable*. There are no equations or models that can tell us precisely what the long-term weather will be—it is something that will emerge in the future.

Stacey suggests that the idea of the future being 'unknowable' applies to organizations. As such, this emergent approach to change dismisses the idea that change is a 'planned' activity where the change manager can work towards a particular desired outcome—the consequences of a change intervention are yet to emerge when action is taken. Rather than being planned, change is unpredictable—its knock-on effects and ultimate outcomes are unknowable.

Managing with emergence

Using the river metaphor, we see the organization as an emergent phenomenon. This presents a picture of knock-on effects of action which become uncontrollable and unplannable, and a murky world of political processes and power struggles lie within this. To plan change precisely becomes impossible, just as it is impossible to predict the weather beyond the very short term.

Does this mean that we can do without management and leadership if they are so evidently powerless to control change? For Jenner (1994), management still have a role in guiding the system; rather than managing change, managers are, in effect, managing *with* change—they are carried along by the flow of the river as much as the rest of the organization.

One value of the emergent approach is simply for management to appreciate the systemic nature of an organization (Stacey, 1992) and the fact that a change will have knock-on effects—an appreciation beyond the simplistic view of change that is simply arranging a set of building blocks.

Furthermore, the emergent approach suggests ways in which management can create opportunities for creativity and innovation among their workforce. Rather than the river being something to be feared and coped with, it is something to be encouraged for the potential that it offers.

Real life case: the Googleplex

Google is a massive multinational organization which also relies on technological innovation. Its headquarters in California, the Googleplex, and similar buildings worldwide, resemble playgrounds in many respects. There are slides linking floors, table football and similar games on offer, and free food in the various canteens around the building. Rules about such things as set office hours are relaxed (imagine how Frederick Taylor, in Chapter 3, with his time and motion study would react to this!). Fixed work spaces, such as offices, are rare. Workers have laptops and are encouraged to roam the building, having impromptu meetings and conversations with co-workers.

Sources: National Geographic, 2012; Google, 2009; Time Magazine, 2006.

The Googleplex creates an environment almost like a river, with workers free to roam the building as they please. In a creative and innovative industry we can see how this might benefit Google. Rather than being stuck in offices behind walls and divided from other workers, the staff can meet and share ideas—even random connections and meetings can occur. In Chapter 10 we saw how learning organizations have an interest in sharing knowledge across the organization so as to promote innovation and the development of new products. The post-bureaucratic (see Chapter 4), river-like form of organization at Google is designed to allow more space and more opportunity for knowledge and new ideas to emerge, rather than being planned from above.

The emergent approach is one which seemingly makes management over an organization a more difficult task to achieve; however, it brings with it opportunities for more creative and innovative approaches to management and organization.

Employability skills: emergent careers and transferable skills

The distinction between planning and emergence is one that is reflected in the nature of contemporary careers. Van Buren (2003) suggests that a 'boundaryless career' is becoming the norm for many workers. Where previously it was possible to plan for a career path within one organization, now many workers move from one job to another on short-term contracts.

For Van Buren, employability is a key issue in such a boundaryless career. A CV needs to demonstrate transferable skills—skills which might have been gained in one job, but which can transfer from one organization to another. An important part of writing a CV is to show how skills and experience gained in one organizational setting are transferable and of value to the organization to which you are applying for a job.

Transferable skills can also enhance employability when applying for your first job. Think about things you do at university and whether they demonstrate skills that would be of value to an employer. Playing in a sports team may demonstrate teamwork. Being the treasurer of that sports team is evidence of managing a budget.

Often, your careers service will be able to help you in teasing out such transferable skills to place on your CV.

Review questions

1. Describe the main features of the emergent approach to change.
2. Explain what is meant by taking a systemic view of an organization.
3. Analyse how the butterfly effect can lead to small changes in an organization leading to unpredictable consequences.

Apply

4. Would the form of organization at the Googleplex be suitable for all organizations? Would it work in a fast-food restaurant, for example?

Chapter summary

Running case: denouement

Back in the present day, Meg Mortimer returns to the boardroom where the party is in full swing and Carl Jones is the man of the moment. He is being feted as a great manager and implementer of change. 'Easy to say once it's all been done and dusted', thinks Meg, 'but if it weren't for me coping with the fall-out it would never have happened'.

Meanwhile, the five 'oldies' have moved away from defacing the picture of Carl Jones. They are in a pub, meeting a representative of an upmarket residential development with gym facilities. They sign on the dotted line to go into partnership to run it themselves as a gym and personal-training business. They too raise their glasses to toast change—and the change they are looking forward to most is going into work the next day to hand in their notices to Carl Jones.

Knowing the full story, how well do you think Carl Jones managed change at the fitness centre. Do you think the change can be described by the naïve, planned, or emergent approach (or any combination thereof?)

Once the upheaval of a period of change is out of the way and a change has been achieved it can often be presented as having been successful. This, however, might mask a lot of upset, resistance, and unintended consequences that have happened along the way.

In this chapter we have seen how change can be a messy process. What might seem like perfectly rational triggers to change from one perspective may cause fear and anxiety from another, leading to resistance to that change.

We have seen that a naïve view of change would ignore this resistance, seeing the organization simply as a set of building blocks that can be rearranged at will. A planned approach to change recognizes this resistance as existing in the 'hidden depths' of the organization, beneath the surface of the organization, and would use techniques based in psychology to overcome that resistance. An emergent approach—the organization as a river—views resistance as part and parcel of the dynamic, interconnected, and political nature of the organization, part of the course of events that managers have to deal with.

While it is argued that the emergent approach is more in tune with the dynamic, changeable nature of our contemporary world, all three approaches contribute to our understanding of the nature of change. The planned approach, for example, is suited to changing deeply-held attitudes and cultures, as found in the police force, and even a building-blocks approach might be appropriate when quick and drastic action is required. All three approaches uncover, and make us aware of, different characteristics of the organization which are important when engaging in change.

Further reading

Burnes, B. 2004. Kurt Lewin and complexity theories: back to the future? *Journal of Change Management* **4(4): 309–325.**
An introduction to the work of Lewin, which is then related to complexity approaches.

Cummings, T.G., and Worley, C.G. 2009. *Organization development and change.* **South-Western/Cengage Learning, Mason, OH.**
A practical overview of a wide range of change management techniques and intervention.

Grugulis, I., and Wilkinson, A. 2002. Managing culture at British Airways: hype, hope and reality. *Long Range Planning* **35(2): 179–194.**
A critical study of change over time at British Airways.

Senior, B., and Swailes, S. 2010. *Organizational Change.* **Pearson Education, Harlow.**
An accessible introduction and overview of the wide field of change management.

Bibliography

Association of Chief Police Officers (ACPO). 2010. *Equality, diversity and human rights strategy for the police service*. ACPO, ISBN: 978-1-84987-031-3.

Beckhard, R. 1969. *Organization development; strategies and models*. Addison-Wesley: Reading, MA.

Bress, E., Gruber, J. 2004. *The Butterfly Effect*. Katalyst Films.

Burnes, B. 2004. Kurt Lewin and the planned approach to change: A re-appraisal. *Journal of Management Studies* 41(6): 977–1002.

Capra, F. 1992. A systems view of the world. *Resurgence Magazine* 151, 34–37.

Collins, D. 1998. *Organizational change: Sociological perspectives*. Routledge: London.

Cooke, B. 1999. Writing the left out of management theory: the historiography of the management of change. *Organization* 6(1): 81–105.

Cummings, T.G., and Worley, C.G. 2009. *Organization development and change*, South-Western/Cengage Learning: Mason, OH.

Darwin, J., Johnson, P., McAuley, J. 2002. *Developing strategies for change*. Financial Times/Prentice Hall: Harlow.

Drafke, M.W. 2009. *The human side of organizations*. Pearson/Prentice Hall: Upper Saddle River, NJ.

Evered, R. 1980. Consequences of and prospects for systems thinking in organizational change. In: Cummings, T.G. (ed.) *Systems theory for organization development*. John Wiley and Sons: New York, pp. 5–13.

Gibson, J., Gibson, O., and Conlan, T. 2008. Puerile prank that left BBC stars and executives on the ropes. *The Guardian*. 30 October 2008. Available at: http://www.guardian.co.uk/media/2008/oct/30/russell-brand-ross-sachs-bbc.

Goodstein, L.D., and Warner Burke, W. 1991. Creating successful organization change. *Organizational Dynamics* 19(4): 5–17.

Google. 2009. Life at the Googleplex. Available at: http://www.youtube.com/watch?v=eFeLKXbnxxg (last accessed 28 November 2012).

Holmwood, L. 2008. Countdown to a PR calamity: how the BBC bungled its way into 'Sachsgate'. *The Guardian*. 21 November 2008. Available at: http://www.guardian.co.uk/media/2008/nov/21/russell-brand-jonathan-ross2?intcmp=239.

Holmwood, L. 2009. Chris Moyles criticises 'weird state' BBC is in following Sachsgate. *The Guardian*. 14 July 2009. Available at: http://www.guardian.co.uk/media/2009/jul/14/chris-moyles-criticises-bbc-compliance-rules.

House of Commons. The Macpherson Report – ten years on. Her Majesty's Stationery Office: London. Available at: http://www.publications.parliament.uk/pa/cm200809/cmselect/cmhaff/427/427.pdf.

Howitt, P. 1998. *Sliding Doors*. Paramount.

Jackson, N., Carter, P. 2007. *Rethinking organisational behaviour*. Financial Times/Prentice Hall: Harlow.

Jenner, R. 1994. Changing patterns of power; chaotic dynamics and the emergence of a post-modern organizational paradigm. *Journal of Organizational Change Management* 7(3): 8–21.

Kanter, R.M., Stein, B., and Jick, T. 1992. *The challenge of organizational change: how companies experience it and leaders guide it.* The Free Press: New York.

King, D. 2001. *Devils and Nazis: Representations of change through postmodern research.* British Academy of Management, University of Edinburgh: Edinburgh.

Lawson, M. 2009. Is censorship taking over the BBC? *The Guardian.* 18 November 2009. Available at: http://www.guardian.co.uk/tv-and-radio/2009/nov/18/bbc-trust-censorship.

Lewin, K. 1943. Defining the 'field at a given time'. *Psychological Review* 50(3): 292.

Lewin, K. 1947. Frontiers in group dynamics. *Human Relations* 1(2): 143–153.

Lorenz, E. 1972. *Does the flap of a butterfly's wings in Brazil set off a tornado in Texas?* Speech before the American Academy for the Advancement of Science, December, 1972.

Macpherson, W. 1999. *The Stephen Lawrence Inquiry: report of an inquiry.* The Stationery Office: London.

Meek, J. 2001. 'Things fall apart'. *The Guardian.* 1 March 2001. Available at: http://www.guardian.co.uk/theguardian/2001/mar/01/features11.g2.

Morgan, G. 2006. *Images of organization.* Sage Publications: Thousand Oaks, CA.

Nakrani, S. 2011. AFC Wimbledon celebrate 'phenomenal' rise to League Two. *The Guardian.* 22 May 2011. Available at: http://www.guardian.co.uk/football/blog/2011/may/22/afc-wimbledon-promotion-luton-town.

National Geographic. 2012. Inside Google. Available at: https://www.youtube.com/watch?v=eC_DvRd-NMs (last accessed 28 November 2012).

National Police Training Magazine. 2000. On your marks – watch your language. *National Police Training Magazine* (8 July 2000).

National Police Training Magazine. 2001. Temple is thanked. *National Police Training Magazine* 12 (August 2001).

Senior, B., and Fleming, J. 2006. *Organizational Change,* 3rd edn. Pearson Education: Harlow.

Senior, B., and Swailes, S. 2010. *Organizational change.* 4th edn. Pearson Education: Harlow.

Stacey, R.D. 1992. *Managing chaos: Dynamic business strategies in an unpredictable world.* Kogan Page: London.

The Guardian. 2004. Wimbledon become MK Dons FC. 21 June 2004. Available at: http://www.guardian.co.uk/football/2004/jun/21/newsstory.mkdons.

The Guardian. 2008. Sachsgate emails. 'I would say take it out but it . . . is VERY funny.' 21 November 2008. Available at: http://www.guardian.co.uk/media/2008/nov/21/russell-brand-jonathan-ross1.

Time Magazine. Life in the Googleplex. Available at: http://www.time.com/time/photogallery/0,29307,1947844,00.html (last accessed 28 November 2012).

Tsoukas, H. 1998. Introduction: chaos, complexity and organization theory. *Organization* 5(3): 291–313.

Tynan, G. 2012. FA Cup: MK Dons book grudge tie against AFC Wimbledon. *The Independent.* 14 November 2012. Available at: http://www.independent.co.uk/sport/football/fa-league-cups/fa-cup-mk-dons-book-grudge-tie-against-afc-wimbledon-8313304.html.

Van Buren, H.J., III. 2003. Boundaryless careers and employability obligations. *Business Ethics Quarterly* 13(2): 131–149.

White, J. 2003. Pitch battle. *The Guardian.* 11 January 2003. Available at: http://www.guardian.co.uk/football/2003/jan/11/clubsincrisis.sport.

Wimbledon Independent Supporters' Association. 2012. WISA – A brief History. Available at: http://www.wisa.org.uk/history/index.html (last accessed 28 November 2012).

Zemeckis, R. 1985. *Back to the Future.* Universal.

Leadership

Life at the top

Chapter overview and learning outcomes

By the end of this chapter you should be able to:

- describe the key leadership theories
- explain why contingency theory sees there is no best leadership style
- explain the differences between leadership and management

- analyse whether there is too much emphasis on the individual leader
- explain the key principles of distributive leadership.

Key theorists

Fred Fielder	One of the founders of contingency theory, he developed the Least Preferred Co-worker model, which assesses an individual's leadership style
Paul Hersey and Ken Blanchard	Key writers who developed situational leadership—a perspective which argues that the appropriate leadership style depends on the situation
James Meindl	A key critic of the heroic leadership perspective, Meindl argues there is a romanticism of leadership
Rosabeth Moss Kanter	A Harvard Business School professor who specializes in leadership for change. Has written widely and is considered to be a highly influential writer

Key terms

Behaviourism	Drawn from psychology, behaviourism is the study of human behaviour
Contingency theory	States that the type of leadership style adopted is dependent (contingent) on the situation
Trait	A characteristic of the person, often considered the behaviour, thoughts, and emotions that the person exhibits considered stable over time
Post-heroic	A perspective which argues that we need to move beyond seeing the leader as hero
Followership	A theoretical perspective which stresses the importance of followers
Glass ceiling	A barrier that a particular group (e.g. women) cannot move beyond

Introduction

Running case: Simon Chance prepares for the day

Sitting in his office Chance gathers together his notes for the day. It's Wednesday and he is due to lead the staff meeting. As Chief Executive Officer (CEO) of the Second-Chance Consortium he feels that it is important—indeed his duty—to give a clear sense of direction to his followers and therefore likes to take the weekly meeting at least once a month. After the meeting he has a one-to-one session with Linda Wilkinson and then Graham Effingham—two interesting and different characters. He is then hosting a small lunch for the local chamber of commerce before spending the afternoon preparing for a big evening meal with potential investors. Getting this right is going to be really critical. 'Another busy day', he thinks to himself. 'Just need to finish my emails first . . .'

Real life case: an interview with the boss of RBS

Stephen Hester is widely acknowledged to have one of the hardest jobs in business. When he took over as the CEO of the Royal Bank of Scotland (RBS) in November 2008 they were facing potential collapse. RBS had become the biggest bank in the world, but had, in his words, 'taken a lot of risks to get there' and, as the financial crisis unravelled, they found 'the world was collapsing around [their] ears in financial market terms'. Massive change was needed to recover from near collapse, which had to be done at the same time as running a normal bank.

These early months were a time of crisis, with a real possibility that RBS could collapse. A lot of very important, long-term decisions had to be taken in a short time period, which Hester describes as 'intense'.

Stephen Hester, CEO of the Royal Bank of Scotland. © Oli Scarff/ Getty Images.

During that early period he says he had to 'provide a strong lead [. . .] because everyone is confused and panicked and they need the reassurance of someone saying 'This is the way we are going.' Secondly you need to get stuff done quickly so you cannot wait around for a consensus to build. There is no point doing things lots of people disagree with, or if you do you'd better get rid of those people. But in an intense situation you have less time to build a careful consensus and you have to more say, 'This is where we are going and here's why.' You are balancing what some people call leadership with consensus building.'

Hester describes his role as providing the vision and the framework. 'I needed to very much lead the strategy and vision of how we were going to get out of this mess, what were all the things we were going to do. What might RBS look like? And obviously get colleagues to buy in.'

A lifetime in business, learning from his and other people's experience led him to the concept underpinning this vision and strategy of dividing the bank into a 'good bank', which were the parts of the business they wanted to keep and the 'bad bank'. On his first day at RBS he laid out a list of five criteria that parts of the bank had to achieve in order to be classed as part of the good bank. He then set ▶

up a team 'whose only job is to get out of the risky bad things' and another focusing on maintaining the current business. At its heart, he states, is dividing problems into manageable pieces, being clear on what is to be done, putting a management structure in place to tackle these problems, and then develop plans and strategies to solve the problems. This is not done alone. 'All I'm doing is bringing in the sum of my business experience and if it is not in my immediate experience, bring in the business experience of other people who surround me in my management team or as consultants.'

He states 'the big vision needs to sound like "that would be good if we could do that" but also you have to explain why it is realistic, why we could do that'. Hester states that this involves winning hearts and minds at the same time—where do we want to be (hearts) and how are we going to get there (minds)—selling the vision that it is going to be a better place in the future than it is now. By doing this even those people that are going to suffer personally are more likely to 'work hard right to the end' if they know that the direction is the right one. This, he states, shows the importance of communication, of selling the vision to the staff, and the centrality of bringing people on board with the decisions. The day before this interview he met a member of staff who was receiving an award for good customer service. In conversation with her he discovered it would be her last event with the Group as her branch was closing. However, because she understood the reason for the changes Hester claims she took it well, which was a credit both to her and the way the vision was communicated.

Being the CEO of RBS is more than just providing this framework and direction as the 'big things [are] made up of 1000s of little things'. To be effective, staff have to have 'pretty good conviction about the piece they are asked to do' and other people's tasks 'need to sound sensible'. One of his early jobs was therefore to 'recapture optimism' throughout the organization.

As CEO, Hester states he only is effective through other people. 'As an individual I can only help RBS to be effective if I stimulate other individuals because it is too big and complicated a company to do everything myself, even if I was capable in doing so. That's why spending time with people is so important.' Consequently, he splits his time equally between internal people, external people, and tackling business problems (Figure 12.1).

Working with, inspiring, and developing people is therefore key to RBS's success. He is also the figurehead of the company and therefore needs to spend time with external people, such as shareholders, the media, investors, and politicians. Just days before our discussion he was interviewed from 7 am, firstly on the BBC's *Today Programme*, then by TV, radio, and print journalists through to the end of the day. The day before that he spent the whole day in meetings and in one-on-one conversations with internal members of staff.

Stephen Hester, though, is most famous for the public debate about his bonus. At the end of January 2012 he turned down a bonus of just under £1 million (BBC News, 2012). However, he believes that there should not be a cap on executive pay. 'If you look around the world at the countries that are doing well you will not find one of them that caps executive pay.' We will have more to say about this issue in Chapter 17; however, for the purposes of this chapter it is

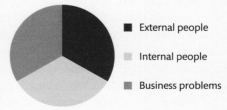

Figure 12.1 Division of Chief Executive Officer (CEO)'s time.

- External people
- Internal people
- Business problems

worth noting the justification for the pay and bonus leaders receive is based on the impact that they can make to the organization. Hester cites the 5% fall in share price when António Horta-Osório, the CEO of LloydsTSB went off sick (Goff and Jenkins, 2011). However, Stephen Hester also acknowledges

> that the impact he can make is 'unknowable' and 'all people are less important than they think they are'. The focus on one individual 'is not in anyway fair, but is the way of the world . . . whatever walk of life you are in individuals are celebrated or vilified. The truth is never as individualistic as that would make out. That's why I think anyone leading an organization or a unit needs to understand they are only as good as the team around them. And that's why you have to spend a lot of time on (a) getting the best team around you that you can and (b) getting them to be more effective.'
>
> **Source:** Author interview with Stephen Hester, Royal Bank of Scotland, February 2012.

Visit the Online Resource Centre to read the rest of the interview and for links to newspaper coverage of Stephen Hester and RBS.

What challenges did Stephen Hester face when taking over RBS? How did he go about it? What do you think are the key aspects of his leadership approach?

Leaders as heroes and villains

We love stories of great leaders, such as Gandhi, Martin Luther King, Julius Caesar, Winston Churchill, Nelson Mandela, Mother Teresa, and John F. Kennedy. They are regularly presented as visionaries, courageous, heroic, and principled individuals who lead their people to better futures; extraordinary people that do extraordinary things.

In the business world, leaders are also presented as having extraordinary powers. Howard Schultz is widely credited with reinvigorating Starbucks by refocusing the company on its core values (Groth, 2011). Jim Sinegal is praised with inspiring the employees of Costco to continued success. His down-to-earth manner (his name badge simply says 'Jim') and restricted earnings of $350,000 a year, when others in his role could get millions, is said to result in his followers loving him (Goldberg and Ritter, 2006). Mark Zuckerberg has become the 'poster boy' for social media. His role in founding and leading Facebook has won him plaudits around the world. Zuckerberg would do well to emulate the affection that was held for Steve Jobs, the co-founder and CEO of Apple. The announcement of his death in October 2011 was greeted by an outpouring of grief worldwide. Customers and employees laid flowers, tributes, and part eaten apples outside their stores, and tweeted and updated their Facebook statuses with details of their affection for the former Apple CEO. Jobs was loved not only for being the inventor of the iPhone, iPod, and iMac, but for rescuing Apple from near bankruptcy in 1997 to become the world's most valuable company by 2011. His importance to Apple was underscored by the drop in share price of 5% when his death was announced (Kollewe, 2011) (although, at the time of writing, it has since risen by 40%).

Yet, leaders can also become the villain. In October 2010, Tony Haywood resigned from his position as CEO of British Petroleum (BP) after being criticized continually in the US press and even by the US president for his handling of the Deepwater Horizon oil spill. It was not only the scale of the disaster (which, at the time of writing, is estimated to cost BP at least £5 bn) or numerous failed attempts to block the leak, but his handling of the media, encapsulated in the widely quoted comment: 'There's no one who wants this thing over more than I do, I'd like my life back' (*The Guardian*, 2010; Durando, 2010). Haywood was seen as out of touch and not sympathetic to the lives of those the oil spill had affected.

In February 2012 James Murdoch, the son of media tycoon Rupert Murdoch, resigned from his position as Chairman of News International, the publishers of *The News of the World* because of the phone hacking scandal that the newspaper became embroiled in. While there was no suggestion that James Murdoch was personally involved in the hacking, it was generally felt that there was too much trouble hanging over his head for him to be a positive influence in the company (Sabbagh, 2012).

Similar vilification has been aimed at Fred Goodwin the former CEO of the RBS. Goodwin had previously been presented as a hero, leading RBS to become one of the biggest companies in the world, and received a knighthood in the process. However, in October 2008, just months before RBS announced the biggest losses in UK corporate history of £24.1 bn, he resigned. In the press he was publically vilified, not only for these losses but for continuing to receive a substantial pension. In February 2012, he lost his knighthood—a very unusual act by the government (Jones, 2012; *The Daily Telegraph*, 2012a). In the weeks following the stripping of his knighthood, debate raged as to whether Fred Goodwin was responsible. He was criticized by a range of politicians, but others argued that it was unfair to attack one individual for the banking crisis and that this approach might put off 'wealth creators' from around the world coming to the UK (*The Daily Telegraph*, 2012b). While what happened at RBS did show signs of failure, it was unfair to single out one man.

Who do you consider a good leader and why? What have they achieved to be seen as a good leader?

Beyond the popular image of leadership: chapter overview

Business leaders are therefore regularly presented as heroes or villains. The business press focuses heavily on the 'man at the top' (and often it is a man), as though they, virtually single-handedly, are the difference between a company's success and failure. For instance, the debate over Stephen Hester's bonus was conducted through the lens that *he* alone is responsible for transforming RBS (and therefore should receive his bonus depending on RBS's success or failure). Faith, it seems, is directed firmly at the leader as the one who can transform the organization.

This has led to substantial interest in investigating the background, leadership style, and personality traits of these *individual great leaders* to understand what makes them excel. Yet, while the individual leader is important, as Stephen Hester states in our interview, leaders need to be humble about how much they personally can achieve. Indeed, as is clear in his interview, in large organizations a leader can only succeed through impacting many other people—Hester states he spends a third of his time with staff. We therefore need to broaden our focus to how leaders can impact their staff, which leads us to **behavioural theory**.

Not all leaders can be effective in all situations. Winston Churchill, so praised for leading Britain through World War II, was not seen to be appropriate in peacetime and did not get re-elected. **Situational leadership** therefore draws attention to the importance of the context for the type of leadership approach used.

Leadership, though, is seen as more than choosing the right style but in transforming the organization. **Transformational leadership** therefore provides the image that leadership offers more than doing deals, and offers a vision of inspiring followers and of a better future.

Behavioural theory
A psychological perspective which seeks to understand and change the behaviour of individuals.

Situational leadership
A theory which stresses the importance of adapting the leadership style to meet the situation.

Transformational leadership A leadership which stresses the leader's ability to transform the organization by offering a better vision for the future.

Post-heroic A collection of theories that argue that traditional leadership over-emphasizes the importance of leaders and under-emphasizes followers.

Social identity theory Drawing from psychological theory, how an individual's identity is derived from being part of a group.

Followership theory Stresses the importance of followers and seeks to emphasize their importance in theory and practice.

Servant leadership theory A bottom-up perspective which sees the leader being the most effective when they support followers to enable them to do their jobs.

Command and control A top-down leadership style that emphasizes the importance of the leader who tells others what to do.

Alternative models of organization Workers cooperatives and mutual organizations which seek for non-hierarchical modes of organizing and not-for-profit objectivities, often to bring about benefits to the members and society.

This view, though, still provides the heroic vision of the leader, one which **post-heroic** leadership theory seeks to challenge. These views argue that there is too much emphasis on a single individual at the top and draws our attention to the process of leading that occurs throughout the organization. Some of these theories, such as Greenleaf's servant leadership, argue for a more bottom-up rather than top-down leadership style. **Social identity theory**, discussed later, also sees the leader less as one standing at the front, but rather helping the group to form a collective identity (for a review see Haslam et al., 2011).

More recently, theories such as **transformative theory**, **followership theory**, and **servant leadership theory** have focused on the *impact* the leader has on their *followers*. They all see that in order to get things done leaders have to build alliances, persuade or encourage, or use coercive tactics in order to get their way. In traditional theories, leadership has, therefore, been about visionary leaders, inspiring others through force of personality or political might in order to get things done. More recent theories have begun to see leadership as more of a *social practice* of bringing others in the organizations with the leader. Rather than the individualized, heroic model, these theories look to the social processes involved in leading, emphasizing the collaborative nature of leadership and the importance of social relations. However, despite these theoretical moves, much of leadership practice and popular media portrayals retain its **command and control** approach where the leader sets the direction of the organization and determines how things are done, and the employees are followers.

Finally, we will turn our attention to **alternative models of organization** which emphasizes alternative modes of decision making which can occur without a leader. While not that common, these approaches offer possibilities to increase engagement, participation, and ideas from throughout the organization.

> **Employability skills:** developing your leadership skills—insights from prominent business leaders
>
> While the early theories saw leadership as something people are born with, increasingly there is attention on how to develop leadership skills. As is apparent from Stephen Hester's interview, he worked on developing his skills over the course of his career. For instance, he realized his 'strongest skills were analytical skills and communication skills, my weaker skills were dealing nicely with people or managing people well. And I got a long way with just analytical and communication skills, but I did not get as far as I wanted to get. So, I needed to spend a point in the middle bit of my career working really hard to improve my ability to manage people.' So how did he go about this? 'Concentrating on it, thinking about it; I actually took on an external coach for a couple of years to help work with me on those things, getting feedback from other people, the same way anyone would learn about anything.'
>
> Joe Greenwell, the Chairman of Ford in Britain echoes many of these sentiments stating you need the capacity to 'learn all the time', to be able to use data well, and understand the marketplace and the customer. Fundamentally, you need to have energy and enthusiasm, a passion for what you do, an acute awareness of your strengths and weaknesses, and an ability to overcome your weaknesses. Listen and learn from others, particularly good leaders. Above all you need to focus on the essentials of the business—revenue costs and profit.
>
> Sources: Author interview with Stephen Hester, Royal Bank of Scotland, February 2012; author interview with Joe Greenwell, Ford in Britain, 2012.

Visit the Online Resource Centre to read the full interviews with Stephen Hester and Joe Greenwell.

What skills and experience do you have of leadership and what areas do you need to improve? Identify one or two areas that you want to work on and spend some time considering how you can develop.

Definitions of leadership

The following are some popular definitions of leadership:

> Leadership has traditionally been seen as the ability and capacity to influence others.
>
> (Bass, 1985)

> The ability of an individual to influence, motivate, and enable others to contribute towards the effectiveness and success of the organisations of which they are members.
>
> (House et al., 2004: 56)

> Managers are people who do things right and leaders are people who do the right thing.
>
> (Bennis and Nanus, 1985: 21)

Differences between leadership and management

Before we begin we need to distinguish leadership from management. While some commentators use these titles interchangeably, Grint and Holt (2011) have recently provided a helpful distinction. **Management** is concerned with organizations running smoothly, creating stability, and following the rules; **leadership** focuses on the vision of the future of the organization and creating new rules. Management is, therefore, business-as-usual, whereas leadership is concerned with the future of the business. These differences are summarized in Table 12.1.

Management The everyday practices of running the organization in a smooth fashion.

Leadership The process of leading or influencing the behaviour of others. In the broadest definition can be carried out by anyone in the organization.

Table 12.1   The differences between leadership and management. Based on Grint and Holt, 2011

	Leadership	Management
Type of problem	Uncertain	Certain, knowable problems
	vu jàdé (never seen this before)	Déjà vu (seen this before)
	Wicked problems (complex problem, not a simple cause and effect)	Tame problems (complicated but it is resolvable through unilinear acts and it is likely to have occurred before)
Response	Ask right questions	Give correct answers
	Innovative response to the novel problem	Same process or standard operating procedure that resolved the problem the last time it emerged
Outlook	Art	Science
	Vision	Operational
Example	Creating a transport strategy	Timetabling the railways

© Grint & Holt, *Followership in the NHS*, 2011. Available at http://www.kingsfund.org.uk/publications/articles/leadership_papers/nhs_followership.html

This definition does not just impact particular organizations, but whole sectors. Grint and Holt cite the US car industry, which they say focused on efficiency of sports utility vehicles (SUVs), which is a tame problem, rather than questioning whether these are appropriate vehicles for the twenty-first century (Grint and Holt, 2011: 90). Thus, leadership is about asking the right questions, and acting with vision and rethinking the status quo. Leadership is not necessarily a position in the organization, but more a way of thinking about how to solve organizational problems.

Individualistic leader: great man theory and trait theory

Running case: Chance looks for inspiration

Chance rises up to begin his speech to the staff at Junction Hotel. He loves these moments—laying out the vision and mission of the hotel, reminding the staff of the direction that they are going in, and rallying the troops. At times like this he imagines what other leaders would do. He loves the innovation of Steve Jobs and his drive and determination, and the passionate outlook of Howard Schultz, but he is happiest and feels most leader-like when he imagines himself as Winston Churchill. As he concludes his speech about how the hotel will overcome adversity and move into a brighter future, particularly if the investors' meal goes well, Chance declares with gusto, in Churchillian tones, that Junction Hotel will never be defeated.

Look at your list of great leaders—what is it that made them great? Are there any common characteristics that made them great? Go to our online site and vote for your favourite leader and join the debate.

A visit to the business section of high-street bookshops quickly reveals our fascination with *great* business leaders. Their shelves are often full of the biographies and autobiographies of some of our most successful leaders, including Richard Branson's *Losing My Virginity* (2009) and *Business Stripped Bare* (2009), Walter Isaacson's *Steve Jobs: The Exclusive Biography* (2012), Alan Sugar's *What You See is What You Get* (2011), and Duncan Bannatyne's *Anyone Can Do It* (2007). These books tantalize the reader with the promise that these leaders will reveal the secrets of leadership.

Our interest in individual leaders is not new. One of the earliest incarnations is **great man** theory, founded by historian Thomas Carlyle. It examines the biographies of great leaders, particularly their background, character, key actions, and philosophy, to learn what made them great. Great man theory often provides hagiographies, heroic accounts of leaders, emphasizing their wisdom, charm, intelligence, insight, or political savvy-ness.

Great man theory presents leaders as born, not made—great men that rise to prominence at times of crisis. Such leaders are rare and cannot be trained, so great man theory is used to identify potential future great leaders before they reach prominence.

Great man A theory that certain individuals are born great and can lead organizations and societies.

Real life case: Winston Churchill—the exemplar of a great man

Winston Churchill is often said to be the UK's greatest statesman of the twentieth century, leading the country in a time of crisis when it 'stood alone' against Nazi Germany. Centres, such as Winston Churchill Leadership, and numerous biographies aim to study the personality, background, and skills of Churchill to uncover his greatness and unique character.

Winston Churchill.

Churchill is widely presented (e.g. Roberts, 2003) as having a 'sense of destiny' and superior insight into the potential danger that Hitler posed. He is described as a visionary: inspirational, courageous, and an innovative leader with good people-management and listening skills. A good public orator, he also impacted those he met, leaving them feeling braver after the meeting.

Some accounts of Churchill (e.g. Roberts 2003; Longstaffe, 2005) try to uncover his key leadership principles and learn from them for today's leaders. They suggest that listening and communication skills coupled with his courage and passion offer an example for modern-day leaders. 'Churchill's leadership principles have proved both timeless and to be a continual source of inspiration to modern-day leaders, in both politics and business at a time when effective leadership has never been more essential' (Longstaffe, 2005: 83).

Sources: Roberts, 2003; Longstaffe (2005) and www.winston-churchill-leadership.com.

What makes great leaders stand out? Focusing on their leadership abilities, personal characteristics, and even physical appearance, **trait theory** aims to provide a list of key characteristics or **traits** that make great leaders great. In his book, *On Leadership*, John Gardner listed the key traits that make for a successful leader, these include:

- Physical vitality and stamina
- Intelligence and action-oriented judgement
- Eagerness to accept responsibility
- Task competence
- Understanding of followers and their needs
- Skill in dealing with people
- Need for achievement
- Capacity to motivate people
- Courage and resolution
- Trustworthiness
- Decisiveness
- Self-confidence
- Assertiveness
- Adaptability/flexibility

Source: Gardner (1989)

Trait theories Nomothetic theories of personality which see individual traits rather than broad personality groups as the foundations of personality.

Trait A characteristic of the person, often considered the behaviour, thoughts, and emotions that the person exhibits, considered stable over time.

Visit the Online Resource Centre to read some leader profiles. What do you think are their most important traits?

Interest in trait theory can be traced to Sir Francis Galton's book *Hereditary Genius*, published in 1869. Galton believed leadership qualities were genetic and that certain people, largely members of the aristocracy, were born good leaders. Leadership traits, therefore, are something you are born with and cannot be learned.

Even today, trait theory presents leaders as superior to ordinary people, often having characteristics such as greater intelligence, self-confidence, determination, integrity, and sociability. In Kirkpatrick and Locke's words 'it is unequivocally clear that leaders are not like other people' (1991: 59). Indeed, these special qualities provided the justification why business leaders earn substantially more than most people (see Chapter 17 for a discussion). More recently, trait theorists have argued that individuals can cultivate certain traits and therefore develop their leadership skills by learning from successful people.

The individualistic (heroic) leader assessed

The focus on individual leaders continues to be popular to this day, with top business leaders celebrated regularly and presented as people to learn from. Leaders are presented as powerful—shaping, and even controlling, the fate of their organization.

However, the assumptions that individualistic leadership theories are based on are problematic. They have tendencies towards elitism, particularly in early versions which saw great leaders coming, almost exclusively, from the aristocracy and being a result of 'breeding'. While few hold such views today the assumption still persists that certain people are born *natural* leaders and stand apart from *normal* people.

Individualistic models also suffer from difficulty in defining what makes a great leader. It is hard to imagine one person having all the traits a great leader should possess. Indeed, as far back as 1948, Stogdill concluded that there was no universal list of traits that could be defined for all leaders, making the concept inconclusive at best and, arguably, meaningless.

Moreover, leadership traits that are successful in one situation might prove counter-productive in another. For instance, Winston Churchill was widely seen as one of the greatest war-time leaders, with approval ratings of over 78%; however, after the war he led the Conservative Party to one of its heaviest defeats (Addison, 2011). His traits, as a strong and determined personality that everyone could rally round may have worked in war-time, but in peacetime, without a clear common enemy or collective vision for the country, his strong-willed personality was unsuited for the more political environment.

Many researchers have also questioned whether these traits are objective and measurable. Complex personalities, they argue, cannot be simply reduced down to a list of definable characteristics (see Chapter 8 on personality). These traits therefore do not actually exist in an objective sense, but are a result of researchers interpreting the actions of the leaders.

Why do you feel the 'romanticism of leadership' has been such an enduring concept?

Many of the key traits such as individualism, assertiveness, and control are often associated with a masculine personality (Calás and Smircich, 1993). Individualistic theory reinforces

> **Research insight:** The romantic view of leadership, Meindl, J. R., Ehrlich, S. B., and Dukerich, J. M. 1985. The romance of leadership, *Administrative Science Quarterly* 30(1): 78–102.
> Pillai, R., and Meindl, J. R. 1991. The impact of a performance crisis on attributions of charismatic leadership: A preliminary study. In: *Proceedings of the 1991 Eastern Academy of Management Meetings*, Hartford, CT.
>
> In a series of influential studies Meindl and colleagues have argued that we overestimate the power and control of leaders. Using attribution theory (how people look for causes for events), they argue that often we over-attribute the success (or failure) of an organization to the leadership.
>
> An early study (Meindl et al., 1985) found when reading 33,248 press articles there was a significant correlation between references to the organizational leader in the article title and strong company performance. They found that in the years that the firms did well these articles emphasized the leader more.
>
> In a later study Pillai and Meindl (1991) gave a group of people an identical CV of a male CEO but different information about the company's success. In the scenario, when there was a sudden increase in performance, the CEO was considered charismatic, but when performance declined, they stated he lacked charisma. In other words, the performance of the firm changed the way the leader's personality was viewed.
>
> The implication is that leaders get credit (or the blame) even when there is little evidence that they have done anything remarkable. The perception of the 'great leader's' personality is thus constructed based on organizational performance and not the cause of it.

dominant, masculine images of the heroic leader (Bryman et al., 1988) and, as Badaracco (2001) argues, downplays the quiet, less heroic, but often more effective, aspects of leadership (Table 12.2).

Table 12.2 Strengths and weaknesses of individualistic leadership theories

Strengths	Weaknesses
Focused research on leadership	Lacks empirical evidence
Some evidence as there are number of great leaders throughout history	Lacks explanatory value
Still popular with some	Masculine and Western bias
	Stogdill (1948) no universal list—inconclusive
	Class bias—breeding
	Not necessarily applicable to work organization
	Post-hoc rationalization
	Dated

Review questions

1. Describe the key principles behind great man and trait theories.
2. Explain why the romantic leadership model believes there is too much emphasis on the individual leader.

Behavioural theory

Running case: the kitchen in preparation for the investors' meal

In the kitchen, Effingham is pacing up and down barking orders like a sergeant major as he knows this meal it critical to the hotel's success. 'Right everyone, we have a big dinner tonight, with members of the board, potential investors, and the press. I don't want anyone to put a foot wrong. Mike start peeling the potatoes and then cut them into chips like I showed you last week; Josh, corkscrew the carrots—I want 100 of them by 4 pm; and, Toby, start dicing the onions. We have to be on the case tonight lads. Mike, come over here and I'll show you how I want the meat prepared.'

How would you describe Effingham's leadership style? Do you think it is appropriate for working in the kitchen?

Behaviourism Drawn from psychology, it looks at behaviours.

Michigan studies Early leadership studies which stressed the benefit of being employee orientated rather than task orientated to improve output.

Ohio State studies Conducted at a similar time to the Michigan studies and also considered leaders to be people- or task-orientated.

As interest in great individual leaders began to wane, attention switched to what a leader actually does. Drawing on **behaviourism**, particularly behavioural psychology (see Chapters 9 and 10), they focused on how leadership behaviour shapes their followers.

Behaviour theories begin with the premise that all behaviour is a result of what they call *conditioning* (Figure 12.2). How we behave is thus a result of learned reacting to positive signs (rewards) or negative ones (punishment), and then adjusting our behaviour accordingly.

Consequently, the actions of followers emerge from how the leader responds to their behaviour and the signals that they exhibit. Leadership, rather than being an innate part of somebody's personality, can, according to a behaviourist, be learned.

One of the earliest focuses of the impact of a leader's behaviour was developed in the late 1940s by the **Michigan studies**, and in the 1950s and early 1960s in the **Ohio State studies**. They stated that leaders are either employee- or task-focused, as shown in Table 12.3.

The Ohio studies have led to the conclusion that *the most effective leaders combine task- and employee-focused approaches*.

This approach was developed in 1964 by Robert Blake and Jane Mouton, who developed the Leadership Grid®. They argued the team management style, which combines a high concern for people and production, was most effective, whereas the worst style is the impoverished management style, which has low concern for both.

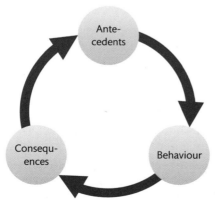

Figure 12.2
Skinner's A–B–C of behaviourism conditioning.

Table 12.3 Differences between employee-centred and task-centred leadership (based on the Ohio State leadership studies)

Overall focus	Employee-centred	Task-centred
Leadership style	Listens to the subordinates, encourages participation, has a friendly manner that aims to enhance self-esteem, and builds an environment of trust, warmth, and concern. Social sensitivity	Focuses on the task, provides clear expectations, instructions, and deadlines, focusing on maintaining standards
Leader's focus	Towards satisfying emotional and social needs of employees	Towards goals
Inspired by	Human relations theory	Taylorism
McGregor's Theory X or Y (see ORC for a discussion)	Theory Y	Theory X
Leader's primary aim	Increased satisfaction	Higher production
Potential problems	Lower production	Increased turnover absenteeism and grievances of employees

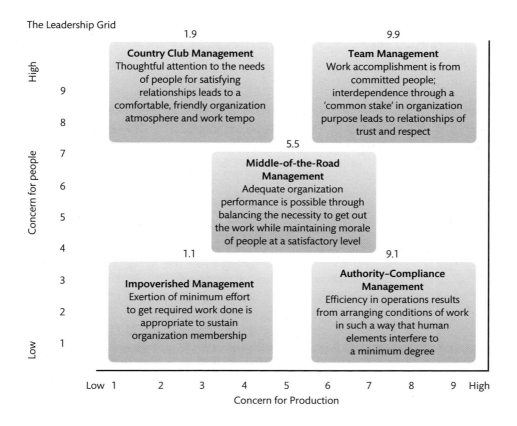

The Leadership Grid

Figure 12.3 Blake and Mouton's Leadership Grid.

© Scientific Methods Inc., from Blake, R. and Mouton, J. (1985). *The Managerial Grid: The Key to Leadership Excellence.*

Blake and Mouton argued that people tend to have one dominant leadership style and a secondary style which the leader falls into if the dominant approach does not work. The Leadership Grid is popular with managers as a way of assessing their leadership style and for diagnosing organizational problems. It is therefore useful for training leaders. However, there is little empirical support for it.

 What is your dominant leadership style? Go to the Blake and Mouton leadership quiz online to find out. What do you need to do to adjust your style to the team management approach?

Autocratic, democratic, and laissez-faire leadership styles

Another approach to leaders' behaviour was developed in the late 1930s by Kurt Lewin and colleagues. They claimed there were three key styles of leadership: **autocratic**, **democratic**, and **laissez-faire**. See Table 12.4 for a summary.

The autocratic style emphasizes *command and control*. All decisions are made by the leader, with little input from the group, one step at a time, so that the followers never know for certain what the next step will be. The leader is personal in his praise and criticism of the followers, but aloof from the group unless demonstrating what the next step is.

While this approach is good for rapid decision making it tends to be dysfunctional, creating discontentment, hostility, scapegoating, and aggression within the group, and a lack of creativity. The group 'develop a pattern of aggressive domination towards one another, and their relation to the leader was one of submission or of persistent demands for attention' (Lewin et al., 1939: 277).

In many senses, the laissez-faire approach offers the complete opposite perspective. The group has *complete freedom to act without any participation of the leader*. The leader provides the resources and information but does not participate or interfere outside of this. Lewin et al. (1939) state that the laissez-faire approach is highly inefficient and unproductive, producing discontent, hostility, scapegoating, and aggression as the groups feel they lack direction.

The democratic approach makes *all policy matters a subject for group discussion*. The leader facilitates group discussions but does not dominate. The aim is to involve all the group members and allow them to make decisions, as they will implement them and be impacted by them. The democratic approach is the most effective. There is less aggression, change is

Autocratic A command and control leadership style.

Democratic A leadership style which encourages the involvement of the group, but the leader ultimately makes the decisions.

Laissez-faire A leadership style which leaves all decisions to the group.

Table 12.4 Lewin's three leadership styles (Lewin et al., 1939)

Name	Decision making	Role of group	Advantages	Disadvantages
Autocratic	Centralized	Followers	Quick decision making	Can hinder creativity
Participative	With group, leader overall	Participating and involved	Involvement and originality	Can be slow in time of crisis
Laissez faire	Left to the group	Have full autonomy	Freedom of group members	Slow decision making and often unproductive

more easily accepted, relations between the group members are friendlier, and the group is more creative. It creates a sense of belonging and participation within the group.

What is your leadership style? Visit the Online Resource Centre to take the Lewin quiz and find out.

Theory in context: Lewin's leadership styles

As with many of the theories that we use in organizational behaviour they did not start out as business and management theories. Lewin's three leadership styles actually started life assessing the reactions of 10-year-old children to a group leader in 'theatrical mask-making for a period of three months' (Lewin et al., 1939: 271). Therefore, it is questionable if this research can be applied easily to understanding management practice, as the context is quite different.

They were also part—Professor Bill Cooke, an expert in Kurt Lewin argues—of Lewin's left-wing political project. Lewin, he claims, saw these three leadership styles as representing three different political systems.

- Autocratic style: Fascism, dictatorship, and control.
- Participative style: social democracy, a left-wing reform movement embracing socialism and government intervention for the good of society.
- Laissez-faire: free-market capitalism.

Lewin, a German Jew who left Germany when Hitler came to power, had an obvious opposition to autocratic leadership styles. As a socialist he was also opposed to the laissez-faire approaches, as he thought that the capitalist market should not be left to itself as the poor and weak suffer in these systems. Lewin wanted to demonstrate that it was 'right, proper and possible to intervene to effect social change on behalf of the disadvantaged' (Cooke, 1999: 92). Therefore, the superiority of the democratic model was, for Lewin, support for the social democratic model of government (Thelen, 1992). This model of leadership, therefore, could be read as a political project to further a more democratic and fairer society rather than simply as three categories of leadership.

Why might the background of theories we use today matter?

Behavioural approaches assessed

The behavioural approaches have focused attention on how the leaders' actions impact followers, bringing in followers to research for the first time. It also offers the potential that leadership skills can be learned and developed over time.

However, they still search for a 'one best way'—an ideal form of leadership that should be used by all leaders in all situations. As with the individualistic focus, it retains a male and Western bias, and over-emphasizes taxonomies (lists). Behaviourism also offers a simplistic and mechanical understanding of followers' behaviour, as simply a reaction to stimulus with little free will. See Table 12.5 for a summary.

Review questions

1. Explain why behaviourists believe the leader's behaviour impacts the followers.
2. Analyse the implications that Lewin's political leanings might have on his theory of leadership.

Table 12.5 Strengths and weaknesses of behaviourism

Strengths	Weaknesses
More subtle than many previous theories	Hard to measure
Examines the interaction of the leader and follower, and the impact the leader has on the group	Presents a 'one best way' approach and does not take into account the situation
Practice of leadership	Male and Western bias
Possibility of training	Validity of research
	Over emphasis on taxonomies
	Simplistic
	Examines only behaviour, not its impact

Contingency leadership theory

Running case: Chance prepares for his one-to-one meetings

As he returns to his office Chance gathers his notes for his one-to-one sessions. First, he is meeting Linda Wilkinson, his keen, committed, but sometimes anxious, domestic manager. Although she is experienced, Chance sometimes feels he has to be careful what he says to her as he feels she has a habit of taking things the wrong way. They have to have a tricky discussion over why the maintenance staff are not fixing rooms up to the standard that some customers require. Wilkinson, though, can be defensive of her team, and Chance wonders quite how to put it.

Being direct with Effingham, though, is never a problem. The boisterous and outspoken chef is the complete opposite and obsessed with the restaurant. However, Chance wonders if this style always works well with others in the hotel, as Effingham has a reputation for falling out with other members of staff. It is this issue that Chance needs to raise with Effingham. He wonders if he should just come out and say it.

How do you think Chance treats these two? Visit the Online Resource Centre to read our online profiles of them and make up your own mind.

Contingency theory
Suggests that the best structure for an organization is determined by factors such as environmental uncertainty, the organization's size, and the technology that the organization uses.

Why are some leaders more effective in some situations and not others? **Contingency theory** argues that the appropriate leadership style depends on the situation, particularly the skills and experience of the followers, the complexity of tasks, the speed of decision making required, and the type of organization. The leader's approach, therefore, needs to fit the context they are facing and they need to adapt their leadership style accordingly (Figure 12.4).

Contingency theory argues that a leader's success is dependent on two factors: (1) the leaders *preferred leadership style*—their typical way of interacting with followers; (2) *situational control*—the degree of control the leader has over the situation. Effective leadership depends on getting the perfect match between the situation *and* the personality.

The Least Preferred Co-worker scale

One of the most famous proponents of the contingency approach was Fiedler. He argued that everyone has a preferred leadership style which is more likely to succeed in certain situations and less likely in others. To understand when you are more likely to succeed, he argued, you need to understand your preferred leadership style.

To diagnose leadership style Fiedler developed the *Least Preferred Co-worker scale* (LPC). This works by asking the user to think of the *one person in their life* they find hardest to work with and rate their characteristics (Fiedler and Chemers, 1984). The test is not about the *Least Preferred Co-worker*, but the motivation and personality of the person filling in the form. The model works on the assumption the LPC is, on average, equally unpleasant—what varies is the perception of the LPC. Fiedler believed task-orientated people tend to see their LPC in more negative terms, whereas people-orientated individuals see the positive factors in the LPC. It claims to reveal the basic goals and priorities in a work setting—what they feel they need to achieve to be satisfied with their performance and themselves.

Fiedler (1967) argued that these responses translate into the respondent's preferred leadership style as either task- or relationships-orientated. So far, the LPC model mirrors the behavioural theories already discussed. However, unlike behavioural theory, Fiedler's contingency theory does not suggest that one LPC style is superior. Rather, he argued, the most effective leadership style is dependent on three factors in order of importance: the quality of the relationship the leader has with the followers; the nature of the task; and the degree of formal authority the leader has (see Table 12.6).

Fiedler argued that it is easier to be a leader when the group accepts and trusts its leader, when tasks are highly structured, and when the leader has formal authority than it is when the group distrusts the leader, tasks are vague, and the leader has little formal authority.

Visit the Online Resource Centre to see the LPC diagram discussed here, take the LPC questionnaire, and discover what your leadership style is.

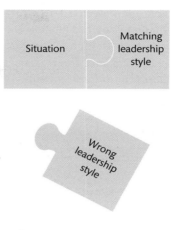

Figure 12.4
Leadership style to match the situation.

Table 12.6 Key factors in Fiedler's (1967) Least Preferred Co-worker scale

Leader–member relations	Good—the group tends to trust the leader and accept them
	Poor—the group tends to distrust the leader and does not accept the leader's position
Task structure	Structured—with clear goals and is highly standardized and predictable with only a few ways to carry it out
	Unstructured—ambiguous goals, many ways of undertaking the task, and unclear criteria to judge success
Leader position power	Strong—the leader has considerable formal authority and has the power to influence the group
	Weak—the leader has little formal authority and little power to influence the group

Task orientated leaders (with low LPC scores) succeed in highly favourable conditions (i.e. quadrant 1 of the LPC diagram) and highly unfavourable conditions (quadrant 8). Relational leaders (with high LPC scores) do better when the factors are more mixed (quadrants 4–7) as they balance the needs between building relations and focusing on the task. Visit the Online Resource Centre to view the table.

> **Real life case:** Formula4Leadership
>
> One of the stated benefits for contingency theory is that it offers practical guidance for leaders to adjust their leadership style to meet the circumstance they face. However, how do you diagnose what state the group is in? An example of a tool marketed to business leaders to do this is *coach on the desktop*. Designed by Formula4leadership, this computer application asks the user a series of questions about the situation that they face. Based on the answers the program offers a diagnosis of the situation and an analysis of the correct response a leader should make.
>
> **Source:** http://www.formula4leadership.com.

Visit the Online Resource Centre for an interview with the owners of Formula4Leadership.

Least Preferred Co-worker scale assessed

The LPC scale offers the opportunity to diagnose what your leadership style is and explore whether it matches the context. As a personality measurement, in common with other psychological perspectives (see Chapter 9), it sees personality as relatively stable over time. Consequently, if the leadership style does not meet the situation either the leader needs to adapt the situation to meet their leadership style (e.g. making the tasks more structured) or a different leader needs to be put in place.

While LPC also moves away from the 'one best way' assumption of leadership theory it still assumes each situation has a best leadership approach. It also assumes that leaders are unable to adapt their style.

Situational leadership

A more flexible contingency leadership theory is offered by Hersey and Blanchard (1988), who see that leaders can be high or low in both task and relationship focus. They state leaders can adapt their style to the situation rather than simply having to match the leader to the appropriate situation. The appropriate style also depends on the maturity of the group. They called this situational leadership.

Hersey and Blanchard presented their model as a four-square matrix. On the horizontal axis is the nature of the complexity of the task (either low or high), and the amount of direction the leader gives to the group. On the vertical axis is the relationship focus, how supportive the leader needs to be. Their model (see Table 12.7) argues that groups go through stages as they mature and the leader needs to adjust their behaviour to match the situation of the group.

- Stage 1 *'telling or directing'*. High task- and low relationship-focused. In this stage the group are new, they are committed (they want to be seen as doing well), but have low levels of competency (do not have many skills). The leader is highly directive, telling the subordinates what to do and how to do it. The leader has very little relationship with the followers.

- Stage 2 *'selling or coaching'*. High task and high relationship. At this stage the group increases their competency (they have started learning to do things), but, as a result, they begin to lose confidence and therefore their motivation drops as they become aware of what they cannot do. In this situation the leader remains quite directive, telling them what to do, but is more encouraging and therefore focused on building up personal relationships.

- Stage 3 *'participating or encouraging'*. Low task and high relationship. As the group develops it increases its level of skill and confidence, the commitment levels begin to rise again. To support this stage the leader becomes less focused on the task and more on helping to support and encourage the group through adopting a facilitation style.

- Stage 4 *'delegating and empowering'*. Low task and low relationship. At this final stage the group have matured, and have high levels of skill and confidence. As a result, the leader can allow them to run things on a daily basis and is only really involved in problem-solving and key decisions.

Visit the Online Resource Centre for a link to the diagram.

Table 12.7 Situational leadership model (based on Hersey and Blanchard, 1988)

	Title	Leaders focus		Followers		Appropriate communication style	Appropriate leadership style
		Task	Relationship	Commitment	Competency		
S1	Telling/ directing	High	Low	High	Low D1	Top-down Announced as the followers are after certainty	Goal focused Clear well-defined task. What is to be done, how to do it, and who is responsible Closely supervised
S2	Selling/ coaching/ explaining	High	High	Lack (lost initial motivation) Aim to build self-esteem	Some competent D2	Two-way to involve and motivate the employees and develop their competency	Leader provides some direction as still relatively inexperienced
S3	Participating/ supporting/ asking	Low	High	Lack (as unsure of their skill)	Moderate to high D3	Facilitation model	Day-to-day decision making by followers as they have experience but involvement by leader to bolster confidence and motivation
S4	Delegating/ empowering	Low	Low	High	High D4	Little support or facilitation needed	Leaders are still involved in decisions and problem-solving, but control is with the follower

How it works

The leader diagnoses the commitment and competency of the followers, and then shapes their leadership style accordingly. For instance, faced with an inexperienced, but highly motivated group (D1), the leader needs to adopt a direct and goal-focused approach, providing clear tasks with clear instructions (S1). The followers with low skill levels will appreciate clear tasks as it removes ambiguity.

As the group learns new skills (D2) they become increasingly uncertain and can thus lose motivation. The leader therefore needs to develop the group's confidence by focusing on relationship and commitment by using two-way dialogue to increase involvement. As their skills increase (S3) the group needs less direction, but more encouragement as they tend to be uncertain of their skills (D3).

An experienced, motivated, and confident group (D4) works best with more autonomy, with the leader only involved in problem-solving and key decisions (S4).

More recently, Hersey and Blanchard have argued the leader also needs to explain to the group why they are changing style otherwise the group can be left feeling isolated, believing that the leader does not care (compare this model to Tuckman's group formation on pp. 177–82).

Study skills: leadership in group work

During your time at university you will probably spend time working in groups. While it is unlikely your group will officially appoint a 'leader', you will, at times, take on leadership roles, both in terms of organizing your group, and by supporting and encouraging other group members. As you read through this chapter consider your own leadership style and how it can be adjusted to meet different situations.

Path–goal and congruence model

Path–goal theory
Developed by Robert House, argues the leader's effectiveness is dependent on the motivation, satisfaction, and performance of her subordinates.

One of the primary problems of early contingency theory is that it sees leadership style as simply matching the leader's focus on task and/or relationships to the followers' commitment and competency, ignoring wider factors, such as culture, power and politics, and identity.

To overcome this narrow perspective, House developed **path–goal theory** (1996), and Nadler and Tuschman (1997) developed the congruence model. These theories broaden the analysis to include factors such as the organization's environment, the resources available to the leader, and the organization's history (see the Online Resource Centre for more details). By taking into account more variables, they offer a more subtle and far-reaching understanding of the environment the leader faces. However, they also become more complicated and mathematical as they try to deal with almost every factor the organization faces.

Situational and contingency leadership theory assessed

Contingency theory has been used regularly in training programmes for future leaders because it offers practical guidelines and tools that help leaders assess and adapt their leadership style to meet followers' needs. It offers a more subtle understanding than individualistic and behavioural approaches as it increases attention on leaders' impact on followers. However, situational theory does little to explain how leaders move from low to high development levels (Northouse, 2009) and there is a lack of empirical evidence to support it (Bryman, 1986).

One underlying problem is that all contingency theories work on the assumption that the context of the group, such as the skill levels, motivation, leader–follower relations, organizational history, etc., is an objective reality which the leader can know 'transparent[ly] through scientific analysis' (Grint, 2005: 1470). However, human behaviour is far more unpredictable and complex than these models suggest.

Also, although these perspectives challenge the notion there is one best leadership style they still assume that each situation demands a particular leadership style, thus moving from the *one best way* to *one best response*. Table 12.8 summarizes the 'pros' and 'cons'.

Visit the Online Resource Centre for more details on these models.

Table 12.8 'Pros' and 'cons' of contingency theory

Pros	Cons
Understand situation	Neat models but applicable to real life?
No ideal leader	Still limited view on the group
Variety of leadership styles	Potentially normative
More flexible models	North-American and gender bias
Impact on followers	Limited look structure, politics, etc.

Review questions

1. Explain what is meant by contingency.
2. Explain why contingency theory offers a more flexible approach to leadership.
3. Analyse why it still represents a 'one best way'.

Transformational and transactional theory

Running case: Linda Wilkinson's one-to-one

As their meeting progresses Simon Chance realizes that Linda Wilkinson is struggling a little with managing the maintenance team. 'They just ignore some of my requests', she says honestly. 'You know, I ask them to do things, try to offer them incentives to fix the rooms but they just don't seem to make it a priority. I've even tried just pulling rank on them and telling them—it works OK for a day or so and then they go back to their old ways.' Chance listens intently and then leans forward. 'You need to inspire them—they need to want to do a good job.' 'Easier said than done', thinks Wilkinson.

Table 12.9 Transactional and transformational leadership styles (based on Burns, 1978)

Transactional	Transformational
Cuts deals with employees	Transform institutions
Exchange with workers	Offer a vision of the future that people want to buy into
Monitor and control workers	Feel part of the solution
Extrinsic motivation	Intrinsic motivation
Short-term self-interest	Long-term substantive goals
Works best with inexperienced followers	Works best with experienced followers
Contingency theory	Charismatic leadership
Manager	Leader
Tame problems	Wicked problems
Preserver/trustee	Insurgent entrepreneur
Organizational man	Maverick

One of the problems with the leadership styles presented so far is there is little uplifting in these models. They tend to focus on either heroic leaders who are born that way or present leadership as a mundane, mechanical model. This concern led Burns (1978) to form his transformative leadership model. Burns argues there are two styles of leadership: transactional and transformative. Transactional leadership operates by trying to control followers and cut deals with them. Transformative, however, is more uplifting. Table 12.9 sums up the main differences between these two approaches.

Transformational leaders lead through inspiring, causing a change in the followers, creating a shared mission and encouraging followers to take ownership of their work. Drawing from the work of Maslow (see Chapter 9), Burns argued that great leaders lift people up through the hierarchy of needs by focusing attention away from low-level needs (met through pay) towards loftier goals, such as self-esteem and self-actualization. According to Tichy and Davanna, transformative leaders are visionary change agents who are courageous, driven by values, have a strong belief in people, can cope with complexity, and are life-long learners. Similarly, Bass (1985) identified the following characteristics of transformational leaders:

- *idealized influence*—high moral and ethical standards, and therefore respected by the followers which creates loyalty
- *inspirational motivation*—strong vision for future based on values and ideals. Build confidence and inspire followers
- *intellectual stimulation*—challenge organizational norms and encourage alternative thinking
- *individual consideration*—recognize unique growth and developmental needs of followers.

Real life case: Howard Schultz's transformation of Starbucks

In 2007 Howard Schultz, then the chairman and former CEO of Starbucks, wrote a highly critical memo to the board. In it he argued that Starbucks was chasing growth for its own sake and felt invincible—it had lost its soul. A year later he seemed correct. Starbucks was closing stores, and campaigners, and even their employees who they call partners, were turning against them. Starbucks seemed to have lost its way (Schultz, 2011: 41).

Schultz then shocked everyone by returning as CEO. He aimed to transform Starbucks by returning to its core values—a focus on people. Schultz enacted many of the key traits of a transformational leader; he offered an inspiring vision for the future. Starbucks, he claimed, not only has to make money, but has also created value for the employees and the wider community. To this end he changed part of the mission statement to 'We want to be invited in wherever we do business. We can be a force for positive action' (Starbucks, 2012).

Sources: Starbucks (2012); BBC Radio 4 (2011) and Schultz (2011).

Visit the Online Resource Centre to read more about Starbucks.

What can a leader do to create passion and zeal in their followers? What would give you passion and zeal for your work?

Transactional leaders, however, believe their followers are motivated by rewards and punishment, so lead through offering exchanges (promises of higher pay, promotion, or status) for increased effort. The primary focus of transactional leaders is to plan, organize tasks, monitor progress, and fix problems as they arise. According to Bass (1985) the following characteristics define transactional leaders:

Transactional leaders Leaders who do deals with employees in order to get the task done. Seen in opposition to **transformational leaders** who offer a better vision of the world that employees can buy into.

- *contingent reward*—tangible or intangible support or resources for effort and support
- *management by exception–action*—monitor performance and take corrective action when necessary
- *management by exception–passive*—monitor performance and only take action when really serious
- *laissez-faire*—avoidance of leadership responsibility.

Transformational leaders, therefore, are best at dealing with wicked problems, whereas transactional leaders are more like managers as they are concerned with finding answers to everyday, tame problems. As Kanter (1992) states, for an organization to be successful it needs a mix of both of these types. Too many questioners and everything gets confused, too many people who follow the same old patterns and organizations get stuck in dead ends; too many chiefs and not enough indians.

Transformative theory assessed

The transformative theory reignites the idea of the heroic leader, often using masculine traits to describe their personality, presenting them as having almost super-human characteristics. However, they are not operating in a top-down, command and control manner, but aim to inspire their followers with passion to go the extra mile.

However, from a critical perspective this could be seen as a form of control, manipulating the workers' desires and interests (see Lukes in Chapter 13) or inspiring them with a vision to get them to work harder against their real interests (see Chapter 7).

Review questions

1. Explain the difference between transactional and transformational leadership.
2. Analyse to what extent a transformational leader is a reincarnation of the heroic leader and how they are different.

Challenging the leader-centric view: the post-heroic perspective and the importance of followers

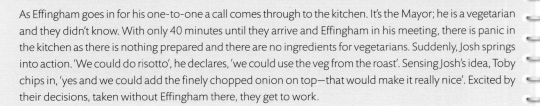

Running case: crisis in the kitchen

As Effingham goes in for his one-to-one a call comes through to the kitchen. It's the Mayor; he is a vegetarian and they didn't know. With only 40 minutes until they arrive and Effingham in his meeting, there is panic in the kitchen as there is nothing prepared and there are no ingredients for vegetarians. Suddenly, Josh springs into action. 'We could do risotto', he declares, 'we could use the veg from the roast'. Sensing Josh's idea, Toby chips in, 'yes and we could add the finely chopped onion on top—that would make it really nice'. Excited by their decisions, taken without Effingham there, they get to work.

Up until now all the theories presented have been leader-centric. They have assumed the leader is central to an organization's success: a superman (and, very occasionally, superwoman), with extraordinary powers to transform the organization virtually single-handedly. They achieve this either through force of character (great man, trait, and trans-formative theory) or by having a perfect insight into the nature of the group (in contingency theory). This leader-centric lens portrays leaders as having free will with the capacity to make choices, whereas the followers are simply passive, merely responding to leaders' actions. The leaders' significance is therefore overstated, producing what Meindl et al. (1985) call a 'romanticism of leadership'.

This romanticism presents leaders as saviours of the organization, solely responsible for its fate, justifying the often incredibly large salaries (and bonuses) and high status which leaders receive (as discussed earlier in this chapter). Indeed, followers often collude in this image, looking to leaders and investing hopes and fears in the leader to be saviours or scapegoats if things go wrong (see Grint, 2010). See, for instance, the interview with Stephen Hester and consider how, in the early days of his leadership, members of RBS were looking for 'strong leadership' because there was a lot of anxiety.

This infatuation with great leaders overshadows followers. Post-heroic theory argues that leaders are nothing without the hard work, imagination, and commitment of their followers. Moreover, followers are not passive, simply responding to the behaviour of the leader, but have their own ways of thinking and acting. Followers, therefore, need to be more prominent in our attention, what Bjerke calls **followership** (1999). As Kelley states, our 'preoccupation with leadership keeps us from considering the nature and importance of followers' (1998: 143).

For an organization to be successful it needs fully engaged followers who are committed to the organization and are willing to put in extra effort on behalf of it. A post-heroic leadership style encourages collaboration and participation. It is also, according to Fletcher (2004), more 'feminine' in nature as leaders need empathy, community, vulnerability, and collaboration (Fletcher, 2004).

> **Followership** In leadership theory: (a) the importance of looking at followers and (b) the ability to follow a leader.

Real life case: followers care about their work but are not engaged

The 2007 *The Global Workforce Survey* canvassed over 90,000 followers in 18 countries and discovered some surprising results. They found employees cared a lot about their work, wanted to learn and grow, wanted stability and security, and cared about their work/life balance, but did not, generally, slack off.

They found that workers wanted to be engaged in their work and had a passion for what they did. However, only 21% were fully engaged and would 'go the extra mile' for their job. More worryingly, 38% were actually disengaged because they did not have an emotional connection with the company (Figure 12.5).

This 'engagement gap', the researchers stated, results because organizations are not tapping into the full potential of their staff or creating an energized workforce. The top driver to increased worker engagement was senior management being interested in employee well-being.

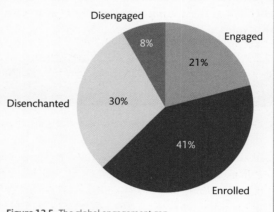

Figure 12.5 The global engagement gap.

Source: *The Global Workforce Study*, Towers Watson. © Global Workforce Study 2010, reproduced by permission of Towers Watson.

Social constructionist theory of leadership

The leader-centric position sees the leader defining and imposing their version of leadership on the followers, who are largely irrelevant to the process. The social constructionist perspective (see the Online Resource Centre for more details) challenges this view. It argues that what counts as good leadership is determined by the followers' perceptions, as well as the intentions of the leader.

Followers hold certain beliefs or expectations of what a good leader should do, and to be successful (or at least accepted) the leader needs to live up to (or potentially redefine) them. For instance, all professions have social and cultural expectations of how they should be treated and led. For example, doctors tend not to respond well to just being told what to do because part of their identity and training is tied up in being autonomous (Dent, 2003). Consequently, a leader needs to respond to these expectations to be accepted.

Acceptance is vital to be successful. While the leader can use their position in the hierarchy through rewards and sanctions, as we argued earlier, to move beyond mere obedience towards inspiring, and creating passion and zeal, the followers have to actually want to follow the leader.

Leadership is a practice

Leadership is not just something for leaders alone, but can be carried out by people throughout the organization. Many engage in acts of leadership—like an administrative assistant 'showing the ropes' to a new employee (Raelin, 2005), a shop worker solving a customer's problem, or an engineer designing a new tool to solve a problem. Everyone has the capacity to take a lead at certain points, which Raelin calls **leaderful** (2005). This perspective shifts the focus to the act of leading instead of the personal characteristics leaders embody.

Consequently, leadership is not simply done by those at the top but throughout the organization. This is particularly important in knowledge-intensive, creative, or customer service-focused industries. Traditional command and control leadership styles are less effective in these environments where everyone, to some extent, needs to take on leadership roles.

Leaderful Where everyone has the capacity to be a leader or take a lead through doing activities.

> **Theory in context:** the changing nature of society needing alternative forms of leadership
>
> Over the last 50 years there have been dramatic changes, particularly in the West, in the nature of society and the economy, which challenge traditional leadership theories. First, since the 1960s there has been a gradual loss of faith in authority figures to solve our problems. Secondly, the shift from manufacturing to the information or knowledge economy has meant that the nature of jobs has changed. Thirdly, these better-educated 'knowledge workers' desire more autonomy and use of their skills. Fourthly, there is a change in organizational structure with flatter organizations based more around teamwork.
>
> The 'knowledge worker' thus holds specialized skills meaning their ideas and input are essential for organizational success. They are employed to think rather than be told what to do. As Niall FitzGerald, Deputy Chairman of Thomson Reuters, puts it: 'the way in which the world has developed means authority is no longer to be given. It must be earned. People will only give their loyalty to those they respect – they will not give it to the position . . . You have to engage people' (Thomson and Lloyd, 2011: 31).
>
> Such shifts require different approaches to leadership. Instead of top-down, command and control leadership, this new economy requires involving the workers by getting their ideas and input. Organizational success is based on building upon the experience and knowledge of the workforce.

The question therefore emerges of how to create the right conditions to encourage and enhance the actions of organizational members. Rather than the leader standing at the front of the organization directing and controlling the passive followers, the leader's role is to create the environment in which followers can flourish.

Servant leadership (Greenleaf, 1970), also known as 'leading up' and 'connective', provides one solution to this. Greenleaf's theory argues for a more bottom-up, equal, and supportive leadership style. The leader should give priority to the needs of their followers and colleagues, aiming to serve rather than to be served. Drawing on the example of Jesus Christ, servant leadership sees the leader more as a steward of the organization than the person leading from the front. The leader takes on a more supportive role, listening to the staff, and building the community and trust within the organization.

This is a dramatic change in the model of leadership, and the leader is humble and acts to bring the best out of the employees:

> The difference manifests itself in the care taken by the servant-first to make sure that other people's highest priority needs are being served. The best test, and difficult to administer, is: Do those served grow as persons? Do they, while being served, become healthier, wiser, freer, more autonomous, more likely themselves to become servants? And, what is the effect on the least privileged in society? Will they benefit or at least not be further deprived?   (Greenleaf, 1970: 7).

Similarly, **environmental leadership** aims to cultivate a self-sustaining group where employees find gratification through the group and task. These perspectives aim to create a more egalitarian and less hierarchical culture where the relationship between the leader and follower are more collaborative in nature.

Other post-heroic leadership theories have questioned the distinction between leaders and followers as somewhat artificial (Collinson, 2005). This view sees leadership as a social practice, a *process* rather than individual characteristics. Leadership is about creating shared meaning and understanding by using symbols, forming shared language, and shaping values (see, for instance, Smircich and Morgan (1982)). The followers are seen not simply as accepting this reality but active participants in its construction.

Another key post-heroic leadership style is **distributive leadership**. This view argues that leadership does not simply follow a formal position in the hierarchy but can be seen throughout the organization. Team working, empowerment, and more participatory approaches are encouraged as they create a more inclusive, motivated, and involved workforce, utilizing everyone's skills and abilities within the organization.

Proponents of this perspective argue top-down leadership can be a source of frustration, particularly for professionals who generally desire autonomy and input into decision-making processes. By not engaging followers or using their passion, ideas and knowledge can be experienced as demotivating, particularly when they feel decisions are being imposed on them.

Rather than being tied to the formal role or position, distributive leadership works on the premise that different people can take on leadership responsibilities at different points, largely linked to their knowledge and expertise. Leadership therefore works on a rotational basis with members of the group stepping forward and leading the group when their specialism or skills demand it and then acting as normal members of the group the rest of the time. This is particularly effective in situations where other members of the group recognize that a particular individual has the knowledge to respond to that particular situation.

Servant leadership
A bottom-up perspective which sees the leader being the most effective when they support followers to enable them to do their jobs.

Environmental leadership A self-sustaining group where employees find gratification through the group and task.

Distributive leadership An approach which emphasizes that leadership can occur throughout the organization by a wide variety of organizational members.

Real life case: distributing the power and getting results

John Timpson is the CEO of Timpson, the UK-based shoe repair and key-cutting business that bears his name. He has a highly participatory form of management, which he calls upside-down management. He describes this style as giving people, who know what they are doing, the power to get on with it. He states that employers should trust their people and give them the power to work in the way that they think is best. They should listen to what the customers want and be free to act in the manner they think is necessary to achieve it. He also claims that you cannot give individual service with standardized rules. Each store can set its own prices. Devolved power means that everyone's brainpower is used. The secret of his success is getting the right people who see it more than just a job (BBC, 2009; Timpson, 2010).

Ricardo Semler was Latin American businessman of the year in 1990. He is widely heralded as leading one of the most innovative and democratic organizations in the world. Semler argues he treats Semco's 800 employees as responsible adults. Workers can set their own hours, chose their own information technology, share all information, and even set their own salary. Semco has three core values: democracy, profit-sharing, and information. Twice a year subordinates evaluate their managers and they even interview their future managers. Key decisions are made collectively via a vote. Letting people participate in decisions that affect their lives has positive effects on their motivation and morale, he claims (Semler, 1999).

Social identity theory
Drawing from psychological theory, how an individual's identity is derived from being part of a group.

The increased focus on team working and flatter organizations has shifted the role of the leader to one in which there is more emphasis on the team. Within the team ideas and skills are shared collectively and come from the team rather than solely from the leader. To make this work effectively **social identity theory** stresses the importance of followers seeing their fate tied to the group rather than simply being personal. We saw this process, which is called depersonalization, earlier in the chapter as group members shift their focus from seeing themselves as individuals to being members of the team. The leader's role in creating the right environment for the group to make this shift in outlook and identity is vital for success.

Consider, for instance, how the iPhone was created. While Steve Jobs might have had a significant input in its inception, the range of technologies, software, and features—a phone, mp3 player, email system, web browser—cannot simply be the product of one person. Indeed, for Apple to survive Jobs' death this creativity needs to be embedded and allowed to flourish throughout the organization. Modern, knowledge-based industries are therefore entirely dependent on releasing the creativity and enthusiasm of the whole organization.

Finally, in recent years, partnership working has become common-place within the public services. This view sees that to meet the needs of their service users, public agencies (such as social workers, schools, hospitals, etc.) have to work more closely together to offer what they call 'joined up services'. The role of the leader therefore changes as they are no longer leading a single organization, but have to work in partnership with others and learn to negotiate across different agendas.

Post-heroic leadership assessed

The post-heroic leadership theory has therefore sought to redress the balance that has over-emphasized the role of individual leaders at the top of the organization's hierarchy by drawing attention to the everyday practices of leadership which occur throughout it.

However, it often ignores issues of gender and race, and does little to really transform the power relations within organizations.

What do leaders actually do? Practice-based theories

Running case: Simon Chance's office

As his meeting with Effingham concludes, Chance hears a knock on the door. 'Come in, David', Chance says, showing Hunter to a seat. 'Have you heard the good news? We've got the Mayor tonight.' 'Yes, that's why I've come', responds Hunter hesitantly. 'I fear it is not good news.' 'What?', asks Chance, somewhat confused. 'Have you not heard the stories?', Hunter continues. 'The Mayor has had a falling out with City Investments.' 'Oh dear, that's one of our top potential investors', Chance responds. 'What are we going to do?'

Another challenge to post-heroic leadership is by investigating what leaders actually do in practice. Our common-sense views, which are derived from writers like Henri Fayol (see Chapter 2) and emphasized in mainstream leadership theory, present leadership and management as a rational activity conducted by heroic characters—reflecting, and having creative visions and strategies. However, as Alvesson and Sveningsson (2003) argue, in practice much of what managers and leaders actually do is mundane, and involves everyday activities, such as listening and chatting, which gains more significance because it is done by the manager.

One of the first writers to bring this to the attention of management theory was Henry Mintzberg. In a famous article in 1975, he compared the folklore (the stories of myths about managers and leaders) to what he called the fact (the actual practices). His theory is summarized in Table 12.10.

He discovered that practice is more messy, confusing, and disjointed than the idealized image presented in leadership theories. Much of leadership and management work is political (see Chapter 13) and involves dealing with competing priorities. He also found

Table 12.10 What managers really do—folklore and fact (based on Mintzberg, 1975)

Folklore	Fact
Systematic, reflective planner	Brevity, discontinuous activity, orientation to action
No regular duties, but is a coordinator and then sits back	Regular duties, such as presiding over rituals, ceremonies, and negotiations
Uses formal management information system	Does not use them but prefers verbal communication instead of documents
Management is a science	Little has really changed over the last 100 years but has become a little more scientific

that, far from the idealized reflective planner, the average day of managers he studied was characterized by brevity and discontinuity. Most of the managers surveyed 'worked without interruption for [only] a half hour or more only about once every two days'. He concluded the current system of 'managing does not breed reflective planners; managers respond to stimuli'.

More recently, a number of researchers have discovered that the overwhelming majority of decisions are taken 'on the hoof' (Chia and Holt, 2006: 643) and therefore leaders need to be 'skilled, [at] improvised in-situ coping' (Chia, 2004: 33). Holmberg and Tyrstrup (2010) argued recently that more of management and leadership activity is event driven—responding to situations rather than future-planning. Classic leadership theory of the reflective planner or heroic visionary could therefore be seen as a romanticized fantasy, as reality is far more messy and confusing (Sveningsson and Larsson, 2006).

While this might come as a disappointment to the classic fantasy view of leaders and managers, the revelation that reality is more messy and confusing can be comforting. Reflecting on Mintzberg's article some 15 years later, one manager stated that it was a relief to discover that most managers do not spend their time planning and coordinating as in the idealized image, but rather were 'keeping a lid on the chaos'.

Review questions

1. Explain the key principles behind post-heroic leadership.
2. Analyse why shifting from command-and-control to distributive leadership could increase productivity in the organization.
3. Explain why it is important to focus attention on followership.
4. Explain why the idealized view of leadership is challenged by seeing what managers actually do in practice.

Breaking the glass ceiling: leadership and gender

Real life case: women in the boardroom

In February 2012, David Cameron, the UK Prime Minister, claimed there is a 'positive link between women in leadership and business performance, so if we fail to unlock the potential of women in the labour market, we're not only failing those individuals, we're failing our whole economy'. He argued this was not only to increase equality but that there is clear evidence it would lead to improved performance and maximizing of the pool of talent. He cited Scandinavian countries as examples that the UK could learn from, where representation of females is higher (Hope, 2012).

Cameron is not the first to raise such concerns. In 2008, 17 leading businessmen wrote a letter published in *The Daily Telegraph* stating 'Women contribute to properly balanced boards . . . their participation has a beneficial impact on the character and culture of the board' (cited in Thomson and Lloyd, 2011: 25). In 2009, Deputy Leader of the Labour Party, Harriet Harman, claimed a 'balanced team of men and women makes better decisions' (Smith, 2009). She also went on to speculate that if ▶

▶ the collapsed bank of Lehman Brothers had had more female representation then their crash would have been less likely to happen. While Harman's views are hard to substantiate there appears to be some support from the conservative MPs Matthew Hancock and Nadhim Zahawi. In their book *Masters of Nothing* (Hancock and Zahawi, 2011) they argue that the male-dominated, 'testosterone-fuelled' world of finance encourages riskier, irrational behaviour that can cause 'market manias' and, ultimately, major crashes. While acknowledging it is a generalization, speaking on BBC Radio 4, they claim women 'find it a lot easier, for example, to sort of ask questions and not to dive straight in with the response'.

In 2011, a government-commissioned report *Women on Boards* (Davies, 2011) called for higher representation of women in the boardroom. The report claimed: 'Evidence suggests that companies with a strong female representation at board and top management level perform better than those without and that gender-diverse boards have a positive impact on performance' (2011: 3). Some of their key claims include:

- women 'take non-executive roles more seriously, preparing more consciously for meetings . . . ask the more awkward questions'
- more diverse boards are less likely to produce 'groupthink'
- having at least one female director reduces the chances of going bust by 20%
- more gender-balanced boards are more likely to follow guidelines when making decisions
- increasing female representation increases the talent pool.

The report recommended that by 2015 the FTSE 100 companies should aim for a minimum of 25% female representation and all chairmen of FTSE 350 companies should set out a percentage of women they aim to have on their boards by 2013 and 2015.

The report cited Norway as the prime example—it has over 44% of positions occupied by women. It was not always like this. In 2002 only 6.8% of posts were filled by women and 18% by 2005. Concerned by this, the Norwegian government drafted legislation giving companies until 2008 to meet their quota with the threat of fines, and even liquidation, if they missed them. Norway had a training programme for women, as well as well-supported childcare, a welfare state, and maternity and paternity leave. With the right pressure, things can change.

Should women be better represented in the boardroom? If they are, would boardrooms be any different? And if they should, how do we get there? Among all the issues on leadership, the role of women at senior levels remains among the most controversial. There is a clear imbalance, as in the UK women occupy 12.5% of positions in boardrooms and only 5.5% of directorships. What is more debatable is whether firms should be forced to change their practices to achieve higher proportions of women on boards (Plimmer, 2012; Hope, 2012).

Over recent years there has been some progress with women's representation growing from 5.8% in 2000 to 12.5% in 2010 (Davies, 2011). However, for many it is not fast enough. In 2008 the Equality and Human Rights Commission (2008) stated that at the current rate of change it would take until 2080 to achieve a gender-balanced boardroom.

Visit the Online Resource Centre for more statistics on the representation of women in companies.

Internationally, the UK is in a weak position with countries like Sweden, France, and Norway being far more successful (Figure 12.6).

Figure 12.6
International
comparison of
percentage of female
new appointees.

© Female FTSE Board Report
2010. Reproduced by kind
permission of Professor
Susan Vinnicombe and
Dr Ruth Sealy at Cranfield
School of Management.

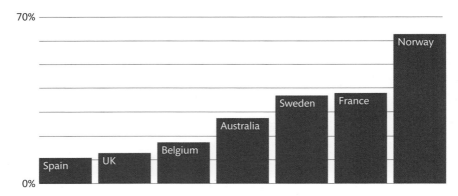

Even below the top positions, women are under-represented, resulting in a 'leaking pipeline'—a reduced supply of women to senior positions (Figure 12.7).

As a result, the number of women, and therefore the talent available, to lead large organizations is diminished.

Figure 12.7
The talent gap.

© Ioannidis, C., and Walter,
N. 2010. *Your Loss: How to
Win Back Your Female Talent,*
Aquitude Press. http://
yourlossbook.com/.

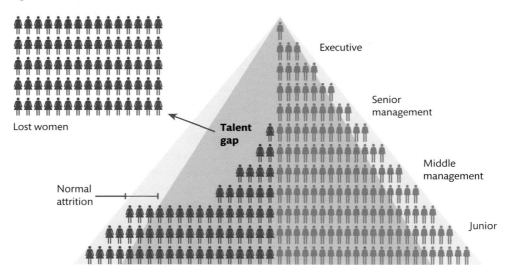

The lack of women in senior positions has long been identified as a problem and has been labelled the **glass ceiling** effect (Davidson and Cooper, 1992; Kanter, 1977), describing how most women are unable to comfortably progress beyond middle management.

Furthermore, men are able to accelerate their careers in female-dominated occupations through the **glass escalator** (Williams, 1992). Female managers, Wood and Newton (2006) have argued, have to work twice as hard to reach the top as they face many challenges within organizations and owing to their position in society, which can limit their capacity to rise up the career ladder. Men, therefore, despite considerable advances by women in junior and middle management, continue to monopolize senior positions of power and authority (Wajcman, 1998), and the women who reach senior positions exist in a male-dominated world.

The *Women in Boards* (Davies, 2011) report identifies reasons for the glass ceiling, including:

- maintaining work/life balance
- masculine culture and poor networks for women

Glass ceiling
An invisible barrier
that minority groups
(particularly women)
cannot pass through to
get to senior positions
in the organization.

Glass escalator
Occurs when men enter
female dominated
professions and glide
past them to more
senior positions.

- maternity issues/leave
- traditional bias
- lack of opportunities
- tendency to recruit men.

To deal with this situation the *Women on Boards* report put forward a number of proposals to equalize opportunities for women, including:

- mentoring and support that helps overcome some of the gender issues
- changing corporate and societal attitudes
- challenging stereotypes about male and female roles (particularly those which suggest women cannot lead)
- childcare, flexible work arrangements, career breaks, and sabbaticals
- affirmative action, creating informal support and providing senior management sponsorship
- working with head-hunters to make women more visible in the recruitment process.

Real life case: improving gender balance on French boards

Diafora are a French company that train and coach young female French managers to develop their 'power, influence, visibility and impact' to rise to the top of large organizations. With only 8% of top management positions occupied by women, Diafora believe that 'companies are better served by diverse leadership and management teams – and that mixity [a French word that means gender balance] is a proven contributor to better corporate performance, better corporate governance and more human workplaces for all'.

They help female managers better understand themselves and the political (see Chapter 13) and cultural (see Chapter 7) environment in which they work. They aim to reveal the 'hidden rules of the game and how to make women's unique qualities visible and valued. They discover a new vocabulary and behavioral style that conveys authentic leadership'.

Source: http://www.diafora-leadership.com/.

A feminine leadership style

Do women act differently on boards and is there a feminine leadership style? This is a complicated question which involves competing assumptions about human nature and also what equality means. The response to this question has also shifted over time.

In the 1970s, the women's movement sought to deny differences between the genders. For instance, Kanter (1977) stated that women can be as successful as men because they are no different. In the 1980s many began to celebrate differences arguing that more women in leadership could offer positive impacts on society and speed up changes in leadership style towards a more inclusive approach. More recent approaches have questioned the boundaries between masculine and feminine, arguing that, in practice, they are not as solid as we tend to think (Billing, 2011). Sara Louise Muhr has recently likened a successful female

Table 12.12 Differences between masculine and feminine leadership styles

Masculine leadership style	Feminine leadership style
Competitive	Collective
Power-orientated	Inclusive
Status	Common understanding
Command and control	Consensus building
Leading	Mentoring
Analytical	Intuitive
Anger when confronted by weakness	Emotionally literate and sensitive to others
Results-orientated	Nurturing
Rights and justice	Care and responsibility

leader to a cyborg: 'Companies want cyborgs in top management, not emotional human women with female leadership skills' (2011: 353).

Hekman argues that for those women that do rise to the top many are forced to adopt masculine leadership styles and to downplay their feminine side (1999). Similarly, Muhr has recently stated 'As leaders, women do not make it to the top by being caring, maternal figures, but by being cold, rational and intelligent machines' (2011: 338).

Leadership theory, as we have seen, has been constructed around a male norm (Billing and Alvesson, 2000; Fournier and Smith, 2006), written at a time when men dominated senior organizational positions, and organizations were hierarchical using command and control. This privileged the masculine leadership style. However, leadership styles are changing. The post-heroic leadership style has emphasized a more inclusive, participative, and involving style which, arguably, should favour more feminine traits (Helgeson, 1995). Feminist organizations which de-emphasize hierarchy and promote more egalitarian decision-making styles are also said to cope with more turbulent and complex environments. Indeed, Pines et al., found that feminine or democratic leadership styles can be found in both men and women (2001). Table 12.12 show a summary of these styles.

To deny the difference is to see leadership as gender neutral and downplay the significance of the limited number of women on organizational boards (and the historical privileging of men). However, to stress these differences could fall into the trap of **essentializing** gender by claiming all women (or men) are the same.

Essentialize
To make one factor indispensable.

Review questions

1. Explain some of the reasons why there is a lack of representation of women in the boardroom.
2. Analyse the consequences of this to organizations and leadership style.

Analyse

3. Do men and women lead in different ways?

Alternatives to leadership

Running case: Effingham returns to the kitchen

'OK everyone, I've just heard we have the Mayor tonight, and he's vegetarian. I want you, Toby, to start preparing another main course and Josh another starter.' Looking up he notices none of them move. 'Come on everyone!' Effingham shouts in exasperation. 'It's OK', Josh smiles, 'we knew about this one as Saffron overheard Hunter on the phone—we've already got it sorted.' Effingham looks confused. 'What's this?', he says pointing at the starter. 'It's meant to be pork.' 'But we knew the Mayor is vegetarian', Toby declares proudly. Josh pipes up confidently: 'Look we have it all under control'. Looking round the kitchen, Effingham is forced to agree.

All the theories mentioned thus far have presented organizational leadership, and with it existing hierarchies and power structures, as inevitable, and, to a certain extent, essential to the success of organizations. Theories deriving from anarchist literature, cooperative movements, and Scandinavian social theory, however, question these assumptions and argue that alternative, non-hierarchical, and non-leader-centred ways of organizing are not only possible, but are preferable. They state that worker-owned and worker-run organizations can not only produce benefits for society, but can also be more effective, creative, and motivational than traditional top-down run organizations (e.g. McAdam et al., 2005; Brown and Hosking, 1986; Reedy et al., 2012).

Such approaches are not new. The Rochdale Pioneers, founded in 1844, were one of the first cooperative organizations and many building societies started as mutual societies. In the UK today the coalition government have called for mutual societies to run public services. However, these organizations still retain the traditional command and control structures.

More radical worker-run organizations do away with formal hierarchy altogether believing that all members of the organization should be involved in decision making as it is more democratic, increases involvement, and results in better, more representative decision making. They are self-managed, built around consensus decision making, and conducted in the interest of the workers and wider society. All members of the organization have their say in how things are run and all have a share of the profits (Parker et al., 2007; Schwabenland, 2006).

This view goes beyond the participative approach of post-heroic leadership (and empowerment, which we will examine in the next chapter) as all the power resides with the members, who, on an equal basis decide how the organization is run and receive the benefits. Generally, these organizations have a social purpose and seek to make products or sell services that people need. They work on a completely different value structure, as shown in Table 12.13.

While small in number, there are many examples of this approach from manufacturing and housing cooperatives, through to youth groups. For example, Woodcraft Folk is an international youth movement based on spreading ideas of cooperation and understanding throughout the world.

One of the key aims for these groups is to change the way that organizations are run based on more democratic, participatory lines with the purpose of social progress.

Table 12.13 Differences between worker-run and shareholder-run organizations

Worker-run organizations	Shareholder management-run organizations
Cooperation	Competition
Collective decision making	Senior management make decisions
Bottom-up decision making	Top-down decision making
Individual freedom	Economic freedom
Network	Command and control
Consensus decision making	Leader decides
Self-governing	Leader governing
Workers' democracy	Share-owning democracy
Self-management	Hierarchical management
Vertical	Horizontal
Socially-driven	Shareholder-driven
Profit-sharing	Profit-driven
Self-help	Economic benefit

One group which aims to develop such an approach is called Radical Routes. They state:

> We want to see a world based on equality and co-operation, where people give according to their ability and receive according to their needs, where work is fullfilling and useful and creativity is encouraged, where decision making is open to everyone with no hierarchies, where the environment is valued and respected in its own right rather than exploited.
>
> http://www.radicalroutes.org.uk/aims-and-principles.html.

Workers take control of the means of production, how they organize themselves, and decide the aims and purposes of the organization. By getting rid of the organization's leader, who makes decisions, they work in a more cooperative, consensus-driven, and democratic manner.

Real life case: Unicorn Grocery Manchester—a food cooperative

Unicorn Grocery offers an alternative form of supermarket based in Manchester. It is run as a workers' cooperative, which means that everyone takes equal responsibility for all the decisions that impact their business, from big strategic plans to the everyday practices. To work like this they need to be able to communicate well and therefore they hold regular meetings so that everyone can know what is going on and have their say.

One of the key features of how it is run is that it is non-hierarchical, which means that there is no top management, but everyone has an equal say. Everyone gets equal pay and input in decision making. This requires them to manage themselves and each other, and requires, as they state, 'initiative, hard work, and trust!'.

They operate through consensus-based decision making. They admit this is not the quickest or most straightforward way, but does result in learning from everyone and enabling them to make 'strong, well-founded decisions upheld by a unified and active membership' that everyone feels they have a sense of ownership over.

Source: http://www.unicorn-grocery.co.uk/co-op.php.

Consensus-based approaches offer alternatives to hierarchical, management-led approaches, aiming towards a shared solution. Consensus-based approaches build on the group's knowledge and insight, founded on learning from each other, and creating a shared understanding of the problem and the solution. The aim is to get the overwhelming agreement and informed consensus, striving for everyone to say yes, but, where not possible, getting support from most of the group. The aim is for informed consent—they can live with the proposed settlement.

There is an obvious challenge in getting more people involved—many reject the potential for large-scale group discussions. However, techniques like *World Café* (Brown et al., 2005) and *Open Space Technology* (Owen, 2008) can be used to hold meetings between only a handful or a few thousand people. They allow members of the organization to propose subjects to discuss, focus on the topics that matter to them, and build consensus through conversations. They have been used for cultural change programmes, business planning, and international conferences in for-profit organizations, social enterprises, and government agencies. Supporters of these systems argue that they are more democratic, participative, and create better decisions that everyone can buy into by engaging with a much wider range of decision making.

Visit the Online Resource Centre for further discussion of these systems.

Review questions

1. Explain why worker-run organizations require different leadership styles and decision-making processes.
2. Analyse why alternative approaches would require a different attitude for everyone in the organization.

Chapter summary

Running case: the evening meal

'Well, I must say', declares the Mayor, 'that is one of the finest meals I have had in a long time. To have produced that at such short notice you must have a wonderful chef.' 'I agree', declares Steph, one of the potential investors, 'it was an individual meal, full of character and style.' Chance feels chuffed to lead Junction Hotel and is pleased to see the team pulling together.

Over the last 100 years, leadership theory has become more advanced, from considering certain individuals are born with innate natural ability to lead organizations through their charisma or strength of personality. The context the leader faces, their behaviour, and, most significantly, the impact they have on their staff has become an increasing focus of research as academics and practitioners try to understand how to lead more effectively to motivate and inspire their followers. More recently a few business leaders have been praised for handing over responsibility to their workers and creating cultures where people can put forward their own ideas.

However, in practice, despite these advances, command and control leadership style is highly prevalent, leaders are still paid substantially more than their subordinates, and often presented as heroes. Women and ethnic minorities are still under-represented at senior level and this is a trend that does not seem to be changing very quickly.

For leaders to really succeed they need to use power—this is the subject of the next chapter.

Further reading

Bass, B. M. 1985. *Leadership and performance beyond expectation*. Free Press, New York.
This is one of the most influential mainstream leadership texts exploring why certain leaders outperform others. This book was central in the establishment of the transformational view of leadership.

Grint, K. 2005. Problems, problems, problems: The social construction of 'leadership'. *Human Relations* 58(11): 1467–1494.
One of the current leading writers on leadership argues that leaders actively construct the situation that they face, proving a fascinating challenge to conventional situational leadership.

Meindl, J. R. Ehrlich, S. B., and Dukerich, J. M. 1985. The romance of leadership. *Administrative Science Quarterly* 30(1): 78–102.
This highly influential article provides a telling critique of the heroic leadership model and provides the opening to post-heroic.

Pettigrew, A., and McNulty, T. 1995. Power and influence in and around the boardroom. *Human Relations* 48(8): 845–873.
This article examines the power and influence of board members of some of the top 200 companies and asks some interesting critical questions about the influence that this elite group have.

Bibliography

Addison, P. 2011. Why Churchill lost in 1945. BBC Online. Available at: http://www.bbc.co.uk/history/worldwars/wwtwo/election_01.shtml (last accessed 30 November 2012).

Alvesson, M., and Sveningsson, S. 2003. Good visions, bad micro-management and ugly ambiguity: contradictions of (non-)leadership in a knowledge-intensive organization. *Organization Studies* 24(6): 961–988.

Badaracco, J. L. 2001. We don't need another hero. *Harvard Business Review* 79(8): 120–126.

Bass, B. M. 1985. *Leadership and performance beyond expectation*. Free Press: New York.

BBC (2009) In Business—Hell for leather (BBC Radio 4, 6 August 2009) [radio interview]. Available at: http://www.bbc.co.uk/iplayer/console/b00lvlv3 (last accessed 5 July 2012).

BBC (2011) Howard Schultz—CEO of Starbucks (BBC Radio 4, 12 May 2011) [radio interview]. Available at: http://www.bbc.co.uk/programmes/p00gwwkb (last accessed 5 July 2012).

Bennis, W., and Nanus, B. 1985. *Leaders: The strategies for taking charge*. Harper Collins: New York.

Billing, Y. (2011) Are women in management victims of the phantom of the male norm? *Gender Work and Organization* 18(3): 298–317.

Billing, Y., and Alvesson, M. 2000. Questioning the notion of feminine leadership: a critical perspective on the gender labelling of leadership. *Gender Work and Organization* 7(3): 144–157.

Bjerke, B. 1999. *Business leadership and culture: National management styles in the global economy*. Edward Elgar: Northampton, MA.

Blake, R., and Mouton, J. 1964. *The managerial grid*. Gulf: Houston, TX.

Brown, J., and Isaacs, D., World Café Community. 2005. *World Café: Shaping Our Futures Through Conversations That Matter*. Berrett-Koehler Publishers Inc.: San Francisco.

Brown, M. H., and Hosking, D. M. 1986. Distributed Leadership and Skilled Performance as Successful Organization in Social Movements. *Human Relations* 39(1): 65–79.

Bryman, A. 1986. *Leadership and organizations*. Routledge: London.

Bryman, A., Bresnen, M., Beardworth, A., and Keil, T. T. 1988. Qualitative research and the study of leadership. *Human Relations* 41(1): 13–30.

Burns, J. M. 1978. *Leadership*. Harper & Row: New York.

Calás, M., and Smircich, L. 1993. Dangerous liaisons: The feminine-in-management meets globalization. *Business Horizons* 36(2): 71–81.

Chia, R. 2004. Strategy-as-practice: Reflections on the Research Agenda. *European Management Review* 1(1): 29–34.

Chia, R., and Holt, R. 2006. Strategy as practical coping: A Heideggerian perspective. *Organization Studies* 27(5): 635–655.

Collinson, D. 2005. Questions of distance. *Leadership* 1(2): 235–250.

Cooke, B. 1999. Writing the left out of Management theory: the historiography of the management of change. *Organization* 6(1): 81–105.

The Daily Telegraph. 2012a. RBS timeline: The Fred Goodwin era. 31 January 2012. Available at: http://www.telegraph.co.uk/finance/newsbysector/banksandfinance/9052427/RBS-timeline-the-Fred-Goodwin-era.html.

The Daily Telegraph. 2012b. You can't have it both ways Mr Osborne. 8 February 2012. Available at: http://www.telegraph.co.uk/comment/telegraph-view/9069273/You-cant-have-it-both-ways-Mr-Osborne.html.

Davidson, M., and Cooper, C. 1992. *Shattering the glass ceiling: The woman manager*. Paul Chapman Publishing: London.

Davies, E. 2011. Women on Boards. Department for Business Innovation and Skills. Available at: http://www.bis.gov.uk/assets/biscore/business-law/docs/w/11-745-women-on-boards.

Davis, G., McAdam, D., Scott, R., and Zald, M. (eds). 2005. *Social Movements and Organization Theory*. Cambridge University Press: Cambridge.

Dent, M. 2003. Managing doctors and saving a hospital: Irony, rhetoric and actor–networks. *Organization* 10(1): 107–127.

Durando, J. 2010. BP's Tony Hayward: 'I'd like my life back' USA Today. 1 June 2010. Available at: http://content.usatoday.com/communities/greenhouse/post/2010/06/bp-tony-hayward-apology/1#.UJzn14beckR.

Equality and Human Rights Commission. 2008. *Sex and Power*. EHRC: Manchester.

Fiedler, F. 1967. *A theory of leadership effectiveness*. McGraw-Hill: New York.

Fiedler, F., Chemers, M. 1984. *Improving leadership effectiveness: The leader match concept*. John Wiley and Sons, Chichester.

Fletcher, J. 2004. The paradox of postheroic leadership: An essay on gender, power, and transformational change. *Leadership Quarterly* 15(5): 647–661.

Fournier, V., and Smith, W. 2006. Scripting masculinity. *Ephemera* 6(2): 141–162.

Gardner, J. 1989. *On leadership*. Free Press: New York.

Goff, S., and Jenkins, P. 2011. Sleep gets Horta-Osório up ready for action. *Financial Times*. 15 December 2011.

Available at: http://www.ft.com/cms/s/0/d50bcc36-2744-11e1-864f-00144feabdc0.html#axzz2DWQIuZUn.

Goldberg, A., and Ritter, B. 2006. Costco CEO Finds Pro-Worker Means Profitability. ABC News. Available at: http://abcnews.go.com/2020/Business/story?id=1362779#.ULJqJYYsL3V (last accessed 25 November 2012).

Greenleaf, R. K. 1970. *The servant as leader*. The Robert K. Greenleaf Center: Newton Centre, MA.

Grint, K. 2005. Problems, problems, problems: The social construction of 'leadership'. *Human Relations* 58(11): 1467–1494.

Grint, K., and Holt, C. 2011. Leading questions: If 'Total Place', 'Big Society' and local leadership are the answers: What's the question? *Leadership* 7(1): 85–98.

Groth, A. 2011. 19 amazing ways CEO Howard Schultz saved Starbucks. *Business Insider*. 19 June 2011. Available at: http://www.businessinsider.com/howard-schultz-turned-starbucks-around-2011-6?op=1.

The Guardian. 2010. BP's Tony Hayward: resignation statement. *The Guardian*. 27 July 2012. Available at: http://www.guardian.co.uk/business/2010/jul/27/bp-tony-hayward-statement.

Hancock, M., and Zahawi, N. 2011. Masters of Nothing: The Crash and how it will happen again unless we understand human nature. Biteback Publishing: London.

Haslam, A., Reicher, S., and Platow, M. 2011. *The new psychology of leadership: Identity, influence and power*. Psychology Press: Hove.

Hekman, S. 1999. *The future of differences: Truth and method in feminist theory*. Polity Press: Oxford.

Helgeson, S. 1995. *The female advantage*. Doubleday Publishing: New York.

Hersey, P., and Blanchard, K. H. 1988. *Management of organizational behaviour: Utilizing human resources*. Prentice Hall: Englewood Cliffs, NJ.

Holmberg, I., and Tyrstrup, M. 2010. Well then—what now? An everyday approach to managerial leadership. *Leadership* 6(4): 353–372.

Hope, C. Plans for women's quotas on company boards dropped. *The Daily Telegraph*. 28 May 2012. Available at: http://www.telegraph.co.uk/news/politics/9293618/Plans-for-womens-quotas-on-company-boards-dropped.html (last accessed 17 July 2012).

House, R. 1996. Path-goal theory of leadership: Lessons, legacy, and a reformulated theory. *Leadership Quarterly* 7(3): 323–352.

House, R. J., Hanges, P. W., Javidan, M., Dorfman, P., and Gupta, V. (eds) 2004. *Culture, leadership, and organizations: The GLOBE study of 62 societies*. Sage: London.

Jones, D. 2012. Fred Goodwin stripped of knighthood. *Investment Week*. 31 January 2012. Available at: http://www.investmentweek.co.uk/investment-week/news/2142732/fred-goodwin-stripped-knighthood.

Kanter, R. 1977. *Men and women of the corporation*. Basic Books: London.

Kelley, R. 1988. In praise of followers. *Harvard Business Review* 66(6): 142–148.

Kirkpatrick, S. A., and Locke, E. A. 1991. Leadership: Do traits matter? *Academy of Management Executive* 5(2): 48–60.

Kollewe, 2011. Apple stock price falls on news of Steve Jobs's death. *The Guardian*. 6 October 2011. Available at: http://www.guardian.co.uk/technology/2011/oct/06/apple-stock-steve-jobs.

Lewin, K., Lippitt, R., and White, R. 1939. Patterns of aggressive behavior in experimentally created social climates. *Journal of Social Psychology* 10: 271–301.

Longstaffe, C. 2005. Winston Churchill, a leader from history or an inspiration for the future? *Leadership; Management skills; Communication skills; Modern History* 37(2): 80–83.

Meindl, J. R., Ehrlich, S. B., and Dukerich, J. M. 1985. The romance of leadership. *Administrative Science Quarterly* 30(1): 78–102.

Mintzberg, H. 1975. The manager's job: folklore and fact. *Harvard Business Review* 53(4): 29–61.

Muhr, S. 2011. Caught in the gendered machine: On the masculine and feminine in cyborg leadership. *Gender Work in Organization* 18(3): 337–357.

Northouse, P. 2010. *Leadership: Theory and practice*. Sage: London.

Owen, H. 2008. *Open space technology: A user's guide*. Berrett-Koehler Publishers Inc.: San Francisco.

Parker, M., Fournier, V., and Reedy, P. 2007. *The Dictionary of Alternatives*. Zed Books: London.

Pillai, R., and Meindl, J. R. 1991. The impact of a performance crisis on attributions of charismatic leadership: A preliminary study. In: *Proceedings of the 1991 Eastern Academy of Management Meetings*, Hartford. CT.

Plimmer, J. 2012. Women on boards boost headhunters. Financial Times. 15 July 2012. Available at: http://www.ft.com/cms/s/0/bee544e8-ce54-11e1-bc0c-00144feabdc0.html#axzz20mlrJApK (last accessed 17 July 2012).

Pines, A. M., Dahan-Kalev, H., and Ronen, S. 2001. The influence of feminist self-definition on the democratic attitudes of managers. *Social Behavior and Personality* 29(6): 607–616.

Raelin, J. 2005. We the leaders: In order to form a leaderful organization. *Journal of Leadership and Organizational Studies* 12(2): 18–31.

Reedy, P., Coupland, C., and King, D. 2012. Freedom is an Endless Meeting: The role of alternative organizations in resisting dominant contemporary discourses of the self. 10th International Conference Discourse and Organization: Amsterdam.

Roberts, A. 2003. *Hitler and Churchill: Secrets of Leadership*. Weidenfeld & Nicolson: London.

Sabbagh, D. 2012. James Murdoch resigns as News International chairman. *The Guardian*. 29 February 2012. Available at: http://www.guardian.co.uk/media/2012/feb/29/james-murdoch-resigns-news-international-chairman.

Schultz, H. 2011. *Onward: How Starbucks fought for its life without losing its soul*. John Wiley and Sons: Chichester.

Schwabenland, C. 2006. *Stories, Visions and Values in Voluntary Organisations*. Ashgate: Farnham.

Semler, R. 1999. *Maverick! The success story behind the world's most unusual workplace*. Random House: London.

Smircich, L., and Morgan, G. 1982. Leadership: The management of meaning. *The Journal of Applied Behavioral Science* 18(3): 257–273.

Smith, J. 2009. Joan Smith: Men, power and a reality check. *The Independent*. 3 August 2009. Available at: http://www.independent.co.uk/voices/commentators/joan-smith/joan-smith-men-power-and-a-reality-check-1766577.html.

Starbucks. 2012. *Our Starbucks Mission Statement*. Available at: http://www.starbucks.com/about-us/company-information/mission-statement (last accessed 25 November 2012).

Stogdill, R. M. 1948. Personal factors associated with leadership: A survey of the literature. *Journal of Psychology* 25: 35–71.

Sveningsson, S., and Larsson, M. 2006. Fantasies of leadership: Identity work. *Leadership* 2(2): 203–224.

Thelen, H. 1992. *Research with Bion's concepts*. In: Pines, M. (ed.) *Bion and group psychotherapy*. Tavistock/Routledge: London.

Thomson, P., and Lloyd, T. 2011. *Women and the new business leadership*. Palgrave Macmillan: Basingstoke.

Timpson, J. 2010. *Upside down management: A common sense guide to better business*. John Wiley & Sons: Chichester.

Towers, W. 2008. Available at: http://www.towersperrin.com/tp/getwebcachedoc?webc=HRS/USA/2008/200803/GWS_Global_Report20072008_31208.pdf.

Wajcman, J. 1998. *Managing like a man: women and men in corporate management*. Polity Press: Cambridge.

Williams, C. 1992. The glass escalator: Hidden advantages for men in the 'female' professions. *Social Problems* 39(3): 253–267.

Wood, G., and Newton, J. 2006. Childnessness and women managers: 'choice' context and discourses. *Gender, Work & Organization* 13(4): 338–358.

Power and politics in organizations

The murky world of organizational life

Chapter overview and learning outcomes

By the end of this chapter you should be able to:

- describe the power as property view
- explain why power and politics exist within organizations
- explain why power and politics challenge the image of organizations as rational places
- explain why Lukes and Foucault believe that power shapes how people see the world
- analyse the different underlying assumptions of power as property, structure as power, and power as productive.

Key theorists

Stephen Lukes	A Marxist theorist who argues that power works in often invisible ways defining the choices that people make in ways they are often not aware of
Jeffrey Pfeffer	US management theorist who has investigated power in organizations and is a leading proponent of the power as property view
John French and Bertam Raven	US social psychologists who argue that individuals can have certain sources of power
Michel Foucault	A French historian and philosopher who presents a challenging interpretation of how power operates, seeing it as productive rather than repressive
Max Weber	A German sociologist who argued there are three categories of authority

Key terms

Power	A highly contested term but can be seen as the capacity to get things done or to influence others
Office politics	Often seen as game-playing or manipulation, but can also be seen as an essential part of organizational life
Influence	The capacity to impact others, directly or indirectly
Emancipation	Literally—freedom from slavery. To free from (often onerous) levels of control
False consciousness	A Marxist term—false beliefs held by the proletariat (workers) who do not know their true position in society as the revolutionary force to overthrow capitalism. Instead, they see the current structure of society as unchangeable and largely fair
Empowerment	To be delegated power or authority to make (some) decisions

Introduction: politics at work

Running case: Linda Wilkinson's new idea

Linda Wilkinson is excited, but nervous, about her idea of introducing a new wedding service for Junction Hotel—a new, comprehensive wedding planner, an upgrade to the bridal suite, and new themed weddings.

She has been working on the idea for weeks, building up the argument by writing a 20-page document with evidence from other hotels, and including a survey of potential clients and information that she gathered at the UK hoteliers' wedding fair.

She is sure that this will be a success and has put together what she thinks will be a convincing case that will bring Junction Hotel into the twenty-first century. All she needs to do now is convince the board.

We like to think of organizations as rational places where decisions are based on merit, follow rational and logical procedures, and are taken in the long-term interest of the organization. Everyone involved in decision making, we hope, leaves aside personal interest and works together for the common good. We also tend to believe that as individual employees we will be judged on our merits based on our hard work and performance, and get promoted or praised accordingly. In our idealized view of organizations they are meritocracies, free of power and politics.

In a recent book, Jeffery Pfeffer (2010) claims this view is a fantasy. 'Power and politics is an essential feature of organizational life. It takes more than good performance to do well in organizations', he states, 'being politically savvy and seeking power are related to career success and even managerial performance' (Pfeffer, 2010: 4). Pfeffer argues that as organizations only have one Chief Executive Officer (CEO), and other senior positions are limited, competition to get to the top can be ferocious and highly politically charged. That can result in 'Some of the individuals competing for advancement bend the rules of fair play or ignore them completely. Don't complain about this or wish the world were different', Pfeffer (2010: 4–5) counsels. 'You can compete and even triumph if you understand the principles of power and are willing to use them' (ibid: 5).

While most managers do not want to admit to being involved in political activity, their regular activities demonstrate a different reality. They include 'showing up opponents at meetings, getting access to some critical information, making a point with the boss . . . forming alliances' (Pfeffer, 1981: 369). Getting resources, such as budgets, staff members, the go-ahead for projects, or being judged as successful are all politically charged. Power and politics are also involved further down the organization, impacting who gets to choose shifts through to big issues, such as increased pay and promotion.

This chapter argues that power and politics are a central feature of organizational life. Like organizational culture, power and politics are subterranean, below the surface, often invisible, but impact everything. It reveals a shadow organization where decisions are made for alternative reasons than those officially stated. If you want to get on in organizations or understand how they work, then you need to understand power and politics.

Consider an organization that you know well, somewhere you have worked, a club or society you have been involved in, or even your family. Are there any features that you would class as political? How did you feel about this?

Often power and politics are portrayed in negative terms, as actions by manipulative individuals for personal financial or status gain. Yet, power and politics could also be seen as essential to the functioning of organizations. Take a charity worker who needs to get food to starving people in a war-torn area. She/he would need to use political skills to negotiate a safe passage for the lorries between the warring factions. It takes power to get things done.

Chapter outline

This chapter starts with defining power and politics before moving on to explore office politics in everyday situations. We will then explore three key theoretical perspectives to understand power, *power as property* (which sees power as the possession of an individual or group), *structure as power* (which sees how the social structure shapes the way people think), and *power as productive* (which examines how power operates within everyday relations between people and organizations). Finally, we will explore how some writers and managers have sought to produce more equal and balanced management practices.

Power and politics thus represent an important field of study for those interested in organizations. However, until relatively recently it did not receive much attention from organizational researchers who preferred to view organizations as rational and bureaucratic (see Chapters 2–4). As a consequence, many of the following theories did not arise from studying management, but rather came from political and social science, and, therefore, ask slightly broader questions about the way that power works in influencing society. However, as many of these writers make clear, it is in organizations that power operates and shapes how we act and behave.

Real life case: the murky world of the 2018 World Cup

In May 2011 Lord Triesman, the former chairman of the Football Association (FA) who led England's failed bid to host the 2018 World Cup football tournament, accused a number of Fédération Internationale de Football Association (FIFA) members of asking for bribes in exchange for votes. His specific allegations included a demand for a £2.5 m education centre in Trinidad with the cash channelled through FIFA's vice-president, Jack Warner; a Knighthood for Paraguay's FIFA member Leoz; and television rights to a friendly between England and the Thai national team given to Thailand's FIFA member, Makudi (Blitz, 2011; Longman, 2011; Zieger, 2011; BBC 2011a, *The Guardian*, 2011).

The allegations put the new FA chairman in a difficult position. David Bernstein made it one of his aims when taking over the chairmanship of the FA to build relations with FIFA, which had become strained by the claims. He argued that England have to work in the existing structures and try to influence things from the inside, build relationships, and understand their needs. However, with 200 FIFA members it will be hard for England to make a deep impact on their own (Wallace, 2011).

How would you advise David Bernstein to rebuild relations with FIFA? What political skills do you think he'll need?

What is power?

While the alleged offer of votes for bribes might be fairly extreme, in everyday organizational life individuals or groups regularly agree to support one group's proposal in exchange for backing their own projects. Power and politics is thus at the heart of much of organizational life.

Politics A process of game playing and tactics that occurs within organizations often where different individuals jostle with each other to gain personal advantage.

Power The capacity to get things done or to influence others.

As with many of the subjects that we cover in this book there is no single definition or even agreement as to what power and politics are. Some define **politics** as the illegitimate, unofficial or unsanctioned behaviour by those who manipulate or control decisions for their own (selfish) interest (Ferris et al., 2005), against formal authority or accepted ideology.

For other researchers **power** is actually used to overcome resistance in order to achieve the desired results (e.g. Pfeffer, 1981). According to this view, power is therefore 'the ability to get things done, to mobilize resources, to get and use whatever it is that a person needs for the goals he or she is attempting to meet' (Kanter, 1977: 166). According to this view, power is therefore *legitimate* and can be 'defined as the capacity to effect (or affect) organizational outcomes' (Mintzberg, 1983).

Does power actually need to be used in order to be classed as power? Robert Dahl believes that power exists only when it is actually used. For him, power only exists through actual actions and observable behaviour. As Henry Mintzberg has argued 'having a basis for power is not enough. The individual must act' (1983: 25). Others, though, argue that it is merely having the potential to use power that counts. For instance, a manager might only threaten to fire someone, so therefore they do not actually use their power, but the threat alone makes the employee work harder.

What is the boundary between power and influence (Figure 13.1)? Some scholars use these terms interchangeably, whereas others see influence as the legitimate activity of managers and power as the illegitimate use to gain personal ends or play the system:

Figure 13.1 Three views of power.

Official sanctioned   Unofficial unsanctioned

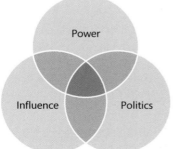

- 'A has power over B to the extent that he can get B to do something that B would not otherwise do' (Dahl, 1957)

- 'Power is the capacity of individuals to overcome resistance on the part of others, to exert their will and to produce results consistent with their interests and objectives' (Huczynski and Buchanan, 2004)

- 'can we subdue the voracious, crafty, and inescapable beast of power?' (Burns, 1978)

- 'Power is a property of the system at rest; politics is the study of power in action' (Pfeffer, 1981: 7).

Therefore, there is no single definition of power and politics as some of the terms used in the debate are used in different ways by different authors. Care should therefore be taken when assessing the different theoretical viewpoints presented.

How would you define power?

Why are there power and politics in organizations?

Running case: Effingham and Mortimer meet to discuss rumours of Linda Wilkinson's wedding plan

'Have you heard about Linda's plans for her new wedding package?', Effingham asks Mortimer. 'Yes, it's a good idea isn't it? I can really see it taking off for the hotel', Mortimer replies positively. 'You think?', scoffs Effingham. 'It's going to be bad news for the hotel. Wedding food is always dire *and* really dull to make—I don't want to be lumbered with stuffing hundreds of tuna *vol-au-vents*. And, have you thought about the hassle it will have on the rest of the hotel—discos until 1 am, drunken uncles setting off fire extinguishers, and the like.' 'Oh', replies Mortimer thoughtfully, 'I see what you mean.' 'Yep', Effingham responds confidently, 'we need to stop this.'

Why are there power and politics in organizations? The answer to this question depends on the theoretical assumptions you take (Figure 13.2).

Those from the **regulation** perspective (functionalist and interpretivist) ultimately believe that conflict is the breakdown of consensus.

The **functionalist** perspective privileges order, consensus, and harmony as it suggests organizations share collective goals (visit the Online Resource Centre). Social scientists like Parsons see power only tied to legitimate authority and therefore argue 'the threat of coercive measures, or of compulsion, without legitimation or justification, should not properly be called the use of power at all' (Lukes, 2005: 331). They believe that everyone in the organization shares the same interests and therefore see politics as the breakdown of this harmony. This perspective suggests that political activity is not productive and is a result of not understanding the reality of the situation.

Regulation The sociology of regulation looks for the sources of stability and order rather than conflict, taking consensus at face value and seeing how social order can be preserved and strengthened. In organizational behaviour this perspective emphasizes the interests of managers and shareholders.

Functionalist A highly pragmatic theoretical perspective which takes an 'objective' view of reality. It looks at the elements that promote stability and within management theory it tends to promote the interest of shareholders and managers with less attention on the potentially negative effects on employees or other stakeholders or opportunities to promote creativity or freedom.

Radical change = Conflict is inevitable

Radical humanism People have different perspectives on the world and each group has no single interest	**Radical structuralism** People have different interests, and workers' true interests are hidden by power	
Interpretivist People have different perspectives but ultimately privilege consensus	**Functionalist** Sees conflict as a breakdown of harmony	

(Subjective ... Objective)

Regulation = Conflict is a breakdown of consensus

Figure 13.2 Burrell and Morgan's sociological paradigms framework.

© *Sociological Paradigms and Organizational Analysis: Elements of the Sociology of Corporate Life*, Burrell, G., & Morgan, G. (1979), Ashgate Publishing

Interpretivist A philosophical approach which seeks to understand how people interpret and make sense of the world.

Radical change A political and theoretical approach which emphasizes the need to radically transform the social and political structure of capitalism to overcome the contradictions of capitalism.

Radical structuralist A radical change perspective which emphasizes the 'objective' contradictions of capitalism between the capitalist (shareholders and managers) and workers and society.

Radical humanist A radical change perspective which emphasizes the 'subjective' contradictions capitalism has on the consciousness of people, often outside their awareness, producing alienation and oppression.

The **interpretivist** perspective sees organizational members holding different views, but, ultimately, still seeking harmony. For these theorists most actions within the organization are bureaucratic or rational, and are, therefore, not political. Political activity is reserved for overcoming resistance: 'the conscious effort to muster and use force to overcome opposition in a choice situation' (Pfeffer, 1981: 7). This perspective would suggest that although members of an organization have different interests, ultimately they can achieve harmony by understanding each other and seeing where their common interests reside.

From the opposite perspective, those that see things through the **radical change** perspective argue that conflict is inevitable because members of the organization share different, often competing interests. While power and politics arise, in part, through personal ambition they are also about seeking to take control and shape the future direction of the organization. Power and politics are inevitable as, in order to get anything done, organizational members have to use scarce resources (time, money, equipment, etc.) and be reliant on other people (who might have different views, belief systems, or priorities). In short, this scarcity and divergent perspectives mean that in order to get things done power and politics are essential. The radical change perspective suggests that the workers and management have different objective interests and use power to further their own interests.

Those from the **radical structuralist** perspective, such as that held by Steven Lukes (see pp. 427–430), argue that power works by the broader capitalist society hiding employees' *true* interests from them. The **radical humanist** perspective takes this argument one step further by arguing that individuals do not have *true* interests. Like the interpretivists, they believe that people have different interests but do not see that this should produce consensus. Instead, they think that power works by shaping the individual's sense of identity and producing what they believe are their interests (Figure 13.3).

Figure 13.3
Power as a product of competing interests.

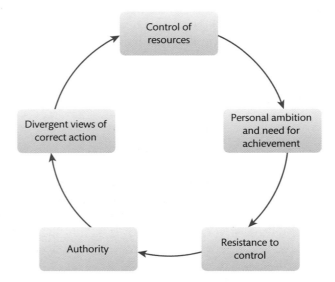

A number of authors from a psychological and philosophical perspective have argued that the need for power is a core part of human identity. Friedrich Nietzsche (1990) called this drive 'the will to power', arguing that the need to expand one's power is the ultimate driver of human actions. David McClelland argued that this drive is an essential motivating force alongside the need for achievement and belonging (1975). According to this view the need for power is seen as an essential human trait.

The individual's power

Running case: Linda turns to help

Dear Sarah

As you know, I have been working on this new wedding project for Junction Hotel, which I am very excited about. However, while it makes perfect sense on paper and is the right thing to do to make Junction Hotel more profitable, all I'm getting are negative reactions and people telling me why it won't work. Meg Mortimer says that it is going to put off our regular clients, Effingham says that he'll need a new kitchen to make it work, and David Hunter thinks that the bridal suite is going to cost too much money and thinks it will only be used at weekends.

On top of all this I seem to really have peeved Graham off as he is now spreading lies about me being incompetent when all I've tried to do is help him. Graham was the one that pushed me into this and now he's deserted me.

I'm really worried that it's going to go horribly wrong at the board meeting next week. I think I'm being stitched up and there is nothing that I can do.

Any advice? I'm feeling desperate and want to give the whole thing up.

Yours, as always

Linda

What advice would you give to Linda?

Office politics—political skills

When we think of power and politics in organizations we often think of manipulation, treacherous personalities, sucking up to the boss, and personal feuds. Stories of managers putting unrealistic pressures on the workers, people with less talent getting promoted over more worthy peers, and favouritism shown by the boss regularly fill the advice pages of the business press as employees try to grapple with a complex political landscape. The common term for this is *office politics*.

Real life case: examples of office politics in the news

- In March 2011, Don Amott resigned as chairman of Derbyshire County Cricket Club after falling out with members of the board and feeling undermined by the changes in the cricket decision-making process (BBC, 2011b).
- In 2010, Michael Geoghegan stepped down as CEO of HSBC holdings after a reported 'unprecedented bout of boardroom back-stabbing, when it became clear that he stood no chance of replacing the departing Stephen Green as HSBC chairman—a role won by the finance director, Douglas Flint' (Moore, 2010).
- Reported 'civil war' in the boardroom of Liverpool FC as owners Gillett and Hicks fall out (Ripley, 2010).
- Reported in-fighting at the board of the Rugby Football Union (Rees, 2011).

Can you think of any examples of office politics that are either in the news or that you have seen at work?

Office politics, although often presented as rife within organizations, rarely makes it into the public arena, as companies and the individuals involved do not want to discuss (or even admit) that there is a problem.

Office politics can take many forms, including being humiliated by one's boss, being subject to gossip, and being offered support that never materializes. Popular management guide books have considerable advice about how to succeed, negotiate, or just survive office politics. These include: learning the unspoken rules of the game, standing up for oneself, being seen in a positive light, being associated with a successful project, and ingratiating oneself to key people, and are all seen to be essential for office politics. Many claim that office politics is at least as important as being good at your job for career progression. Table 13.1 lists some examples and suggested solutions.

Visit the Online Resource Centre to see more examples of office politics.

Table 13.1 Office politics and suggested solutions

Examples of office politics	Suggested solutions
Regularly falling out of favour with the boss or with colleagues	Think about how you present yourself at work and how others might interpret your comments
Being the scapegoat for decisions	Build alliances with others and get a mentor
Swamped with work while a colleague slacks	Be more assertive at work and ask your colleague politely, but firmly, to take on some tasks
Having a boss that does not solve problems in a team and instead follows the line of least resistance	Do not expect the boss to be the saviour and try to tackle the problem yourself

Niccoló Machiavelli's *The Prince*

Running case: Linda gets her answer

Dear Linda

Many thanks for your letter. Your wedding plan seems a really good idea—well done for coming up with such a good initiative. It seems, though, that office politics are getting in the way of your plans. You need to accept that office politics exists and you cannot go it alone.

It sounds to me that you need to start working with the other senior members of Junction Hotel. Have a think about what is in it for them and why they would want to back your wedding scheme. Even if it is good for the hotel you need to show how it is good for them. What are the buttons you need to press to convince them that it's a good idea? Don't forget the rest of your staff as well—you will need them on board if it is going to work.

I enclose a book on dealing with office politics at work. It has some good exercises in it and advice as to how to increase your power base and personal style at work. It might be worth having a read.

Good luck and keep in touch

Sarah

Those involved in office politics are often accused of being manipulative, dishonest, controlling, cunning, and duplicitous. Such people are often labelled 'Machiavellian'. Based on Italian philosopher Niccoló Machiavelli's work *The Prince* (1532/1984), someone who is Machiavellian is seen as an unscrupulous character who stops at nothing to gain, and retain, power and influence.

Machiavelli, however, is subtler than his popular portrayal. He provided one of the earliest accounts of how power actually works in organizations. Rather than taking an idealized view (what we would like to happen) of the leaders as good people annointed by God or born with authority, Machiavelli took a realist view (a description of what really happens) of how power was actually gained (and lost) by the elite.

Machiavellian office politics.

He therefore challenged the view that leaders are necessarily good, simply because of their position (a dominant view at that time). Rather, he argued, to get to the top and maintain their power, leaders need to perform sometimes ethically questionable activities.

A key question for Machiavelli (1532/1984) is: Is it better to be loved or feared? He replied:

> The answer is that one would like to be both the one and the other; but because it is difficult to combine them, it is far safer to be feared than loved if you cannot be both.

He argued that people obey because they fear the consequences of not doing so. Therefore, the leader should use coercive power and be prepared to do evil; to produce good, sometimes the leader has to do evil. For Machiavelli, the end justifies the mean.

Real life case: Jack Welch

Between 1981 and 2001 Jack Welch was the CEO of General Electric, one of the world's largest companies. He was highly successful and named CEO of the year on numerous occasions, taking GE to the top of most of the markets it competed in. He had a relentless drive to improve shareholder value.

To achieve this outcome Welch sacked the worst-performing 10% of his staff every year. He was thus nicknamed 'Neutron Jack' because the people disappeared but the buildings were left standing.

> Welch was considered a demanding boss and was prominently listed on Fortune's list of the most difficult bosses to work for. He certainly appeared to use subordinates, if not solely as a means for his own end, then solely as a means to increase the wealth of GE shareholders.   (Bowie, 2000: 186).

Sources: O'Boyle (1998), Tichy and Stratford (1993), Bowie (2000).

Have you met someone who you would describe as Machiavellian? How would you describe them? Did they get what they want?

What do you think of Machiavelli's question—is it better to be loved or feared? Are there times when you have to do things that you think are wrong in order to get the right outcome?

Employability skills: enhance your political skills

Even if you do not want to be Machiavellian, political skills are very important to success within organizations. Consequently, it is necessary to understand what skills an individual might need in order to survive. Political skill has been defined as 'the ability to effectively understand others at work, and to use such knowledge to influence others to act in ways that enhance one's personal and/or organizational objectives' (Ferris et al., 2005: 127).

Academic articles (see Ferris et al., 2007), popular business books, newspaper columns (for instance *The Guardian*'s 'Work' section), and websites offer advice as to how to be a good political operator or just how to survive at work. Some of the overall advice is included in Table 13.2.

Table 13.2 Ways to build your political skills. Adapted from Ferris et al., 2007, www.office-politics.com, and Yeung (2009)

Political skill	Description	Example
Accept that office politics exists	Accept and understand that organizations are not meritocracies, but office politics exists and is vital for survival (and career)	Understand the political landscape and informal rules of your organization
Develop social skills	Listen to, and be sensitive to, others and adapt your ideas to fit their worldview	Have a convincing personal style that influences others and elicits the desired response from others
Networking ability	Develop diverse contacts within, and outside, the organization that are useful for personal and organizational purposes	Attach oneself to potential high-flyers and get a mentor to support your development. Go to lunch with people and for a drink after work
Appearing sincere	Appear authentic, sincere, genuine, and as though you have no ulterior motives	Make sure that you do not appear to have political motives for your actions
Political nous	Learn how things really work	Watch what is deemed acceptable and unacceptable behaviour, and the unwritten rules of what is a success
Personal characteristics	Self-confidence, self-awareness, with a strong locus of control and an outgoing and likeable personality	Have the type of personality that others want to be with and charm people
Self-promotion	Demonstrate how accomplished you are, presenting yourself, and your successes, in the best possible light	Get on flagship projects that the boss pays attention to. Appear in company newsletters, etc.
Building coalitions	Build power bases either with peers (alliances) or subordinates (empire-building)	Bring a range of people on to your side and make them feel they will benefit from your projects

Are you skilled in any of these areas and are there some that you would like to improve? From what you have read, what advice would you offer Linda Wilkinson in dealing with her situation?

Implications of office politics at work

Running case: Linda Wilkinson decides what to do

Reading Sarah's letter, Linda Wilkinson feels a little despondent. Surely she should have her ideas judged on their merits alone. But she has noticed that some members of Junction Hotel seem to get their own way far more than they should. Are they better at playing the politics, she wonders?

Certainly, she will need to get Simon Chance and the board to like the idea. This should be possible as the figures add up and it will generate good public relations for the hotel. However, she will also need the senior management team to like it. Effingham seems to have the ear of Meg Mortimer and Phil Weaver, and he seems to be against the idea. She will also need to show that she will be able to get her team to back it, otherwise it will not run smoothly. 'How do I go about this?', she wonders.

'Hi Graham, can we have a chat?', asks Wilkinson. 'Not really', responds Effingham, 'I'm busy'. 'OK', continues Wilkinson uncertainly, 'I wanted talk to you about the menu plans for the wedding proposal'. Effingham does not respond. 'Well, I think this is a great opportunity to really develop the restaurant and get us lots of new customers', continues Wilkinson, undeterred. 'You do a great job and I think the wedding service could really be the making of the restaurant.' 'Serving *vol-au-vents*', mutters Effingham. 'Not at all', replies Wilkinson, grabbing her chance. 'I think that we—well, you actually—could invent a really exciting new way of doing wedding food.' Effingham looks up. 'I mean', Wilkinson continues, 'the new wedding service is about redefining what Junction Hotel is about and the type of service we can offer. If it goes through we will all get the chance to be genuinely innovative and creative', Wilkinson continues positively, thinking about Effingham's trigger words, 'putting Junction Hotel above the rest. Look, I know you're busy now, but when you have some time I would be ever so grateful if you could give me an hour of your time to put forward some menu ideas that will make Junction Hotel really stand out.' Effingham looks up again. 'Oh, on another note', states Wilkinson, pretending it to be an afterthought, 'you know that we are meeting next week about the kitchen upgrade. A better kitchen will help make the business case for this.'

The existence of office politics alerts us to the fact that work is not always a meritocracy and decisions are sometimes made on political grounds. Organizations are, therefore, sites of contests between competing individuals (and groups) with different interests, goals, and visions of the future of the organization. Individuals and groups also have a need for power and desire to control their own futures. In short, power and politics are essential parts of organizational life.

However, the Machiavellian image of office politics tends to present political activity as a result of individual manipulation, selfishness, careerist focus, or incompetency. In particular, this view of power sees it as a result of the activity and mindset of particular individuals. Politics, therefore, is seen as a something to be downplayed or, ideally, eliminated, as it distracts the organization from making decisions that are in the interests of everyone. This perspective reduces it to the actions of individuals and ignores wider structural reasons that might produce power and politics. It is to this topic that we now turn.

Review questions

1. Define Machiavellianism.
2. Explain why office politics happens in organizations.
3. Describe some of the key strategies for dealing with office politics.

Levels of power in organizations

When we think of power in organizations we immediately think of senior members making decisions, controlling the resources, setting the organization's strategic direction, and having the possibility of hiring and firing employees. Yet, when we look a little closer we come to realize that it is not as clear-cut as this. Management, at both operational and executive

Table 13.3 Levels of power

Executive power	Management power	Worker power
Set wider operational goals	Operational decisions	Specialist knowledge that managers or co-workers do not have
Strategic direction of the company	Individual career progression	Specialist skills that make the employee valuable
Set key overall policies	Appraisals	Implement management requests
Hire and fire key management	Work allocation	Work-to-rule and go-slow, do the job poorly
Open and close key stores/factories	Set targets/pace of the machine	Withholding information
Agree major purchasing decisions (e.g. a new information technology (IT) system)	Rewards and punishment	Resist management control

level, are reliant on the workers in order to put their plans into operation. Power, therefore, could be seen as distributed across the organization rather than held in the hands of the leaders or managers (see Table 13.3).

However, while employees potentially have substantial power (e.g. withhold their labour, quit, withhold information) in comparison with managers' power (e.g. give or withhold rewards), except in times of dispute (e.g. in strikes), it could be said that they rarely use it. As Jeffery Pfeffer argues 'most of the time in most work settings the authority of the manager to direct the work activities is so legitimated and taken for granted, that issues of relative power and sanctions seldom become consciously considered' (1981: 5–6).

Equally, it could be argued that managers rarely use their power to fire employees or impact their promotion opportunities. Most of the time managerial authority is taken for granted. Therefore, while power is essentially operating in organizations, the dynamics of the labour–capital relationship (see Chapter 3) are often not visible to the participants (Figure 13.4). To understand why this is the case and how power operates in organizations, we need to explore deeper theoretical perspectives.

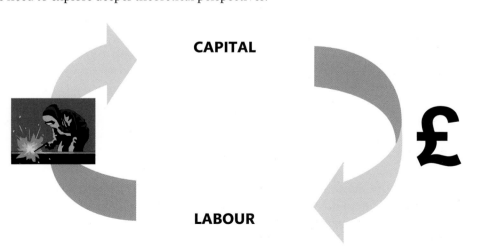

CAPITAL

LABOUR

Figure 13.4 The capitalist wage–labour relationship.

Theoretical interpretations of power

In the following section we will discuss the three main ways of looking at power:

- *power as possession*—sees power as something that is owned or possessed by individuals or groups
- *power through structure*—sees power as something that is a product of the social structure
- *power as productive*—sees power as something that produces new ways of thinking and acting, rather than a negative force which prevents action.

They each present alternative views of what power is and how it impacts organizational members. They come from different ideological viewpoints and are therefore not only different views of power, but also the type of society that they want to produce. As perspectives, they each have their strengths and weaknesses, allowing us to see different ways in which power can impact how people see and experience work.

Power as a possession

Running case: Linda Wilkinson tries convincing Effingham

'You need me', thinks Effingham as he listens to Linda Wilkinson's suggestion. 'I am the only one who can come up with ideas for the menu that will rescue the new wedding service. However, I'm liking the idea of inventing a new wedding menu—could be a good chance to experiment, though I'm not telling her yet. And, if the restaurant is busier then maybe I could use it to help boost the kitchen and get the new refit we want?'

Who has power in this situation and why? Visit the Online Resource Centre to read an analysis of the situation.

When we think about power our common-sense reaction is to think that power is something that belongs to an individual, a position (e.g. CEO), or group (e.g. human resources department) who use this power to further their own interests and get things done.

The underlying metaphor for this view of power belongs to an individual or group who use it to gain advantage over others. Consequently, Steven Lukes states, this view leads people to 'discuss its location and its extent, who has more and who less, how to gain, resist, seize, harness, secure, tame, share, spread, distribute, equalize or maximize it, how to render it more effective and how to limit or avoid its effects' (2005: 61).

So how do individuals acquire power? Jeffery Pfeffer argues it is by 'having something that someone else wants or needs, and being in control of the performance or resources so that there are few alternative sources, or no alternative sources, for obtaining what is desired' (1981: 99). This can include doing *jobs important to the organization* and having the skill to do them properly, particularly if there are few people who have that particular ability; *controlling resources*, however small, in a strategic way, to get others to be *dependent* on you; being good at *solving problems* that the organization considers important or *reduces the organization's uncertainty*; controlling information that others have; and having the ability to *control the information about alternatives* and the premise upon which decisions are made. The key underlying principle of Pfeffer's view is that power is created by having something that others need without a suitable alternative and being able to withdraw this at any given point.

Personal characteristics such as *energy and endurance*, an understanding of the political dynamics in the organization, and a willingness to use this insight all further someone's power. This is easier for those higher up as those 'with relatively more power are better able to get their perception of the problem and the environment accepted' (Pfeffer, 1981: 141).

French and Raven: bases of power

Running case: David Hunter's office

'Damn', exclaims Hunter, 'blasted printer has run out of ink again. Does anyone know where the toner is? The cupboard seems to be locked.' 'You have to call out Frank, the maintenance guy now', Meg Mortimer responds wearily. 'Effingham put a new toner in a month ago and a bit leaked out so Frank says none of us are to be trusted to do it.' 'But that's silly', Hunter responds crossly, 'we've always been able to do it before.' 'Well you can phone him and ask', responds Mortimer.

'Why should I phone him? He's only maintenance', huffs Hunter. However, compliantly, he picks up the phone. 'Hi Frank, it's David here. The printer has run out of ink and we really need it replacing.' 'Oh', responds Frank gruffly, 'no can do. I've got this shower to mend in room 17 and then there is that toilet in room 12. After that I have the curtain rail in room 10.' 'Can't they wait?', Hunter replies exasperatedly, 'I've got to print this to give to Chance in an hour! Can't you just give me the key?'. 'Look we can't afford for another error with the printer again', Frank responds, 'I've had the training and the engineer said I am the only one who can change the printer toner or it will invalidate the warranty.'

Who has the power in this situation? Is that power reflected in their positions in the hierarchy?

Another view that sees power as possession was developed by John French and Bertram Raven (1958), who explore the sources or, as they put it, the 'bases of power' that individuals can hold. Although, they state, there can be many, there are five common sources that are seen across most organizations, which are described in Table 13.4.

While, in this model, the power is possessed by particular individuals, for it to be effective what really matters is if the powerless person perceives the powerful person has power. For instance, it does not matter if the leader actually has the power so long as the follower believes that they do. The strength of the power base is dependent on the extent to which the follower desires the item on offer. A threat to sack someone will hold far less sway over an employee who does not really want the job and believes that they will have better job prospects elsewhere.

The follower's perception is produced mainly by two things. First, the follower's upbringing and socialization shapes the way that they perceive the power base. For instance,

Table 13.4 French and Raven's five bases of power (based on French & Raven, 1958)

	Type	Description	Example
Hierarchical	Legitimate	The extent to which an individual is socialized and has internalized the belief that certain groups (e.g. managers) have a legitimate right to command. This belief is set by cultural values and acceptance of current social structure	You respond to a request because it is a manager telling you rather than because you think it is a good idea
	Reward	Extent to which an individual can use rewards from the organization. The employee must desire the reward in order for it to work. If they do not want the reward it will have no sway over them	You take on a task because you believe that you will get a promotion out of it
	Coercive	Perception that one's boss has the power to punish. This can be strong punishments, such as sacking, through to more symbolic forms such as withdrawing positive interaction. The more legitimate this approach the more it will be accepted	You aim to hit your sales targets because they are part of your appraisal and you do not want to fail
Personal	Expert	Knowledge that another person needs, but does not have. For instance, following a lawyer's advice as to whether an advertising campaign is legal. What is essential for it to be valid is that the recipient trusts the advice of the giver	You require an IT specialist in order to fix your computer
	Referent	To be the type of person that others want to emulate. Be friendly/supportive towards others	A colleague you want to emulate asks you to take on a task which you do not want to do but, because you want to emulate them, you do it anyway

some followers will believe that the management have an automatic right to lead and will accept their authority unquestioningly, whereas others will believe that the leaders need to earn this right or even be hostile to leaders. This perception is a product of socialization, such as the follower's schooling, previous experiences, and the wider culture they are a part of. For instance, in the 1950s, when French and Raven were writing, authority was accepted more readily than it is today. Secondly, this perception is dynamic and changes over time based on experience of the actions of an individual. Therefore, if a person uses expert power, but is proved to be wrong on a number of occasions, this form of power will diminish over time.

The basis of power can also be divided up into that which is hierarchical, derived from the leader's position in the organization, and that which is more influenced by the perception of personal skills and characteristics. Therefore, while someone can be senior in the organization, if they lack the skill or knowledge the 'expert holds', then they can be beholden to that person.

Weber's three ideal types of authority

Our final individualistic view on power is developed by Max Weber (2004) (whose views on bureaucracy we saw in Chapter 3). He argued there are three ideal types of authority.

- Charismatic—based on a heroic leader (see pp. 378–381) where people unquestioningly follow the leader. One of the problems with this type is that it relies on a single leader for its survival. The followers also become subservient.
- Traditional—based on tradition or custom. The leader holds their authority based on the status they are given or inherited (such as the monarchy).
- Rational–legal—based on formalized laws and regulation, and is akin to bureaucracy. Weber saw this form as superior as it does not rely on the charisma of a single leader or the unquestioning following of tradition.

Therefore, while bureaucracy sometimes has a bad reputation, Weber considered that well-constructed rules can produce the best form of authority.

Power is property assessed

While the perspective that power is the property of an individual or group is intuitively appealing, it does suffer from some key problems. First, it tends to individualize power—seeing it as something that is solely in the possession of an individual or group. Power is therefore considered a zero-sum game, where some people have power (often the managers) and others do not. In reality, power is not something that an individual holds nor is there a fixed quantity of it. Secondly, this perspective ignores more societal reasons for why people think how they do. Although French and Raven describe how individuals are socialized into seeing the world in a particular way, this view of power downplays issues such as gender and the labour–capital divide, which others, such as Steven Lukes, feel is essential. It is to this perspective that we now turn.

Review questions

1. Explain the key principles of the power as possession perspective.
2. Describe French and Raven's five bases of power.

Power as structure: Steven Lukes's three dimensions of power

In 1974 Steven Lukes, a Marxist political scientist, wrote a highly influential account of power (republished and updated in a second edition in 2005). He aimed to offer a more comprehensive view of how power operates—offering three dimensions or faces of power. Drawing on Marxist theory, Lukes was particularly interested in asking why do the powerful, i.e. managers or leaders, achieve compliance by the less powerful, i.e. the workers? The first two dimensions, he concluded, were inadequate in answering this question and, therefore, the third dimension offered a deeper understanding of how power operates in practice.

Dimension 1 is direct observable conflict and still sees power as a possession. This perspective draws from the political theorist Robert Dahl, who defined power as: 'A has power over

B to the extent that he can get B to do something that B would not otherwise do'. Dahl (1957: 202–3) focused on decision making by the US political elite and provided one of the first rigorous explorations of how power works in practice. For Dahl 'who[ever] prevails in decision making [provides] the best way to determine which individuals and groups have more power' (1958: 4, cited in Lukes, 2005: 18). Dahl, who had a pluralist outlook, saw different groups having preferences which can lead to conflict when they clash. Dahl argued the one who comes out on top has the power. While Dahl believed power can occur even when no opposition appears, his methods and assumptions only focus on overt, observable behaviour and, therefore, when there is actual, visible conflict.

Dimension 1 assessed: the advantage of dimension one is that it focuses on the actual processes involved in decision making. However, according to Lukes, this perspective is too narrow as it only focuses on observable aspects of power and ignores many covert, less observable aspects. This aspect is examined by dimension two.

Dimension 2 sees power as the ability to set what can or cannot be spoken about—what Lukes calls behind-the-scenes agenda setting. Those with power limit the range of topics that can be discussed and, by doing so, keep certain controversial issues 'off limits'. This gives them power as certain things, such as pay for employees, incompetence by a manager, or a proposal by a competing group, are not spoken about, and therefore cannot be decided upon. Leading supporters of this view, Bachrach and Baratz, state a person or group has power to the extent he or she 'consciously or unconsciously—creates or reinforces barriers to the public airing of policy conflicts' (1970: 8, cited in Lukes, 2005: 6). Dimension 2 thus broadens the definition of power away from purely observable conflict to non-decision processes where the powerful can ignore the grievances of the less powerful.

Real life case: limiting the agenda—the Hutton Inquiry

After the second Iraq war, Tony Blair's government set up the Hutton Inquiry into the death of the government scientist Dr David Kelly. Many criticized this inquiry, arguing that they limited the scope of decision making to a far too narrow remit and therefore did not examine fairly the real reasons behind the war or Dr Kelly's death. This could be seen as a classic example of keeping certain controversial issues off the agenda.

Sources: Wheeler (2006); Runciman (2004); *The Daily Telegraph* (2003).

How did the government keep certain issues off the agenda? Can you think of any examples you have seen in organizations where someone more powerful has kept issues off the agenda?

Dimension 2 assessed: This view of power is more subtle and demonstrates a deeper understanding of how power actually operates in practice. Power can be covert (concealed), allowing the powerful to maintain their position through establishing the 'rules of the game' that privilege certain groups at the expense of others. However, it still assumes that if there is no conflict or grievance then there is consensus and therefore no use of power. According to Bachrach and Baratz 'if there is no conflict, overt or covert, the presumption must be that there is consensus on the prevailing allocation of values, in which case non-decision-making is impossible' (1970: 49, cited in Lukes, 2005: 23).

Dimension 3 states that power not only shapes our behaviours, but also our desires and beliefs. Therefore, while it might appear that there is consensus or certain individuals and groups have no grievances, dimension 3 argues that this gives a false perception of harmony. Workers, owing to their position in the capitalist working relationship, are often not conscious of their *true* interests and therefore this conflict between labour and capital (the workers and managers) rarely materializes. It remains latent—present but rarely visible.

Dimension 3 assessed: this dimension goes beyond behaviouralism (Lukes, 2005) as it argues that just because you cannot observe the conflict it does not mean it does not exist. Rather the powerful (i.e. management) influence, shape, or determine the very wants of the less powerful (i.e. workers), distracting them from their true interests. The conflict, therefore, does not materialize (become visible) because the workers have been socialized (taught) to believe that they do not have different interests. This is achieved through processes of socialization, such as schooling, company induction programmes, and wider culture, where the worker is taught to see their interests as the same as the organization's. To quote Karl Marx (1859/2012: 11–12): 'It is not the consciousness of men that determines their existence, but, on the contrary, their social existence determines their consciousness' (*A Contribution to the Critique of Political Economy*). In other words, how people see the world (their consciousness) is shaped by the society in which they live and its values, a process influenced by economic interests of the powerful. Consequently, according to Lukes (2005), not only do workers not know that they are oppressed, but they enthusiastically participate in their own oppression.

For further information on Lukes' three dimensions see the Online Resource Centre.

⊸○ Running case: Linda Wilkinson meets her team in the dining room

Having spoken to Effingham, Linda Wilkinson decides that she needs to get her team on board.

'As you know, we are developing this exciting new wedding package which will provide lots of great opportunities for Junction Hotel with more weddings, the new bridal suite, and a new exciting menu with the big, sit down meal in the evening. Now, as you might have heard, some of the board are sceptical about this and I need to be able to convince them at next week's board meeting. I want to know that I have your backing. We are all in this together. If it goes well then we will all benefit. It will really put Junction Hotel on the map. There will be a lot more shifts, working 12–3 pm to prepare for the wedding and then 5–11 pm for the evening function. We will have new uniforms and will be doing silver service. I think we can make Junction Hotel a really special place for people's special day, but I need your support.'

Are the *true* interests of the workers being served by this deal?

Power as structure assessed

Lukes's theory is helpful because he alerts us to the often invisible processes of power within organizations, providing a compelling explanation of how the more powerful can gain compliance over the less powerful (Figure 13.5). He thus moves power beyond individualistic power to explore the wider structural aspects.

As with any Marxist (radical structuralist) analysis of its type, Lukes believes employees suffer from 'false consciousness'. This creates a state of mind where workers do not recognize their 'true' interests, oppression, and exploitation because they get distracted by everyday issues. Workers are thus unable to think of alternative ways of doing things

Figure 13.5 Lukes's (2005) three levels of power.

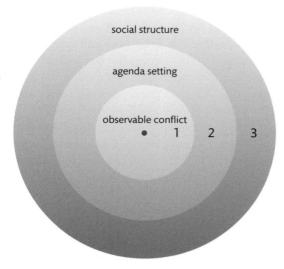

social structure

agenda setting

observable conflict
•   1   2   3

(i.e. self-management) because they are socialized into believing the current way society runs is fixed (management-led organizations).

However, this view is based on the assumption that employees, collectively, have 'true' interests which they are not aware of, but, presumably, the Marxist theoretician is. Many, particularly from the post-structuralist viewpoint, have argued that there is no universal interest that all employees share and the Marxist theorist in not necessarily better placed to identify what these interests are. As a response in the more recent edition, Lukes recognizes that he implied that everyone of a particular class has the same interest, whereas he now argues that workers have multiple, and sometimes contradictory, interests and needs.

Have you ever considered the alternatives to capitalism in depth?

Review questions

1. Explain why Lukes considers the first two dimensions inadequate.
2. Explain why he considers the third dimension to capture the true nature of power.

Analyse

3. Do workers really know their true interests?

Power as productive: French philosopher Michel Foucault

Running case: Linda Wilkinson plans her next steps

Linda Wilkinson sits down to read the book Sarah sent her on gaining power at work. She completes the self-diagnostic test and decides that she needs to be more confident and assertive. She is excited by the possibilities that this offers, but is still scared of tackling Effingham. That will be a real test of the new, confident Linda.

She finds an assertiveness quiz online and starts to work through the program. Her results show that she is quite assertive, but not as much as she could be. Looking at these results she starts to read more on assertiveness training. Breath deeply, relax, don't apologize for having an opinion . . . 'This is going to be good', she thinks to herself.

Visit the Online Resource Centre to try the assertiveness quiz. How do you feel about completing it?

In his most recent edition of *Power: A radical view*, Lukes argues that Michel Foucault's work is the fourth dimension of power (Lukes, 2005). Foucault was a French philosopher and historian who aimed to rethink our assumptions about how power operates. In doing so he provides a radical departure from the theorists discussed previously in this chapter. His views on power, however, are complex and he never came up with a full theory of power. Rather, his views are general in theme and are presented in Table 13.5.

Foucault (1977) asks us to think about power and how it operates in a markedly different manner to traditional perspectives. Power is not something that one group possesses and which forces others to do things against their own interests. Rather, for Foucault, power is a creative, positive force that brings certain ways of thinking and behaving into being and, through that, introduces a new reality. He offers this view as a result of three key theoretical perspectives.

- *Power/knowledge*—for Foucault, knowledge is intertwined with power. He argued the 'human sciences', like sociology and psychology (which feature heavily as the underpinnings of

Table 13.5 Foucault's reconceptualization of power (drawn from Foucault 1981 and 1971)

Classic view	Foucault's view
Power is a repressive, coercive, controlling, authoritarian force	Power is also productive and creative. It produces new knowledge and behaviours, and, through this, new realities
Power forces people to do things that they do not want to do	Power also works in a positive fashion by guiding individuals, giving them choices, shaping how they see things, and their identity
Power is a property, a thing that certain groups possess	Power has no essence—it is not a thing that one group possesses and other (weaker) groups do not possess. Rather, for Foucault, power is relational—it exists in the relationship between people and only when it is exercised (i.e. used)
Power is top-down, possessed by an elite and held over the powerless (such as the workers)	Power also is bottom-up. Rather than possessed by a small elite, for Foucault, power is everywhere—it is like a net, a system of relations spread throughout society. It is also constantly shifting. One group does not always hold it—it changes over time
Power crushes resistance	Where there is power there is resistance. Resistance for Foucault is the production of alternative discourses. If there is no possibility of resistance then there is no power as this is domination
Control through direct repression	Control through invisible strategies of normalization
Knowledge is seen as either objective and disinterested—it does not take sides (mainstream view)—or emancipatory (critical view), freeing people from power	Knowledge is linked fundamentally to power. New knowledge (such as sociology) produces new techniques of power. Foucault used the phrase power/knowledge to indicate this link
Individuals or groups have true interests that exist outside of power	Who we think we are—our identity—is a product of knowledge and of power. Power is everywhere and in all relations with people
Asks who has power, and how they gain and maintain their position, and use or abuse power	Investigates specific techniques and practices through which power operates

many of the theories in this book (see Chapter 1), produce new techniques of power. For instance, psychology creates personality tests used in recruitment and selection, and Belbin's teamwork framework (see Chapter 6). These techniques are powerful, not only by helping management, but also, they claim, in enabling us to discover the truth about ourselves. Knowledge, therefore, for Foucault, cannot be thought of as a neutral technique, but is linked fundamentally to power. This extends the investigation of power to the role that knowledge plays in how we understand ourselves at work.

- *Power-relations*—for Foucault (1981), power exists in relations between people and occurs when it is exercised (used). He sees power as a relationship where both sides have some power and each person has some choice in what they do. Therefore, for Foucault, there must always be the opportunity for **resistance**, otherwise it is domination.

  For example, a manager might ask one of their team to write a report which is additional to their existing workload. The employee has a number of options, including completely ignoring the request, doing it very slowly, or not writing it in the way the manager would like. The important point here is that both the employee and the manager have a range of options available to them and therefore power is more a relationship than a one-way process. The employee can always resist the manager's request.

- *Disciplinary power and normalization* provides the third area where Foucault (1977) rethought power. Disciplinary power operates through hierarchical observation, normalizing judgement, and examination—observing people, judging them against a series of norms, standards and values, which separates the normal from abnormal. These norms provide the standards by which we learn to judge ourselves. We do this in many areas of life from 'levels'—we judge ourselves at school and compare averages for height and weight, such as the Body Mass Index (BMI), through to sales targets that workers judge themselves by. Power through normalization is often not conducted in a domineering or controlling manner. Rather, it can be experienced as positive in that we decide how to engage with it. For instance the 'five-a-day' campaign to get people eating more fruit and vegetables encourages people to eat more healthily, while failing to eat healthy is seen as a moral failure for which the individual is blamed. This form of power is invisible as we tend to treat these norms as unquestionable facts, designed by experts for our own good. Foucault's view reveals how power shapes seemingly neutral everyday practices that are missed by other approaches.

We can see all three of these accounts of power at work in Foucault's most famous book, *Discipline and Punish* (1977). This book examines the history of prison and starts with a graphic scene of the botched torture and execution of 'Damiens the regicide'. Foucault describes how this criminal was placed on a scaffold, his 'flesh torn from his breasts, arms, tights and calves with red-hot pincers . . . [and] his body drawn and quartered by four horses and his limbs and body consumed by fire' (1977: 3). Ultimately, six horses were needed to pull Damiens apart and still the executioner struggled to tear his limbs off him, requiring the executioner to cut his limbs off.

Foucault then presents a description of a criminal who is being reformed, which takes place a mere eight years later. His day includes getting up at 6 am, working for 9 hours, and receiving 2 hours of schooling (reading, writing, drawing and arithmetic, and then listening to an instructional text). The aim of this style of punishment is to reform the prisoner, i.e. to make them a better person.

Resistance Drawn from critical theory, where marginalized and oppressed groups (such as workers and minorities) resist the aims and requests of more powerful groups, such as management.

When thinking about the form of power in the two accounts of the prisoners our initial reaction is that the first one is brutal and the second is more humane. These cases provided not only two different styles of punishment, but also two types of power—the public (force) and the timetable (reform). However, Foucault questions the view that the second is better. He argues that while the first prisoner had violence (and power) directed on the body, the second has this internalized on him, with the punishers seeking to control the values and the beliefs of the prisoner; in short, their soul. The second form of power is a key example of what Foucault called disciplinary power, which was most evident in his discussion of the Panopticon.

Visit the Online Resource Centre for pictures of the Panopticon.

The Panopticon (which literally means all-seeing-eye) was a prison devised by English philosopher and social theorist Jeremy Bentham (see Chapter 4) for the purposes of reforming the prisoner in a cost-effective manner. It achieved a high level of efficiency as in the centre of the prison stood the prison guard who could see into every prison cell at all times. In theory, therefore, it only required one prison guard who could watch all the prisoners at one time. This was achieved because the prisoner was unable to tell if they were being watched and therefore had to always assume that they were. There are two key implications for this.

First, this image of the Panopticon has been used to make the claim that a key area of modern power is through **surveillance**. The power of the Panopticon was that the prisoner never knew if they were being watched and therefore they had to act in the right way at all times. It is therefore used to render (make) visible key aspects of someone's behaviour. A modern example of this is the call centre, where all of the call-centre operatives are monitored constantly for things like their call length and success rates, through to the time taken between calls and even toilet breaks. They can also be listened into at any stage of their call, meaning that they always need to perform because they never know when they might be being heard. Similarly, shop workers can be investigated by mystery shoppers who judge whether they are smiling at the right point (see Chapter 16). Even university lecturers are now increasingly subject to surveillance practices like student feedback and evaluation surveys, or fellow staff members watching a lecture or seminar.

> **Surveillance** The observation, either overt or covert, of people to gain information about them or to exert order and control over them.

The second key development of this form of power is how it is used to reform the prisoner through a series of routines and practices in order to make them a better person. Seemingly everyday practices, such as timetables, filling in forms, or types of training, are used to change the prisoner in how they understand themselves and the way that they act. This form of power is at its strongest when it is internalized by the prisoner as a form of **self-discipline**. Rather than forcing them to change through coercive force, reform and self-discipline is used to train the prisoner to change their behaviour and become a better person. A series of experts (social workers, probation officers, mentors, etc.) work with the prisoner to transform themselves. It works best where the prisoner wants to become a better person. This occurs when the prisoners internalize the power and monitor themselves against these particular standards. In this sense discipline does not just mean punishment, but comes from the Latin and means training to produce a specific character or pattern of behaviour, particularly a form of training that produces moral or mental improvement.

> **Self-discipline** The process by which an individual trains and controls themselves usually for the purposes of self-improvement .

This form of self-discipline is often seen as essential for those who want to be successful. For instance, a successful boxer needs to follow a strict timetable, with set times for exercise and rest, needs to eat particular types of food, and avoid certain activities. They will follow the advice of experts (trainers, nutritionists, psychologists) and work on particular areas of physical and mental development (power/knowledge). By following this regime and being self-disciplined (discipline and normalization) the boxer is able to develop certain capabilities and skills, and is moulded into becoming a particular type of person. However, they are also limiting the development of other skills and outlooks. By going through this training the boxer is transformed and could, arguably, become a different person. Power therefore works in a positive way—creating a new type of person—but it also stops other possibilities that the individual could develop.

Study skills: the power of university

Going to university to gain your degree is another example of this form of self-discipline. By going to university, studying the subjects that you do, and meeting new people, many claim university changes who they are—that they come out as someone not necessarily recognizable from the person that went in. Part of this will involve reading certain texts and debating particular ideas that might change the way that you think. To do well will also mean having to train yourself to go to the library regularly, turn up to

Self-discipline.

9 am lectures, read around the subject, plan your assignments, and do your work on time. It is likely that you will not have someone watching over you telling you what to do; rather, you will have internalized the power and disciplined yourself. This form of power should not necessarily be seen as something oppressive—forcing you to do work against your will. Rather, you may begin to identify yourself as a different person who studies hard to get good grades.

At work this form of power operates on us through processes, such as training, appraisal, and management development. The power of normalization is most evident in appraisal systems where employees are asked to, 'confess' their strengths and weaknesses, and judge themselves against a series of categories of what is considered normal behaviour. In particular, they are asked to define areas they do well in and those that require development. They are then made responsible for their own improvement by putting themselves forward for development. In this sense employees engage in their own self-surveillance, judging themselves against these set categories (power/knowledge) with the view to self-improvement. Employees, therefore, act as their own overseers—they monitor and judge themselves against particular norms, often with the view to self-improvement (Townley, 1994).

The same argument could be made about management. We might find some of the techniques used by Taylorism controlling, oppressive, at times brutal, and often dehumanizing (see Chapter 3). However, workers are not expected to actually believe in the cause of the organization. In contrast, the so-called more humane developments of the human relations school (see Chapter 5) appear more sympathetic to the interests of the staff, as people feel that they belong. However, through Foucault's reading of power they are actually more controlled. Through processes such as teamwork, motivation, and culture, workers are expected to act as though they believe in the purpose of the organization, and want to progress and develop themselves into better forms of employees. Employees are more controlled because they believe in the organization and therefore have no possibility to resist it.

Therefore, like Lukes, Foucault argued that people actively participate in practices which involve invisible power. However, unlike Lukes, Foucault does not necessarily see this form of power as coercion—forcing people into changes against their will. Rather, they participate actively in practices which result in them being new types of people. The question is: Do we like the people that we have become?

The power as productive view assessed

Running case: Linda Wilkinson reviews her progress with Sarah

Linda Wilkinson decides to phone Sarah. 'Hi Sarah, it's Linda. Is now a good time to talk?'. 'Sure', Sarah replies. 'I have ten minutes before my next appointment, but, until then, I'm all yours. How was the book?'. 'Brilliant . . .', enthuses Linda, 'amazing. It really made me think—I feel like a new me!'. 'That's great, replies Sarah. 'It works, doesn't it?' 'Yes,' acknowledges Linda, 'I did the assertiveness quiz you recommended and I came out OK, but not that strong, so I started work on those exercises and have changed the way that I speak to people. I'm much more direct, but not aggressive. I learned those phrases and I'm using them all the time.' 'How have people reacted to you?', asks Sarah. 'I'm amazed . . . really differently. Effingham . . .' replies Linda. 'The bully guy?', Sarah interjects. 'Yes, him', answers Linda, 'well, I stood up to him yesterday and asked, I mean I requested, him to deliver the new menu for the weddings by midday. And guess what? He did it!'. 'Fantastic!', exclaims Sarah. 'Yes, it is,' continues Linda. 'I feel like a different person. I've still got work to do and I'm working through the exercises, but I feel transformed.'

According to Foucault, how might power/knowledge, power-relations, and normalization be occurring in this case?

While Foucault has produced a powerful re-reading of power, his theories have been criticized for a number of reasons. First, because Foucault sees power everywhere critics (e.g. McNay, 1994; Thompson and Ackroyd, 1995), have argued that he considers there is no escape from it. Foucault, they claim, presents a world of complete domination without the hope for a better world and therefore creates despair. Secondly, Foucault's theory seems to discount human agency (i.e. the capacity of individuals to exist independently of the social structure). There is little account in Foucault's theory for those that can resist power. Finally, because Foucault does not offer a set of values by which to judge the use of power, many have questioned the political benefits of his work. Without a clear set of values to judge power, Foucault's critics argue that he does not give us the capacity to resist (e.g. Callaghan and Thompson, 2001).

Review questions

1. Describe what is meant by the term Panopticon.
2. Explain the principles of Foucault's view on power.
3. Analyse why Foucault sees power as productive rather than repressive.

Obedience to authority

Would you electrically shock someone just because a scientist told you to? The infamous experiment by Stanley Milgram (1974) predicts that you probably would. Conducted in 1961, in what remains one of the most controversial experiments in history, Milgram devised a scientific study of obedience to authority. He wanted to find out whether normal, law-abiding citizens would give a lethal electric shock because they were following authority. He discovered almost two thirds of people would.

The participants were university students who thought they were taking part in a study of memory and learning, and received a small payment for their participation. When they joined they were met by a scientist and another 'volunteer' (who actually worked for the experiment), and were told they were studying the effects of punishment on learning (a behaviourist approach). They drew lots, with one person acting as the learner who would receive shocks and the other as the teacher who applied the shocks. While it appeared random it was actually a fix so the person who had the experiment done to them ended up as a teacher.

The teacher then saw the learner strapped to an electric shock device and the generator, which had power up to 450 volts. They were then told that the learner had been given a list of word-pairs to memorize. Whenever they got it wrong they had to administer electric shocks, which were small at first, starting at 15 V. Every time the learner made a mistake they were increased, all the way up to 450 V (which is twice the household level). When they administered the shock they could hear what they thought was the learner (but what was actually a tape recording) shouting things like 'I cannot go on'. Two thirds continued to do this past the switch marked 'fatal'.

The results shocked Milgram. Indeed, before the experiment all the psychiatrists that Milgram questioned stated most people would stop early. The results were disturbing, as most people gave an electric shock of 450 V. Why did they do it? The answer, for Milgram, lay in their acceptance of authority. After a while the screams became very loud and the teacher would often voice their concerns that they were harming the learner, but, usually, the scientist would reassure them that they were not doing any real harm or simply say 'the experiment requires it'. It was not that they were uncaring; indeed, many of the experimenters voiced concerns, but they were willing to obey the commands of the scientist over their own judgement.

Another experiment which revealed how people respond to authority was Zimbardo's prison experiment. Zimbardo wanted to test good people versus an evil situation. Unfortunately, he found that the unpleasant situation won (Zimbardo, 2007).

Zimbardo set up a mock jail and selected twenty-one normal, healthy, and emotionally stable men and placed them into two groups: ten as prisoners and eleven as guards. The guards wore uniforms, including special glasses to prevent eye contact. Unexpectedly, the prisoners were picked up from home, put in a police car, finger-printed, blindfolded, placed in prison uniforms, and had nylons put on their head to give the appearance of baldness. They were also given identification numbers instead of names.

After only six days into the fourteen-day experiment, it was abandoned. The relationship between the guards and the prisoners was vicious, with the guards using their power in sadistic ways, developing techniques to break the prisoners, and making them feel worthless. They wanted to show their power over the prisoners. The prisoners felt dehumanized and some even had breakdowns. They also accepted their roles. When their appeals for parole were turned down they merely returned to their cells, seemingly accepting their role and identity as prisoners.

Zimbardo's experiment further questioned the impact of power and authority. Merely being given the label prisoner or guard shaped the way individuals behaved, demonstrating the power of the social environment (in this case the prison) on individual behaviour, and even on Zimbardo himself, as running the experiment pushed his power too far by allowing the experiment to continue beyond what was acceptable (2007).

Both these experiments show (as well as the insights of Zygmunt Bauman, 1989) the potentially dangerous effects of people following authority unquestioningly. Instead of using their own judgement, people regularly defer to authority figures (Milgram, 1974), who, when in this position, can abuse their power (Zimbardo, 2007) or simply say they are following the rules (Bauman, 1989). Critical theorists therefore look for less hierarchical and more empowering organizations.

Empowering workers

Running case: numbers are short for the bar

Mark, the bar supervisor, needs to find someone to work tonight's shift as the other staff are unavailable. Mark knows that Carole never wants to work on Tuesday evenings as it is her salsa dancing night and she is training for a competition; however, he gives her a call.

'Hi Carole, it's Mark. Look I know it is short notice but I really need you to come in tonight. Sue has just phoned in sick and Jim is away at the moment.' 'But Mark', Carole huffs, 'you know I can never work Tuesdays, it's my one night out to enjoy myself.' 'Yes, I know', Mark butts in anxiously, 'but I really need you this once. Please do this for me.' 'Go on then', Carole relents, 'as it's you, but you can't let this happen again.'

How could Mark be more empowered in this situation? What do you think will be the consequences of this?

So far in this chapter we have focused on how people gain and use power in organizations. However, many workers feel powerless and unable to make key decisions that impact their work. Heavily bureaucratic organizations create systems and cultures in which workers must follow prescriptive rules over which they have little say (see Chapter 4). Heroic leadership styles (see Chapter 12) concentrate power in the leaders' hands. They then dictate decisions, resulting in many employees having little authority or control, and, consequently, they feel powerless. This can be frustrating—not only do they feel dehumanized (see Braverman's critique of Taylorism in Chapter 3), it can be counterproductive as it could be argued that workers often have better ideas of how to complete a task than their managers.

Supervisors, in particular, suffer from this position. As Kanter states, supervisors are 'caught in the middle' between the managers that demand their targets to be met and the workers who 'have the power to slack, to slouch, to take too much time' (a supervisor quoted in Kanter, 1977: 187). The supervisor in this position has little power to actually influence the work because they do not have access to rewards or punishment that can influence the employees' behaviour or the processes that shape how the activities occur.

Kanter argues this feeling of powerlessness significantly impacts people's mindset. Drawing on psychoanalysis by Karen Horney, Kanter claims that powerless people tend to become 'critical, bossy, and controlling' (1977: 189) and neurotic (excessively anxious about everything), and therefore attempt to dominate (control) everything around them. In doing so they act rationally because this is the only power available to them. Such behaviour, though, can result in more controlling leadership behaviour creating a 'vicious cycle: powerless authority figures who use coercive tactics, provoke resistance and aggression, which prompts them to become even more coercive, controlling, and behaviourally restrictive' (1977: 190).

Powerlessness can make people overly focused on rules. As we saw in Chapter 2, highly bureaucratic organizations can lead people to remove themselves from taking personal responsibility and follow the rules, regardless of the effect on customers or clients. They therefore only do the minimum they need in order to get things done. Finally, those with less power guard their territory more jealously as they seek to protect their domain. This can result, Kanter argues, in competitiveness, sectarianism, and hostility between sections. As a result, they are less effective and less satisfied.

To tackle this situation she argues that workers should be empowered. Empowerment distributes power away from being solely in the hands of managers to the people actually doing the job. They get to define how they should achieve their tasks and, in negotiation with their manager, what overall goals they are trying to achieve. Consequently, 'when more people are empowered – that is, allowed to have control over the conditions that make their actions possible – then more is accomplished' (Kanter, 1977: 166).

Empowerment is a post-bureaucratic form of management as it aims to move away from command and control to more participatory forms of management and decision making (see Chapter 17). Empowered workers have the capacity to make on the spot decisions that can satisfy customers rather than having to refer to managers or the rule book, have more opportunities to participate in decision making, and can be more self-determined. It therefore frees people up to do their jobs in response to customer needs, which is particularly important in the service sector (see Chapter 16).

Empowerment is said to increase commitment because employees feel that they have more control over their destiny and the decisions that impact their work. They also work harder because they feel more engaged in the process and are often implementing their own ideas. By being empowered proponents state employees quickly take responsibility, have increased motivation, commitment, and skills, and move away from a blame culture, resulting, therefore, in a more positive outlook.

In order for empowerment to work, three key factors are often considered important. First, they require employees to understand the production process or how things currently operate (with a view to changing them); secondly, it requires trust from management to give over key information; and, thirdly, it requires a high level of teamwork and cooperation among the members.

Quality circles provide an example of empowerment in action. They started in the Japanese car industry where they began as a grass-roots movement of workers who wanted to take more responsibility for their work. A quality circle often has around ten volunteers who come together to solve a problem of mutual concern, such as how to improve their products, the production process, or other related aspects. The members aim to identify the root of the problem, devise solutions, and disseminate them to the relevant people in the organization. Rather than seeking to produce large-scale changes, these are often incremental (step-by-step) changes designed by the people that will implement them (see Chapter 11). Workers in these situations have been very successful not only in empowering themselves, but in improving the production line.

However, they have been less successful in the UK. Some have put this down to the cultural difference between Japan (which is more collectivist) and the UK (which is more individualistic; see Chapter 15 for more details on national cultural differences). Often, empowerment programmes are said to fail because senior management fail to let go of control or to trust the workers to make decisions. Similarly, employees can be resistant to change as they do not want to take on the extra responsibility that the empowerment programme produces. As a result, empowerment programmes sound very good in principle, but, in many cases, they do not live up to the hopes that their supporters suggest they should achieve (Cunningham and Hyman, 1999).

Critique of empowerment

Writers from the critical management studies perspective have argued that while empowerment sounds positive in principle, rather than giving workers more autonomy it could, in fact, be seen as a more subtle form of control (Alvesson and Willmott, 1992a). They argue that most empowerment programmes increase the workers' responsibility, but do not give them the power to set the overall aims and objectives of the organization. Therefore, they are made responsible for all aspects of the implementation so, instead of blaming management, workers internalize the blame, believing that if they do not achieve the task they need to adjust their own behaviour. According to this view, empowerment therefore gives the illusion of autonomy, but actually elicits a more subtle form of control as employees become their own supervisors (think back to the image of the Panopticon earlier in the chapter).

Emancipation

For Rosabeth Moss Kanter, empowerment was important not simply in giving the powerless more discretion and influence in what they do, but as a wider part of changing the 'fabric of job relationships' (1977: 11). Kanter argued that although empowerment on its own is limited, it provides a step in the right direction towards broader changes in how work is organized. She argued that to produce real change a more substantial overturning in the way organizations, and society, operates needs to occur to produce a truly equal and fair workplace.

Marxists, such as Lukes, would agree. Within their perspective they argue that capitalist working relationships always produce power dynamics which act in the favour of management. Therefore, while systems such as empowerment might produce changes that have benefits for the workers, they will always ultimately favour the management. They argue that in order to produce more substantial changes the entire basis of capitalism needs to be overthrown and a new society with a new economic system created. It is only when this change happens and power is truly in the hands of workers who can determine their own ends that a more equal, fair, and effective distribution of power can occur.

Those of the critical management studies perspective are generally not optimistic that the whole of capitalism will be overthrown. Alvesson and Willmott (1992b) argue that a more realistic objective is what they call 'microemancipation'. Microemancipation involves small-scale changes that help the individual or group to take control of their own destiny. For these writers 'emancipation is not a gift bestowed upon employees; rather it necessitates the (often painful) resistance to, and overcoming of, socially unnecessary restrictions' (1992b: 433). In other words, power cannot be given by managers (because it always comes with strings attached); rather, it needs to be fought for actively to produce a fairer system.

According to this view, workers therefore need to try to achieve microemancipation by working on small-scale changes that they choose themselves. Workers (and indeed management) can, therefore, temporarily escape from domination and control through small changes in how they work. 'Inherent in the concept of microemancipation is an emphasis on partial, temporary movements that break away from diverse forms of oppression, rather than successive moves toward a predetermined state of liberation' (1992b: 447). Microemancipation therefore aims for little breaks with the normal ways of doing things to think and act differently.

Microemancipation, however, does not come without a cost. It might mean a reduction in production, workers might be less work focused, and, therefore, might not get promotions or may even lose their jobs. Therefore, microemancipation has its benefits, as well as costs.

Review questions

Describe

1. Define empowerment.

2. Explain what negative reactions feeling powerless can produce.

Analyse

3. Is empowerment increasing control for workers or control over them?

Chapter summary

Running case: Wilkinson enters the boardroom

Linda presents to the board. She feels more confident about the proposal and feels that she has the backing of her team. As she looks up, she sees Effingham give her a smile. Or is it a smirk? 'I can do this', she thinks to herself. 'Breathe deeply, believe in yourself, be confident . . .'

While we often do not like to think about it, power and politics are central parts of everyday organizational practice. It impacts individuals' careers, decision-making processes, and organizational effectiveness. Power can be seen as one of the drivers of organizational life, propelling people's actions, thinking processes, and even belief systems. While for some power and politics are just on the surface, seen in decision making and conflict, writers like Lukes and Foucault offer a deeper view of power that shapes our fundamental ways of thinking and acting in the world.

It might be nice to think of a world where power does not exist, but as theorists as diverse as Jeffery Pfeffer and Michel Foucault have demonstrated, such a view is impossible. Power is with us in all situations in our lives. The real question that power raises is: How do we use it in ways that are positive and productive?

Further reading

McNay, L. 1994. *Foucault: a critical introduction*. Blackwell, Cambridge.
A very readable introduction to Foucault's work which provides a good explanation of his views on power.

Lukes, S. 2005. *Power: a radical view*. Palgrave Macmillan, Basingstoke.
This gives a good overview of the issues of power and politics—particularly the three faces of power. It presents an interesting Marxist view of power that demonstrates how it is structural and often invisible.

Pfeffer, J. 1992. *Managing with power: politics and influence in organizations*. Harvard Business School Press, Boston, MA.
Pfeffer is in the power as a possession camp and this book is his key text on the subject. It explores how managers can use power and politics in organizations.

Townley, B. 1994. *Reframing human resource management: power, ethics and the subject at work*. Sage, London
A challenging, but very interesting, account of how Michel Foucault's work can be applied to real-life organizations. It gives good examples, such as the role of appraisal systems as a form of power.

Pettigrew, A., and McNulty, T. 1995. Power and influence in and around the boardroom. *Human Relations* 48(8): 845–873.
This article examines the power and influence of board members of some of the top 200 companies and asks some interesting critical questions about the influence that this elite group have.

Bibliography

Alvesson, M., and Willmott, H. 1992a. *Making Sense of Management*. Sage: London.

Alvesson, M., and Willmott, H. 1992b. On the idea of emancipation in management and organization studies. *Academy of Management Review* 17(3): 432–464.

Bauman, Z. 1989. *Modernity and the holocaust*. Polity Press: Cambridge.

Bauman, Z. 2000. *Liquid Modernity*. Polity Press: Cambridge.

BBC. 2011a. Triesman claims four Fifa members sought 2018 bribes. Available at: http://news.bbc.co.uk/sport1/hi/football/9481461.stm (last accessed 9 July 2012).

BBC. 2011b. Don Amott stands by Derbyshire resignation decision. Available at: http://news.bbc.co.uk/sport1/hi/cricket/counties/derbyshire/9439012.stm (last accessed 9 July 2012).

Blitz, R. 2011. Fifa set to probe fresh bribery claims. *Financial Times*. 10 May 2011. Available at: http://www.ft.com/cms/s/0/f652298c-7b0d-11e0-991a-00144feabdc0.html" \l "axzz2CqqNNoqi (last accessed 24 November 2012).

Bowie, N. 2000. A Kantian theory of leadership. *The Leadership & Organization Development Journal* 21(4): 185–193.

Burns, J. 1978. *Leadership*. Harper & Row: New York.

Callaghan, G., and Thompson, P. 2001. Edwards Revisited: Technical Control and Call Centres. *Economic and Industrial Democracy* 22(1): 13–37.

Cunningham, I., and Hyman, J. 1999. The poverty of empowerment? A critical case study. *Personnel Review* 28(3): 192–207.

Dahl, R. 1957. *The concept of power, behavioral science*, 2: 201–125; reprinted in Scott (1994) *Power: critical concepts*, 3 vols. Routledge: London.

Dahl, R. 1958. A Critique of the Ruling Elite Model. *American Political Science Review* 52: 463–469.

The Daily Telegraph. 2003. The truth about Dr Kelly. 22 July 2003. Available at: http://www.telegraph.co.uk/comment/telegraph-view/3594099/The-truth-about-Dr-Kelly.html (last accessed 24 November 2012).

Ferris, G., Treadway, D., Kolodinsky, R., Hochwarter, W., Kacmar, C., Douglas, C., and Frink, D. 2005. Development and validation of the political skill inventory. *Journal of Management* 31: 126–152.

Ferris, G., Treatway, D., Perrewé, P., Brouer, R., Douglas, C., and Lux, S. 2007. Political skill in organizations. *Journal of Management* 33(3): 290–320.

Foucault, M. 1977. *Discipline and Punish; The birth of the prison* (A. Sheridan, trans.). Penguin Books: London.

Foucault, M. 1981. *The History of Sexuality: The Will to Knowledge*, vol 1. Penguin: London.

French., J., and Raven, B. 1958. *The bases of social power*. In Cartwright, D. (ed.) *Introducing social psychology*. Institute for Social Research, University of Michigan Press: Ann Arbor, MI, pp. 150–167.

The Guardian. 2011. Lord Triesman accuses Fifa executives of 'unethical behaviour'. 10 May 2011. Available at: http://www.guardian.co.uk/football/2011/may/10/lord-triesman-fifa?INTCMP=ILCNETTXT3487 (last accessed 9 July 2012).

Huczynski, A., and Buchanan, D. 2004. *Organizational behaviour*. Pearson Education Ltd: Harlow.

Kanter, R. 1977. *Men and Women of the Corporation*. Basic Books: London.

Longman, J. 2011. Six From FIFA Are Accused in Bribery Case. *The New York Times*. 10 May 2011. Available at: http://www.nytimes.com/2011/05/11/sports/soccer/six-top-fifa-officials-named-in-bribery-investigation.html?_r=0 (last accessed 24 November 2011).

Lukes, S. 2005. *Power: a radical view*. Palgrave Macmillan: Basingstoke.

Machiavelli, N. 1532/1984. *The Prince*. Oxford University Press: Oxford.

Marx, K. 1859/2012. *A Contribution to the Critique of Political Economy*. Forgotten Books: London.

McClelland, D. 1975. *Power: the inner experience*. John Wiley & Sons Inc.: Chichester.

McNay, L. 1994. *Foucault: A Critical Introduction*. Polity Press: Cambridge.

Milgram, S. 1974. *Obedience to authority: An experimental view*. Travistock: London.

Mintzberg, H. 1983. *Power in and around organizations*. Prentice Hall: Englewood Cliffs, NJ.

Moore, J. 2010. HSBC still out of Africa after walking away from Nedbank takeover. *The Independent*. 16 October 2010. Available at http://www.independent.co.uk/news/business/news/hsbc-still-out-of-africa-after-walking-awayfrom-nedbank-takeover-2108256.html (last accessed 9 July 2012).

Nietzsche, F. 1990. *Beyond Good and Evil*. Penguin Books: London.

O'Boyle, T. 1998. *At any cost: Jack Welch, General Electric, and the pursuit of profit*. Knopf: New York.

Pfeffer, J. 1981. *Power in organizations*. Harper Collins: New York.

Pfeffer, J. 2010. *Power: Why some people have it – and others don't*. Harper Collins: New York.

Rees, P. 2011b. Twickenham braced for new bout of infighting a week before World Cup. *The Guardian*.

1 September 2011. Available at http://www.guardian.co.uk/sport/2011/sep/01/rugby-football-union-england-rugby-union-team (last accessed 9 July 2012).

Ripley, D. 2010. The five ways Tom Hicks and George Gillett got it wrong at Liverpool. *The Daily Mail*. 11 October 2010. Available at http://www.dailymail.co.uk/sport/football/article-1319463/Tom-Hicks-George-Gillett--waysgot-wrong-Liverpool.html (last accessed 9 July 2012).

Runciman, W. 2004. *Hutton and Butler: Lifting the Lid on the Workings of Power*. Oxford University Press: Oxford.

Thompson, P., and Ackroyd, S. 1995. All quiet on the workplace front?: A critique of Recent Trends in British Industrial Sociology. *Sociology* 29: 615–33.

Tichy, N., and Stratford, S. 1993. *Control your destiny or someone else will: how Jack Welch is making General Electric the world's most competitive company*. Doubleday: New York.

Townley, B. 1994. *Reframing Human Resource Management: Power, Ethics and the Subject at Work*. Sage: London.

Wallace, S. 2011. Bernstein in tight spot over Fifa president vote. *The Independent*. 12 May 2011. Available at http://www.independent.co.uk/sport/football/news-and-comment/bernstein-in-tight-spot-over-fifa-president-vote-2282545.html (last accessed 24 November 2012).

Weber, M. 2004. *The Essential Weber*, (ed. S. Whimster). Routledge: London.

Wheeler, B. 2006. MP investigates Dr Kelly's death. BBC News. Available at: http://news.bbc.co.uk/1/hi/uk_politics/4995076.stm (last accessed 24 November 2012).

Yeung, R. 2009. *Office politics: the new rules*. Marshall Cavendish: London.

Yrle A., Hartman S., and Payne, D. 2005. Generation X: acceptance of others and teamwork implications. *Team Performance Management* 11(5/6), pp. 188–199.

Ziegler, M. 2011. New Fifa bribe allegations over Qatar World Cup bid. *The Independent*. 10 May 2011. Available at: http://www.independent.co.uk/sport/football/news-and-comment/new-fifa-bribe-allegations-over-qatar-world-cup-bid-2281847.html (last accessed 24 November 2012).

Zimbardo, P. 2007. Revisiting the Stanford Prison experiment: a lesson in the power of situation. *Chronicle of Higher Education* 53(30): B6–B7.

Part 5
Contemporary trends

14

Information, communication, and technology

Chapter overview and learning outcomes

By the end of this chapter you should be able to:

- describe theories and processes of communication in organizations

- explain how technology mediates communication, producing a trade-off between efficiency and richness of communication

- explain how technology produces information within the organization, especially when it is used to perform bureaucratic tasks

- analyse the effects of the Internet and computer networks upon organizations.

Key theorists

Albert Mehrabian	Noted the important role of non-verbal communication in organizational settings
Richard Daft and Robert Lengel	Devised media richness theory which examines the abilities of different media to communicate rich information and meaning
Shoshana Zuboff	Wrote about the 'informated' organization, which generates a large amount of computerized activity about its own activities
Frank Blackler	Noted the simultaneous nature of organizations 'imploding' into computer code and 'exploding' into computer networks
Gilles Deleuze and Felix Guattari	Philosophers who devised the concept of the rhizome, which has been used to describe organizations which operate through computer networks
Saskia Sassen	Noted how the control of the Internet and organizations within the Internet mirror wider control structures in society

Key terms

Communication	The transfer of meaning or information from one person, or several, to another
Noise	Anything which disrupts and distorts communication so that the perceived meaning of the recipient is different to the intended meaning of the sender
Information, communication, and technology (ICT)	A set of contemporary electronic technologies which facilitate communication between people and the sharing of information
Social presence	The degree to which the physical presence of the sender of a message can be felt in a particular communications medium

Media richness	The ability of different communications media to communicate rich, personal meanings rather than lean, impersonal information
Informating	Where a large amount of an organization's activity and knowledge is stored as computer code in a database
Network	Where organizations are linked by sharing data through computer networks or through the Internet
Rhizome	A mass of random, tangled connections which some people suggest is similar to the nature of the Internet and cyberspace

Introduction

Running case: 'Guests First'

From: simon_chance@junctionhotel.co.uk
To: senior_management_team@junctionhotel.co.uk

Dear colleagues

As you are aware we have been facing a tough time economically, leading to some efficiencies being made in work processes and staff numbers. At the same time, we face the challenge of maintaining our position as a luxury hotel.

It is my belief that we can achieve this balancing act if we recognize that the key factor which adds value and luxury status to the hotel is our people and the attention to customer service that they provide.

For this reason, I am introducing our new 'Guests First' initiative. It means that, for all of us, whatever our role in the organization, we need to perform our roles with the recognition that without our guests we have no income. It is through you putting the guests first that we can maintain our status as a luxury experience.

Could you all, as senior managers, please cascade this down to the people in your departments and we can all start putting the guests first as soon as possible!

Many thanks

Simon

Information, communication, and technology (ICT) refers to a raft of contemporary computer technologies which facilitate communication and the sharing of information. It is an ever-present part of our daily lives. Think of a commonly-used device, such as a smartphone. It is a form of communications technology, allowing us to communicate by phone, text, or email. It also allows us to manage information, such as our personal diaries, or access information through the Internet.

ICT is also an important part of organizational life, with whole departments devoted to running and maintaining the communication technologies that an organization uses. In this chapter we suggest that communication is not only an important process within organizations, but also that ICT has had a profound impact on the nature of what organizations do and, indeed, on what organizations *are*.

Familiar communications technology

- First, we examine theories of communication within organizations—the way in which information and meaning is transferred from one person to another. Communication is an important part of managerial activity, but one which is prone to being disrupted by *mis*communication—what a person sending a message means may not be the same as how the person receiving that message understands it.

- Secondly, we examine how technology, such as email, facilitiates communication. In particular, we see that while technology can make communication more efficient, different media convey different degrees of the richness that comes from face-to-face communication.

- Thirdly, we examine how information is communicated between organizations, especially as more and more organizational activity takes place through computer code.

The final point brings us to the nature of organizations which operate through global, electronic networks, including the Internet. We see how this changes both the nature and activity of organizations, but, at the same time, brings particular challenges of maintaining the boundary of the organization in order to keep its valuable data safe.

Communication in organizations: getting the message through

Effective **communication** is an important part of organizational success. It means that the wishes, desires, and orders of those at the top have been successfully transmitted to, and understood by, all people within the organization who will then act upon them. Communication is therefore important for the exercise of managerial power, but is it something which always takes place flawlessly?

In this section we examine some of the main features of communication between people in organizations, but also the ways in which **miscommunication** can occur. We see how **noise** can interfere in the communication process, resulting in its original, intended meaning being distorted and, potentially, a completely different message being received. As such, we question the amount of power that management actually have over the communication process and the degree to which communication allows managerial power to be exerted.

Communication
A process whereby information is transferred from a sender (or senders) to a receiver (or receivers).

Miscommunication
Where some of the meaning of a communication is distorted.

Noise Anything which distorts the transfer of a message from source to recipient so that the intended and perceived meanings differ.

Features of communication

Message An item of communication sent from a sender to a recipient.

Rather than being a simple transfer of a **message** from a sender to a recipient, communication has many facets and features which mean that the nature of any one communication, or the way in which we pass on a message, will be different to another. We begin this section by examining four particular features which make up the nature of communication:

- Is it formal or informal?
- What channel does it take—is it spoken, written, symbolic, or expressed in the form of gestures?
- How long does it take to reach its intended recipient and for a reply to be received?
- Is it between individuals or between many people?

Formal and informal channels of communication

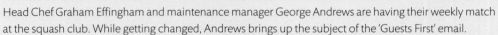

Running case: at the squash club

Head Chef Graham Effingham and maintenance manager George Andrews are having their weekly match at the squash club. While getting changed, Andrews brings up the subject of the 'Guests First' email.

'Have you seen that latest rubbish from Chance? Does he have nothing better to do with his time?', asks Andrews. 'Tell me about it', replies Effingham. 'It's not as if we're not busy enough already. And doesn't he think my waiters are trained in customer service?'

'Why is he doing it—does he think it will make any difference?', asks Andrews.

'Well, word on the street is that Chance is coming under a lot of pressure from the consortium. They are seeing the hotel as a bit of a loss-making distraction and they want to concentrate money and efforts on the football club. This is Chance trying to show he's serious about the hotel', replies Effingham. 'Interesting . . .', replies Andrews, 'I heard Chance has been arguing with that business manager—Weaver. This should have been Weaver's initiative, but they disagreed, and now Chance has taken it on himself to launch the initiative by himself.' 'Well, he probably needs the distraction', replies Effingham. 'From what?', asks Andrews. 'Have you not heard? His wife walked out on him last week . . .'

Formal communication Official communication within an organization, following authorized pathways.

Organization chart A diagram of the structure of an organization.

Hierarchy The levels and ranks of an organization. Any one level reports to the level immediately above and commands the level immediately below.

Matrix structure An organizational structure that combines a traditional functional hierarchy with separately-managed project teams that draw people from across different functional departments.

When you think about communication in organizations, do you think of it as something official, signed by the managing director and sent on company letter-headed paper, or do you think of the conversations and gossip between workers in the staff canteen? The first feature of communication that we examine is its formal and informal aspects.

Formal communication is the official communication from management downwards, such as memos and commands, that follow formalized channels. These channels can be represented by the **organization chart** (Figure 14.1), which was presented in Chapter 2 as a diagram of hierarchical structure which facilitated organizational control. However, the chart can also be seen as a map of organizational communication, showing who communicates with whom as orders and messages are passed up and down from one level to the next throughout the **hierarchy**.

As seen in Chapter 4, this form of hierarchical bureaucracy has been superseded in many organizations by more flexible structures, such as the **matrix structure** (Figure 14.2, see Chapter 4 for more explanation). Formal communication channels are thus not just

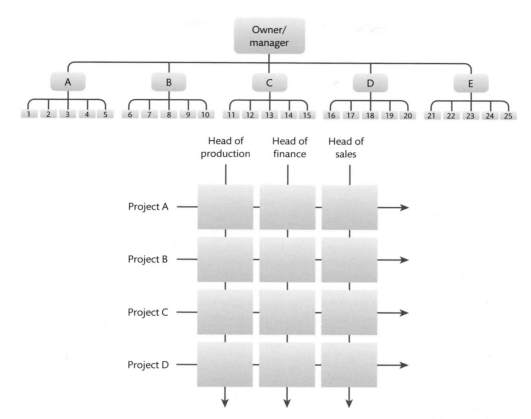

Figure 14.1 An organizational hierarchy.

Figure 14.2 A typical matrix structure.

vertical, as with the organizational hierarchy, but can also be horizontal—with communication flowing across the organization through formally-constituted project teams.

Alongside formal channels of communication, however, are the **informal communications** that take place: the 'water-cooler' conversations and quick chats at the photocopier, for example. Such communication is not part of the organization's authorized, formal communication, but information about the workplace is, nevertheless, shared.

For example, a workplace football team may bring together people from different parts of the organization—sales, accounting, production, etc., and even from different levels in the hierarchy. Conversation in the bar after a match is likely, at some point, to turn to work-related issues. People get to learn about what is going on in other parts of the organization—information that they might not hear otherwise. And a football team is just one of potentially many informal, social groups that may exist in an organization.

It is here that organizational issues might be discussed in ways that would not be mapped out by the formal organizational channels of the organization chart. There is a 'suppleness of communication' (Deleuze and Guattari, 1987: 214) that bypasses official bureaucratic structures and communication channels.

Such communication is sometimes linked with **gossip**, where people get to find out work-related information to which they would otherwise not be party. Gossip in organizations is an area of study in itself and has been analysed as not just a form of informal communication, but also a source of power and a means of maintaining the cohesion of groups within organizations (e.g. Kurland and Pelled, 2000; Noon and Delbridge, 1993).

Visit the Online Resource Centre for more analysis of gossip in organizations.

Informal communications Communication in an organization not following official and formal guidelines.

Gossip Rumours and information communicated through informal means.

Management are able to control the content of formal communications, such as memos and emails. To what extent can they control both the content and accuracy of informal communications, such as gossip?

In more recent theories of organization, the distinction between formal and informal communication can become blurred. For example, **post-bureaucratic organizations** (Chapter 4) minimize structure and formal roles, and, instead, emphasize dialogue between people as the main feature of an organization. Models of **organizational learning** also emphasize the importance of sharing work-related knowledge through conversations, as with the case of the Xerox photocopier engineers (Chapter 10).

Rather than communication being a discrete feature of the organization, mapped out by the organization's structure, communication is a big part of what the organization actually *is*:

> It is through the telephone calls, meetings, planning sessions, sales talks and corridor conversations that people inform, update, gossip, review, reassess, reason, instruct, revise, argue, debate, contest and actually *constitute* the moments, myths and, through time, the very *structuring* of the organization.   (Boden, 1994: 8, original author's emphasis)

Communication, whether formal or informal, is thus a continual and ongoing process in organizations, or, as Broekstra (1998) states, the organization *is* a conversation.

Channels of communication

Post-bureaucratic organization A trend away from rigid, bureaucratic rules and structures in organizations towards more flexible, and less hierarchical and rule-driven organizations.

Organizational learning Sharing and transfer of individual knowledge so that it becomes a collective property of the organization.

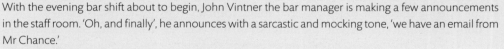

Running case: raising the bar

With the evening bar shift about to begin, John Vintner the bar manager is making a few announcements in the staff room. 'Oh, and finally', he announces with a sarcastic and mocking tone, 'we have an email from Mr Chance.'

'Ooh', reply the bar staff in mock fascination, before descending into giggles.

'We have a new initiative for customer service', announces Vintner, his voice both grandiose and mocking. Vintner continues to read out the email, strutting around the staff room, making grand sweeping gestures with his arms, his voice becoming more mocking in tone as he continues. Each mention of the phrase 'Guests First' is telegraphed with ever more exaggerated facial mugging and, as the announcement continues, the staff fall more and more into hysterical laughter.

Finally, Vintner returns to his normal tone of voice. 'Well, guys, as far as I'm concerned you've been putting guests first for years—so off you go and do the same as always.'

What is the bar manager communicating through his gestures and tone of voice over and above the words that he is reading out?

Have you ever found yourself giving directions to somebody while speaking on the telephone, only to realize that you are pointing and tracing out the directions with your free hand, even though the other person cannot see you? Such gestures show how communication involves factors beyond the words themselves—much of what we understand from a conversation comes from non-verbal body language.

> **Research insight:** Mehrabian's 55–38–7 ratio, Mehrabian, A. 1971. *Silent messages*. Wadsworth Pub. Co., Belmont, CA.
>
> Albert Mehrabian (1971) studied communication among workers in a laboratory and was particularly interested in how people communicated emotions and attitudes. While we might think that the information conveyed in a conversation would be from words alone, Mehrabian's study discovered that much more is communicated through body language, such as hand gestures, comportment, and eye contact. The 55–38–7 ratio suggests that:
>
> - 55% of communication is from body language
> - 38% of communication comes from the tone of voice
> - just 7% of communication is from the actual words.
>
> Mehrabian's work has implications for communication that does not take place in a face-to-face setting—how much meaning is lost if 55% of communication is from bodily gestures?

Channels of communication are the means by which a communication is transferred or mediated from a sender to a recipient. As we will see later in the chapter, different channels are seen to have different degrees of richness, i.e. the amount of information that they can communicate. Four general types of channel through which communication in organizations takes place are:

- verbal communication is through spoken words: conversations, meetings, briefings, negotiations, phone calls, etc.
- bodily, non-verbal communication is the gestures, facial expressions, and body language that convey meaning beyond the actual words spoken
- written communication takes place through words on paper, or on a computer or telephone screen. Examples include letters, memos, emails, text messages, a newsletter, or a noticeboard
- symbolic communication uses signs and symbols, e.g. drivers understand that a symbol such as a red circle with a white horizontal line through the middle means 'no entry'.

> Channels of communication Ways in which a message is expressed, e.g. verbally or in written words.

Which examples of the four channels of communication have you engaged in—either as a sender or receiver—today?

Synchronicity and feedback

A conversation is generally a two-way process—we take it in turns to say something, listen to the response, and then respond accordingly. We also understand how a person feels about our words from the bodily, non-verbal reactions—the look on their face and their body language. This process of receiving a response to communication is **feedback**.

However, not all feedback is as instantaneous as it is with a conversation. Many of us may have experienced the frustration of sending an email or a letter only to be left waiting for a response. **Synchronicity** describes the amount of delay between sending a message and that message being received, and gives a further facet of communication:

> Feedback Reaction or response to a message.
>
> Synchronicity The degree to which something happens immediately or after a delay.

- synchronous communication is where transmission of the message, by the sender, and receipt of the message happen simultaneously, and there is thus the possibility for feedback to be instant. Examples include face-to-face conversations, phone calls, and video calls
- asynchronous communication is where there is a delay between the sending and receiving of the message. Thus, feedback is not instantaneous—the sender may have a long delay before getting a response to their communication. Examples include letters, emails, and text messages.

Focus of communication

A final facet of communication is the focus of the message— whether is it directed to one person or is a more impersonal form of communication directed to many people, even the whole organization. Table 14.1 shows a number of different types of focus of communication that may take place in organizations.

Table 14.1 Different types of focus of communication

Focus	Description	Examples
One-to-one	Personal communication between two individuals	Conversation, personal email, personal letter, phone call
One-to-many (broadcasting)	One person sends a communication to many people (even a whole organization)	Bulk email, speech at a staff meeting, memo
Many-to-many	A communication to many people that doesn't come from one personal, identifiable source (e.g. it might come from the board or a marketing department)	Newsletter (although there may be individual items within this, e.g. an address from the Chief Executive Office (CEO))
Many-to-one	A group of people communicate to just one person	A project group might have a single email address and communicate their results collectively through this to one individual within the organization

Communication and miscommunication

Running case: misinterpretation

Chance's email is one of many in the inbox of fitness manager Carl Jones. With a busy workload to deal with, he only has time to glance at the email, picking up on the phrase 'Guests First.'

From: fitnessmanager@junctionhotel.co.uk
To: fitness_staff@junctionhotel.co.uk

Guys,

Quick message to pass on from Simon Chance—we now have to put guests first.

Carl

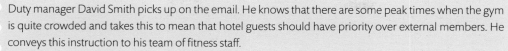

Duty manager David Smith picks up on the email. He knows that there are some peak times when the gym is quite crowded and takes this to mean that hotel guests should have priority over external members. He conveys this instruction to his team of fitness staff.

Come Monday evening at 6 pm, when the gym is usually busiest, the staff are asking paying gym members to make way on the equipment for hotel guests. This leads to arguments between staff and customers, and between customers. It continues throughout the week and ten members cancel their memberships.

Noticing this exodus, Chance makes his way to the fitness centre to confront the manager.

'What's the issue here—the members are leaving in their droves?', asks a panicked Chance. 'I'm implementing just what you asked for—putting guests first. The members aren't happy being asked to make way for hotel guests you know—what did you expect?', replies Smith.

'What?' asks a puzzled Chance, before realization dawns. 'No—that's not what I meant in the email. What I meant was . . . oh . . . tell you what, do you have five minutes for a quick chat?'

The four features of communication that we have examined all play a role in an overall model of the communication process. A simplified version of this model is shown in Figure 14.3.

Communication passes through the following stages, as illustrated in the model:

- the communication begins with the **source**, be this one or many people, who have a particular intended meaning that they wish to communicate to one or many people
- the source **encodes** the communication, i.e. they form a message using a verbal, bodily, written, or symbolic channel
- the message is sent, using either formal or informal means of communication
- the **recipient** (or recipients) receives and **decodes** the message, and perceives a particular meaning from it before providing feedback, either synchronously or asynchronously.

Source The sender or originator of a message.

Encodes Convert the intended meaning of a communication into a form that can be sent as a message.

Recipient The person or persons that receives a message.

Decodes Convert a received message into the meaning perceived by the recipient.

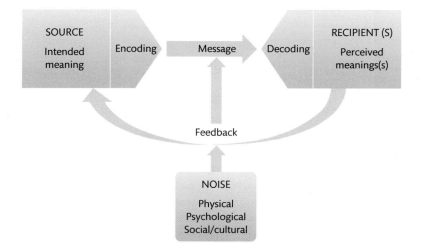

Figure 14.3 A model of the communication process (based on Shannon et al., 1949).

Table 14.2 Examples of noise in the communication process

Type of noise	Examples
Physical noise	Background noise getting in the way of a conversation
	Interference on a phone line
	Corruption of data in a computer file
Psychological noise	Semantics—people interpret words in different ways, attach their own meanings to subjective ideas, such as 'good', 'dedicated', etc.
	Perception—people may attach different degrees of importance to different parts of a message
	Attention—people may not give their full attention to a message, being distracted by other things
Social/cultural noise	People may speak a different language to the original communication, thus mistranslations may occur
	Different cultures may interpret messages differently (see Chapter 15 for examples of cultural misunderstandings and differences)

Noise and miscommunication

Messages are open to misinterpretation. The intended meaning of the sender and the perceived meaning of the receiver can differ, sometimes vastly. Where there is more than one recipient, each recipient may have their own different perception of the meaning.

Anything which intervenes in the communication process and alters the original intended meaning of a message is termed noise (Shannon et al., 1949). We think of noise in physical terms, such as someone shouting over a conversation so that it can't be heard perhaps, but, in the communication process, noise can take a number of forms. Examples of noise are shown in Table 14.2.

Noise exists as a barrier to communication and the effective transfer of meaning from the sender to the recipient. The model in this section shows noise intervening in a single communication. In the next section we see how the potential for noise increases as the number of stages of communication of a message increases.

 Have you ever had a situation where something you have said or a message that you have sent has been misinterpreted? What do you think was the cause of that misinterpretation?

Communication and power

Many of you will have played the party game where a message is whispered from person to person, often with a wildly different message to the original appearing at the end of the line. Noise interferes as the message is passed from one person to the next and this can happen at any stage along the way. Now think about the power that the first person in the line has, to control the final message that appears at the end of the line. They can say the message very clearly to the next person along, but, after that, they have no control over what miscommunication and noise may happen further down the line.

A similar problem faces a manager trying to communicate a message across an organization—it has to pass from person to person and, at any stage, there is the potential for noise and miscommunication. Nichols (1962) suggested that, from top management at board level down to operators on a factory floor, only 20% of the meaning of an original message remains. It would seem that management have very little **power** over how their communication is interpreted and acted upon.

Power The capacity to get things done or to influence others.

Theory in context: 'There she goes'

Who has power over the meaning of a song? Do the songwriter's intentions and thoughts when writing a song dictate the meaning of the song or is the meaning open to interpretation by people when they listen to the song?

For example, the song *There She Goes* by The La's, has a bright, jolly tune with lyrics suggesting some form of yearning for unrequited love. Other interpretations, however, suggest that the song is about drugs. But this, possibly less agreeable, interpretation didn't put off a travel agency in the UK from using the song as background music in a television commercial for tropical beach holidays, conjuring up images of clear blue seas and golden sands.

There is no one 'fixed' meaning of the song that the original songwriter can control. Once unleashed, the song is open to multiple interpretations. In other words, what is communicated is open to interpretations that are beyond the power and control of the original sender.

Visit the Online Resource Centre for links to the song and the lyrics.

This lack of power over meaning and interpretation of communication is compared by Latour (1986) to a passing move in a rugby game. As players throw the ball to each other they each have to receive it and, with a new exertion of force, throw it to the next player. It is a fragile exercise which can fail if one player should drop the ball or throw it in the wrong direction. The power of the initial throw only lasts until the first person who catches the ball—how it is then passed on is literally 'in the hands' of the next person along the line.

How is this view of power and communication similar with the whispering game described earlier?

Latour uses this rugby metaphor to understand the movement of power in social settings such as organizations. We generally think of power being held by managers at the top of an organization and which can be exerted across the organization (see Chapter 13 for a discussion of this). Latour's rugby ball metaphor suggests that, in fact, the successful exercise of power is 'in the hands' of others. Each person who receives a managerial command, order, or similar communication of power will, in some way, have to interpret it or decode it in their own mind. Management can never be certain just how their acts of power, their words, commands, and deeds will be interpreted and acted upon by individuals within the organization (Gergen, 1992).

Latour's rugby ball metaphor illustrates how noise can disrupt communication at many levels within an organization as messages are passed from person to person and department to department. The official, formal communications of the organization through which orders and power are carried out are open to being modified and disrupted in the day-to-day informal conversations and communications that take place throughout the organization.

In the next section, we see how such issues of miscommunication and noise affect an organization as it uses technology to communicate across the whole organization.

Review questions

1. Describe the four main features of communication in organizations.
2. Explain how noise can alter the intended meaning of a message.
3. Analyse the ways in which management lack power to ensure consistent communication of a message across an organization.

Apply

4. What examples of noise and miscommunication can you identify in the running case throughout the chapter so far?

Technology and communication: the medium is the message

Running case: email exchange

From: lindawilkinson@junctionhotel.co.uk
To: reception_staff@junctionhotel.co.uk; porters@junctionhotel.co.uk

Subject: Guests First

Hi everyone

I hope you are all well. We have a new initiative beginning this week called 'Guests First'. The aim is to make guests feel like they are the most important part of our business and, as reception area staff, you will be at the front line of this.

It's vital that we do this to maintain our reputation for customer service in these difficult times. So, can we all make that extra effort from now on to put the guests first!

Many thanks

Linda

....

From: suesmith@junctionhotel.co.uk

To: lindawilkinson@junctionhotel.co.uk

cc: reception_staff@junctionhotel.co.uk; porters@junctionhotel.co.uk

Subject: RE: Guests First

Dear Linda

I read with interest your email and I would be grateful if you could clarify what you mean by 'extra effort'. In particular, it implies that my effort in the job up until now has been insufficient—could you please point out the faults that you seem to think exist in my work.

Best wishes

Sue

....

From: lindawilkinson@junctionhotel.co.uk

To: suesmith@junctionhotel.co.uk

cc: reception_staff@junctionhotel.co.uk; porters@junctionhotel.co.uk

Subject: RE: RE: Guests First

Dear Sue

I wasn't implying that there's anything wrong with your work, but, in times like these, we all need to go that little bit further . . . We really need to pull together in these difficult times rather than engaging in internecine discussions such as these.

Best

Linda

....

From: suesmith@junctionhotel.co.uk

To: lindawilkinson@junctionhotel.co.uk

cc: reception_staff@junctionhotel.co.uk; porters@junctionhotel.co.uk

Subject: RE: RE: RE: Guests First

Linda

I see—so now I'm the problem then and I can't even raise a point without being branded a troublemaker. Ten years I've been here with no one saying a bad thing about my work—now it seems I don't put in enough effort and I'm a troublemaker!

Sue

....

From: janedavies@junctionhotel.co.uk
To: lindawilkinson@junctionhotel.co.uk
cc: reception_staff@junctionhotel.co.uk; porters@junctionhotel.co.uk

Subject: RE: RE: RE: RE: Guests First

Sue—come on give Linda some slack. We need to try everything we can to keep afloat in this recession.

Jane

....

From: bobjones@junctionhotel.co.uk
To: janedavies@junctionhotel.co.uk
cc: reception_staff@junctionhotel.co.uk; porters@junctionhotel.co.uk

Subject: RE: RE: RE: RE: RE: Guests First

Could you all have this discussion in private and not use reply all—I'm fed up of seeing this nonsense in my inbox.

Thanks

Bob.

....

From: gailwilliams@junctionhotel.co.uk
To: bobjones@junctionhotel.co.uk
cc: reception_staff@junctionhotel.co.uk; porters@junctionhotel.co.uk

Subject: RE: RE: RE: RE: RE: RE: Guests First

Looks like a few people have gotten out of the wrong side of bed this morning :)

....

From: suesmith@junctionhotel.co.uk
To: gailwilliams@junctionhotel.co.uk
cc: reception_staff@junctionhotel.co.uk; porters@junctionhotel.co.uk

Subject: RE: RE: RE: RE: RE: RE: RE: Guests First

OH SHUT UP. THIS ISN'T A JOKE

....

From: lindawilkinson@junctionhotel.co.uk
To: suesmith@junctionhotel.co.uk
cc: reception_staff@junctionhotel.co.uk; porters@junctionhotel.co.uk

Subject: RE: RE: RE: RE: RE: RE: RE: Guests First

Look everyone—we need to calm down a bit. This doesn't help anything at all. Maybe we need to sit down and have a face-to-face meeting about this. Let's say my office at 10.30 am.

Thanks

Linda

Imagine you are a chief executive wanting to communicate an important message to all 1,000 members of your organization. How would you go about doing this? You could speak to each worker individually—but that would take a long time, especially if the message was complex. **Communication technology** might help the chief executive to communicate their message more efficiently, for example:

- a simple technology, like a microphone, would allow the CEO to address all staff at once in one large auditorium
- printing/photocopying technology would allow a letter to be sent to all employees conveying the message
- even more efficiently, the message could be sent instantly as an email to all employees.

However, while each of these communications **media** allow the message to be delivered more efficiently (think of the difference in time between speaking to each employee individually, and composing and sending a mass email) this efficiency comes with a loss of **richness**—much of the information gained from the body language of a face-to-face conversation is lost, for example.

How many types of communications technology can you think of? Which do you use in your daily life? Do you use different technologies for different tasks?

> **Research insight:** What is technology? Cooper, R. 1993. Technologies of representation. In: Ahonen, P. (ed.) *Tracing the semiotic boundaries of politics.* Mouton de Gruyter, Berlin, pp. 279–312.
>
> We tend to think of technology in terms of the latest gadgets—smartphones, games consoles, etc.—or perhaps in terms of heavy machines. Cooper (1993) however, suggests a wider view of technology—it is any form of tool that turns a human weakness into an advantage. In other words, it facilitates human action, opening up new possibilities and potential.
>
> Think of a communication tool like a microphone. It is developed from the fact that the human voice is too weak to address a large crowd, but turns that weakness to an advantage whereby one speaker has the ability to communicate with many people at once. Technologies such as email allow a person to be able to communicate not only with many people, but also over a global geographical reach. Again, human potential is increased by technology.

In this section we first examine how communications technology enhances the abilities of people to communicate in organizations, both efficiently and over geographical distance. We then examine examples of how such technologies not only communicate information, but they in fact *create* information. The organization is **informated** (Zuboff, 1988)—in effect becoming a giant computer database.

Communication technology Technologies which facilitate communication between people and the sharing of information.

Media A specific form of technology or technologies which convey and carry information, e.g telephone, letter, email.

Richness The amount and quality of information conveyed by any one message.

Informated The process whereby information about an organization's activities is created.

Efficiency and richness: a trade-off

In recent years, email has come to dominate communications both within and outside organizations, replacing many forms of communication like telephone calls and things that previously might have been written on paper (e.g. a memo).

The convenience of email can be seen by the fact that it allows global communication without the expense of telephone conversations, or the delay and expense of postage. It also means that, unlike a telephone conversation, the recipient does not have to be there physically—they can pick up emails as and when they log on to their computer network.

When was the last time you wrote a letter?

In this section we use email as an example to examine the trade-off that communications technology brings between efficiency and richness. Email certainly allows for efficient communication—a message can be sent to an entire workforce across the whole globe with just one click of a button. Using **social presence theory** and **media richness theory**, we examine the extent to which this is at the expense of the richness of the message and the amount of information that it can convey.

Social presence theory

Social presence theory is the degree of perceived immediacy of a person in a communication. What sense does a particular communications medium give of the person writing the message actually being there (physically present) in the room with you (Rice, 1992; Short et al., 1976)?

The most obvious form of social presence is a face-to-face conversation. As with Mehrabian's study, it is from this that important non-verbal aspects of communication, such as gestures and facial expressions, are gleaned. With an email, the sender is absent, and so the communication that comes from their physical presence—body language and tone of voice—is missing. In Mehrabian's analysis, this would leave just the words, which communicate a meagre 7% of intended meaning.

Many of you will use particular tactics in emails which increase social presence and give more communications clues. **Emoticons**—facial expressions created out of punctuation marks, such as a smiley face (e.g. ☺)—are often added to emails or similar text-based communication methods, such as text messages and Twitter. Emoticons are a surrogate for the physical facial expression that would be seen if the person typing the email were actually present—they make up for some of the non-verbal meaning that has been lost (Lo, 2008).

The degree to which smiley faces can be used in professional workplace communication is debatable, but signatures on emails with links to web pages or that contain personal information are other examples of bringing social presence into this largely written form.

To what extent do profiles on social media sites, such as Facebook, increase social presence by including photos and other informal aspects of the person's life?

Social presence theory Examines the degree to which the physical presence of the sender of a message can be felt in a particular communications medium.

Media richness theory Examines the ability of different communications media to communicate rich, personal meanings rather than lean, impersonal information.

Emoticon Punctuation marks used in electronic communications, designed to simulate facial expressions.

Media richness theory

The amount of social presence desirable in a particular communication depends on what is being communicated, for instance think about the following items of information that might need to be communicated at different times within an organization:

- a single piece of data, a figure

- a summary of data, e.g. a table of a chart

- a fact

- an instruction or order

- an item of tacit knowledge about how to perform a particular task (cf. knowledge transfer in Chapter 10)

- an emotion or feeling ('I'm trying to communicate my feelings about this deal').

In some cases, basic facts are all that need to be communicated. For others, a richer, more personal form of communication that puts across information, such as a person's feelings and attitudes, is required. Daft and Lengel's (1986) theory of media richness recognizes two particular contingencies of information which might make different communications media more or less appropriate at different times.

- **Uncertainty** relates to an absence of information. This uncertainty can be reduced by providing basic facts and data. For example, a head of sales looking to produce a sales forecast would reduce uncertainty by receiving an email with sales figures for the past year. The lack of gestures and facial expressions does not alter the value of information in this email for someone who simply needs to know the basic facts.

- **Equivocality** is the amount to which a communication is open to interpretation. It involves attitudes, feelings, items of disagreement, something which can't be resolved by the provision of basic facts alone. For example, an email to workers which outlines complaints about customer service might need to be carefully worded. Workers could misinterpret it, a member of staff who is working well might think it applies to them, for example, and take unnecessary offence. A manager may decide that email is not the best way to communicate such a complex message that might affect people emotionally and instead have a quiet word with a few individuals.

Uncertainty A lack of knowledge about a particular factual issue.

Equivocality Situations where meanings are ambiguous and open to interpretation.

Daft and Lengel (1986) provide a continuum between rich and lean media (see Figure 14.4). Richer media are those which provide more of the personal, face-to-face qualities of communication, which might be needed in situations of equivocality where feelings and attitudes are being expressed, while leaner media provide more basic information and facts.

The amount of richness of a particular medium can be described in terms of the four features of communication explored in the previous section. For example, are verbal, bodily, or written channels used?; Is the communication personal or addressed to many people?; Is feedback immediate or is the communication synchronous? From Figure 14.4 we see the different levels of richness in different media with aspects of richness lost as the diagram moves down towards leaner, more efficient modes of communication.

Figure 14.4 Media richness theory.

Based on Daft and Lengel (1986: 560).

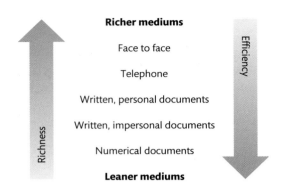

- Face-to-face communication is the richest form of communication. It is personal, contains bodily gestures and vocal tone clues, and provides immediate feedback.

- A telephone conversation is personal and may give rich communication information and feedback from the tone of voice, but it lacks the bodily gestures of a face-to-face conversation.

- An email addressed to a specific person is an example of a written personal document which lacks the richness of communications forms, such as a conversation face to face or by telephone. The sender has to formulate the words in such a way as to best convey their intention, but it might be difficult to interpret by the reader, for example if a comment is made as a joke or seriously. Furthermore, there is no opportunity to clarify the meaning of a communication through feedback, thus misunderstandings, for which there is already more potential, may go uncorrected.

- Bulk emails, those sent to a group of recipients, are an example of a written, impersonal document. Richness is lost further as the communication moves from being personal to impersonal. Think about how many bulk or 'spam' emails you receive—do you even open all of them, let alone read the message contained within?

- Numerical documents, such as spreadsheets or a set of accounts are the leanest and least rich medium, containing basic facts and information.

Think about specific communications technologies that you use—email, SMS, social media. Where would you place them on the media richness continuum in Figure 14.4?

We can see in this model the trade-off between efficiency and richness of communication, for example while a bulk email may be an efficient form of communication, it lacks richness—some people may not even open and read the email. Conversely, while a face-to-face conversation may provide rich communication, useful in situations of an equivocal nature, it is time-consuming and inefficient if communication needs to be over a wide scale.

The importance of media richness theory is not necessarily to choose the richest medium for all communication, but to choose the medium appropriate for what is being communicated.

The medium is the message

Real-life case: fired by email

In 2011 a number of British Army officers, some of whom were serving, or had recently served, in Afghanistan, were informed by email that they were being made redundant. They were informed that their contracts would end in a year and that they should begin to plan for their future careers.

The case attracted a lot of press coverage, not only because of the redundancies themselves, but because of the manner in which the communication was made—by email rather than in person, which was seen to be insensitive for such potentially upsetting news.

Sources: The Independent (2011a), Quinn (2011); BBC News (2011).

The case of the army redundancies shows the importance of using the right medium of communication for the purpose. Furthermore, the choice of communication medium might in and of itself contribute to the message and how it is perceived, as Marshall McLuhan (1964) stated: 'The medium is the message'. Thus, a letter might seem too formal as way to ask a friend out for a night out, when a text message might suffice. Likewise, an email might be too distant as a means to deliver bad news when a face-to-face conversation might communicate more sincerity and concern.

While face-to-face conversations might be the richest form of communication, it doesn't follow that it is the most appropriate form of communication in all cases. Think about getting driving directions—would you prefer someone to tell you every twist and turn of the journey face to face or would you prefer to simply look at it on a map. The map might be a leaner form of communication—it is impersonal, with symbols, but it gets the message across concisely and efficiently.

Thus, on occasions leaner forms of communication might be more appropriate for communicating information in organizations—it is simpler to see a summary of sales figures as a table than have somebody recite them face to face.

What do you think would be the most appropriate ways to communicate the following within an organization?

- Facts about a project.
- Figures, such as accounts.
- Instructions for repairing a piece of machinery.
- Directions to the head office.
- Feedback to members of a project team.
- Praise to an individual who has secured a new contract.
- Anger at a colleague who is stirring up trouble.
- An idea for a new product.
- A new culture.

Research insight: Communicating a culture, Gergen, K.J., and Whitney, D. 1996. Technologies of representation in the global corporation: power and polyphony. In: Boje, D. M., Gephart, R. P. Jr, and Thatchenkery, T. J. (eds) *Postmodern management and organization theory*. Sage, Thousand Oaks, CA, 331–357.

Gergen and Whitney's (1996) study of culture change in a recently merged multinational firm, Sloan Becker, highlights the relevance of media richness in communicating something as open to interpretation as an organizational culture.

In a bid to integrate the two newly-merged firms and their cultures, it was decided to implement a common set of principles or a common culture. This came under the slogan 'Simply Better', summing-up the idea that workers should improve their 'performance' continually to reach the potential and promise within Sloan-Becker. The new culture would be disseminated globally through a printed booklet.

However, as a relatively lean medium, lacking the richness of information that would come from the presence of the original authors, much of the culture was left open to the interpretation of the workers receiving and reading the booklet. Terms such as 'performance' are equivocal—they mean different things to different people; however, there was no opportunity for feedback for workers to ask about, and clarify, the meaning of terms and statements in the booklet.

The recipients were left to make their own interpretations of the culture, in discussion with familiar people around them. What emerged at Sloan-Becker was not the one unified culture that management desired, but a whole patchwork of different cultures and meanings across the organization.

Gergen and Whitney's case highlights the problem of using a relatively lean medium, like a text, to communicate richer, more equivocal ideas, such as culture and corporate values. The leaner medium cannot communicate every nuance of the culture, and allows more possibility for noise to intervene in the communication process and for people's perceived meanings of the culture to be different to the original intended meaning. As we saw earlier with the example of a song, the original author lacks the power over the interpretation that others will make—the meaning of the culture here is passed on by others and redirected in a manner similar to Latour's rugby ball metaphor.

Employability skills: communication

When advertising a vacancy many employers call for good 'communication skills.' We might think of this as equating to good interpersonal skills—being able to engage in conversation, for example.

While this is a part of communication, effective communication skills are about putting a message across in the most appropriate manner for what is being communicated. It is about making the message as clear as possible, and not open to misinterpretation and miscommunication. As we have seen in this section, on occasions the most appropriate communication might be a face-to-face conversation and at other times it might be sending figures in an email.

Think about your own experience of communication and how you might be able to demonstrate skills to a potential employer. It might be from collaborating on a project with other students. What variety of communication methods did you use and which did you find most effective? How did you overcome any areas of confusion or miscommunication?

The informated organization

So far, in examining communication, information has been seen largely in terms of communications such as words, gestures, and diagrams, etc. Leaner communications media gain efficiency at the expense of richness. However, in this section we see how the creation of information by such lean media, often as a result of organizational techniques, such as **bureaucracy**, is an important aspect of the nature of organizations which use information and communications technology.

Zuboff's (1988) concept of the informated organization suggests that more and more of what an organization actually does—its processes and the information that it holds—is stored as computerized information, to the extent that the organization becomes like a computer **database**.

The nature of such information, however, derives from technologies and tools that pre-date the use of information and communication technology in organizations.

Bureaucracy and information technology

We may not think of something like a form as a piece of technology. However, think back to the analysis of the UCAS form for university admissions in Chapter 2. Using Cooper's (1993) earlier definition of technology, it emerges from a human inadequacy—people are unable to process the applications of thousands of university students in person. The form is the tool which makes this processing possible—it standardizes information in a manner which can then be processed more easily, and communicated and shared within the organization.

For Cooper and Burrell (1988) this at the heart of what bureaucracy does. It is not simply a structure—it is a technology of classifying and ordering people. Forms, records, and paperwork all are used for ordering organizational populations by not only storing information, but also using that information to create further information. For example, with the UCAS form it is easy, given the standard nature of the form, to create information such as the average age of applicants, the number of people applying for business degrees, and the average qualifications, etc.

Bureaucracy records thus not only store lean information—facts and figures about people—they go on to create further lean information from the analysis of data that is already stored. In Zuboff's terms bureaucratic records are a basis for *informating* the organization.

The organization as a database

Where bureaucratic records are stored in computer databases, the potential for information processing and sharing, and creating, new information is increased. Given the processing power of information technology and computers, a greater amount of information can be stored and processed. More and more of what the organization actually is comes to be stored within a computer system.

Think about how your bank knows you. Rather than the rich, face-to-face version of you, they will know you as a leaner entry on a database. It is a 'highly caricatured' (Poster, 1995: 91) version of you that boils you down to a few database fields, such as name, address, and account number, etc.

Bureaucracy From the French *bureau*, meaning office; bureaucracy covers official, formal elements of rational organizational design, such as the hierarchical organization structure, the rules and procedures, and the official paperwork, which exert impersonal control over the organization.

Database A computerized store of structured, organized data.

What other 'highly caricatured' forms of you are held by other organizations?

It is not just you, and all of the other customers that are held on a database by your bank, financial and account information will also be held in various computer systems; indeed, the whole bank operates by updating various entries on the different databases. When you withdraw an amount of money it is deducted on the database field relevant to your account.

For Zuboff (1985: 10), it is not that banks simply use databases, banks are 'becoming more like databases'. So much of their activity is done through the computer data that they hold it is as if the database is the equivalent of the bank itself.

Chapter 4 shows how information technology and computer records can be used to intensify control and surveillance over workers, as seen in call centres. Do you think such technology brings any advantage to workers?

Rather than being a second-class form of communication compared with richer communications media, leaner forms of communication are the means by which organizations are informated and through which database information is held. In other words, the organization becomes almost purely information. In Blackler's terms (1995: 1032) it has 'imploded' into code. The possibilities for communication using such code are enhanced when, as we see in the next section, organizations communicate through electronic networks, such as the Internet.

Review questions

1. Describe the main features of media richness theory.
2. Explain how different communications media convey the social presence of the sender of the message.
3. Analyse how communication is a trade-off between efficiency and richness.

Apply

4. How can the miscommunication in the email chain in the running case be analysed in terms of media richness and social presence theories?

Organizations and networks

Much of our experience of contemporary organizations is mediated through the Internet. We manage our money through online banking, log on to our university emails, and order shopping from numerous online retailers. While the previous section showed us how much of organizational activity is represented as computer code, in this section we see how this code is communicated through computer **networks**—between people and organizations, and between organizations.

Networks The sharing of data through linked computer systems or through the Internet.

When did you last access any data through a computer network or the Internet—either on a phone or a computer, or any other device? Or, alternatively, when was the last time you went for a day without accessing information in such a way?

The section begins by examining the nature of organizations as they operate more and more through global networks, which can be summarized by two potentially contradictory trends:

- on the one hand, organizations become more of a 'free-for-all', with boundaries between organizations becoming less obvious and organizations operating globally on an almost random basis. The concept of the **rhizome** is introduced as a means to understand this particular nature of the contemporary organization

- on the other hand, we see how structures of control exist within the Internet and how these structures both affect, and are used by, organizations.

Rhizome A mass of random, tangled connections which some people suggest is similar to the nature of the Internet and cyberspace.

The 'implosion' and 'explosion' of organizations

Frank Blackler (1995: 1032) suggests that contemporary organizations have undergone two simultaneous processes. On the one hand organizations have imploded into computer code, on the other hand they have simultaneously exploded out into computer networks.

This implosion and explosion metaphor encapsulates two consequences of the informating of organizations. Much more of what an organization does is stored as electronic data—the organization becomes a database (implosion). At the same time, the very nature of that data means that it can be shared in global computer networks, such as the Internet (explosion). Rather than ICT being a tool that facilitates communication in the organization, the technology becomes the very medium through which the organization operates and exists.

In this section we examine the implications of this. If technology is the very medium of organizing, what implication does this have for the nature of the organization itself? In a global, networked world, what exactly is an organization?

Blackler (1995: 1033) states that, through computer networks, organizations can 'operate relatively independently from geographical location, thereby blurring the boundaries between one organization and another'. We examine these ideas of

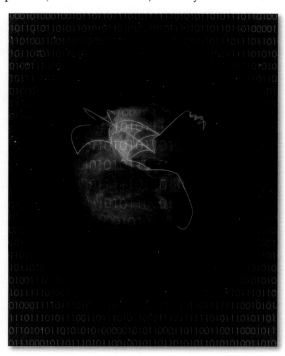

The implosion and explosion of contemporary organizations.

Placelessness Where organizations exist in networks and seem to have no one fixed geographical location.

Boundarylessness Where the extent of sharing and dispersal of an organization's computer data gives a sense that there is no boundary to the organization.

placelessness and **boundarylessness** in turn, examining how contemporary organizations both increase their geographical reach and have blurred boundaries between each other.

Organizations and geographical reach

Where are you when you interact with your university, performing actions such as emailing a tutor, submitting an essay, or renewing a library book, etc.? Do you do it on the premises or elsewhere, through a computer network? Much interaction with our universities is often done from home or from a computer somewhere outside the university. We have even received emails from students on the other side of the planet while they have been on holiday.

For many tasks, it is not necessary to be within the physical boundaries of the organization geographically. It could be argued that the university has extended its geographical reach—if the organization is imploded into its database, that database is being interacted with in some way from a student's living room, from a cyber café, or from a hotel room in the Caribbean. *It becomes difficult to draw the boundary around the organization in geographical terms. Where exactly does the organization end?*

Similar interactions can be seen to take place with other organizations, for example online banking and ordering online shopping, etc. all take place in geographical locations beyond the organization itself.

Global village A metaphor to describe a perception of the globe shrinking in size as a result of the speed and global reach of transport and communications technologies.

For Latour (1997: 4), closeness is no longer defined in terms of geography, but in terms of how people are linked together through a network. Two people separated by a large geographical space are still close together in network terms if they are having an online conversation. In Chapter 15 we examine a similar idea with McLuhan's (1964) **global village**. While people may be far away geographically, communication technologies make people feel much closer together. Such technologies contribute to processes of globalization—even the smallest organization can now use the Internet to operate on a global basis.

When you use the Internet, how many different global locations do you interact with?

Teleworking, telecommuting Working away from a place of work by logging into a workplace's computer network.

Real life case: teleworking and telecommuting

An example of where the increased geographical reach of organizations has an effect on working practices is with **teleworking** or **telecommuting** (Nilles, 1975). Computer technologies allow a worker to work from home, accessing organizational databases and their email through the Internet.

As such, the worker at home becomes a part of the organization's computer network—the home is connected directly to the organization. Where an organization's network may encompass geographically dispersed organizational premises, the worker's home effectively becomes one of such premises. With mobile and wireless technology, and the use of laptop or tablet computers, it's not just from home that a worker may telecommute, but also a café, waiting at a train station or anywhere in reach of a wi-fi or mobile Internet signal.

Castells (1996: 394) suggests that it is only people who substitute work done in the workplace for work done at home who are true teleworkers. For example, a writer is not a teleworker—writers have always worked at home, the only difference is that now they can email work to a publisher rather than send it by post. However, a lawyer who is able to retrieve case notes from their firm's server, comment upon them, and circulate those comments to other members of the legal team—all from home—is doing work that would previously have to be done in the office. They are telecommuters in the true sense.

What do you think are the advantages and disadvantages for both workers and employers of teleworking?

Teleworking leads us to question when a worker is actually 'in' the organization for which they work. Is it when they are physically within its premises or is it when they are connected to the organization through a network? Teleworking also blurs the distinction between home and work life. If working from home but logged into our organization's network, we are at once both at home and at work. This blurring of boundaries is further examined in the next section.

Organizations and the blurring of boundaries

In addition to making organizations 'placeless' by extending their geographical reach beyond their physical boundaries, computer networks also blur the boundaries *between* organizations. While organizations hold data in computer systems about their own operations, this data is shared between organizations through networks.

Let us take two examples that we have used previously. In this chapter we have seen how banks are effectively databases of customer and financial data. In Chapter 4 we saw how supermarkets operate in a similar way—barcodes are the key to organizational databases of stock levels and the like.

Now, imagine a customer at the supermarket checkout pays for their goods using their debit card. This sets off a number of interactions between data across computer networks, and which blur the distinctions between the supermarket and the bank (based on Lawley, 2006: 105–106):

- the supermarket's computers link to those of the bank, which checks its own database to ensure that the card is valid and that there are sufficient funds in the customer's account

- the customer may ask for 'cashback' with their transaction. The supermarket cashier hands the requested cash over to the customer. The cashier, although an employee of the supermarket, is also, in effect, playing the role of that customer's bank teller

- the economy doesn't just have one supermarket and one bank—it has many retail outlets and many financial institutions. Many transactions similar to the one above will be carried out throughout the day. To minimize the number and complexity of transactions, the Bankers Automated Clearing Service (BACS) (Boddy and Gunson, 1996: 173) acts as an umbrella organization, mediating transactions between the different banks and settling indebtedness between them at the end of each day. The databases between banks and retail outlets are thus in constant communication and interacting from second to second.

The link between supermarkets and banks is just one example of interactions that blur the boundaries between organizations. Think, for example, of hotel booking sites, such as Expedia, which interrogate the computer networks of individual hotels and hotel chains in response to a customer enquiry, and make bookings on those networks on behalf of the customer.

Can you think of any other examples where computer networks blur the boundary between different organizations?

Organizations as rhizomes

We usually think of an organization as some form of structure, but organizations that are mediated through computer networks perhaps challenge our traditional views of what an organization actually *is*. As we have seen, computer networks both remove the geographical boundaries of organization and blur the distinctions between organizations. It is as if an organization can pop up anywhere and at any time within a computer network. Organizations become a constant and unpredictable movement of data, making multiple connections between networks which appear and disappear throughout the course of a day, and through which data is shared.

The tree and rhizome.

Deleuze and Guattari's (1987) concepts of the 'rhizome' and the 'root-tree' are a useful means of examining these two contrasting views of the organization . These are botanical metaphors which illustrate contrasting types of structure—as Jackson and Carter (2007: 306) suggest, they explore different ways that we might be 'rooted to the spot'.

- A tree always grows in relation to a central structure—its roots and trunk—from which other outgrowths 'branch out'. In this respect, it is similar to the more traditional view of an organizational structure, as represented by the organization chart (see Figure 14.1), where different parts of the organization 'branch out' from the level above.

- The rhizome, however, is an underground root system typified by the random movement of grass. It develops in a random fashion and is not constrained by any central structure or root system, it is '. . . a tangled mass of randomly developing connections following no logical pattern. It is always connecting points to other points' (Jackson and Carter, 2007: 306).

Cooper (1998: 126) sees cyberspace as a rhizome, seeking to 'expand its possibilities of unconstrained freedom'. Data moves freely around the Internet, seemingly moving around networks and making infinite connections and combinations. Given that organizations use the electronic networks of cyberspace, the links between the organization and the rhizome become apparent, for instance Sean Cubitt notes:

> The new transnational companies are themselves placeless creatures. In Deleuze and Guattari's terms they are 'rhizomes' . . . The old companies were sedentary and rooted to a specific spot. But we can no longer picket the typical new company's headquarters, because there is none: only the shifting, headless rhizome of connections between its executives and their employees.
>
> (Cubitt, 2001: 129–130)

Cubitt suggests that the nature of organizations is thus a shifting random set of data connections. The rhizome certainly has some explanatory power in mapping the movement and communication of organizational data, and where people and other organizations interact with an organization in myriad different connections and combinations.

The rhizome is sometimes used to suggest that the Internet is completely unstructured—a free-for-all. Certainly, there are cases where the unrestricted nature of the Internet has had an impact upon organizations. For example, the Internet has made the illegal downloading of music possible and this has had an impact on recording companies who have had to explore new ways of operating as a response, for example through legal downloads and music-streaming services, such as Spotify (Sweney, 2012; Kusek and Leonhard, 2005).

It may be tempting to view cyberspace as a 'free-for-all'—an uncontrollable frontier whereby all manner of illegal activities take place, for example illegal downloading, pornography, and leaks of confidential information, and these are, perhaps, at the less murky end of what goes on. For some people, the Internet allows laws to be bypassed, but we should be careful about seeing it as a complete free-for-all. As Hardt and Negri (2001) note correctly, the Internet has both its rhizomatic and root-tree elements—there is a flow of data between networks within the Internet, but, at the same time, this is controlled and structured. In the next two sections we examine this control and structure in terms of the organization of the Internet and how organizations structure themselves within the Internet.

The organization of the Internet

There is a great deal of *control* and *organization* within cyberspace and the Internet. While there are many hyperbolic and somewhat utopian views of cyberspace as being some entity separate to the real world, as Sassen (2000: 28) points out, 'digital space . . . is partly embedded in actual societal structures and power dynamics. Its topography weaves in and out of non-electronic space'. By this, Sassen means that cyberspace interacts with and is, indeed, controlled by existing structures within society, where 'recurrent attempts to control its data and steer its data flows have been made' (Röhle, 2005: 404). In other words, organizations exert control over the Internet.

Lawley (2006) suggests that the Internet, and the networks and technologies through which it operates, are controlled and organized at four particular levels (see Figure 14.5):

- computer and network hardware
- Internet access and **Internet service providers (ISPs)**

Internet service provider (ISP) An organization which provides a link to the Internet.

Figure 14.5 Levels of Internet organization (based on Lawley, 2006).

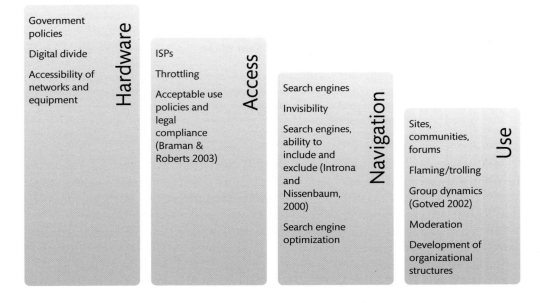

- navigation within the Internet
- the use of the Internet through forums and communities.

Internet hardware

Real life case: cutting the cable

In 2011, a woman in Georgia who was scavenging for copper cut through an underground wire. Unfortunately, this was the wire which carried Internet data to the neighbouring country of Armenia. The whole of Armenia was cut off from the Internet for five hours while the cable was being repaired.

Source: Parfitt (2011).

The nature of the Internet is put into perspective when we realize that, rather than being a random free-for-all, it has to travel through cables and physical **hardware**. This can be seen when national regimes may wish to restrict their population's access to the Internet. Recent years have seen stories in the news of dictators in various countries under threat from revolution. One of their first responses is to cut off access to the Internet within those countries so that people are unable to access information about what is happening.

Access to networks and computer equipment to use them is pertinent to discussion of a so-called **digital divide** between an infrastructurally-rich developed world and a developing world which has little access to such technology (see, e.g. Munro (2000) and Sassen (2002)). In the UK, there has been a debate recently about the widespread availability of broadband, with areas that do not have access to broadband being seen to be at a disadvantage in an information-rich economy (BBC News, 2012).

Hardware Computer equipment and infrastructures through which computer networks operate.

Digital divide A divide between people who have access to computer hardware and network infrastructures, such as the Internet, and those who do not.

Internet access and Internet service providers (ISPs)

Even with access to digital networks and hardware, a level of Internet organization can be found in the way that people connect to the Internet. ISPs are companies which provide a service for users to connect to the Internet and, in doing so, are able to control and regulate how people use the Internet.

For Braman and Roberts (2003) it is the 'terms of service' and 'acceptable use policies' of ISPs, to which users must sign-up, which effectively become the law of the Internet. While people may wish to download masses of files, ISPs may engage in **throttling**—slowing down the rate of data transfer for those who they deem do it in excess.

ISPs have the power to block access to certain sites. This is done, for example, with a child pornography blacklist—such sites are blocked before they can be accessed (BBC News, 2010). An ongoing debate in the UK is whether or not ISPs should also enforce laws such as illegal downloading by monitoring what their customers download and reporting it to relevant authorities (e.g. Halliday, 2011).

> **Throttling** Where an ISP deliberately reduces the speed at which a client can download data.

Internet navigation and search

While the previous section explored the rhizomatic nature of the Internet, if the Internet were completely random and unstructured it would be unusable. How would you find relevant sites for example? It would just be a sea of unstructured data.

Search engines, such as Google, organize the data on the Internet, making it navigable for users. However, this can affect organizations in different ways. An organization which appears at the top of search lists will be seen by many more people than one which is down on the fifth page. As such, through their ability to include and exclude, search engines have the power to make sites 'disappear' (Introna and Nissenbaum, 2000: 180).

> **Search engine** A website which allows users to search for items on the Internet.

As a result of this, an industry which has appeared in recent years is one which offers **search engine optimization** (SEO). Consultants offer to examine clients' webpages and structure them in such a way that they will appear higher up on search engine results.

> **Search engine optimization** Techniques to increase the rank of a website on search engine results.

Study skills: literature searching

The organization of information which is available through computer networks is of direct relevance to your studies, for example when you search for literature for a piece of coursework or an exam. There is a vast amount of potential sources available—books, journal articles, and databases, to name but a few, and knowing how to go about finding relevant information for your work can be confusing and daunting.

Many university librarians nowadays refer to their job as 'information management'. They know the best ways to search for, and find, information relevant to a particular academic subject, understanding how such information is organized, categorized, and catalogued. As part of your induction to university they will pass on some of this information to you, highlighting the databases and search facilities that will best help you to find information that you need.

Searching for information is a skill in itself—knowing the right databases and catalogues to use, and how to use the appropriate search terms within them. A further skill is knowing which are appropriate academic sources to use. A general search on a commonly-used search engine, such as Google or Bing, will give all manner of results, many of which are unsuitable for academic work. Knowing the right databases and search facilities to use, and how to use them, will help greatly in sourcing relevant academic material.

Structuring Internet forums and communities

Many of you will use or read Internet forums and discussion boards, or be a member of **Internet communities** where people interact. You may be used to moderators who delete unsuitable posts and even ban members who engage in disruptive acts, such as **flaming** or **trolling**. A final level of organization of the Internet is at the level of individual sites and communities which develop their own rules and terms of usage.

We suggest that many online communities, in fact, take on structures that are familiar in other organizations. While they may begin as fairly unstructured, as they grow they need to maintain order so that they can continue to operate without unwelcome disruptions. Online communities thus take on bureaucratic forms (see Chapter 2), such as hierarchies (through various levels of moderators), and rules and procedures.

Further organizational characteristics can be seen in terms of the social interactions in such sites, linking with the dynamics of groups and teams and organizational cultures (see Chapters 6 and 7). Gotved (2002) suggests that online communities develop their own norms and values, just as with social groupings in the 'real world'.

With online communities becoming structured like their 'real-world' counterparts, we now turn to how real-world organizations structure themselves within the Internet.

Internet communities A group whose main form of interaction is through the Internet.

Flaming Abusive messages sent to Internet forums and communities.

Trolling Messages sent to Internet forums and communities which deliberately aim to disrupt their normal functioning and norms of behaviour.

Organizations within the Internet

While the previous section has shown how the Internet is structured and organized at various levels, the final issue that we address is how organizations within the Internet are structured. If, as Blackler suggests, organizations are imploded and exploded into code simultaneously, then this computer code is a valuable asset of the organization—it is essentially what the organization *is* and the medium through which it operates.

The rhizomatic nature of the Internet means that, as we have seen, organizations can use this data to communicate through networks, expanding their geographical reach and interface with other organizations. However, it is this same rhizomatic nature that poses a threat to organizations and this valuable code. Organizations are vulnerable to their networks being accessed for a number of malicious purposes, for example:

- hacking—unauthorized people gaining access to a computer network to view confidential data, stealing valuable data, or vandalizing a company's data

- computer viruses—malicious programs that enter a computer network and destroy data within that network

- denial of service attacks—multiple and repeated attempts to access the network of a particular organization which overloads the network and makes it unusable.

Rather than being boundaryless in cyberspace, organizations need to engage in forms of electronic boundary maintenance in order to keep their data secure.

The 'Janus face' of organizations

Janus is a figure from Roman mythology. His role was that of a gatekeeper—to maintain border and boundary controls within ancient Roman walled cities. Janus's two faces looked simultaneously inwards to protect what was within the walls and outwards to look out for any impending hostile threats from outside (Burchett, 1918).

In a similar manner, an organization looks inwards to protect the database that makes up so much of what it is—the valuable computer code into which it has imploded. At the same time, it looks outwards to the networks in which it operates so as to be alert to hostile threats from outside, such as hackers and viruses.

The Janus figure is used here as a metaphor for organizational 'gatekeeping' and boundary maintenance within cyberspace. However, unlike the entrance to an Ancient Roman walled city, there is not one gateway, but a multitude of ways in which data can be shared across an organization's boundary. Organizations, thus, put in place a number of 'border controls' and security measures across their network boundaries. Examples include:

JANUS.

The Janus face.

- passwords—giving different levels of access to different people
- firewalls—a technology which screens data entering a network for potential threats, preventing hostile data from entering
- filters—either as part of a network or on an individual computer, filters can screen emails and similar communications for harmful viruses and can also be used to screen out bulk email, so called 'spam', or even content and language that an organization deems to be unacceptable.

The Janus face of organizations thus refers to the multiple levels of access and boundary maintenance—passwords, firewalls, etc. that regulate the data flow necessary for an organization to operate, while maintaining data security.

Have you ever found email difficult to use because the inbox is over-run with spam messages. Or, on the contrary, have you ever found perfectly reasonable emails being directed to a spam folder?

This is a tricky balance that organizations need to maintain. On the one hand they need to keep data moving so that business is actually taking place, but not have that movement so free that any malicious entry can be obtained. Make the barriers too tough, however, and genuine interactions will not be able to take place—throwing the baby out with the bath water.

For example, let us return to the example of the bank. While you might want access to your bank account from home, you would not want any other random person having that access. Indeed, if the bank did not maintain adequate levels of security then they would find all of their accounts emptying into the wrong hands pretty rapidly. However, if there was a password regime that took five minutes to gain access to online banking, many people would give up and the activity would simply not take place.

The communication of data between organizational networks, and how that communication is structured and regulated, is thus a major component of what makes up the structure and nature of contemporary, network-mediated organizations.

Review questions

1. Explain what is meant by organizations 'imploding' into code and 'exploding' into global networks.
2. Describe the four ways in which the Internet is structured.
3. Analyse the need for organizations to maintain a balance between data security and data flow.

Apply

4. Can you think of examples of organizational 'border controls'—electronic or physical—that you have encountered?

Chapter summary

In this chapter we have examined the nature of communication in organizations and, in particular, how this is mediated by contemporary ICT. Technology can affect the richness and degree of social presence in communications within an organization, and can affect the nature and structure of organizations as they communicate information through networks, such as the Internet.

ICT is a contemporary topic and, as such, it is one which is also constantly changing in terms of the latest technologies available and the ways in which they affect, and are used by, organizations.

For example, at the time of writing, three ongoing issues which relate to organizations and ICT were:

- various high-street retailers in the UK were entering administration, closing down, or experiencing difficult sales figures. While this might be attributable to difficult economic conditions, a challenge also comes to the traditional high-street model or organization from online retailing (Davis, 2011)

- it is suggested that email is falling out of favour in some workplaces, with instant messaging systems or group communication forums similar to social media platforms being favoured (Sherwin, 2011)

- there remain debates about control over the Internet—either by governments limiting access to the Internet or private companies, such as Google and Facebook, holding data within the Internet (*The Guardian*, 2012).

Visit the Online Resource Centre for further discussion of these ongoing issues.

Looking back at this chapter, are there any more recent developments in the use of ICT by organizations that you can identify?

In this chapter, changes that ICT bring to the nature of organization as more and more of its activities are codified and mediated through global networks have been identified. As such, these technologies also play a major part in the subject of the next chapter—globalization.

Further reading

Rollinson, D. 2008. *Organisational behaviour and analysis: an integrated approach*. Financial Times/Prentice Hall, Harlow.
Many textbooks have a chapter on communication; Chapter 15 is recommended in particular.

Rice, R.E. 1992. Task analyzability, use of new media, and effectiveness: A multi-site exploration of media richness. *Organization Science* 3(4): 475–500.
Introduces and critiques social presence theory and media richness theory.

Zuboff, S. 1985. Automate/informate: the two faces of intelligent technology. *Organizational Dynamics*,14(2): 5–18.
Although written in 1985 it still makes relevant points about the informated organization and the organization as a database.

***The Guardian*. Battle for the Internet. Available at: http://www.guardian.co.uk/technology/series/battle-for-the-internet (last accessed 9 July 2012).**
A useful series of current newspaper articles examining issues of control over the Internet.

Bibliography

BBC News. 2010. Internet porn block 'not possible' say ISPs. 20 December 2010. Available at: http://www.bbc.co.uk/news/technology-12041063.

BBC News. 2011. Army job loss e-mails: Soldiers get apology. Available at http://www.bbc.co.uk/news/uk-12461211 (last accessed 17 July 2012).

BBC News. 2012. Rural communities 'at risk' without broadband access. 24 September 2012. Available at: http://www.bbc.co.uk/news/uk-19696904.

Blackler, F. 1995. Knowledge, knowledge work and organizations: an overview and interpretation. *Organization Studies* 16(6): 1021–1046.

Boddy, D., and Gunson, N. 1996. *Organizations in the network age*. Routledge: London, New York.

Boden, D. 1994. *The business of talk: organizations in action,* Polity Press: London, Cambridge, MA.

Braman, S., and Roberts, S. 2003. Advantage ISP: Terms of service as media law. *New Media & Society* 5(3): 422.

Broekstra, G. 1998. An organization is a conversation. *Discourse and Organization*. Sage: London, pp. 152–176.

Burchett, B. 1918. *Janus in Roman life and cult: A study in Roman Religions*. George Banta Publishing Company: Menasha, WI.

Castells, M. 1996. *The rise of the network society*. Blackwell: Malden, MA.

Cooper, R. 1993. Technologies of representation. In: Ahonen, P. (ed.) *Tracing the semiotic boundaries of politics*. Mouton de Gruyter: Berlin, pp. 279–312.

Cooper, R. 1998. Assemblage notes. In: Chia, R. (ed.) *Organized worlds: explorations in technology and organization with Robert Cooper*, vol. 2. Routledge: London.

Cooper, R., and Burrell, G. 1988. Modernism, postmodernism and organizational analysis: An introduction. *Organization Studies* 9(1): 91–112.

Cubitt, S. 2001. *Simulation and social theory*. Sage: London, Thousand Oaks, CA.

Daft, R.L., and Lengel, R.H. 1986. Organizational information requirements, media richness and structural design. *Management Science* 32(5): 554–571.

Davis, E. 2011. Is the High Street doomed? BBC Online. 29 August 2011. Available at: http://news.bbc.co.uk/today/hi/today/newsid_9573000/9573436.stm.

Deleuze, G., and Guattari, F. 1987. *A thousand plateaus: capitalism and schizophrenia*. University of Minnesota Press: Minneapolis.

Gergen, K.J. 1992. Organization theory in the postmodern era. In: Reed, M., and Hughes, M. D. (eds) *Rethinking organisation: new Directions in Organization Theory and Analysis*. Sage: London, pp. 207–226.

Gergen, K., and Whitney, D. 1996. Technologies of representation in the global corporation: power and polyphony. In: Boje, R., Gephart, R. Jr, and Thatchenkery, T. (eds) *Postmodern management and organization theory*. Sage: London, pp. 331–357.

Gotved, S. 2002. Spatial dimensions in online communities. *Space and Culture* 5(4): 405–414.

The Guardian. 2012. Battle for the Internet. Available at: http://www.guardian.co.uk/technology/series/battle-for-the-internet.

Halliday, J. 2011. Digital Economy Act: further delay to illegal downloading measures. *The Guardian*. 28 March 2011. Available at: http://www.guardian.co.uk/technology/2011/mar/28/digital-economy-act-illegal-downloading.

Hardt, M., and Negri, A. 2000. *Empire*. Harvard University Press: Cambridge, MA.

The Independent. 2011. Soldiers' email sackings condemned. 15 February 2011. Available at: http://www.independent.co.uk/news/uk/home-news/soldiers-email-sackings-condemned-2215368.html (last accessed 17 July 2012).

Introna, L.D., and Nissenbaum, H. 2000. Shaping the Web: Why the politics of search engines matters. *The Information Society* 16(3): 169–185.

Jackson, N., and Carter, P. 2007. *Rethinking Organisational Behaviour*. Financial Times/Prentice Hall: Harlow.

Kurland, N.B., and Pelled, L.H. 2000. Passing the word: Toward a model of gossip and power in the workplace. *Academy of Management Review* 25(2): 428–438.

Kusek, D., and Leonhard, G. 2005. *The Future of Music: Manifesto for the Digital Revolution*. Berklee Press: Boston, MA.

Latour, B. 1986. The powers of association. *Psychological Review* 32: 264–280.

Latour, B. 1997. On Actor-network theory; A few clarifications. Working paper for Centre for Social Theory and Technology, University of Keele. Archived at http://www.nettime.org/Lists-Archives/nettime-I-9801/msg00019.html.

Lawley, S. 2006. Accelerating organisations through representational infrastructures: the possibilities for power and resistance. *Advances in Organization Studies* 19: 91–118.

Lo, S.K. 2008. The nonverbal communication functions of emoticons in computer-mediated communication. *CyberPsychology & Behavior* 11(5): 595–597.

McLuhan, M. 1964. *Understanding media; the extensions of man*. McGraw-Hill: New York.

Mehrabian, A. 1971. *Silent messages*. Wadsworth Pub. Co.: Belmont, CA.

Munro, L. 2000. Non-disciplinary power and the network society. *Organization* 7(4): 679–695.

Nichols, R.G. 1962. Listening is good business. *Human Resource Management*, 1(2): 1–10.

Nilles, J.M. 1975. Telecommunications and organizational decentralization. *IEEE Transactions On Communications* 23: 1142–1147.

Noon, M., and Delbridge, R. 1993. News from behind my hand: Gossip in organizations. *Organization Studies* 14(1): 23–36.

Parfitt, T. 2011. Georgian woman cuts off web access to whole of Armenia. *The Guardian*. 6 April 2011. Available at: http://www.guardian.co.uk/world/2011/apr/06/georgian-woman-cuts-web-access (last accessed 9 July 2012).

Poster, M. 1995. *The second media age*. Polity Press: Cambridge.

Quinn, B. 2011. MoD 'clerical error' results in soldiers being sacked by email. *The Guardian*. 15 February 2011. Available at: http://www.guardian.co.uk/uk/2011/feb/15/mod-clerical-error-sacked-email (last accessed 17 July 2012).

Rice, R.E. 1992. Task analyzability, use of new media, and effectiveness: A multi-site exploration of media richness. *Organization Science* 3(4): 475–500.

Röhle, T. 2005. Power, reason, closure: critical perspectives on new media theory. *New Media & Society* 7(3): 403.

Sassen, S. 2000. Digital networks and the state. *Theory, Culture & Society* 17(4): 19–33.

Sassen, S. 2002. Towards a sociology of information technology. *Current Sociology* 50(3): 365–388.

Shannon, C.E., Weaver, W., and Blahut, R.E. 1949. *The Mathematical Theory of Communication*, vol. 117. University of Illinois Press: Urbana.

Sherwin, A. 2011. Are we facing the death of email? *The Independent*. 7 December 2011. Available at: http://www.independent.co.uk/life-style/gadgets-and-tech/features/are-we-facing-the-death-of-email-6273170.html (last accessed 17 July 2012).

Short, J., Williams, E., and Christie, B. 1976. *The social psychology of telecommunications*. Wiley: London, New York.

Sweney, M. 2012. Downloads, Spotify and Napster help offset UK CD sales slide. *The Guardian*. 16 February 2012. Available at: http://www.guardian.co.uk/media/2012/feb/16/downloads-spotify-napster-cd-sales.

Zuboff, S. 1985. Automate/informate: the two faces of intelligent technology. *Organizational Dynamics* 14(2): 5–18.

Zuboff, S. 1988. *In the age of the smart machine: the future of work and power*. Heinemann Professional: Oxford.

Globalization

Managing between the global and the local

Chapter overview and learning outcomes

By the end of this chapter you should be able to:

- describe the key features of globalization
- explain how contemporary globalization can be described as giving a sense of being in a 'global village'
- explain how organizations operate on a global scale
- explain how national and local cultures affect the ways in which organizations operate globally
- analyse how global inequalities are caused by globalization.

Key theorists

Marshall McLuhan	A theorist of media who first described the effects of globalization as a 'global village'
Roland Robertson	A sociologist who has analysed globalization from the perspective of global consciousness and the relationship between the global and the local
Geert Hofstede	Attempted to outline national managerial cultures on a set of four numerical scales
Naomi Klein	Author of 'No Logo', one of the earliest and most popular manifestos of the anti-globalization movement

Key terms

Globalization	Activities, both organizational and in wider society, taking place on a global scale
Global village	A perceived shrinking of the globe and increased sense of global proximity due to the effects of transport and communications technologies
Global culture	A homogeneous, worldwide culture that emerges as a result of globalization and the activities of global organizations
National culture, local culture	Individual and distinct cultures as seen in individual nations or territories
Glocalization	Adapting global practices to local cultures and contexts
Anti-globalization movement	A collective term for protestors and critics of globalization and its perceived inequalities

Introduction

> ### Running case: 'Junction International'
>
> Simon Chance is discussing Junction Hotel's global ambitions with his team of investors. The hotel has joined up with an online booking website, which means that it is showing up on global searches resulting in an increase in the number of guests coming from across the globe.
>
> In response to this, Chance has tried to give the hotel a more international feel. So far, it has all been fairly superficial—hanging welcome signs on the doors in different languages, displaying a set of clocks showing different world times behind reception, and a providing a selection of international newspapers in the hotel lobby.
>
> Chance sees an opportunity in the global market and wants to take his international strategy further. As an independent hotel, it doesn't have the global presence of some of the big-name hotel chains, but nevertheless, Chance still wants the hotel to be an international player.
>
> At the meeting, it is decided to work towards an internationalization plan, codenamed 'Junction International.'

You may often hear that we live in a 'globalized' society and that contemporary business takes place within global horizons. The global nature of our own existence, and the array of products and services that we consume is, perhaps, summed up in the following popular statement circulating the Internet:

> Being British is about driving in a German car to an Irish pub for a Belgian beer, then travelling home, grabbing an Indian curry or a Turkish kebab on the way, to sit on Swedish furniture and watch American shows on a Japanese TV. And the most British thing of all? Suspicion of anything foreign (quoted in Wooley, 2010).

Although humorous in its intent, the quote highlights not only the global nature of the economy, but also how this global variety can be seen in the goods and services available within one particular country, in this case the UK.

Furthermore, as individuals we are more aware and in touch with the globe as a whole. Films and television programmes bring to life situations from other countries, and the Internet allows us to communicate directly with people in those countries.

?!

In your day-to-day Internet and media activity, which countries do you come into contact with?

Globalization
Defined in many different ways, globalization is where activities take place on an increasingly global scale.

This chapter examines two broad issues related to **globalization**—which might be seen as complementary or contradictory—and how they relate to organization and management issues on a global scale, especially as it relates to individual national issues:

* on one hand, the world is organized into nation states, but it is suggested that these are becoming less relevant—globalization suggests we are one globe and features of globalization make individual nations less relevant. We examine the move towards what McLuhan (1964) termed a 'global village' and the features of globalization that contribute to this trend, and the role of organizations in contributing to this

- on the other hand, it is suggested that, despite trends towards globalization, individual nations, and the differences between them, are still important—their laws, cultures, and customs, etc. still exert an influence on how management is practised within their borders. We thus look at the implications of national and cultural differences for managing and organizing on a global basis.

Within the debates on globalization, we also see a number of perspectives critical of the effects of globalization, suggesting that it perpetuates inequalities on a global scale rather than being a uniformly global process.

Globalization is a complex and multifaceted process which commands full books in its own right. In this chapter we examine some of the key features of the process, beginning with its early development.

Review question

Apply

1. Do an inventory of all the goods that you own or have in your house—clothes, food, electronic goods, white goods, and transport, etc. Where was each made? Think also about companies whose services you use—banks, insurance, utilities, etc. Who owns these companies and in what country are they based?

The development of globalization

Running case: globally connected

Chance has been examining ways for Junction Hotel to have a presence on a global scale while remaining independent. A particular trade association—Global Luxury—catches his attention. Membership of Global Luxury is exclusive and subject to a number of stringent tests to earn the label of 'luxury hotel'.

While hotels in this association remain independent, they meet regularly to discuss common issues. Furthermore, the hotels engage in cross-promotion, producing a joint brochure and website, from which bookings for any of the hotels can be made. Marketing and booking is thus pooled between the member hotels, while each individual hotel remains independent.

Regular meetings are held between the members of the chain, both at continental and, for top representatives, at global levels. For European meetings, Chance leaves on the 6 am flight to Amsterdam and is in a meeting room at the airport for 8.30 am. Representatives from other European hotels in the network will also be there. None of them will actually leave the airport during the day. Instead they will get on their return flights in the early evening and Chance will be back home in time for supper.

Global meetings are rare, at least in person, as there are greater distances to travel. Meetings tend to take place by phone or videoconferencing—even then the time has to be chosen carefully, as morning in the USA can be the middle of the night elsewhere.

Chance feels much more globally connected than he was in his previous life as a football club chairman. Looking at his email inbox, he used to have a list of clubs from various small-sized English towns. Now his inbox spans the globe, with messages from Australia, Germany, Brazil, and China, amongst others, sitting next to each other.

When globalization is mentioned, we tend to think of it as a relatively recent phenomenon, one which is a part of our modern era of international travel and instant global communication through the Internet. However, instances of individuals, organizations and nations operating on an international or global stage can be witnessed throughout history.

- In the 1500s, explorers from European countries, such as Francis Drake and Walter Raleigh, travelled the high seas, circumnavigating the globe to discover 'new' lands, such as the Americas.

- The discovery of new worlds opened up the possibility of international trade, bringing back newly-discovered goods to European markets. Founded in 1600, the East India Company is one of the earliest global companies as they traded cotton, tea, and opium on a global scale, moving goods between China, India, and the UK (Chaudhuri, 1965).

Colonization Invasion and conquering of land, and enslavement of people, in Africa, the Americas and Asia from the 1500s to the 1900s by European countries, such as England, Spain, Belgium, Portugal, France, and the Netherlands.

- Exploration and trade led to European countries developing global empires, **colonizing** countries in Africa, Asia, and the Caribbean, exploiting the natural resources of those countries and reducing their inhabitants to slavery. While attention is often focused on acts like slavery, colonialism was connected implicitly with the expansion of global markets and the collection of resources. While we tend to think of colonialism as something historic, as recently as the beginning of the twentieth century Western colonial empires covered 84.6% of the global economy (Loomba, 1998).

- It is not just organizations that operate globally, workforces, too, may move across the globe in search of work. In Chapter 2, we saw that Henry Ford's factory was made up of a multinational workforce, many of whom did not speak English. This was typical of the **migration** to the USA of people in search of work opportunities in the early 1900s from countries such as Poland, Italy, and Ireland (see LeMay, 1987).

Migration Leaving one country or area to move to another—possibly for reasons of finding work, or, alternatively, for avoiding oppressive regimes.

- Multinational organizations are often thought of as commercial trading enterprises. However, major religions are another example of organizations which operate globally— and have done so for centuries—often with recognizable organizational structures that divide up the hierarchy by continent and country (see Chapter 2).

- Many sporting events are global in scale (see Maguire, 1999) and the reach of participating nations (see the example later in this chapter) is not, again, necessarily a development of the past few decades. The modern Olympics were first held in 1896, for example, and the football World Cup was first held in 1930.

While these examples show that global organization and activity is not a new phenomenon, in this section we examine how the globalization that we experience today is qualitatively different, that is to say we experience globalization differently now than in the past. In particular, there is a feeling that the world is a lot smaller and more immediate.

The global village

Real life case: a cricket tour to Australia

Since 1882, England and Australia have regularly contested a cricket contest called the Ashes. When the Ashes began, there were no aeroplanes and the only way to go to Australia was by boat—a journey lasting six weeks. Now, a direct plane journey can take 24 hours. Where previously an English touring party (or anyone wishing to visit Australia for other reasons) would be cut off from home for the three months' journey time plus the time of the tour, now it is not uncommon for England players to return home, mid-tour, for family events, such as childbirths (England and Wales Cricket Board, 2012).

Similarly, communication has become much more immediate. If the only form of communication available is a letter, which has to be transported by boat, then the time between sending a message and receiving a reply would be a frustrating and impractical three months. Now, rather than waiting three months for a reply, telephones and the Internet can be used to communicate instantaneously in real time. So, when an England player returns to the tour from the birth of their child, they can still see the newborn in real time over the Internet using videoconferencing software, such as Skype.

Compared with the time when a boat was the only means of transport, it is as if the distance between the UK and Australia has shrunk.

How might the changes in transport and communications described in the Real life case facilitate trading and business between the UK and Australia? What types of business and organizational activity are possible now that would not have been when the Ashes began in 1882?

When people say that the world is becoming a smaller place, it does not mean that it is literally shrinking in size. Rather, it means that the world *feels to us* as if it is getting smaller. It takes less time to travel across the globe than it did even a few decades ago and we can communicate instantly with people on the other side of the planet.

Marshall McLuhan (1964) described the world as a **global village**. When he was writing in 1964, this related to the role of the media in particular. Films and television brought images from across the world to our attention—we could see other people and cultures as if they were our neighbours, as if the

The global village.

Global village A metaphor to describe a perception of the globe shrinking in size as a result of the speed and global reach of transport and communications technologies.

globe were a village. Thinking about the case of Australia, much of Australian life feels familiar to UK consciousness through soap operas, such as *Neighbours* and *Home and Away*. And it is not just Australia that is brought to our consciousness—US life is familiar through its extensive film and television industry. Global problems, such as war and famine, and global issues and events are also made familiar through news broadcasts.

Perhaps the world is now, almost 50 years since McLuhan first used the term, even more of a global village. News broadcasts switch seamlessly between live images from different parts of the globe, budget airlines make international travel available to more of us, and the Internet allows us not just to communicate instantly across the globe, but to see the minutiae of everyday life across the planet through applications such as Google Street View and videos posted on YouTube.

How many people do you communicate with globally, either personally, through email and messaging services, or through online discussion boards and similar forums?

Intensification of consciousness Alongside the global village, an increased awareness of events and people worldwide.

Robertson (1992: 8) describes globalization as 'the compression of the world and the **intensification of consciousness** of the world as a whole'. This captures the idea of the compression or shrinking of journey times, and times for communicating with people, alongside people having a greater awareness and perception of what goes on elsewhere within the globe (see Figure 15.1).

Figure 15.1
Robertson's (1992) 'intensification of consciousness'.

Based on Robertson, *Globalization*, 1992.

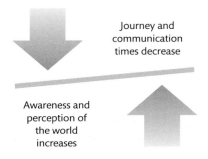

Journey and communication times decrease

Awareness and perception of the world increases

In a similar vein, Waters (2001: 5) defines globalization as 'a social process in which the constraints of geography on social and cultural arrangements recede and in which people become increasingly aware that they are receding . . .'. Again, this encompasses the idea that geography (physical space) is less of an issue in separating people across the globe and that we are aware of the world feeling much more immediate to us. We live in a global village and we are more than aware that we live in that global village.

Aspects of globalization

Waters's definition highlights globalization as a 'process' rather than a distinct 'thing'. It would be difficult to pin down globalization as one single phenomenon. It is multifaceted and encompasses a number of different trends and phenomena. Furthermore, globalization is an evolving and interdisciplinary field of study, that is to say it is ever changing and combines insights from a number of different academic areas.

Parker and Clegg (2006) suggest six main aspects (see Figure 15.2) which together contribute to the multifaceted nature of globalization or, more specifically, 'global interconnectedness' (ibid: 655).

Each of these in themselves do not constitute globalization, rather they are inter-related aspects which together combine towards the processes of globalization that we experience today and within which organizations operate. We therefore use these headings as a basis to give an overview of aspects of globalization that affect contemporary organizations. In this section we examine how four of these—the economy, politics, technology, and the natural environment—contribute to globalization. Later in the chapter we examine the specific importance of global business and organizations, and of global culture.

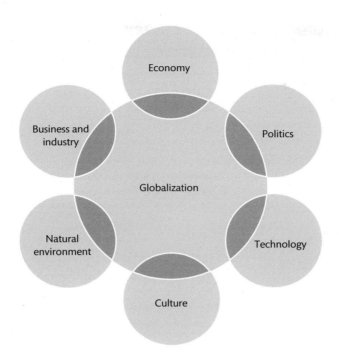

Figure 15.2 Parker and Clegg's (2006) six aspects of global interconnectedness.

Based on Parker & Clegg, 'Globalization' in *Handbook of Organizational Studies*, 2006.

The global economy

There is a saying that 'When America sneezes, Britain catches cold'. The USA is the world's largest economy (although China is rapidly catching up) and is also the largest purchaser of UK exports (see Table 15.1). A recession or other economic problem in the USA will thus affect the demand for UK exports and affect UK businesses that export to the USA—global economies are interconnected.

Furthermore, as Table 15.1 shows, the UK is not only dependent on the state of the economy in the USA, but in many other countries. Ireland accounts for almost half as many exports as those to the much larger USA, for example. Most other countries will have a similar set of global dependencies for their export trade.

Recent events in the global economy have demonstrated that interdependency is not just about trading and exports, but also about the global interconnectedness of financial institutions and financial products. The 2008 financial crisis was a global phenomenon which hit countries and continents across the globe.

Table 15.1 UK exports 2011

	Exports (£ milliions)
USA	38,949
Germany	33,038
France	23,056
Netherlands	22,671
Irish Republic	17,219
Belgium	15,354
Italy	9,888
Spain	9,449
China	8,773
Sweden	6,141

Source: HM Revenue and Customs (uktradeinfo.com).

Real life case: the global financial crisis

This financial crisis began in the so-called subprime mortgage market in the USA. Lehman Brothers, one of the world's oldest financial institutions collapsed, impacting its operations across the globe overnight (Osborne, Aldrick and Quinn, 2009). The panic quickly spread to other banks, many of which had interests tied to the financial products of Lehman, with many around the world bailed out and nationalized (Cooper 2010: 54), and it also led to a global rise in food and other commodity prices.

World leaders came together in numerous emergency meetings at institutions such as the World Economic Forum to work out how to recapitalize the banks. As banks stopped lending to each other the global economy faltered. Stock markets were extremely volatile, with crashes in one stock market affecting others internationally.

Some small economies were hit particularly hard. Iceland, whose economy was little over $10 bn a year, had an astronomical debt of around $100 bn, with the stock market crashing by 77% within three days; Ireland and Singapore both reported a fall in gross domestic product (GDP) of around 9%, and in China an estimated 10 million people lost their jobs through the slowdown in trade (Ferguson, 2011). The Euro suffered substantial problems with whole countries, such as Greece, needing to be bailed out and strong financial controls placed on them (Castle, 2012).

The speed and devastation that this crisis caused shows the interconnected nature of the economies and financial markets of the world, and the impact that a problem in a seemingly small area can make globally.

Global politics

Politics is often seen as an activity which takes place at a national level—general elections, national prime ministers, and presidents, etc. However, politics also takes place at increasingly international levels, partly because of the global nature of the economy and its importance to individual nations.

Real life case: the European Union

The European Union (EU) is a political entity made up 27 European nations. It began life as a free-trade area (the European Economic Community) before taking on its current title in 1993.

The activities of the EU have effects on businesses and organizations within its constituent nations—both as a result of economic activity and policy. While not an exhaustive list, examples of how the EU affects organizations in its member states include:

- single currency (the Euro) means no exchange rate fluctuations—makes exporting and importing more stable and predictable
- removal of trade/labour barriers—companies can trade freely across borders and, likewise, there are no restrictions on where people may work within the EU
- employment law—harmonizes some conditions of employment, e.g. maximum working hours per week, legislation on workplace discrimination
- investment—regeneration or investment to particular areas, especially where unemployment might be a problem.

Many global political groupings and agencies have an effect upon the global economy and the conditions for individual organizations within that economy. For example, the World Trade Organization (WTO) in effect sets the rules and regulations for world trade (and, as we will see later in the chapter, comes under criticism for how it does this).

Global technology

Global technology refers to those technologies which contribute to the aforementioned 'global village', that is to say they allow barriers of geography to be overcome so that people can travel the globe or communicate globally with much more ease. Examples of such technologies include:

- transport—cars, planes, trains, etc. and their associated infrastructures, such as roads and railway lines
- communications technologies—e.g. the telephone and the infrastructure through which it works
- media technologies—television transmitters, satellites, etc. which allow the dissemination of words and images, such as news, film, and television shows
- computer networks—the Internet allows an instantaneous transmission and reception of images, words, data, and communication, etc.

Such technologies obviously have an impact on what organizations can do on a global scale. The Internet and computer networks, and how they affect organizations, are examined in more detail in Chapter 14.

Globalization of the natural environment

Real life case: global oil production

The Druzhba pipeline is the one of the longest in the world, connecting Eastern Russia with much of Europe. Running through some of the most politically unstable countries in the world it has suffered numerous disputes with countries such as Ukraine threatening to pull out (Parfitt, 2007).

Several wars, such as in Iraq and Libya, have been seen by some as wars over control of oil (Bignell, 2011). There are predictions that as a result of climate change in the future there will be wars over water (Pederson, 2012). Golan Heights, which borders Israel, Lebanon, and Jordan is a cause of considerable political tension as it contributes a significant proportion of Israel's water supply (Asser, 2010).

A final aspect of globalization is that of the natural environment and its resources—the resources of the earth become commodities to be traded on a global basis. Such resources are of importance because of their value and, in many cases, their finite nature—think of the importance of fuel to the world economy, for example.

Depletion of natural resources and climate change are aspects of damage to the environment that are viewed as global problems. Workers, too, can be seen as natural resources that are now employed on a global scale. For example, a global division of labour has emerged because in the developing world, where manufacturing now tends to be concentrated, labour is cheaper—in some cases employed in sweatshop conditions. Such problematic issues have fuelled an anti-globalization movement, which is examined towards the end of this chapter, and issues of corporate social responsibility with respect to workers and the environment are further examined in Chapter 17.

Physical and intangible spaces of globalization

Earlier in this section, it was suggested that there is a difference in the experience of globalization today to forms of globalization that went before—that we now experience a 'global village' where the world feels smaller and more immediate. We suggest that this difference comes about from the nature of globalization having shifted from a globalization primarily of physical space to one which is supplemented by a global, intangible space:

Physical space Aspects of globalization that involve goods and people moving across land.

Intangible space Aspects of globalization that take place through intangible means such as media transmissions, data in computer networks, and imagery.

- globalization of **physical space** refers to the actual land of the globe itself—the *terra firma* on which we stand. Early globalization was thus about discovering new lands, physically moving products across the globe to trade them, and conquering land to create empires

- global **intangible space** is that which brings about some form of global connectedness without movement over actual land—data in computer networks and television signals, etc. It is these abstract elements which bring about global consciousness, the immediacy of communication, and global images that we are now afforded.

Globalization has both physical and abstract elements, and these are reflected in Parker and Clegg's aspects of globalization that we have used in this section. For example:

- the global economy has physical aspects—the physical goods which are produced and then exported across land and sea. Equally, it has intangible elements, the 'symbol economy' (Clegg and Gray, 1996: 303) of financial transactions and data flow between financial institutions

- global technology has physical aspects (transport which crosses land) and intangible aspects (the signals and data which are beamed through communications, computer and media networks).

Among these various physical and intangible elements lie organizations. While organizations are affected by the aspects of globalization listed previously, Parker notes that they are not simply passive bystanders, rather they play their part in making globalization happen:

> Organizations are not simply affected by globalization: the combined activities of all kinds of organizations stimulate, facilitate, sustain and extend globalization.   (Parker, 1996: 484)

We now turn to organizations themselves—their role in both the global economy and global culture, noting how they contribute to physical and intangible elements of globalization.

Review questions

1. Describe some examples of globalization from history.

2. Explain what is meant by the phrase 'global village'.

3. Analyse what is meant by globalization being experienced as an 'intensification of consciousness'.

Apply

4. Think of an organization that you know. How do Parker and Clegg's aspects of globalization affect this organization?

5. Analyse the key differences between physical and intangible aspects of globalization.

Global organizations

Running case: part of a franchise?

Simon Chance is enjoying the new status of Junction Hotel being part of Global Luxury group, but feels that while it has brought an undoubted cachet to the hotel, it is not paying off in terms of revenue. Indeed, it is creating extra cost and expense to keep up to the luxury standards required to stay within the group.

Chance wonders whether there are other ways to have a global reach but to also maintain the efficiency and cost-competitiveness necessary for the current economic conditions. Will it even be possible to survive as an independent hotel?

At his regular meeting with the board of investors, an option put on the table is to buy a similar hotel that is up for sale in France. While the board of investors like the sound of 'Junction Paris' and see it as a possible start for a whole chain of Junction Hotels, they soon realize that the costs for this form of expansion will be prohibitive.

Another option presented is to become a *franchise* of a global hotel chain. A number of such franchises exist, the one with the best reputation for quality is the US Luxonational chain.

Luxonational don't own their own hotels; instead, independent hotels apply to become franchise holders, which they would get subject to passing a set of standard requirements. The business belongs to the franchise holder in return for an annual fee, based on the size of the hotel, being paid to Luxonational in return for the right to run the franchise. The franchise has to be renewed annually, subject to maintaining the standard requirements.

Being part of the Luxonational franchise will certainly make the hotel part of a global chain, but at what cost to the hotel? Chance is asked to investigate and bring his findings to the next board meeting.

When we think of global organizations, we tend to think of huge companies with recognizable brands. Certainly, a glance (CNN Money, 2012) at the world's top multinationals by their annual income shows some familiar names, which tend to be concentrated in a number of industries:

- energy companies, such as Royal Dutch Shell (Netherlands), Sinopec (China), and BP (UK)

- automobile companies, such as Toyota (Japan), Volkswagen (Germany), and Ford (USA)

- finance companies, such as AXA (France), Bank of America (USA), and HSBC (UK)

- telecommunications and electronics companies, such as Verizon (USA), Siemens (Germany), and Samsung (South Korea).

Is there anything in the nature of the products and services in the list here which makes them more likely to be traded on a global scale? Would they benefit from economies of scale?

Such organizations can be so huge as to be bigger than the economies of individual nations. For example, US retailer Walmart, the largest multinational by income, has an income larger than individual medium-sized nations, such as Belgium and Sweden (CNN Money, 2012; Nationmaster, 2012).

Visit the Online Resource Centre for a full list of the top multinational companies and a comparison of the largest with national economies.

It would seem, then, that being a global organization is about size. Such massive conglomerates, however, are just one example of how organizations may operate on a global scale. In this section we will see different ways in which organizations are able to grow their operations to become global players, including possibilities for small-scale organizations to use technology to operate globally.

Using the terminology of the previous section we see how global organizations move from being achieved through physical means, such as goods, people, and premises, to being achieved through more intangible means, such as brands, licences, and computer networks.

Employability skills: international credentials

Many organizations promote themselves as 'international' or 'global' organizations, the terms bringing a certain cachet, even glamour, to the organization. Demonstrating international credentials can enhance employability in such organizations. Overseas placement experiences, languages learned, experiences of travel, and evidence of working with people from different international backgrounds are all good additions to your CV to enhance the international aspects of your employability.

The structure and spread of global organizations

Organizations are not born global, but, instead, extend and expand their activities through a number of different types of multinational activity. This section outlines examples of structures and activities that organizations use to increase their activity on an international scale.

Exporting

This is perhaps the most basic form of international activity—selling a product to another country and shipping it to that country. In its simplest form this would mean a company operating in just one country selling goods that it distributes to other countries while not having any premises or operations in those countries. In practice, **exporting** may be combined with some of the activities discussed next.

Exporting Selling and distributing a good to another country.

Overseas investment and expansion

If an organization exports frequently to a particular country or area, it may find a benefit in setting up premises in that area. For example, to generate exports a company may open sales offices in different countries or operate after-sales service centres for different national markets.

Foreign direct investment is an example of overseas investment where, rather than exporting goods, an organization sets up a production plant in an overseas territory directly. Examples of this might be car firms setting up production plants closer to different markets globally. This happened in the 1980s when a number of Japanese firms, such as Sony and Nissan, set up production plants in the UK.

> **Foreign direct investment** Setting up a production or office facility in another country.

Mergers, acquisitions, and joint ventures

Rather than setting up brand new operations in overseas territories, another way of expanding operations globally is by buying, or **acquiring** companies overseas. This might be by buying a similar organization so as to expand operations internationally (e.g. a supermarket chain buys a supermarket chain in another country) or it may involve buying an organization at another point in the production chain (e.g. a food manufacturer buys an overseas supplier or a film company buys an overseas distributor).

> **Acquisition** The purchase of another company or business.

In some cases, two companies may feel it in their best interests to **merge**, perhaps to gain economies of scale by pooling certain operations. In 2011 British Airways and Iberia merged to form International Airlines Group (*The Guardian*, 2010). This allows some ground operations to be merged, for example check-in desks, and also cooperation and efficiency in terms of scheduling the routes that the two airlines fly, and removing flights that duplicate each other, thus gaining efficiencies.

> **Merger** Two companies joining together to become one single entity.

Sometimes organizations in different countries find it in their best interests to cooperate in some way without merging their own operations—a **joint venture**. US electronics retailer Best Buy expanded its brand into the UK, but the stores were managed and products supplied by existing UK company Carphone Warehouse (Rushton, 2012).

> **Joint venture** Cooperation between two or more companies on a particular project.

> **Real life case:** the overseas expansion of Tesco
>
> The UK supermarket Tesco has used a number of different methods to expand into international territories. In the USA it engaged in direct investment, setting up a new 'Fresh & Easy' chain (*The Economist*, 2007). In Thailand it set up a joint venture with a local firm (BBC News, 2006), while in the Czech Republic (Thompson, 2010; Tesco plc, 2012) and Turkey (Treanor, 2003; Tesco plc, 2012) it acquired, or bought out, existing chains of stores. (For more information about Tesco's overseas businesses, see Tesco plc, 2012.)

Franchising and licensing

A company might not want the upfront expense that direct investment or an acquisition might necessitate. **Franchising** is where a company allows another organization to operate its business on its behalf using its brand and products. This will be for some form of fee, and will come with specific conditions as to how the franchisee operates and uses the brand.

> **Franchising** Granting the right to another company to operate an outlet or branch of a particular organization, subject to adhering to standards and conditions of the franchising company.

McDonalds, for example, do not own their restaurants. Their global expansion has come from their restaurants being run independently by franchise holders, albeit franchise holders who have to adhere to numerous conditions. For example, a franchise holder could not, of their own volition, change the menu offered.

Sometimes in a McDonalds restaurant, the name of the actual business holder—the franchisee—will be on display in the restaurant.

Licensing Granting the right to another company to produce a particular branded good.

Licensing is similar to franchising; however, here, a company grants a licence to produce its good (and sell it under their brand) in another territory. For example, adverts for Fosters beer play very much on the Australian origin of the product, but a small caption at the bottom of the advert indicates it to have been 'brewed under licence in the UK'. The strategy makes sense—it would be impractical to brew beer in Australia and export it to the UK. Licensing is a means to expand the brand globally. This is how Coca-Cola operates on a global scale—by licensing its syrup to overseas plants who then produce and sell it in their local markets.

Subcontracting

Subcontracting Hiring another person or company to perform a particular process or service for an organization.

With **subcontracting** an organization employs the services of another organization to conduct an aspect of its work. This has become a global activity whereby an organization not only subcontracts, but does so to an organization in a different country—often where the costs of this are cheaper. Clothing and manufacturing organizations subcontract production of their items to a factory in a different country, leading to criticism in instances where the cost of labour is so cheap that people are employed in 'sweatshop' conditions (see Chapter 17).

Real life case: call centres in India

The Indian call centre industry is a well-known example of subcontracting on a global scale, handling calls for credit card companies, insurance companies, technical helplines—any organizations that use a call centre to handle enquiries. Organizations will exist purely as subcontractors—an organization could run contracts for firms across the globe (UK, USA, Australia) in one building, for example.

While global technology allows for such calls to be handled on the other side of the planet instantly, in India the call centres try to create an illusion of being in the same country. Training in accents, pronunciation, and culture is given, for example by teaching about UK food, sport, or television programmes.

While workers on the UK contract will be learning about UK culture and current events, workers in a neighbouring room working on a US contract can, similarly, be learning about US culture.

Visit the Online Resource Centre for detailed commentary on this case study.

Sources: Harding (2001); Deb (2004); BBC News (2011).

Global technology has allowed for administration tasks, in addition to manufacturing, to be subcontracted globally. The operation of call-handling centres in India is one example of this; others include handling paperwork, such as the typing up of medical notes which are scanned and emailed to workers performing the task.

Global industries and labour markets

Subcontracting shows that it is not just organizations that are globalized—labour markets, too, are global. In the case of manufacturing and call centres, cheaper labour elsewhere in the world is used by global organizations. Global labour markets could also refer to large multinationals hiring their top staff or valued knowledge-workers with key skills (see Chapter 10) from a global pool of labour. A university department, for example, will often be made up of an international variety of leading professors.

Industries, too, can be seen as global, with different organizations within that industry contributing to that globalization in different ways. These forms of global activity show that both physical aspects (setting up premises, exporting goods, etc.) and more intangible aspects (e.g. licensing a brand) both contribute to organizations and industries extending their activities globally.

Real life case: sport as a global industry

Sport is an industry which, when taken as a whole and by looking at some of its individual aspects, can be seen as a global industry, demonstrating some of the features examined thus far in this chapter:

- global competitions and events take place between national teams, such as the Olympic Games and the football World Cup

- furthermore, events such as Formula One are a global travelling show, with rounds in different countries across the globe, and teams themselves made up of an international mix of drivers, engineers, and sponsors

- such events are also global in that they are viewed globally through the media

- sports are governed by global governing bodies, e.g. the International Olympic Commission or Fédération Internationale de Football Association (FIFA)

- such bodies bring an element of global politics to sport. Furthermore, bidding processes for global events can include contributions and influence from politicians

- individual sports teams can become global brands, e.g. clubs such as Manchester United are popular in the Far East. Such brands are extended through licensing and franchising deals

- furthermore, global brands are involved in sport through sponsorship

- large multinational brands are also involved in the production of sporting goods and clothing, e.g. Nike, Adidas

- the existence of global labour markets can be seen in some elite level clubs, especially in football, where players will be from a variety of countries and continents

- global labour markets are also in evidence, from a different perspective, in the production of sporting goods, many of which are produced on assembly lines in the developing world. (See Maguire, 1999, for more on sport as a global phenomenon.)

Technology and the potential for globalization

While global organization tends to be associated with large-scale global expansion, as described in the previous section, another aspect of global organizational activity worthy of mention is the ability of small-scale organizations, even individuals, to have a global presence. This is made possible by global technology, in particular that provided by the Internet.

Real life case: *Angry Birds*

Many of you will have played the game *Angry Birds* on a smartphone or tablet computer. The game, and its variants, have had hundreds of millions of downloads worldwide—it is a global phenomenon.

The organization that produces the game, however, is small in scale. Rovio Mobile, based in Finland, had just over 40 employees at the time of writing (although it was expanding). *Angry Birds* demonstrates how a small-scale organization can be global in its reach. (See Cheshire, 2011, for more information.)

The example of *Angry Birds* shows how larger scale organizations—in particular those which provide some form of global network infrastructure—facilitate the global spread of smaller organizations. The global scale of the downloading comes from the intangible global technologies of computer networks and, furthermore, from being available through existing organizations, such as mobile phone download stores. It is as if a form of 'piggy-back' is provided by the larger organization—itself global—to enable the smaller organization to also achieve a global presence (see Chapter 14 *Information, Communication, and Technology* for more on the merging of an organization's operations through computer networks).

At an individual level, a similar situation exists with a site such as eBay—itself a global organization which allows a variety of smaller organizations to piggy-back on its infrastructure to achieve a global presence. As a sole trader on eBay, you can reach a, potentially, global audience for the goods that you are selling. It's a situation similar to the simple exporter mentioned earlier in this chapter, but now an exporter who, no matter how small-scale, can export globally.

Global organizations tend to be large in scale, but can, in some instances, have a global reach on a small scale. In the next section we see how organizations contribute to what is sometimes described as a global culture.

Review questions

1. Describe the different ways in which organizations might extend their activities internationally.

2. Explain how global technology allows small-scale organizations to operate on a global scale.

3. Analyse the advantages and disadvantages of the different types of international organizational activity, such as franchising or subcontracting.

Apply

4. Look at websites for a number of small and large organizations. In what ways do those specific organizations operate globally?

Organizations and global culture

From: simon_chance@junctionhotel.co.uk
To: board_members@junctionhotel.co.uk; senior_management_team@junctionhotel.co.uk

Subject: Re: Franchising

As requested, I've done some research into what becoming a franchise of Luxonational would entail. Here are the main points:

- *Branding.* Junction Hotel would lose much of its identity. Instead, it would be rebranded as 'Luxonational Nottingham'. All marketing and logos to be replaced by those of Luxonational.

- *Booking and marketing.* Common booking and marketing procedure with other franchises in the Luxonational chain. We would be marketed through the international Luxonational website and appear in their marketing materials—a much wider reach than before. We would do some local marketing, but this would have to adhere to a Luxonational 'template'. Information technology upgrade needed at reception to fit in with the standard booking procedure.

- *Hotel furnishings.* Standard Luxonational 'look'. Furniture in rooms, carpets, curtains, the reception layout—all fixtures and fittings would be those supplied by Luxonational. This will cost, but we are due for a refurbishment. Taking the standard Luxomania items will be cheaper owing to their bulk purchasing power.

- *Staff procedures.* Just like the furnishings, the staff will be branded as Luxonational staff, with new uniforms provided similar to the rest of the chain. Furthermore, certain staff procedures would be expected to be brought into line with the rest of the chain, including human resources issues, such as pay and holiday entitlements (not quite as generous as currently operating at Junction). Training provided by Luxonational manual or at a number of regional training centres that the head office run. Expectation of certain cultural behaviours and a brand 'look' that the workers will embody.

- *Purchasing.* Items such as towels, toiletries for rooms, toilet paper, pens, and many other consumables bought on a regular basis would have to be purchased from Luxonational. Restricts choice, but would bring economies of scale as such items are produced for the global range of hotels. Furthermore, the drinks in the bar, food supplies, and many other catering items would have to be sourced from Luxonational's preferred suppliers—this would give discount but dictates to the hotel what drinks and food they can serve.

From: meg_mortimer@junctionhotel.co.uk
To: simon_chance@junctionhotel.co.uk

<Subject: Re: Re: Franchising

Simon, I've stayed at one of those Luxonational places before: identikit, sterile, characterless, bland—need I go on?

So far in the chapter we have seen how multinational companies are able to extend their reach across the globe, to dominate the globe in economic and business terms. In this section we examine claims that this dominance is also cultural, to the extent that there is a global culture that overrides cultures at a national and local level.

Cultural homogenization A tendency for culture to become the same globally.

The media is seen as one aspect in this **cultural homogenization**. Across the globe we all watch the same films and television shows, listen to the same music, and play the same computer games. In many cases, these reflect a Western, predominantly US, culture. Such a global culture is shown by the following statement made in 1998 by Michael Eisner, then Chairman and Chief Executive of Disney:

> It doesn't matter whether it comes in by cable, telephone lines, computer, or satellite. Everyone's going to have to deal with Disney.
>
> (quoted in *New Internationalist* 1998)

Eisner is speaking here about the global prevalence of Disney films, media, and even imagery through merchandising. It is a global cultural presence and the means by which this is achieved is not through physical globalization, but intangibly through the satellites, television signals, and computer networks that he mentions.

Given that such media are usually presented in English, it is not surprising that a further element of global culture is the emergence of English as a global language (Bryson, 1990). While English is not the most widespread language by first speakers (indeed, it is not even second —the top three languages are Mandarin, Spanish, and then English) it, nevertheless, has a position of the second language of choice in many business and cultural areas. For example:

- the international language of air travel is English, in particular all communications between pilots and air traffic controllers, wherever they may be in the world, are in English. This is even the case where the participants share a common language, thus a Spanish pilot will speak to a (Spanish-speaking) Argentinian air-traffic controller in English

- international conferences, more often than not, choose English as their language of business. An example of this is academic conferences. Conferences set in a non-English speaking country will transact their proceedings in English. Speeches, presentations, handouts, email communications, and websites are all in English, regardless of the native language of the host country.

Global brands

Real life case: I'd like to buy the world a Coke

Coca-Cola is a brand which enjoys a global reach and recognition, its brand being named the most valuable global brand of 2012 (Interbrand, 2012). Its global reach comes about, as we have seen, from licensing to licensees in different territories the right to use the Coca-Cola syrup to then produce, bottle, and sell the drink.

However, its global reach is also achieved by the power of the brand itself. Having been developed in the late 1800s, such was the global reach of the product by the 1970s that it embarked on the first ever global advertising campaign. A popular song of the time—*I'd Like to Teach the World to Sing* by the New Seekers—was re-recorded as 'I'd Like to Buy the World a Coke'. People of different races and nationalities were shown in the advert, standing on a hillside, smiling and in harmony, all drinking Coca-Cola.

The implication of the advert is not just that Coca-Cola is a global product and a global brand, but that Coca-Cola unites the globe.

Visit the Online Resource Centre for a link to a video of the advert on YouTube.

Beyond the media and the use of English, multinationals can be seen to contribute to global culture through their brand imagery. Brands are viewed as 'icons of culture and signifying devices' (Yakhlef, 2004: 238), that is to say they give an identity to an organization, even create a meaning to people who consume them (as may be the case when people buy a particular pair of trainers for the brand).

Where brands create meaning and identity, they also contribute to global culture. Disney is, again, significant here. As we will see in Chapter 16, Bryman (2004) suggests that the Disney theme park, and the way it creates particular imagery that is experienced within that organization, is a model for other types of service and leisure organizations. Organizations want to create a particular feeling that reflects their brand through the decoration, atmosphere, and even the behaviour of the staff within their premises (Witz et al., 2003; Yakhlef, 2004).

In Chapter 4 we saw how the 'McDonaldization of Society' (Ritzer, 2011) brings about standardization on a global scale. Thus, the predictability element of McDonaldization is global predictability—there is a standard global product range (a Big Mac can be bought in McDonalds restaurants worldwide), and a standard brand and layout of the restaurants (the McDonalds arches have, in some surveys, been deemed to be a global symbol recognized more than the Christian cross). McDonaldization can also be seen in the worldwide spread of such places as shopping malls, multiplex cinemas, and hotel chains, etc.

Taken together, McDonaldization and Disneyization are representative of organizations with a standard experience and atmosphere on a global scale. One hotel, fast-food restaurant, airport, or multiplex cinema feels the same wherever in the world you happen to be. It is as if, when in these organizational spaces, one could forget which country lies outside—such is their standardized nature—there is a global homogenous space created within organizations. Many of these spaces are branded and, as such, global brands contribute to a standardized global culture not just through the ubiquitous presence of those brands, but also through the organizational environments that they create.

The standardized airport.

Review questions

1. Describe what is meant by global culture.

2. Explain the ways in which global organizations contribute to global culture.

3. Analyse the role that brands play in global culture. How do they help to create standardized organizational spaces?

Apply

4. What are the advantages and disadvantages that Junction Hotel should consider in thinking about becoming a franchise of Luxonation?

Globalization and national differences

The franchise idea has been rejected—it was felt that it would create a bland space that would lose the distinctiveness of Junction Hotel. The international strategy continues, however, and even being on a few booking websites has brought in more international visitors to Junction Hotel.

This includes a group of Japanese tourists who had booked through the website and are trying to check in. They speak little English and the receptionists don't speak a word of Japanese between them. Even basic cultural niceties, such as greetings, are not understood between the two and gestures are being misunderstood. Flustered, the receptionist has asked the guests to sit in the bar and wait for a while. This leaves the reserved and polite guests feeling uncomfortable as another of Chance's rowdy football weekend parties also enters into the same area of the bar, chanting loudly.

Simon Chance goes into the bar to smooth over the situation, and thinks to himself that a bit of cross-cultural training for the staff might be needed. A global strategy will have to start much closer to home—within the hotel itself.

There is a saying that 'travel broadens the mind' and, certainly, any of you that have visited countries either near to, or far away from, home will have experienced different ways of life. It's not just the language that might be different—the food, mannerisms, and daily routines may also seem unfamiliar. It can take time to adjust to, and understand, the cultural differences between life at home and life in the new country. There might even be cultural misunderstandings—what is considered acceptable at home may offend people in other cultures or be seen as inappropriate behaviour.

Anyone experiencing such cultural differences might, understandably, be sceptical about the idea that we live in a globalized world with a standard, homogenized global culture. In this section we examine the extent to which national differences are still noticeable and still exert an influence on the way business is done, and the challenges of **cross-cultural management** that this creates for organizations operating in a global environment.

> Cross-cultural management Managing a workforce from different national and cultural backgrounds.

In the European Union, the Schengen Agreement, signed in 1985, dismantled border controls between most of its member countries, allowing people to pass freely between countries. However, while the border might not contain and constrain the movement of people as it did previously, it can still be seen to demarcate differences between neighbouring countries.

This photo shows the border between Ahlbeck, Germany and Swinoujscie, Poland on the Baltic coast, with the stone between the two poles marking the exact border. Given the history of World War II, this is a border that has been contested previously and was heavily secured. In the next photo, looking back from the beach, we see the remnants of a fence, and a loop which held barbed wire to

A border between Germany and Poland.

▶ maintain the border along the beach, backed up by a watchtower in the distance. Now, it is possible to walk freely along the beach between the two Schengen countries.

Barbed wire fence replaced by an open border.

However, the border still demarcates certain differences, not least *linguistically*, with German and Polish being spoken on either side. Crossing the nearby road border further on, one is faced with a long roadside market on the Polish side with most stalls offering 'Billige Zigaretten' (cheap cigarettes—not the German language being used on the Polish side). This shows economic and political (e.g. levels of taxation) differences between the two countries that result in different prices being charged.

Furthermore, there are *cultural* differences that are still maintained. Sensitivities and values on the Polish side were offended by the tendency of German bathers towards naturist bathing. When the border was first opened up, this led to a spat between representatives from the two towns; the Poles bemoaning German permissiveness, the Germans amused by Polish 'puritanism' (France 24, 2008).

This example shows that, despite economic, political, and cultural globalization, there still exist differences between nations. Policies, laws, and economic circumstances can exert an influence; indeed, in Chapter 14 we saw how national laws could also have an influence on how organizations use global technologies, such as the Internet. Furthermore, linguistic and cultural differences can begin to take effect, even just a few footsteps over the border. It is to these linguistic and cultural differences, and their effects upon organization and management, that we now turn.

From linguistic to cultural differences

A key aspect of national and cultural difference is that people speak different languages. As explored earlier, English is widely used as a global *lingua franca* for business and organizations; however, linguistic differences—and the difficulties in translating between languages—are evident.

For example, while we have examined the presence of global brands and global advertising campaigns, their ability to convey a global message or identity can be undermined by mistranslations, for example:

- the French pronunciation of the Toyota MR2, 'MR Deux', sounds like a vulgar word in the French language (CNN Money, 2008)

- Coors advertising slogan 'Turn it loose' was translated into Spanish as 'Get loose bowels' (CNN Money, 2008)

- KFC's slogan 'finger licking good' was translated into Chinese as 'eat your fingers off' (Adler, 2003).

Translation is a major issue in global organizations. For example, we suggested earlier that the European Union (EU) is part of global politics. Much of its energy is put into translation —both simultaneously through headphones at European Parliament meetings and in the reams of official documentation translated into all of its member languages. National differences through language are thus still important—English does not dominate as a language of the EU.

Furthermore, translation brings its own issues. Try using an online translation service or translation software. Put a paragraph in your own language, translate it to another language, then translate that back into your own language. The chances are that what you will have is clumsy—at times incomprehensible, at times amusing like the mistranslations listed earlier—but certainly not a perfect rendition of your original paragraph.

> **Research insight:** Lost in translation, Blenkinsopp, J., and Pajouh, M.S. 2010. Lost in translation? Culture, language and the role of the translator in international business. *Critical Perspectives on International Business* 6(1): 38–52.
>
> Blenkinsopp and Pajouh (2010) suggest that a 'mechanical perspective' on translation—translating word for word often misses out on the cultural meaning of what was originally said.
>
> For Blenkinsopp and Pajouh (ibid.), words can be embedded in the culture from which they come. This can lead to some 'untranslatable' words, for example the German word *schadenfreude*. This means a sense of pleasure in the misfortune of others; however, there is no equivalent word in English that conveys such an idea. As such, it is untranslatable; indeed, in English the original German word is used.
>
> That words can be laden with untranslatable cultural values also has an effect in the business sphere. Blenkinsopp and Pajouh offer two 'untranslatable' words, Guanxi in Chinese, often translated as 'relationship' into English, and a Persian word 'Tarouf', which refers to a form of superficial politeness. However, rather than simplistic translations, both words refer to particular types of behaviours, trust, politeness, and relationship-building that are particular to their own culture and impact how business relationships are carried out. The cultural and interpersonal behaviours suggested by these words in their original cultural context would be missed if relying on a simplistic, mechanistic translation of the words.

Blenkinsopp and Pajouh's work on translation suggests that differences between nations are more than linguistic—there is a cultural element. What might work in business in one cultural context, may not cross into other cultures.

For example, the opening of Eurodisney in Paris was seen to have been hampered by different cultural outlooks, from a view of Disney being an icon of US global culture, to a cynical viewpoint in France of its cultural inferiority—a 'cultural Chernobyl' (Hamnett, 1999). Such differences in cultural perspective could also be found among workers. Disneyland relies on a very American form of service culture, where workers are almost putting on an act in front of theme park guests (see Chapter 16). Curwen suggests that, again, a cultural mismatch led to high labour turnover at Disneyland Paris where '. . . French youth refused to see the need to cut their hair, dress uniformly and smile incessantly' (Curwen, 1995: 17).

Similar cultural mismatches have been suggested in the business world, for example Al-Husan et al., (2006) examine cultural differences in transferring Western human resources management practices to the Middle East, and there are suggestions that Japanese management techniques do not function as effectively outside of the specific Japanese cultural context from which they emerge.

Real life case: cultural differences and teamwork

In the 1980s Japanese car manufacturers started to build factories in the UK (e.g. Nissan in Sunderland) introducing management practices such as *Kaizen*, a system of continual improvement; *quality circles*, a small team dedicated to finding improvements where workers spend four hours a month looking how to improve their work; *Just-in-time production* where parts arrive just when they are needed rather than being stockpiled in the factory; and more fluid boundaries so that people do not just work in one team but throughout the whole organization. All these approaches required strong levels of teamwork (Imai, 1986).

They found that practices that worked very well in Japan struggled in the UK context. UK workers liked to have more fixed teams and did not engage initially in the continuous improvement approach. The problem was trying to import practices that worked well in the collectivist Japanese culture—where the workers and management were extremely loyal to the organization rather than themselves or their immediate team—into the more individualistic UK—where workers saw themselves as individuals first rather than forming their identity as members of the organization and where they had more fixed views of their team.

So, instead, they developed a hybrid system, taking elements from both UK and Japanese culture. 'It is the accumulation of the little ideas that bring the big benefits in manufacturing', Mr Gibson (the plant deputy managing director) said. 'And here the changes have been made by the workers themselves. None of them came because some engineer was standing around with a stopwatch and a clipboard.' (Lohr, 1987.) In short, they developed systems that worked well by adapting UK notions of teamwork to Japanese styles.

Can national cultures be measured?

Dutch researcher Geert Hofstede (1980) saw national cultures in a similar manner to organizational cultures (see Chapter 7) in that they demonstrated a set of values, attitudes, and sensitivities that amounted to the 'wiring of the brain' (Hofstede, 1980). As such, he suggested that differences between national cultures, and specifically national management cultures, could be measured and quantified.

Hofstede's study comes from a large-scale attitude survey of managers in the many national offices of computer firm IBM. From this, he devised a formal, numerical means of identifying and describing individual management cultures, which were plotted out on four **dimensions of culture** (adapted from Hofstede, 1986).

- Power distance concerns the mobility of people with regard to positions of power. Does power come from social status—who you are, who you were born to, and who you know—or is promotion more about merit, your proven abilities, and 'what you know'? This also covers the way in which managers and subordinates interact—is a lot of deference shown to authority, or do management and workers interact more as equals.

- Uncertainty avoidance is the amount to which people are comfortable with risk and insecurity, or whether or not they tend to prefer stability and predictability.

- Masculinity/femininity concerns the level of assertiveness and aggressiveness within the organization, which Hofstede saw as a masculine trait, as opposed to a more feminine view of the organization based around concepts of welfare and nurture. It is also reflected in the level of equality between the genders.

Hofstede's dimensions of culture Four numerical scales on which national management cultures can be located.

Table 15.2 Selected results of Hofstede's (1986) dimensions of national culture

	Power distance	Uncertainty avoidance	Masculinity	Individualism
USA	40	46	62	91
UK	35	35	66	89
Japan	54	92	95	46
Sweden	31	29	5	71
France	68	86	43	71
India	77	40	56	48
Top-ranked	Malaysia	Greece	Japan	USA
Bottom-ranked	Austria	Singapore	Sweden	Guatemala

Source: Based on Hickson and Pugh (1995: 33–35).

- Individualism/collectivism is the extent to which the organization is seen as a community or a family to which a worker 'belongs' and has loyalty, or do people work more as individuals, more interested in a sense of getting ahead than a sense of belonging?

Table 15.2 gives some examples of the results from Hofstede's survey. Some particular cultural features of different countries highlighted by these scales are (adapted from Hickson and Pugh, 1995):

- the UK and USA are seen to have very similar characteristics. The two countries have very highly individualistic approaches to work—workers are there for their own career rather than a sense of loyalty to an organization. Low power distance suggests that promotion on merit to the top of organizations is possible, perhaps reflected in the 'American dream' that anyone can become president. Both countries are also comfortable with risk and uncertainty. Overall, it suggests a forward-looking, individual achievement-based culture.

- France has much higher power distance and uncertainty avoidance. A characteristic of the latter is a large amount of bureaucracy in French public and organizational life. Combined with high power distance, this brings about a more formal working environment with greater deference to seniority and perhaps explains the lack of willingness to engage in more informal service interactions, as highlighted earlier in the chapter.

- a notable feature of Swedish management culture is its high femininity. Sweden is known for its egalitarian work legislation and practices between the genders; however, femininity also feeds into a management style that is less aggressive and abrasive, and more nurturing, cool-headed and focused on practical outcomes.

- Japan is seen to have a unique set of characteristics, contributing to its very culturally-specific management style. There is very high uncertainty avoidance—decision making is time-consuming, conservative, and avoids risk (Kono, 1982). Individualism is low—Japanese workers have very high loyalty to the organization and will work long hours of unpaid overtime. Masculinity is also high—there are few women in senior management positions.

- Indian management has very high power distance and low individualism. It is characterized by 'paternalistic centralization'—managers will exert strong, centralized control in a way that shows concern for workers, too. There is loyalty to the workplace, but not in the sense of devotion found in Japan.

Hofstede's findings have attracted considerable critique. We might question whether culture is something that can be reduced to numbers (cf. critiques of numerical personality scales in Chapter 8; whether surveys adequately measure rich and complex phenomena, such as cultures, and, indeed, whether a view of an overall national culture can be gained from a survey of just one organization—IBM). McSweeney (2002) gives a thorough critique of the methodology and conclusions of the work of Hofsetede, and his 'limited characterization' (2002: 112) of the concept of culture.

Managing across the global and the local

While the rigid numerical calculation of Hofstede's scales should be treated with caution in terms of giving an absolute mapping of national managerial cultures, it suggests that national differences and cultures are important and exert an effect on how business and management operate. In the final part of this section we examine two particular ways in which organizations manage globally, but taking account of the local; namely managing people and cultures, and managing strategies.

Managing people and cultures

The first implication of national cultural differences is that, in a multinational workforce, they might impact differently on how individuals are managed. For example, an assertive, ambitious, individualistic worker might be motivated differently to one whose culture suggests loyalty to the organization and belonging.

Real life case: managing across cultures in a football team

Top level football teams are an example of a multinational workforce. Players will be from many different countries and continents. Sir Alex Ferguson, manager of Manchester United, has noted how sensitivity to different cultural backgrounds is needed in managing across cultures within a team, where people not only have a different way of seeing the world, but also even basic things, like times for eating and sleeping, may be different (BBC Sport, 2011).

Cultural differences can, however, have more serious consequences. A recent, upheld case of alleged racist abuse in the English Premier League against Uruguayan player Luis Suárez hinged around his defence that there was a misunderstanding caused by cultural differences (Taylor, 2011).

The Football Association (2011) investigation into the incident went into meticulous detail about the differing meanings and use of racially-sensitive words between the UK and South America. Suárez was fined and served a ban following the investigation; however, the report highlights a confused picture of cross-cultural differences that can revolve even around the meaning of a single word (see also Chapter 14, on cross-cultural issues in miscommunication).

These differences extend to the management of culture across organizations. Gergen and Whitney (1996) argue that the implementation of a global culture is simply impossible given the effects of different cultures in national context; instead, culture is seen through the lens of local cultures at a national level.

Furthermore, personal cultural differences extend beyond management over the organization, to relationships across organizations—dealing with clients, customers, and colleagues in different countries. Crace (2003) outlines the role of 'cultural consultants' in advising firms on cultural differences that might cause problems from seemingly innocuous behaviours: for example, a polite enquiry about somebody's family might be seen in Arab countries as planning an affair with a customer's wife; and putting a business card into a back pocket would cause offence in Japan.

Study skills: working with students from other cultures

Universities are usually international, multicultural environments and, in project work, you may well find yourself working with people from other cultures. The cultural differences outlined in this section relate to the workplace, but apply equally to project teams and groups at university.

Crace (2003) outlines that even email communication, as is often used in project work, can lead to cultural differences. For example, some cultures tend to be very abrupt and curt in their use of email, which can upset people from other cultures not used to such directness.

 What cultural differences do you notice between students at your university? Does this affect the way that you might work together on a project?

Managing structure and strategies

Real life case: the limits of McDonaldization

While McDonalds and its brand is globally ubiquitous, and employs global standardized practices, it is not true to say that McDonalds, as it exists from country to country, is uniformly global, for example:

- in France beer is served in restaurants as local culture associates dining out with drinking (Audi, 2009)
- in parts of India, beef cannot be eaten because of religious laws and so mutton is used in the burgers (Harding, 2000)
- in many Far Eastern countries, McDonalds is not viewed as a place to eat quickly, instead it is seen as place where people will sit and socialize for long periods of time (Watson, 1997).

Glocalization Adapting global practices and products to local conditions.

Glocalization (Robertson, 1995) is a term which captures both the global activities of multinational firms and, at the same time, their adaptation of strategies for local markets as discussed in the previous section—at once acting globally and locally.

The highlighted case shows how an organization like McDonalds, while seemingly a contributor to a global, standardized culture, in fact adapts for local tastes, sensitivities, laws, and cultures. There are adaptations to McDonalds' menus in different national markets.

Similarly, in a set of adverts, the global bank HSBC describes itself as 'The world's local bank'. The suggestion is that, while it operates on a global scale, it understands and responds to different national markets. Indeed, many of the national subsidiaries operate independently, with a knowledge of their national market, while carrying the global HSBC branding.

Different degrees of glocalization are encompassed in Bartlett and Ghoshal's (1989) model of multinational structures and strategies, based around two particular dimensions:

- corporate integration—the extent to which the organization is standardized and controlled across its global operations. Is it an integrated, bureaucratic whole, or do individual, national units operate relatively independently?

- responsiveness to local markets—to what extent are the goods, services and branding of an organization standardized globally, or are they adjusted to be more responsive to local needs and requirements?

Figure 15.3 shows different types of organization along the dimensions suggested by Bartlett and Ghoshal. This gives four particular types of global firm.

- Global firms benefit from high economies of scale through a globalized and highly standardized offering. There is a great deal of standardized control across the globe and little alteration of products to suit local markets. This is found in consumer electronics, for example an iPad is the same standard product wherever it is sold. Look also at the international website of Swedish clothes retailer H&M—the websites for each national territory where it operates offer the exact same range of (mass-produced) clothing.

- Transnational firms have economies of scale, especially through standardized control mechanisms; however, there is some responsiveness to local markets, e.g. by adapting products, services, or marketing strategies. The organization is seen as a set of international subsidiaries with some independence, but also a sharing of learning across the global organization. The standardized bureaucratic control of McDonalds, coupled with its responsiveness to local markets, as described previously, would be an example of this.

- A multinational or multidomestic firm is a global organization which runs more like a set of independent national subsidiaries. Different national subsidiaries may have different identities or product ranges, e.g. it is the national context which is important rather than standardized, global control. The example of Tesco would fit into this category—it runs a number of differently branded chains in different countries.

- An international firm uses knowledge from head office, but in a more autonomous way. People might be trained at head office, but are then free to operate relatively autonomously once they have that knowledge.

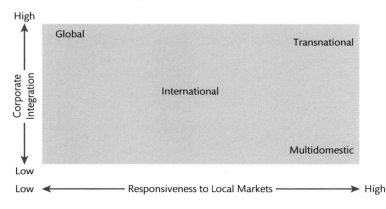

Figure 15.3 Bartlett and Ghoshal's (1989) model.

Based on Bartlett and Ghoshal, *Managing Across Borders*, 1989.

In this section we have seen that national and cultural difference do have an impact on the ways in which people and organizational strategies are managed. In the next section we see how these differences, on a global scale, can become global inequalities.

Review questions

1. Explain what is meant by cultural differences.

2. Describe Hofstede's dimensions of national culture.

3. Analyse how organizations respond to national and cultural differences in managing people and strategies.

Apply

4. How would you advise Junction Hotel on dealing with cultural differences?

The inequalities of globalization

The previous section has shown that, rather than a uniform, standardized global culture, globalization still has to account for national differences. Differences within globalization can also be seen in its inequalities. Rather than being an even process, it can be seen as one which benefits some parts of the globe and not others; in particular, it is seen to benefit the developed, Western world at the expense of the developing world. In this respect, globalization has been the object of considerable protest and critique.

Real life case: the anti-globalization movement

Anti-globalization movement A collective term for protestors and critics of the power and effects of multinational corporations which they see as making the world less fair and more homogenized.

Over the last two decades the so-called **anti-globalization movement** has become increasingly vocal, involved in often violent protests at meetings of global political and economic institutions, such as the World Bank and the G8 group of eight leading world economies. The anti-globalization protestors have sought to challenge the 'Washington Consensus' of free-market capitalism that they argue is sweeping the world.

While the media often focus on the violence that can accompany these protests their real message can get lost. For instance, in 2005 over 200,000 protestors, many of them families with young children, came together under the banner *Make Poverty History*, campaigning for *trade justice*, to make the trading laws fair for poor countries (Jeffery and Tempest, 2005), *drop the debt*, to cancel unaffordable international debts for developing countries, and *more and 'better' aid*, with rich countries giving a small percentage of their gross domestic product (GDP) to aid poor countries (Make Poverty History, 2012).

The central focus for much of the protests was the pro-capitalist policies of the World Bank, International Monetary Fund, and G8 which, the protesters claim, force poorer countries to privatize essential services, such as water, telecommunications, and energy production to 'liberalize' their economies and make them more competitive. The protestors argue that, in reality, these moves serve the interests of global elites as they are often sold to rich multinationals who cream off the profits and move them out of these countries. They also argue that trade laws promote the free movement of capital, but protect the interests of the richest nations.

They argue these polices have 'left a trail of destroyed economies, ruined nations and marginalized people' (Brahm, 2009: 16).

Inequalities of the global economy

Inequalities in the world economy can be seen through a calculation of GDP per capita, i.e. national income per person.

Figure 15.4 shows that this income is unevenly distributed—the higher incomes per person are enjoyed mainly in North America, Western Europe, and other developed counties. There are much lower incomes, in some cases below the poverty line, in Africa, large parts of Asia, and South America.

The economic divide is further illustrated when looking at the distribution of headquarters of the top fifty multinational companies worldwide (see Figure 15.5). This mirrors the inequalities shown by GDP per capita distribution.

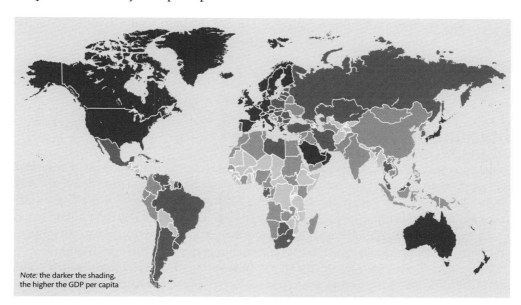

Note: the darker the shading, the higher the GDP per capita

Figure 15.4 Gross domestic product (GDP) per capita 2007–11.

Based on data from the World Bank, http://data.worldbank.org

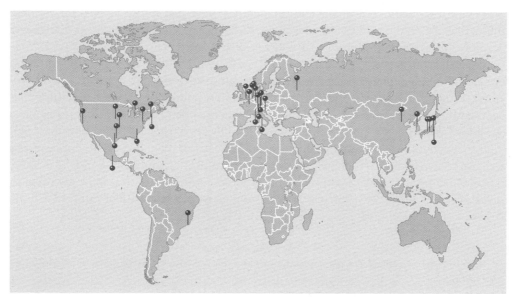

Figure 15.5 Location of headquarters of top fifty multinational companies. (Based on CNN Money, 2012.)

A central criticism made by anti-globalization protestors is that global politics reinforces and, indeed, creates inequalities within the global economy. Institutions such as the World Trade Organisation (WTO) and the World Bank are dominated largely by rich countries who can decide on policies which tend to suit their purposes. As Laurence Brahm puts it, 'the WTO has come to be seen as a forum for the G8 to extract trading conditions from less-developed nations' (2009: 71) for their own benefit. This view is even more strongly expressed by anti-globalization campaigner Walden Bello, who states the WTO is 'patently a method for the US and the EU to institutionalize their hegemony [leadership/power]' (cited in Brahm, 2009: 72).

Anti-globalization campaigners therefore state that these institutions promote and, indeed, force countries to adopt a free market model by, for instance, only lending money when an individual country promises to sell off formally nationalized industries. In doing so, not only are they promoting a particular form of capitalism, but they also erode the power of the nation state (i.e. an individual government's options and choices) by imposing sanctions if they do not act in the required way, therefore reducing their autonomy as they need to work in accordance with the rules and regulations of institutions, such as the International Monetary Fund.

Inequalities in global culture

Walk along your local high street and you will probably see the same shops as in any other high street in the country. You drink coffee in Starbucks, get your food from Tesco, and buy clothes from H&M. Indeed, if you travel abroad many of the shops and products inside them will be very familiar to you. Naomi Klein (2001) suggests a return to colonization under the dominance of global brands. This is not so much of physical space, but more of an intangible cultural space, and it is the large brands performing this colonization.

George Rizter, who we saw in Chapter 4 and who argued that society had become McDonaldized, extends this thesis to state that the whole world has become globalized, centralized, and standardized. Through this process, Ritzer (2007) argues that local products, with their distinctive character and qualities, have become swallowed up by these standardized global products. As a result, distinctiveness (*something* in Ritzer's language) becomes lost to standardization (which Ritzer calls *nothing*).

Klein (2001) uses Starbucks as an example of a firm that hastens this standardization by setting up their coffee shops in every community, squeezing out alternative, local providers. While their supporters argue that this is simply a result of offering something that people want—good coffee in a pleasant environment—their critics claim that they have developed tactics of flooding the market to drive local coffee shops out of business and then they reduce their number of shops once they control the market. This criticism was recognized by Howard Schultz who, when taking control of Starbucks as chief executive officer (CEO), stated that they should only work in communities that welcome them in (see discussion on p. 393) for fear that customers would reject them outright (Shultz 2011).

Inequality and global problems

Chapter 17 examines corporate social responsibility, an imperative for organizations to act in a way which is responsible to society, indeed to the globe. Part of the impetus for this has come from problems associated with globalization, such as:

- global warming and environmental problems, which are treated as global political issues
- sweatshop labour conditions, often arising from global brands subcontracting manufacturing labour to the third world
- global commodity chains, dominated by Western multinational firms, which pay below subsistence prices to third world suppliers.

These arguments are taken up in Chapter 17, alongside some potential global solutions to such problems, for example the Fairtrade movement, which aims to pay fair prices to suppliers in the third world.

An overall argument is that, at the start of this chapter, a precursor of globalization was seen to be the colonization of and slavery in Africa, Asia, and South America. While such a level of colonization of physical territory does not exist, the level of control of both physical and intangible aspects of globalization that Western governments and multinationals have amounts to a modern-day form of colonization. Indeed, it is not just Western countries that extend their reach in this way. More recently, China has placed considerable investment in Africa, and similar, albeit contested suggestions of empire building have been made. (See *The Guardian*, 2012 for more discussion.)

Review questions

1. Describe the inequalities of the global economy.
2. Explain the main arguments of the anti-globalization movement.
3. Analyse what problems you think global politics and global culture might create in the global economy.

Chapter summary

Globalization is a complex process, involving both physical and intangible spaces, and encompassing areas of society such as the economy, politics, culture, technology, and the natural environment. Organizations play a role in this, using a number of strategies to act on a global scale, whether on a large or small scale.

On the one hand, there is an argument that globalization is a process that brings us together as a 'global village', leading to a homogeneous global culture with the differences between individual nations and their cultures becoming less and less pronounced. On the other hand, these national and cultural differences can be seen to still exist and, indeed, influence the global strategies that organizations undertake.

Furthermore, globalization can be seen to perpetuate inequalities between nations and problems on a global scale. Recent financial crises have highlighted not only the global nature of our society, and organizations within this, but also how problems, too, are global issues requiring a global response.

Further reading

Hickson, D.J., and Pugh, D.S. 2001. *Management worldwide: Distinctive styles amid globalization.* **Penguin Books Ltd, London.**

A good introduction to Hofstede's scales, with examples of national cultures in a wide variety of countries worldwide.

Parker, B., and Clegg, S. R. 2006. Globalization. In: Clegg, S.R., Hardy, C., Lawrence, T., and Nord, W. R. (eds) *The SAGE handbook of organization studies.* **Sage, London, pp. 651–674.**

An introduction and overview of globalization, including the six aspects of global interconnectedness outlined in this chapter.

Klein, N. 2001. *No logo: no space, no choice, no jobs.* **Flamingo, London.**

An accessible introduction to the main arguments of the anti-globalization movement.

Waters, M. 2001. *Globalization,* **2nd edn. Routledge, London, New York.**

An introduction to globalizaiton as it affects organizations and society more widely.

Bibliography

Adler, C. 2003. Colonel Sanders' march on China. *Time Magazine.* 17 November 2003. Available at: http://www.time.com/time/magazine/article/0,9171,543845,00.html.

Al-Husan, F.Z.B., Brennan, R., and James, P. 2009. Transferring Western HRM practices to developing countries: The case of a privatized utility in Jordan. *Personnel Review* 38(2): 104–123.

Asser, M. 2010. Obstacles to Arab-Israeli peace: Water. BBC News. 2 September 2010. Available at: http://www.bbc.co.uk/news/world-middle-east-11101797 (last accessed 26 November 2012).

Audi, N. 2009. France, land of epicures, gets taste for McDonald's. *New York Times.* 25 October 2009. Available at: http://www.nytimes.com/2009/10/26/world/europe/26mcdonalds.html.

Bartlett, C.A., and Ghoshal, S. 1989. *Managing across borders: the transnational solution.* Harvard Business School Press: Boston, MA.

BBC News. 2006. Tesco's Thai plans under threat. 27 September 2006. Available at: http://news.bbc.co.uk/1/hi/business/5384494.stm.

BBC News. 2011. India's call centre growth stalls. Available at: http://www.bbc.co.uk/news/magazine-15060641 (last accessed 10 July 2012).

BBC Sport. 2011. In-depth interview – Sir Alex Ferguson on TV, youth policy, hairdryers and more. Available at: http://www.bbc.co.uk/sport/0/football/15064028 (last accessed 10 July 2012).

Bignell, P. 2011. Secret memos expose link between oil firms and invasion of Iraq. *The Independent.* 19 April 2011. Available at: http://www.independent.co.uk/news/uk/politics/secret-memos-expose-link-between-oil-firms-and-invasion-of-iraq-2269610.html (last accessed 26 November 2012).

Blenkinsopp, J., and Pajouh, M.S. 2010. Lost in translation? Culture, language and the role of the translator in international business. *Critical Perspectives on International Business* 6(1): 38–52.

Brahm, L.J. 2009. *The anti-globalization breakfast club manifesto for a peaceful revolution.* John Wiley & Sons (Asia): Singapore.

Bryman, A. 2004. *The Disneyization of society.* Sage: London.

Bryson, B. 1990. *Mother tongue: the English language.* Penguin: London.

Castle, S. 2012. With details settled, a second Greek bailout is formally approved. *New York Times.* 14 March 2012. Available at: http://www.nytimes.com/2012/03/15/business/global/greece-gets-formal-approval-for-second-bailout.html?_r=0 (last accessed 26 November 2012).

Chaudhuri, K. N. 1965. *The English East India Company: The Study of an Early Joint-Stock Company, 1600–1640.* Cass: London.

Cheshire, T. 2011. In depth: How Rovio made Angry Birds a winner (and what's next). *Wired.* 7 March 2011. Available at: http://www.wired.co.uk/magazine/archive/2011/04/features/how-rovio-made-angry-birds-a-winner?page=all.

Clegg, S.R., and Gray, J.T. 1996. Metaphors of globalization. *Postmodern Management and Organization Theory.* Sage: Thousand Oaks, CA, pp. 293–307.

CNN Money. 2008. How not to sell abroad. Available at: http://money.cnn.com/galleries/2008/fsb/0807/gallery.bad_translations.fsb/index.html (last accessed 26 November 2012).

CNN Money. 2012. Global 500. Available at: http://money.cnn.com/magazines/fortune/global500/2010/full_list/ (last accessed 26 November 2012).

Cooper, J. 2010. *The Origin of Financial Crises: Central Banks, Credit Bubbles and the Efficient Market Fallacy.* Harrman House: London.

Crace, J. 2003. Crossing cultures. *The Guardian* (14 October 2003).

Curwen, P. 1995. EuroDisney: the mouse that roared (not!). *European Business Review* 95(5): 15–20.

Deb, S. 2004. Call me. *The Guardian.* 3 April 2004. Available at: http://www.guardian.co.uk/theguardian/2004/apr/03/weekend7.weekend2 (last accessed 10 July 2012).

The Economist. 2007. Fresh, but far from easy. 21 June 2007. Available at: http://www.economist.com/node/9358986.

England and Wales Cricket Board. 2012. Smith celebrates birth of first child. Available at: http://www.ecb.co.uk/news/england/investec-tests/smith,318922,EN.html (last accessed 28 November 2012).

Ferguson, C. 2011. Inside Job. Song Pictures: New York.

The Football Association. 2011. The Football Association and Luis Suarez. Available at: http://www.thefa.com/TheFA/Disciplinary/NewsAndFeatures/2011/~/media/Files/PDF/

TheFA/Disciplinary/Written%20reasons/FA%20v%20
Suarez%20Written%20Reasons%20of%20Regulatory%20
Commission.ashx (last accessed 10 July 2012).

France 24. 2008. German nudists versus Polish puritans.
6 August 2008. Available at: http://www.france24.com/
en/20080803-usedom-island-baltic-sea-border-germany-
nudists-poland-puritans (last accessed 28 November 2012).

Gergen, K., and Whitney, D. 1996. Technologies of representation
in the global corporation: power and polyphony. In: Boje, D.,
Gephart, R. P., and Tatchenkery, T. J. (eds) Postmodern
management and organization theory. Sage: London,
pp. 331–357.

The Guardian. 200,000 form Edinburgh human chain. The
Guardian. 2 July 2005. Available at: http://www.guardian.co.uk/
world/2005/jul/02/g8.uk (last accessed 26 November 2012).

Hamnett, J.L. 1999. Euro Disney: a cross-cultural
communications failure? In: Goodman, R. A., Atkin, I., Barry,
J., and Pettersen, E. (eds) Modern organizations and emerging
conundrums: exploring the postindustrial subculture of the third
millennium. Lexington Books: Lanham, MD, p. 240.

Harding, L. 2000. Give me a Big Mac—but hold the beef. The
Guardian (28 December 2000).

Harding, L. 2001. Dehli calling. The Guardian. 9 March 2001.
Available at: http://www.guardian.co.uk/g2/story/
0,3604,448955,00.html (last accessed 10 July 2012).

Hofstede, G.H. 1980. Culture's consequences: international
differences in work-related values. Sage: Beverly Hills, CA.

Imai, M. 1986. KAIZEN – the key to Japan's competitive success.
Random House: New York.

Interbrand. 2012. Best global brands 2012. Available at: http://
www.interbrand.com/en/best-global-brands/
2012/Best-Global-Brands-2012-Brand-View.aspx
(last accessed 26 November 2012).

Klein, N. 2001. No logo: no space, no choice, no jobs. Flamingo:
London.

Kono, T. 1982. Japanese management philosophy:
can it be exported? Long Range Planning 15(3): 90–102.

LeMay, M.C. 1987. From Open Door to Dutch Door: An Analysis of
US Immigration Policy since 1820. Praeger
Pub Text: Westport, CT.

Lohr, S. 1987. Nissan's Revolution In Britain. The New York Times.
2 June 1987. Available at: http://www.nytimes.
com/1987/06/02/business/nissan-s-revolution-in-britain.
htmlpagewanted=all&src=pm (last accessed
26 November 2012).

Loomba, A. 1998. Colonialism-postcolonialism. Routledge:
London, New York.

Maguire, J. 1999. Global Sport: Identities, Societies, Civilizations.
Polity Press: Cambridge.

Make Poverty History. 2012. Available at: http://www.
makepovertyhistory.org/takeaction/ (last accessed
26 November 2012).

McLuhan, M. 1964. Understanding media; the extensions of man.
McGraw-Hill: New York.

McSweeney, B. 2002. Hofstede's model of national cultural
differences and their consequences: A triumph of faith-a
failure of analysis. Human Relations 55(1): 89–118.

Nationmaster. 2012. GDP (2010) by country. Available at: http://
www.nationmaster.com/graph/eco_gdp-economy-
gdp&date=2010 (last accessed 26 November 2012).

New Internationalist. 1998. The mousetrap – Inside Disney's
dream machine. Special edition, 5 December 2008.
Available at: http://www.newint.org/issues/1998/12/01/.

Osborne, A., Aldrick, P., and Quinn, J. 2009. Lehman collapse: the
drama of a mad 48 hours that will never fade. The Daily
Telegraph. 13 September 2009. Available at: http://www.
telegraph.co.uk/finance/financialcrisis/6179138/Lehman-
collapse-the-drama-of-a-mad-48-hours-that-will-never-
fade.html (last accessed 26 November 2012).

Parfitt, T. 2007. Belarus cuts off Russian pipeline in bitter gas war.
The Guardian. 9 January 2007. Available at: http://www.
guardian.co.uk/business/2007/jan/09/oilandpetrol.russia
(last accessed 26 November 2012).

Parker, B. 1996. Evolution and revolution: From international
business to globalization. In: Clegg, S.R., Hardy, C., and Nord,
W.R. (eds) Handbook of organization studies. Sage: London,
pp. 484–506.

Parker, B., and Clegg, S.R. 2006. Globalization. In: Clegg, S.R.,
Hardy, C., Lawrence, T., and Nord, W.R. (eds) The Sage
handbook of organization studies. Sage: London,
pp. 651–674.

Pederson, I. 2012. Central Asia could go to war over water.
Business Insider. September 15 2012. Available at: http://
www.businessinsider.com/central-asia-really-could-go-to-
war-over-lack-of-water-2012-9#ixzz2DLumadrE (last
accessed 26 November 2012).

Ritzer, G. 2007. The globalization of nothing 2. Pine Forge Press:
Thousand Oaks, CA.

Ritzer, G. 2011. The McDonaldization of Society 6. Pine Forge
Press: Thousand Oaks, CA.

Robertson, R. 1992. Globalization: social theory and global
culture. Sage: London.

Robertson, R. 1995. Glocalization: time-space and
homogeneity-heterogeneity. In: Featherstone, M., Lash, S.,
and Robertson, R. (eds) Global Modernities, Sage: London,
pp. 25–44.

Rushton, K. 2012. Carphone Warehouse likely to buy Best
Buy out of European joint venture. The Daily Telegraph.
14 November 2012. Available at: http://www.telegraph.co.uk/
finance/newsbysector/retailandconsumer/9678947/
Carphone-Warehouse-likely-to-buy-Best-Buy-out-of-
European-joint-venture.html.

Schultz, H. 2011. Onward: How Starbucks Fought for its Life
without Losing its Soul. John Wiley and Sons: Chichester.

Taylor, D. 2011. Luis Suárez-Patrice Evra racism case may hinge
on cultural differences. The Guardian. 15 December 2011.
Available at: http://www.guardian.co.uk/football/2011/
dec/15/luis-suarez-patrice-evra-case (last accessed
10 July 2012).

Tesco plc. 2012. Our business. Available at: https://www.
tescoplc.com/index.asp?pageid=8 (last accessed
November 28. 2012).

Thompson, J. 2010. Tesco bags stores in Czech Republic. The
Independent. 24 December 2012. Available at: http://www.
independent.co.uk/news/business/news/tesco-bags-stores-
in-czech-republic-2168380.html.

Waters, M. 2001. Globalization, 2nd edn. Routledge: London,
New York.

Watson, J.L. 1997. Transnationalism, localization, and fast
foods in East Asia. In: Golden Arches East: McDonald's
in East Asia. Stanford University Press: Stanford, CA,
pp. 1–38.

Witz, A., Warhurst, C., and Nickson, D. 2003. The labour of
aesthetics and the aesthetics of organization. Organization
10(1): pp. 33–54.

Yakhlef, A. 2004. Global Brands as Embodied 'Generic Spaces'.
Space and Culture 7(2): 237–248.

The service and leisure economies

Organizations as an experience, work as a performance

Chapter overview and learning outcomes

By the end of this chapter you should be able to:

- describe the main features of 'Disneyized' organizations (Bryman, 2004) within the service sector and leisure industries

- explain how many service sector organizations create an 'experience' rather than a product which is consumed

- explain what is meant by performative labour as an aspect of the service sector labour process

- describe the main features of emotional and aesthetic labour

- analyse how emotional and aesthetic labour impact workers differently depending upon their gender.

Key theorists

Alan Bryman	Developed the idea of the 'Disneyization of society' to suggest that characteristics of Disney theme parks are widespread in other service and leisure organizations
Arlie Hochschild	From research into the work of air hostesses, developed the term 'emotional labour' to show how workers are expected to manage their emotions in return for a wage
Pierre Bourdieu	Used the term 'habitus' to suggest that people have deeply-held dispositions which they demonstrate unwittingly in their behaviour and which are difficult to change
Erving Goffman	Used theatrical analogies in his 1959 book *The Presentation of the Self in Every Day Life* to suggests that people put on different performances in different social contexts
Anne Witz, Chris Warhurst, and Dennis Nickson	Identified aesthetic labour in customer-facing service industries, where people manage their appearance and behavioural dispositions in return for a wage

Key terms

Disneyization (of society)	As noted by Alan Bryman, the adoption of certain characteristics of the Disney theme park in a large number of service and leisure organizations, especially in organizations which are experienced by consumers as destinations in their own right
Performative labour	Cited by Bryman as an aspect of Disneyization whereby workers are on show in front of consumers and are required to put on some form of performance. Such performance encompasses both emotional and aesthetic labour
Emotional labour	Workers managing the emotions that they display in front of customers and clients in return for the wage that they are paid
Aesthetic labour	Workers adhering to certain requirements of appearance and comportment in return for the wage that they are paid

Introduction

Running case: a bar at the Junction Hotel

Jane Grimes, a local university student, has recently started part-time bar work at Junction Hotel. At the weekend, Grimes likes to go out around town with friends. This Friday, however, she is on the rota to work evenings.

Édouard Manet's *A Bar at the Folies-Bergeres*.

© The Samuel Courtauld Trust, The Courtauld Gallery, London.

At 7 pm, the bar is quiet. Grimes catches sight of the painting hanging on the wall—Édouard Manet's *A Bar at the Folies-Bergeres*. It has become a favourite of Grimes's, and, after several weekend shifts in the bar she realizes why. The facial expression on the painting sums up Grimes's feelings—she is bored. She would much rather be having a laugh with her friends than being stuck behind the bar.

To compound matters, unlike the barmaid in the painting, she isn't allowed to look bored for too long. However she feels—bored, sad, angry . . . whatever—she has to put on a show—a smile, being pleasant, showing interest in the customers. As the bar manager keeps reminding her, she is a part of the decoration in here and an unhappy face spoils things for customers.

Keeping a happy face becomes more and more of a test as the night wears on and the punters drink more.

The first man to arrive tells her 'how lovely' she looks. She smiles and says 'thank you', but, inside, feels disgust. Her skin crawls at the thought that she is some sort of object for him to ogle at. Besides, she doesn't feel 'lovely' at all. The bar has a dress code, which includes a uniform that she hates, and rules on make-up and hair that she feels make her look like a doll rather than a real person.

As the night continues and customers drink more, they become ruder and the compliments on her looks become more suggestive. The regular bar-room bore sits at one end of the bar, unburdening his tales of marital woe to Grimes. She wants to tell him what a sad individual he is, but, instead, she has to smile and humour him. This is particularly difficult for her because his drawling, incoherent sentences are keeping her from serving others, and these gaps in service will show up on the printout from the till at the end of the shift.

Jane Grimes looks up again at the woman in the painting and the bored expression on her face. 'If only I could show my true feelings like she does; just drop the mask for a while', she thinks, 'instead, I have to keep up this performance for the rest of the shift'.

What aspects of this case do you recognize from your own experiences of work?

Service sector work will be familiar to many readers of this book. As a student you may well work part-time in a shop, bar, restaurant, or call centre. It is also likely that, upon graduating, you will also be employed in the service sector, which has replaced manufacturing as the dominant focus of many Western economies. In the UK, for example, service industries are estimated to account for over three quarters of economic activity (Office for National Statictics, 2012).

Many types of work are included in the measurement of the service sector used by the Office for National Statistics, including transport, communications, media, finance, and government services, such as defence. In this chapter, we are particularly interested in aspects of service work defined variously as front-line, customer-facing, or **interactive service work**. This might include retail work or leisure work, such as bars and restaurants, but can include any job where work is performed in front of customers or clients.

The service sector: from rationalization to performance

When rational management techniques, such as Taylorism, Fordism, and bureaucracy (see Chapters 2 and 3) were developed, manufacturing dominated the economy. An important issue in this chapter is whether the shift towards services and away from manufacturing diminishes the importance of rationalization to management and organization.

The organizations examined in Chapter 4 would suggest not. Call centres, supermarkets, budget hotels, and the fast-food restaurant are all contemporary examples of efficient, rationalized organizations, and all are located in the service sector. Indeed, Ritzer's (2011) McDonaldization not only examines service sector industries, but also shows explicitly how they employ bureaucratic, Taylorist, and Fordist techniques—the fast-food restaurant being compared with an assembly line for producing and serving food.

While service-sector organizations employ rationalized techniques, they also display their own particular characteristics, which we suggest are linked to work and the consumption of that work taking place *at the same time*. Think about a trip to a restaurant—it is not just the food that determines your enjoyment of the visit, but also the atmosphere, the décor, and the attitude of the waiting staff, etc. We examine how it is the organization itself and the nature of the service work performed that are as much part of the experience for customers as the product and services offered.

- Service sector organizations, such as bars, restaurants, and shopping malls often create their own particular theme, environment, or experience for the consumer in a similar way to the experience created by a Disney theme park. Bryman (2004) thus uses the term 'Disneyization' to describe characteristics of Disney theme parks which can be found in contemporary service and leisure organizations.

- If a theme or experience is part of what an organization is selling, then workers play a role in creating that experience. Unlike workers on a manufacturing assembly line, service workers are 'on show' to customers. Gabriel (2005) uses the metaphor of the 'glass cage' to at once invoke the McDonaldized, rationalized nature of much service work (alluding to Weber's iron cage of bureaucracy as discussed in Chapter 2), and similarly, to highlight workers being constantly on display as if they were in a glass cabinet.

Organizations become almost like theatres, with workers putting on a performance in front of customers and clients. Indeed, Bryman (2004) suggests that workers are specifically paid to undertake **performative labour** in exchange for the wages they are paid. In this chapter we examine two particular aspects of how workers might be expected to engage in performative labour:

- **emotional labour** (Hochschild, 1983) is concerned with expectations of how workers will behave and interact with customers and clients. In many cases this might be by smiling

---

Interactive service work Jobs where the worker deals directly with a customer or client, found especially in the service and leisure industries.

Performative labour Paid interactive service work where the worker is engaging in some form of performance, as if on stage. Refers, in particular, to emotional and aesthetic labour.

Emotional labour Work where, in exchange for a wage, the worker is expected to manage their emotions to put on a particular emotional performance in front of customers or clients, especially in interactive service work.

and being pleasant to customers, but we will see that other service work might demand different types of emotional display

- **aesthetic labour** (Witz et al., 2003) is concerned with aspects of appearance, e.g. through dress codes, and how workers present and 'carry' themselves in front of cutomers.

While these aspects of performative labour can be found in many aspects of customer-facing service work, we conclude the chapter by suggesting that emotional and aesthetic labour are not gender neutral. The burden of peformative labour falls disproportionately upon women, to the point where women are seen to be objectified or sexually 'commodi-fied' (Adkins, 1994) in service work.

> **Aesthetic labour** Usually found in customer or client-facing service work where, in exchange for a wage, the worker is expected to manage their appearance and comportment in a manner directed by the organization.

Review questions

1. Describe how service sector work is rationalized (you may wish to look back at Chapter 4).
2. Explain what is meant by 'putting on a performance' at work.

Apply

3. What characteristics of customer-facing service work can you identify in the Junction Hotel case?

The organization as an experience

We may think of the Disney theme parks as a place to visit on a special occasion—a land where we can experience spectacular images and sights before returning home to our more ordinary lives. Bryman (2004), however, suggests that the characteristics of Disney theme parks are more commonplace; indeed, they can be found in one form or another in many everyday service and leisure organizations. Bryman suggests four characteristics which make up this **Disneyization** of society:

Disneyland.

> **Disneyization** Term coined by Bryman which describes characteristics of the Disney theme parks that can be seen in other service and leisure organizations.
>
> **Theming** As with a theme park, this is where the image and identity of an organization, and the experience that it provides for consumers, is based around a particular theme.
>
> **Hybrid consumption** Different types of consumption activity, which might otherwise take place in separate organizations, appearing together in one organization.

- as with theme parks, there are examples in service and leisure organizations of **theming**. Pubs are presented as sports bars or Irish pubs. Restaurants are themed around the food they serve (e.g. Chinese or Indian) or take on other themes, e.g. the Hard Rock Café themed around music (Beardsworth and Bryman, 1999). Even geographical areas are themed for the purposes of the tourist industry, e.g. 'Shakespeare country' around Stratford-upon-Avon, England, or Santa Claus Land in Finland (Pretes, 1995)

- a theme park encompasses a number of different types of consumption—shops, restaurants, leisure rides, etc. Such **hybrid consumption**, whereby a number of different types of consumption activity take place under the same roof, is also found in service and leisure organizations. Shopping malls are often combined with other leisure activities, such as bars, restaurants, and cinemas. New football stadia developments may encompass hotels, fast-food restaurants, and may be built as part of a retail park

- goods are produced using the name or image of a particular organization. Disney **merchandizing** (films, soft toys, etc.) is familiar and there may even be cross-promotion with, for example, a new Disney film being promoted at a fast-food restaurant. Top sports clubs also produce merchandizing—think of a Manchester United duvet or a Chelsea pencil case

- as we will see later in the chapter, workers are expected—through the management of emotion and appearance—to engage in performative labour as if they were on a stage.

Merchandizing The image or brand of one company or organization appearing on other products.

> ### Real life case: West Edmonton mall
>
> The West Edmonton mall, in Alberta, Canada, is a giant shopping mall, but encompasses many other attractions. Within its walls are a water park, cinemas, restaurants, an ice rink, a marine life centre, a miniature golf course, and even an indoor fairground with roller coasters. It has themed areas with attractions based around Chinese, European, and New Orleans themes.
>
> The mall also has hotels and is so much of a destination in its own right that its website suggests taking a three-day stay at the hotel, with an itinerary for each day composed of activities to do purely within the mall itself.
>
> **Source:** West Edmonton mall (2012).

The example of the West Edmonton mall shows at least three examples of Disneyization. There is theming of some of the areas, there is hybrid consumption with different types of consumption in one place, such as retail, entertainment, and hotels, and with interactive service work in the various attractions within the mall, we can presume that performative labour takes place too. There is no merchandizing of the mall as such—although a Disney store within the mall means that merchandizing is not entirely absent!

Not all service and leisure organizations will exhibit all of the characteristics of Disneyization, some will exhibit more than others; however, a common theme that we take forward is that these factors combine in different organizations in different ways as a means for the organization to create a particular **experience** for its consumers.

Experience Where consumption is of the organization itself rather than any product or service that it provides.

Production The work done in an organization by the workers within that organization.

Consumption The purchase and use by customers and clients of goods and services created by an organization.

From consuming products to consuming organizations: the organization as an experience

When we buy manufactured goods, such as a television, we don't actually see the work that has gone into making them. It is highly unlikely that we will have stood and watched the television being assembled in a factory—**production** took place in another place at another time and our enjoyment of the product is none the worse for this.

In manufacturing, production takes place in one particular place (the factory) whereas **consumption** of that product—using and enjoying the product—takes place elsewhere (the

customer's home) and at a different time. There is a 'temporal and spatial buffer' (Korczynski and Ott, 2004: 576) between the labour performed in producing the item and the consumption of that item (see Figure 16.1).

At a Disney theme park, the product on offer is not a tangible good, such as a television, it is the experience of the time spent at the theme park which is consumed. The temporal and spatial buffer that exisited with manufacturing has disappeared in service industries, such as Disney. The experience produced by the theme park *is consumed by the visitors at the same time and in the very same place.*

While there may be products sold in the theme park which were produced elsewhere, in terms of the experience that it provides, production and consumption are intertwined, both happening simultaneously (see Figure 16.2).

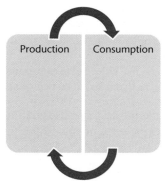

Figure 16.2 Simultaneous production and consumption in the 'experience' of service and leisure organizations.

In that consumption takes place within the organization itself, a characteristic of many service and leisure organizations is that they are created as locations in their own right, to be experienced by consumers. As seen with the West Edmonton mall, shopping malls are destinations to be experienced for themselves rather than simply a place to shop. For Gottdiener (1998) the mall has to advertise itself as an attractive location or experience to compete with the town centre that it aims to replace and, increasingly, to compete with other shopping malls.

> As a result, almost every mall has an overarching motif that attempts to convey it as a unique and desirable location for its own sake . . .
> (Gottdiener, 1998: 80)

Real life case: the Black Country Living Museum

The Black Country Living Museum, in Dudley, England, is an outdoor museum where, brick-by-brick, buildings of historical significance from the surrounding area have been moved and set up—a church, a pub, a nailmaker, and various shops, etc. The exhibits are working exhibits with which vistors can interact. So, visitors can have a drink in the pub, buy sweets from the confectionery shop, and ride on the working tram line within the museum. School parties can even experience Victorian-style teaching in the working classroom on the site.

Source: Black Country Living Museum (2012).

Museums are another type of organization that can be seen to be geared towards providing an experience. Featherstone (1991: 102) and Kirstenblatt-Gimblett (1998: 138) suggest that this is a shift in emphasis. Once museums concentrated on the product—think of dusty artefacts on shelves with 'do not touch' signs—but now they concentrate on the visitor 'experience'. People are encouraged to touch and interact with exhibits as part of that experience.

What organizations do you visit as a destination or experience in their own right?

Controlling organizational realities

When we enter a theme park, museum, shopping mall, or similar organization, we are effectively leaving our everyday lives behind for a few hours and immersing ourselves in the experience that they create. It could be said that these organizations create their own particular 'realities', especially so in a themed environment where that reality is meticulously created to match with the theme.

In fact, it is not just that organizations create their own realities, the experience that they create is so much *better* than the reality it is meant to imitate that it has been described as **hyper-reality** (Baudrillard, 1983; Eco, 1986). Referring to the painstaking recreation of a tropical rain forest at Disneyland, Eco states:

> A real crocodile can be found in the zoo, and as a rule it is dozing or hiding, but Disneyland tells us that faked nature corresponds much more to our daydream demands.   (Eco, 1986: 44)

Hyper-reality An artificial reality which is better than anything that could be experienced in the reality that it aims to reproduce.

We might expect something spectacular, better-than-reality from a theme park, but the experience of something more mundane, such as a shopping centre, also aims to create something of a 'perfect world'. For example, in a town centre the weather can provide all manner of unpleasant surprises—rain, snow, and cold temperatures. In shopping centres, technology provides a constant perfect climate within its walls—much better than that of a 'real' climate outdoors (Ritzer, 2011: 112–113).

Technology and organizational control can also help to make the mall better than the world outside by reducing the instances of crime. Surveillance technology, such as closed circuit television (CCTV) cameras, along with private security forces, are designed to ensure that the mall remains a safe space.

In such organizations, the environment is totally organized or 'climatized'—a 'total conditioning of actions and time' (Baudrillard, 1970: 23–24, author's translation). The better-than-perfect experience comes from very tight levels of organizational *control*:

> The shopping mall exerts great control over shops and shopkeepers. Before allowing shops to open, mall developers often must approve their design, logo, colours, and even names. Once open, mall managers proliferate rules and regulations and enforce them on shopkeepers. Security people inspect shops and take note of those that violate the rules (for example, opening or closing a few minutes early or late). Persistent violators may be expelled from the mall. Efforts are also made to exclude controversial groups.   (Ritzer, 1996: 116)

Bryman (1995: 181) notes how the themed experience and hyper-reality created by Disney theme parks also comes about as a result of tight levels of control over workers and over the organization itself. Many of the techniques used are familiar teachniques of rational management, including manuals to control the work process, job roles delineated by different uniforms, and highly structured work routines. The magical experience of the theme park would seem to bear the rationalized hallmarks of Taylor and Ford.

Review questions

1. Describe the four main features of Disneyization.

2. Explain how the nature of consumption differs between manufacturing and service environments.

3. Explain how organizations create 'hyper-real environments'.

4. Analyse how the environments that organizations create come about as a result of tight levels of control.

Work as a performance: the service sector labour process

Real life case: the bar till

At one time in the UK, pubs tended to be small-scale 'locals', where the landlord and landlady would know most customers personally. Now many pubs are larger in size and part of national chains. The changing nature of pub work towards one that is more rationalized can be evidenced in the typical till found in such a busy establishment.

The till is very similar to that found in a fast-food restaurant (see Chapter 4). It has a button on the screen for each particular product, so there is no need to think about the prices for different items and add them up. The transaction becomes a matter of pushing three or four buttons for a round—the process of serving becomes much more efficient which is, of course, useful for a packed, busy bar.

The till also allows for control to be exerted over bar staff. A staff member swipes a card into the till before processing their transaction. This identifies the member of staff to the till (or, more precisely, to the computer system working behind the till); it may even inform the customer of this on the receipt—'you were served by X'. It also means that the number, time, and amount of transactions for each member of staff can be recorded and examined at a later date—just like in a call centre staff can be monitored by the data held on them in the computer system. So, even without a supervisor around, the data can reveal when people take breaks (which can be assumed by an absence of any transactions in that time period) and can also be used to compare the efficiency with which people work—the number of transactions they make per hour, for example.

The bar till seems to be a perfect tool for the service sector manager wishing to bring elements of rationalization, as seen in Chapter 4, into their organization. It combines the efficiency of service of a fast-food restaurant with the surveillance and control of the call centre.

While rationalization is commonplace within the service and leisure sectors, the nature of work is much more than McDonaldization alone. Indeed, Korczynski and Ott (2004: 578) suggest that while rationalization is undoubtedly present in service work, there is little evidence of pure McDonaldization or Taylorism in practice; instead, rationalization is blended with customer-focused work.

It perhaps sounds obvious to say that service work should be customer-focused, but looking back at Figures 16.1 and 16.2 gives us an idea of why this is the case. In manufacturing work, the customer is distant from the worker on the assembly line: as long as the product is in good condition the customer has no interest in the worker's name, appearance, and mannerisms, etc.

In a service organization, production, and consumption take place at the same time. Workers in the service sector interact directly with customers—there is no distance in time or space between the work done and the consumption of that work. While a bar worker and a worker on an assembly line might both be subject to rationalization, a bar worker is also on show to the customers at the same time. Whether they are friendly, rude, well-groomed, or unkempt, they are a part of the customer's 'experience' of the organization.

Have you ever complained about the service you have received in an organization or maybe even not gone back to that organization because of bad service?

Performative labour

In organizations such as the theme park there is no tangible product to sell, such as a television or a pint of beer, it is purely the experience that is consumed. Thus, Disney views its staff as an important part of the experience that the organization creates, and exerts considerable control over their behaviour and appearance to ensure their 'performance' as a standardized 'product'.

While rationalization exerts considerable control over workers at Disney, a further aspect of control over workers in service sector industries is shown in the final aspect of Disneyization— that of performative labour. This is where, in Disney and in other customer- and client-facing service indus-

Performance time.

tries, work is '. . . akin to a theatrical performance in which the workplace is construed as similar to a stage' Bryman (2004: 104). Work is a performance, and managers are the directors of that performance.

Performative labour draws together two strands of control over the service sector labour processs which we examine in the remainder of this chapter: emotional labour, where people control their behaviour and feelings in front of customers, and aesthetic labour, where workers adhere to particular requirements of dress, appearance, and comportment.

The presentation of the self

Goffman (1959) applied metaphors of theatre and performance to analyse how people present themselves in different social situations, including the workplace. He noted how people put on different emotional and behavioural 'performances', including their use of dress, props, and appearance, depending on the situation.

For Goffman, a team refers to a set of individuals with a common interest—a group of workplace colleagues might be one such team. In life we are members of different teams at different times. Goffman suggested that in different teams we might offer a different 'presentation of the self', that is to say we may modify our behaviour and appearance accordingly.

Think about how you behave in different social circumstances—in a university seminar, in church, at work, at a rugby club social, etc. Do you act differently in these different situations? How do you *know* the appropriate performance to maintain in each?

Crucial to Goffman's (1959) work are three areas, which retain the theatrical metaphor:

- frontstage—where members of a team are involved in a performance and must maintain that performance

- backstage—where the team is out of view of the performance. The performance does not need to be maintained, but issues relating to the performance might be discussed among the team (similar to the wings or the rehearsal room in a theatre)

- outside—away from the situation completely.

It is not difficult to see how Goffman's theatrical metaphor resonates with the service industry; indeed, similar metaphors are even used in some service organizations. Disney, for example, refers to theme park workers as 'cast members' and speaks of **frontstage** areas

Frontstage A theatrical metaphor to represent areas of the organization where workers are in contact with customers and clients.

Backstage A theatrical metaphor to represent areas of the organization where workers are out of view of customers and clients.

as being in front of theme park visitors and **backstage** areas being out of view of the visitors. Similarly, service organizations, such as cinemas or hotels, have 'front-of-house staff' who deal directly with customers and 'backroom staff' who work out of view of customers in offices or kitchens, for example.

We can thus make a direct link between Goffman's theatrical metaphors of society and the workplace, especially in the service sector:

- frontstage areas would be any areas where workers are facing and interacting with customers, and where some form of performance might be expected—at the counter, in the aeroplane cabin, on the gym floor, or on the phones in a call centre, for example

- backstage areas are in the workplace but out of view of customers—the offices, the staff room, the smoking area at the back of the building, or the galley in an aeroplane, for example

- outside areas would be away from work—at home, out with non-work friends; in other words, it represents private life rather than working life.

Performance and the wage–labour relationship

It is worthwhile to outline here the specific meaning of labour as it applies to these performance aspects of work. Recall the following diagram from Chapter 3 which outlines the nature of the capitalist wage–labour relationship.

Workers receive a wage and, in return, provide their labour. So, labour has a specific meaning: it is that which is provided (or done) by workers in exchange for the wage paid to them. There are two types of labour with which we are familiar:

- manual labour involves using physical abilities in return for the wage paid. It could be argued that Taylor and Ford's factory techniques relied on manual labour as they reduced work to simplistic, repetitive tasks

- intellectual labour is where a worker uses their knowledge, skill, or some other similar intellectual ability in order to carry out a task for which they are paid a wage.

Figure 16.3
The capitalist wage–labour relationship.

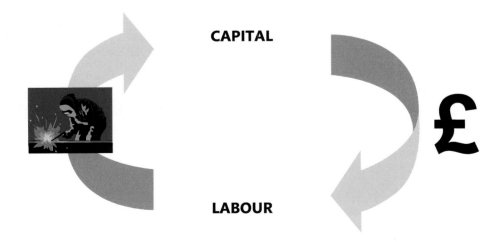

While both of these types of labour might be required in service sector work, performative labour is where a particular emotional performance or standards of appearance are prescribed as part of what the worker does in return for their wage, or where there is an expectation that they will be performed as a part and parcel of the job.

So, while a member of bar staff may have to carry crates up from the cellar (physical labour) and operate till equipment (intellectual labour), they also have the additional burdens of smiling at customers (emotional labour) and adhering to a particular dress code (aesthetic labour). Performance is, thus, a further aspect of labour expected in exchange for the wage paid in service sector work.

From the iron cage to glass cages

Frontstage performances therefore become important to the organization—the service interaction is a part of what the organization offers, and emotional and aesthetic performances of workers are a part of this. The emotional and aesthetic labour of the workers have a direct and immediate impact on the experience consumed by the customer *at the same time and in the same place*.

Gabriel (2005) adapts Weber's concept of the iron cage of society to take account of this immediate visibility of people's work. The iron cage (see Chapters 2 and 4) suggested that bureaucracy and rationalization were so commonplace that they trapped people in their monotonous routines. Ritzer (2011) later developed the iron cage metaphor to describe the prevalence of McDonaldization in contemporary society.

Gabriel's **glass cage** metaphor recognizes this iron cage aspect of rationalization in contemporary service work. The visibility of being behind glass equates to the visibility that rational forms of surveillance bring to the work that people do. The bar till, for example, records every transaction made by a worker and when it took place. The transparency of glass also refers to the further visibility of constantly being on show—working in an organization is like being on display behind a glass cage.

On the one hand, this could be seen as a further level of control in the capitalist wage–labour relationship. Performative labour can be seen as an extra level of control, with emotional and aesthetic performances being demanded on top of rationalized efficiency as part of the wage–labour relationship.

However, as we will see with emotional labour, the nature of this part of the relationship, of performing a show front of stage, also creates spaces where resistance against that control may take place.

> **Glass cage** Gabriel's metaphor to represent the visibility of workers in service sector organizations, both from the surveillance of rational organizational control and the visibility of being 'on show' in front of customers and clients.

Review questions

1. Explain what it means for work to be a 'performance'.

2. Using Goffman's concepts, explain what is meant by front- and backstage areas of an organization.

3. Analyse how performative labour works alongside rationalization in the service sector labour process, and how this affects the nature of the wage–labour relationship.

Apply

4. How can you see aspects of the glass cage metaphor in bar work?

Emotional labour

Anybody who has had to work in front of clients or customers will be familiar with the mantra that 'The customer is always right'. No matter how wrong, impatient, rude, or downright abusive the customer might be, you treat them as if they are right—the customer is king. You might want to shout or swear at the abusive customer, but these feelings and behaviours have to be suppressed—the expectation is that you will smile and remain pleasant.

You may have your own feelings that you have brought into work that particular day—personal events may have made you sad, upset, or angry. But, while in front of customers, you will again be expected to put these personal emotions into the background and perform the emotional display required by the organization.

Such a performance, where emotions are managed to project a particular set of feelings, potentially different to the feeling being held deeply within, is what Hocshchild (1983) termed emotional labour, defining it as '. . . the management of feeling to create a publicly observable facial and bodily display [which] is sold for a wage . . .' (Hochschild, 1983: 7).

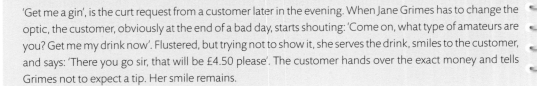

Research insight: Emotional Labour: Hochschild, A.R. 1983. *The managed heart: commercialization of human feeling.* University of California Press, Berkeley, CA.

Arlie Hochschild's concept of 'emotional labour' derived from her research into the work of air cabin crew. Hochschild noted how the smile of the air hostess was something that seemed to be 'bought' by the airline as part of the wages paid. Maintaining a particular emotional display—the smile—was a part of the wage–labour relationship as much as other aspects of the work of cabin crew, such as pushing trolleys and performing safety demonstrations.

Cabin crew are thus, when in front of passengers and throughout a flight, expected to maintain the appearance of a particular set of feelings—smiling and being pleasant to passengers, no matter how rude they may be. This management of feeling and emotion as part and parcel of paid employment thus gives the title of Hochschild's (1983) text *The Managed Heart*.

A genuine smile?

The nature of cabin-crew work, where emotions and feelings have to be controlled in front of passengers as a part of the work done for wages will be familiar to many people who have worked in customer-facing jobs. It is often characterized as retaining a smile in the face of the abusive customer, but there are a variety of ways in which workers might be expected to manage their emotions to give a particular form of emotional display.

- *Smiling and being pleasant to customers.* This is the type of behaviour that people most associate with emotional labour—shop workers, bar staff, cabin crew, any job where workers maintain a smile and pleasant manner in front of customers, no matter how rude or abusive the customer may be.

- *Presenting an upbeat, motivational personality.* Gym instructors (Bryman, 2004: 120), tour reps (Guerrier and Adib, 2003), and teachers are all examples of workers who may have to put on an upbeat performance at work to motivate and interest others.

- *Presenting a respectful and sombre personality.* While emotional labour is often characterized as putting on a smile, in some work very different displays are needed. Nurses delivering bad news are discussed later in this chapter; funeral directors and social workers (Karabanow, 1999) are examples where, even if a worker is personally happy, they may need to manage emotions to put on a more serious display.

- *Remaining calm during tense situations.* Police officers and nightclub bouncers often have to deal with situations that could be inflamed easily. They may even be on the receiving end of verbal abuse or physical threats. Emotions have to be managed so as not to retaliate to such threats, but to stay calm and not let the situation get out of hand.

What other examples of work that requires emotional labour could you add to this list?

Theory in context: Fawlty Towers

To understand the concept of emotional labour, we could, perhaps, turn to an example of emotional labour *not* being performed. In the BBC hotel-based comedy *Fawlty Towers*, John Cleese plays hotel owner Basil Fawlty.

The comedy in the programme comes from a mis-match of our *expectations* and the actual *behaviours* within a hotel setting. We would *expect* a hotel owner to be pleasant and polite to guests, as these guests may bring repeat business or make recommendations to other people. If guests have a complaint, no matter how trivial or incorrect it may be, the management and hotel staff will deal with it politely and attempt to 'smooth over' the situation.

The actual *behaviour* in Fawlty Towers stands in marked contrast, Basil Fawlty is rude and will even shout at guests. It stands as an example of how not to perform emotional labour.

Visit the Online Resource Centre for a link to a clip of the show.

Deep and surface acting

In that emotional labour involves putting on some form of act, it fits in with the performance and theatrical metaphors discussed earlier in this chapter. As customers we may sometimes be well aware that an act is taking place. When we are encouraged to 'have a nice day' accompanied by a toothsome, sickly grin, it can feel fake and inauthentic.

In *The Managed Heart*, Hochschild (1983) noted that such a distinction between fake and authentic also exists in how emotional labourers themselves approach their work.

Surface acting
Emotional labour that is performed by workers conscious of the fact that they are engaged in an artificial performance.

Deep acting
Emotional labour where the worker internalizes and believes in the performance in which they are engaged.

- **Surface acting** is where the emotional display is fake and superficial—the smile and pleasantness are deliberately put on, like a mask. The worker is not acting as their 'authentic self' and, instead, is consciously acting and putting on a display in front of customers.

- **Deep acting** is, in Hochshild's words, where a worker is deceiving themselves as much as they are the customer. The feelings being displayed are much more authentic—the display is coming from within. This might mean that the worker is displaying their authentic feelings, or that they have taken on board the performance so much that it has become their authentic behaviour rather than a superficial performance.

A distinction between the two is not necessarily clear cut—a receptionist might come across to customers as warm, genuine, and authentic but out of view in the back office they drop the mask and act as themselves. Being a better actor in front of customers does not necessarily mean that deep acting is being undertaken.

Furthermore, think of a situation where a nurse has to deliver bad news. On the one hand, if the nurse appeared superficial and artificial in delivering the news (i.e. surface acting), it could come across as crass and insensitive. A nurse would be expected to display genuine sensitivity and empathy in delivering such news, i.e. there is an expectation of acting with much more depth.

But this in itself is fraught with difficulties—if a nurse were to get emotionally involved at a deep level in all cases that they handled, it would have a detrimental effect on their own ability to cope with the job: the emotion would overwhelm them. There is thus a delicate balance between displaying deep emotional sensitivity but keeping this at such a surface level that it allows the nurse to remain unaffected while not appearing artificial.

Such difficulties in maintaining a balance of appropriate emotional performances, while maintaining a suitable distance so as not to be personally affected, means that the performance of emotional labour is often associated with stress.

Stress, coping, and emotional labour

Running case: 'all kicking off'

Simon Chance has arranged, through his football club directorship, some deals at the hotel for travelling away supporters. Jane Grimes can hear a set of supporters in the restaurant being drunk, loud, and generally abusive to the waiting staff—as if the waiters didn't get enough abuse from the Head Chef.

After dinner, the football party makes their way into the bar area. At first, the raucous behaviour—singing, chanting, and dancing on the table—is confined to their corner of the bar. Then, two of the party stagger up to the bar to buy a round.

As they slump against the bar, Grimes feels intimidated. They start to make lewd suggestions about what she might like to do once her shift has finished. She tries as hard as she can to smile and humour them, but, as it becomes obvious she will not be acquiescing to their requests, things turn nasty. Pointing at her, one of the men starts yelling at the top of his voice, shouting a stream of the worst insults and expletives possible.

Grimes can take it no longer, bursts into tears, and runs behind the bar into the staff room.

Imagine performing a job, day in, day out, where you are required to remain calm and pleasant in the face of abusive customers—a constant onslaught of unpleasant remarks, swearing, and even violent threats. How much of this could you take before you snapped back at the customer? How would you cope if you were not able to snap back for fear of how managers might react?

Visit the Online Resources Centre to listen to a recording of such a phone call in a call centre.

Real life case: emotional labour in call centres

In a study of an airline sales call centre, Steve Taylor (1998) notes the difference between 'hard' and 'soft' targets that workers have to meet. Hard targets are the familiar numerical targets of calls handled per hour, for example, which can be monitored using the surveillance afforded by computerized monitoring of workers.

Soft targets relate to the way in which operators speak, and respond, to customers during calls. It is stated that agents should respond '. . . in a manner which upholds the commercial interests of Flightpath, rather than in a manner which expresses their own perception and feeling' (Taylor, 1998: 91). The targets can be monitored by listening into conversations—staff will be found out if they let their emotions get the better of them, and shout or snap back at rude or abusive callers.

As described earlier, emotional labour often accompanies service sector jobs which are already subject to intensified forms of rationalization, such as the numerical targets in the case of the call centre. Pugliesi (1999: 134) describes this emotional labour as a 'hidden workload' on top of existing work.

Pugliesi (1999) further suggests that emotional labour is stressful, lowering job satisfaction and increasing psychological distress.

To what extent workers are expected to deal with unpleasant behaviour, even abuse, as part of their work, varies in different professions.

Korczynski and Bishop (2009) highlighted how workers in UK job centres faced regular threats, abuse, and often violence in their work. This, however, was 'normalized and routinized' (ibid: 84) with neutral, euphemistic language used in training and by management—abusive customers became 'challenging customers', for example. At the same time, the workers were expected to perform emotional labour. Requirements to be helpful and friendly could be enforced by 'mystery shopper' visits.

In other cases, management might intervene more in protecting front-line staff. In UK railways stations, posters can be seen which uphold the right of staff to work 'without fear', stressing to passengers the unacceptability of abusive behaviour.

What responsibility do you think management have to help workers manage and cope with stress caused by performing emotional labour?

Running case: backstage

Jane Grimes is in tears in the staff room, with a small group of staff gathered around to comfort her.

'Poor you', said one of the bar staff, 'you're new aren't you—not had anything like that before. Don't worry, you'll get used to it, you'll be able to keep that smile fixed pretty soon'.

'But why should I have to put up with that?', blubs Grimes. 'They were just horrible to me.'

'We shouldn't have to put up with it, but unfortunately we have to, otherwise we'd be out of a job', is the reply. 'Look, we get no help on this from the management, so we have to help each other and help ourselves—don't let the punters get the better of us. When we are back here we can help each other and be ourselves—remember out there it's all an act.'

'Look over there', says one of the bar staff, pointing at the now highly-inebriated man who had been making suggestive comments to Grimes earlier on, 'I mean, as if someone as gorgeous as you would go near him. He's in here a lot—we've all had those approaches from him. We're convinced that's a wig he wears.' Grimes peers through a gap in the staff room door to see another member of staff clearing glasses next to the supporter. She smiles at him as she takes the glass, then turns to the staff room, touches the top of her head as if to indicate a wig, and winks towards the others in the staff room.

Grimes starts to laugh and the women in the staff room join in, pulling apart the character of the football fan and imagining the inadequacies that lead him to behave in such a way. Feeling better, she thanks the other staff for helping her to cope.

'Don't worry', replies one, 'we all have our ways of dealing with it.' 'Just remember', adds another waitress, 'they have no idea who you are so don't take it personally. In fact, most of us put on an act, almost taking on a different personality in front of the punters. As long as you don't lose sight of who you are when you get back here then you'll be OK. Just think of yourself as an actor, and out there is your stage, and you can even begin to enjoy it, let alone cope with it.'

Rather than management helping workers to cope with the stress of emotional labour, a number of studies have shown how workers help each other on a more informal basis. Such emotional support among colleagues that takes place is often focused around camaraderie and the use of humour as a means of coping with the stress of such work (Bolton, 2005; Bolton and Boyd, 2003).

- Hochschild (1983) noted the use of 'upbeat banter' among cabin crew when in 'backstage' areas, out of sight of passengers. This may be to offer support to each other or may be to make jokes at the expense of passengers to help 'laugh off' the stresses of abusive or rude behaviour.

- Korcynski (2003: 58) studied emotional labour in call centres and used the term **communities of coping** to describe informal, backstage groupings that provide mutual emotional support and which become a '. . . crucial part of the social relations of the service workplace'.

Communities of coping Mutual support among co-workers to cope with stress and other negative factors of emotional labour.

- Livesy (2000) notes similar forms of 'reciprocal emotion management'—colleagues listening and offering emotional support—among paralegals in private law firms.

There would seem again to be a distinction between 'frontstage', where workers are in front of customers and required to perform emotional labour, and 'backstage', where workers are not on show and are thus more at liberty to 'be themselves'. However, as we will see, this distinction between front and backstage is not always so clear cut.

> ### Employability skills: service sector experience
>
> In Chapter 11 we examined transferable skills and how identifying such skills from your experience of work can enhance your employability. For many students, the service sector will be the main experience of work undertaken, with part-time and vacation jobs in bars, shops, and the like. Think about the extent to which skills of emotional and aesthetic labour can be shown as transferable skills on your CV—dealing with people, for example. Furthermore, in interviews you may be asked to give examples of where you have solved a problem or worked under pressure—aspects of emotional labour that you have encountered in your own work may provide you with examples that you can present as evidence for these.

Emotional labour and emotion management

The management of our emotions is not confined to what happens in the workplace when serving customers. When a casual acquaintance passes in the street and enquires how we are, we may smile and say 'very well, thank you', rather than reveal all of our tales of woe.

Hochschild (1983) made a distinction between emotional labour and other, wider forms of emotion work or **emotion management**. When saying 'very well' to an aquaintance, we are engaging in the management of our emotions, but we are not performing emotional labour—the reason being that we are not receiving a wage for that particular performance.

Earlier in the chapter we saw performative labour, of which emotional labour is an example, located within the capitalist wage–labour relationship. Hochschild, too, located emotional labour within this relationship—it is work performed *specifically and explicitly for a wage*.

Emotion management is thus a general term for the control of emotions, of which emotional labour is one specific type that has an exchange value—it attracts a wage (Callahan and McCollum, 2002). The backstage banter and mutual coping strategies seen previously are a form of emotion management, but they are not emotional labour as they are not done for a wage. However, it is not a clear-cut distinction to say that emotional labour is that which takes place frontstage and emotion management is a coping strategy which takes place backstage.

Bolton and Boyd (2003), drawing from Goffman's earlier terminology, use the term 'presentational self' to describe the sort of emotion management that takes place not only backstage, but occasionally front of stage too—the nudges and winks that workers use to help each other cope with stresses of emotional labour: 'A put down comment, a secret smile—these are small, but important moments . . . offering important intervals in organizational control for the maintenance of organizational identities' (Bolton and Boyd, 2003: 102).

While such emotion management does not attract a wage, it does, nevertheless, play a part in the wage–labour relationship in the sense that it affects the balance of control in

Emotion management Any management of personal emotional displays inside or outside of a working relationship.

that relationship. The organization 'no longer controls the emotional agenda' (Bolton and Boyd, 2003: 291).

While management may wish to control workers into particular emotional performances in exchange for a wage, the emotion management of the workers can be seen as a form of coping with stress and, furthermore, as a form of collective resistance aganst these organizationally prescribed 'feeling rules' (Bolton and Boyd, 2003).

Taylor and Tyler (2000), like Hochschild, studied air cabin crew and noted a number of individualized acts of coping and resistance. Some attendants spoke of faking smiles, deliberately maintaining a personal level of distance behind the look that the organization required of them—a psychological act of distancing in order to maintain their own identities. The suggestion is that workers maintain a degree of control, even when frontstage, such that control of emotions by management is not total.

By bringing in the role of emotion work in backstage areas, and its slippage into the behaviour and gestures of the team while in frontstage areas, the boundaries between frontstage and backstage are not necessarily permanent. As Goffman (1959: 78) states:

All the world is not, of course, a stage, but the crucial ways in which it is are not easy to specify.

Review questions

1. Describe what is meant by emotional labour.

2. Explain the difference between deep and surface acting.

Apply:

3. How does backstage emotion management help workers in the bar at Junction Hotel cope with the stress of their work?

4. Analyse how emotional labour can be used as form of resistance by workers.

Aesthetic labour

Running case: dress code

From: simon_chance@junctionhotel.co.uk

To: bar_staff@junctionhotel.co.uk; restaurant_staff@junctionhotel.co.uk; reception_staff@junctionhotel.co.uk; porters@junctionhotel.co.uk

Subject: New uniforms

Dear colleagues

I am writing to you all as valued members of hotel staff, particularly as you are our front-line stars, the people that are on show to our customers. I know that your standards of service are great, but now we really want you to look the part, too.

Tomorrow, new uniforms will arrive for all customer-facing staff. I hope that you will like them and, when wearing the Junction Hotel uniform, feel that you are a living, breathing part of the brand itself.

It's not just the uniform which is important here—it's the way you are the look of the hotel. Service is sleek and professional, polite and unhurried, yet efficient.

May I here remind you of other aspects of our dress code which have been slipping recently, but which are important in presenting the look of Junction Hotel that you are here to perform.

- Women: wear make-up to be elegant—it is there to enhance your professional image. Too little and you look unkempt, but, at the same time, don't lay it on with a trowel. Hair is to be in a neat, professional style—nothing too extreme in colour or styling. Some jewellery looks good, but, as with the make-up, not too much.

- Men: hair should be neatly styled and short—full stop. Facial hair is absolutely discouraged. This is a slick, luxurious hotel, not a gathering of geography teachers. No jewellery is the preferred option—it is a distraction.

- For both men and women it goes without saying that basic levels of hygiene are required—nails and the like are to be clipped to appropriately professional lengths. And remember—absolutely no tattoos to be on show at all.

You will be called out from shifts tomorrow to collect your new uniforms—wear them proudly and exude the Junction Hotel image throughout your working day!

Best wishes,

Simon

Performance aspects of service work involve not just the management of emotions, but of appearance too—if work is like a stage, then costume is a part of the performance. An example might be dress codes, which specify what workers should wear, and other aspects of appearance, such as hair or fingernail length.

Witz et al., (2003) coined the phrase aesthetic labour to describe those demands upon a worker's appearance, which form part of the wage–labour relationship—just as there are demands on emotional performances front of stage in service industries, so it is that workers are also expected to dress and look the part. However, they go beyond surface appearance—clothes and grooming—to bodily movements and comportment, almost the way that the look and image of an organization is performed.

Workplace dress codes

Uniforms are common in many workplace environments. We might not think of a police officer, a professional footballer, or a nurse as adhering to a dress code, but they are being instructed what to wear while undertaking paid employment. At the most basic level, uniforms are thus an aspect of aesthetic labour.

However, **dress codes** often go further than just providing a particular set of clothes to wear. They provide guidance as to how a uniform should be supplemented with particular aspects of grooming. Thus, Lainsbury (2000), quoted in Bryman (2004: 124) notes appearance standards that might supplement uniforms at Disneyland Paris:

Dress code Standards of dress and appearance prescribed by an organization to its workers.

We have appearance standards that are a condition of being hired. For men it means no facial hair, a conservative haircut with no hair over the ears or the collar, no earrings, no exposed tattoos, and no jeans. For women, no extremes in dying hair or in makeup, and no long fingernails. We want a conservative, professional look; we want our employees to be warm, outgoing and sincere. We don't want guests to be distracted by oddities or mannerisms of the cast members.

With these conditions, would you be eligible to be employed at Disneyland Paris?

Even without there being a specified uniform, guidance on the type of clothing to wear, as well as grooming standards might be given. This might be in routine service work or in professional jobs where workers deal with clients.

Real life case: UBS dress code

Swiss Bank UBS hit the news after publishing a 44-page dress code (BBC News, 2010), giving advice on appearance to its client-facing staff, both male and female. The guide was notable for its precise attention to detail (Bolshaw, 2010; *The Guardian*, 2010a). It also outlines reasons for a dress code, suggesting that the UBS dress code is there to communicate their professional values and culture (*The Guardian*, 2010a).

Such a professional image would be conveyed by women wearing a plain tailored suit in dark charcoal, black, or dark blue, with a white blouse or shirt (*The Guardian*, 2010a). The code then goes into detail on the length of skirt (it should be mid-knee length) and how the jacket should remain smooth when seated. It should not rise up when walking (*The Guardian*, 2010a).

Further advice within the code, among many other points, suggests:

- shoes should fit properly as tight shoes create a 'twisted smile' (BBC News, 2010)
- wristwatches should be worn to signal trustworthiness and punctuality (*The Daily Telegraph*, 2011)
- glasses should be kept clean for the sake of optimal vision (*The Daily Telegraph*, 2010)
- detailed advice on how to apply make-up and the type of perfume to wear (*The Daily Telegraph*, 2011).

After giving advice on other pertinent topics, such as maintaining fresh breath, the code turns its attention to men. A similar professional style of dress is encouraged, with daily shaving recommended, and certainly no stubble over three days old (Bolshaw, 2010). Detailed instructions, including a diagram, on how to put on a tie were also included, with advice that a tie should complement the bone structure of the face (Kellaway, 2010).

The extent of detail in the dress code led to negative press coverage. UBS stated that it would review the code and, while a dress code for men, for example, of dark suit, white shirt, and red tie would remain, the extent of detail of other recommendations would be reviewed (BBC News, 2011; *The Daily Telegraph*, 2011).

Why do you think this dress code attracted so much negative publicity? Do you think this was deserved or do you think the dress code is useful?

While dress codes can set standards and advice for workplace appearance, they may also be used both to *preclude* people from gaining employment and *exclude* people from current employment. Nickson et al., (2003: 193) give a list of reasons for dismissal from work or the refusal of employment in the first place. They included a man refused bar employment for having a pony tail, people being dismissed for appearing too old, and a designer boutique manager not employing women who wore larger than a dress size 16. Such stories often form the basis of legal action.

- In the USA a woman employed in a property firm took action after claiming to have been sacked for refusing to dye her grey hair and wear 'younger, trendy suits' (Pilkington, 2011).

- In the upmarket Harrods store in London, a female member of staff took legal action after being sacked for refusing to wear make-up in line with the store dress code (Davies, 2011).

Dress codes, thus, make up an initial aspect of aesthetic labour and, as we will see later in the chapter, often these impinge unequally on women and the standards of appearance by which they are judged compared with men.

Aesthetic skills and embodiment

While dress and appearance form a part of aesthetic labour, Witz et al., (2003), who originally coined the term, suggested that it is about more than just surface 'costume'. Rather, aesthetic labour is about how we 'embody' deep down a particular 'look' or aesthetic.

The suggestion is that service work requires more than the robotic fast-food worker repeating phrases at the till. Service work involves a lot of feeling in the interaction, for example in a hotel or restaurant the interaction is judged a lot more and it is in movements and looks, as well as costumes, that this is demonstrated—it comes from much deeper within the body.

Theory in context: Pierre Bourdieu and habitus

The idea of embodiment, or **embodied dispositions**, derives from Pierre Bourdieu (1984), whose concept of **habitus** described how aspects of our social being are deeply ingrained and are manifested in such things as our dispositions—the way we instinctively act and react in social situations. This is not just a product of the feeling and emotional mind, nor reducible to a product of learning—it is a product of much deeper levels of socialization.

Bourdieu's work is most strongly associated with social class. He suggests that our upbringing creates deeply embodied markers of class that are shown in our mannerisms and dispositions. It is when we try to adopt the mannerisms of a different class group that we betray our background.

You may hear people pour scorn on people for being 'new money'—lottery winners or self-made business people, for example. The implication is while they have the money, they do not have the 'breeding'—the tastes and mannerisms associated with the upper class. Despite having the money being associated with the upper class they give away their working class origins in their tastes and behaviours.

Such examples illustrate the idea of habitus—the social signs of class are so ingrained that it is difficult to achieve mobility between the classes while not betraying class origins in mannerisms and behaviour in our embodied dispositions.

Embodied dispositions/habitus Our natural way of acting and reacting—a deeply held repertoire of instinctive behaviours.

The concept of aesthetic labour, as outlined by Witz et al., (2003), suggests that aesthetic labourers do more than put on an act, but begin to embody the dispositions as demanded of them by their workplace.

Real life case: *Ladette to Lady*

The idea of whether or not people can adopt and embody the appearance, behaviour, and mannerisms of a different class is tested in television 'reality' programmes, such as *Ladette to Lady* (ITV/RTF Media) or *Australian Princess* (Network 10/Granada Productions).

The concept of such programmes is that a group of women, whose behaviour is deemed to be loud, raucous, uncouth, and of a lower class, is taken through a set of tasks which train them to adopt the mannerisms of the upper class. The competition is to see which of the contestants does this the most convincingly.

The degree of embodiment of class-related habitus is shown in the range of tasks and instruction that the contestants receive—dress, speech, and deportment (posture, walking, getting in and out of cars, etc.), for example. Using habitus we could debate what is achieved at the end of such a series. Has the winning contestant fully embodied the behaviours of a different class, or are they simply putting on the best act—a form of class transvestitism where the surface apperarance is adopted, but the mannerisms do not really reach deep down?

Think of nightclub bouncers. They don't just have to dress the part—wearing a dark suit and tie maybe—a key skill of their job is that they also have to *embody* the part. Thus, we would not only expect a bouncer to have certain physical characteristics—emphasizing size and strength—we would also expect them to 'carry' that body in a certain way, with an authoritative demeanour. Such a demeanour would also be carried through in interactions—the way in which a situation is responded to, for example—in the face of a fight a calm authority can be displayed through bodily movements and mannerisms as much as words. Of course, such a performance also links with emotional labour, as described earlier. The bouncer would be expected to remain calm, even if others were in a heightened emotional state and, perhaps, being abusive.

 Can you think of any other jobs where you would have expectations of the appropriate demeanour that a worker would display?

The suggestion of Witz et al., is that a similar set of embodied dispositions are expected more and more in service work—workers are expected to embody the image or 'look' of the company in their actions and movements. Workers arrive with a set of 'embodied dispositions'—those which are desirable will have been encouraged, for instance, through imagery in recruitment advertising. Such dispositions are never a completed project and so, through training, workers are 'corporately made up' (Witz et al., 2003: 37)—trained not just in appearance and social/emotional interaction, but also in the style of the service encounter or 'specific modes of embodiment' (ibid: 44). Thus, the workers themselves become part of the organizational aesthetic that is presented to customers, part of the 'experience' created by service and leisure sector organizations examined earlier in the chapter.

Thus, this embodied notion of aesthetic labour draws both on Bourdieu, to show the deep nature of embodied dispositions, and Goffman, to demonstrate how these are presented in 'action' when front of stage.

Nickson et al., (2003) note specific class issues in this type of aesthetic labour in service encounters, namely that the types of dispositions sought are increasingly those typical of the middle class. In areas where manufacturing industry has declined, those made unemployed, generally from a working-class background, have found themselves at a disadvantage in gaining employment in service work, where it is the characteristics of students from middle-class backgrounds performing part-time service work which are valued more by employers.

Class is not the only area where aesthetic labour has a disproportionate impact. In the following section we see how both emotional and aesthetic labour have a different impact when gender is considered.

Review questions

1. Explain how aesthetic labour is about more than surface-level appearance.
2. Analyse how embodied dispositions might be part of creating the experience or image of an organization in the sevice industry that guests consume.
3. Explain how aesthetic labour might exclude people from certain jobs.

Performative labour and gender

Running case: sexing up

Staff reactions to the new uniforms are mixed. The receptionists have business suit outfits, whereas in the bar and restaurant women are expected to wear outfits described by one waitress as 'a bit revealing'.

'Lucky you', replies a receptionist, 'you get to be feminine, do yourself up a bit. We have to stand behind reception looking like we're working in a bank.' 'No, lucky you', replies the waitress, 'those customers are like rampant tom-cats at the best of times—we're just going to be objects for their desires in these outfits.'

In contrast, the male staff in all areas have the same outfit: a regular fitting shirt, trousers and tie, with a jacket for any staff on duty in the reception area—certainly not an outfit that could also be described as 'revealing'.

In the bar, the first shift wearing the new uniform starts. While the male bar staff are allowed to get on with their work, Simon Chance calls Jane Grimes over. 'Come on love, do the outfit some justice', he says in an encouraging tone. 'Go and have a bit of banter with them—it will make their night. You've got the outfit—go and sex it up a bit with them.'

Grimes has had enough—she already has to deal with the unpleasant behaviour of customers that often borders on harassment, now she is expected to positively encourage it. She removes her name badge and throws it on to the floor in front of Simon Chance. 'I quit', she shouts. 'I thought I had come to work in a hotel, but it seems like I'm working in a brothel!'

Statistically, service work is gendered (Kerfoot and Korczynski, 2005: 389) and the types of performative labour demanded in service work suggest that the burden of emotional and aesthetic labour impinges unequally on women rather than men.

Are there any jobs where you would more than likely expect the person doing that job to be one gender rather than another?

For Steve Taylor (1998) the increase of women in the service workforce has been paralleled by an increase in emotional labour. As Hochschild suggests:

> Schooled in emotion management at home, women have entered in disproportionate numbers those jobs that call for emotional labour outside the home.   (1983: 181)

Within the wage–labour relationship, emotional labour is not rewarded financially to the same extent as other workplace competencies. A worker might expect a qualification, such as a degree, to be rewarded financially as part of the wage–labour exchange, but emotional skills seem to be considered merely a natural part of being female, learned as a part of growing up. Women are employed as 'women' with various assumed natural resources (Adkins and Lury, 1999), but these resources are not rewarded in the market place.

As with emotional labour, many of the requirements of aesthetic labour seem to impinge more on women. Studies on appearance at work have focused on how it is often an unrewarded burden that falls upon women as part of a perceived 'natural femininity', an embodied knowledge, or habitus, about what 'feminine' behaviour and aesthetics entails. Taylor and Tyler (2000: 86) note how, in addition to norms of feminine 'aesthetically pleasing' appearance, flight attendants' emotional work in caring for and interacting with people were seen as 'natural' feminine abilities or as 'women's work'.

Gender and sexual commodification

Furthermore, aesthetic labour, with its concerns with appearance, can lead to demands which lead to the sexualization and objectification of women in service work. Sexual attractiveness becomes a part of what is expected in return for a wage; in other words, sex sells. Examples of such uneven demands between the genders in different jobs include:

- emphasis on the physical attractiveness of (female) betting shop cashiers, enhanced by the uniform, in the face of (mainly male) clients (Filby, 1992)
- in tourist and hotel industries standards of attractiveness may even be stipulated in person specifications in job advertisements, but tend to apply only to female employees (Adkins, 1995)
- grooming and weight checks being performed regularly on air cabin crew, but only on female staff (Tyler and Abbott, 1998).

In her original work, Hochschild (1983: 181) noted how female flight attendants were expected to embody both 'motherly' emotional qualities and more appearance-bound 'sexual' qualities. Or, as Tyler and Abbott (1998: 440) state more bluntly, the air stewardess combines three emotional, aesthetic, and sexually-commodified roles—'part mother, part servant, part tart.' Hochschild repeats a quote from one air hostess in her original study:

You have a married man with three kids getting on a place and suddenly they feel anything goes. It's like they leave that reality on the ground, and you fit into their fantasy as some geisha girl.

(Hochschild, 1983: 93)

In such professions where smiles, ego massaging, and 'entering into the spirit' take place, Adkins suggest that women are being expected, as part of their paid work, to enter into a form of 'sexual servicing' of men. This involves not only maintaining an attractive appearance and complying with a dress code, but also engaging in sexualized jokes and banter, or 'giving men what they want' (1985: 133). In this respect, Adkins states that women become **sexually commodified**—it is part of the 'arrangement of service labour' (Adkins, 2000: 207). Brewis and Linstead (2000: 172) suggest that in some areas of service work, women may 'genuinely prostitute' themselves.

> **Sexually commodified**
> The sexual attractiveness or desirability of a worker is used as part of the work they perform for customers or clients.

Real life case: Hooters

The marketing of theme restaurant Hooters is based around the attractiveness and sex appeal of the Hooters girls. This is stated on their own website, where they suggest that 'The element of female sex appeal is prevalent in the restaurants, and the company believes the Hooters Girl is as socially acceptable as a Dallas Cowboy cheerleader, Sports Illustrated swimsuit model, or a Radio City Rockette.' (Quoted in Ferrell and Hartline, 2011: 520). However, this aspect of marketing female sex appeal has lead to protests when new Hooters restaurants have been proposed in both the UK and the USA (*The Guardian*, 2010b; Brown, 2008; Bindel, 2008; MSNBC, 2006).

The issue revolves around the role of the 'Hooters girls', waitresses who are expected to wear a revealing outfit (MSNBC, 2006) based on the image of an American cheerleader. A contract from Hooters in the USA was leaked on to the Internet, which emphasized just how much such Hooters girls were expected to see their 'sex appeal' as a part and parcel of their everyday job for which they are paid, including signing an acknowledgement that they accept an amount of joking, banter, and sexual innuendo based upon this (Hyde, 2008; Bindel, 2008).

It is this explicit drafting of sexualized appearance and sex appeal into the labour process that angers protestors, with one commentator (Bindel, 2008) suggesting that the sexualized atmosphere is more akin to a 'strip club' than a restaurant.

Hooters, on their website, disagree with this, noting a vigorous anti-harassment policy. Furthermore, they suggest that the marketing or use of sex appeal in work is justified and not limited to Hooters: 'Claims that Hooters exploits attractive women are as ridiculous as saying the NFL exploits men who are big and fast. Hooters Girls have the same right to use their natural female sex appeal to earn a living as do super models Cindy Crawford and Naomi Campbell. To Hooters, the women's rights movement is important because it guarantees women have the right to choose their own careers, be it a Supreme Court Justice or Hooters Girl' (quoted in Ferrell and Hartline, 2011: 520–510; and *The Guardian*, 2010b).

Do you think that it is legitimate for a company to expect people to perform the type of work described at Hooters for a wage?

While Hooters might be a one-off case, women's aesthetic and emotional performances are commodified in frontstage service work, with differing degrees of sexualization required as part of the wage–labour relationship, in a way that is not expected of men.

Review questions

1. Explain how both emotional and aesthetic labour are expected more from women than they are from men.

Apply

2. Are there jobs where emotional and aesthetic labour are expected mainly of men?

3. Explain what is mean by sexual commodification.

Analyse

4. What do you understand by Brewis and Linstead's (2000) statement that some women 'genuinely prostitute' themselves in service work?

Chapter summary

This chapter has examined emotional and aesthetic 'performances' that take place in customer-facing service work in order to contribute to the 'experience' that is consumed in many service sector organizations. Such work sits alongside rational management techniques as part of the service sector labour process. Both rationalized working techniques and performances where the worker is 'on show' are aspects of the service sector working relationship for which a wage is paid. Such performative labour creates inequalities in terms of class and gender, for example, and can be seen as an extra element of control over workers by management. At the same time, it is also an area where worker resistance, which starts with strategies of coping in backstage areas of the organization, can find its way into frontstage workplace performances.

Further reading

Bryman, A. 2004. *The Disneyization of society*. Sage, London.
Covers all aspects of Disneyization; the chapter on performative labour looks at both emotional and aesthetic labour.

Grugulis, I. 2007. *Skills, training and human resource development: a critical text*. Palgrave Macmillan, Basingstoke.
Chapter 6 covers emotional and aesthetic labour from a workplace and worker perspective.

Nickson, D., Warhurst, C., and Cullen, A. M. 2003. Bringing in the excluded? Aesthetic labour, skills and training in the 'new' economy. *Journal of Education and Work* 16(2): 185–203.
A case study of how aesthetic labour excludes certain sections of the workforce from service sector work.

Adkins, L. 1995. *Gendered work: sexuality, family and the labour market*. Open University Press, Buckingham.
Two service sector case studies, from a hotel and a theme park, which show the uneven impact of service work on women.

Bibliography

Adkins, L. 1995. *Gendered work: sexuality, family and the labour market*. Open University Press: Buckingham.

Adkins, L. 2000. Mobile desire: aesthetics, sexuality and the 'lesbian' at work. *Sexualities* 3(2): 201–218.

Adkins, L., and Lury, C. 1999. The labour of identity: performing identities, performing economies. *Economy and Society* 28(4): 598–614.

Baudrillard, J. 1970. *La société de consommation: ses mythes, ses structures*. Denoël: Paris.

Baudrillard, J. 1983. *Simulations*. Semiotext(e) Inc.: New York.

BBC News. 2010. UBS dress code scrutinizes staff underwear. 17 December 2010. Available at: http://www.bbc.co.uk/news/business-12023033.

BBC News. 2011. UBS to revise 44-page dress code. 17 January 2011. Available at: http://www.bbc.co.uk/news/business-12207296.

Beardsworth, A., and Bryman, A. 1999. Late modernity and the dynamics of quasification: the case of the themed restaurant. *The Sociological Review* 47(2): 228–257.

Bindel, J. 2008. It's more like a strip club than a restaurant. *The Guardian*. 11 April 2008. Available at: http://www.guardian.co.uk/lifeandstyle/2008/apr/11/women.business.

Black County Living Museum. 2012. Available at: http://www.bclm.co.uk. (last accessed 29 November 2012).

Bolshaw, L. 2010. La DressCode revisited. *Financial Times*. 23 December 2010. Available at: http://blogs.ft.com/women-at-the-top/2010/12/20/la-dresscode-revisited/#axzz2DLktqGZ6.

Bolton, S. 2005. *Emotion management in the workplace*. Palgrave Macmillan: Basingstoke.

Bolton, S. C., and Boyd, C. 2003. Trolley dolly or skilled emotion manager? Moving on from Hochschild's Managed Heart. *Work, Employment & Society* 17(2): 289–308.

Bourdieu, P. 1984. *Distinction: a social critique of the judgement of taste*. Harvard University Press: Cambridge, MA.

Brewis, J., and Linstead, S. 2000. The worst thing is the screwing (2): context and career in sex work. *Gender, Work and Organization* 7(3): 168–180.

Brown, J. 2008. Hooters: over the top, underdressed and over here. *The Independent*. 12 April 2008. Available at: http://www.independent.co.uk/life-style/food-and-drink/features/hooters-over-the-top-underdressed-and-over-here-808160.html.

Bryman, A. 1995. *Disney and his worlds*. Routledge: London, New York.

Bryman, A. 2004. *The Disneyization of society*. Sage: London.

Callahan, J. L., and McCollum, E. E. 2002. Obscured variability: The distinction between emotion work and emotional labor. In: Rafaeli, A., Ashkanasy, N. M., Zerbe, W. J., and Hartel, C. E. J. (eds) *Managing emotions in the workplace*. Sharpe: Armonk, NY, pp. 219–231.

The Daily Telegraph. 2011. Swiss bank UBS changes much-mocked dress-code. 17 January 2011. Available at: http://www.telegraph.co.uk/finance/newsbysector/banksandfinance/8265124/Swiss-bank-UBS-changes-much-mocked-dress-code.html.

Davies, C. 2011. Harrods 'ladies' code' drives out sales assistant. *The Guardian* (1 July, 2011).

Eco, U. 1986. *Travels in hyper reality: essays*. Harcourt Brace Jovanovich: San Diego.

Featherstone, M. 1991. *Consumer culture and postmodernism*. Sage: London.

Ferrell, O. C., and Hartline, M. D. 2011. *Marketing Strategy*, 5th edn. South-Western Cengage Learning: Mason, OH.

Filby, M. P. 1992. The figures, the personality and the bums: service work and sexuality. *Work, Employment & Society* 6(1): 23–42.

Gabriel, Y. 2005. Glass cages and glass palaces: images of organization in image-conscious times. *Organization* 12(1): 9–27.

Goffman, E. 1959. *The presentation of self in everyday life*. Doubleday: Garden City, NY.

Gottdiener, M. 1998. Themed environments of everyday life: restaurants and malls. In: Berger, A. A. (ed.) *The Postmodern Presence: Readings on Postmodernism in American Culture and Society*. Alta Mira: Walnut Creek, pp. 74–87.

The Guardian. 2010a. UBS demands 'well groomed' employees, right down to their pants. 17 December 2010. Available at: http://www.guardian.co.uk/money/blog/2010/dec/17/ubs-well-groomed-employees.

The Guardian. 2010b. Feminist activists protest against Hooters in Cardiff. 11 August 2010. Available at: http://www.guardian.co.uk/cardiff/2010/aug/11/cardiff-feminist-network-say-no-to-hooters-campaign-city-centre-protest.

Guerrier, Y., and Adib, A. 2003. Work at leisure and leisure at work: a study of the emotional labour of tour reps. *Human Relations* 56(11): 1399–1417.

Hochschild, A. R. 1983. *The managed heart: commercialization of human feeling*, University of California Press: Berkeley, CA.

Hyde, M. 2008. Buffalo duck wings and a dash of orange tempt Beijing palates. *The Guardian*. 12 August 2008. Available at: http://www.guardian.co.uk/sport/2008/aug/12/olympics20081.

Karabanow, J. 1999. When caring is not enough: Emotional labor and youth shelter workers. *Social Service Review* 73(3): 340–357.

Kellaway, L. 2010. Better to waste time at the office. *Financial Times*. 19 December 2010. Available at: http://www.ft.com/cms/s/0/6240fe56-0a30-11e0-84bc-00144feabdc0.html#axzz2DLkxbaax.

Kerfoot, D., and Korczynski, M. 2005. Gender and service: new directions for the study of 'front-line' service work. *Gender, Work & Organization* 12(5): 387–399.

Kirstenblatt-Gimlett, B. 1998. *Destination culture: tourism, museums and heritage*. University of California Press: Berkeley, Los Angeles.

Korczynski, M. 2003. Communities of coping: collective emotional labour in service work. *Organization* 10(1): 55–79.

Korczynski, M., and Bishop, V. 2009. Abuse, violence and fear on the front line: implications of the rise of the enchanting myth of consumer sovreignty. In: Fineman, S. (ed.) *The emotional organization: passions and power*. Blackwell Publishing, Oxford, pp. 74–87.

Korczynski, M., and Ott, U. 2004. When production and consumption meet: cultural contradictions and the enchanting myth of customer sovereignty. *Journal of Management Studies* 41(4): 575–599.

MSNBC. 2006. Hooters to change – but not what works. 14 December 2006. Available at: http://www.msnbc.msn.com/id/16209446/ns/business-us_business/t/hooters-change-not-what-works/#.ULOvZ2f_1M4.

Nickson, D., Warhurst, C., and Cullen, A.M. 2003. Bringing in the excluded? Aesthetic labour, skills and training in the 'new' economy. *Journal of Education and Work* 16(2): 185–203.

Office for National Statistics (ONS). 2012. *Index of Services: December 2011*. ONS: Newport.

Pilkington, E. 2011. Woman 'sacked for having grey hair'. *The Observer* (10 July 2011).

Pretes, M. 1995. Postmodern tourism: The Santa Claus Industry. *Annals of Tourism Research* 22(1): 1–15.

Pugliesi, K. 1999. The consequences of emotional labor: Effects on work stress, job satisfaction, and well-being. *Motivation and Emotion* 23(2): 125–154.

Ritzer, G. 1996. *The McDonaldization of society: an investigation into the changing character of contemporary social life*. Pine Forge Press: Thousand Oaks, CA.

Ritzer, G. 2011. *The McDonaldization of society 6*. Pine Forge Press: Thousand Oaks, CA.

Taylor, S. 1998. Emotional labour and the new workplace. In: Thompson, P., and Warhurst, C. (eds) *Workplaces of the Future*. Palgrave Macmillan: Basingstoke, pp. 84–103.

Taylor, S., and Tyler, M. 2000. Emotional labour and sexual difference in the airline industry. *Work, Employment & Society* 14(1): 77–95.

Tyler, M., and Abbott, P. 1998. Chocs away: weight watching in the contemporary airline industry. *Sociology* 32(3): 433–450.

West Edmonton mall. 2012. Available at: http://www.wem.ca (last accessed 29 November 2012).

Witz, A., Warhurst, C., and Nickson, D. 2003. The labour of aesthetics and the aesthetics of organization. *Organization* 10(1): 33–54.

17
Corporate social responsibility, sustainability, and business ethics
Can businesses act sustainably, ethically, and responsibly?

Chapter overview and learning outcomes

By the end of this chapter you should be able to:

- describe some of the key principles of corporate social responsibility, business ethics, and sustainability

- explain why Milton Friedman considers firms should have no corporate social responsibility
- explain the principles behind shareholder capitalism
- analyse what the key critiques of capitalism are.

Key theorists

R. Edward Freeman	Freeman is one of the leading proponents of stakeholder theory. His theory argues successful businesses build their strategy around their relationships with key stakeholders
Karl Marx	Philosopher, economist, activist, and revolutionary, Karl Marx is famous for his hard-hitting critiques of capitalism and support for communism. His works continue to be widely read and debated today
Milton Friedman	The Nobel prize-winning economist who famously argued corporate social responsibility as 'unethical'

Key terms

Free market	A philosophy and economic system which argues that business works at its most efficient when open exchange can happen between businesses with minimal government interference
Business ethics	The application of ethical principles to organizations to either understand, judge, or direct individual and organizational ethical decision making
Corporate social responsibility	A perspective which stresses the responsibilities that corporations have towards society and other stakeholders
Sustainability	A complex term, but often stresses the long-term viability of both the environment and the corporation
Capitalism	The dominant economic system which is based on private ownership of the means of production of goods and services for the purposes of making profit
Philanthropy	Originally meaning 'for the love of humanity' it is now taken as meaning the giving of time or more commonly money for good causes

Introduction: corporations in the news

Running case: expansion plans

With Junction Hotel now finally doing well Simon Chance begins to think about expansion. Booking rates are near capacity, the hotel now regularly holds five weddings a weekend with, on average, 150 people for a full sit down meal, and the bar takings have doubled. Profits are increasing and, for the first time, he is looking forward to writing the yearly report.

With this success Chance has started to consider building an extension at the front of the hotel. A new conservatory would add much needed space and allow them to host 250 people per wedding and for the big Christmas parties—boosting potential profit. An architect has said it should be feasible, as long as they can get planning consent.

Flicking through his emails he notices a couple from Linda Wilkinson entitled 'Complaints from local residents'. In the email she explains how two of the local residents came in over the weekend, while the wedding was in full swing, complaining about the noise. Another email—'More complaints'—was, this time, about the aggressive behaviour of the guests as they left the wedding. While he wished things didn't happen, he thinks 'What can Junction Hotel do? People come to the hotel to have a good time and it is our job to give it to them.' With that, he went back to the architect's plans.

Bankers bonuses, Ponzi schemes, insurance mis-selling, sweatshop labour, bribery scandals, oil leaks, and suicidal workers are just some of the stories to have hit the headlines over the last few years. They have raised questions over the ethical status of businesses today. These stories have led many to argue they have damaged the image and trust in large corporations. As Andrew Witty, Chief Executive Officer (CEO) of the pharmaceuticals giant GlaxoSmithKline puts it, 'Trust in business has clearly eroded and needs to be reconstructed. It's very dangerous if a country doesn't trust the private sector' (cited in High Pay Commission, 2011). The financial crisis has now put the social responsibility of business firmly in the spotlight, and with climate change and human rights in developing countries, such concerns can be expected to exist for many years to come. Indeed, as we will contend in this chapter, corporate reputation is likely to form one of the biggest contemporary issues throughout your career.

Real life case: KitKat and palm oil

For many, having a KitKat represents little more than a harmless pleasure. Nestlé produce over a billion KitKats annually in the UK, representing 23% of confectionery sales. A KitKat is an item that many people buy without a second thought.

In March 2010, Greenpeace launched a campaign claiming a key ingredient, palm oil, was killing orang-utans. They stated it was sourced unsustainably from areas which cut down rainforests to produce the oil, destroying the orang-utans' natural habitat. Indeed, the oil was often from Indonesia which, over the last 60 years, has lost a portion of rainforest three times larger than the size of the UK and, according to the UN, was a significant reason why Indonesia is the third largest emitter of carbon in the world.

> To highlight the issue, Greenpeace produced a short advert of an office-worker biting into a KitKat finger in the shape of an orang-utan, which then dripped blood on to his computer keyboard. The advert went viral on Facebook and YouTube, with tens of thousands of hits. Greenpeace campaigners posted messages on Nestlé's Facebook page and dressed as orang-utans to meet shareholders at the Annual General Meeting (AGM).

At first Nestlé, Greenpeace claim, tried to censor the advert, but, within three months, and after substantial public pressure, they promised to change. Nestlé now state 'the destruction of tropical rainforests and peatlands in the production of ingredients such as palm oil, is one of the most serious environmental issues facing us today' (Nestle, 2012). From January 2012 all palm oil in KitKats will be from responsible sources and by 2015 or earlier they will only source from sustainable sources. KitKats are also Fairtrade—and so maybe it is now acceptable to eat them with a clear conscience.

Sources: Nestle (2012); Greenpeace (2012); Hickman (2009); Tabacek (2010).

Why do you think Nestlé felt the need to respond to this campaign? Look through other ingredients of your food, and even cleaning products. Do they include palm oil? How do you feel about this?

The humble KitKat, therefore, connects us to many of the key features that this chapter examines.

- Nestlé are not alone at being the subject of campaigns; indeed, recent years have seen numerous corporations under scrutiny about their practices. At stake is their corporate reputation and brand image, prevention of increased legislation, and maintenance ties with key stakeholders.

- Getting these features wrong, as we will see, can cost firms millions of pounds in fines and, more significantly, goodwill from customers, suppliers, and the government. Getting it right can open up new customers or give the firm a competitive advantage.

- For virtually all companies, charities, and public sector organizations their reputation and ethical standing is now a vital issue and one that is achieving increased attention throughout the organization.

- As we will see later in the chapter, corporate social responsibility (CSR) statements have become standard practice and many organizations are now also producing sustainability reports. Business ethics and sustainability have become core aspects on many business degrees and are increasingly seen as critical competences for business leaders.

A word on definitions and terms

Attentive readers will have noticed that so far we have used three key phrases: business ethics, sustainability, and CSR (Figure 17.1). We could also have used, among others, the phrases 'stakeholder theory', 'corporate governance', and 'global citizens'. Each phrase captures a particular aspect of business practice.

Business ethics deals primarily with the principles that should be used to govern business conduct, how people should act, and the underlying philosophies behind ethical actions.

Business ethics A form of ethics applied to business. It is the study and evaluation of decision making within businesses through various moral concepts and judgements.

Figure 17.1 The three overlapping theoretical frameworks. CSR, ethics and sustainability.

Corporate social responsibility A contested term with different interpretations but generally taken to be social and environmental responsibility corporations have towards their stakeholders.

Sustainability The long-term stewardship and maintenance of the environment and the prospects of the firm.

Often taught using case studies, one of its central aims is to sensitize students to the need for ethical awareness in business and (in some versions at least) is the attempt to lay out a moral code of conduct for business people.

CSR, also known as **corporate social responsibility** looks at the wider responsibilities that businesses have and how they should meet them. Based on stakeholder theory (see pp. 559–563), the CSR perspective argues that it is often in the firms interest to meet the needs of its stakeholders in order to achieve its long-term survival.

Sustainability has come into vogue recently, in part because of increasing concerns with the environment (particularly climate change), but it has the wider meaning of the long-term sustainability of the firm itself. This can lead to confusion, but does demonstrate the challenges of balancing environmental and profit concerns.

While each has their different meaning and focus, for the purposes of this chapter we will not spend too long distinguishing between them, rather drawing on the ideas from each area where appropriate.

Chapter outline

This chapter will begin by laying out why ethics matters before moving on to examine the four key ethical perspectives. This discussion will then lay the foundation for the central questions which preoccupy this chapter: Should privately-owned, profit-seeking companies be concerned with acting in a socially responsible, moral, and humane way?; Should they exist for their own purposes or for the good of society? The response one makes to this question is moral and depends, to a large degree, on one's beliefs as to the central purpose and responsibility of businesses, which we have summed up in the following five categories:

- shareholder capitalism
- stakeholder capitalism
- ethical capitalism
- ethical within capitalism
- against capitalism.

Heuristic device Used to help simplify a theory and make it more understandable.

While each category covers a particular perspective, they also overlap and do not, necessarily, capture all the views of each perspective. They, therefore, should be seen as **heuristic devices**, which broadly capture these positions rather than fixed categories.

The need for business ethics

Real life case: corporate scandals

The last few decades have seen a large number of corporate scandals, the most famous being Enron, which was made (in)famous in the film *Enron: The Smartest Guys in the Room* (Gibney, 2005). Enron were the largest seller of natural gas in North America and covered many other markets, too. To most outsiders Enron was considered a miracle, seemingly able to make money regardless of how the financial markets were doing; however, they achieved this growth through 'clever' accounting and finding loopholes in the system that meant they made a profit on paper, but, in reality, they were getting into debt. In the end they were declared bankrupt, causing substantial losses for their shareholders, many of whom were employees.

More recently, Bernie Madoff and Allen Stanford have both been found guilty of creating 'Ponzi schemes'; complicated, but fraudulent, investment schemes which report to make profits but really are simply bringing in new investors to pay existing shareholders dividends. Eventually, they cannot be sustained and collapse.

Both these sets of corporate scandals were caused, in part, by the investors not wanting to ask tough ethical questions about how the unrealistically large reported profits were made.

Sources: The Economist (2008), Teather (2009); Rushe (2012); BBC News (2012).

If you have a cynical attitude then you might expect this chapter to be a very short one—business ethics, there are none. Ethics and business could be seen as **oxymorons**. You might think that businesses are just worried about making a profit. Indeed, the phrase 'business is business' is often used to suggest that you have made a 'hardnosed', 'rational' decision where morals and feelings did not come into it.

But, on closer examination, all business, at its most basic level, requires some degree of ethical behaviour, otherwise it will quickly break down. What would happen, for instance, if you knew that your university canteen, to save costs, were using ingredients that might kill you? Similarly, how likely would a business be to sell to someone they believe has no intention of paying? Also, given the choice, would you want to work for a company that you knew treated it workers badly and even physically abused them? All business activity, to be able to survive, requires a level of trust and moral action, otherwise the entire system disintegrates quickly.

The question, therefore, does not become whether firms should act in an ethical way, rather what is the ethical basis for their actions and how do they balance wider social responsibilities with concerns for profit?

> Oxymorons
> Incompatible phrases that contradict each other.

An ethical framework

The following sections will introduce the main ethical theories. The business ethics literature is diverse, but is summarized neatly in Figure 17.2.

Figure 17.2
An ethical framework.

© *Business Ethics & Values:*
Individual, Corporate and
International Perspectives,
Fisher, C. & Lovell, A., Pearson
Education Limited, 2006

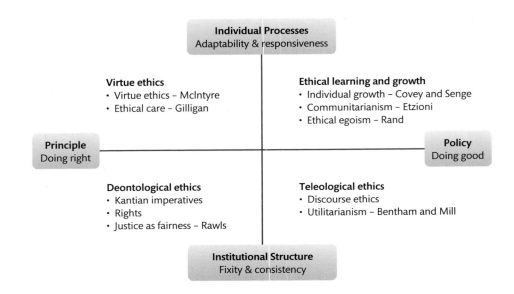

Principle ethics: beliefs not shaped by those involved

Teleological ethics

Taken from the Greek *telos* meaning ends, teleological ethics states an action can only be judged by its consequences. For our purposes the most important teleological perspective is utilitarianism, which was summed up by Jeremy Bentham (the inventor of the Panopticon (see Chapters 4 and 13)) as 'The greatest happiness of the greatest number is the foundation of morals and legislation' (cited in Fisher and Lovell, 2009: 129).

Within this view actions are not good or bad because of their character or intention, rather it is their effect on how much overall benefit they produce. For utilitarians something is good if it increases the overall well-being of people. A moral act is thus one that increases pleasure (good) more than it produces pain (bad). Utilitarians therefore argue you can calculate the cost–benefit of a particular action. Bentham assumed all humans are motivated by the desire to create pleasure and avoid pain, therefore they will do things that increase pleasure.

In a business sense, pleasure is often equated with profit maximization and is used to justify shareholder capitalism (see following sections); the belief being that if everyone follows their self-interest, overall it will benefit the whole of society. A fuller reading, however, might be used to justify stakeholder capitalism (see later in the chapter) as the impact on the whole of society needs to be calculated.

Consider an ethical dilemma you had recently. How easy would it be to do a cost–benefit analysis?

Deontological ethics

Taken from the Greek *deon*, meaning duty, deontological ethics asks whether the action is right, fair, and honest. It is not concerned with the consequences of an action, but the reasons behind it. Within this perspective, acts are only ethical if they are conducted based on duty and not if there is a reward.

The deontological perspective looks to create universal rules and sees ethics as an end in itself. Ethical principles, particularly for the philosopher Kant, exist *a priori*; in other words, they exist independently of the particular circumstance or the outcome and are worked out on the basis of pure reason, and there is one universal code, regardless of culture, and belief that everyone should follow. Kant, in what he called the 'categorical imperative', argued you should always act based on the assumption your action will become a universal law of human behaviour. (For a review, see Fisher et al., 2013.)

A priori Independent of experience.

Would you act any differently if all your actions became universal laws for human behaviour? Might you, for instance, recycle more or reduce your carbon emissions?

While this view might seem appealing, it is also seen as very rigid. For instance, while most of us would consider lying as wrong, what if you had to lie to save someone's life? For Kant this then raises the question over which duty should come first (such as lying or preserving someone's life). However, it becomes difficult to come up with universal laws that fit all circumstances.

Another deontological perspective is that of justice and rights. The **libertarian** view, particularly as developed by Robert Nozick, argues that the essential right people have is for freedom, particularly freedom from government interference and for property rights. People, he argued, have the right to free choice and to act how they want so long as they are not breaking the law. In business, this justifies shareholder capitalism as shareholders are seen as having the right to use their property in whatever way they like providing they act within the law (see pp. 551–560).

Libertarian A perspective that stresses individual freedom above all other concerns.

An alternative deontological perspective is social justice. This perspective is most strongly associated with John Rawls and linked to communitarianism (see p. 555). He asks us to imagine what a 'just' society would look like if we did not know our position in the world. In other words, you could be anyone, rich or poor, male or female, in the developed world or from a developing nation. From this position of 'total ignorance' we then need to imagine what we would like the world to be like. Believing that we are risk-averse individuals, Rawls thinks we would design a world of fairness based upon the same civil and political rights for all and a system of meritocracy (this supports the stakeholder approach).

Virtue ethics

Real life case: the MBA oath

In light of the financial crisis, questions began to emerge about the ethical and moral role that business leaders played in creating the crisis and, consequently, the type of education they received (Currie et al., 2010). MBA students from Harvard Business School (widely acknowledged to be one of the leading business schools in the world and a centre for training future leaders) began to ask: 'How did we get into this crisis? Why didn't business school professors sound the alarms in advance of the meltdown? Why were so many MBAs involved in the decisions leading up to the crisis? Are MBAs so concerned with increasing their personal wealth that they ignore ethics and their responsibilities to society?' ▶

> As a response to these questions the graduates of the 2009 MBA created the MBA oath. Modelled on the Hippocratic oath, which doctors swear, its stated 'mission is to facilitate a widespread movement of MBAs who aim to lead in the interests of the greater good'. Among the pledges were to be aware of the impact the organization had beyond the business itself, to not be corrupt or do practices harmful to society, to provide economic and environmental sustainability for future generations, and to set an example to followers.
>
> **Source:** http://mbaoath.org/about/.

Visit the Online Resource Centre to read the MBA oath in full. Would you pledge an oath like this? Do you think that saying an oath will make you behave in a more ethical manner?

Virtue-based ethics focuses on the individual, particularly their personal characteristics. Drawing on Aristotle it looks at the individual character—how it is formed and develops to achieve 'eudaimonia' (life-long development of well-being or human flourishing). (For a review, see Fisher et al., 2013.) It focuses on means, not ends (unlike teleological ethics), and personal characteristics rather than rules (unlike deontological ethics). Advocates of virtue-based ethics believe that if practised in the right way it will lead the individual to make the right choices.

In the business context virtue ethics focuses on the character of the individual and their capacity to make the right choices (see MacIntyre, 1967). Proponents would argue that the moral education of managers is therefore vital to help them cope with the ethical complexity of modern life.

A related concept, drawing on feminist philosophy, is the 'ethics of care'. It argues that most philosophy (and therefore ethics) are written by, and based on, male ideals. For instance, Gilligan (1982) argues that women demonstrate a different way of moral reasoning, particularly due to early socialization, and tend to seek compromise and ways of avoiding blaming one side exclusively in a dispute so that everyone gets something, rather than looking for the black and white morals that men tend to look for (see, for a review, Fisher and Lovell, 2009: 107).

Virtue ethics, however, can overemphasize the importance of the individuals, either by praising heroic individuals or blaming **bad apples** for immoral actions.

Bad apples A phrase that dismisses an occurrence as just down to a few bad people or organizations, while claiming that others should not be judged as the same.

Individual growth and organizational learning

Our final ethical perspective emphasizes the importance of learning and development (see Chapter 10) as part of ethical development. It focuses on how to be more effective, not only in doing one's job but in developing an ethical character. A particularly popular (and inspiring) example is provided by Stephen Covey's *The 7 Habits of Highly Effective People* (2004). On the surface this book appears to be a conventional time-management and self-help book, with charts for how to plan a week and habits to be successful. However, it goes further by asking the reader to define what they consider being successful really means, and what sort of character and life they want. This stresses a number of things, including the importance of having a personal vision. This is important, not just in work, but also in terms of balancing personal, family, and professional responsibilities. At the heart is developing an ethical character and focusing on priorities based upon principles rather than quick fixes. Having sold over 15 million copies, Covey's book has proved highly influential, particularly during the 1990s. It does, however, reinforce the image of the heroic ethical individual able to overcome all adversity.

What are your personal values and how important are they in your daily decision making? What would you like others to say about your moral character?

The second individual growth perspective is communitarianism. This perspective argues the community should be considered more important than individuals or the state. Communitarianism stresses the importance of social relations and suggests that human life will improve if the community and public values guide our decision making. In other words, we do things for the good of the community rather than for ourselves. We will have more to say on communitarianism later in the chapter.

Study skills: research ethics

Research ethics is becoming an increasingly important aspect of university life for both lecturers and students. Any significant piece of research now has to be passed beforehand for its ethical credentials, either by a supervisor (in the case of undergraduate students) or a committee (for most academics). Aspects like how the data is collected, stored, and used all need to fit ethical guidelines. The primary aim is to reduce the risk of harm to participants and make sure that the data is not used in the wrong way.

Undoubtedly, this has brought a lot of benefits as it requires the researcher to consider the impact their research can have on their participants before the research is conducted. However, it might stifle some research. For instance, it is unlikely that some innovative research like Zimbardo's Stanford Prison experiment would be allowed to occur today due to the harm it might cause to the participants (Wilson and Hunter, 2010), (see Chapter 13).

Review questions

1. Describe the key principles of each of the ethical frameworks.
2. Evaluate their strengths and weaknesses.

Analyse

3. Which of these ethical frameworks do you feel more drawn to and why?
4. Evaluate which you consider more useful when tackling business dilemmas, and why.

The economic framework for ethical action

While ethical frameworks are important in guiding individual and organizational behaviour, the choices that we have, and the possibilities for ethical action, are also shaped by the economic system in which we live. For the rest of the chapter we will examine the five main perspectives that exist currently, at least within Western countries.

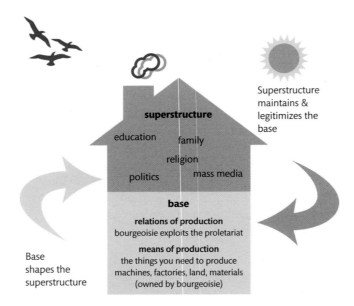

Figure 17.3 The base and superstructure model (based on Marx, 1859/2012).

Karl Marx (1859/2012) argued that the economic structure (which he called the base) shapes the nature of society (which he called the superstructure), and society exists to maintain and legitimize the economic system (Figure 17.3). For instance, this Marxist framework argues that within our society schooling exists primarily to support the economy, not only in providing skilled workers, but also in establishing the values and attitudes these workers should have (to accept authority, turn up on time, want to achieve high grades (promotion at work), and accept discipline).

Consequently, for ethics, our central ideas are a product of the superstructure (our family, education, religion, reading of mass media, politics, etc.) and our actions are constrained by the base—the economic system in which we operate. According to this view, while it is important to look to individual organizations and people, our ethical beliefs and the choices that we have, are more political or ideological in nature.

The first three frameworks accept the economic system of capitalism as their basis, although they have different interpretations and emphasis within it. The latter two could broadly be said to be against capitalism as an economic system, but offer two different responses to the problems they perceive that capitalism creates (Figure 17.4).

Figure 17.4 The five frameworks featured in this chapter.

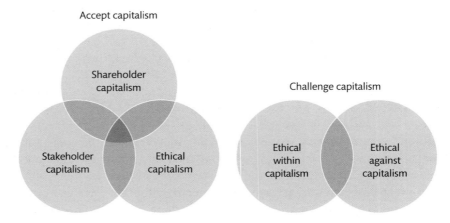

For the purposes of this chapter capitalism is understood as the economic system in which we (in the West) live, where one group—the capitalists (shareholders or owners of the firm)—owns the means of production, and another group—labour (workers)—sell their labour. We have featured this in the capitalist working relationship (see p. 63).

Shareholder capitalism

Running case: hitting the headlines

While still musing his hotel expansion plans, Linda Wilkinson comes rushing into Simon Chance's office looking flustered. 'Do we have an appointment?', Chance looks at her quizzically and with a slight sense of annoyance. 'Look at this', Wilkinson cuts across him, pointing to the front page of the local paper, 'it's worse than I predicted'. Still not really understanding what is going on, Chance snatches the paper from her. 'What are you talking about . . . oh, I see', Chance says seeing the headline 'Junction Rubbish' accompanied by a big photo of the hotel with litter strewn across the road. '"Weddings at local hotel are causing mayhem, say local residents"', Chance reads to Wilkinson, '"drunken yobs making noise throughout the night . . . traffic blocking up local streets . . . guests being sick in neighbour's front garden . . . litter being dumped on the street"'. 'This is not good', Chance declares, looking up from the paper. Chance's office door opens and in comes Weaver. 'Have you seen this?', Chance asks, handing the paper to Weaver. With only a quick glance, Weaver hands the paper back. 'Newspaper tittle-tattle', Weaver declares. 'Look, the weddings make us a lot of money. Sure, they make a lot of noise, but, then, they are having fun.' Wilkinson looks shocked: 'But, it's a really bad story—front page, too.' Weaver smiles at her. 'It's just paper talk. It will all blow over in a week and be forgotten about. News today, but tomorrow it's just fish and chip paper. You have to be strong and withstand these stories. When the profits come through the investors will be thanking you.'

Milton Friedman: the social responsibility of business is to increase its profits

Nobel prize-winning economist Milton Friedman is the most prominent and outspoken critic of corporate social responsibility and a defender of shareholder capitalism. In a 1970 article he claimed 'there is one and only one social responsibility of business – to use its resources and engage in activities designed to increase its profits so long as it stays within the rules of the game, which is to say, engages in open and free competition without deception or fraud' (Friedman, 1970: 126). Anything else, he states, not only is not the purpose of organizations, but is actually unethical.

Drawing on libertarianism, Friedman argues that companies are the shareholders' property and therefore should be run exclusively in their interest. This interest, he stated, is 'to make as much money as possible while conforming to their basic rules of the society'. For instance, a company should not spend money 'on reducing pollution beyond the amount that is in the best interests of the corporation or that is required by law' as it would lower profit for the shareholders.

This libertarian perspective also calls for less control by the government, as people (including shareholders and therefore corporations) should be free to live their lives in a way that maximizes freedom. Finally, Friedman also argues that because managers are not trained in solving social problems they should not be required to tackle them. Businesses, therefore, should not have responsibilities for solving society's problems because it dilutes what they are good at—being run in an efficient and profitable manner.

Visit the Online Resource Centre to read more about Milton Friedman's theories.

Do you think companies should be run exclusively in shareholders' interests?

Adam Smith: the invisible hand

Ethical egoism
People acting in their own best interest is the best way to get a good society.

The shareholder capitalism perspective also takes a particular reading of utilitarianism, using **ethical egoism**. This perspective claims that you should act in your own self-interest as doing so is the best way of promoting the maximum overall level of happiness. 'It is not from the benevolence of the butcher, the brewer, or the baker, that we expect our dinner, but from their regard to their own interest. We address ourselves, not to their humanity but to their self-love, and never talk to them of our own necessities but of their advantages' (*Wealth of Nations*, I.ii.2 (Smith, 1776/2012)). Because trading is beneficial to both parties it will increase the good for all. Collective interest, it is claimed, is best promoted through self-interest. Intentions reached individually will be the best decisions for the entire society.

Smith argues that you are more likely to work harder, spend your money more carefully, and invest it more wisely if it is for your own interest. Similarly, workers will seek to maximize their skills and work as hard as possible to maximize their wages, buyers will look to purchase goods for the lowest amount possible, and sellers will thus be forced to compete with each other to offer the best goods at the lowest price. Self-interest supports society as a whole, 'led by an invisible hand to promote an end which was no part of his intention . . . By pursuing his own interest he frequently promotes that of the society more effectually than when he really intends to promote it' (*Wealth of Nations* IV.ii.9 (Smith, 1776/2012)). According to this view the market, therefore, has an 'invisible hand' that promotes the greatest good for all.

Economic growth is good for all: the rising tide raises all ships

Real life case: Stephen Hester's bonus

In January 2012 Stephen Hester, the CEO of Royal Bank of Scotland (RBS), turned down a bonus of just under £1 million. Hester had come under considerable public and political pressure, particularly because RBS are predominately a government-owned company. Many members of the public considered his pay excessive, particularly at a time of austerity that meant the majority of public and private sector workers were experiencing pay freezes and even job cuts (Neate, 2012).

In our interview Hester said that although it 'may not be the job of a business person specifically' everyone needs to understand the issues surrounding high pay and inequality. However, he argues ▶

that capitalism is 'the most effective way of increasing the wealth and opportunities of most people'. It is effective because it increases the size of the 'economic pie' which 'unleashes different people's motivations and talents in different ways, which can accentuate financial differences. The biggest income differences on the planet at the moment are in China and India today, which are the fastest-growing, biggest producers of economic pie growth out there'.

'If you want, as a society, to have some wealth to go round, you need to allow, or even encourage, the efforts that lead to some people having a lot more money than others because of their business success. And then you need to reign some of that back through taxation in order to make acceptable to everyone the way that the pie is ultimately distributed . . . and that is the trick. So, if we were to instigate a rule that said that pay differences cannot be more than X, then, simply, we will be less successful economically and there will be less of the pie to go round for everyone. But, equally, if the people that do well out of the current system are ignorant of everyone else and offensive, then the system won't last either.'

Source: Author interview with Stephen Hester, Royal Bank of Scotland, February 2012.

Visit the Online Resource Centre to read the full interview.

Hester's arguments can be interpreted as being drawn from utilitarianism and libertarianism. Both hinge on the assumption that shareholder capitalism is the most effective way of increasing overall wealth and in doing so they produce increased benefits for all. This argument, sometimes known as the 'trickle-down effect' or, in former US President Franklin D. Roosevelt's metaphor, 'the rising tide raises all ships'. This argument claims that although capitalism might produce more inequality (as the rich will get proportionally richer than the poor), it will 'drag up the poor people, because there are the resources to do so' (Robinson, 2012: 204), as Margaret Thatcher once famously claimed. According to this view the goal of the economy should be wealth creation rather than wealth redistribution as, in the long-run, everyone will benefit.

Philanthropy: giving something back to society

What do you think of Andrew Carnegie's statement: 'The man who dies rich, dies disgraced'? (in Partington, 1998: 181).

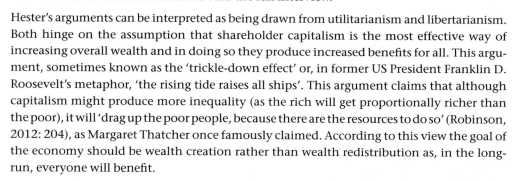

Real life case: world's richest man gives away his fortune

In 1999, Bill Gates, the founder of Microsoft, and his wife, announced he would give away most of their $100 billion fortune. (In 2006, Warren Buffett joined them, giving away about $31 billion (99% of his wealth).) The charity they set up, The Gates Foundation, according to their website, has a mission to: 'Increase opportunities for people in developing countries to overcome hunger and poverty'. They apply business techniques to invest in high impact (therefore, they state, efficient) projects, looking for 'high-impact, sustainable solutions that can reach hundreds of millions of people'.

In 2010, Gates and Buffett launched a campaign called *The Giving Pledge* 'to invite the wealthiest individuals and families in America to commit to giving the majority [at least half] of their wealth to philanthropy'. Many have signed up.

Visit the Online Resource Centre for more detail about the campaign.

Source: http://www.gatesfoundation.org/global-development/Pages/overview.aspx

Why do you think these billionaires are giving away much of their fortunes?

The shareholder capitalism model argues that individual shareholders have the right, indeed in countries like the USA, almost a duty, to give some of their wealth away. Gates and Buffett are not the first. Henry Ford, who set up one of the first *foundations*, and David Packard, the founder of Hewlett Packard, gave money to set up a hospital, university, and aquarium (Ford Foundation, 2012; Packard Foundation, 2012).

Philanthropy was at its strongest in the UK in the Victorian era when many successful business people were often driven by Christian belief that money is the root of all evil, and a necessity to help the poor. Many were Quakers, such as the founders of banks Barclays and Lloyds, and chocolate manufacturer, Cadbury's. They gave away vast fortunes to help the needy and also set up schools, hospitals, and funded the arts (Ackrill and Hannah, 2001; Dellheim, 1987).

Today, many corporations have a philanthropic arm, giving money back to society, investing in the arts, in local community projects, in sponsoring local sports teams, and allowing staff to volunteer their time and skills to local charities.

Real life case: how much do corporations give?

The Committee Encouraging Corporate Philanthropy (CECP) surveyed 184 companies and discovered:

- median total giving in CECP's sample was $22.10 million in 2010
- 94% of companies offered at least one matching gift programme in 2010
- 89% of companies had a formal domestic employee volunteer programme
- 81% of companies reported having a corporate foundation
- health, education, and community and economic development were top priorities for the typical company.

The report made clear that they did not just give cash, but also gave free advice and support, matched employee donations, and gave volunteers' time.

Source: Committee Encouraging Corporate Philanthropy (2012).

While such actions are highly commendable, questions remain about the role of philanthropy. First, there is a concern that it is undemocratic as certain causes might be more appealing to rich people, giving them more power than if the money was distributed through general taxation (BBC Television, 2011a). For instance, Victorian philanthropist George Peabody, who helped the poor of London to have somewhere to live, only wanted people he considered of 'excellent moral character', who he thought were worthy of help (BBC Television, 2011b).

Secondly, by giving these large amounts it diverts attention away from some of the potentially less ethical activities, for example donating money to a local good cause to gain public support for a potentially controversial activity. For instance, one of us went on a training day for artists in business, and was told of a business that put on an arts event to give them some positive publicity when applying for planning permission. The impression they gave was that using the arts was a cheap way of buying public support for their new development.

Problems with the shareholder capitalism model

While shareholder capitalism has been very popular with many politicians and business leaders, substantial questions remain over its ethical status and the assumptions on which it is based. First, it is based on the assumption of the 'economic person' who always acts in a rational manner. As we covered in Chapter 5, people do not always act rationally or seek to maximize their own interests. Secondly, it assumes that self-interest is good for all—an assumption of the 'tragedy of the commons' questions. Thirdly, it assumes that acting in self-interest has no negative effects on others, something economists call *externalities*. Fourthly, challenges have been presented to the rising tide thesis by arguments that income inequalities produce social problems. Finally, the supreme rights of shareholders are being challenged by placing more attention on them.

Assumption 1: self-interest is good for all

Research insight: The tragedy of the commons, Hardin, G. 1968. The tragedy of the commons. *Science* 162(3859): 1243–1248.

In this seminal article, ecologist Garrett Hardin describes a fictional situation where cattle herders graze their cows on common land. Hardin states that, unconsciously, each herdsman will ask 'What is the **utility** *to me* of adding one more animal to my herd?'. By putting another cow on the land a herdsman increases his personal wealth as he benefits from the proceeds of the sale of the cow, but it has a negative effect on the grass that will be spread across all the herdsmen. Therefore, by acting in his individual interests each herdsman will add more

Self-interest versus common interest.

Utility The benefit that an individual might gain.

cattle to the land that will ultimately destroy the quality of the land—thus the tragedy of the commons.

While widely criticized for, among other things, historical inaccuracies (Hawkshaw et al., 2012), Hardin's work provides a powerful repost to the utilitarian argument that everyone should act in their own self-interest as it demonstrates that if they do, our common interests are not always served. Hardin's work has been most influential in the ecology and sustainability movement.

As Hardin's article illustrates, if everyone acts in their self-interest then this does not necessarily create the best outcome for all. As the KitKat example which opened this chapter demonstrates, while it might have been in Nestlé's private interest to obtain supplies from the cheapest possible source, the long-term interests of the whole of humanity would be better served by maintaining the rainforest. Such failures are sometimes called 'market failures', when negative effects of a transaction can fall on a third party—an occurrence economists call *externalities* (Bakan, 2005).

Assumption 2: individuals should be free to pursue their own interests

The premise of shareholder capitalism that business leaders only have responsibilities to shareholders is justified on the ground that business activity is positive—creating jobs, goods, and services—or, at best, benign (not harmful) for society. However, upon closer examination, this position is hard to sustain in every instance.

To maximize profits, critics argue, businesses, in fact, transfer the *true* cost of transactions to society. For instance, firms do not pay for the pollution they cause, the unemployment benefit of workers made redundant, the building of new roads needed for a new factory, or the extra health costs caused by their products, e.g. smoking. These other costs fall on a third party who is not involved in the decision-making process.

Economists call these costs externalities or spillover costs. These are the side effects—positive or negative costs on society, on other people, who have no part in the decision-making process (see Bakan, 2005).

Real life case: The Stern Report

Notwithstanding that human-made climate change is contested, there is increasing acceptance that human activity (including business) is a significant cause of climate change. As the Intergovernmental Panel on Climate Change (IPCC) and similar research bodies have demonstrated, global temperatures have risen steadily since 1880—the birth of the industrial revolution (Figure 17.5).

A rise in global temperatures of 2°C above pre-industrial levels might trigger the collapse of the Amazon rainforest, resulting in the release of trapped carbon, and the thawing of the permafrost, releasing trapped methane, which might start a potentially irreversible process of temperature growth. A rise of 3°C would lead to temperatures not seen for 3 million years. Lord Stern, from the Grantham Research Institute on Climate Change, argues that this could have profound effects on human life, causing droughts, famines, and mass migration (Schäfer, Goff and Parker, 2012).

In 2006 he released a report for the UK Government declaring climate change to be the 'greatest and widest-ranging market failure ever seen' (Schäfer, Goff and Parker, 2012). Not only could it ▶

Figure 17.5 The average rise in global temperatures.

Source: Based on research by the Intergovernmental Panel on Climate Change (IPCC).

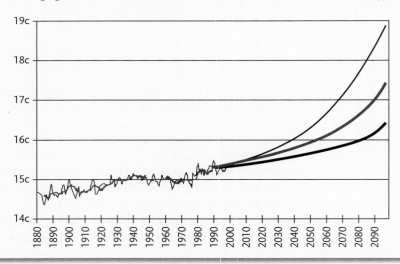

> have a devastating impact on the environment, but also on long-term business survival. Lord Stern claimed the impact of climate change could result in a global reduction of consumption of 20% per year. To overcome this market failure he called for 1% of gross domestic product (GDP) investment now to shift to a low carbon economy. This would need to be imposed on governments and businesses globally in order to be effective.
>
> **Source:** Stern (2006).

As the Real life case illustrates, governments are faced with the need to deal with externalities, such as reducing carbon emissions back to the socially-optimal level. Either the government could impose regulation to overcome any negative effects on society, for instance making it more expensive to emit carbon by imposing a carbon tax, or it could make firms internalize the negative costs, e.g. the clean-up costs, which is an incentive to reduce pollution.

Assumption 3: economic growth is good for all

Real life case: executive pay

In recent years one of the strongest areas of criticism of large corporations has been the levels of executive pay. In a recent report by the High Pay Commission (2011), it is argued that some bosses' pay has risen more than 4,000% since the 1980s.

In the USA the top 0.1% take home over 7.5% of gross domestic product (GDP), whereas in Sweden it is less than 2.5%. Other statistics from the report include:

Table 17.1 Percentage of UK national wealth received

Top percentage earners	1979	2007
0.1%	1.3%	6.5%
1%	5.93%	14.5%
10%	28.4	40%

- the average income of a FTSE 100 CEO is estimated at £4.2m
- the CEO of BP earns over 63 times that of the average employee; in 1979 it was 16.5 times
- the former CEO of Barclays, Bob Diamond, earned over 75 times the average employee; in 1979 it was 14.5 times. In 2011, he received £16 million in salary, benefits, and previous years' share awards. He even had his £5.75 million tax bill paid (Schäfer, Goff and Parker. 2012)
- they predict, at current levels of increase, that by 2035 the top 0.1% will take home 14% of national income.

The High Pay Commission report called for greater fairness and transparency in executive pay. In opposition to the report, Dr Heather McGregor, who herself earns £108,000 per annum, argued, in the BBC Today programme (BBC News, 2011a) that you cannot have executive pay that is too high or too low. She went on to say that shareholders, not the public, should set the pay of CEOs, and people who complain about high pay are childish and should live in the real world. She stated that putting an employee on a remuneration committee (to decide the level of CEO pay) was 'barking mad'. In her view, remuneration is only the business of shareholders and she likened workers on remuneration committees to children deciding their parents' allowance. She claimed, if you want workers to run companies you should go and live in Cuba.

Source: High Pay Commission (2011); BBC News (2011a).

Listen to 'Bosses' pay too high? Then move to Cuba' on the BBC's Today programme, which is available on the Online Resource Centre and make up your own mind.

The belief that as long as everyone gets richer the level of inequality does not matter has been challenged in a recent book *The Spirit Level: Why Equality is Better for Everyone* (Wilkinson and Pickett, 2009). Drawing on large amounts of statistical evidence, Wilkinson and Pickett (2009) argue that it is not the overall level of wealth which matters (as shareholder capitalism has it), but the level of inequality.

Looking at societal issues, such as physical health, mental health, drug abuse, imprisonment, obesity, trust, and violence, they found that the countries with the highest levels of social inequality fared worse in these measures. For instance, on one hand, the USA is the world's richest country; they have vast inequalities of income, high crime, and even high infant deaths per head of population (see Figure 17.6). On the other hand, Scandinavian countries have greater equality and lower social problems. Wilkinson and Pickett therefore conclude the greater the gap between the rich and the poor, the higher the levels of crime, health problems, unhappiness, drug addiction, and environmental problems.

Wilkinson and Pickett therefore argue that developed countries have achieved about as much as they can from growth. Indeed, increasing growth now contains the potential to harm the planet as it requires more resources. Consequently, the goal of society should therefore be to increase equality rather than focus on economic growth.

 Does the amount of money you have matter more, or the gaps between rich and poor? How might equity theory (which we examined in Chapter 9) apply here?

Figure 17.6 The impact of income inequality on child mortality. (From Wilkinson and Pickett, *The Spirit Level*, 2010. Allen Lane, Penguin.)

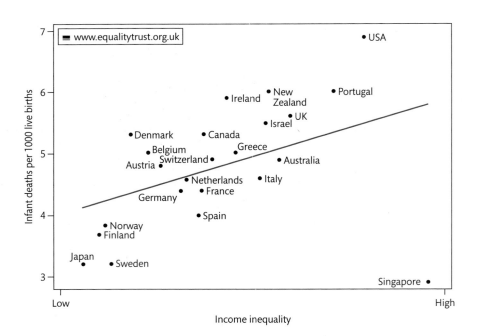

Assumption 4: shareholders' interests are the only important ones

The final underlying assumption of shareholder capitalism is that because they (the shareholders) own the firm, it is their property to do with as they like. The business should be run exclusively in shareholders' interests and the consequences for others are, at best, secondary and, at worst, disregarded if they harm the shareholders interest. As we will see later, however, it could be argued that from a moral point of view such a perspective is problematic and can even be detrimental to the long-term interests of the shareholders.

Cases of harm to stakeholders

In recent years there have been numerous cases of the harmful impacts that large (and sometimes small) organizations have had—see Table 17.2 for details. Business supporters, however, often reject them as examples of a few bad apples and state that we should also be aware of the vast amount of good that businesses do (primarily in supplying jobs, goods and services that people need, and also giving things back into society). However, for campaigners and anti-capitalism protestors, such cases are examples of fundamental problems with the structure of capitalism.

Table 17.2 Corporate social responsibility in the news

Category	Headline	Description	Key details	Sources
Harm to workers	Olympic uniforms come from unethical sources	Just 100 days before the start of the 2012 London Olympics an investigation by *The Independent* revealed that the British Olympic team uniform and that worn by the helpers came from unethical sources	• Widespread violations of workers' rights in Indonesia • Forced overtime—working 65 hours a week • Factory workers not on a living wage • Intensive working conditions • Workers suffered physical and verbal abuse • Being called 'dog', 'brainless', 'uneducated' • Even claiming 'It's hard to get permission even to go to the bathroom'	*The Independent* (2012), Nelson (2012), TUC (2012)
Suicidal workers	Xbox and iPad workers threaten mass suicide	Recent reports about the Foxconn factories in China have alleged that the working conditions are so bad that 300 workers threatened to commit mass suicide. Another report has stated the workers even had to sign pledges that they will not kill themselves	• At least 14 workers have killed themselves in 16 months • They are paid only 65p an hour • Excessive overtime—98 hours instead of the legal maximum of 36 hours a month • Sleeping in dormitories of 24 people • Badly-performing workers were humiliated in front of colleagues • The factories say that the suicides were not linked to the conditions, and both Microsoft and Apple are investigating the issue	*The Daily Mail* (2011), *The Guardian* (2011), CBS News (2012)

Table 17.2 (*cont'd*)

Category	Headline	Description	Key details	Sources
Harm to customers	Car explosion	In *The Corporation* Joel Bakan (2005) describes a court case where car manufacturer General Motors (GM) were sued after a car exploded. During the court case they discovered not only had GM put the fuel tank in a dangerous position to save costs, but they had calculated that the savings outweighed the risks of getting sued by 500 fuel-related fatalities they thought might occur each year. This produced a potential saving of $2.40 per car. The judge concluded GM's behaviour was 'morally reprehensible and against applicable laws because it had put profits above public safety' (2005: 63).	Bakan (2005), Geyelin (1999), Pollack (1999)
Harm to animals	Mega-cowshed	While we often like to think of our milk coming from cows happily grazing in the countryside, the reality can be very different. A mega-cowshed proposed in Nocton, Lincolnshire, was originally planned to house 8,100 cows (but was reduced to 3,770 after protests) who would have 'little access to pasture or sunshine'. With two milking cycles a day, they aimed to produce 387,000 pints of milk each day. The owners argued they would produce milk more efficiently while still maintaining welfare standards. Responding to public concerns, Nocton Dairies stated: 'We do not feel there is a nutritional benefit for the cows to go outside. But we have listened to the concerns of welfare groups, the RSPCA and the public of what they feel is better for the dairy cows. If they feel happier with cows allowed to go outside we are going to offer our cows outside space' (BBC News, 2010). Despite these changes, at the time of writing, the planning application had been turned down.	*The Daily Mail* (2010), BBC News (2010), *The Daily Telegraph* (2011)

Visit the Online Resource Centre for links to further examples.

These sorts of cases challenge Milton Friedman's and Adam Smith's argument that unfettered self-interest produces good for everyone. They demonstrate that firms have an impact on, and, many would argue, a responsibility to, wider society. This is where stakeholder perspective comes in.

Review questions

1. Describe the key arguments for shareholder capitalism.

2. Explain what the key critiques of this perspective are.

Analyse

3. What are your views? Can you support your views with the ethical frameworks discussed here?

Stakeholder capitalism

Running case: the letters column

Having hoped that the media storm would blow over, Chance is horrified to see that in the following day's paper the letters column is full of letters from the local community complaining that Junction Hotel is affecting their lives. Oliver Price from the local neighbourhood committee writes to complain of the 'loutish' behaviour of wedding guests and the 'excessive noise' made at weekends. Ronald Farley also wrote in complaining that, despite his emails, the management of the hotel do not seem to care.

Thinking that nothing else could go wrong Chance picks up his ringing telephone. On the other end is Ian Terry, one of Second-Chance Consortium's biggest investors and a local in the town. Terry has also seen the letters column in the paper and says that he is horrified that the hotel is receiving such negative publicity. Recalling Weaver's words, Chance tries to calm his fears by saying that the storm will quickly blow over and once the profits come in from the larger weddings all of this will be forgotten. 'I live in this community', Terry protests, 'and, anyway, do you really think that we have a chance of getting the extension through planning with stories going on in the press like this? We will get kicked out at the first stage if this is kept up. You need to sort it out, and fast.' With that, he slams the phone down.

It is quickly apparent that the shareholders are not the only ones to be affected by an organization's actions. Many groups or individuals have a **stake** in the actions that a business takes and therefore, it could be argued, need to be considered when decisions are made. For instance, a full-time employee spends a large part of their waking hours at work and is, generally, financially dependent on the job, so, arguably, has more at stake than an individual shareholder who might only have some of their savings tied up in the company. Similarly, many customers rely on the services a company offers. For instance, when care home provider Southern Cross ran into financial difficulties after their rents increased not only were staff going to, potentially, lose their jobs, but the accommodation of thousands of vulnerable pensioners was at risk, causing anxiety for them and their families (Snell, 2011; BBC News 2011b). Equally, local communities can be impacted by issues such as noise pollution or an increase in traffic. In short, many other parties are impacted by the actions of a single organization. These groups include, but are not limited to, those shown in Figure 17.7.

> **Stake** A claim or interest.

Within academic literature and business terminology these groups are often called **stakeholders**. A stakeholder is a person or group who could be impacted by the actions of the organization. The challenge is to identify who the stakeholders are, what responsibilities the organization has to them, and balance the competing interests of these stakeholders.

> **Stakeholder** Someone who has an interest or claim in the activities of the organization.

Some stakeholder theorists go further, arguing that firms have to act within the interests of society otherwise society will withdraw its support and prevent them from existing. As Davis argues 'Society gave business its charter to exist, and that charter could be amended or revoked at any time that business fails to live up to society's expectations' (1973: 314). Furthermore, governments impose or loosen controls, set investment in infrastructure, provide workers through training and education, and provide healthcare for sick employees and regulation against unfair competition. Indeed, in recent years, throughout the world,

Figure 17.7
Organizations'
stakeholders.

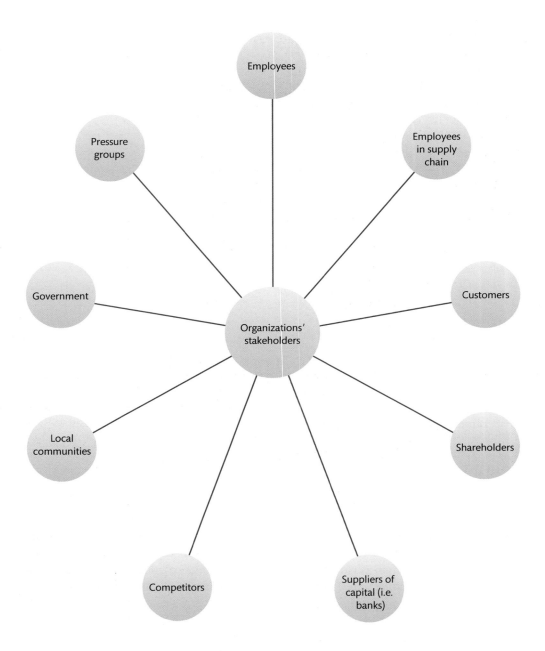

governments have even been bailing out banks because of the negative impact that their failure would have had on other businesses. As a consequence, businesses must maintain enough trust in order to not be put under extra legislation.

One of the central challenges, therefore, is to define who are stakeholders and how much to privilege them. Different versions of stakeholder theory present alternative approaches to this issue. The legal view presents a narrow list of only the legal duties a firm has, the strategic view stressing what is good for the firm, therefore privileging the importance of customers or those whose actions will impact trade (e.g. maintaining a good relationship with a key supplier and paying them on time), whereas the full stakeholder view looks at everyone the firm can impact, even if they are not likely to trade. Even this wider view can have business benefits (Figure 17.8). Consider the KitKat case from the beginning of the chapter. The orangutan is not a consumer of Nestlé products and the activists who campaigned against them were still a small minority of consumers, but the wider impact of this campaign had the potential to damage Nestlé's long-term reputation.

Figure 17.8 How wide should stakeholder theory go?

Consider a company that you know well and try to list all the stakeholders that you can think of (remember to include those in the supply chain and those who are indirectly impacted by the organization or might have an interest in it). Using the three models listed, which ones would fit in a legal, strategic, or wide definition of stakeholders? Which would you consider the most important and why?

Stakeholder theory also draws on business ethics. From a social justice (deontological) viewpoint it argues that business actions should be fair. Drawing on communitarian ethics it stresses the importance of placing the community above individual interests.

Certainly, from an ethical viewpoint stakeholder theory offers the potential for a more well-rounded view of the ethical responsibilities than the rather narrow definition of shareholder capitalism because it asks businesses to consider the overall benefits to society. Yet, questions remain about how much organizations fully apply these principles.

Corporate social responsibility (CSR)

Few people and, in particular, few large-scale organizations today (at least publicly) support Friedman's claim that the only responsibility businesses have is to their shareholders. Increasing attention by the press, public awareness, and campaign groups has meant that firms have to respond to issues like sweatshop labour and environmental pollution to protect their reputation and brand image. Consequently, it is increasingly important to consider CSR (Freeman and Liedtka, 1991).

Companies, like Ford, now stress the CSR credential. In our interview, Joe Greenwell, the Chairman of Ford in Britain states that Henry Ford saw his purpose as 'broader than just making money', but in 'serving mankind' (source: Author interview with Joe Greenwell, Ford in Britain, 2012). He paid for schools and hospitals, and got involved in the local community—something that lives on in Ford as a company. Greenwell states that all leaders within Ford throughout the world are engaged in some aspect of CSR. Ford, Greenwell states, 'clearly went beyond Milton Friedman' as he 'wanted to make the world a better place'. The pillars of Ford today—'quality, green, safe and smart'—carry on this legacy. 'Ford has given us such good opportunities and we want others to think well of it'. This is not just to do social good, but there 'is a certain amount of enlightened self-interest about it'.

Visit the Online Resource Centre to see the full interview with Ford's Joe Greenwell.

Why might it be in Ford's interest to be seen in a good light?

Indeed, Adam Smith, who we met earlier, alongside writing *The Wealth of Nations* (1776/2012) also wrote *The Theory of Moral Sentiments* (1759/1976), a book which called on combining ethics with capitalism. In the Victorian era many business owners, particularly because of their Christian faith, became concerned about the ethics of their wealth, resulting in them setting up charities or, like Cadbury's, running their firms in a way that also looked after their workers. However, it was not until the 1950s that CSR became a serious concern within business and academia, starting with Howard Bowen (1953).

Bowen is considered the founder of CSR (Carroll, 1999). He argued that because business leaders have decision-making power which impacts citizens, they have a responsibility to act in ways beyond money making but 'which are desirable in terms of the objectives and values of our society' (Bowen, 1953: 6). Interestingly, when surveyed, 93.5% of businessmen agreed with this statement (Bowen, 1953).

Over the last sixty years CSR has grown enormously as an academic discipline and business practice. Most businesses now consider it an important part of their practice (Carroll, 1999)—essential for building (or protecting) their reputation and demonstrating the positive impact they can have on society. Thus, it has now become almost an obligatory requirement for most medium and large companies to issue CSR statements, reports, and even departments dedicated to it.

Visit the Online Resource Centre to see some examples of CSR statements and reports.

CSR draws on the ideas of Scottish industrialist and philanthropist Andrew Carnegie, the founder of US Steel. He believed that business is a positive force as it increases society's wealth. However, it required two key principles to be in place in order to work: (i) the charitable principle, where the more fortunate help the less fortunate; and (ii) the stewardship principle, where the rich hold the wealth 'in trust' for the rest of society (Fisher et al., 2013). The belief that these basic principles, combined with the belief that acting appropriately, result in limited government intervention (particularly rules and regulations) has given CSR considerable credence in business circles (Freeman and Liedtka, 1991).

Think of a medium-to-large-sized company that you know well and search on the Internet for '[company name] CSR statement' and see the result. What do you find out?

While there is no agreed definition of CSR (Carroll, 1999), there are a few common themes (Figure 17.9). Most definitions argue that businesses have obligations (something that an organization has to do) beyond their legal (following the law) and economic obligations (making money for shareholders), towards society. (For a discussion, see Carroll, 1999.)

In this section we will argue that there are two main forms of enlightened self-interest. First, the damage limitation model, which sees CSR as a way of limiting the negative side-effects of the firm's activity. This view sees CSR coming into play only when there is a potential impact on the firm. Secondly, the view that we have called **ethical capitalism** (see pp. 569–570) tries to integrate CSR into the heart of the firm's activities and trade on the benefits

Ethical capitalism
A business approach which seeks to integrate CSR as central to the purpose and activity of an organization.

(Figure 17.10). Firms like Innocent Smoothies, Yeo Valley milk, and Ben and Jerry's ice cream set themselves up as being more ethical in their approach with the intention of customers buying into (and paying a premium) for more ethical and sustainable products.

These two positions can really be seen on a continuum, with many firms operating somewhere between them.

The minimal CSR perspective argues it is in a firm's self-interest to act in a responsible way because it will save money, avoid legislation, and prevent the brand being stained. For example, the cost of BP's oil spill in 2010 was not only for the clean-up, but for the reputational implications (*The Guardian*, 2012).

Figure 17.9 Carroll's (1991) levels of corporate social responsibility (CSR).

Figure 17.10 Minimal and integrated corporate social responsibility (CSR).

Real life cases: Enlightened self-interest; companies responding to criticism

Many clothing retailers, such as Primark and GAP, have been accused of using sweatshop labour to provide cheap goods. As a response they formed the Ethical Trading Initiative. They state: 'Our vision is a world where all workers are free from exploitation and discrimination, and work in conditions of freedom, security and equity. This year our corporate members' ethical trade activities touched the lives of over 9.8 million workers' (Ethical Trade Initiative, 2012).

TV celebrity chef Hugh Fearnley-Whittingstall launched a fishing campaign. He found that half of fish caught were thrown back, often nearly dead; there was over-consumption of cod, prawns, salmon, haddock, and tuna; and there were unsustainable practices for catching the tuna. The largest single tuna company, John West, was singled out from the rest of the industry for their use of fish aggregating devices (FADs) which indiscriminately catch sharks, rays, and endangered sea turtles. They recently announced they were stopping the use of FADs and would only use pole and line by 2016 (Greenpeace 2012; John West, 2012).

Supermarkets like Sainsbury's have conducted a campaign to get people to eat alternative forms of the big five fish (cod, prawns, salmon, haddock, and tuna).

Marks and Spencer's have launched a campaign 'Forever Fish—a major new campaign to help customers and their children learn more about fish, clean our British beaches and protect UK marine life' (Greenpeace, 2012; FishFight, 2012).

Sources: Ethical Trade Initiative (2012); Greenpeace (2012); John West (2012); FishFight (2012).

The rise of corporate social responsibility is said to produce numerous benefits for the firm. This is sometimes called the self-enlightened interest model. These benefits include:

- *better employees*—as companies compete on a 'war for talent', top employees are more likely to go to a company with good CSR credentials. In a recent survey almost 90% of respondents said they would be more likely to work for an organization that is considered ethically and socially responsible. Around 50% said they would be willing to forgo pay or promotion to work for a company with a good reputation and 33% said global warming issues were 'very important' when deciding where to work (Kelly Global Workforce Index, 2012).

Would working for a more ethical company be important for you?

- *gaining more affluent customers*—having products that are Fairtrade, more sustainable, and ethically supported is often seen as attracting more affluent customers who can afford to pay more for ethical products.
- *attracting shareholders* who do not want to be associated with unethical companies. In recent times ethical investment funds have emerged, for instance those that do not invest in arms companies or tobacco producers.
- *long-term reputation*—speaking on BBC Radio 4 in 2011, Sir Martin Sorrell argued that if businesses are only interested in short-term profit then CSR does not matter. However 'if you are in the business of building brands in the long-term . . . you will not do things that offend society, the environment and other stakeholders'. CSR should not be an add-on or a separate department or statement. CSR should be 'embedded in the strategy of the company. CSR therefore is an essential prerequisite for the success, ensuring that the firm continues to be trusted by the public'.
- *avoiding legislation*—for instance firms avoid giving off too much pollution in order to prevent more stringent legislation from occurring. This is a critical reason for putting CSR in place and is seen in the long-term as a way of reducing costs.

Does being ethical reduce profits?

CSR scholars (e.g. Aras and Crowther, 2012) argue that CSR and profitability is not only compatible, but essential. While unethical practice might, in the short-term, produce a profit, in the long-term it can have devastating impacts on the firms through negative implications on reputation, legislation, and employee commitment. Selfish interests and ethics coincide.

What evidence seems to suggest (see Capaldi, 2005) is that firms that apply *some* CSR to their practices do better than those that are completely unethical, but also do better than those that really try to integrate their ethical practices. Melvin Tumin calls this the 'principle of least morality' (1964). It costs to be seen as really bad, but it is also expensive to do very good activity. The most financially prudent and successful way is to do just enough to be seen as not negative.

It is arguable that enlightened self-interest is not really ethical at all. According to this view, doing a good act because it is for your own benefit could simply be considered as self-interest and does little to challenge the dominance of large-scale corporations (Banerjee, 2008).

Greenwashing: do CSR statements really result in ethical practice?

While CSR statements are popular, there are substantial questions over whether companies are more concerned with presenting a positive image than changing their practice. This concern is illustrated by the next Real life case.

Real life case: the corporate social responsibility of Walmart

Walmart is one of the world's largest companies (in the UK they own Asda) with a revenue of $418,952 million (Walmart, 2011). The supermarket is famous for selling food, clothes, and many other consumer goods at low prices.

In recent years they have become increasingly focused on presenting a positive image about their CSR. Their CSR statement states they have a positive impact on society and many of their adverts stress the benefits to the customers' family, the community, and their employees. They state that they seek to integrate sustainability into every aspect of their business and are taking a global outlook on their responsibility to communities throughout the world. They now publish a Global Responsibility Report (Walmart, 2012a) detailing their activities. These include working towards zero landfill waste globally, expanding the use of local produce, commitment to sourcing $20 billion of products from women-only businesses, donating millions of dollars to support those experiencing natural disasters, and clearer labelling to help customers make more healthy choices.

They also state that integrity is at the heart of what they do. For instance, they state that they treat their employees, who they call associates, and all suppliers, with respect and dignity. All new associates have to complete e-learning modules in ethics, which takes four hours. The company also complete global ethics education, which they are now rolling out throughout the world.

They also engage directly in philanthropy, giving $958 million annually ($500 million in-kind within the USA) and plan, by 2015, to donate $1.1 billion of food.

Robert Greenwald's documentary *Wal*mart: The High Cost of Low Price* (2005) argues Walmart are not as ethical as they present themselves. The film shows Walmart's CEO, Harold Lee Scott, speaking about the great economic and social benefits that the company brings, creating jobs and opportunities not only in the USA, but throughout the world. However, Greenwald argues the reality is somewhat different. He accuses Walmart of driving down wages, resulting in the employees being forced to rely on the state to support their families; promoting only part-time working, thereby avoiding the cost of benefits paid to full-time workers; union-busting activities; demanding unpaid overtime from staff; and lobbying for tax cuts.

One of the most notable examples in the film was an interview conducted with Jim Bill Lynn, their former Global Services Operations Manager. His job was to make sure that the factories making Walmart products in Mexico, and Central and South America complied with the code of conduct that Walmart had to provide clean, safe and human working conditions. Bill Lynn stated he was very loyal to Walmart, claiming if you cut him he 'would have bled Walmart blue blood'.

During his inspections, he states that he found 'female workers subjected to mandatory pregnancy testing, padlocked fire doors, a lack of available drinking water, workers that were locked in factory compounds until released by management, and other shocking conditions'. He also observed threats by management against employees for revealing these conditions. After his first factory inspection, he went home to his hotel room, phoned his wife and 'wept' (Greenwald, 2005).   ◗

He believed once aware of these violations, Walmart, would 'do the right thing' and enforce the code. However, rather than welcoming this information, for doing his job, Jim Bill claims they, in fact, sacked him. This, Greenwald implies, challenges Walmart's CSR claims.

Walmart rigorously attacked the film arguing it is biased and misinformed, and was created by anti-Walmart activists. Walmart stress how they are making positive impacts on the lives of people in developing countries. They cite interventions like the Women's Economic Empowerment Initiative in Bangladesh where they support 60,000 women with basic numeracy and literacy schemes so they can calculate their overtime (Walmart, 2012b) and a scholarship in India where women can develop retail skills to become more independent (Walmart. 2012c).

See the film for free at http://topdocumentaryfilms.com/wal-mart-the-high-cost-of-low-price/ to make up your own mind.

Visit the Online Resource Centre for links to the claims Walmart make and the criticisms that campaigners make about their impact, and make up your own mind.

Sustainability

In recent years, particularly reflecting the concerns over climate change, sustainability has risen on the agenda. While this is, in part, an environmental concern (using the earth's natural resources in a sustainable manner) it has also come to mean sustainability of the organization. It has therefore become quite a woolly concept and means different things to different people, as the recent debate in the UK over 'sustainable planning' has demonstrated. However, a good working definition has been provided by former Norwegian Prime Minister Gro Harlem Brundtland: 'meeting the needs of the present without compromising the ability of future generations to meet their own needs' (World Commission on Environment and Development, 1987: 43).

Real life case: Ford's EcoBoost

While for most environmental campaigners the car is the symbol of pollution and the destruction of the environment, over the last few years car manufacturers have increasingly been designing cars that have better environmental credentials. They have been working on cars that have lower fuel consumption, lower carbon dioxide (CO_2) emissions per mile, the production of hybrid cars, and, in the long-term, fuel cell technology so that by 2050 we will have zero-emission cars (Greenwell, 2011).

The Ford Focus Econetic.
© Ford in Britain.

Every car manufacturer is now producing more environmentally-friendly cars. Joe Greenwell, Chairman of Ford in Britain argues that the car industry 'bought the science [on climate change] a while back' and has been working on reducing the CO_2 emissions of cars for many years.

It is necessary to comply with European legislation, but in our interview, Greenwell states that it is 'not a compliance issue but a competitive race . . . as the customer in general sees the benefits'. He says he sits on climate change groups who see the automobile industry as a good example of where 'regulation has been useful in encouraging us as a manufacturing group to compete with each other to get CO_2 emissions down'.

Customers, however, have not bought into all eco-cars, largely because some are expensive, and Greenwell states the industry believes there is more that it needs to do to convince them. 'The

> ▶ customer has to see value.' It has moved from compliance to competitive advantage as customers become more interested in eco-cars. He argues that low carbon technology is a tremendous opportunity for growth for car manufacturers.
>
> **Source:** Author interview with Joe Greenwell, Ford in Britain, 2012.
>
> Visit the Online Resource Centre for the full interview with Joe Greenwell, Chairman of Ford in Britain.

Triple bottom line

Whereas shareholder capitalism only looks to 'the bottom line' of profit, triple bottom line extends the organization's focus to include 'people' and the 'planet' (Figure 17.11).

Developed by John Elkington of consultancy firm SustainAbility, it works on the basis that by measuring performance it improves the focus on people and planet. Its aims to create a set of measures, called metrics, for all firms' activities. By measuring them the belief is that it will change their behaviour. While profit is easy to measure, the impact on people and the plant is harder. Balancing the different bottom lines is also a challenge. However, it does represent an interesting way of putting into 'hard' terms (i.e. numbers) many of the social and environmental concerns that CSR and sustainability raise.

Figure 17.11 The triple bottom line.

Ethical capitalism

> **Running case:** Chance needs to decide between money and reputation
>
> Chance realizes that he is on the horns of a dilemma. Yes, the weddings are making a lot of money, but they are beginning to create a bad reputation for Junction Hotel, and this is hitting the business. He had heard that at a recent wedding fair at least two couples had said they did not want to get married at the hotel because of what they'd read in the papers about people getting drunk and aggressive. 'We need to turn this around', he thinks, 'but how?' So, he calls in Linda Wilkinson for a meeting.
>
> 'We need to grab hold of the agenda and show that we are putting something back into the local economy', Wilkinson suggests. 'How about we get all our food locally—sustainably, and seasonally. You know, local beef and pork, freshly-picked vegetables . . . people really go for that sort of thing. We could buy in local beer from the microbrewery and also start offering eco-weddings. Then, get it out in the paper to show that we are doing good things for this area—creating jobs and supporting the environment. You never know, we might even get a better class of customer and not have the same problems.'

Our third perspective extends the CSR/sustainability issue by arguing that rather than being an add-on to existing practice, ethics needs to be at the heart of business. A firm can no longer simply 'appear' ethical—they have to actually practise it; otherwise, in the world of social media, they will be found out. For instance in *Who Cares Wins* David Jones claims 'Consumers now know more about companies and expect more of them' (2012: 4). He argues that in the world of social media greater attention is placed on companies' ethical standards. It is not enough to simply appear ethical—they need to be ethical.

Similarly, in *Screw Business As Usual* Sir Richard Branson (2011) argues that businesses should be a force for good in the world. He asks his reader to imagine the potential of all the businesses in the world coming together to do good for society. He claims the boundaries between doing good and doing well are becoming merged. He writes that if he had 'one message' to help the next generation of entrepreneurs it is 'doing good can help improve your prospects, your profits and your business; and it can change the world' (2011: 2). Profits and being ethical is a 'false dilemma', Branson claims; 'business as usual isn't working. In fact, it's "business as usual" that's wrecking our planet. Resources are being used up; the air, the sea, the land – are all heavily polluted. The poor are getting poorer'. While capitalism has 'created economic growth in the world and brought many wonderful benefits to people [it has] come at a cost that is not reflected on the balance sheet' (2011: 20–21). Being ethical and making money is therefore seen as not only possible, but as desirable.

Jones (2012) provides a number of fascinating examples, including Levi's Water<Less Jeans, Marks & Spencer's Plan A, and Dove's Campaign for Real Beauty, as examples which have sought to put ethics at the heart of their actions.

Visit the Online Resource Centre for more examples.

Employability skills: put ethical actions on your CV

Both David Jones (2012) and Richard Branson (2011) argue that ethical capitalism is on the rise and, in the future, numerous jobs and businesses will focus on this emerging area of business. Branson claims that successful entrepreneurs will combine ethics and business, and Jones claims that consumers are driving businesses to greater social responsibility. These views are backed up by the professional services company KPMG, who state 'Business leaders are increasingly realizing the need to integrate environmental and social issues within the business strategy' (KPMG, 2011: 1). As we saw in the KitKat example and the MBA oath, many feel that there is a need for businesses to be more aware of the ethical actions of the firm. Therefore, CSR and employability do not, necessarily, have to be seen in opposition.

As you develop your CV, having something that demonstrates a good understanding of CSR can be very useful. As Lord Michael Hastings (2008), Global Head of Citizenship and Diversity states: 'I think that any of the big FTSE 100 companies is utterly and expectantly approachable on CSR'. He goes on to say that when putting together your CV highlight things that you have done that have done good, not as extras under CSR, but that are integral to your CV. In doing so you will demonstrate that you 'love making a difference'. Finally, find a job where you feel you can make a positive impact on the world. This will turn your job from being a 'duty' to 'an opportunity to make a powerful difference in the world' around you.

Review questions

1. Describe the key principles behind stakeholder capitalism.
2. Explain why stakeholder and ethical capitalism see shareholder capitalism as unsustainable, both for the planet *and* for the businesses concerned?
3. Analyse which position you consider stronger and why.

'Ethical within capitalism'

While CSR and ethical capitalism has brought with it a number of benefits, for many academics and campaigners it does not go far enough. They state that organizations' primary purpose should not be to make money, but to do social good. Often, this social good is to help particular communities and the environment, promote particular causes, or to create more humane work practices.

Real life case: Sound Bites

Sound Bites in Derby are a local, organic, and wholefoods shop that specialize in providing sustainable and ethical food. Not only are the products they sell seeking to be ethical—organic, Fairtrade, and ecological—but the way that they run the business is integral to what they do. They are a workers' cooperative, which means that the workers run the shop—managing it day to day and through a weekly co-op meeting. Instead of having a boss that tells them what to do, they take collective decisions. They aim to bring about 'positive social change', not only through the things that they sell, but also by being involved in boycotts and campaigns, being a hub for the community to promote social projects, and being a catalyst for increased support of socially and environmentally responsible producers and distributors.

As Ruth Strange, one of their founders, states: 'We set up Sound Bites to make it easier for people shopping in Derby to support projects they could believe in, rather than increasing the wealth of the dominant and destructive food corporations.' (Author interview with Ruth Strange via email, April 2012.)

Source: Soundbites (2012).

Many of these alternative organizations are run on a not-for-profit basis, either reinvesting their surpluses back into the community or running things on a cost-only basis. Many are run as workers' cooperatives, which seek to make the workers central to the decision-making processes (Parker et al., 2007; Radical Routes, 2009).

Cooperatives have a long tradition. One of the most famous are the Rochdale Pioneers, a group of textile and other workers who came together to pool their resources in order to buy food and other household items. They were responding to the high prices that the mill owners charged and came together with a common goal of good service over profit. Their aims (BBC Manchester, 2010) were to have:

- open membership
- democratic control
- dividend on purchase
- limited interest on capital
- political and religious neutrality
- cash trading
- promotion of education
- sell pure, unadulterated goods.

The Rochdale Pioneers were working-class people who came together to offer self-help and tackle their own problems (rather than receiving handouts from middle-class philanthropists). They offered an alternative model of production and exchange.

Real life case: UK building societies

It is interesting to note that in the UK much of the financial services were run through mutual organizations called building societies and friendly societies. These were local, mutual societies where people would club together, often meeting in pubs, to buy their own houses. They would be run in the interests of their members, offering fairly cheap mortgages and reasonable savings rates. They were also very cautious with their lending. In the 1980s the UK Conservative government relaxed the laws to allow them to be converted into banks. Many did, as members would receive a pay-out of thousands of pounds, particularly as 'carpetbaggers' (opportunists) joined them for as little as £100. Some of those that demutualized—Northern Rock, Bradford & Bingley, Halifax, Bank of Scotland (HBOs), and Alliance & Leicester—have struggled in the financial crisis.

Sources: Newcastle Building Society (2012); Nationwide Building Society (2012); Bowers (2008); BBC News (1999); Pollock (2008); Klimeckî and Willmott (2009).

While it is impossible to predict what would have happened, many have argued that had the building societies stayed mutual then they would have had the cash reserves and safer lending policies to have weathered, or not even have landed in, the credit crisis of 2008. Have customers sacrificed long-term security for short-term profit?

'Ethical within capitalism' organizations are not only driven by social purpose, but they are also run in a different way. Often, one of their key principles is to be run in a non-hierarchical way in which power is distributed throughout the organization and decisions are based upon consensus rather than through orders from the leader. Consensus-based decision-making is not based on voting, but in reaching a genuine, informed agreement which everyone supports or can live with. It aims to weave together the best ideas to allow the group to collectively formulate the most creative solutions (see pp. 405–407). *Seeds for Change* is one of the key trainers and proponents for consensus-based decision making. They describe its aims as:

- *Common goal*: that everyone wants to be a part of.
- *Commitment to reaching consensus*: by honestly listening to each other and being willing to shift your position to accommodate others.
- *Trust and openness*: everyone respects each other's opinions and right to express them.
- Sufficient time given for consensus making so that the right decisions are made.
- *Clear process*: making sure everyone understands the process.
- *Active participation*: create a situation where everyone can feel involved.

Source: Adapted from http://seedsforchange.org.uk/free/shortconsensus

In doing so, these alternative organizations provide a direct challenge to many of the 'mainstream' practices that we have covered in this book. It turns the pursuit of profit on its head by making the ambition for the organization to work for social good or to create employment opportunities where, in conventional terms, they would not exist.

Real life case: *The Take*

At the height of the Argentinian economic collapse in 2001 numerous factories were closed resulting in job losses and massive unemployment. Avi Lewis and Naomi Klein's film *The Take* (Lewis, 2004) tells the dramatic story of how one set of workers from the Forja car factory start occupying the factory in which they used to work and make it function again. Whereas the managers and accountants had abandoned it as a going concern, seeing it only for its scrap metal value, the workers started cleaning up the machines and turning it into a working plant again. They set up a workers cooperative, run on democratic lines, with the aim of giving them a livelihood (see also Magnani, 2009 and Lavaca Collective, 2007).

The film is fascinating in showing how motivating this struggle for workers control is and how shop-floor democracy works in practice (cf. Taylorism in Chapter 3), but also how challenging it is to run things in this way when it works against the interests of the banks and former owners who see the factory for its scrap metal value rather than as an opportunity to create jobs.

Visit the Online Resource Centre for a link to clips of the film.

'Ethical within capitalism' models do not, therefore, focus primarily on what is most effective or efficient in traditional management terms (i.e. profit), but, instead, direct their attention to what maximizes human freedom, growth, and personal autonomy. They therefore offer a different model not only of what organizations can be, but also of the type of society and culture that they would like to create. The focus on mutual aid, community, personal growth, expression, and empowerment is often seen by their members as working in direct opposition to the consumerism of much of Western society (Parker et al., 2007; Radical Routes, 2009).

While small in number in comparison with the power and influence of large corporations that tend to dominate society and business, they do cover a wide variety of areas from housing, food, transport, and even construction. Many work in education, often teaching people long-forgotten skills to help them become more independent in their lives and build up community bonds to become less reliant on large-scale corporations. In doing so they aim for more sustainable and ethical organizations, and, with it, a reform of society.

Visit the Online Resource Centre for a list of alternative organizations.

'Ethical within capitalism' assessed

Non-capitalist organizations often aim for highly progressive principles. Their emphasis on community, empowerment, personal growth, and social change offers a fascinating and exciting vision of how organizations and society could be. However, sometimes they fail to live up to their ideals, with their own prejudices and blind-spots. For instance, Sherryl Kleinman (1996) describes a holistic health centre which, while run on alternative grounds, allegedly ends up reproducing the same practices of exclusion, power, and gendered relations that many accuse mainstream organizations of doing. This shows the challenges of really acting in an alternative way—at least within the existing capitalist society.

Often, things like organic, Fairtrade, or local and craft products are more expensive than their less ethical counterparts and sometimes only available for those who have more money.

'Ethical against capitalism'

Running case: Chance tries to balance ethics and profits

Chance considers Wilkinson's views—they make sense. The more he thinks about it the more he begins to see possibilities for environmental and social improvements within the hotel. Some, he comes to realize could actually save money, like better loft insulation, eco-lights, reduction of food waste, key-cards for rooms to switch off electric, and reducing the washing of towels. Others, though, might be more expensive, like trying to get the hotel to reach zero carbon emissions would require refitting the whole hotel, insulating the whole building, and buying all the food as organic. 'There's only so far I can go really . . .', Chance thinks to himself, 'it is a challenge balancing profits with ethics'.

While alternative business practices offer another, potentially more sustainable, humane and ethical approach to running organizations, for many campaigners and some academics, particularly those of the critical management and Marxist perspectives, it is the economic system itself that is destructive and needs overturning. They argue that the problem is not individual people or even organizations, but capitalism as an economic system. They believe we cannot simply try to reform the system—we need to overthrow it.

Inspired by critics of capitalism, such as Marx and Engels, and anarchists, such as Proudhon (2011), many thinkers from Marxist, the Frankfurt School, post-structuralist tradition, and the libertarian tradition have long argued that the capitalist system is fundamentally exploitative and destructive. As an economic system, with its relentless focus on growth and profit, they argue that it is destructive to the environment, to people, and to society. It breeds inequality, exploitation and social division, and, through this, makes everyone poorer. It makes humans compete with each other, rather than cooperate. According to this view, we are all trapped into an economic system that we have very little control over. It also holds us back from reaching our true human creative potential. Capitalism also perpetuates inequality by drawing wealth towards the rich and away from the poor.

Real life case: 'Occupy' and other protest movements

The 'Occupy' movement has sought to expose not only the vast profit and greed of the 'city', but the way that these institutions are intertwined to perpetuate the existing order. Proponents of this movement argue that the current economic system takes power, control, and money away from local communities and places it in the hands of large corporations, leaving individuals and communities feeling largely powerless.

They argue for alternative economic systems, like local money spendable only in local communities so that they can be allowed to flourish; local businesses rather than large-scale corporations; and economic activities to support human need, rather than the other way round (OccupyLondon, 2012; How to Occupy, 2012).

Central to their activity is to introduce more democratic and accountable ways of acting. They therefore operate without leaders, but work in a collective way focusing on collective decision making and empowering members to take ownership and control where they are. While they might not be overthrowing capitalism, they do offer a powerful image of an alternative (McDonald, 2006).

Such theorists argue that it is impossible, even when one sets out with good intentions, to act in a fully ethical manner (such as 'ethical within capitalism' models) because they exist within the current economic system—they do not challenge capitalism as a system and therefore face the dangers of being dragged back in. Business ethics, it is therefore suggested, acts as little more than a mask, deflecting attention away from what should be the actual target of capitalism as an economic system itself. It allows businesses to carry on in their usual practices without changing their underlying structure from a for-profit structure.

For instance, making more environmentally sustainable products might be commendable in that they are more sustainable and ethical; however, it could be argued that this does not overcome the deeper problem of consumerism and the pursuit of profit by capitalist firms. Capitalism as an economic system still drives firms to need to produce and sell more products, expand their sales, and have an economy based on increased growth. Anti-capitalists argue that capitalism as an economic system is therefore a driver towards economic growth rather than human need, and more sustainable products do not really solve the problem. In other words, it is not just making products in a more sustainable way, but really our desire (created by marketing) for more products that we do not really need that is the problem (McDonald, 2006; Parker, Fournier and Reedy, 2007; Radical Routes 2009).

Such views, while very interesting, require a fundamental overthrowing of the capitalist system which, except for the most optimistic of campaigners, does not seem that likely in the short-term (although the 'Arab Spring' of 2011 shows how quickly things can change). It does not remove the ethical, social, and environmental challenges that exist today and therefore the need to still consider business ethics.

Chapter summary and reflections for the future

It is easy to be cynical about the ethical and sustainable credentials of businesses, but, as we have seen, it is an area that has become increasingly high on the media, consumer, and business agenda. While shareholder capitalism is a powerful force, stakeholder theory—particularly through CSR and sustainability—is now a mainstream force within business and society as most people expect businesses, at least to some extent, to hold a certain level of responsibility.

Others, though, would like businesses to go further, arguing that the pace of change is too slow and that businesses largely act in order to protect their own interests. Ethical capitalism might present a growth area for the economy as increasing attention is placed on local, sustainable, and ethical products. However, these are often quite expensive and out of reach of poorer consumers.

Therefore, substantial questions remain about the nature of capitalism and whether businesses should be governed for the interests of the shareholders, consumers, and society as a whole. These are personal, as well as societal issues, and worthy of strong debate.

Review questions

1. Describe some of the key objections to capitalism that the 'ethical within' and 'ethical against' capitalism models hold.

2. Analyse the different responses these two positions make to their critique of capitalism.

Analyse

3. What are your views on these positions? Is an alternative to capitalism possible and desirable?

Further reading

Boje D.M. 1998. Nike, Greek goddess of victory or cruelty? Women's stories of Asian factory life. *Journal of Organizational Change Management* 11(6): 461–480.

In this controversial article, David Boje describes some of the key criticisms made of a factory making Nike products, including physical and verbal abuse of the workers, long hours, and low pay. What is most fascinating is that it was originally withdrawn by the Journal—visit the Online Resource Centre for links to Boje's own explanation of what happened and for links to the original article.

Bakan, J. 2005. *The corporation: the pathological pursuit of profit and power.* **Constable and Robinson, London.**

In this book, which also lead to a popular documentary film, Bakan provides a challenging analysis of the legal foundations of the modern corporation, arguing that if judged against the World Health Organization's mental health criteria the corporation is a psychopath. This readable and interesting book provides some excellent case studies, as well as good theoretical contributions.

Ngai, P. 2004. Women workers and precarious employment in Shenzhen Special Economic Zone, China. *Gender and Development* 12(2): 29–36

This interesting article describes the difficult working conditions of garment workers in China. While a little dated, recent case studies have shown these conditions continue in many developing countries.

Fisher, C., and Lovell, A. 2009. *Business ethics and values: individual, corporate and international perspectives.* **Prentice Hall, Harlow.**

This business ethics textbook provides an excellent introduction to many of the key business ethics theories with a number of interesting case studies.

Bibliography

Ackrill, M., and Hannah, L. 2001. *Barclays: The Business of Banking, 1690–1996.* Cambridge University Press: Cambridge.

Alvesson, M., and Willmott, H. 1992. *Making Sense of Management.* Sage: London.

Aras, G., and Crowther, D. (2012) *Governance and social responsibility: international perspectives.* Palgrave: London

Bakan, J. 2005. *The corporation: the pathological pursuit of profit and power.* Constable and Robinson: London.

Banerjee, S. 2008. Corporate social responsibility: The good, the bad and the ugly. *Critical Sociology,* 34(1), pp. 51–79.

BBC Manchester. 2010. How Rochdale Pioneers changed commerce forever. Available at: http://news.bbc.co.uk/local/manchester/hi/people_and_places/history/newsid_8838000/8838778.stm (last accessed 24 November 2012).

BBC News. 1999. Building Society offers £1000 windfall. Available at: http://news.bbc.co.uk/1/hi/business/your_money/523936.stm (last accessed 24 November 2012).

BBC News. 2010. Nocton super dairy cow numbers to be cut. Available at: http://www.bbc.co.uk/news/uk-england-lincolnshire-11747601 (last accessed 11 July 2012).

BBC News. 2011a. Bosses pay too high? The move to Cuba? BBC Radio 4, Today. 22 November 2011. Available at: http://news.bbc.co.uk/today/hi/today/newsid_9645000/9645038.stm.

BBC News. 2011b. Southern Cross set to shut down and stop running homes. Available at: http://www.bbc.co.uk/news/business-14102750 (last accessed 24 November 2012).

BBC News. 2012. Allen Stanford jailed for 110 years for $7bn Ponzi. Available at: http://www.bbc.co.uk/news/world-us-canada-18450893 (last accessed 17 July 2012).

BBC Radio. 2011. Desert Island Discs. *Martin Sorrell.* BBC Radio 4. Available at: http://www.bbc.co.uk/radio/player/b017vjlw (last accessed 28 November 2012).

BBC Television. 2011a. Newsnight. BBC 2, 13 June 2011.

BBC Television. 2011. When Bankers Were Good. BBC 2. 23 November 2011.

Bowen, H. 1953. *Social responsibilities of the businessman.* Harper & Row: New York.

Bowers, S. 2008. Bradford & Bingley: Cast of characters, from demutualisation to nationalisation. *The Guardian.* Available at: http://www.guardian.co.uk/business/2008/sep/30/bradfordbingley.banking?INTCMP=SRCH (last accessed 24 November 2012).

Branson, R. 2011. *Screw business as usual.* Virgin Books: London.

Capaldi, N. 2005. Corporate social responsibility and the bottom line. *International Journal of Social Economics* 32(5): 408–423.

Carlyle, E. 2012. Forbes. Meet the Eight Forbes 400 Billionaires Who Just Signed the Giving Pledge. Available at: http://www.forbes.com/sites/erincarlyle/2012/09/18/forbes-400-billionaires-whove-signed-the-giving-pledge/ (last accessed 24 November 2012).

Carroll, A. 1991. The pyramid of corporate social responsibility: Toward the moral management of organizational stakeholders. *Business Horizons* 34: 39–48.

Carroll, A. 1999. Corporate social responsibility: evolution of a definitional construct. *Business Society* 38: 268–295.

CBS News. 2012. Xbox 360 workers reportedly threaten mass suicide. Available at: http://www.cbsnews.com/8301-205_162-57357444/xbox-360-workers-reportedly-threaten-mass-suicide/ (last accessed 11 July 2012).

Committee Encouraging Corporate Philanthropy. 2012. Giving In Numbers. New York. Available at: http://www.corporatephilanthropy.org/pdfs/giving_in_numbers/GIN2012_finalweb.pdf (last accessed 28 November 2012).

Covey, S. 2004. *The 7 habits of highly effective people.* Simon and Schuster: London.

Currie, G., Knights, D., and Starkey, K. 2010. Introduction: A Post-crisis Critical Reflection on Business Schools. *British Journal of Management* 21(s1): s1–s5.

The Daily Mail. 2010. Battery farm for cows: 8,000 animals to be housed in milk factory. Available at: http://www.dailymail.co.uk/news/article-1254467/Battery-farm-cows-8-000-animals-housed-milk-factory.html (last accessed 11 July 2012).

The Daily Mail. 2011. You are NOT allowed to commit suicide: workers in Chinese iPad factories forced to sign pledges. Available at: http://www.dailymail.co.uk/news/article-1382396/Workers-Chinese-Apple-factories-forced-sign-pledges-commit-suicide.html (last accessed 11 July 2012).

The Daily Telegraph. 2011. Plans for 'mega dairy' scrapped amid fears for the environment. Available at: http://www.telegraph.co.uk/earth/earthnews/8328927/Plans-for-mega-dairy-scrapped-amid-fears-for-the-environment.html (last accessed 11 July 2012).

Davis, K. 1973. The case for and against business assumption of social responsibilities. *Academy of Management Journal* 16(2): 312–322.

Deakin, S. 2003. After Enron: An Age of Enlightenment? *Organisation,* 10, 583–587.

Dellheim C (1987) The creation of a company culture: Cadburys, 1861–1931. *The American Historical Review* 92(1): 13–44.

The Economist. 2008. Con of the century. Available at: http://www.economist.com/node/12818310 (last accessed 17 July 2012).

Ethical Trading Initiative. 2012. About ETI. Available at: http://www.ethicaltrade.org/about-eti (last accessed 24 November 2012).

Fisher, C., and Lovell, A. 2009. *Business ethics and values: individual, corporate and international perspectives.* Prentice Hall: Harlow.

Fisher, C., and Lovell, A. 2010. *Business ethics and values: individual, corporate and international perspectives.* Pearson Education Limited: London.

Fisher, C., Lovell, A., and Valero-Silva, N. 2013. *Business Ethics and Values,* 4th edn. Pearson: Financial Times.

Fishfight. 2012. Available at: http://www.fishfight.net (last accessed 23 November 2012).

Ford Foundation. 2012. History. Available at: http://www.fordfoundation. org/about-us/history (last accessed 23 November 2012).

Freeman, E., and Liedtka, J. 1991. Corporate social responsibility: a critical approach, *Business Horizons* 34(4): 92–98.

Friedman, M. 1970. The social responsibility of business is to increase its profits. *New York Times Magazine* (13 September 1970).

Geyelin, M. 1999. How a Memo Written 26 Years Ago Is Costing General Motors Dearly. *Wall Street Journal*. Available at: http://online.wsj.com/ article/SB9385366607816889.html (last accessed 28 November 2012).

Gibney, A. 2005. *Enron: The Smartest Guys in the Room*. Jigsaw Productions: New York.

Gilligan, C. 1982. *In a Different Voice: Psychological Theory and Women's Development*. Harvard University Press: Cambridge, MA.

The Giving Pledge. 2012. Available at: http://givingpledge.org/ (last accessed 24 November 2012).

Greenpeace. 2010. Ask Nestlé CEO to stop buying palm oil from destroyed rainforest. Available at: http://www.youtube.com/ watch?v=1BCA8dQfGi0 (last accessed 28 November 2012).

Greenpeace. 2012. Available at: http://www.greenpeace.org.uk/blog/ oceans/and-then-there-were-none-john-west-changes-its-tuna-20110726 (last accessed 23 November 2012).

Greenwald, R. 2005. Wal*Mart: The High Cost of Low Price. Brave New Films: Culver City.

Greenwell, J. 2011. *Responding to the Twin Challenges of Global Motor Industry – Sustainability and Gridlock*. Lecture at Nottingham Trent University: Nottingham, UK.

The Guardian. 2011. Apple's Chinese workers treated 'inhumanely, like machines'. Available at: http://www.guardian.co.uk/technology/2011/ apr/30/apple-chinese-workers-treated-inhumanely (last accessed 11 July 2012).

The Guardian. 2012. BP adds $847m to Deepwater Horizon costs. Available at: http://www.guardian.co.uk/business/2012/jul/31/deepwater-horizon-bp-847m-dollars (last accessed 24 November 2012).

Hardin, G. 1968. The tragedy of the commons. *Science* 162(3859): 1243–1248.

Hastings, M. 2008. Everyone's taking about Corporate Social Responsibility. YouTube. Available at: http://www.youtube.com/ watch?v=TNKn93VViUc (last accessed 24 November 2012).

Hawkshaw, R., Hawkshaw, S., and Sumaila, U.R. 2012. The Tragedy of the 'Tragedy of the Commons': Why Coining Too Good a Phrase Can Be Dangerous. *Sustainability* 4(11): 3141–3150.

Hickman, M. 2009. Have a break—have an ethical Kit Kat. *The Independent*. 2009. Available at: http://www.independent.co.uk/life-style/food-and-drink/news/have-a-breakndash-have-an-ethical-kit-kat-1835608.html (last accessed 11 July 2012).

High Pay Commission. 2011. *Cheques with Balances: Why Tackling High Pay is in the National Interest*. Final Report of the High Pay Commission.

How to Occupy 2012. A quick guide to revolution. Available at: http:// howtocamp.takethesquare.net/2012/09/05/quick-guide-for-a-revolution-multi-language/ (last accessed 24 November 2012).

The Independent. 2012. Exposed: the reality behind London's 'ethical' Olympics. Available at: http://www.independent.co.uk/news/world/ asia/exposed-the-reality-behind-londons-ethical-olympics-7644013. html (last accessed 11 July 2012).

John West. 2012. Available at: http://www.john-west.co.uk/sustainability (last accessed 23 November 2012).

Jones, D. 2012. *Who cares wins: Why good business is better business*. FT Publishing: London.

Kelly Global Workforce Index. 2012. The Modern Workforce: Acquisition and retention in the war for talent. Available at: http://www.kellyocg. com/uploadedFiles/Content/Knowledge/Kelly_Global_Workforce_ Index_Content/Acquisition%20and%20Retention%20in%20the%20 War%20for%20Talent%20Report.pdf.

Kleinman, S. 1996. *Opposing Ambitions: Gender and Identity in an Alternative Organization*. University of Chicago Press: Chicago.

Klimecki, R., and Willmott, H. 2009. From demutualisation to meltdown: a tale of two wannabe banks. *Critical Perspectives on International Business*. 5(1/2), pp.120–140.

KPMG. 2011. *Corporate Responsibility Survey 2011: Marching towards embracing sustainability development*. KPMG: India. Available at: http:// www.kpmg.com/IN/en/IssuesAndInsights/ArticlesPublications/ Documents/Corporate-Responsibilty-Survey-Report.pdf (last accessed 24 November 2012).

Lavaca Collective. 2007. *Sin Patrón: Stories from Argentina's Worker-Run Factories*. Haymarket Books: Chicago.

Lewis, A. 2004. The Take. Barna-Alper Productions: Canada.

MacIntyre, A. 1967. *A short history of ethics: a history of moral philosophy from the Homeric age to the twentieth century*. Routledge: London.

Magnani, E. 2009. *The Silent Change: Recovered Businesses in Argentina*. Editorial Teseo: Buenos Aires.

Marx, K. 1859/2012. *A Contribution to the Critique of Political Economy*. Forgotten Books: London.

McDonald, K. 2006. *Global Movements: Action and Culture*. Blackwell: Malden, MA.

Nationwide Building Society. 2012. Membership matters. Available at: http://www.newcastle.co.uk/help/mutuality.aspx (last accessed 24 November 2012).

Neate, R. 2012. RBS boss Stephen Hester waives bonus: reaction. *The Guardian*. 30 January 2012. Available at: http://www.guardian.co.uk/ business/2012/jan/30/rbs-stephen-hester-bonus-reaction (last accessed 26 November 2012).

Nelson, D. 2012. Cambodian workers on £10 a week making Olympics 'fanwear'. *The Daily Telegraph*. Available at: http://www.telegraph.co.uk/ sport/olympics/news/9399363/Cambodian-workers-on-10-a-week-making-Olympics-fanwear.html (last accessed 24 November 2012).

Nestlé. 2012. Response to author query from Nestlé Customer Services. Enquiry 003072121A, March 2012.

Newcastle Building Society. 2012. Mutuality. Available at: http://www. newcastle.co.uk/help/mutuality.aspx (last accessed 24 November 2012).

OccupyLondon. 2012. Initial Statement. Available at: http://occupylondon. org.uk/about/statements/initial-statement (last accessed 24 November 2012).

Packard Foundation. 2012. Our history. Available at: http://www.packard.org/ about-the-foundation/our-history/ (last accessed 24 November 2012).

Parker, M., Fournier, V., and Reedy, P. 2007. *The Dictionary of Alternatives*. Zed Books: London.

Partington, A. 1998. *The Oxford Dictionary of Quotations*. Oxford University Press: Oxford.

Pollack, A. 1999. $4.9 Billion Jury Verdict In G.M. Fuel Tank Case. *The New York Times*. Available at: http://www.nytimes.com/1999/07/10/us/ 4.9-billion-jury-verdict-in-gm-fuel-tank-case.html (last accessed 28 November 2012).

Pollock, I. 2008. Not such a good idea after all? BBC News. Available at: http://news.bbc.co.uk/1/hi/business/7641925.stm (last accessed 24 November 2012).

Proudhon, P. 2011. *Property is Theft!: A Pierre-Joseph Proudhon Reader*. AK Press: London.

Radical Routes. 2009. Aims and Principles. Available at: http://www. radicalroutes.org.uk/aims-and-principles.html (last accessed 24 November 2012).

Robinson, N. 2012. *Live From Downing Street: The Inside Story of Politics, Power and the Media*. Bantam Press: London.

Rushe, D. 2012. Allen Stanford sentenced to 110 years in jail for $7bn investment fraud. *The Guardian*. Available at: http://www.guardian.co.uk/ world/2012/jun/14/allenstanford-110-years-jail (last accessed 17 July 2012).

Schäfer, D., Goff. S., and Parker, G. 2012. Barclays paid chief's £5.75m tax bill. *Financial Times*. Available at: http://www.ft.com/cms/s/0/e1115196-69d8-11e1-8996-00144feabdc0.html (last accessed 26th November 2012).

Smith, A. 1759/1976. *The Theory of Moral Sentiments*. Clarendon Press: Oxford.

Smith, A. 1776/2012. *The Wealth of Nations*. Wordsworth Editions Ltd: Ware.

Snell, J. 2011. The Guardian. Why a critic of institutional care is taking over from Southern Cross. *The Guardian*. Available at: http://www.guardian. co.uk/society/2011/oct/19/interview-anne-williams-hc-one?newsfeed=true (last accessed 24 November 2012).

Soundbites. 2012. Soundbites Home. Available at: http://www. soundbitesderby.org.uk/. (last accessed 27 November 2012).

Stern, N. 2006. *Stern Review on the Economics of Climate Change*. Her Majesty's Treasury: London.

Strange, R. 2012. Author interview via email. 2 April 2012.

Sunderland, R. 2008. Were our mutual friends a safer bet? *The Guardian*. Available at: http://www.guardian.co.uk/business/2008/jun/08/banking. demutualisation, (last accessed 24 November 2012).

Tabacek, K. 2010. Nestle stars in smear campaign over Indonesian palm oil. *The Guardian*. Available at: http://www.guardian.co.uk/sustainable-business/nestleindonesian-palm-oil (last accessed 11 July 2012).

Teather, D. 2009. Bernard Madoff receives maximum 150 year sentence. *The Guardian*. 2009. Available at: http://www.guardian.co.uk/business/ 2009/jun/29/bernard-madoff-sentence (last accessed 17 July 2012).

TUC. 2012. Fair Games? Human Rights of workers in Olympic 2012 Supplier Factories. Available at: http://www.tuc.org.uk/tucfiles/291.pdf

Tumin, M. 1964. Business as a social system. *Behavioral Science* 9(2): 120–130.

Walmart. 2011. *2011 Annual report*. Available at: http://www.walmartstores. com/sites/annualreport/2011/letter.aspx (last accessed 12 July 2012).

Walmart. 2012a. *Beyond 50 Years: Building a Sustainable Future*. Walmart Stores Ltd: Bentonville, Arkansas.

Walmart. 2012b. Bangladesh. Available at: http://corporate.walmart.com/ global-responsibility/womens-economic-empowerment/bangladesh-anju-ara (last accessed 25 November 2012).

Walmart. 2012c. India. Available at: http://corporate.walmart.com/global-responsibility/womens-economic-empowerment/india-amandeep-kaur (last accessed 25 November 2012).

Webb, J. 2007. Seduced or sceptical consumers? Organised action and the case of Fair Trade coffee. *Sociological Research Online* 12(3), p. 5.

Wesseling, C., Ahlbom, A., Antich, D., Rodriguez, A., and Castro, R. 1996. Cancer in Banana Plantation workers in Costa Rica. *International Journal of Epidemiology* 25(6): 1125–1131.

Wilkinson, R., and Pickett, K. 2010. *The Spirit Level: why equality is better for everyone*. Allen Lane, Penguin: London.

Wilson, J., and Hunter, D. 2010. Research exceptionalism. *The American Journal of Bioethics* 10(8): 45–54.

World Commission on Environment and Development (WCED). 1987. *Our Common Future*. Oxford University Press: Oxford.

18

Conclusion
Fond farewells

Chapter overview and learning outcomes

By the end of this chapter you should be able to:

- explain the importance of connecting the theories together

- describe some of the changes that have occurred in organizations over the last forty years

- analyse why it is important to develop your lifelong learning skills.

Chapter overview

This chapter draws together some of the key themes of the book. Organizational behaviour (OB) should not be seen as a series of discrete topics, but as interlinked themes. Therefore, as we will see, in order to really understand it, and to write strong essays or perform well in exams, it is important to understand how the themes connect together.

This chapter also asks you to consider how organizations could change in the future. As we will see, the last forty years have seen considerable change in the nature of organizations and jobs, and the next forty years are therefore equally unpredictable. With the developments in technology, the rise of countries like China and India, and the emerging green economy, the nature of jobs is likely to change dramatically, with many occupations that will be common in the future not even existing in the present.

Pulling things together

'It is 6 am and you are listening to Smooth FM', Meg Mortimer's radio blurts out in the same way as it has every morning for the last forty years. 'The headlines today . . .', the presenter drones on in his usual way, with Meg playing little attention. For her, today there is only one headline . . . it is her last day at work.

It feels surreal knowing that this routine, which she has come to know so well, is going to be her last: getting up at 6 am and having breakfast—two slices of toast; shower at 6:20 am; walking the dog at 6:40 am; driving to work at 7 am (she'll be pleased not to have to battle through the traffic and that queue on London Road again); in the cubbyhole-cum-office at 7.45 am reading her emails, seeing the reception girls, and catching up with the gossip with the cleaners; beginning her daily inspection at 9 am; looking at the daily statistics for room bookings at 10 am; attending the daily senior management meeting at 10.30 am; attending the restaurant meeting at 11.30 am; and having lunch at 12:30 am. Then, in the afternoons, tackling emergencies, dealing with maintenance issues, having meetings with staff to solve their problems, and—the bit that she really likes—listening to them as people. Today, though, will be different. Today she is having her leaving party.

Mortimer begins to reflect on the last year. It has been a year of changes, what with the new structure, all the new procedures, and the culture that the Second-Chance Consortium has tried to bring in.

She is surprised at how successful they have been. Occupancy rates are up, cleaning times are down, the restaurant has gone from strength to strength, and the new staff are certainly professional and hard-working. Yet, some of the magic, of the things that she really used to love about the hotel, seems to have been lost. Yes, they are more effective and efficient, more business-like in their approach, and have clearly-stated objectives, but it is somehow different.

With all these changes she wonders whether Junction Hotel, the one that she really loves, is still there.

Sometimes work and organizational life is presented as a dreary, rational place—devoid of emotions or feelings—where people only go to work to be paid, longing for the weekend, and, eventually, retirement. Yet, as we have seen repeatedly throughout this book, organizational life is far more complex that it appears. The informal, or what is sometimes referred to as the hidden organization, can have dramatic repercussions on organizational practice.

The challenges of managing people and organizations

Running case: Simon Chance reflects on a year in charge of Junction Hotel

Today is also a strange day for Simon Chance as it has been a year since he officially began running Junction Hotel. 'How time flies', he thinks. It only seemed yesterday that he sat in this office and began what has proved to be one of his hardest, but also most interesting, years in management. Chance looks around his office again. 'Those wooden panels are still loose', he thinks to himself, 'it is about time that I got them fixed.'

This last year has been hard—harder than he had ever imagined. It began with such optimism, a real sense of adventure. They had made all these plans, Weaver's A3s, new work processes, business reports, and targets for every departments. They had worked—well, if he was honest, they had sort of worked. The new systems for cleaning had certainly been successful. A few people had left, but you don't make an omelette without breaking eggs, as his mother used to say. Yet, so much of what they had tried to do had seemed so much harder than they had thought it would be. When he and Weaver had worked on their plans prior to buying the hotel, he had thought there would be a few quick fixes by bringing in a few tools he had used elsewhere and off they would go—the hotel would become profitable again; another dose of the Second-Chance magic.

Yet, in practice, it all seemed so much harder. Things just did not fit the masterplan. Indeed, things rarely seemed to go to plan. Numerous issues that disrupted things kept popping up that he and Weaver had not even considered. People did not react how they expected, systems that had worked so well elsewhere seemed to fail here, and the usual ways they had used to get people motivated before seemed to stutter at Junction Hotel.

At first, he had got really frustrated with this and blamed the staff for not wanting to change. But, gradually, his respect for them began to grow. They cared about the hotel, he realized, not just their jobs. They just had different values and objectives than his.

At the heart of this was Meg Mortimer. At first, Chance had thought Mortimer was a silly old fool with all her talk that Junction Hotel was special. However, now, a year on, he really feels that he is beginning to understand what she meant. He has grown to love the place. Yes, it is a business, but he feels increasingly that it is more than that—that it has something special.

Ever since Fredrick Taylor and Henri Fayol, the belief that managers do the planning and create systems, and the workers just follow orders, has persisted. This has given the impression that organizational problems are fairly easy to solve—implement a few simple procedures, steps, or theories, and all the organizational problems will be solved. However, as we have seen throughout this book, in practice it can be far harder to do this.

We have sought to stress how complicated and multifaceted management and working in organizations really is. To even get the seemingly simplest change through can involve working with numerous personalities with their own agendas, groups with their established hierarchies and potential groupthink, working through political agendas, and within (or sometimes even against) the established organizational culture. These are the sorts of realities that people working in organizations face on a daily basis. Therefore, as we have seen, it is the informal, or hidden, organization that often largely shapes the decisions and actions that people make within organizations.

To really understand what goes on within organizations and, importantly, to be able to implement change you need to be able to appreciate the interconnected nature of OB. For instance you cannot hope to understand motivation separately from individuals and personality, culture or responses to leadership. OB is a highly connected discipline.

Study skills: the importance of connecting the themes together

It is tempting when completing an essay or exam question to just look at the topics closely associated with that particular question and only read the chapter concerned. However, in practice, and, indeed, to really understand the theory, it is important to understand how each aspect of organizational behaviour (OB) connects to other aspects. Strong answers show an awareness of the connection between themes. Intelligent management understands the connections between one intervention and other aspects of the organization.

It is therefore essential to appreciate the connections between the themes. By showing these connections you are able to present a stronger level of understanding of the particular topic as it demonstrates an awareness of how the individual theory is impacted by the wider field of OB and the deeper issues that theorists are seeking to explore. Therefore, when you come to write an essay or study for an exam, do not simply focus on one topic alone, but try to make connections back to other themes.

Review questions

1. Explain why it is important to link the key themes together.
2. Analyse the significance of the informal organization.

The changing nature of organizational behaviour

Running case: Meg's leaving do

As Meg walks nervously into the conference room she is greeted by a massive round of applause from Junction Hotel staff—past and present. 'Grab yourself a drink', Simon Chance declares in a jovial way, greeting his adversary and friend. 'I want you to enjoy today.' It seems odd, but in many ways comforting to Mortimer, that through all their disagreements, at least Chance is nice to her as a person—their disagreements are largely professional rather than personal.

As she picks up a glass of Merlot she looks around the room. 'I'm going to miss you lot', she thinks. Sam from reception comes up to her and they exchange pleasantries for a while. 'I bet you can't wait to retire,' Sam beams, 'particularly putting up with him', she says looking in the direction of Weaver. Weaver had certainly been difficult, or, in his management speak, 'a challenge', with all his systems and efficiency practices. Yet, she must concede the hotel is now running better that it had ever done. However, in some areas it has gone too far. The changes to the fitness centre are certainly a step too far. If Weaver had had his way then the whole hotel would have been running on a great big flow-chart.

Then there was Chance himself. Meg has grown to respect him over the year. They did not see eye to eye on a lot of things and it had felt as though he was taking her hotel away from her. But, she has to admit it: ultimately, the guy seems to care about what goes on here. The way he tried to change the culture of Junction Hotel and get them working in teams was different to how she would have done it, but at least it showed some awareness of the importance of people.

'I don't know how I feel about retiring', Meg says more to herself than in response to Sam. 'I thought I would. I've been dreaming, longing for this day for a while. But now it's here I've come to realize that I like it here. I'm good at what I do, I know how everything works here, and I feel respected. Does that sound odd?', she said noticing Sam. 'Now I'm retired, who am I?' Sam smiles in a puzzled, but sympathetic, way. Suddenly, she notices Simon Chance standing at the podium.

'Hello . . . hello everyone—if I could have your attention for only a few minutes.' A couple of people sigh, but in a friendly way. 'Today', begins Chance, 'we are celebrating two major events: our long-serving and esteemed colleague Meg's retirement and the first anniversary of the Second-Chance Consortium buying Junction Hotel. Now, we have been through a lot, all of us together, over the last year and I wanted just to say a few words about what we have achieved, as well as how important Meg has been to this.

'When I walked into Junction Hotel for the first time just over a year ago I thought that we were buying just another hotel. How wrong I was.' Some of the audience laugh. 'You are unique and I mean that in a good way. We have been though a challenging journey over the last year and I am sure that we have all learned a lot. I thought I would share with you today a few things I have learned.

'Things have been tough and some tough decisions have been made. I know that they have not always been popular, but I think time will prove them to be correct.

'However, I have learned never to judge things by appearances. While this hotel might look ordinary, there are some extraordinary and talented people here. I have learned that what works well in other places will not necessarily work well here. I really hope that we can all grow together. Junction Hotel is a special place.

'Finally, I want to say a few words about Meg. As many of you will know, Meg began her life here as a cleaner and has worked her way up to the top of her profession. It is this attitude of hard work, customer care, and dedication to her staff that has made her the model professional and I, for one, will be sad to see her go. Although we have not always seen eye to eye on everything, I know that she is Junction Hotel through and through and you can never doubt her dedication to the cause.

'So from all of us to you I would like to give you this . . .' At this point Chance hands over an enormous leaving card, a big bunch of flowers, a cheque, and, finally, a mug with a picture of Junction Hotel on the front' . . . for your world cruise, so you can never forget us.' 'And the mugs that work here!', Effingham pipes up to much laughter.

Then Meg begins to speak. She says how proud she had been to work at Junction Hotel and how much it has meant to spend so much of her time there. She is leaving with a heavy heart and thanks them for the great support she has received. 'Lots of things have changed over the last forty years', she says. 'Who would have thought that we would now have all this technology and bookings coming from all over the world.' Then, with a subtle passing shot directed at Chance, Meg ends by saying 'Yet, some things never change— the basics, listening to people, and good service—remember, keep the Junction Hotel spirit alive'. With that Mortimer sits down to her second round of rapturous applause of the day.

In many senses the nature of work has changed dramatically over the last forty years. Western economies have moved from manufacturing to a predominately service-led industry, creating jobs and numerous firms that would have been unthinkable in the 1960s and 1970s. The rising importance of information technology is an obvious one. The mobile phone in your pocket is more powerful than many of the computers that took up whole floors in offices only a few decades ago, and your laptop can store and process more information than the computers that first sent man into space. But there have been numerous social changes as well.

The number of young people going to university has risen dramatically throughout the world. For instance, in the UK it has increased from around 400,000 in the 1960s to over 2,000,000 today (Greenaway and Haynes, 2003; Elias and Pucell, 2004). The types of jobs have also shifted as the 'knowledge economy' has taken off. However, with it, the hours that people work has increased, particularly, with the advent of mobile phones, the feeling that you never really leave the office.

Our relationship with our jobs and employers has also altered significantly. Our grandparents' or great-grandparents' generation often went into their first job thinking that they would have a job for life and many stayed with the same employer throughout their entire career—such an occurrence is almost unthinkable in today's world. For some so-called 'portfolio workers' (Handy, 1984), even having one employer is not the case, as they work for two or three different employers at the same time, juggling different jobs (Van Buren, 2003).

There have certainly been some significant social advancements over the last forty years. The number of women in the workplace has dramatically increased and there has been some development in the number of women in senior positions. However, as we have seen, there is still a long way to go on this issue, as women and people from minority groups face significant hurdles on their way to the top of organizations.

This changing nature of the workforce has created the need for workplaces to be more flexible in their hours, as there is increasing recognition of the challenges that women *and* men face juggling family commitments alongside their work responsibilities. Work–life balance is, consequently, becoming a more significant issue as many workers have caring responsibilities (not only with young children, but, as we face an ageing population, elderly parents).

For all these changes, some of the optimism that existed in the 1960s, 1970s, and 1980s seems to have waned. Women and ethnic minorities still represent a relatively small minority on the boards of companies, social equality still seems a distant aspiration, and social mobility is still largely static (Hope, 2012; Thomson and Lloyd, 2011).

Real life case: technology—the promise that was never delivered

As we have seen throughout this book, over the last 100, and particularly the last 40 years the rate of technological progress has been enormous as production processes have become more efficient and effective. One significant change has been the decline in numbers employed in agriculture from about 80% in 1900 to around 2–3% in 2000 (Jacques, 1996). This rate of change and the increasing efficiency elsewhere brought with it a concern that there would not be enough jobs to go round. So strong was this belief that in the 1970s and early 1980s, particularly with the birth of the 'micro-computer' (the forerunner to today's laptop and PC), many theorists were concerned about a workerless economy (Jenkins and Sherman, 1979; Rifkin, 1996) as production was taken over by robots (Levitan and ▶

Johnson, 1982). The concern, these theorists tried to explore, is how would people of the future (i.e. now) cope with how they are able to express their abilities through what they called 'serious leisure' (Stebbins, 1982).

Of course things have not turned out this way, with a long-hours culture continuing to be a major issue within the UK. Managers work an average 46 days a year longer than in their contract (Worrall and Cooper, 2012). Jobs that barely existed in the late 1970s have become commonplace and technology seems to make more jobs, rather than reducing them. Moreover, as a way of covering pensions and the increased debt that people face, we are also working longer—into our late 60s and, potentially, early 70s. Interestingly, as a response to the recent economic downturn the *New Economics Foundation* (Coote, 2010) has even proposed that the three-day week would be a viable alternative to distribute jobs more widely, and create a fairer and more balanced economy. It would require a reduction in income but, they argue, a substantial increase in quality of life. Only time will tell if such a vision will be realized.

Would you sacrifice a lower income for a higher quality of life and more leisure time? Do you think that it is possible to really predict the future?

The world of employment has, therefore, changed dramatically in the last few decades, bringing with it major changes in expectations, roles, and skills for graduates entering the workplace for the first time. The recent economic downturn has also played a significant role meaning that many graduates are entering employment taking on quite different jobs to those that they were expecting when they started university, as a survey from PricewaterhouseCoopers demonstrates.

Real life case: What do Millennium graduates want from work?

In late 2011, the accountancy and consultancy firm PricewaterhouseCoopers surveyed over 4,000 recent graduates throughout the world. Their results saw some interesting trends, particularly as a result of the recent global economic downturn. Their key findings were:

- loyalty-lite—a quarter expect to work for six or more employers over their lifetime, up from 10% in 2008
- 72% said that they have been forced to compromise in order to get a job
- 66% said they need international experience to further their career
- 18% say that they expect to stay in their current job for the long-term
- development and work–life balance are more important than financial reward
- graduates want a good work-life balance, but 28% thought it was worse than they had expected
- 41% would rather communicate electronically than face to face
- CSR has decreased as a factor that graduates look for when searching for a job.

Source: PricewaterhouseCoopers (2008).

 What do you think are going to be the most significant changes over the next forty years and why? How likely is it that your predictions will come true? What skills do you think you will need?

We can see here that the recent economic downturn has made it difficult for graduates to find the jobs they want, with many having to compromise and take jobs quite different in level and type than they originally intended, sacrificing location, pay, or even the level of job, just to get their first step on the career ladder. When the economy picks up such compromises might not been needed; however, there are more substantial long-term shifts also occurring. The increasing expectation to travel, to work for various employers, and also to be flexible in how they work, but needing a better work–life balance, are all trends that have been growing over the last few decades. The way that we treat work is changing.

Indeed, it is not just our attitudes to jobs that are changing, but the nature of the jobs themselves. As Vanessa Gough, Professional Development Manager for IBM, states 'most of the jobs that you will work in do not even exist yet'. She states that it is important to be open to the types of jobs that you will take in the future (author interview with Vanessa Gough via telephone, January 2012). This view is supported by Deborah Henretta, Group President, Asia & Global Specialty Channel, Procter & Gamble. She states:

> The workplace and workforce are going to change pretty dramatically as we look forward. The entire concept of work is going to become more flexible. The skills needed in the workforce are going to be less about IQ and a little bit more about EQ [**emotional quotient**], because if you think about it, a lot of IQ knowledge is going to be available at our fingertips through hand-held devices and the computer and technologies that we have at our disposal.
>
> Source: PricewaterhouseCoopers, 2011: 6

Emotional quotient (EQ), emotional intelligence The ability to assess the emotions of yourself and others.

So, with this dramatic change in the nature and types of jobs that are available, and the skills and attitudes that will be needed to meet them, what can you do now to get ahead and how can your study of OB help?

One of the most significant factors is that you will not simply be able to learn a set of skills that you can then just import into your work. As we argued in Chapter 10, we cannot only learn a set of skills and techniques from university to import into the workplace as the nature of employment is likely to undergo substantial change over the next few decades. Any skills that you might learn could well be obsolete within the next few years. Rather, what you can learn is the process of learning how to learn—of being able to respond to new situations, and analyse and think critically about them.

Employability skills: learning to learn—the importance of continuous learning

As we have seen, the types of jobs that you are likely to be involved in and do over the course of your career may not even exist yet. Therefore, you cannot assume that at university you will learn a series of skills or gain knowledge that you can take into your job. If that was the case then within a few years your skills would become obsolete and you would, therefore, become ineffective in your job. Consequently, rather than learning facts, knowledge, or set skills that you can then use directly in your job, what university can most effectively give you is the capacity to learn. Learning to learn, developing the skills to develop yourself, identifying and building on your strengths and overcoming your weaknesses will, therefore, be vital throughout your career.

Predicting future trends

Running case: Meg looks to the future

Meg's replacement, so she is told, is beginning on Monday. A business graduate who has had five years' experience in an international chain of hotels, has worked throughout the world, and has a 'really good track record' of successful management. 'All very well', thinks Meg, 'but he will not know the staff as well as I do or know what makes them tick'.

Reflecting on her time at Junction Hotel she wonders what the next forty years will be like for her replacement. Certainly, it is unlikely that he will be able to retire at 60 like she has been able to—will it be 67 or even 70 by then? She certainly hadn't even thought of the iPad, email, or Skype when she began working. 'What new technology will be in place when my replacement retires?', she thinks—'Something we cannot even imagine now'.

Meg has been working for Junction Hotel all her adult life. She wonders whether Steve, her replacement, will do that. 'Not likely', she thinks, 'young people don't seem to stick to firms like we did, but then there are far more opportunities than we ever had. Apparently, this guy, Steve, has just come back from working in America. America! Wow, I'd never have thought of working out there. Life for Steve will certainly be different than it has been for her', she thinks.

As we have already seen, it is notoriously difficult to predict the types of changes that will be happening over the next few years as things rarely work out as we expect. However, there do appear to be a few trends on the horizon that might become key areas for your future working life.

- Increased concerns over climate change have led to many calls to shift to a low-carbon economy (Stern, 2006). This may cause dramatic changes in the nature of the economy and with it the way that organizations need to operate (European Commission, 2011). It also has the potential to produce new jobs in areas that do not exist yet (BIS, 2012). Companies, such as Ford, are preparing themselves by developing products that can begin to respond to these challenges (Source: Author interview with Joe Greenwell, Ford in Britain, 2012). If carbon emissions continue as a factor it will not only be in manufacturing and design, but also in the way the workplace is focused that will need changing. The move to a low carbon economy will be a source of jobs and new ways of living that we are only beginning to imagine (Harvey, 2012).

- Another major change on the horizon is the rise of China and the potential decline of the West. As the recent 'credit crunch' has revealed, many commentators say that we are currently witnessing a dramatic realignment of the world's global economy from the West (USA, Europe) towards the East (China), and, with it, the shift in power and economic influence. This will bring with it new opportunities for Western companies as a new, emerging middle-class in China will be interested in the products and services that the West provides, but it will also bring new competition and the need for other ways of working to respond to a different type of client group and culture.

- Similar to the previous point, as we saw in Chapter 15, the world has been getting smaller and the issues of globalization and greater connectivity are becoming more important. This is reflected in the PricewaterhouseCoopers (2011) survey where 71% said that they felt they needed international experience to further their career.

- The changing nature of technology will also open up new possibilities for employment, as well as destroying existing ones. New technologies can now quickly emerge making predictions difficult to make.

However, many of the fundamentals remain. Central skills will include communication—listening to, understanding and responding to people—working in teams, and being self-motivated.

Review questions

1. Describe what changes might occur in organizations over the next forty years.
2. Analyse what the implications of this are for you throughout your career.

Concluding remarks: the more things change, the more they stay the same

Running case: Meg writes a letter to her replacement

Dear Steve,

I am writing to you on my last day at Junction Hotel and you will read this on your first. I have had forty long, but happy, years at Junction Hotel. Along the way I've met some amazing and interesting people (as well as some difficult ones) and generally had a positive experience here. I hope that you have as positive a time as I have had.

As we may never actually meet I thought I would take this opportunity to write and tell you a little about why this is a special place and means so much to me. I really hope that you come to love the hotel in the same way as I do and come to appreciate why it is such a unique place.

This hotel means a lot to me; indeed, it has been my life. It has a character and charm that you can only really see from the inside. While on the surface they may have made a lot of changes, I hope that the spirit of Junction Hotel will live on long beyond me.

You see, Steve, what makes Junction Hotel special is that we care. We care about keeping the rooms clean, that the guests have a good stay, and that the food is made well. But, most of all, we care about each other. This place has been like a second family to me. When my son died five years ago, these were the people that cared for me and helped me get through the days. With all the talk of profit margins and room occupancy rates, the things that really matter are people.

I know others here might say that I am old-fashioned and sometimes do not keep up with the modern ways of doing things. Well that might be the case, but this is because I believe that it is important to keep certain values alive. In our non-stop world of iPads, email, and the like I wonder if we are losing something important—the ability to really listen and respond to people, to care for them, and treat them as individuals. You might think I'm naïve or a relic from the past, but, to me, for all the changes that have happened in the last few years, the people are at the heart of this business. While Chance and Weaver might have all these systems and grand ideas, the real thing that keeps this hotel going, through the good and bad times, are the people. So, when you come in and make changes please be aware that, ultimately, people's lives are at stake. I have many good friends here; I hope that you look after them well.

And, most of all, I really advise that you enjoy your job. Money, status, and power are all well and good, but remember the key thing in the end is that you enjoy what you do. We spend so much of our time at work it is important that you feel you are enjoying it.

Yours
Meg

And, with a tear in her eye, Meg seals the envelope, puts it on the keyboard of her—well what will soon be Steve's—computer.

What do you think of Meg's views? Do you feel that these values are realistic in the modern world?

As she does so, Meg wonders what her career has really achieved. She is proud to have made it all the way from the position of cleaner to the top of Junction Hotel—'I wonder if anyone will manage that again', she muses. She is also proud of the way that she has held the hotel together at times of crisis. But, she also feels a little frustrated. The last ten years felt a little like treading water, going through the same routines day in, day out with little new to show for it.

Opening her leaving card, Meg is taken aback by the comments in it. There are more than the simple platitudes that one normally writes in leaving cards, but comments of genuine warmth and sincerity. Reading and re-reading, the recurring comments are of how much she has influenced the people around her, the little tricks of the trade that she had taught them, acts of kindness that she had long forgotten, and actions that she had performed which had helped them through difficulties. 'This is it', she thinks, 'this is what the last ten years have been about—helping others'. Realizing that she has made a difference, she wells up. 'Yes, that's it. It was helping out those around me, that's what really counts. That's my legacy.'

What do you want to achieve in your career? What would you count as success? What sort of person do you want to be known as at work?

This chapter has sought to make two key arguments. First, it is important, when studying OB, to understand that it is not a series of isolated topics, but is an interconnected discipline. To gain a strong understanding it is vital to explore how the topics connect together. This will give you a deeper appreciation of the subject, as well as the potential of a better grade.

Secondly, we have looked forward to the changing nature of organizations and, consequently, work, over the next forty years. As we have seen, the nature of work has changed in unimaginable ways over the last forty years and it is quite likely that the next forty years will be equally unpredictable. Therefore, instead of feeling that you can learn a series of skills or techniques of how to work in, and manage, organizations, it is more important to develop the capacity to learn, reflect, develop, and grow. Learning to learn, to think analytically and critically, will be more important to your future career than simply digesting a series of simple techniques.

A final note in our experience of having taught OB to thousands of students is that the issues that we have covered in this book are best understood when connected to actual practice. We have had many students approach us after a placement year or at graduation saying that the issues we have covered here have only really made sense to them after seeing them in practice. They have been grateful for the insights that they have gained, which have helped them understand themselves and others better, and enabled them to cope with the complexities of organizational life.

Bibliography

Coote, A. 2010. New Economics Foundation. 21 Hours: A new norm for the working week. Available at: http://www.neweconomics.org/blog/2010/02/15/21-hours-a-new-norm-for-the-working-week (last accessed 25 November 2012).

Elias, P., and Purcell, K. 2004. Is mass higher education working? Evidence from the labour market experiences of recent graduates. *National Institute Economic Review* 190(1): 60–74.

European Commission. 2011. A Roadmap for moving to a competitive low carbon economy in 2050. *COM (2011)* 112(4).

Gough, V. 2012. Author interview via telephone, 17 January 2012.

Greenaway, D., and Haynes, M. 2003. Funding Higher Education in the UK: The Role of Fees and Loans. *Economic Journal* 113, F150–F167.

Handy, C. 1994. *The Empty Raincoat*. Hutchinson: London.

Harvey, F. 2012. Switching to a green economy could mean millions of jobs, says UN. *The Guardian*. 31 May 2012. Available at: http://www.guardian.co.uk/environment/2012/may/31/switching-green-economy-jobs-un.

Hope, C. 2012. Plans for women's quotas on company boards dropped. *The Daily Telegraph*. 28 May 2012. Available at: http://www.telegraph.co.uk/news/politics/9293618/Plans-for-womensquotas-on-company-boards-dropped.html.

Jacques, R. 1996. *Manufacturing the employee: management knowledge from the 19th to 21st centuries*. Sage: London.

Jenkins, C., and Sherman, B. 1979. *The Collapse of Work*. Eyre Methuen: London.

Levitan, S.A., and Johnson, C.M. 1982. The Future of Work: Does It Belong to Us or to the Robots? *Monthly Lab. Rev.* 105: 10.

PricewaterhouseCoopers. 2008. Managing tomorrow's people: Millennials at work: Perspectives from a new generation. Available at: http://www.pwc.com/gx/en/managing-tomorrows-people/future-of-work/pdf/mtp-millennials-at-work.pdf (last accessed 25 November 2012).

PricewaterhouseCoopers. 2011. Millennials at work: Reshaping the workplace. Available at: http://www.pwc.com/gx/en/managing-tomorrows-people/future-of-work/download.jhtml (last accessed 25 November 2012).

Renner, M., Sweeney, S., and Kubit, J. 2008. *Green Jobs: Towards a Decent Work in a Sustainable, Low-Carbon World*. UNEP/ILO/IOE/ITUC: Geneva.

Rifkin, J. 1996. *The End of Work*. Putnam Books: New York.

Stebbins R.A. 1982. Serious leisure: A conceptual statement. *Pacific Sociological Review* 251–272.

Stern, N. 2006. *Stern Review on the Economics of Climate Change*. Her Majesty's Treasury: London.

Tselichtchev, I. 2012. *China Versus the West: The Global Power Shift of the 21st Century*. John Wiley and Sons: Chichester.

Thomson, P., and Lloyd, T. 2011. *Women and the New Business Leadership*. Palgrave Macmillan: Basingstoke.

Van Buren, H.J. 2003. Boundaryless careers and employability obligations. *Business Ethics Quarterly* 13(2): 131–149.

Worrall and Cooper. 2012. *The Quality of Working Life 2012: Managers' Wellbeing, Motivation and Productivity*. Chartered Management Institute: London.

Glossary

16 personality factor A personality test which measures personality on a set of 16 scales of opposing character traits.

A *priori* Independent of experience.

Acquisition The purchase of another company or business.

Aesthetic labour Usually found in customer- or client-facing service work where, in exchange for a wage, the worker is expected to manage their appearance and comportment in a manner directed by the organization.

Alienation In capitalism, the estrangement of people from a number of human qualities, noted particularly by writers such as Marx and Braverman as a consequence of rational work design.

Alternative models of organization Workers cooperatives and mutual organizations which seek for non-hierarchical modes of organizing and not-for-profit objectivities, often to bring about benefits to the members and society.

Analyse Widely associated with deeper intellectual thinking, it is process of breaking things down into their constituent parts, investigating the underlying cause or basic principles.

Anti-globalization movement A collective term for protestors and critics of the power and effects of multi-national corporations which they see as making the world less fair and more homogenized.

Assembly line An automated conveyor that moves a product in front of workers who perform a small, repetitive task to each product that passes before them.

Assessment centre A recruitment strategy where different selection techniques are blended in a selection process.

Autocratic A command and control leadership style.

Aversion therapy A type of classical conditioning whereby a particular behaviour is continually accompanied by a punishment so as to discourage that behaviour.

Backstage A theatrical metaphor to represent areas of the organization where workers are out of view of customers and clients.

Bad apples A phrase that dismisses an occurrence as just down to a few bad people or organizations, while claiming that others should not be judged as the same.

Banking education Freire's critique of learning and teaching styles which see learners as being like bank accounts to be 'deposited' with amounts of knowledge.

Behavioural psychology/behaviourism An area of psychology which suggests that learning can be managed through the use of rewards and punishments.

Behavioural theory A psychological perspective which seeks to understand and change the behaviour of individuals.

Big five personality scale A personality test which measures personality according to a set of five traits: openness, conscientiousness, extraversion, agreeableness and neuroticism.

Binged A phrased used during the Hawthorne studies meaning flicking the ear or arm of the person working too hard.

Bolshevik An insult indicating that a person is a Russian communist; in other words, that they are troublemakers who want revolution.

Boundarylessness Where the extent of sharing and dispersal of an organization's computer data gives a sense that there is no boundary to the organization.

Bureaucracy From the French *bureau*, meaning office; bureaucracy covers official, formal elements of rational organizational design, such as the hierarchical organization structure, the rules and procedures, and the official paperwork, which exert impersonal control over the organization.

Bureaucratic The process of bureaucracy, sometimes used in a derogatory sense.

Bureaucratic personality A tendency to follow rules to the letter rather than seeing the wider picture and making more common-sense judgements.

Business ethics A form of ethics applied to business. It is the study and evaluation of decision making within businesses through various moral concepts and judgements.

Buzzword A phrase which is a fad for a period of time.

Call centre An organization or department set up to handle a large volume of telephone calls, often managed efficiently using rationalized techniques.

Camaraderie A sense of togetherness and bonding.

Capital Investment in a business to set up the means of production, often used as a term to refer to business owners or capitalists who make that investment.

Capitalist wage–labour relationship The relationship between capitalists, who pay wages; and labour, who work in return for those wages.

Ceremonies A public act, often planned and formal, which celebrates a particular event, achievement or anniversary, largely planned by senior management or part of the organizations established calendar. They often have symbolic meaning that emphasizes important aspects of the organizations culture.

Change The process by which an organization changes in practices, processes, culture etc. in a planned or emergent fashion.

Change agent A manager, consultant, or other person who instigates and manages change.

Change management Ideas and techniques which are used to help manage periods of change within an organization.

Channels of communication Ways in which a message is expressed, e.g. verbally or in written words.

Chaos theory A branch of science which sees natural systems as both ordered, but, at the same time, unpredictable.

Classical conditioning A type of conditioning of behaviour where a reward or punishment accompanies and reinforces every instance of the behaviour to be conditioned.

Classical Management School A set of theories of management which draws upon rational methods of managing and organizing. Having developed from the early 1900s, it encompasses a number of theorists and practitioners who advocated 'one best way' of management. Examples of management styles and techniques which the school draws upon include Fayol and Frederick Taylor.

Cliques Exclusive groups.

Coercion Behaviour that arises from being forced in some way into performing that behaviour.

Collective action Any form of resistance against management taken by a group of workers.

Colonization Invasion and conquering of land, and enslavement of people, in Africa, the Americas and Asia from the 1500s to the 1900s by European countries, such as England, Spain, Belgium, Portugal, France, and the Netherlands.

Command and control A top-down leadership style that emphasizes the importance of the leader who tells others what to do.

Communication A process whereby information is transferred from a sender (or senders) to a receiver (or receivers).

Communication technology Technologies which facilitate communication between people and the sharing of information.

Communities of coping Mutual support among co-workers to cope with stress and other negative factors of emotional labour.

Communities of practice Social groupings based around a common occupational practice and set of knowledge, who develop and share that knowledge among themselves.

Complexity theory The application of chaos theory to social systems, such as organizations, suggesting that small changes can have unpredictable and potentially limitless consequences.

Conditioning A change in behaviour brought about using stimulus–response techniques typical of behavioural psychology.

Conformity Everyone in the group thinking and acting in the same way.

Congruence To correspond or match.

Consumption The purchase and use by customers and clients of goods and services created by an organization.

Content theories Theories of motivation which suggest that the content of work should be designed so as best to meet the needs which motivate workers.

Control group Used in scientific research, a control group does not receive any intervention and therefore is thus seen as representing the population as a whole. The control group is used as a standard of comparison to the research group who do receive intervention.

Contingency Dependent on the situation.

Contingency theory Suggests that the best structure for an organization is determined by factors such as environmental uncertainty, the organization's size, and the technology that the organization uses.

Corporate social responsibility A contested term with different interpretations but generally taken to be the social and environmental responsibility corporations have towards their stakeholders.

Cost The amount in wages and materials that it costs to produce a good or provide a service.

Craft knowledge Knowledge of a particular skill, often the result of a long period of training or apprenticeship.

Critical (as in 'critical management studies') A critical perspective, among other things, draws on Marxist theory and seeks to challenge the assumptions of mainstream management theory by stressing the impact that it has on employees and society.

Critical analysis To question the underlying assumptions of a perspective. In OB this may have particular emphasis on how power and inequality occur.

Critical perspective A perspective, drawing on Marxist theory, which seeks to challenge the assumptions of mainstream management theory by stressing the impact that it has on employees and society.

Cross-cultural management Managing a workforce from different national and cultural backgrounds.

Cultural homogenization A tendency for culture to become the same globally.

Database A computerized store of structured, organized data.

Dataveillance Surveillance brought about by examining electronic data which is held about individuals.

Decoding Converting a received message into the meaning perceived by the recipient.

Deep acting Emotional labour where the worker internalizes and believes in the performance in which they are engaged.

Deep learning Learning that tries to achieve a deeper understanding of, and engagement with, the material being learned.

Dehumanization Work that reduces people to part of a machine-like process, ignoring their human attributes. Widely associated with rational work design that was criticised by Harry Braverman.

Delegation Passing a job, task, or order down to lower levels of a hierarchy.

Democratic A leadership style which encourages the involvement of the group, but the leader ultimately makes the decisions.

Description A piece of writing that describes the theory or case study with little attempt at providing analysis. Often considered more superficial and therefore in student coursework results in lower grades.

Deskilling The obsolescence of workplace skills caused by rational work design or the introduction of new technology.

Deutero learning Bateson's conception of a higher level of learning whereby people are aware of how they 'learn to learn'.

Digital divide A divide between people who have access to computer hardware and network infrastructures, such as the Internet, and those who do not.

Direct control Face-to-face control of workers by a manager or owner.

Discretion The ability of an individual to act according to their own independent judgement, rather than being told exactly what to do.

Discrimination Where a person is treated negatively and unfairly because of their membership of a particular social group, e.g. because of race or gender.

Disenchantment For Max Weber this was a loss of 'magical elements' in society, and suggests some of the dehumanizing elements of bureaucracy.

Disneyization Term coined by Bryman which describes characteristics of the Disney theme parks that can be seen in other service and leisure organizations.

Distributive leadership An approach which emphasizes that leadership can occur throughout the organization by a wide variety of organizational members.

Division of labour Breaking down a job into more simplistic, individual tasks.

Double-loop learning Learning in organizations which goes beyond achieving a goal to question assumptions behind the goal being set, and that questions assumptions, values, and strategies more widely in the organization.

Downsizing Reducing the size of the workforce.

Dress code Standards of dress and appearance prescribed by an organization to its workers.

Dysfunctions of bureaucracy Unintended consequences of bureaucracy which lead to it not functioning in the efficient manner for which it is designed.

Economies of scale Cost reduction that comes from producing a product in large amounts.

Efficiency The minimization of cost, doing the same for less input of time and money.

Electronic Panopticon The ability to monitor our lives through the amount of electronic data and records held about us.

Embodied dispositions/habitus Our natural way of acting and reacting—a deeply held repertoire of instinctive behaviours.

Emergent approach to change An approach to change which sees the organization as being like a river, in constant flow, and suggests that in such an environment change emerges in the course of events rather than being planned in advance.

Emotion management Any management of personal emotional displays inside or outside of a working relationship.

Emotional labour Work where, in exchange for a wage, the worker is expected to manage their emotions to put on a particular emotional performance in front of customers or clients, especially in interactive service work.

Emotional quotient (EQ), emotional intelligence The ability to assess the emotions of yourself and others.

Empowered The process by which the workers are given greater power and autonomy. Critics suggest this approach also places a greater burden on workers.

Encoding Converting the intended meaning of a communication into a form that can be sent as a message.

Environment The world outside of an organization which can have an impact upon that organization.

Environmental leadership A self-sustaining group where employees find gratification through the group and task.

Equity theory A process theory of motivation which suggests that people are either motivated or demotivated depending on how they are rewarded in the workplace compared with others.

Equivocality Situations where meanings are ambiguous and open to interpretation.

Ergonomics The design of workplace environments and tools to best fit the movements of the human body.

Ethical capitalism A business approach which seeks to integrate CSR as central to the purpose and activity of an organization.

Ethical egoism People acting in their own best interest is the best way to get a good society.

Evidence In academic writing, support for claims made.

Expectancy theory A process theory of motivation which suggests that people will be motivated into actions and behaviours that they can link with them achieving goals and rewards that they desire.

Experience Where consumption is of the organization itself rather than any product or service that it provides.

Experiential learning Learning which comes from experiences and reflecting on those experiences.

Explanation In academic writing the ability to explain a theory or perspective.

Explicit knowledge Knowledge which can be expressed to other people as a set of words, facts, diagrams, or instructions.

Exporting Selling and distributing a good to another country.

Extinction Where a conditioned behaviour dies out because the reward or punishment is no longer provided.

Extraversion A tendency to focus and gain energy externally rather than within the self.

Extrinsic reward A reward that a person receives which is provided by somebody else.

Feedback Reaction or response to a message.

Fixed reinforcement A reward or punishment provided at fixed time intervals or fixed instances of a behaviour to be reinforced.

Followership In leadership theory (a) the importance of looking at followers and (b) the ability to follow a leader.

Followership theory Stresses the importance of followers and seeks to emphasize their importance in theory and practice.

Force-field analysis A technique whereby triggers and resistance to change are plotted on a diagram in order to identify areas to focus a change-management programme.

Formal communication Official communication within an organization, following authorized pathways.

Four humours The four elements that Hippocrates suggested made up the human body and which also divided into four personality types.

Fordism The use of a moving assembly line to mass produce goods.

Foreign direct investment Setting up a production or office facility in another country.

Formal rationality Technically efficient means of achieving particular ends without thinking of the human or ethical consequences.

Founder The person who established the organization.

Franchising Granting the right to another company to operate an outlet or branch of a particular organization, subject to adhering to standards and conditions of the franchising company.

Frontstage A theatrical metaphor to represent areas of the organization where workers are in contact with customers and clients.

Functionalist A highly pragmatic theoretical perspective which takes an 'objective' view of reality. It looks at the elements that promote stability and within management theory it tends to promote the interest of shareholders and managers with less attention on the potentially negative effects on employees or other stakeholders or opportunities to promote creativity or freedom.

Gaia hypothesis A theory popular in environmental movements where the whole world is seen as an interconnected system.

Gestalt psychology An area of psychology which suggests that we perceive things as forms, patterns, and connections rather than as a set of discrete individual items.

Glass cage Gabriel's metaphor to represent the visibility of workers in service sector organizations, both from the surveillance of rational organizational control and the visibility of being 'on show' in front of customers and clients.

Glass ceiling An invisible barrier that minority groups (particularly women) cannot pass through to get to senior positions in the organization.

Glass escalator Occurs when men enter female dominated professions and glide past them to more senior positions.

Globalization Defined in many different ways, globalization is where activities take place on an increasingly global scale.

Global village A metaphor to describe a perception of the globe shrinking in size as a result of the speed and global reach of transport and communications technologies.

Glocalization Adapting global practices and products to local conditions.

Gossip Rumours and information communicated through informal means.

Great man theory A theory that certain individuals are born great and can lead organizations and societies.

Group A collection of people with a sense of shared identity and something in common but *not* with a shared purpose.

Group dynamics The processes involved in interaction between group members, with particular emphasis on the tensions, conflicts and adjustments that occur.

Group norms The unwritten rules that shape behaviour.

Halo/horns effect The tendency for people to continually reaffirm their initial impressions of a person, whether good or bad.

Hawthorne effect The very act of observation changes behaviour.

Hawthorne studies A series of studies which ran from 1924 into the late 1930s.

Widely credited with discovering the human side of the organization.

Heuristic device Used to help simplify a theory and make it more understandable.

Hierarchy The levels and ranks of an organization. Any one level reports to the level immediately above and commands the level immediately below.

Hierarchy of needs Maslow's theory which shows that individuals have a set of needs in hierarchical order, whereby people are motivated by the most immediate unsatisfied need.

Hofstede's dimensions of culture Four numerical scales on which national management cultures can be located.

Horizontal/functional differentiation The process whereby different parts of the hierarchy are grouped according to criteria, such as the function performed, the geographical area served, or the product or service provided.

Horizontal loading Increasing the scope of a job by adding elements of work of a similar nature and at the same level of hierarchical responsibility.

Human Relations A movement emerging out of Organisational Development that studies the behaviour of people in groups.

Human resource management (HRM) The part of an organization, and the study of organization, which concentrates on policies and procedures relevant to the management of people within the organization (sometimes known as personnel management).

Hybrid consumption Different types of consumption activity, which might otherwise take place in separate organizations, appearing together in one organization.

Hygiene factors For Herzberg, characteristics of a job which cannot bring about increases in the job satisfaction and motivation of workers, but which can cause

demotivation if they are not addressed sufficiently.

Hyper-reality An artificial reality which is better than anything that could be experienced in the reality that it aims to reproduce.

Hypothesis A proposition that needs to be tested.

Ideographic approach An approach which sees personality as complex, unique to each individual, and dynamic.

Impersonal control Control of workers that is not done face to face, for example through delegation or through rules and procedures.

Impersonal fairness The idea that standardized bureaucratic procedures treat people equally and avoid the personal prejudice and preferences that individual managers might have.

Implosion Where a large amount of an organization's activity takes place through computer systems and is stored as computer code.

Industrial action Any action taken by workers in a dispute between capital and labour.

Inertia A tendency for an organization as a whole to resist change.

Informal communication Communication in an organization not following official and formal guidelines.

Informal/unofficial culture Culture that is often not known or supported by management but one that many of the employees share. It can be in opposition to official, management-led culture.

Informated organization Where a large amount of an organization's activity and knowledge is stored as computer code in a database.

Inputs In equity theory, efforts and contributions made by an individual to their work.

Intangible Something that you cannot touch.

Intangible space Aspects of globalization that take place through intangible means such as media transmissions, data in computer networks, and imagery.

Intensification of consciousness Alongside the global village, an increased awareness of events and people worldwide.

Interactive, customer-facing, front-line service work Work in the service and leisure industries where the worker interacts with the customer or client, either face to face or by telephone.

Interdisciplinary team/multifunctioning team A team of people that is comprised of people coming from different disciplines. This approach can produce a wider perspective and knowledge but can also produce greater conflict.

Internet community A group which communicates together regularly on the Internet.

Interpersonal perception The way in which one individual perceives the personality of another.

Interpersonal relationships The way group members relate to each other.

Interpretivist A philosophical approach which seeks to understand how people interpret and make sense of the world.

Intrinsic reward A reward that a person senses for themselves, rather than it being provided by someone else.

Introversion A tendency to focus and gain energy more from within the self rather than externally.

Iron cage of bureaucracy Max Weber's observation of the increased presence of bureaucracy in society and its potential to trap people in its routines and procedures.

Job description A document which outlines the formal duties and activities that the holder of a particular office will be expected to perform, and their place within the overall organizational structure.

Job enlargement Where the elements of an immediate task are increased to take in further elements of a similar nature.

Job enrichment Where the quality of work is increased through the provision of increased responsibility, autonomy, and variety of tasks.

Job rotation Where workers alternate between different tasks of a similar nature.

Job simplification Where a job is broken down into simplistic tasks, as with Taylorism or Fordism.

Joint venture Cooperation between two or more companies on a particular project.

Just-in-time management A form of management that tries to promote efficiency by reducing the amount of stocks that an organization holds, with components delivered as and when needed.

Keirsey's temperament sorter A personality-testing instrument which relates personality types to suggested occupational roles.

Knowledge and learning An aspect of organizational behaviour which emphasizes the importance of information, understanding and practical skills for organizational success. In particular it examines the capacity of the organization to share this knowledge in effective ways.

Knowledge clusters Geographical areas where a number of knowledge-intensive organizations in a particular industry are congregated in close proximity.

Knowledge-intensive firms Organizations whose main business involves the development and innovation of knowledge.

Knowledge workers Workers employed for their specific knowledge and their ability to use this knowledge to innovate, and develop new ideas and products.

Kolb's learning cycle A model of experiential learning which suggests that people learn through different stages of experience and reflection, and which suggests that people have particular learning style preferences for different parts of that cycle.

Labour Any person who works in return for a wage; the term is used to refer to such workers collectively.

Labour process How work is designed and controlled by management.

Laissez-faire A leadership style which leaves all decisions to the group.

Leaderful Where everyone has the capacity to be a leader or take a lead through doing activities.

Leadership The process of leading or influencing the behaviour of others. In the broadest definition can be carried out by anyone in the organization.

Lean management A contemporary form of Taylorist rational organization that attempts to eliminate waste or anything that does not add value from organizational processes.

Learning organization An organization which is set up so as to facilitate continual learning at individual and organizational levels.

Learning styles questionnaire Based on Honey and Mumford's development of Kolb, a questionnaire which ascertains people's preferred learning styles.

Libertarian A perspective that stresses individual freedom above all other concerns.

Licensing Granting the right to another company to produce a particular branded good.

Liquid modernity Bauman's characterization of modern day society as dynamic, changeable, and flexible.

Lottery question A question which asks whether people would give up work if they had enough money to live on without having to work.

McDonaldization (of society) The principles of efficiency, calculability, predictability, and control by which fast-food restaurants are managed and organized, as applied by Ritzer to other contemporary organizations.

McJobs Deskilled jobs found particularly in service industries, such as the fast-food restaurant.

Mainstream The dominant or accepted view that emphasizes managers' right to manage and the central objective of organizations to make profits for shareholders.

Management The everyday practices of running the organization in a smooth fashion.

Mass consumption Large-scale purchasing of a product by consumers within society.

Mass production The production of a large volume of a standardized product, often making use of an assembly line.

Matrix structure An organizational structure that combines a traditional functional hierarchy with separately-managed project teams that draw people from across different functional departments.

Means of production Tools, premises, and other property used to manufacture goods.

Media richness theory Examines the ability of different communications media to communicate rich, personal meanings rather than lean, impersonal information.

Medium, media A specific form of technology or technologies which convey and carry information.

Merchandizing The image or brand of one company or organization appearing on other products.

Merger Two companies joining together to become one single entity.

Message An item of communication sent from a sender to a recipient.

Metaphor A figure of speech whereby we try to understand something by suggesting a resemblance to the characteristics of something else.

Michigan studies Early leadership studies which stressed the benefit of being employee orientated rather than task orientated to improve output.

Miscommunication Where some of the meaning of a communication is distorted.

Mock bureaucracy A situation where policies and rules exist, but are ignored.

Motivating factors For Herzberg, characteristics of a job which can bring about increases in the job satisfaction and motivation of workers.

Motivation The will and desire that a person has to engage in a particular behaviour or perform a particular task.

Multiple intelligences Gardner's theory that there are different types of intelligence that people possess in different combinations.

Myers–Briggs Type Indicator A personality testing instrument based on the personality types of Carl Jung.

Naïve approach to change An approach to change which sees the organization in simplistic terms, as if it were a set of building blocks which can be rearranged easily.

Neo-Fordism A form of rational organization which combines Fordist efficiency and control with the ability of computer technology to introduce flexibility into the work process.

Neuroticism Emotional instability.

No-frills A model of organizational cost reduction which offers a basic product, charging customers for anything extra to this basic offering.

Noise Anything which distorts the transfer of a message from source to recipient so that the intended and perceived meanings differ.

Nomothetic An approach which views personality as a set of measurable traits or types.

Office A defined role within an organization.

Official A person who fills a particular role in an organization. When working in that role, a person is said to be working in an official capacity.

Ohio State studies Conducted at a similar time to the Michigan studies and also considered leaders to be people- or task-orientated.

One best way Rational management techniques that propose one most efficient way to perform any task.

Open source A form of knowledge sharing and collaboration where computer code is made publicly available and developed collaboratively.

Operant conditioning A conditioning of behaviour which recognizes that rewards and punishments do not need to be continuous, but can be scheduled in a way to still condition behaviour.

Organization chart A diagram of the structure of an organization.

Organization development A wide-ranging set of change management techniques, including techniques which derive from behavioural and Gestalt psychology.

Organizational behaviour modification The use of operant conditioning techniques in a workplace setting.

Organizational knowledge Knowledge which is a collective property of an organization rather than belonging to an individual.

Organizational learning Sharing and transfer of individual knowledge so that it becomes a collective property of the organization.

Organizational structure The roles and positions in an organization, often organized horizontally and vertically in the form of an organization chart diagram.

Orientations to work A perspective which suggests that people have a predisposition to work that is influenced by our lives outside work and the meaning that we attach to work.

Outcomes In equity theory, the rewards and results of a person's inputs.

Oxymorons Incompatible phrases that contradict each other.

Panopticon A prison design that allows surveillance to take place efficiently over all prisoners, used as a metaphor for surveillance and control in organizations as a whole.

Path-goal theory Developed by Robert House, this theory argues that the leader's effectiveness is dependent on the motivation, satisfaction, and performance of her subordinates.

Paperwork Official documentation and record keeping within an organization.

Performative labour Paid interactive service work where the worker is engaging in some form of performance, as if on stage. Refers, in particular, to emotional and aesthetic labour.

Person specification A formal list of the main requirements for a successful candidate for a particular job.

Personality A set of characteristics of behaviour displayed by any individual.

Personality types Broad personality groupings which are associated with a set of particular traits.

PEST model A model which breaks an organization's environment into four sectors: political, economic, social, and technological.

Physical space Aspects of globalization that involve goods and people moving across land.

Placelessness Where organizations exist in networks and seem to have no one fixed geographical location.

Planned approach to change An approach to change which sees change as planned over a series of long-term steps. Pays attention to human and social aspects of change, which are seen as 'hidden aspects' below the surface, as if the organization were an iceberg. Closely linked with organization development.

Politics A process of game playing and tactics that occurs within organizations often where different individuals jostle with each other to gain personal advantage.

Post-bureaucracy/post-bureaucratic organization A trend away from rigid, bureaucratic rules and structures in organizations towards more flexible and less hierarchical, rule-driven organizations.

Post-Fordism A break away from Fordism and towards management techniques which use the skill of workers and grant autonomy to workers, emphasizing communication and competencies, rather than command and control.

Post-heroic leadership theory A collection of theories that argue that traditional leadership over-emphasizes the importance of leaders and under-emphasizes followers.

Post-industrial A move in society and economy away from the dominance of manufacturing, towards a more flexible, service-based economy.

Power The capacity to get things done or to influence others.

Power games and politics The process where one individual or group tries to gain advantage or get another individual or group to do things that they might otherwise not intend to do.

Process theories Theories of motivation which suggest that motivation is a result of individual processes of perception, comparison, and calculation.

Processual Always in a process of changing and developing.

Processual approach to change An approach to change which emphasizes the messy and political nature of change.

Production The work done in an organization by the workers within that organization.

Professional knowledge A common body of knowledge relevant to a particular profession or occupation.

Pro-forma A type of paperwork, sometimes called a form. It is a blank template with standard fields for different types of relevant information, which is filled in as a means of capturing information for the records of an organization.

Psychodynamic A description of Freud's approach to personality which sees personality as continually being developed and changed by various influences.

Psychological Arising from the mind or emotions.

Punishment In behaviourism, a negative response that is received for performing a particular behaviour.

Quality circles A group of workers who come together, often under the supervision of a leader, to identify, analyse and solve organizational problems.

Radical change A political and theoretical approach which emphasizes the need to radically transform the social and political structure of capitalism to overcome the contradictions of capitalism.

Radical humanist A radical change perspective which emphasizes the 'subjective' contradictions capitalism has on the consciousness of people, often outside their awareness, producing alienation and oppression.

Radical structuralist A radical change perspective which emphasizes the 'objective' contradictions of capitalism between the capitalist (shareholders and managers) and workers and society.

Rationalization Work that is designed to achieve maximum efficiency and reduce costs, encompassing aspects of bureaucracy and the scientific design of work.

Rational-legal authority According to Max Weber this is power that is legitimated by rules and procedures associated with an office rather than by traditional or charismatic means.

Rational organizational design The design of organizational structures and activities in order to achieve the organization's goals in the most technically efficient manner. Rational organization suggests an organization which is designed logically and systematically, even scientifically, so as to achieve its aims.

Rational work design The design of work tasks to achieve maximum efficiency and reduce costs.

Recipient The person or persons that receives a message.

Records Information held by the organization relevant for bureaucratic functioning, including information about workers.

Recruitment The process of attracting a pool of candidates for a particular job vacancy.

Red tape An unintended consequence of bureaucracy, where rules and paperwork get in the way of work and activities, rather than helping tasks to be performed efficiently.

Reflective practice A form of professional development and training where workers reflect on actual workplace experiences and events.

Reflexivity Where an individual is connected in some way to a text they are reading about or writing, rather than simply looking at a text to which they are completely disconnected.

Regulation The sociology of regulation looks for the sources of stability and order rather than conflict, taking consensus at face value and seeing how social order can be preserved and strengthened. In organizational behaviour this perspective emphasizes the interests of managers and shareholders.

Reinforcement In behavioural psychology, the continued encouragement of a behaviour by the provision of a particular reward.

Resistance Drawn from critical theory, where marginalized and oppressed groups (such as workers and minorities) resist the aims and requests of more powerful groups, such as management.

Resistance to change Forces which resist a change taking place.

Reward In behaviourism, a positive response that is received for performing a particular behaviour.

Rhizome A mass of random, tangled connections which some people suggest is similar to the nature of the Internet and cyberspace.

Richness The amount and quality of information conveyed by any one message.

Rite A solemn act or procedure to observe an event or occasion.

Rituals Everyday habits that individuals do without thinking, which once had meaning but have gradually become part of the everyday activities of the organization.

Rules, policies, and procedures Formal instructions that govern how particular activities in an organization are to be performed.

Search engine A website which allows users to search for items on the Internet.

Search engine optimization Techniques to increase the rank of a website on search engine results.

Selection The process of selecting the most appropriate candidate from a pool of applicants for a particular vacancy.

Self-managed teams A team, often of professionals or highly qualified people, who manage themselves.

Schedules of reinforcement A blend of fixed and variable reinforcements designed so as best to reinforce desired behaviours.

Scientific management The use of scientific techniques to design work to be as efficient as possible.

Scientific selection Defining the precise characteristics of the ideal candidate for a job.

Self-actualization For Maslow, a realization, or actualization, or an individual's ultimate human and creative potential.

Self-discipline The process by which an individual trains and controls themselves usually for the purposes of self-improvement.

Separation of planning and doing Tasks designed by management, with workers having no input other than to perform those tasks.

Servant leadership theory A bottom-up perspective which sees the leader being the most effective where they support followers to enable them to do their jobs.

Service sector Non-manufacturing industries, such as retail, leisure, transport, finance, and media.

Sexually commodified The sexual attractiveness or desirability of a worker is used as part of the work they perform for customers or clients.

Shirking or **free-riding** An individual who does not pull their weight but is carried by other members of the group.

Single-loop learning Learning in organizations which merely adapts to achieving a particular goal.

Situational leadership A theory which stresses the importance of adapting the leadership style to meet the situation.

Social The human side of the organization, in particular the relations between people at work.

Social facilitation The tendency that individuals have to work harder when being watched by others, particularly on simple tasks.

Social identity theory Drawing from psychological theory. How an individual's identity is derived from being part of a group.

Social loafing A term which describes people who, when working in groups, do not work as hard because, often unconsciously, they rely on others to do the task.

Social presence theory Examines the degree to which the physical presence of the sender of a message can be felt in a particular communications medium.

Social–radical approach The view that organizations have an effect on the personality of their members.

Social reward A reward that comes from the feeling of being part of a group or team.

Soldiering Techniques used by workers to create time for themselves during the working day. Soldiering means that workers are not working at the most efficient level possible.

Source The sender or originator of a message.

Span of control The number of workers controlled by a manager at any one particular level in a hierarchy.

Stake A claim or interest.

Stakeholder Someone who has an interest or claim in the activities of the organization.

Stereotype Where a characteristic is attributed to a person because of their membership of a particular social group, e.g. because of race or gender.

Stimulus–response The underlying relationship of behaviourism, whereby a particular response, or behaviour, is the result of a particular stimulus—either a reward or punishment.

Strike A form of collective action where workers withdraw their labour.

Structured interview An interview with a set format and standard questions, based around job-specific questions.

Subcontracting Hiring another person or company to perform a particular process or service for an organization.

Subculture A localized culture with its own set of values and behaviours that reflects, but is distinct from, the wider culture.

Substantive rationality Rationality from a human and ethical perspective—if something is formally rational and efficient it does not make it substantively rational when considering its human and ethical consequences.

Surface acting Emotional labour that is performed by workers conscious of the fact that they are engaged in an artificial performance.

Surface learning Learning a set of facts in themselves, possibly for the purposes of a test or exam, rather than with any additional depth.

Surplus value Profit that capitalists gain over and above the wages they pay to workers.

Surveillance The observation, either overt or covert, of people to gain information about them or to exert order and control over them.

Sustainability The long-term stewardship and maintenance of the environment and the prospects of the firm.

Synchronicity The degree to which something happens immediately or after a delay.

Systemic approach to change An approach to change which recognizes the organization as an interconnected system whereby change in one area can have consequences and knock-on effects in other areas.

Tacit knowledge Knowledge which is personal, a form of second nature or knowing things 'off by heart', and which is difficult to explain to others.

Task orientation Focusing on tasks rather than on people.

Taylorism The work process designed by Taylor, associated with the division of labour into small tasks, which are then redesigned to be performed as efficiently as possible.

Team A group who meet together with a common purpose and some degree of mutual interdependence.

Teleworking, telecommuting Working away from a place of work by logging into a workplace's computer network.

T-group (training group) An activity which aims to get a group to understand and change its dynamics and attitudes.

The butterfly effect The suggestion in chaos theory that a small action can have unpredictable knock-on effects of a greater magnitude.

Theming As with a theme park, this is where the image and identity of an organization, and the experience that it provides for consumers, is based around a particular theme.

Therapy groups A group who meet together with a trained counsellor or facilitator where the group members decide what to talk about.

Three-step model of change Lewin's model whereby a process of change goes through three stages of unfreezing, movement, and freezing.

Time and motion study Rational work design where tasks are measured and timed, and redesigned to maximize efficiency.

Trade unions Membership organizations which collectively represent the interests of a group of workers.

Trained incapacity Where people are so used to their behaviour being controlled by bureaucratic rules and procedures that they become inflexible and unable to think for themselves and show initiative.

Trait A characteristic of the person, often considered the behaviour, thoughts, and emotions that the person exhibits, considered stable over time.

Trait theories Nomothetic theories of personality which see individual traits rather than broad personality groups as the foundations of personality.

Transactional leaders Leaders who do deals with employees in order to get the task done. Seen in opposition to transformational leaders who offer a better vision of the world that employees can buy into.

Transformational leadership A leadership theory which stresses the leaders ability to transform the organization by offering a better vision for the future.

Triggers Factors which push towards a change taking place.

Triggers to change Forces which provide an impetus for an organization to change.

Trolling Messages sent to Internet forums and communities which deliberately aim to disrupt their normal functioning and norms of behaviour.

Typologies A system of classification of traits that organizations have in common.

Uncertainty A lack of knowledge about a particular factual issue.

Unconscious From psychology, particularly psychoanalysis, the area of thinking that is not directly available to the conscious mind, and is below the level of personal awareness.

Unstructured interview An interview with no preset formal structure.

Utility The benefit that an individual might gain.

Value engineering A form of cost analysis that compares the cost of an item or process against its perceived value.

Variable reinforcement A reward or punishment provided at varying time intervals or varying instances of a behaviour to be reinforced.

VARK model A model and questionnaire which places individuals into one of four preferred learning styles—visual, auditory, reading and writing, or kinesthetic.

Vascular skin reaction A white line on the wrist created by a blunt instrument which disappears more quickly when the person is fatigued.

Vertical differentiation The process whereby a hierarchy creates a number of different layers of management within an organization.

Vertical loading Where a job is enriched by adding tasks which would normally be associated with elements of responsibility linked to positions higher in an organizational hierarchy.

Work–life balance A balance between work and career on one hand, and wider aspects of life, such as family and leisure time on the other.

Work to rule A form of industrial action where workers follow rules, regulations, and instructions precisely—this often results in the speed of work slowing considerably.

Index